English Language

English Language

Description, Variation and Context

Edited by

Jonathan Culpeper

Francis Katamba

Paul Kerswill

Ruth Wodak

Tony McEnery

palgrave macmillan

LANCASTER UNIVERSITY
Department of Linguistics and English Language

First published 2009 by
PALGRAVE MACMILLAN

Palgrave Macmillan in the UK is an imprint of Macmillan Publishers Limited,
registered in England, company number 785998, of Houndmills, Basingstoke,
Hampshire RG21 6XS.

Palgrave Macmillan in the US is a division of St Martin's Press LLC,
175 Fifth Avenue, New York, NY 10010.

Palgrave Macmillan is the global academic imprint of the above companies
and has companies and representatives throughout the world.

Palgrave® and Macmillan® are registered trademarks in the United States,
the United Kingdom, Europe and other countries.

ISBN-13: 978–1–4039–4589–1 hardback
ISBN-10: 1–4039–4589–6 hardback
ISBN-13: 978–1–4039–4590–7 paperback
ISBN-10: 1–4039–4590–X paperback

This book is printed on paper suitable for recycling and made from fully
managed and sustained forest sources. Logging, pulping and manufacturing
processes are expected to conform to the environmental regulations of the
country of origin.

A catalogue record for this book is available from the British Library.

A catalog record for this book is available from the Library of Congress.

10 9 8 7 6 5 4 3 2 1
18 17 16 15 14 13 12 11 10 09

Printed and bound in Great Britain by
CPI Antony Rowe, Chippenham and Eastbourne

Contents

Preface

We believe this book to be distinct in a number of respects – and not just because all the contributors are based in the Linguistics and English Language department at Lancaster University! (To be precise, Dawn Archer and Arfaan Khan are not currently based in the department, but were previously). One motivation for writing it in the first place was that we were unable to find a textbook with the kind of coverage we wanted. Too often, studying the English language is restricted to structural topics (e.g., phonology, morphology, syntax) and traditional approaches. Of course, these areas are important, but they are not the be all and end all. Fields of inquiry that have come to prominence in recent decades concern language use in context (e.g., language and power, politeness, language and politics), and these have an equally important role to play, not least because they enable us to tap into the social consequences of English. Furthermore, we firmly believe that even the most introductory textbook should be research-led, just as our own teaching is. There is no reason why students cannot be given a glimpse of the very latest developments, nor why those developments cannot shape what we write. The trick, of course, is to do this, yet still make what we write accessible to those with little or no background in linguistics.

Above all, we would like to thank all contributors for helping us to make this volume what it is. We are particularly indebted to Gerard Hearne for attending to all of our stylistic infelicities and for creating the index. Also, we are grateful to Brian Walker and John Heywood for helping us iron out inconsistencies in the bibliography. At Palgrave, we thank Kate Wallis for supporting this project from the beginning, and Kitty van Boxel for providing patient and good-humoured support in the closing and crucial years of the project. Finally, we would like to thank Penny Simmons for going well beyond the call of duty in her meticulous copy-editing work and careful supervision of the production of the final book.

JONATHAN CULPEPER, FRANCIS, KATAMBA, PAUL KERSWILL,
TONY MCENERY AND RUTH WODAK
Lancaster University, 2009

Acknowledgements

The authors and publisher wish to thank the following for permission to use copyright material:

Blackwell Publishing Ltd., for the figure 'Regional Varieties of English', in *The Dialects of England*, 2nd *edition*, by Peter Trudgill (Blackwell: Oxford, 1999).

Brad Shorr and Word Sell Inc. for the cartoon 'Fire Hydrant and Mailbox' © Word Sell Inc/ Brad Shorr.

Carcanet Press, for the poem 'Flying Crooked', by Robert Graves, in *Complete Poems in One Volume*, edited by Patrick Quinn (Carcanet Poetry, 2000).

Cambridge University Press, for permission to use the following figures: Figure 5.1 from J. Cheshire, P. Kerswill and A. Williams, 'Phonology, grammar and discourse in dialect convergence', in *Dialect Change: Convergence and Divergence in European Languages,* edited by Peter Auer, Frans Kinskens and Paul Kerswill (2005); Figure 2, 'The Variable by Class and Style in Norwich' in *The Social Differentiation of English in Norwich*, by Peter Trudgill (1974); a table entitled 'Wells's (1982) lexical sets' and figure entitled 'Vowels in Received Pronunciation, Popular London and Cockney showing the Diphthong Shift in Cockney' from *Accents of English* by John C. Wells (1982).

Fallon London, and Skoda Auto UK, for kind permission to reproduce the text of the 'Factory Tour' advertisement (Director: Lawrence Green, Writer: Andrew McLeod and Agency: Fallon London, 2001).

Guardian News and Media Ltd, for the article entitled 'Bullied teacher wins £230,000', by Rebecca Smithers, published 5 October 2002 © Guardian News and Media Ltd 2002.

International Phonetic Association, at the Department of Theoretical and Applied Linguistics, School of English, Aristotle University of Thessaloniki, for the reproduction of The International Phonetic Alphabet (2005).

Merriam-Webster Inc., for the entry 'shlumpadinka' from the Merriam-Webster Online Dictionary © 2008 by Merriam-Webster, Incorporated (www.Merriam-Webster.com).

Mouton de Gruyter, for a figure from 'New towns and koineisation: linguistic and social correlates, by Paul Kerswill and Ann Williams (2005) in *Linguistics*, 43 (5): 1023–48.

Pearson Education Ltd for the figure 'The use of ain't for auxiliary verbs be and have' from J. Cheshire, in *Dialects of English: Studies in Grammatical*

Variation, edited by P. Trudgill and J. Chambers, (New York: Longman, 1991), pp. 54–73.

Penguin Books Ltd, for the figure 'Social and regional accent and variation' in *Sociolinguistics: An Introduction to Language and Society*, by Peter Trudgill (Penguin Books, 1974, Revised edition 1983) Copyright © Peter Trudgill, 1974, 1983.

Telegraph Media Group Ltd, for the article entitled 'Actors say they are alarmed by obsession with regional accents', by Chris Hastings in *The Daily Telegraph*, 31 October 2004.

The New Yorker, for the cartoon "On the Internet, nobody knows you're a dog" © Peter Steiner/Condenast.

United Syndication Incorporated, for the 'Peanuts' cartoon strip © 1971 United Syndication Inc.

Introduction

CHAPTER 1

Studying the English Language

JONATHAN CULPEPER, PAUL KERSWILL, RUTH WODAK, FRANCIS KATAMBA AND TONY MCENERY

What does the study of the English language involve? Any book on the English language must address this question, as the answer will determine its contents. This, however, is a very tricky question to answer. A glance at the contents lists of other books on the English language will find variation, and sometimes quite dramatic variation. Perhaps it may seem self-evident and unproblematic to you that studying the English language is simply that – studying any aspect of the English language. However, 'the English language' is not in itself a neatly identifiable entity: what counts as English is not straightforward. Consider the view 'English is the language of England'. As we shall see in this book, the roots of English are not in England at all, but in the old dialects of what is now north-western Germany. Once it became established in Britain, it was relatively restricted geographically: in the sixteenth century there were approximately 3 million speakers of English, nearly all indeed based in England. However, today there are well over 300 million native speakers of English, not to mention a further 300 million regularly speaking it as a second language (i.e., in addition to their native language), and the huge number of people learning it as a foreign language, mainly to communicate with other non-native speakers of English (there are more Chinese people learning English than there are native speakers of English in the United States!). Thus, most English is produced, heard and read outside England. Take the example of the Egyptian airline pilot landing at Frankfurt airport in Germany, and talking to air traffic control in English. For that pilot, English is the language used for communication in that context – it has nothing to do with England (except for its distant historical connection). English has emerged as a global **lingua franca**, that is, a language used throughout the world as a means of facilitating communication between speakers of different languages. Consider the view 'English has a common core of words and structures that are recognized as being English'. In fact, not everybody would recognize the same things as being English, something which we will discuss and illustrate in Chapter 12. One might appeal to some notion such as **Standard English**, claiming it represents the common core. However, most English is **spoken**: accents vary and, in a global perspective, they vary widely. At best we can say that certain groups of English accents tend to share certain features. And there is the issue of what is meant by 'standard'. Appeals to such notions frequently slide from talk of a uniform set of features to talk of a set of features which a particular group considers best. For example, whilst it may indeed be possible to identify a set of standard grammatical and spelling features for British written English, that set would not be the same for American written English. So, which Standard English should we follow? Answers to that question typically involve the social evaluation of language (e.g., British people tend to think that the British 'standard' is 'best').

To study anything requires that there be an object to study. If we cannot agree about what constitutes English, how can we study it? The answer is simply to accept that there are various views as to what counts as English. Although there is often considerable agreement within these views, flowing from them are different conceptions as to the boundaries of English, how the language is constituted, and also how we might study it. These views fall into three groups, the second of which contains a number of notable sub-groups (our use of the word 'English' below denotes a language that might be labelled as such by a community of people):

1   **The folk view.** In fact, we have already touched on folk views about English in our first paragraph. There, we expressed beliefs about English in quotation marks. Many such beliefs have a prescriptive quality – they are beliefs about how English should be. For example, people tend to believe that English pronunciation, or a least the best English pronunciation, should reflect spelling. As we shall see in Chapters 2 and 12, nobody speaks English in a way which corresponds with spelling in a simple manner: even Queen Elizabeth II herself would not pronounce the <d> of the word *and* in the phrase 'fish and chips', and it is in fact speakers of *less* prestigious regional accents (in England, at least) who would pronounce the <r> in words like *sort*. Studying English from the point of view of folk beliefs and 'correctness' not only involves examining the truth of a particular belief (i.e., whether it is a myth), but also considers the real effects that having that belief in the first place can have on the language, its social contexts and the people who speak it. We will do this at various points in this book.

2   **The academic views.** These can be considered under four headings:

- **The comparative view.** In this perspective, any study that reveals similarities or differences between English and another language can contribute to an understanding of how it is constituted (i.e., its distinctive nature). Many studies focus on formal structures (e.g., the grammar, semantics and phonology) of English in comparison with those of other languages, but it is also possible to study the use of language in English-speaking countries or cultures and contrast it with the use of language elsewhere (contrasting, for example, how people are 'polite' in different languages and cultures).
- **The variational view.** In this perspective, any study that considers the nature of the varieties of English can contribute to an understanding of how it is constituted. Such varieties can be distinguished **synchronically** (i.e., how they vary at one point in time, for example, how they make up different accents or written genres) or **diachronically** (how they vary over time, thus

feeding into the history of English). It is worth noting here that English, as with other languages, is made up of its own distinctive varieties, especially spoken varieties (e.g., accents), and has its own distinctive history.

- **The structural view.** In this perspective, any study that considers the nature of the specific structures (e.g., words, sounds) of English can contribute to an understanding of how it is constituted. This view is a relatively weak view of the study of English in the sense that some of the phenomena discussed may also be characteristics of other languages. Thus, for example, a study of nouns using English data (perhaps for reasons of convenience) may reveal certain characteristics of English nouns, but it may well be the case that at least some of those characteristics are shared with other languages. In this respect, this view differs from the comparative view.

- **The social (context) view.** In this perspective, any study that considers the nature of the specific social contexts in which English occurs (and with which it interacts) can contribute to an understanding of how English is constituted. Here, the focus is on the *use* of English and its associated social contexts, including both how English is shaped by the social contexts and how English shapes social contexts. For example, there are linguistic differences which relate to the formality of a situation (a job interview vs. family chat) and the roles speakers have (the defendant vs. the judge). As speakers, we can completely change the context through our choice of words – for example, the decision to swear could reduce formality (and have other far-reaching consequences). This view is also a relatively weak view of the study of English in the sense that some of the social and interactive phenomena discussed may also be the same for other languages.

3 **The educational view.** For millions of people around the world, studying English does not mean enhancing one's abstract understanding of English, as with academic views, but enhancing one's ability to put it into practice – to speak it, write it and understand it. 'It' here, as propagated in textbooks and educational materials, is usually a standard written English and a prestigious accent (e.g., Received Pronunciation). Enhancing readers' abilities in this way is not the prime focus of this book. However, it is important to note that a further academic perspective pertains here, namely, studying the teaching and learning of English, particularly, but not exclusively, in educational contexts. We will address this area in the final section of this book.

All the above views overlap. Note, for example, that the academic study of folk views could be considered a sub-category of the social (context) view. Our book does not espouse one particular view, but embraces all of them. That way, we hope that our understanding of English is enriched.

Where does English language study take place? Addressing this question can help reveal other things about the subject. In the UK, North America, Australia and New Zealand, it typically takes place in departments of English, English literature, linguistics or linguistics and English language; in other countries, it also appears in departments of English linguistics or English philology. These labels reflect two pertinent issues. The first issue concerns a terminological problem: does the word 'English' encompass English literature,

English language or both? Some departments labelled 'English' are relatively little concerned with language, focusing mainly on English literature in terms of literary theory. This does not mean simply analysing a certain body of texts, but considering who wrote them, who they are written for, the social and political contexts in which they were written, and so on. There is no denying that English literature is worth studying, if only on the grounds that the works studied are generally considered to have cultural value. However, English literature accounts for only a relatively small proportion of the language that people consider to be English – it can hardly represent the English language as a whole. The language of English literature is represented in this volume (see Chapter 26), as are the many other varieties that comprise the English language. The second issue concerns the relationship between English and linguistics. Linguistics, in its broadest definition, is the study of language or languages, along with phenomena pertinent to language(s). So, linguistics as a discipline is clearly broader than the study of English language. Most obviously, it is not primarily focused on language that people would label English. Moreover, it is focused on the fundamental – and in some cases perhaps even universal – mechanisms of language, often drawing theoretical backing from cognitive or social sciences. Consider, for example, the fact that research has revealed that bilinguals store the lexical inventories of the languages they speak in different parts of the brain. This runs counter to what one might imagine to be a more efficient arrangement, whereby particular concepts (e.g., a 'table') are straightforwardly 'hot wired' to one 'lexicon' (or dictionary) containing all the possible words (in the languages known to the particular speaker) for each concept. This fact in itself has no particular bearing on the nature of English, or indeed any other specific language: it is an insight into a general linguistic mechanism. Having said that, to study the English language is also to study a language. In our view, it is impossible to study the English language without also doing linguistics. We need to be aware of how language works in general, and we need to be able to evaluate our frameworks and tools for language analysis in particular, if we are going to investigate a language and in particular to address the issue of why it is as it is. We should stress that we are not attempting to cover all of linguistics as a discipline, but rather we emphasize areas of linguistics pertinent to the study of the English language.

The up-coming chapters

The chapters are organized under six major headings. The first group appears under English: Structure. This section includes many of the traditional areas of linguistics relating to, for example, English phonology, grammar and semantics. One of the functions of these chapters in Part 1 is to provide you with a basis in language description, which will set you up for later chapters in the book that draw upon aspects of that description. The second group, Part 2 under English: History, addresses diachronic variation in English; in other words, the history of English. This is organized according to linguistic area, rather than periods in the history of English, for the reason that this better suits the focus of this book. The following two groups of chapters appear under English Speech: Regional and Social Variation in Part 3 and English Writing: Style, Genre and Practice in Part 4. These focus on synchronic variation in English. The chapters dealing with genre and practice pave the way for a transition to Part 5 and the next group of chapters, which appear under English: Communication and Interaction. Here, the focus is on the use of English in social context(s). The final group of chapters, in Part 6 under English: Learning and Teaching, considers the learning and teaching of English, both outside and inside educational contexts.

The chapters are written so that they should be understandable by a first year undergraduate, but there is plenty of potential for the content of the chapters to support courses pitched at more senior undergraduates, or even as preliminary steps for postgraduates, to whom the research-led nature of the chapters should appeal. With a few exceptions, each chapter has the same structure. In particular, chapters typically conclude on a more research-oriented note. Each chapter contains one or more boxes, which may be of two kinds. **Advances Boxes** are like an aside. If you decided to skip them, the rest of the text will still make perfect sense. They are pitched at a somewhat higher-level readership, or at least contain a particularly close focus that you would not expect in an introductory text. They are designed to give readers a sense of controversies and debates, complications and problems, further research, and so on. **Illustration Boxes** contain extended examples (or a set of shorter examples), additional examples (plus, optionally, some analysis of them), and sometimes further elaboration on an issue. Each chapter ends with some recommendations for further readings.

PART 1

English: Structure

EDITED BY FRANCIS KATAMBA

CHAPTER 2

Phonetics

Kevin Watson

2.1 Introduction

One of the first things we human beings do when we are born is make noise, and we rarely stop. As soon as we begin to master our native language, we turn our gurgles and cries into meaningful utterances and begin to talk. It is fitting, then, that we begin this book about the English language by exploring the primary medium through which humans communicate: **speech**. The study of speech belongs in the branch of linguistics called **phonetics**. Phoneticians study how speech sounds are produced by speakers and perceived by listeners, and how sound travels through the air. In this chapter, we will focus on speech production, by situating ourselves in the realm of **articulatory phonetics**. An understanding of how speech works is crucial for many aspects of English language study. For example, before we can understand how sounds pattern together in English and in other languages, or investigate how speech varies across different regions of a country, or think about how speech is different from writing, we must have a thorough understanding of what speech is, how it works and how we can describe it. Furthermore, an understanding of speech production is also vital to many professional applications of linguistics. Speech therapists, for example, cannot diagnose and treat patients with speech difficulties without a detailed knowledge of the workings of the vocal tract, speech technologists working in spoken language recognition cannot make computers interact with human talkers without understanding how the speech signal travels through the air, and forensic phoneticians cannot pass judgement on issues of speaker identity in criminal cases without an understanding of how speech varies. Knowledge of phonetics is the cornerstone of these activities.

The main aim of this chapter is to provide the background and technical terminology necessary to understand how speech is made and how linguists describe it. By investigating how the consonants and vowels of English are articulated, we will see exactly why speech has been called 'the most highly skilled muscular activity that human beings ever achieve' (Laver, 1994: 1). Readers should note that the Appendix of this book contains a comprehensive display of phonetic symbols, as produced by the International Phonetics Association (IPA). This IPA chart is not for the beginner; instead, this chapter will provide introductory lists, and we will build on those in the following two chapters. However, the chart puts together all that we use and more. It may also prove useful for those wishing to explore other languages.

2.1.1   Making and hearing noise

All noise travels through the air to the human ear in the same way. When noise is generated, air particles close to its source vibrate. These particles nudge neighbouring particles, which nudge neighbouring ones, and so on, until they run out of energy and stop vibrating. The vibrations are picked up by the human eardrum and perceived as sound. When someone talks, the air particles close to the mouth vibrate, and affect neighbouring particles, and this chain is eventually picked up by a listener.

Sounds are perceived differently according to how the air particles vibrate, or according to the shape of the space around which they vibrate. If you were to blow a stream of air across the top of an empty milk bottle, for example, you would produce a sound with a fairly low pitch. Fill the milk bottle half full with water and do the same, however, and the pitch would be higher. Each time, the **source** – the stream of air – is exactly the same, but the space in which the air vibrates is a different shape. Speech production works on exactly the same principles. Speech sounds differ when the space inside the mouth differs. For example, dentists typically ask patients to 'say aahh'. This ensures the patient's tongue moves to the lower back region of their mouth and creates lots of space further forward. If a dentist asked a patient to 'say eee', the tongue would be further forward and this would create a much smaller space in the mouth, generating a different sound (and also, unhelpfully for the dentist, obstructing the teeth).

In order to be able to understand and describe how the shape inside the mouth changes during the production of sounds, we must examine the workings of the vocal apparatus used in speech production. We begin to do this in the next section.

2.1.2   The human vocal tract

Studying phonetics requires you to get intimate with your **vocal tract** – the parts of the body used for producing speech. You will already be perfectly familiar with some of these parts, but others will be new to you. We will take each part in turn, starting from the front of the mouth where you will find the more familiar pieces of your anatomy.

Figure 2.1 illustrates the parts of the vocal tract we will consider here. First, right at the front of the mouth, we have the **lips**. The lower lip moves upwards and downwards according to the movement of the lower jaw, but the upper lip is non-mobile. Next are the **teeth**. Like the upper lip, the upper teeth are non-mobile. The teeth near the very front of the mouth are used in speech production but, of course, the teeth extend further back along the sides of the mouth too. Moving further back, we start to reach the parts of the vocal tract that cannot easily be seen without a mirror. Try putting the tip of your tongue at the front of your mouth, so that it is touching the back of your top teeth. Move it slowly backwards, so that it strokes the roof of your mouth as

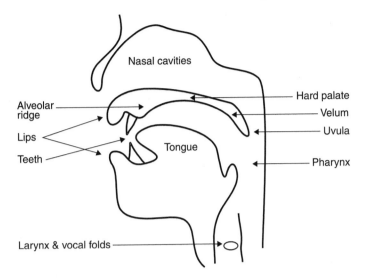

The human vocal tract   *FIGURE 2.1*

it goes. Quite soon, before you move your tongue very far, you will feel a hard bump, which, when you move over it, will feel like your tongue is going down a hill and rolling onto the roof of your mouth. This bump is the **alveolar ridge**. Continuing to move the tip of your tongue backwards, you will feel what most people know as the **roof of the mouth**. This is the hard area behind the alveolar ridge, which is called the **hard palate**. It is slightly curved, and you can feel this curve as you move your tongue over it. If you move the tip of your tongue even further back, beyond the hard palate, you will suddenly feel a patch of soft tissue. This is the **velum** (it is also called the **soft palate**). Further back from the velum is the **uvula,** a fleshy cone-shaped pendulum which stops bits of food going up the nose during swallowing and is also used for speech. Next is what most people call 'the throat': the **pharynx**. The top of the pharynx, near the velum, splits into the oral cavity (the mouth) and the **nasal cavities** (the nose). The velum acts like a valve to control the flow of air into the nasal cavity. When the velum is raised, it blocks access to the nose and air is directed into the mouth. When the velum is lowered, air is free to enter the nasal passages. Near the bottom of the pharynx is the **larynx,** made of cartilage, muscle and tissue. The front part of the larynx, which is usually more protruded in males than females, is sometimes called the 'Adam's apple'. Inside the larynx are the **vocal folds** (or **vocal cords**), which are ligament-covered membranes that open and close to modify the size of the space between them (which is called the **glottis**). The vocal folds act to modulate air as it is pushed out from the lungs. We will revisit the larynx in some detail in Section 2.2.

We have left until last the most mobile of all articulators – the **tongue**. In phonetics, the tongue is usually divided up into a number of sections, as Figure 2.2 shows.

The **tongue root** is furthest back, opposite the pharynx. Further forward is the **back** of the tongue, which can make contact with the velum. Then we

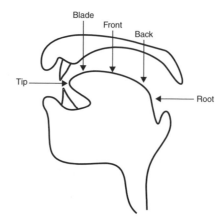

FIGURE 2.2   The tongue

have the **front** of the tongue, approximately under the hard palate. The **blade** of the tongue, also called the **lamina**, sits between the front and the **tip**, also called the **apex**, which is furthest forward. We will revisit these terms in Section 2.2, and see that particular parts of the tongue are involved in making particular sounds.

2.1.3 Writing speech down

In Section 2.1.1, we encountered the sound that dentists often ask patients to make, which was written as 'aahh'. It should be obvious that writing down the sound in this way is not very helpful because it is not very accurate and is open to interpretation. Indeed, using the conventions of English spelling to record pronunciation is fraught with problems. One such problem is that the same speech sound can be spelled in a number of different ways. For example, the first sound of the word *fish* is [f], which is straightforwardly spelled with the letter <f>. However, consider the words *affect* and *bluff*, which have one [f] sound each, but are spelled with not one but two <f> letters. Furthermore, consider the words *cough* and *trough* or *Phillip* and *graph*, which all have [f] sounds in their pronunciation but no letter <f> in their spelling. Another problem is that the same letter or combination of letters can represent different sounds. For example, in the word *cough* the letters <gh> represent the [f] sound. However, in the word *ghost*, the same letters represent the [g] sound. Plenty more examples abound in English: compare the words *script* and *receipt* – in the former the letters <pt> are pronounced as the sounds [pt], but in the latter the [p] sound is missing.

Another problem is related to English speakers rather than English spelling. Take, for example, the words *finger* and *singer*. Everyone pronounces the word *finger* with a [g] sound in the middle and, if you come from the north of England, *singer* may be pronounced in this way too. However, if you come from the south of England, *singer* will probably not have a [g] sound. Of course, when you write *singer* and *finger*, the letter <g> is always present. This is because

ILLUSTRATION BOX 2.1

What's a ghoti?

One of the most well-known examples of the problematic nature of English spelling, often attributed to the playwright George Bernard Shaw, is the fact that the word *fish* could reasonably be spelt <ghoti>. This works because the <f> of *fish* sounds the same as the <gh> in *cough*, the <i> is the same as the <o> in *women*, and the <sh> is the same as the <ti> in *motion*. We can show this more clearly using symbols from IPA:

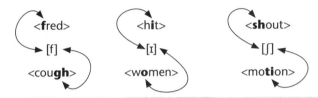

spoken English is highly variable, for a variety of reasons, including regional accent (see Chapter 18). However, written English, on the whole, does not vary to the same degree, because it is governed by the rules of standard spelling (see Chapter 13).

These complications mean we cannot rely on the spelling system when we are trying to represent a speaker's pronunciation. In linguistics, another system is used to represent the sounds of language: the **International Phonetic Alphabet (IPA)**. The IPA consists of a range of symbols – some similar to ordinary letters and some more distinct – which allow us to write down sounds accurately. The main principle behind the IPA is that one symbol represents one sound. This means that, unlike in English spelling, whenever a particular symbol is used it always represents the same speech sound. In the case of *finger* vs *singer* above, we can say that if you are from the north of England you might pronounce *finger* as [fɪŋgə] and *singer* as [sɪŋgə], in each case pronouncing [g]. But, if you are from the south of England you might pronounce *finger* as [fɪŋgə], with [g], but *singer* as [sɪŋə], with no [g].

As you will see in the examples above, there is a convention in linguistics to use angle brackets < > when referring to letters. In phonetics, square brackets [ ] are used to distinguish letters from speech sounds. Thus, we can say that although the words *rice* and *pass* end with different letters, <ce> and <ss>, they are spoken with the same final sound, [s]. Throughout this chapter, where appropriate, we will continue to represent IPA symbols using square brackets.

2.2 Initiating speech

We saw in Section 2.1.1 that noise is generated by manipulating a flow of air. The first thing we must do when we talk, then, is initiate the air flow. To do this, we breathe in, and then we slowly exhale as we speak. This initiates a

pulmonic air stream, so called because it begins in the lungs. The air stream makes its way through the larynx and towards the nose and mouth. The outwards direction of the airflow means it is called **egressive**. The egressive pulmonic airstream is used for speech in all languages of the world, and English is no exception. For a good discussion of other airstream mechanisms, see Rogers (2000: 251–60) and Laver (1994: ch. 6).

When the air has left the lungs, the first obstacles it hits are the larynx and vocal cords, and in the remainder of this section we will examine their roles.

2.2.1 Voicing

When the air from the lungs reaches the larynx, it is affected in different ways according to the size of the glottis (which, recalling Section 2.1.2, is the name given to the space in-between the vocal folds). If the glottis is open, meaning the vocal folds are wide apart, air can flow freely from the lungs up towards the mouth. This is the case for normal breathing. It is also the case for speech sounds such as the first ones in *see*, *she* and *fee*, which are called **voiceless** sounds. If the glottis is narrow, meaning the vocal folds are close together, the airflow forces its way through the gap and causes the vocal folds to knock together and vibrate. You can feel this vibration if you put your fingers on your Adam's apple and say 'aahh' (and compare it, for example, to a long 'sss' sound, in which there will be no vibration). Sounds produced when the vocal folds are vibrating are called **voiced** sounds. The different positions of the vocal folds for voiceless and voiced sounds are shown in Figure 2.3.

2.2.2 Pitch

Each voice quality described above was a result of the type of constriction in the glottis. The larynx has another function which is not related to the type of constriction, but instead to how fast the vocal folds vibrate: the creation of **pitch**. When the vocal folds vibrate quickly, they produce a high pitch. Conversely, when the vocal folds vibrate slowly, a low pitch is produced. Pitch is also connected to the size of the larynx. For example, on the whole, the male larynx is larger than that of the female, and one result of this is that male speakers typically have a lower pitch than female speakers.

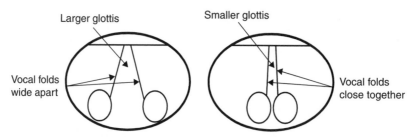

FIGURE 2.3   *The position of the vocal folds for breathing and the production of voiceless sounds (left) and for the production of voiced sounds (right)*

ADVANCES BOX 2.1

The vocal folds and voice quality

As well as being wide apart and close together, the vocal folds have a number of intermediate states which can be used to modify what is called a speaker's **voice quality**. Three quite common voice qualities in English are: **whisper**, **creaky voice** and **breathy voice**.

You probably already know what the voice quality of 'whisper' is like. It is a voice quality which has turbulent airflow but in which no sound is voiced, because the vocal folds are too far apart to vibrate. The vocal folds are slightly closer together for a whisper than they are when producing voiceless sounds.

A voice quality in which the vocal folds are much closer together, but are not tightly shut, is 'creaky voice'. Creaky voice is a very low-pitched quality, in which the individual vibrations of the vocal folds can be heard. It is often used in English to signal the end of a speaker's turn.

'Breathy voice' is a combination of whisper and voicing. It can occur when speakers who are out of breath try to talk. The glottis is open, but the rush of air causes intermittent vibration in the vocal folds (as Catford (1994: 55) nicely describes, the folds 'are set flapping in the breeze').

For more detailed discussion of voice quality, see Laver (1994: ch. 7).

ADVANCES BOX 2.2

Can you hold a tune?

Imagine the tune of your favourite song, and then try to hum along to it whilst whispering. Can you do it? Not really. It is impossible to hum a tune whilst whispering because the different levels of pitch required to create the tune are produced as a result of the different speed of vibration in the vocal folds. During a whisper, the vocal folds do not vibrate and, as a consequence, no pitch can be generated.

2.3 Articulating English consonants

We saw in Section 2.2.1 that consonant sounds are said to be voiced or voiceless, according to whether or not the vocal folds are vibrating. But how can we distinguish between sounds such as [s], [t] and [f]? These sounds are all voiceless, but they are still very different from each other. In order to distinguish between sounds that are similar in terms of voicing or voicelessness, we must consider other aspects of their articulation. The best way to begin to do this is to say certain words aloud whilst thinking carefully about what your articulators are doing, as in Illustration Box 2.2.

As you articulate these sounds, you should notice a number of things. First, when you articulate the sounds at the beginning of the words *bee*, *tea*, *key*, [b], [t] and [k] respectively, you should notice that you use both lips in the production of [b], but not for [t] or [k]. Second, although you use the tongue

---

ILLUSTRATION BOX 2.2

Articulating sounds

Say the words *bee, tea, key* aloud and repeat the sequence a number of times. As you say the words, think about how your articulators are moving in order to articulate the sounds at the beginning of each word. For example, are your lips involved in the articulation of all the sounds? Do you use your tongue? If so, is it the front of the tongue, or the back?

Say the words *tea, see* aloud and repeat the sequence a number of times. This time, as you say the first sound in each word, think about how much contact your tongue makes with the upper front region of your mouth. Is there a complete blockage between the tongue and the mouth? Or is there a small gap allowing air to escape?

---

for both [t] and [k], you should notice that it makes contact with a different region of the mouth for each sound: when you produce [t], the tip or blade of the tongue moves towards the alveolar ridge, while for [k] the back of the tongue moves towards the velum. Third, when you articulate the sounds at the beginning of the words *tea* and *see*, [t] and [s], you should notice that the front of the tongue moves to the same part of the mouth – the alveolar ridge – for both of these sounds. However, for [t] the tongue makes complete contact with this area, allowing no air to escape at first, but for [s] air can continually squeeze through a small gap, meaning complete contact has not been made.

There are two key differences here. The sounds [b], [t] and [k] are different because they are produced in different places in the mouth, with different articulators. In phonetics, we say they have a different **place of articulation**. The sounds [t] and [s] are different not in terms of where they are produced, but in terms of how they are articulated, that is, how the airflow is impeded during their production. This is called the **manner of articulation**. Every consonant sound, then, as well as being labelled either voiced or voiceless, also has a label for its place of articulation and manner of articulation. We explore place and manner in turn below.

2.3.1 Place of articulation

When we describe a consonant's place of articulation, we are most concerned with labelling the articulators that are used in its production. For each sound, the articulators involved can be divided into two categories: **active** articulators, which are mobile, and **passive** articulators, which are stationary. Passive articulators act as the target towards which the active articulators move. For example, when you say the word *alter* you will notice that for the articulation of [l] and [t], the tongue moves (and so is the active articulator) towards and makes contact with the alveolar ridge (the passive articulator). In fact, the tongue is the active articulator for most of the consonants of English. A consequence of this is that in most cases it is the passive articulator which

ILLUSTRATION BOX 2.3

[s] and [ʃ]

Produce an elongated [s] sound, followed by [ʃ], followed by [s], followed by [ʃ] and keep alternating these sounds for a few seconds. What do you feel? You should feel that the tongue moves back towards your hard palate for [ʃ], and moves forward again towards your alveolar ridge for [s]. Your tongue moves back for [ʃ] because it is moving to the post-alveolar region.

provides the label for a consonant's place of articulation. We will now examine the most common places of articulation for English consonants, and explore some other, more 'exotic' sounds later.

Sounds made with both lips, such as the [p] of *pop*, are called **bilabial** sounds. The bottom lip moves towards the upper teeth to produce **labiodental** sounds, such as the [f] of *fish*. Sometimes, bilabial sounds and labiodental sounds are grouped together into a single category, called **labials**. Sounds which are produced by having the tip or blade of the tongue near the teeth, such as the final sound in *bath*, [θ], are called **dental** or **interdental**. When the tongue tip or blade is at or near the alveolar ridge, the sounds produced are **alveolar**, such as the [t] in *top* and the [s] in *see*. Sounds produced with the tongue blade just behind the alveolar ridge, but not quite as far back as the hard palate, such as the first sound in *ship*, [ʃ], are called **post-alveolar** or **palato-alveolar** sounds, as in Illustration Box 2.3.

Sounds made with the front of the tongue at or near the hard palate are **palatal**, such as the first sound of *yes*, [j]. Moving further back, sounds produced when the back of the tongue approaches or makes contact with the velum, such as the [k] of *kiss*, are **velar**. Sounds can also be produced with the uvula, with a **uvular** place of articulation, although they are not very common in English. Sounds produced furthest back, just using the glottis with no other obstruction further forward, are **glottal** sounds, as in the [h] of *house*.

2.3.2 Manner of articulation

When we describe a consonant's manner of articulation, we are concerned with how much obstruction there is in the vocal tract. This obstruction is referred to as **stricture**, and can be of three types, as Ladefoged succinctly summarizes, '[t]he articulators may close off the oral tract for an instant or a relatively long period; they may narrow the space considerably; or they may simply modify the shape of the tract by approaching each other' (2001: 8). Put another way, there can be (i) a complete stricture, if there is a full blockage, or (ii) a partial stricture, if a sound is made with what is called **close approximation**, or (iii) not much stricture at all, if a sound is made with **open approximation**. We will take each one of these categories in turn below and, at the same time, make connections to the places of articulation introduced earlier in order to starting building up a full picture of English consonants.

If a sound is made with complete stricture, the air is completely blocked inside the vocal tract. A number of sounds in English are produced in this way. First, there are **plosives**, which are also called **stops**. Plosives take their name from the fact that the air trapped in the mouth during their production is abruptly and forcefully released, causing audible noise called **plosion**. All plosives are usually considered to have three stages: a **closure, hold** and **release**. In the closure phase, the articulators move together and create a blockage. Then, in the hold phase, the blockage is held to allow the pressure to build up, which is then released during the release phrase. The air can be stopped at the lips for a **bilabial plosive**, [p, b], at the alveolar ridge for an **alveolar plosive**, [t, d], or at the velum for a **velar plosive**, [k, g]. A **glottal plosive**, or **glottal stop**, [ʔ], is a plosive made with complete closure between

---

ADVANCES BOX 2.3

The patterning of plosives

We have just seen that there are seven frequent plosive sounds in most varieties of English [p t k b d g ʔ]. If we consider some words in which these sounds occur, certain differences will be apparent in terms of how they behave. First, consider the following data:

[pɪp] is the word *pip*
[pɪt] is the word *pit*
[pɪk] is the word *pick*
[pɪʔ] is the word *pit*

It should be clear that the glottal stop behaves differently from the other plosives. Changing the final sound from [t] to [p] or [k] changes the meaning of the word, but changing [t] to [ʔ] does not. The transcriptions [pɪt] and [pɪʔ], then, are two different ways of saying the same thing. This means that a glottal stop, in many varieties of English at least, is another way of pronouncing [t]. The technical way to state this is to say that /t/ has two **realizations**: [t] and [ʔ]. Notice that we have now used a different set of brackets, /.../. Slanted brackets denote **phonemes**, categories of sounds, which are explored further in Chapters 3 and 4. Next, consider the following data:

[tɑːt] (*tart*), [stɑːt] (*start*), [dɑːt] (*dart*), *[sdɑːt]
[pɛə] (*pair*), [spɛə] (*spare*), [bɛə] (*bear*), *[sbɛə]
[kuːl] (*cool*), [skuːl] (*school*), [guːl] (*ghoul*), *[sguːl]

Notice how the voiceless plosives, [p t k], can occur at the beginning of a word and can be preceded by [s]. Their voiced counterparts, [b, d, g], whilst they can occur word-initially, cannot be preceded by [s] (the convention in linguistics is to signal something is unacceptable by prefixing it with an asterisk). There is no word in English which starts with [s] followed by a voiced plosive. This is called a **phonotactic restriction**. The phonotactics of languages govern the order in which phonemes appear, see Chapter 4.

ADVANCES BOX 2.4

More manners

There are two other types of sound which are made with complete stricture but which are not very frequent in English. These are the **tap** and the **trill**. A tap (also called a **flap**) is quick ballistic constriction of the articulators. For an **alveolar tap**, for example, the tip of the tongue connects rapidly with the alveolar ridge. The symbol for the alveolar tap is [ɾ], and it is quite common in American English as a way of pronouncing /t/ and /d/ (e.g., *city* [sɪɾi] and *muddy* [mʌɾi]). The trill is a series of taps. For example, for an **alveolar trill**, [r], the tip of the tongue repeatedly taps against the alveolar ridge, creating what is sometimes called the 'rolled r'.

the vocal folds (the glottis). The glottal stop is always voiceless because the vocal folds are held firmly together and so are not able to vibrate while it is being made.

Other sounds produced with complete stricture are **affricates,** such as the sounds at the beginning and end of *church*, [tʃ], and *judge*, [dʒ]. Affricates are similar to plosives in that a complete blockage is created in the mouth, but in the release stage, instead of the air being released quickly, a slower period of friction is produced.

One other type of sound produced with complete oral closure is the **nasal**. For nasal sounds, such as initial and final sounds of *man*, [m] and [n], the velum is lowered to direct airflow into the nose.

Next we will consider sounds made with partial stricture, or close approximation. This means that although the articulators are quite close together, they do not form a complete blockage, instead the air escapes through a narrow gap. As it passes through this gap, it produces friction. For this reason, sounds made in this way are called **fricatives**. There are a number of fricatives in English. For example, a narrow constriction can be made between the lips and teeth, producing the **labiodental fricatives** in *leaf*, [f], and *leave,* [v], between tongue and the teeth, producing the **dental fricatives** in *three,* [θ], and *this,* [ð], or between the tongue and the alveolar ridge, producing the **alveolar fricatives** in *see,* [s], and *zoo,* [z]. If the constriction is made just behind the alveolar ridge, **post-alveolar fricatives** are produced, as in *wash* [ʃ] and *measure* [ʒ]. Finally, a constriction can be made by narrowing the glottis, producing the **glottal fricative** in *house*, [h].

Finally, we consider sounds which are made with open approximation, in which the articulators come together but no frication is produced because the space between them is too wide. These sounds are called **approximants**. There are four frequently occurring approximants in English: [ɹ] in *red*, [j] in *yes*, [w] in *wet* and [l] in *loud*. For [ɹ], the tongue bunches up towards the alveolar ridge, so [ɹ] is an **alveolar approximant**. For [j], the tongue bunches up further back towards the hard palate, so [j] is palatal. The articulation of [w] is slightly more complex than [ɹ] or [j], because [w] has what is called a

Table 2.1   *Common consonants in English*

IPA symbol	Example words	Description	Notes
p	*peace, shop, happy*	Voiceless bilabial plosive	
t	*tea, lot, better*	Voiceless alveolar plosive	
k	*case, back, school*	Voiceless velar plosive	Remember the sound [k] can be spelled with a <c> or a <k>
b	*bad, sob, baby*	Voiced bilabial plosive	
d	*door, bad, ladder*	Voiced alveolar plosive	
g	*goat, log, tiger*	Voiced velar plosive	
tʃ	*church, watch, chat*	Voiceless post-alveolar affricate	
dʒ	*judge, join, wedge*	Voiced post-alveolar affricate	
n	*neat, pen, pond*	Voiced alveolar nasal	Nasals are always voiced
m	*mat, hem, drummer*	Voiced bilabial nasal	Nasals are always voiced
ŋ	*thing, think, singer*	Voiced velar nasal	Nasals are always voiced
f	*free, laugh, photograph*	Voiceless labiodental fricative	
v	*vet, leave, heavy*	Voiced labiodental fricative	
θ	*three, healthy, month*	Voiceless dental fricative	Sometimes called **interdental**
ð	*this, that, brother*	Voiced dental fricative	Sometimes called **interdental**
s	*see, last, rice*	Voiceless alveolar fricative	
z	*zoo, rise, fizz*	Voiced alveolar fricative	
ʃ	*sheep, wash, machine*	Voiceless post-alveolar fricative	Sometimes called palato-alveolar fricatives
ʒ	*leisure, measure, vision*	Voiced post-alveolar fricative	Sometimes called palato-alveolar fricatives. In English, this sound never occurs at the beginning of a word.
h	*house, happy, ahead*	Voiceless glottal fricative	Many speakers 'drop their aitches' and, when they do, [h] should not be transcribed.
l	*leave, like, letter*	Voiced alveolar lateral approximant	
j	*yes, yellow, yacht*	Voiced palatal approximant	This sound also appears in words like *news, music* and *computer*.
ɹ	*red, trap, very*	Voiced alveolar approximant	
w	*well, word, newer,*	Voiced labial-velar approximant	
ʔ	*department, football, butter, cat*	Glottal stop	
ɾ	*city, letter*	Voiced alveolar tap	This sound is found in American Englishes, as a way of pronouncing /t/ and /d/.
r	*red, trap, very*	Voiced alveolar trill	This symbol denotes what is sometimes called the 'rolled <r>'. It is also the symbol for the **phoneme** /r/ (see Chapter 3)

double articulation. For [w], the back of the tongue moves up towards the velum and, at the same time, the lips move into a rounded position. For this reason, [w] is a **labial-velar approximant**. The final approximant, [l], is also produced at the alveolar ridge, but it is its particularly distinctive tongue shape which proves the label for its manner of articulation. For /l/, the tip of the tongue makes contact with the alveolar ridge, but the sides of the tongue bend downwards, allowing air to escape. Sounds with this tongue shape are called **lateral** sounds, so /l/ is a **lateral approximant**.

2.3.3   Putting the descriptions for consonants together

Now we can begin to combine the labels we have considered so far to produce detailed descriptions of English consonants. The usual practice is to begin by stating whether a consonant is voiced or voiceless, and then provide its place of articulation followed by its manner. So, for example, [p] is a voiceless bilabial plosive, and [z] is a voiced alveolar fricative. The most common consonants in English are presented in Table 2.1.

2.4   Describing English vowels

When we talk about English vowels from a phonetic perspective, we are not referring to the five vowel letters of English spelling, <a e i o u>. There are many more vowels in spoken English, such as the final sounds of *bee*, *bay*, *buy*, *bow* and *boy*. When we describe sounds like these, we cannot use the same terminology as we would use in the description of consonants. This is because whilst we can use the degree of stricture in the oral cavity to distinguish between particular consonants, all vowels are made with open approximation, so this criterion becomes redundant. Also, all vowels are voiced, so we cannot refer to the voicing distinction to distinguish between them either. In this section we will explore how vowel sounds are articulated, and how we can describe them.

2.4.1   The vowel space

Whilst consonants are described in terms of the articulators with which the tongue comes into contact, for vowels we are more concerned with the space between the articulators. This space, called the **vowel space**, shown in Figure 2.4, represents the entire space in which it is possible to articulate a vowel. If the tongue moves any further forward than the top left corner, it will begin to form a constriction with the top teeth. If it moves any further back, it will begin to make contact with the velum or pharynx. As soon as contact is made, the sound being produced stops being a vowel and becomes a consonant. The space itself is really an oval shape, but it is often stylized in phonetics into what is called a **quadrilateral** or **vowel trapezium.**

2.4.2   Describing vowels

The position of the tongue inside the vowel space determines the vowel sound that is made. Three criteria are important here: the tongue's vertical position

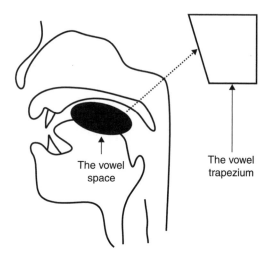

FIGURE 2.4   *The vowel space and the vowel trapezium*

ILLUSTRATION BOX 2.4

The tongue's vertical position

Produce the vowels [iː], [ɛ] and [a] in succession (the vowels of *seat, set* and *sat* respectively). Repeat the sequence a few times.

(how high or low it is), its horizontal position (how far forward or back it is), and whether it moves or not. Also important in vowel articulation is whether the lips are rounded or unrounded. We will explore these criteria in turn below. First, we will consider the vertical position of the tongue. Consider Illustration Box 2.4.

You should notice that during the articulation of [iː] the tongue is in a high position, near the alveolar ridge, but for [a] the bottom jaw lowers, so that the tongue is quite far away from the roof of the mouth. [ɛ] is somewhere in the middle. This shows that [iː] is a **high** vowel and [a] is a **low** vowel. Low vowels are also called **open** vowels, because of the open jaw and, conversely, high vowels are also called **close** vowels, because the tongue is close to the roof of the mouth. [ɛ] is a mid-vowel, but because it is closer to [a] than to [iː], it is called a **low-mid** (or **open-mid**) vowel. A mid-vowel closer to [iː] would be called **high-mid** (or **close-mid**). We will see examples of all of these vowels in Figure 2.5, but first, consider Illustration Box 2.5.

Notice here that during the articulation of [iː] the tongue is near the front of the mouth, but for the articulation of [uː] it is much further back. This shows that [iː] is a **front vowel** and [uː] is a **back vowel**. As another example, compare the front vowel [ɛ] (in *egg*) with the back vowel [ɔː] (in *or*). As with vowel height, there is an intermediate position for vowel frontness. Vowels

ILLUSTRATION BOX 2.5

The tongue's horizontal position

Produce the vowels [iː] and [uː] (the vowels in *seat* and *soup* respectively), but try not to move your lips. Repeat the sequence a few times.

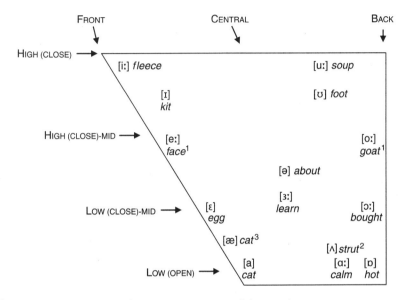

The vowel trapezium and some common English vowels   FIGURE 2.5

Notes: (1) The vowels [eː] and [oː] for *face* and *goat* respectively occur in many parts of the north of England, such as Lancashire and Yorkshire, but in the south of England these words have diphthongs. (2) The vowel [ʌ] is absent for most speakers in the north of England, who instead use [ʊ] in *strut*. (3) RP speakers could use [æ] for *cat*, but other speakers typically use [a].

can be front, back or **central**. The vowel sound in *learn*, [ɜː], for example, is a **central vowel**. The positions of vowels typically found in varieties of English English are shown in Figure 2.5 (see also Table 2.2 below for further illustration).

The vowels we have considered so far all have something in common – once the tongue has moved to the appropriate position in the vowel space, it stays there, without moving, for as long as the vowel is produced. Vowels in which the tongue does not move are called **monophthongs** (they are also called **steady-state vowels**, see e.g., Collins and Mees, 2003: 64). For some vowels, however, the tongue begins in one position and then moves to another. For example, in the word *eye*, which consists of only a vowel, the tongue begins quite low down in the vowel space (the mouth might be slightly open), but by the time the vowel ends, the tongue is closer to the roof of the mouth (and the mouth will be more closed). This vowel is transcribed with two IPA symbols, [aɪ], to highlight the fact that there are two parts to its articulation. Indeed, the symbols provide clues as to how the vowel is articulated – it begins with [a], a low front vowel, and ends in [ɪ], a high front vowel. Vowels in which the tongue moves, which are identifiable by having two symbols in transcription rather than one, are called **diphthongs**.

Next we will examine the role of the lips in vowel production. For any vowel, the lips can be rounded or unrounded. Compare, for example, the unrounded vowel [iː] in *sheep* with the rounded vowel [uː] in *soup*. A useful test for this is to consider whether it is possible to produce a given vowel whilst smiling. For example, it is entirely possible to spread your lips into an exaggerated smile and still articulate the vowel [iː], but it is much more difficult to say the vowel [uː] in this way.

The final criterion we will consider for describing the articulation of vowels is not related to the position of the tongue or lips, but to duration. Vowel duration is a relative measure, of course, and in order to make sense of it in English we need to consider the system of vowels as a whole. Monophthongs can be categorized into two types: **short vowels** and **long vowels**. Unsurprisingly, short vowels, such as [ɪ], are shorter in duration than long vowels, such as [iː], (long vowels are marked as long in transcription by being followed by the symbol [ː]), but there is also a functional difference between them. Monosyllabic words with short vowels must end in a consonant, but, if the vowel is long, no final consonant is necessary (e.g., [bɪt] *bit* and [biː] *bee* are perfectly acceptable words in English but *[bɪ] is not). Diphthongs pattern with the long monophthongs in this respect, allowing an optional final consonant (e.g., [baɪ] *buy* and [baɪt] *bite*).

2.4.3 Putting the descriptions for vowels together

Now we can begin to put all this information together and provide accurate descriptions of English vowels. The usual practice is to label duration (short or long) only when describing monophthongs, because diphthongs are always long. Then, for monophthongs, the label for vowel height is followed by vowel frontness, which is followed by lip shape. For example, [ɪ] would be described as a short, close (or high), front, unrounded vowel, and [ɔː] would be described as a long, open-mid (or low-mid), back, rounded vowel. The description of a diphthong should be in two parts. First, we describe the starting position of the tongue (represented by the first vowel in the pair), and then its ending position (represented by the second vowel in the pair). For example, we could say the [aɪ] vowel begins with an open, front, unrounded vowel and ends with a close, front, unrounded vowel. We conclude this section by listing the most common vowel sounds in English, in Table 2.2 (NB: descriptions for diphthongs are not provided, as they can be deduced from the properties of each vowel in the pair).

2.5 'Exotic' sounds in English

Throughout this chapter we have described sounds that can be found in a number of English accents. Of course, spoken English varies widely. In this

Common vowels in English   *Table 2.2*

IPA symbol	Example words	Description	Notes
ɪ	*kit, hip, lid*	Short high front unrounded	
ɛ	*dress, egg, hem*	Short low-mid front unrounded	
a	*trap, cat, bag*	Short low front unrounded	Sometimes this vowel is transcribed as [æ]. Speakers of older varieties of Received Pronunciation uses [æ], as do many speakers of American English, but [a] is much more common in the accents of England.
ɒ	*lot, hop, odd*	Short low back rounded	This vowel does not exist in American English.
ʌ	*strut, putt, bus*	Short low-mid back unrounded	This vowel is not usually used by people from the north of England.
ʊ	*foot, put, wolf*	Short high-mid back rounded	This vowel also appears in words like *strut, putt* and *bus* in speakers from the north of England.
ɑː	*calm, large, start*	Long low back unrounded	Speakers in the south of England, and people who speak RP, also have this vowel in words like *bath, dance* and *glass*. Speakers from the north of England, however, have the same vowel in *bath, dance* and *glass* as they have in *trap, cat* and *bag* (see above).
ɜː	*nurse, learn, worm*	Long mid central unrounded	
iː	*fleece, heal, eat*	Long high front unrounded	
uː	*soup, pool, news*	Long high back rounded	
ɔː	*thought, morgue, or*	Long low-mid back rounded	
aɪ	*price, like, sky*		
eɪ	*face, lake, play*		Speakers from the north of England may use a different vowel, [eː], in these words.
ɔɪ	*choice, boy, void*		
aʊ	*mouth, house, out*		Speakers from London may use a different vowel in these words, [aː], which is a longer version of the vowel of *trap* and *cat*.
əʊ	*goat, nose, beau*		Speakers from the north of England may use a different vowel, [oː], in these words.
ɪə	*near, here, beer*		
ɛə	*square, hair, bear*		Speakers from parts of the north of England may have the same vowel in these words as they have in *nurse, learn* and *worm*.
ʊə	*cure, tour, poor*		Many speakers have [ɔː] in these words, the same vowel as in *thought* or *morgue*.
ə	*about, letter, comma*		This vowel has a special name: **schwa**. It is a very frequent vowel of English, and occurs only in unstressed syllables.

final section, we will examine sounds which are less common in order to exemplify some of the symbols of IPA which we have not yet encountered.

2.5.1 Fricatives in Liverpool English

We saw in Section 2.3.1 that in most varieties of English there are no fricatives produced in-between the post-alveolar region (where [ʃ] is made) and the glottis (where [h] is made). In Liverpool, in the north-west of England, fricatives can be produced at the hard palate, [ç], at the velum, [x], and at the uvular, [χ]. In Liverpool English, these fricatives are all different ways of pronouncing syllable-final /k/. The palatal fricative is most likely to occur when /k/ is preceded by a high front vowel (such as *week* [wiːç], *like* [laɪç]), and the velar or uvular fricatives are likely when /k/ is preceded by a low or back vowel (e.g., *shark* [ʃɑːx], *dock* [dɒx]). This is because the fricative's place of articulation is influenced by the preceding vowel: a fricative produced further forward is likely when the vowel is front, but a retracted fricative is likely with a back vowel. For more information about Liverpool English fricatives, see Chapter 18 and Watson (2007)

2.5.2 Retroflex consonants in Indian Englishes

A **retroflex** place of articulation means the underside of the tongue makes contact with the alveolar ridge or palate. Whilst retroflex consonants are uncommon in British English, they are very common Indian Englishes, and are usually used where the alveolar consonants in English English would be. In transcription, all retroflex symbols have something in common: they each have a hook, pointing to the right. So, the alveolar plosive is [t], and the retroflex plosive is [ʈ].

2.5.3 The lateral fricative

We have already seen one lateral sound in English, the lateral approximant, [l]. In varieties of Welsh English, there is another: the voiceless lateral fricative [ɬ]. This sound occurs, for example, in place names beginning with <ll> such as *Llandudno* and *Llanelli*. To produce this sound, the tongue is in the same place as for [l], but instead of voicing and allowing the air to escape slowly, the air is pushed out forcefully, with no voicing, creating friction. For more examples see Collins and Mees (2003: 48–9).

2.5.4 The labiodental approximant

We considered two English labiodental sounds in Section 2.3.1, [f] and [v]. There is one more sound, which is less common: a labiodental approximant, [ʋ]. For this sound, like for [f] and [v], the bottom lip approaches the top teeth but, unlike for [f] and [v], never reaches close approximation and so never causes friction. The labiodental approximant is usually a realization of /r/ (e.g., *red* [ʋɛd], *mirror* [mɪʋə]) and is sometimes incorrectly considered to be a speech impediment. On the contrary, the labiodental approximant is a feature which has been found to be spreading amongst varieties of English in Britain (Foulkes and Docherty, 2000).

2.5.5 The long high front *rounded* vowel

In Section 2.4.2 we saw that it is common for front and open vowels to be unrounded, and back vowels to be rounded. In an increasing number of varieties of English, however, we find that the vowel in *goose* or *food* is pronounced as a front rounded vowel, [yː]. (A central rounded vowel, [ʉː], is also common.) Like the labiodental approximant as a realization of /r/, this is an innovation which is spreading amongst varieties of English (see e.g., Kerswill and Williams, 2005).

2.6 Advice for transcribing sounds using IPA

An important part of understanding phonetics is understanding phonetic transcription. Indeed, the IPA is crucial not just for phonetics but for many other areas of linguistics, too. It may not come easily at first but, as your confidence grows, the IPA will make more sense. Because every phonetician makes the same kinds of mistakes in transcription when they start out, this chapter concludes with some advice:

- **Don't be fooled by the spelling.** Just because a single sound is spelled with two letters (e.g., the /t/ and /d/ in *bottle* and *ladder*) does not mean it should have two IPA symbols. Remember, if there is one sound, there should only be one symbol.
- **Think carefully about rhymes.** Words that rhyme, or at least share some similarity, can provide clues about how you should transcribe them. If they sound the same in some way or another, they should have the same symbols. If they sound entirely different, they should have different symbols.
- **Do not use punctuation.** Punctuation such as exclamation marks and commas are features of orthography, not IPA transcription. Do not use punctuation in transcription. (You should not omit the 'length' mark, though, which looks a bit like a colon, [ː] – it might look like one, but it isn't.)
- **Don't forget to use brackets – but only one set.** Brackets are important for making clear exactly what sort of transcription you are producing. Phonetic transcription needs [...]. However, you only need one set of brackets per transcription. You do not need to have a pair of brackets for each word you transcribe.

Recommended readings

A good introduction to English phonetics (and phonology) is Carr (1999). More phonetic detail can be found in Ladefoged (2001) and, if you want to find out more about sounds in languages other than English, Ladefoged and Maddieson (1996). An excellent and very detailed tome, likely to be useful even as your experience with phonetics increases, is Laver (1994).

CHAPTER 3

Segmental Phonology

FRANCIS KATAMBA

3.1 What is phonology?

Building on the last chapter which introduced you to phonetics, the study of the articulation of speech sounds and of their physical properties, this chapter introduces you to **phonology**. Phonology is the study of the systems, patterns and functions of sounds in human language and English phonology is the study of the sound structure of English. The investigation of English phonology will start in this chapter and be continued in the next. In the present chapter we will focus on **segmental phonology**, that is, the study of individual vowel and consonant sounds. (Individual consonants and vowels are referred to as segments.) Segmental phonology is distinguished from **suprasegmental phonology** or **prosodic phonology** which is the subject of the next chapter. The latter treats properties such as stress and intonation which extend over more than a single consonant or vowel.

3.2 Phonemes and distinctiveness

Let us start by considering the notion of distinctiveness which has a pivotal role in phonology. Consider the words in (3.1):

[3.1]   [pɪn] pin   [bɪn] bin
           [peg] peg   [beg] beg
           [pʊʃ] push   [bʊʃ] bush

We can tell these words apart because those in the column on the left begin with [p] and those on the right begin with [b]. Sounds or **phones** that are used in this way to contrast word meaning in a particular language are called **phonemes**. So, /p/ and /b/ are distinct phonemes in English. (Recall from the last chapter the convention of putting phonemes between slashes / / and phonetic representations between square brackets [ ].)

Identifying phonemes: the minimal pair test

Phonemes are identified by applying the **minimal pair test**, which is a **substitution test**. The words in the rows in [3.1] are examples of **minimal pairs**. Words constitute a minimal pair if they are identical in all respects except one, that is, if substituting just one sound for another in the same position signals a difference in meaning, as is the case in [3.1]. Where there are three or more words that differ in meaning due to a difference in one sound, as in the case of [pen], [men], [den], we refer to those words as a **minimal set**. On the evidence of [pen], [men], [den], /p m d/ are separate phonemes.

Again using minimal pairs, we can establish that voiced and voiceless stops, affricates and fricatives are separate phonemes:

[3.2] a. **Voiceless stops**   **Voiced stops**

[peg]	peg	[beg]	beg
[tiːm]	team	[diːm]	deem
[kɒt]	cot	[gɒt]	got

    b. **Voiceless affricate**   **Voiced affricate**

[tʃɑː]	char	[dʒɑː]	jar

    c. **Voiceless stops**   **Voiceless stops**

[faɪl]	file	[vaɪl]	vile
[θaɪ]	thigh	[ðaɪ]	thy
[suː]	sue	[zuː]	zoo

The procedure can be continued to identify the remaining phonemes of English.

Major classes of sounds: obstruents and sonorants

All speech sounds can be classified as either **obstruents** or **sonorants**. Plosives, affricates and fricatives are obstruents. Obstruents are produced by getting the articulators to severely obstruct the air and disrupt its outward flow as it goes past the obstacles placed in its path. All other sounds, that is, vowels, glides, liquids and nasal consonants are sonorant (i.e., non-obstruent). The articulation of sonorants does not involve significant obstruction of the air as it flows out of the mouth. The nasals are non-obstruent because although the outgoing air is blocked in the mouth, it finds an alternative escape route through the nose and escapes virtually unimpeded.

Much of the behaviour of a sound in the phonology of a language is grounded in phonetics. Sounds sharing particular phonetic properties tend to display similar phonological behaviour. Thus, the distinction between obstruents and sonorants is important when it comes to considering the phonological distribution of voicing in English. Phonologically, all sonorants are voiced. There are no voiceless vowel, glide, nasal or liquid (i.e., [l] or r-like sounds) phonemes. But voicing is contrastive in obstruents. As seen above in [3.2], there is normally a voiceless obstruent phoneme that contrasts with its voiced counterparts, for example, voiceless and voiced plosives /p/ vs. /b/; voiceless and voiced fricatives, for example, /s/ vs. /z/; voiceless and voiced affricates, for example, /tʃ/ vs. /dʒ/.

Free variation

So, far the substitution test has reliably revealed phonemic contrasts. Look back at the examples in [3.1] and [3.2]. Minimal pairs have provided us with what appears to be a litmus test for determining if two sounds are separate phonemes. But the minimal pair test is not quite a litmus test. It fails us occasionally. This is the case where a word has two alternative pronunciations, for example, *either* [aɪðə] ~ [iːðə], *economic* [iːkənɒmɪk] ~ [ekənɒmɪk], *eclectic* [eklektɪk] ~ [ɪklektɪk]. (The symbol '~' means 'or', 'alternates with'.) Sounds are said to be in **free variation** if they normally contrast meaning and are therefore separate phonemes, but, very occasionally, they are used interchangeably without affecting meaning.

Now read aloud the words below and group together words which start with the same consonant sound. What does this tell you about the letter–sound correspondence in the standard orthography?

[3.3] Canada city kilt citizen khaki   cinnamon Chris   quay
      Charisma cattle quilt key   chemistry quick   Cyprus cool

The aim of this exercise is to focus on how words actually sound when we say them. The English spelling system is often quite inconsistent as was noted in the last chapter. On the one hand, the same phoneme can be represented in the orthography in a variety of ways, and on the other hand, different sounds may be represented by the same letter. Thus, the words *Canada, kilt, quilt, khaki, Chris, quay, charisma, cattle, key, chemistry, quick* and *cool* all start with the phoneme /k/ though their initial letters are any one of <c, k, kh, ch, qu>. The words *Cyprus, city, citizen* and *cinnamon* start with the letter <c> followed by <i> or < y> but in that case <c> stands for the phoneme /s/. Clearly, describing speech sounds in terms of the letters of the alphabet with which we spell them would be misleading.

A special transcription system is needed to represent phonemes more accurately. Such a transcription system uses the symbols of the International Phonetic Association (IPA), some of which were introduced in the last chapter, and is called **phonemic transcription** or **broad phonetic transcription**. Phonemic transcription overcomes the problem we have identified by always using the same symbol to represent the same phoneme. So, words in the *Canada* group all start with /k/ in phonemic transcription and words in the *Cyprus* group all start with /s/. A complete IPA chart is provided in the Appendix.

Allophones

Sounds that are phonetically different in some respects, but which are not used to contrast word meaning, are said to be **allophones** of the same phoneme if they are phonetic variants of each other, and if they are in **complementary distribution**. If sounds are in complementary distribution, each sound is restricted to certain contexts and cannot be substituted for the other. For instance, English has various types of alveolar voiceless plosives, including rounded [tʷ] which occurs when the phoneme /t/ precedes a rounded vowel as in *took* ([ʷ] indicates lip rounding) and its unrounded counterpart [t] that is found elsewhere (e.g., *take, tally, Tim*). It is impossible to replace [t] with [tʷ] in an English word. Hence there are no minimal pairs distinguished by substituting [t] with [tʷ]. So, [t] and [tʷ] are allophones (i.e., variants) of the phoneme /t/.

Assimilation

One reason for phonemes having allophones is **assimilation.** Assimilation is the phonetic accommodation of sounds to their neighbours. The motivation for this is ease of articulation, a factor of considerable importance especially in fast speech. What we have just observed is, indeed, a good example of assimilation. The roundedness of the vowel rubs off on the consonant which is also uttered with pursed lips. This particular type of assimilation is called labialization (see below).

Distinctive features

We have established that phonemes are the contrastive sounds of a language. But they aren't the smallest contrastive units. They can be decomposed into more basic elements called **distinctive features.** Each feature corresponds to an independent articulatory gesture, for example, [voice], [alveolar], [stop], etc. Occurring together, these features make up a phoneme. The convention is to put features in square brackets. The presence of a feature is indicated by a '+' and its absence by a '−'. Thus, phonological features are regarded as **binary** because when it comes to distinguishing words, it is always a simple two-way decision that has to be made. Is this particular feature present or absent? For instance, although phonetically there may be many degrees of voicing, for the language hearer it always comes down to a two-way decision. Was the word I heard, [sæt] or [sæd]? As you can see in Table 3.1, although phonemes may have much in common, it is what distinguishes them that matters with regard to their distinctive function.

A feature matrix is used to represent a phoneme, as seen in Table 3.2 which lists some of the features for [t, d, n].

Distinctive features as basic contrastive elements   Table 3.1

/t/	/d/	/m/
[t]	[d]	[m]
[+stop]	[+stop]	[+stop]
[+alveolar]	[+alveolar]	[+alveolar]
[−nasal]	[−nasal]	[+nasal]
[−voice]	[−voice]	[+voice]

Partial distinctive feature matrix   Table 3.2

	stop	alveolar	nasal	voice
[t]	+	+	+	−
[d]	+	+	−	+
[n]	+	+	+	+

Table 3.3   *Examples of natural classes*

Feature(s)	Natural class	Examples of members of natural class
[+voice]	Voiced sounds	[eɪ æ ɑː j ɹ g m z]
[+back]	Back sounds	[g k ŋ ɔ ɒ ʊ uː]
[+vowel, −round]	Unrounded vowels	[e ɑː ʌ iː]
[+vowel, +high]	High vowels	[iː ɪ ʊ uː]
[−voice, +stop]	Voiceless stops	[p t k ʔ]
[+consonant, +nasal]	Nasal consonants	[m n ŋ]
[+obstruent, −voice]	Voiceless obstruents	[p t k f θ s ʃ h tʃ]
[+vowel, +back, +round]	Back, rounded vowels	[ɔː ɒ ʊ uː]

Natural classes

In addition to their crucial role in marking contrastive differences, features are also important in accounting for phonological patterns through their role in characterizing **natural classes**. A natural class is a group of sounds that share one or more phonological features and which consequently display similar phonological behaviour. (Refer back to Chapter 2, Section 2.3 for the articulation of consonants.) Natural classes are introduced in a preliminary way here and will be revisited in more detail in Sections 3.3.1 and 3.3.2 when consonants and vowels are discussed respectively. Some natural classes are illustrated in Table 3.3.

Much of the allophonic variation that is encountered in any language is due to assimilation. It is helpful to examine assimilation in the context of natural classes. Frequently, a feature characterizing a set of sounds belonging to a given natural class spreads to a set of sounds belonging to a different natural class that are near it. This makes the task of articulating sounds easier.

Labialization

Let us survey briefly some common types of assimilation found in English. First, let us revisit **labialization** (lip rounding). As observed in Chapter 2, to produce an alveolar sound, for example, [t, d, n, s, z, l, ɹ][1] the primary articulation is alveolar. The blade of the tongue is the active articulator and the alveolar ridge is the passive articulator; the lips remain in neutral position. However, if an alveolar consonant is followed by a vowel belonging to the natural class [round] for example, [ɔː ɒ ʊ uː], the alveolar consonant is normally realized with a degree of lip-rounding marked by [ʷ]. Such supplementary lip-rounding is referred to as a 'secondary articulation'. Compare [3.4a] with [3.4b]:

[3.4] a. **Unrounded alveolar consonants precede an unrounded vowel**

teeth	[tiːθ]
tell	[tel]
tack	[tæk]

b. **Rounded alveolar consonants precede a rounded vowel**

tool	[tʷuːl]
toll	[tʷɒl]
talk	[tʷɔːl]

Labialization is not a peculiarity of alveolars. Whatever a consonant's primary articulation may be, it undergoes labialization before rounded vowels as seen in *pool* [pʷuːl], *poll* [pʷɒl], *call* [kʷɔːl], *cool* [kʷuːl], etc. The kind of detailed transcription exemplified above, which may use diacritics like [ʷ], is called 'narrow phonetic transcription'. It shows details of allophones and closely reflects pronunciation. It is different from broad transcription, which only shows those sounds that are phonemic and ignores non-contrastive details.

Palatalization

Palatalization is another type of secondary articulation. It involves accommodation to a neighbouring front vowel, especially a high front vowel like ([iː] or [ɪ]) or the palatal glide [j]. As such sounds are made by raising the tongue towards the hard palate, a consonant adjacent to them assimilates some of their palatal characteristics. Thus, the primary articulation of palatalized [p t k] is labial, alveolar and velar respectively, but each one of these consonants also has a secondary articulation in the form of a short [j] off-glide as seen in [3.5]. Palatalization is marked by the diacritic [ʲ]:

[3.5] pew   /pjuː/   [pʲjuː]
       student /stjuːdənt/   [stʲjuːdənt]
       cupola   /kjuːpələ/   [kʲjuːpələ]
       kit   /kɪt/   [kʲɪt]
       keen   /kiːn/   [kʲiːn]

The plain counterparts of palatalized consonants are found elsewhere when there is nothing to trigger palatalization for example, /kɑːpət/ [kɑːpət] 'carpet'; /kʌl/ [kʌl] 'cull', etc.

Velarization

Velarization marked by [~] going across a phonetic symbol is another type of secondary articulation found in English. Its production involves the raising of the back of the tongue towards the soft palate. The only velarized sound in English is the phoneme /l/. Velarized [ɫ] is also known as 'dark l' and non-velarized [l] is called 'clear l'. The two sounds are allophones of the same phoneme. Their distribution is as follows:

[3.6]	**Dark [ɫ] allophone follows vowel of the syllable**		**Clear [l] allophone precedes vowel of the syllable**	
	[mɪɫk]	milk	[liːk]	leek
	[heɫpɪŋ]	helping	[lʊk]	look
	[weɫθ]	wealth	[slæm]	slam
	[kɔːɫz]	calls	[dɪpliːt]	deplete
	[fuːɫ]	fool	[fuːlɪŋ]	fooling
	[æpɫ]	apple	[æplət]	applet
	[weɫbred]	well-bred	[mɪlɪpiːd]	millipede
	[seɫdəm]	seldom	[əsliːp]	asleep

The generalization can be stated thus, in Figure 3.1:

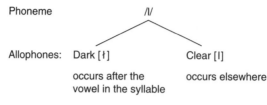

FIGURE 3.1   *Allophones of /l/*

3.3 The phonemes of English

In this section we will consider the phonological properties of vowels and consonants, focusing on Southern Standard British English (SSBE) (usually called RP) but always mindful of the fact that the English language is not monolithic (see Chapter 12, and also Chapters 2 and 18). As we saw in Chapter 2, different dialects and accents have somewhat different phoneme systems (see Gimson, 2001: 149–219, McMahon, 2001: 36–51). Frequently the same words will be transcribed using different IPA symbols in order to reflect differences in pronunciation among dialects. IPA symbols enable us to represent each dialect's actual sounds much more accurately than the standard orthography ever could. This makes the hassle of learning them worthwhile.

3.3.1 Consonant phonemes

Chapter 2 introduced a system for describing the phonetic properties of consonants. The consonant phonemes of SSBE are listed in Table 3.4.

To understand the phonological behaviour of consonant phonemes, it is best to approach the task in terms of natural classes. The first class we will consider is obstruents. As we noted earlier, a significant generalization can be made about obstruents with respect to voicing. Typically, only obstruents may be distinguished by voicing in English. Each voiceless obstruent normally has a voiced counterpart (see /p b, t d, k g, f v, θ ð, s z, ʃ ʒ, tʃ dʒ/). By contrast, all sonorant phonemes (nasals and approximants (i.e., liquids, glides) and vowels) are voiced.

What follows is a closer examination of English consonants based on the natural classes outlined above. Starting with various types of obstruent (plosives, affricates, fricatives), we will go on next to consider sonorants in turn (nasals and approximants (i.e., liquids and glides)). For ease of reference Table, 3.5 lists and exemplifies the consonant phonemes of SSBE.

Plosives

Many phonemes are realized by a variety of allophones in different contexts. We shall now consider the rules that predict the distribution of the allophones of English consonants, starting with the plosives (/p b, t d, k g/). But first, I will digress and explain what is meant by a rule. A 'rule' is a general statement expressing regular patterns observed in a language. The linguist's rules aren't prescriptions of how words and sounds should behave any more than the rules

English consonant phonemes in SSBE   *Table 3.4*

	Plosive (Stop)	Affricate	Fricative	Nasal	Approximant
Bilabial	p, b			m	w
Labiodental			f, v		
Dental			θ,ð		
Alveolar	t, d		s, z	n	l
Post alveolar					ɹ
Palato-alveolar		tʃ, dʒ	ʃ, ʒ		
Palatal					j
Velar	k, g			ŋ	w
Glottal			h		

Note: /w/ appears under both labials and velars because it is both labial (you round the lips to produce it) and velar (you also raise the back of the tongue, bringing it very close to the velum (soft palate).

Exemplification of English consonant phonemes   *Table 3.5*

Phoneme symbol	Word		More examples
/p/	/pæt/	pat	pet, upon, soup, spell
/b/	/bæt/	bat	Bede, abound, sublime, sob
/t/	/tɪl/	till	Tartar, stark, boot, attend
/d/	/dɪl/	dill	daughter, addenda, pride add
/k/	/kɪlt/	kilt	kilo, occult, cattle, sack, quake
/g/	/gɪltl/	guilt	ghoul, against, aggression, bag
/tʃ/	/tʃuː/	chew	child, chess, Thatcher, watch
/dʒ/	/dʒest/	jest	jar, gaol, beige, major, magic
/f/	/fiː/	fee	fish, Philadelphia, tough, stuff
/v/	/væn/	van	vague, sieve, oven, avalanche
/θ/	/θaɪ/	thigh	thermostat, both, think, through
/ð/	/ðaɪ/	thy	the, them, this, those, though
/s/	/set/	set	soon, perceive, city, pass
/z/	/zuː/	zoo	azalea, Wesley, cans, buzz
/ʃ/	/ʃuː/	shoe	sharp, chic, ocean, cash, Chicago
/ʒ/	/ʒ/	pleasure	azure, genre, gigolo, measure
/h/	/hen/	hen	hill, horn, hand, behind
/m/	/muːn/	moon	map, smile, simple, roam
/n/	/nuːn/	noon	now, knot, sign, annul
/ŋ/	/wɪŋ/	wing	bang, singing, single, longer
/l/	/lɪp/	lip	land, wilt, allow, bull
/ɹ/	/ɹɪp/	rip	ripe, rake, spray, bright
/j/	/jel/	yell	yet, yam, young, lawyer
/w/	/wel/	well	Wales, whales, bow, cow

Note: /w/ is labio-velar and not simply velar. It is produced by rounding the lips and simultaneously raising the back of the tongue towards the soft palate.

of physics are diktats ordering matter to behave in certain ways. The theory of gravity explains (among other things) why apples fall to the ground and don't whizz skyward when they get detached from apple trees. But Newtonian physics can't be blamed for gravity causing apples to fall to the ground. Likewise, the phonologist's rules do not make speakers behave the way they do. Thus the rule governing h-dropping, which yields *an ill* (from *a hill*), is not the cause of h-dropping. **Phonological rules** are general predictive statements of how speech sounds behave. Just as Newtonian physics attempts to explain why gravity affects all apples (not just those in farmer Nathaniel Cowperthwaite's orchard in Woodplumpton in Lancashire), phonological rules attempt to broadly predict the behaviour of various types of speech sound. The main task of the phonologist is to show what lies behind the big picture; it is not enough to list idiosyncratic attributes of this or that sound. With this in mind, the discussion that follows will show the pivotal role of phonetics and natural classes in predicting the patterning of phonemes. To begin with, we will consider plosives, focusing on the variation occurring during their release phases.

When a voiceless plosive occurs at the start of a syllable with primary (i.e., main) stress in a word, it is 'aspirated', that is, its release is accompanied by a puff of air that is released audibly before the onset of voicing of the next segment. **Aspiration** is indicated with [ʰ] following the consonant. Primary stress in marked by the diacritic ['] placed before the syllable with the only stress of a word:

[3.7] **Aspirated plosives**   **Unaspirated plosives**

pot	['pʰɒt]	span	['spæn]
tot	['tʰɒt]	Stanley	['stænli]
cot	['kʰɒt]	scan	['skæn]

However, a voiceless plosive that is in a stressed syllable but doesn't occupy the initial position of that syllable is unaspirated. That is the case when the plosive is preceded by [s] as in the examples in the right-hand column.

Being initial in a stressed syllable rather than being word-initial is what is crucial for triggering aspiration. If a word contains more than one voiceless plosive, only the plosive that is at the start of the syllable with primary stress (i.e., the most salient stress) is aspirated:

[3.8]
purport	[pə'pʰɔːt]
purpose	['pʰɜːpəs]
perpetuate	[pə'pʰetʃʊeɪt]
titanium	[tɪ'tʰeɪnɪəm]
cacophony	[kə'kʰɒfəni]
coquetry	['kʰɒkɪtri]

The actual amount of aspiration varies, with some dialects, for example, SSBE, displaying stronger aspiration than others, for instance, Lancashire and Scottish English.

Aspiration teaches us another valuable lesson. Differences that are allophonic in one language may be phonemic in another. Aspiration is not

Rule formalisms   *Table 3.6*

Rule writing formalisms

As a linguist, your task is not merely to provide long lists of patterns found in the language that you are investigating. Rather, your task is to posit general rules that identify the common thread that runs through the patterns that you observe. Some of these generalizations may be peculiar to one language and others may be applicable to many or even all languages. Rules are stated using the formalisms below and each rule is given a concise prose label.

a.   A → B/ X__ Y   Input A undergoes the change specified in B if it occurs in an environment where it is between X and Y.

b.   A → B/ Y__ X   Input A undergoes the change specified in B if it occurs in an environment where it is between Y and X.

c.   A → B/ X__   Input A undergoes the change specified in B if it occurs in an environment where it is preceded by X.

d.   A → B/ __Y   Input A undergoes the change specified in B if it occurs in an environment where it is followed by Y.

e.   A → B/ X __ $\begin{Bmatrix} Y \\ Z \end{Bmatrix}$ Input A undergoes the change specified in B if it occurs in an environment where it is preceded by X and followed by either Y or Z.

f.   A → αF/ __ $\begin{bmatrix} Y \\ αF \end{bmatrix}$ Input A acquires αF (i.e., the same features) that are present in Y if it precedes Y which has those αF (i.e., those same) features). In other words, copy or spread the specified features of Y on to A.

g.   A → B/ X __ C_0 Input A undergoes the change specified in B if it occurs in an environment where it is preceded by X and optionally followed by one consonant or none.

Notes:

→	is re-rewritten (or expanded) as
/	in the environment
_____	'focus bar' stipulates the location of the item affected by the rule
	Alternatives: one of the items between braces must be selected
σ	syllable
#	word boundary
+	morpheme boundary
$_σ[$ __	at the start of a syllable
__ $]_σ$	at the end of a syllable
$_#[$ __	at the start of a word
__ $]_#$	at the end of a word
C_0	one consonant or none
α	same
( )	element appearing in parenthesis is optional
{}	choose one of the items in curly brackets

contrastive in English but in Sotho, a language of South Africa, it is contrastive cf. [pula] *rain* vs. [pʰula] *vale*; [taba] *affair* vs. [tʰaba] *mountain*, etc. For a phonological property to be phonemic, what is crucial is not what it is physically like but how it is used in a particular language – or dialect, or accent.

English aspiration which is exemplified in [3.7] and [3.8] can be formally stated by the rule in [3.9]. The rule says that a voiceless plosive is aspirated if it occurs at the start of a syllable with a vowel receiving primary stress:

[3.9] **Aspiration**

$$\begin{bmatrix} +\text{consonant} \\ +\text{stop} \\ -\text{voice} \end{bmatrix} \rightarrow [+\text{aspirated}] \,/\, _\sigma[\underline{\quad} \begin{bmatrix} +\text{vowel} \\ +\text{stress} \end{bmatrix}$$

Apart from aspiration, there are other ways in which the air trapped in the mouth in producing a stop may be released. Release of the air may be through the nose. This is called **nasal release**. It occurs if the plosive is 'homorganic' with the following nasal. By homorganic is meant 'sharing the same place of articulation'. This can be seen with labial plosives and labial nasals, for example, [b m] as in *gibbon* [ɡɪbm̩], [p m] as in *open* [əʊpm̩]. **Lateral release** is also encountered. It occurs when the alveolar stops [t, d] are followed by the homorganic lateral (i.e., [l]). The plosives are released by lowering the sides of the tongue and allowing air to escape over the sides rather than the centre of the tongue as in *little* [lɪtɬ], *mantle* [mæntɬ], etc. Note in passing that nasal release, (cf. *open* [əʊpm̩]) and lateral release (cf. *mantle* [mæntɬ]) gives rise to syllabic consonants, indicated by the diacritic [ˌ] beneath a consonant if the nasal or lateral is in word-final position. Syllabic nasal and liquids are investigated further on p. 46 below.

Glottalization is another major feature of voiceless stop consonants in many varieties of British English – including 'RP – but not "refined" RP' (Gimson, 2001:159). It takes a variety of forms. First, there is the **pre-glottalization** of syllable-final voiceless stops and affricates which is shown in [3.10] (with the diacritic [ʔ] indicating glottalization). (Revisit Chapter 2, Section 2.3.2 to remind yourself of the articulation of glottal sounds.)

[3.10] /net/   [neʔt]   net
        /bæt/   [bæʔt]   bat
        /netbɔːl/   [neʔtbɔːl]   netball
        /bætmən/   [bæʔtmən]   batman
        /brestpleɪt/ [bresʔtpleɪt]   breastplate
        /læstdiːtʃ/   [læsʔtdiːtʃ]   last-ditch

In fact, the glottalization doesn't always come before the voiceless stop. Rather, it may overlap with it. For this reason many linguists prefer to label this phenomenon 'glottal reinforcement' and not pre-glottalization. Glottal reinforcement is captured by the rule in [3.11] which inserts a glottal stop before a syllable-final stop:

[3.11]   **Glottal reinforcement**

$$\varnothing \rightarrow \begin{bmatrix} +\text{consonant} \\ +\text{stop} \\ -\text{voice} \\ +\text{glottal} \end{bmatrix} / \underline{\hspace{1em}} \begin{bmatrix} +\text{consonant} \\ +\text{stop} \\ -\text{voice} \end{bmatrix}]_\sigma$$

Glottal replacement is also common. In many British English accents, but not in RP, the glottal stop replaces /t/ in certain environments. In [3.12a] the glottal stop is substituted for /t/ where /t/ is preceded by a stressed syllable and it is at the start of a syllable with an unstressed vowel. In [3.12b] the glottal stop is substituted for /t/ where /t/ is preceded by a stressed syllable and it is at the start of a syllable with a syllabic consonant nucleus:

[3.12]   a.   /ˈweɪtə/   [ˈweɪʔə]   waiter
              /ˈlɪtə/   [ˈlɪʔə]   litter
              /ˈmʌtən/   /ˈmʌʔən/   mutton
         b.   /ˈlɪtl̩/   [ˈlɪtl̩]   little
              /ˈmɪtən/   [ˈmɪʔn̩]   mitten

In a nutshell, /t/ is realized as [ʔ] at the start of an unstressed syllable preceded by a stressed syllable and followed by either an unstressed vowel or syllabic consonant (which is always unstressed):

[3.13]   **Glottal replacement**

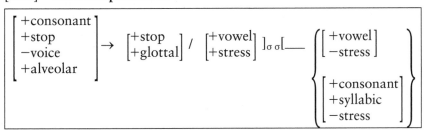

Many speakers also have a glottal replacement rule applying if /t/ is at the end of a syllable that is at the end of a word as in [3.14a] or inside a word, if it is syllable-final and followed by a consonant as in [3.14b]:

[3.14]   a.   **Glottal replacement of word-final and syllable-final /t/**
              /net/   [neʔ]   net
              /sɪt/   [sɪʔ]   sit
              /ɡreɪt/   [ɡreɪʔ]   great
         b.   **Glottal replacement of syllable-final /t/ followed by a con-**
              sonant within a word
              /netbɔːl/   [neʔbɔːl]   netball
              /bætmən/   [bæʔmən]   Batman

/brestpleɪt/	[bresʔpleɪt]	breastplate
/læstdɪːtʃ/	[læsʔdɪːtʃ]	last-ditch

Thus, in many accents of British English (but not RP) the words in [3.14] can be realized with a glottal stop replacing the syllable-final /t/. We see this happening in [3.14a] in word-final position (as in *net* [neʔ]) and in pre-consonantal position in [3.14b] (as in *batman* [bæʔtmən]). This is accounted for by the rule in [3.15]:

[3.15] **Glottal replacement of word-final and syllable-final /t/**

$$
\begin{bmatrix} +\text{consonant} \\ +\text{stop} \\ -\text{voice} \\ +\text{alveolar} \end{bmatrix} \rightarrow \begin{bmatrix} +\text{stop} \\ +\text{glottal} \end{bmatrix} / \underline{\quad} \left\{ \begin{matrix} \# \\ ]_\sigma \end{matrix} \right\}
$$

Replacement of other voiceless stops with a glottal stop is more unusual. It occurs, for example, in Cockney *cup of coffee* [ˈkʌʔə ˈkɒfi], *get back* [geʔ bæʔ] and *mucky* [ˈmʌʔi] where all the voiceless stops [p t k] are substituted for by [ʔ].

Affricates

English has only two affricate phonemes, namely /tʃ/ as in /tʃaɪnə/ *China* and /dʒ/ as in /dʒɔɪnə/ *joiner*. They are both palato-alveolar and are distinguished by voicing. Both affricates are allowed to occur word-initially as in the above examples; word-medially as in [etʃɪŋ] *etching*, [eɪdʒɪŋ] *ageing*; and word finally as in [bætʃ] *batch*, and [bædʒ] *badge*. However, in any syllable, an affricate occurring before the vowel of the syllable cannot be part of a consonant cluster. It must be immediately followed by the vowel. Thus, whereas [tʃʌg] *chug* and [dʒʌg] *jug* are permitted *[tʃmʌg] and *[dʒlʌg] are not.

Fricatives

Most varieties of English have the fricative consonant phonemes /f v, θ ð, s z, ʃ ʒ/ which come in pairs that are distinguished by voicing. In addition, they have a glottal fricative /h/ which has no voiced phoneme counterpart. But allophonically, a weakly voiced glottal fricative [ɦ] is used by some speakers when /h/ occurs in inter-vocalic position. This is quite common when it is at the start of a stressed syllable as in *behave* [bɪˈɦeɪv]. But the realization of /h/ with a degree of voicing is occasionally also found when an intervocalic /h/ is at the start of an unstressed syllable (cf. *rehab* [ˈɪːɦæb].)[2]

The non-glottal fricatives (i.e., /f v, θ ð, s z, ʃ ʒ/ can appear in initial medial and final position in a word. Many of them can also generally combine with other consonants to form clusters (e.g., [stem] *stem*, [flaɪ] *fly*, [θɹiː] *three*, [ʃɹɪŋk] *shrink*, etc.). However, unlike other fricatives /h/ is a rather marginal phoneme. It is marginal with respect to its distribution. It is only found in word-initial position as in *hen, house, hill, hate*, etc., and word-internally between vowels as in *perhaps, apprehend, behead*, etc. It is not allowed to cluster with any other consonant (*/hti:f/ *hteef*); nor can it appear word-finally (*/dreh/ *dreh*).

The phoneme /h/ is also marginal in the sense that its realization is not always assured. It is usually dropped from word-initial position in most non-standard varieties of English spoken in Britain (with the exception of Scotland). Due to h-dropping, in Cockney, Northern English, Welsh English, to name but a few British accents, /h/ is only pronounced in word-medial position between vowels (as in *behind, cahoots*, etc.). As a result, words like the following which are contrasted in Standard English *hat* vs. *at, heat* vs. *eat, hill* vs. *ill, hit* vs. *it, here* vs. *ear* sound exactly the same. They are pronounced as [æt], [iːt], [ɪɫ], [ɪt] and [ɪə] respectively. Because /h/-commencing words like *hat, hill* and *house* have no trace of an initial consonant in these dialects, the indefinite article is realized as *an* when it precedes them, for example, *an handle* [ən ændɫ], *an ill* [ən ɪɫ], *an house* [ən aʊs], etc. instead of Standard English *a handle* [ə hændɫ], *a hill* [ə hɪɫ], *a house* [ə haʊs]. H-dropping isn't a new phenomenon; it started 1000 years ago in Old English.

H-dropping tends to attract negative social evaluation and is often associated with being uneducated. However, it is in fact not confined to non-Standard English. All dialects, including the most conservative RP allow some h-dropping. First, when /h/ is at that start of an unstressed function word like a pronoun or an auxiliary verb, the norm is to drop the /h/ as in *They've not seen him in her house* [ðeɪv nət ˈsiːn ɪm ɪn ə ˈhaʊs]. In addition, there is a group of words (mainly nouns and adjectives that originally were borrowed from French which have an <h> in the spelling which is normally silent, for example, *historian, hotel*, and the like. These words are pronounced with an initial /h/ in present-day English by all speakers, except for a dwindling population of conservative older RP speakers who stay close to the original French pronunciation (see Gimson, 2001:192). One can speculate that because h-dropping is a shibboleth that plays an important role in identifying speakers as members of prestigious and non-prestigious social classes, strong social pressure to avoid h-dropping has resulted in near-universal pronunciation of word-initial orthographic <h> among speakers of Standard English. In fact, recent research has shown that h-dropping is rapidly disappearing even among working-class speakers in the London area (Kerswill, Torgersen and Fox, 2008).

Let us now turn to the dental fricatives /θ/ and /ð/. These require special mention for two reasons. First, they are not realized as [θ] and [ð] in words like *teeth* /tiːθ/ and *bothered* /bɒðəd/ in several accents and dialects including African American Vernacular English, Cockney and Estuary English. The dental fricatives are fronted and are pronounced [f] and [v] respectively. Thus *teeth* comes out as [tiːf] and *bothered* as [bɒvəd] (*Am I bovvered* as in the BBC Comedy *The Catherine Tate Show*) (see p. 284).

Nasals

English has three nasal consonant phonemes, namely /m n ŋ/. They differ in their distribution. Whereas /m n/ occur in any syllable position, /ŋ/ is only encountered in the tail of the syllable, following a vowel as in [sɪŋ] *sing* and [sɪŋ.ɪŋ] *singing*; [lɒŋ] *long* [lɒŋ] and [lɒŋ.gest] *longest* (the dot marks a syllable boundary). In earlier English, [ŋ] was pronounced as [ŋg]. The [ŋg] cluster arose from /ng/ when the alveolar nasal assimilated the velar place of articulation of the following /g/. Subsequently, /g/ was dropped. This resulted in [ŋ] becoming phonemic /ŋ/. There were now minimal pairs like *sun* /sʌn/ vs. *sung* /sʌŋ/. The earlier pronunciation of [ŋg] still survives in the dialects of south Lancashire, Cheshire, Staffordshire and parts of Derbyshire where *singing* and *bringing* are pronounced as [sɪŋg.ɪŋg] and [bɹɪŋg.ɪŋg].

In addition, the velar nasals are subject to a constraint affecting the vowels that can precede them. Unlike other nasals, /ŋ/ is only licensed to appear after short vowels (cf. [lɒŋ] *long*, [bæŋ] *bang* and [lʌŋ] *lung*). Putative words with a long vowel or a diphthong preceding /ŋ/, for example, *[lɔːŋ]; *[siːŋ], *[pæɪŋ], etc. are prohibited.

Nasals are very prone to the assimilation of the place of articulation of a following consonant. Observe, for example, the articulation of the final nasal of the prefix *con–* in [3.16]. As you will see, this nasal always takes its cue for place of articulation from the first consonant of the stem:

[3.16] **Homorganic nasal assimilation: the case of /kən/ con–**

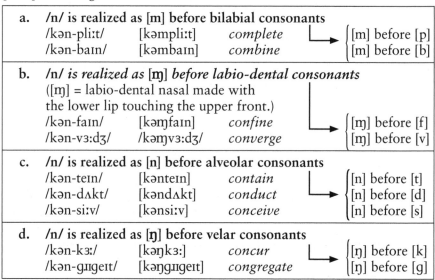

a.	**/n/ is realized as [m] before bilabial consonants**
	/kən-pliːt/ [kəmpliːt] *complete* → [m] before [p]
	/kən-baɪn/ [kəmbaɪn] *combine* → [m] before [b]
b.	**/n/ is realized as [ɱ] before labio-dental consonants**
	([ɱ] = labio-dental nasal made with the lower lip touching the upper front.)
	/kən-faɪn/ [kəɱfaɪn] *confine* → [ɱ] before [f]
	/kən-vɜːdʒ/ /kəɱvɜːdʒ/ *converge* → [ɱ] before [v]
c.	**/n/ is realized as [n] before alveolar consonants**
	/kən-teɪn/ [kənteɪn] *contain* → [n] before [t]
	/kən-dʌkt/ [kəndʌkt] *conduct* → [n] before [d]
	/kən-siːv/ [kənsiːv] *conceive* → [n] before [s]
d.	**/n/ is realized as [ŋ] before velar consonants**
	/kən-kɜː/ [kəŋkɜː] *concur* → [ŋ] before [k]
	/kən-gɹɪgeɪt/ [kəŋgɹɪgeɪt] *congregate* → [ŋ] before [g]

The patterns in [3.16] are captured by the rule in [3.17] which states that the nasal has the same place of articulation (i.e., [αplace]) as the consonant that follows it:

[3.17] **Homorganic nasal assimilation**

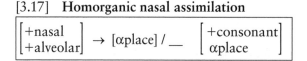

$$\begin{bmatrix} +\text{nasal} \\ +\text{alveolar} \end{bmatrix} \rightarrow [\alpha\text{place}] / \_\_ \begin{bmatrix} +\text{consonant} \\ \alpha\text{place} \end{bmatrix}$$

This rule also applies word-internally where there is no prefix for example, [mp] in *simple*, [nd] *candle*, [ŋg] *single*, etc.

Assimilation is characterized in terms of directionality. If the sound that triggers the assimilation follows the sound that undergoes modification, as in the case of homorganic nasal assimilation, the process is called **regressive assimilation**. If, conversely, the trigger comes before the sound that is modified we call this **progressive assimilation**. This is exemplified by the approximant devoicing rule described below.

Approximants

The natural class of approximants contains the glides /w j/ and the liquids /ɹ l/. Approximants are allowed to occur in various positions in syllables and words and they are also allowed to cluster with stops, for example, *play*, *swell*, *cute*, *drink*, etc. But the freedom of combination that they enjoy is not absolute. The clustering of labial obstruents with the labio-velar approximant /w/ is prohibited. Hence the putative words **fwen *pwine *mwilk*, etc. are disallowed.

When they cluster with a preceding voiceless obstruent, approximants undergo partial or even total devoicing. The **devoicing** is most noticeable if the obstruent-approximant cluster is in onset position in a stressed syllable. Devoicing is indicated by [̥]:

[3.18] **Approximant devoicing**

[twɪn]	twin	[twenti]	twenty
[tɹiː]	tree	[tɹaɪp]	tripe
[θɹet]	threat	[fjuːz]	fuse
[pjuːɹɪtən]	puritan	[pjuːk]	puke
[sliːp]	sleep	[slæb]	slab
[pleɪs]]	place	[pliːz]	please

Approximant devoicing is an example of progressive assimilation as the trigger precedes the sound that is modified. The rule is formalized in [3.19]:

[3.19] **Approximant devoicing**

$$[+\text{approximant}] \rightarrow [-\text{voice}] / \begin{bmatrix} +\text{obstruent} \\ -\text{voice} \end{bmatrix} \underline{\quad}$$

The approximant devoicing rule predicts where voiceless allophones of approximants occur. But it would be wrong to assume that voicelessness among all approximants is always predictable and hence allophonic. In some Scottish, Irish, American and New Zealand accents the voiced labio-velar approximant /w/ is a separate phoneme from its voiceless counterpart /ʍ/ (also written as /hw/). In the dialects of England this opposition has been lost and consequently, *which* and *witch* are both pronounced as /wɪtʃ/; *whales* and *Wales* are both pronounced as /weɪlz/, etc. Accents mentioned above that have a phonemic contrast between voiceless /ʍ/ with voiced /w/ have minimal pairs such as *which* /ʍɪtʃ/ (/whɪtʃ/) from *witch* /wɪtʃ/ and *whales* /ʍeɪlz/ (/wheɪlz /) vs. /weɪlz/.

Syllabic nasal and liquid consonants

Typically, a syllable contains a vowel, which serves as its nucleus. But occasionally we encounter syllables that contain no vowel and which use a syllabic nasal or a syllabic liquid consonant as their nucleus. When a consonant is syllabic it is longer and is more salient than normal. (Recall the diacritic [ˌ] below a consonant indicates that a consonant, is syllabic.) A nasal is syllabic if it occurs word-finally and follows another consonant. Examples of syllabic nasal consonants include labials, for example, *gibbon* [gɪbm̩], *open* [əʊpm̩]; alveolars, *sudden* [sʌdn̩], *smitten* [smɪtn̩] and velars for example, *token* [təʊkŋ̩], *bacon* [beɪkŋ̩]. There is some variation. Some speakers, instead of using a syllabic nasal, have a schwa followed by a nasal consonant, for example, [əʊpən], [sʌdən], etc.

Liquid consonants can also be syllabic, in which case they are also longer than normal. The lateral liquid is generally realized as a syllabic [ɫ̩] when it occurs in word-final position following a consonant, for example, *little* [lɪtɫ̩], *mantle* [mæntɫ̩], *settle* [setɫ̩] and *peddle* [pedɫ̩]. Syllabic [ɹ̩] may also be attested in some peoples' pronunciation of words like *dinner* [dɪnɹ̩] (or [dɪnɚ]) and *sender* [sendɹ̩] (or [sendɚ]) in those accents of English that are described as **rhotic**. They include Scottish English, East Lancashire, West Country (spoken in south-west England) and General American English (GA). GA is widely regarded as the standard variety of American spoken English. It is the accent of well-educated speakers from the mid-west and west of the United States. To say that an accent is rhotic simply means that postvocalic-r is pronounced in words like [fɑ˞ː] *far* and *farm* [fɑ˞ːm] – and may cause **rhotacization** (i.e., r-colouring) of a preceding vowel. (Rhotacization is indicated by [˞].) In non-rhotic varieties, post-vocalic-r is dropped, leaving no trace. However, in rhotic dialects, if [ɹ] occurs in word-final position, following a consonant, it is syllabic (cf. *baker* [beɪkɹ̩] and *temper* [tempɹ̩]). But in non-rhotic dialects [ɹ̩] is vocalized in this context, that is, it becomes a vowel and is pronounced as schwa (e.g., *baker* [beɪkə] and *temper* [tempə]. The differences between rhotic and non-rhotic accents are very important in English phonology. It is one of the key distinguishers of English dialects. We will return to this topic for more detailed discussion below.

Vocalization of a liquid is not limited to [ɹ]. The lateral liquid /l/ may also be vocalized. Recall that /l/ is subject to a velarization as we saw in Figure 3.1 above. The velarization rule is presented in [3.20]:

[3.20]   **/l/ velarization rule (yielding 'dark l'**

> [+lateral] → [+velar] / [+vowel] ___ C_0]$_\sigma$
> Note: C_0 = one consonant or none

In precisely those contexts where the velarization rule applies, in Cockney the dark [ɫ] undergoes 'vocalization' (becomes a vowel) to give [mɪʊk] *milk*, [seʊ] *sell*, etc.

Rhotics

The term 'rhotic' refers to r-like sounds. English has a phoneme (/ɹ/) that is normally spelled using <r>. This phoneme displays considerable variation in

English rhotic consonants   *Table 3.7*

Realization of /ɹ/		Examples
[ɹ]	**Alveolar/post-alveolar approximant** In its production the tongue blade approaches the alveolar ridge (extending slightly beyond it in some cases) while at the same time ensuring that a sufficiently large gap is left between the articulators to allow the air to escape quietly, without audible turbulence.	In most varieties of English spoken in England	*red* [ɹed]
[r]	**Alveolar/post-alveolar trill** It is made by the tongue blade hitting the alveolar ridge repeatedly.	In some traditional Scottish dialects	*red* [red]
[ɾ]	**Alveolar tap** The tongue blade hits the alveolar ridge once (the resulting sound is like a very short [d]).	In Newcastle, Liverpool and sometimes in 'refined RP' between vowels when followed by a non-stressed vowel	*very sorry* [veɾi sɒɾi]; a Liverpudlian shouting *shurrup!* [ʃʊɾəp] *'shut up'*
[ɻ]	**Retroflex approximant** The tip of the tongue is pulled back so that it approaches the rear of the teeth ridge, while at the same time ensuring that a sufficiently large gap is left between the articulators to allow the air to escape without audible turbulence.	In many American and Canadian and English West Country accents	*red* [ɻed]

its realization (see p. 284). To reflect this, different IPA symbols are used to represent <r> in different accents. See Table 3.7.

In North America and some other parts of the English speaking world the voiced tap [ɾ] is used to represent both /t/ and /d/ in these contexts:

[3.21] **North American tap**

a. /t/ or /d/ occurs between a stressed vowel and an unstressed vowel. latter ['læɾɚ] ladder ['læɾɚ]	b. when /t/ is preceded by a stressed vowel followed by a sonorant (i.e., a nasal or liquid) and when /t/ is itself is in turn followed by an unstressed vowel. centre ['seɾ̃ɚ] party ['pæ˞ɾi]

Notes:
(i) [ɚ] stands for schwa with r-colouring.
(ii) In *centre* the nasal assimilates to the following and causes its nasalization; in *party* the 'r' is assimilates to the preceding vowel and leaves a trace of r-colouring on it.

FIGURE 3.2   *Phonemic overlapping: neutralization*

This is a classic case of neutralization of a phonemic contrast. Though /t/ and /d/ are separate phonemes they 'overlap' in ['læɾɚ] which may represent either *latter* or *ladder,* depending on the wider context. The same sound [ɾ] can represent either phoneme /t/ or phoneme /d/. In other words, the opposition between /t/ and /d/ is suspended, neutralized.

We will return to rhotics presently when we investigate the vowel system because they play a very important role in the patterning of vowels.

3.3.2   The vowel phonemes

The articulation of vowels was presented in Chapter 2, Section 2.4. In this section we will explore the very rich vowel system of the English language, focusing on how they are deployed in words. The discussion will focus primarily on SSBE (Standard Southern British English) and will also include, but not be restricted to, vowels in GA (General American) and NE (Northern English, spoken in the north of England). We will explore simple vowels (monophthongs), which may be long or short vowels, as well as complex vowels (diphthongs). The vowel phonemes of various accents as well as the behaviour of vowels in a number of important phonological processes will be investigated. Often the vowels in the same word sound different from one accent or dialect to the next, for example, *bus* is [bʊs] in NE but [bʌs] in SSBE and GA. Transcriptions using appropriate IPA symbols capture these differences; the standard orthography masks them.

A good starting point is to classify vowels in terms of their complexity. The simplest vowels are the monophthongs (i.e., pure vowels). They have almost the same vowel quality from start to finish. But they may differ in duration. Some are short and others are long. There is great deal of variation in the vowel system of English (see Giegerich, 1992: 43–88; Gimson, 2001: 91–148; McMahon, 2001: 79–91). For illustrative examples, the vowel system of SSBE is given in Figure 3.3 and those of NE and GA are given in Figures 3.5 and 3.6.

SSBE also has the following diphthongs:

[3.22]   /eɪ, aɪ, əɪ, aʊ, əʊ, ɪə, eə, ɔə, ʊə/

Diphthongs are classified on the basis of their second element. Those diphthongs whose second element is a high vowel [ɪ] or [ʊ] are called closing diphthongs; those diphthongs that end in [ə] are called centring diphthongs. Consider Figure 3.4.

Conservative RP speakers have all these diphthongs but the language is changing and in the speech most speakers of British English today, the

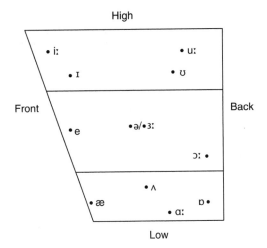

High

Front   Back

Low

The monophthongs of SSBE   *FIGURE 3.3*

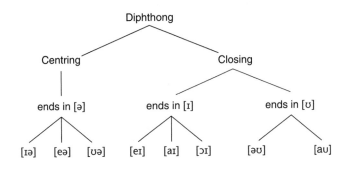

SSBE diphthongs   *FIGURE 3.4*

centering diphthongs /ɔə/ as in *pour* /pɔə/ and /ʊə/ as in *poor* /pʊə/ have merged with /ɔː/. As a result these words rhyme with *paw* /pɔː/. The /eə/ diphthong has also been simplified and is realized as /ɛː/ in words like *air* /ɛː/ and *pair* /pɛː/. This change is called monophthongization.

The inventory of SSBE vowel phonemes, with key words illustrating each vowel phoneme is given in Table 3.8.

The [ə] of centring diphthongs arose from the vocalization of post-vocalic [ɪ] which yielded schwa in words like *near* and *here* in some accents, for example, SSBE and most other dialects found in England, hence the presence of <r> in the spelling. Rhotic dialects such as Scottish English and General American English that retained post-vocalic-r did not develop these centring diphthongs.

Let us briefly consider the vowels of Northern English. Northern English (NE) has the monophthongs listed in Figure 3.5.

Northern English also has the following diphthongs:

[3.23]   /eɪ, aɪ, əɪ, aʊ, əʊ, ɪə, eə, ɔə, ʊə/

Table 3.8   SSBE vowels

Short vowels			Long vowels			Diphthongs		
/ɪ/	/wɪti/	witty	/iː/	/siːn/	seen	/eɪ/	/keɪk/	cake
/e/	/wet/	wet	/uː/	/suːn/	soon	/aɪ/	/kaɪt/	kite
/æ/	/mæt/	mat	/ɑː/	/bɑːd/	bard	/ɔɪ/	/tɔɪl/	toil
/ɒ/	/lɒt/	lot	/ɜː/	/wɜːk/	work	/əʊ/	/təʊ/	toe
/ʊ/	/pʊl/	pull	/ɔː/	/wɔː/	war	/aʊ/	/haʊs/	house
/ʌ/	/nʌt/	nut				/ɪə/	/fɪə/	fear
/ə/	/miːtə/	me*ter*				/eə/	/keə/	care
						/ʊə/	/pʊə/	poor
						/ɔə/	/ʃɔə/	shore

Note: /ɪ/ has allophone [i] in word-final position in many contemporary varieties of English so that /wɪtɪ/ is realized as [wɪti]; Conservative RP has [ɪ] in in word-final position.

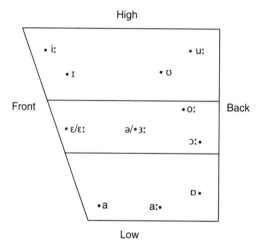

FIGURE 3.5   *The monophthongs of NE*

The inventory of NE vowel phonemes, with illustrative examples, is given in Table 3.9.

Compare Table 3.9 with Table 3.8. You will observe that Northern English has a vowel system that is significantly different from that of SSBE. The first key thing to note is the absence of /ʌ/, normally, where SSBE (and other accents) have this sound NE uses /ʊ/ – or /ə/ in the case of some NE speakers whose accent is relatively close to RP. Furthermore, the list of diphthongs is reduced but the list of long vowels is expanded. Instead of /eɪ/, /əʊ/ and /eə/, NE usually has /eː/, /oː/ and /ɛː/.

There are also realizational and distributional differences between SSBE and NE with respect to the phonemes /æ/ and /ɑː/ (/aː/). In SSBE the vowel /ɑː/ (as in *bard* /bɑːd/ and *card* /kɑːd/ is realized as a very low, very back vowel, but in NE a more central low vowel /aː/ is used (you hear /baːd/ [baːd] (for SSBE /bɑːd/ *bard*) and /kaːd/ [kaːd] (for SSBE /kɑːd/ *card*) in Yorkshire and

The vowels of Northern English (NE)   *Table 3.9*

Short vowels			Long vowels			Diphthongs		
/ɪ/	/wɪt/	*wit*	/iː/	/siːn/	*seen*	/eː/	/keːk/	*cake*
/ɛ/	/wɛt/	*wet*	/uː/	/suːn/	*soon*	/aɪ/	/kaɪt/	*kite*
/a/	/mat/	*mat*	/aː/	/baːd/	*bard*	/ɔɪ/	/tɔɪl/	*toil*
/ɒ/	/lɒt/	*lot*	/ɜː/	/wɜːk/	*work*	/oː/	/toː/	*toe*
/ʊ/	/bʊs/	*bus*	/ɔː/	/wɔː/	*war*	/aʊ/	/haʊs/	*house*
/ə/	/miːtə/	*met<u>er</u>*				/ɪə/	/fɪə/	*fear*
						/ɛː/	/kɛː/	*care*
						/ʊə/	/pʊə/	*poor*
						/ɔə/	/ʃɔə/	*shore*

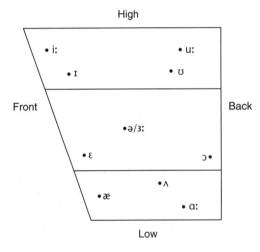

The monophthongs of GA   *FIGURE 3.6*

Lancashire. The SSBE vowel /æ/ as in *bad* is realized with a lower front vowel (/bad/) in Northern English. Also, many lexical items with long /ɑː/ followed by a fricative (and occasionally a nasal) which are pronounced with a long very low back vowel in SSBE (cf. SSBE *laugh* /lɑːf/, *path* /pɑːθ/, *dance* /dɑːns/) are rendered with a short, low front /a/ in NE (cf. *laugh* /laf/, *path* /paθ/, *dance* /dans/). In fact, not only does NE have a short vowel where SSBE has a long vowel in this instance, it does also have a very short [a] , especially where [a] is followed by a voiceless plosive as in *cat* [kat]. This is one of the hallmarks of the Northern English accent (see also Chapter 18, Section 18.4.2).

Let us now turn to General American English. GA has the monophthongs listed in Figure 3.6.

The inventory of GA vowel phonemes, with illustrative examples, is given in Table 3.10.

As we noted earlier when we discussed rhotic (r-like) consonants, rhotacization, that is, r-colouring of vowels, is a major distinguishing feature of several dialects of English, including American English, Scottish English and

Table 3.10   The vowels of General American English (GA)

Short vowels			Long vowels			Diphthongs		
/ɪ/	/wɪt/	wit	/iː/	/siːn/	seen	/eɪ/	/keɪk/	cake
/ɛ/	/wɛt/	wet	/uː/	/suːp/	soup	/aɪ/	/kaɪt/	kite
/æ/	/mæt/	mat	/ɑː/	/dɑːg/	dog	/ɔɪ/	/kɔɪl/	coil
/ʊ/	/pʊl/	pull	/ɔː/	/wɔː/	war	/oʊ/	/toʊ/	toe
/ʌ/	/nʌt/	nut				/aʊ/	/haʊs/	house
/ə/	/əgeɪn/	again						

Table 3.11   The vowels of GA

[ɑ˞ː]	[bɑ˞ːd]	bard
[ɝː]	[wɝːk]	work
[ɚ]	[miːɾɚ]	meter
[ɪ˞]	[fɪ˞]	fear
[ɛ˞]	[kɛ˞]	care
[ɔ˞]	[pɔ˞]	poor, shore

West Country English. All rhotic dialects have rhotacized vowels. The rhotacized vowels of GA are listed and exemplified in Table 3.11. (Recall that [˞] marks rhotacization.)

An obvious difference between GA and other dialects is the absence of a contrast between [ɑː] as in *card* and [ɒ] as in *cod*. Both are pronounced [kɑːd]. But an even more prominent and pervasive difference among varieties of English is whether they are rhotic or not. Rhotic dialects such as GA and Scottish English retain [r] or [ɹ] (or a residue of it) when this sound occurs in the tail of the syllable immediately preceded by a vowel, as we have already noted. In traditional Scottish accents, words like *fear* and *care* are pronounced as [fɪɹ] and [keɹ], with a clearly sounded [ɹ]. In GA the situation is more complex. The [ɹ] is much reduced; but some remnant of it left behind which causes the r-colouring of the preceding vowel which can be heard in the pronunciation of *fear* [fɪ˞] and *care* [ke˞], etc. By contrast, in non-rhotic accents such as Australian, New Zealand and most English accents of England, the [ɹ] is vocalized and becomes a schwa, leaving no trace. The result is a centring diphthong for example, *fear* [fɪə] and *care* [keə]. Clearly, the loss of post-vocalic-r has had a big impact on the vowel system of English. It is the source of the four centring diphthongs /ɪə, eə, ʊə, ɔə/ found in non-rhotic accents like SSBE (see Table 3.9). In West Country and American English the retention of a residual [ɹ] produces the large number of rhotacized vowels found in these dialects (see Table 3.11). Conservative Scottish English, which faithfully keeps the original [ɹ], has a relatively simple vowel system.

English vowels and phonological rules

Let us now consider more closely some of the constraints on the behaviour of vowels in English phonology. This task is best approached in terms of natural classes. The vowels fall into two broad natural classes. One class contains short vowels and the other long vowels and diphthongs (see Table 3.9).

Distribution of long and short vowels

There are some interesting restrictions on where vowels may occur which are based on length differences. First, observe that only short vowels precede the velar nasal [ŋ] as seen in [3.24]; long vowels and diphthongs are excluded from that position as [3.24b] shows:

[3.24] a. wing   bang   long   strength   hung
            [wɪŋ]   [bæŋ]   [lɒŋ]   [streŋkθ]   [hʌŋ]

        b. *weeng   *barng   *laung   *stayngth   *herng
            [wiːŋ]   [baːŋ]   [lɔːŋ]   [streɪŋkθ]   [hɜːŋ]

Rule [3.25] predicts this:

[3.25] **Vowels must be short before [ŋ]**

$$[\text{+vowel}] \rightarrow [\text{--long}] \ / \_\_ \begin{bmatrix} \text{+nasal} \\ \text{+velar} \end{bmatrix}$$

Long vowels have their privileges too. It is only long vowels and diphthongs that can occur in monosyllabic content words (i.e., nouns, adjectives, verbs and adverbs) with open syllables (i.e., ending in a vowel) as seen in [3.26a]:

[3.26] a. see   bar   law   stray   shoe
            [siː]   [baː]   [lɔː]   [stɹeɪ]   [ʃuː]
        b. *si   *ba   *lo   *stre   *pu   *pu
            [sɪ]   [bæ]   [lɒ]   [stre]   [pʊ]   [hʌ]
        c. sip   bat   lock   stress   put   putt
            [sɪp]   [bæt]   [lɒk]   [stres]   [pʊt]   [pʌt]

The made-up forms in [3.26b] above are not potential English words. They are disallowed because they have short vowels. They can be repaired by adding a consonant to yield the well-formed words in [3.267c].

Vowel reduction

The interaction between vowel quality and duration with stress is particularly important. A stressed vowel normally retains its underlying quality and is quite long. But an unstressed vowel is shortened and reduced to schwa by the rule in [3.27]. It states that a vowel with the property [-stress] is realized as schwa:

[3.27] **Vowel reduction**

$$[\text{+vowel} \rightarrow [\text{ə}] \ / \begin{bmatrix} \_\_\_ \\ \text{--stress} \end{bmatrix}$$

This can be seen in *photograph* [ˈfəʊtəɡɹɑːf] vs. *photography* [fəˈtɒɡɹəfi]; *library* [ˈlaɪbɹəɹi] vs. *librarian* [laɪˈbɹeəɹɪən]. Vowel reduction has important consequences for the rhythm of spoken English as we shall see below.

Vowel nasalization

In some English dialects, most notably in American and Canadian English, vowels assimilate the nasalization of a following nasal consonant where they precede a nasal that is both syllable and word-final (as in *pen* [pɛ̃n], [bæ̃n] *ban*, [kɑ̃ːn] *con*) or where the vowels occur before a nasal that is followed by a consonant (e.g., *pansy* [pæ̃nzi], [sæ̃ndbæ̃ŋk] *sandbank*, [kɑ̃ŋɹəs] *Congress*:

[3.28]   **Vowel nasalization**

$$[+\text{vowel}] \rightarrow [+\text{nasal}] \ / \ \underline{\quad} \ [+\text{nasal}] \left\{ \begin{matrix} \# \\ [+\text{consonant}] \end{matrix} \right\}$$

Nasalization is one of the most salient differences between American English and Canadian English on the one hand and most other accents on the other.

3.4   Conclusion

To sum up, phonology is the investigation of the functions and patterns of speech sounds. The focus has been on segmental phonology (i.e., vowels and consonants). Their key function is contrasting word meaning. The contrastive sounds of a language are called phonemes; they are decomposable into distinctive features. These are the most basic contrastive elements. The behaviour of English phonemes can be largely explained in terms of distinctive features and the natural classes defined by them. Members of a natural class are phonetically similar and display similar behaviour. Furthermore, many phonemes have allophones. Allophones are usually the product of assimilation. The consonant and vowel phonemes have also been examined from the perspective of accent and dialect variation. Major differences between dialects have been highlighted. As speech is not made of isolated phonemes but typically involves strings of phonemes, the next chapter explores how phonemes behave when they are combined.

Recommended readings

Two good simple introductions to English phonetics and phonology are Carr (1999) and McMahon (2001). If you want to explore the sound–symbol relationship in the International Phonetic Alphabet, you should visit the IPA website (http://www.arts.gla.ac.uk/ipa/ipachart.html). At that web site, and the links it contains, you will be able to listen to sound clips illustrating the sounds represented in the IPA chart. You should also read Ladefoged (2001) and follow this up with a visit to http://www.phonetics.ucla.edu/, the website that supports Ladefoged's textbook. There you will be able to listen to audio files and see excellent, illustrated descriptions of speech sounds.

Notes

1   The symbol /ɹ/ represents the typical post-alveolar approximant 'r' sound in *red*.
2   For the sake of completeness, we should also mention the voiceless velar fricative /x/ found in Scottish English in a word like *loch* /lɒx/.

CHAPTER 4

Phonology: Beyond the Segment

FRANCIS KATAMBA

4.1 Introducing prosodic phonology

This chapter goes beyond vowel and consonant systems, that is, beyond **segmental phonology**. It considers **prosodic phonology** (or **suprasegmental phonology**). Prosodic phonology is the study of the properties of speech, such as stress and intonation, whose domain extends beyond individual phonemes, in other words, those aspects of speech not normally represented by the letters of the orthography. The suprasegmental segmental nature of stress can be demonstrated by minimal pairs that are distinguished not by consonant or vowel phonemes, but by the relative prominence of the different syllables in a word, for example, 'produce (noun) has a more salient first syllable than pro'duce (verb) which has a stronger second syllable. Intonation is also suprasegmental as it involves pitch modulation over a whole utterance. Depending on circumstances, *When will you start looking for a job?*, said with falling intonation, may be a genuine enquiry, whilst *When will you start looking for a job?*, with rising intonation, might be an indirect rebuke for being jobless.

An unsophisticated analogy may clarify matters. Stress and intonation don't hover above segments. Rather, they ride piggyback atop them (and thus are in contact with them) when phonemes are combined to form words and phrases. The frame that enables prosodic properties to link up with the vowels and consonants is the syllable. So, it is with the syllable that the discussion will begin.

4.2 The syllable

This section introduces you to the syllable, its structure and role in phonology. We will begin by sketching syllable structure. The organization of the syllable is shown in Figure 4.1 and is exemplified with the monosyllabic English word *peg*.

Each position in the syllable tree is a slot that can be occupied by a variety of fillers. The slots can be simple, as in the above example where they are each filled by a single sound, or complex, with more than one element filling a particular slot. See Figure 4.2.

The **nucleus** can be simple, consisting of just a short vowel, in the syllable tree its nucleus doesn't branch; or complex, with a diphthong as in *lay* or a long

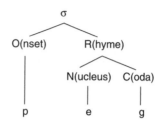

FIGURE 4.1   *Internal structure of a syllable*

Note: σ = Syllable; O = Onset ; R = Rhyme ; N = Nucleus ; C = Coda

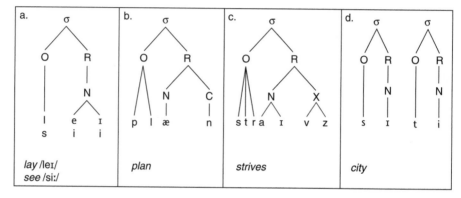

FIGURE 4.2   *Some examples of English syllables*

Note: V: (a long vowel) is represented as VV (i.e., two identical vowels occupying adjacent vowel positions in a syllable nucleus as in the representation of *see*).

vowel as in *see* /siː/ where long [iː] is made up of two identical /i/ sounds. The nucleus is the head of the syllable. That means that its presence is mandatory in all syllables. Other syllable constituents are optional. Words like [ɑː] *are* and [aɪ] *eye* have a bare nucleus. Words like *lay, see* and *city* have syllables with an **onset** and **rhyme** but no **coda**. Words like *eat* and *oil* have a nucleus and coda but no onset. Words like *plan* and *strives* have an onset, nucleus and a coda.

The structure of the rhyme is especially important. If the rhyme doesn't fork out anywhere, which is the case if it contains a nucleus with a short vowel not followed by a consonant, we have a **light syllable**, as in *city* in Figure 4.2d. However, if the rhyme has more than one constituent, as in the remaining examples, we have a **heavy syllable**. That's the case where the rhyme contains a complex nucleus with a long vowel or diphthong as in *lay* and *see*, or where it contains a nucleus and at least one coda consonant, as in *plan* and *strives*. Thus branches reflect the complexity of the rhyme. The distinction between light and heavy syllables is at the core of the notion of **syllable weight** which will be investigated below.

Traditionally a distinction is drawn between open and closed syllables. Open syllables end in a vowel. Consonant positions in a syllable are symbolized by C and vowel positions by V. Open syllables may just contain V (a lone vowel) for example, *awe* /ɔː/ or a vowel preceded by one or more consonants, for example, *see* /siː/ (CV), *blue* /bluː/ (CCV) or *spree* /spriː/ (CCCV). On the other hand, closed syllables end in one or more consonants, for example, *at* /æt/ (VC), *and* /ænd/ VCC, *ants* /ænts/, etc. Of course, onsets of open and closed syllables can also vary in complexity. This gives English a rich syllable inventory. English syllable types include CVCC (e.g., *pants* /pænts/), CCVCCC (e.g., *blends* /blendz/), CCCVCC (e.g., *strips* /strɪps/). We will return to this below.

Syllable division

Recognizing syllables is an important part of doing phonological analysis as many generalizations about the phonology of English (and for that matter many other languages) are stated in terms of syllable structure. For instance, rules that determine whether /l/ is clear or dark, whether /ɪ/ is pronounced or dropped in a rhotic accent, whether a plosive is aspirated or not all refer to syllable structure. In this subsection we will look at the principles used to segment words into syllables.

To be able to identify syllable boundaries we need to understand first the notion of **sonority**. Sonority denotes the relative loudness of speech sounds. Phoneticians have shown that vowels are generally louder than consonants; certain vowels are inherently louder than other vowels (e.g., other things being equal, [ɑː] is louder than [iː]) and certain consonants are inherently louder than other consonants (e.g., [m] is louder than [p]), and so on. To capture this fact, phonologists have proposed a principle referred to as the **Sonority Sequencing Generalization** (also known as the **Sonority Hierarchy**). The Sonority Sequencing Generalization is depicted in Figure 4.3 which is based on Selkirk (1984). Sounds are ranked on a scale of 1 (for voiceless plosives, which are the least sonorous) to 11 (for open vowels which are the most sonorous). English only allows sounds with a score of 7 or above on the sonority scale to function as syllable nuclei (i.e., to be **syllabic**). Vowels are always syllabic and, in certain circumstances, consonants with a score of 7 or above on the sonority scale function as syllable nuclei. Each syllable has just one sonority peak which functions as its nucleus. So if two sonority peaks are encountered, as in *sending*, we recognize two syllables uncontroversially. The only problem is to determine where to place the boundary between them. This is what we will be considering in the following paragraphs.

Syllable structure is governed by two universal principles, namely the **Sonority Sequencing Principle** which is stated in [4.1] and the **Onset Maximalization Principle** which will be discussed presently:

[4.1] **Sonority Sequencing Principle**
Sonority increases moving from the left-hand margin of the onset of the syllable and peaks on the nucleus; then it declines going from the nucleus to the right-hand margin of the coda.

Normally English syllables obey the Sonority Sequencing Principle. This is exemplified by words like *seek* and *grant* which are depicted in Figures 4.4 and 4.5.

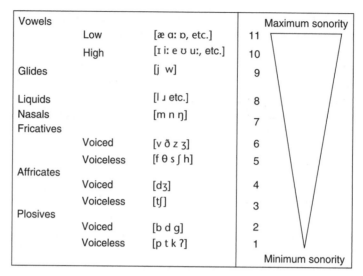

Vowels			
	Low	[æ ɑː ɒ, etc.]	11
	High	[ɪ iː e ʊ uː, etc.]	10
Glides		[j w]	9
Liquids		[l ɹ etc.]	8
Nasals		[m n ŋ]	7
Fricatives			
	Voiced	[v ð z ʒ]	6
	Voiceless	[f θ s ʃ h]	5
Affricates			
	Voiced	[dʒ]	4
	Voiceless	[tʃ]	3
Plosives			
	Voiced	[b d g]	2
	Voiceless	[p t k ʔ]	1

Maximum sonority

Minimum sonority

FIGURE 4.3   The sonority hierarchy

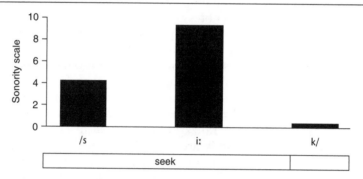

FIGURE 4.4   Sonority sequencing in seek

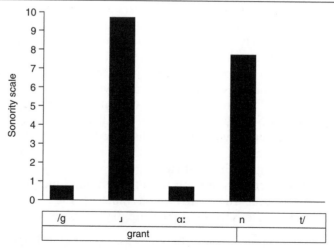

FIGURE 4.5   Sonority sequencing in grant

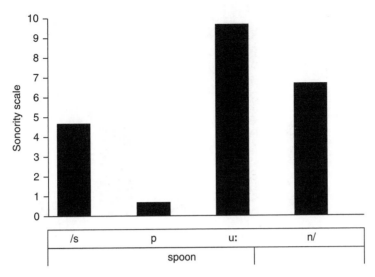

Sonority sequencing in spoon

FIGURE 4.6

However, there are two serious violations of the Sonority Sequencing Principle. First, English allows syllables with /s/ in the onset, followed by a stop which has less sonority than /s/, for example, *spoon* (also, *strip, sky*). Figure 4.6 shows the problematic nature of words with /s/+stop onsets in which sonority decreases going from /s/, the first sound of the onset to /p/, the second sound, before normality is restored going from /p/ to /uː/.

As we noted earlier, English only allows sounds with a score of 7 or above on the sonority scale to function as syllable peaks. So, /s/ must be assigned to the syllable onset in these words as it only has a score of 5 on the sonority scale and hence can't be treated as a syllable in its own right.

Second, in codas too we sometimes find counter-examples to the Sonority Sequencing Principle. One type of counter-examples consist of words with a voiceless stop, that has minimum sonority, which is followed by an alveolar fricative that outranks it in sonority, as in /fɪkst/ *fixed*. The sonority sequencing in *fixed,* is shown in Figure 4.7.

As English only allows sounds with a score of 7 or above on the sonority scale to function as syllable peaks, /s/ must be assigned to the syllable coda in words of this type. Thus, in Figure 4.7, although there is a surge in sonority when /s/ appears flanked by /k/ and /t/, it cannot be treated as a syllable nucleus. It is too low down on the sonority scale. The /kst/ consonants cluster is treated as a coda. Likewise, when /z/ follows a plosive in the syllable coda, for example, /sændz/ *sands*, /legs/ *legs*, it is not isolated as a syllable, rather it is allocated to the coda as it has insufficient sonority to function as a stand-alone syllable.

By contrast, in words like /petl/ *petal* and /bʌkl/ *buckle* where again a voiceless stop precedes a consonant that outranks it in sonority, we recognize the final /l/ as a syllable peak and treat the word as disyllabic. It is proper to do this because /l/, being a liquid, with a score of 7 on the sonority scale,

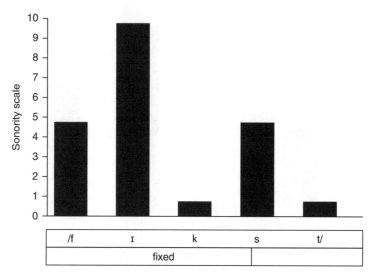

FIGURE 4.7   Sonority sequencing in fix *(one syllable)*

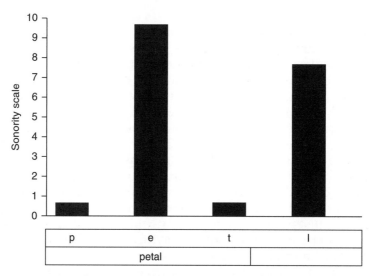

FIGURE 4.8   Sonority sequencing in petal *(two syllables)*

has sufficient carrying power to be a syllable nucleus and can therefore stand alone as a syllable. See Figure 4.8.

A similar analysis would apply to words like [flɪpɹ̩] *flipper* in rhotic dialects where the final [ɹ] is syllabic (see p. 46 above.)

The other constraint on syllable structure is the **Onset Maximalization Principle** which is stated in [4.2]:

[4.2] **Onset Maximalization Principle**

Other things being equal, prioritize the allocation of consonants to onsets rather than codas.

In other words, normally onset creation takes precedence over the creation of codas. There are two factors that may sway us to do otherwise. First, the satisfaction of the Sonority Sequencing Generalization should be maximized: as seen above with the exception of /s/-commencing syllables, onsets have increasing sonority going from left to right, and codas decreasing sonority going from left to right (with the exception of codas where /s/ or /z/ follows a stop). Consonants should normally be allocated to syllables, bearing in mind the need to conform to the Sonority Sequencing Generalization. Second, satisfaction of the Onset Maximalization Principle is overlooked if there is persuasive evidence that the syllable that would be created by following this is not viable. A viable syllable onset is one that is also found at the start of some words of the language; a viable syllable coda is one that is also found in word-final position. We will now survey a number of cases which illustrate these points.

Take the word *problem*. It is divided into two syllables as /pɹɒb.ləm/ (. indicates a syllable boundary). The first syllable satisfies the Sonority Sequencing Generalization as sonority rises in the onset /pɹ/, peaks on the nucleus /ɒ/, and then falls on the coda /b/. In the second syllable, again the Sonority Sequencing Generalization is satisfied by /ləm/ as sonority increases going from the onset to the nucleus and falls going from the nucleus to the coda. The alternative of dividing up the word as /pɹɒbl.əm/ is not a good idea. The initial syllable has a complex coda /bl/ which has increasing sonority going from left to right. This violates the Sonority Sequencing Generalization which stipulates falling sonority in codas. Moreover, the Onset Maximalization Principle has also been violated. Priority has been given to creating a coda at the expense of the onset. Consequently the second syllable lacks an onset.

The Onset Maximalization Principle is also useful for analysing words with a consonant in inter-vocalic position such as *melon*, *hurry* and *singing*. *Melon* is divided up as /me.lən/ rather than /mel.ən/ by applying the Onset Maximalization Principle. Similarly, *hurry* is divided up as /hʌ.ɹi/ rather than /hʌɹ.i/ in order to satisfy the Onset Maximalization Principle. In the case of inter-vocalic /ɹ/ we have additional evidence in support of our decision. Speakers of non-rhotic dialects who drop the coda /ɹ/ do pronounce the /ɹ/ in this word. (They don't say *[hʌ.i] for *hurry*.) This indicates that /ɹ/ is in the onset. Finally, *singing* could be divided up into /sɪŋ.ɪŋ/ or /sɪ.ŋɪŋ/. The latter syllable division is motivated by the Onset Maximalization Principle. An inter-vocalic consonant has been assigned to the second syllable which has been given an onset as a result. This has been at the expense of the first syllable which has not been given a coda. But in this instance, this is a bad decision. No English word ever begins with /ŋ/. This is a powerful argument against assuming that a syllable could begin with /ŋ/ – and that */ŋɪŋ/ is a viable syllable. Therefore, the alternative analysis where the word is divided up into /sɪŋ.ɪŋ/ must be the correct one. The Onset Maximalization Principle may have to play second fiddle to language-specific constraints on the distribution of phonemes.

Now consider syllable division in words that present somewhat different problems. Consider *sending*. Should it be divided into two syllables as /send.ɪŋ/ or /se.ndɪŋ/ or /sen.dɪŋ/? I hope you agree that dividing it up as /send.ɪŋ/ should be dismissed as this flouts the Onset Maximalization Principle.

Both word-medial consonants have been allocated to the coda of the first syllable, leaving none for the onset of the second. Dividing the word up as /se.ndɪŋ/ satisfies the Onset Maximalization Principle but creates a syllable */ndɪŋ/ that violates the Sonority Sequencing Generalization as the nasal /n/ is followed by a plosive which it outranks in sonority. Moreover, a quick check shows that */ndɪŋ/ has an unacceptable onset. No word commencing with a nasal followed by a consonant is found in this language. As we noted above, viable syllable onsets must also be viable word-initial phoneme sequences. The correct syllable division is /sen.dɪŋ/ which violates none of the constraints and contains sequences attested to at the beginning and at the end of English words. Likewise, *melted* /meltɪd/ is divided up as /mel.tɪd/. This satisfies both the Onset Maximalization Principle and the Sonority Sequencing Generalization without yielding a combination of phonemes not found at the start or end of real words. Dividing *melted* up as /me.ltɪd/ wouldn't do as /lt/ is a disallowed onset which has decreasing sonority going from left to right. No English word ever begins with /lt/. If /lt/ were a permissible syllable onset it would be found at the start of some words. The only place /lt/ is allowed to occur in is the coda (as in *bolt, salt,* etc.) where falling sonority is expected.

Syllable weight

We have established the procedures for identifying syllable boundaries. Let us now revisit the idea of **syllable weight** that was introduced earlier. (See Figure 4.2 and the related discussion.) Rhymes and rhymes alone determine syllable weight; onsets are irrelevant. Rhythmically, **light syllables** have a single beat. **Heavy syllables** are longer and have two beats. Table 4.1 summarizes the patterns.

The generalization is that syllables with complex rhymes are heavy. Why should we care about this? Because syllable weight plays a key role in stress placement. For example, a disyllabic verb with a light second syllable is normally stressed on the first syllable for example, *offer, scupper, enter.* But, a disyllabic verb with a heavy second syllable is normally stressed on the second syllable, for example, *review, assume, repeat, attack, pretend.*

The syllable is also important because of its pivotal role in **phonotactics**, the study of permissible combinations of sounds. Some combinations of phonemes are permitted while others are forbidden. We saw this earlier on pages 43–4 when we considered the distribution of /ŋ/. Recall that in English, nasal clusters are disallowed in syllable onsets. Putative words like *[ŋgel] *[mpʌvəd] are not acceptable.

How should the words in [4.3] be divided up into syllables? Why is the sound [p] pronounced in the words in [4.3a] but silent in those in [4.3b]?

[4.3] a. helicopter b. Ptolemy
           captain   ptyalin
           apt   ptarmigan

I hope, like me, you think this is the explanation: in English the consonant cluster [pt] is forbidden in syllable onsets. Hence the dropping of initial [p]

Syllable weight   Table 4.1

Light syllable	Heavy syllable

has a simple, non-branching rhyme, with just a short vowel, e.g.:
 	
[ɹɪ . fə] *refer*
[sɪ . ti] *city*
	has a complex, branching rhyme (which is underlined) belonging to one of the types below:
	
	i) VC (C) (C) (C) vowel followed by at least one consonant and at most four consonants, e.g.:
	  lag [l<u>æg</u>] (VC rhyme)
	  band [b<u>ænd</u>] (VCC rhyme)
	  scents [s<u>ents</u>] (VCCC rhyme)
	  glimpsed [gl<u>ɪmpst</u>] (VCCCC rhyme)
	ii) a long vowel regardless of whether it is followed by a consonant, e.g.:
	  foolhardy [f<u>uː</u>l . h<u>ɑː</u> . di]
	  sleepwalker [sl<u>iː</u>p . w<u>ɔː</u> . kə]
	iii) a diphthong (regardless of whether it is followed by a consonant), e.g.:
	  payday [p<u>eɪ</u> . d<u>eɪ</u>],
	  bright [br<u>aɪt</u>]

in [4.3b] in these Greek loanwords. What is phonotactically acceptable in one language may not be in another. But in [4.3a] this cluster is allowed as it either occurs in syllable final position as in *apt* or where [p] and [t] belong to two separate syllables as in *he . li . cop . ter* and *cap . tain*.

When describing phonotactics, constraints can be stated for each of the units that occupy the onset, nucleus and coda. For instance in English, as we saw above, only short vowel nuclei are allowed to precede a coda velar nasal, see [3.24] on page 53. Onsets are also subject to similar constraints. Whereas *splash, stream, scratch, stupid* and *squeal* have well-formed onsets, *fplash, *znkveam, *wrgatch, *stnupiff and *skfeal do not. The first segment of a syllable-initial three-consonant cluster in English is always /s/; the second consonant in the series is always a voiceless stop, and the third is an approximant (i.e., either a liquid or a glide) as seen in Table 4.2.

Note that some combinations are forbidden and others are marginal. There are no syllables starting with /spw/, /stl/, or /stw/. A /skl/ onset is barely legal; it only occurs in *sclerosis* and related words (*sclerotic, sclera, sclerotic*, etc.).

Phonotactic constraints are language-specific. A phoneme sequence allowed in one language may be prohibited in another. For instance, [pt] onsets are allowed in Greek but not in English as we noted above. Likewise, in French onsets, labial consonants can be followed by [w] as in *mois* 'month' and *poids* 'weight' but such sequences are forbidden in English where *fwen, *pwat and *mwice are barred.

Finally, all non-occurring words are not equal. Combinations of phonemes that are legal, for example, *glack, lipe* and *swall,* but which do not correspond

Table 4.2   *Permissible three-consonant clusters in onsets*

	Voiceless stop	Approximant		
σ [s	p t k	l ɹ w j		
		Examples		
/s	p	l/	splash	/splæʃ/
/s	p	ɹ/	spring	/spɹɪŋ/
/s	p	j/	spew	/spjuː/
/s	p	w/	*spwan	/spwæn/
*/s	t	l/	*stlenk	/stlenk/
/s	t	ɹ/	stream	/stɹiːm/
/s	t	j/	stew	/stjuː/
/s	t	w/	*stwop	/stwɒp/
/s	k	l/	sclerosis	/sklerəʊsɪs/
/s	k	ɹ/	scream	/skɹiːm/
/s	k	j/	squeal	/skjuː/
/s	k	w/	skew	/skwiːl/

to actual words are regarded as 'accidental gaps' in the lexicon. They must be distinguished from phonotactically aberrant phoneme combinations that couldn't be words for example, *spwand, *stlenk, *stwop, *pwend, *kgopick and *gversy which are referred to as 'systematic gaps'. Some accidental words can become real words if a meaning is found for them. A new shampoo could be called *lipe*.

The syllable as the domain of phonological rules

It will have become obvious by now that many generalizations about English phonology that we have examined so far are best made with reference to syllable structure. For instance, the aspiration rule, see [3.9] on page 40, applies to a voiceless stop if it is initial in a stressed syllable. We have noted also that the creation of centring diphthongs in non-rhotic accents and the r-colouring of vowels in rhotic accents only takes place in codas. Turning to /l/, we again have found that the syllable plays a key role in the distribution of its allophones. Briefly, we have seen that /l/ has three allophones whose selection is determined by the place in the syllable where /l/ occurs. 'Clear l' is used in syllable onsets and 'dark l' in codas (see [3.6]). To further clarify this point, let's consider the pronunciation of a word like *call* [kɔːɫ] which has 'dark l' since /l/ occurs in word and syllable-final position. But when a vowel-commencing suffix is added, as in *calling*, /l/ now finds itself in syllable-initial position and the clear allophone is selected ([kɔː . lɪŋ] not *[kɔː . ɫɪŋ]). The 'approximant devoicing rule' that produces voiceless allophones of approximants, including /l/, when they follow a voiceless obstruent that is in syllable onset position is yet another rule that is sensitive to syllable structure (see [3.19] on page 45). In this section we continue to explore the impact of syllable structure, focusing on 'connected speech', that is, utterances containing at least two words.

Many connected speech phenomena can best be interpreted in terms of optimizing CV syllable structure (exemplified by *ba . na. na*). CV, a syllable with an onset consonant followed by a vowel, is the ideal syllable in any language. Many processes alter syllables to turn them into CV syllables or make them approximate to that ideal form.

Consider **liaison** (**linking**). This is motivated by the constraint on syllable structure that requires, wherever possible, to have a consonantal onset in every syllable. When an onsetless syllable follows a syllable ending in a vowel, usually speakers insert a consonant that links the two syllables and functions as an onset for the second syllable. Such a linking consonant is relatively short. It is represented by a superscript consonant symbol. The linking consonant inserted is [ʲ] if a high front vowel is followed by another vowel, as in *seeing* [siːʲɪŋ] and *weighing* [weʲɪŋ]. (Saying these words as [siːɪŋ] and [weɪŋ] is hard work.) Where a high back vowel is followed by another vowel, the linking consonant inserted is [ʷ], as in *rowing* [rəʊʷɪŋ] and *doing* [duːʷɪŋ]. Finally, linking-r ([ʳ]) is employed if a non-high vowel is followed by another vowel within a word as in *barring* [bɑːʳɪŋ] (cf. *bar* [bɑː]), *sharing* [ʃeəʳɪŋ] (cf. *share* [ʃeə]). Linking-r is also used if a non-high vowel is followed by another vowel across a word boundary in connected speech as in *bar is* [bɑːʳɪz] (as in *the bar is packed*). Linking-r reflects coda <r> present in the spelling. It was historically always pronounced, and it still is in rhotic dialects. However, as we have already seen, in non-rhotic dialects, /ɹ/ is not pronounced if it occurs in coda position in a syllable (as in *bar* [bɑː]). But it is re-syllabified as a syllable onset and pronounced, if it is followed by a vowel within a word following the addition of a suffix (as in *barring*) or across a word-boundary as in *bar is* [bɑːʳɪz] and *share again* [ʃeəʳəgeɪn].

Linking-r should not be confused with **intrusive-r** which is also only found in non-rhotic accents in words like *sawing* [sɔːʳɪŋ] and *drawing* [drɔːʳɪŋ]. It appears out of the blue and has no historical source. Its function is to provide onset for an onsetless vowel following another vowel in a word. This discussion has prepared the ground for a closer look at sounds in connected speech, the subject of the next section.

4.3 The phonological phrase: sounds in connected speech contexts

So far we have focused on speech sounds in single words in citation forms – the way words are enunciated in a wordlist. But, the phonology of words in citation forms may differ substantially from the phonology of words when they are actually used in utterances in connected speech (cf. Gimson, 2001: 249–55; Roach, 2001: 156–203). In the lexicon we have ideal segments, syllables and words. In connected speech non-canonical forms are often produced. For instance, while words listed in the lexicon must obey the canonical syllable constraints of the language, words occurring in phrases in connected speech may violate these constraints. Consider the following:

[4.4] Orthographic representation	Lexical representation	Citation form representation	Connected speech representation	
to get	/tʊ get/	[tʊ get]	[tget]	(*[tg] syllable onset)
it is cold	/ɪt ɪz kəʊld/	[ɪt ɪz kəʊld]	[tskəʊld]	(*[tsk] syllable onset)

Sounds frequently change so as to fit in with their neighbours in connected speech, which makes articulation easier. Assimilation, and, in particular, place of articulation assimilation resulting often in homorganic consonants, is especially common. In the following examples the assimilation is **regressive**. The first sound changes in anticipation of the next sound. Note especially how an alveolar consonant assimilates to the place of articulation of the following dental fricative ([θ] or [ð]). To indicate the fact that the alveolar consonant has assimilated the dental property of the following sound, we write the alveolar symbol with a little 'tooth' [ˌ] diacritic under it.

[4.5]	/ðæt pleɪs/	[ðəp pleɪs]	that place
	/ðæt kiːn/	[ðək kiːn]	that keen
	/kwaɪt klɪə/	[kwaːk klɪə]	quite clear
	/hɔːs ʃuː/	[hɔːʃ ʃuː]	horse shoe
	/tenθ/	[ten̪θ]	tenth
	/eɪt θɜːti/	[eɪt̪ θɜːti]	eight thirty
	/wɪdθ/	[wɪd̪θ]	width
	/welθ/	[wel̪θ/	wealth
	/ɪn ðæt/	[ɪn̪ ðæt]	in that
	/wɪl ðiːz/	[wɪl̪ ðiːz]	will these

Manner of articulation assimilation (as in [ðəs siːn] *that scene*, [gʊn njuːzpeɪpə] *good newspaper*) is less common. The assimilation is again regressive.

Alternatively, modification may, involve **elision** (i.e., deletion). For instance, a reduced vowel after a voiceless stop is elided in [4.6]:

[4.6]	[pteɪtəʊ]	potato
	[tmɑːtəʊ]	tomato
	[kɹekt]	correct
	[pkɒz]	because

The example of *because* /bɪkɒz/, which has [bɪkɒz] as its citation form, requires a special mention. The voicelessness of /k/ is assimilated by /b/ when the two sounds come next to each other following the elision of the vowel. Simplification of word-final codas also takes place as part of a strategy for avoiding complex consonant sequences. Word-final dentals and alveolars are the most likely candidates for elision.

[4.7]	Orthographic representation	Lexical representation	Citation form representation	Connected speech representation
	last person	/lɑːst pɜːsən/	[lɑːst pɜːsn̩]	[lɑːs pɜːsn̩]
	Fifth Street	/fɪfθ striːt/	[fɪfθ striːt]	[fɪf striːt]
	twelfth's throne	/twelfθ θɹəʊn/	[twelfθ θɹəʊn]	[twelf θɹəʊn]

Weak forms in connected speech

A key feature of English connected speech is the use of weak, unstressed forms of grammatical function words like articles, pronouns, prepositions and auxiliary verbs, etc. (see Chapter 6, Section 6.7) where those words are not emphasized. The most salient features of weak forms are summarized in Table 4.3.

Weak forms   *Table 4.3*

In the case of function words, for example, pronouns, the negative adverb 'not', auxiliary verbs, etc. (see Chapter 6, Section 6.7) there are established contracted weak forms that are normally used when such words are unstressed. Such weak forms are called **clitics**. They have a status intermediate between a word and an affix. The source is an independent word, for example, a negative adverb like *not* or an auxiliary verb like *will, have*, etc., but when used as weak forms they are appended to a host, just like affixes, as in *aren't, I'll, you've*, etc. A word to which a clitic is attached is called a host. A host and its clitic together constitute a 'clitic group'. Forms such as *aren't, isn't, must've, you've, I'll, you've* are examples of clitic groups.

Examples of weak forms

not	[nt]	after vowels, e.g., *you aren't* [jʊ ant]
	[n̩t]	after consonants, e.g., *he isn't* [hɪ ɪznt]
are	[ə]	after vowels, e.g., *you are* [jʊə]
had, would	[d]	after vowels, e.g., *he'd* [hɪd] (he had done it, he would do it)
	[əd]	after consonants, e.g., *Jack'd* [dʒækəd] (Jack had done it, Jack would do it)
have	[v]	have [v] after vowels, e.g., *I've* [aɪv] (I have)
	[əv]	after consonants, e.g., *must've* [mʌstəv] (must have) (often confused with *of* as in **I should of done it*)
has, is	[s]	after voiceless consonants (e.g., *Jack has* [dʒæks])
	[z]	[z] after vowels and voiced consonants, e.g., *Jane has* [dʒeɪnz]
	[ɪz]	[z] after sibilants e.g., *Alice is, Alice has* [ælɪsɪz]
will	[l]	will [l] after vowels, e.g., *you will* [jʊl]
	[l̩]	after consonants, e.g., *Jane will* [dʒeɪnl̩]

4.4 The metrical foot and word stress

Stress, the relative prominence of one syllable compared to its neighbours, is very important in English. In a word of two syllables this is easy to see. For instance, in *PRINter* the first syllable is more prominent but in *huMANE* it is the second syllable that stands out (prominence is marked by capitalization here). The more prominent syllable is said to be stressed and the weaker one is said to be unstressed. The main phonetic ingredients that produce this prominence, ranked in order of importance, are higher pitch (or pitch movement), greater duration, full vowel quality (i.e., not being reduced to schwa) and greater relative loudness.

Metrical feet

Sometimes, there may be a syllable which is not the most prominent but still isn't totally lacking in salience. In such cases we need to distinguish between primary and secondary stress. **Primary stress** (also called main stress) is marked by ['] and weaker **secondary stress** by [ˌ], for example, ˌcross-'country, ˌpano'ramic, etc. A strongly stressed syllable is referred to as Strong (s) and an unstressed one or one with weaker stress is referred to as Weak (w). A stressed syllable and normally any unstressed syllables that occur following it, until another stressed syllable is reached, constitutes a 'metrical foot'. A word may contain one or more metrical feet (see Carr, 1999: 99–106).

Tree diagrams are a useful way of representing metrical structure as they show graphically the relative prominence of syllables. For instance, in the word *huMANE* a weak syllable (which is dominated by w in the tree diagram in Figure 4.9) is followed by a strong syllable (which is dominated by s in the same tree diagram). Such a foot is called an 'iambic foot'. The word *PRINter* contains a metrical foot with a strong syllable followed by a weak syllable. This type of foot is called a 'trochaic foot' and can also be seen in the tree diagram in Figure 4.9.

It is important to remember always that stress is a matter of relative salience. A syllable that is more prominent in its foot may be overshadowed by another syllable when feet come together to form a word. If a word has both primary and secondary stress, the syllable with primary stress is more prominent. We show this by having it dominated by more s-nodes than its weaker counterpart as you can see in Figure 4.12. The first syllable of ˌsenti'mental has secondary stress. So, it has just one s-node above it. But the third syllable

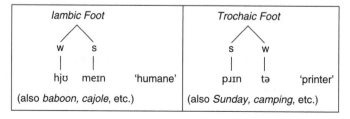

FIGURE 4.9   *Metrical feet*

ADVANCES BOX 4.1

Odd metrical feet

As all the examples discussed so far indicate, a metrical foot must have a stressed syllable as its head. A weak syllable on its own cannot constitute a foot. Normally there is just one weak syllable in a foot. This happy situation does not always prevail. Sometimes there is no one-to-one pairing of weak and strong syllables. If two weak syllables are next to a strong syllable they are both adjoined to the foot containing the strong syllable as shown in Figure 4.10.

Moreover, it is also possible to have a foot consisting of a lone stressed syllable with no attendant unstressed syllables. Such a foot is called a **degenerate foot**. That's what we see in a monosyllabic word like *scout* which is represented in Figure 4.11.

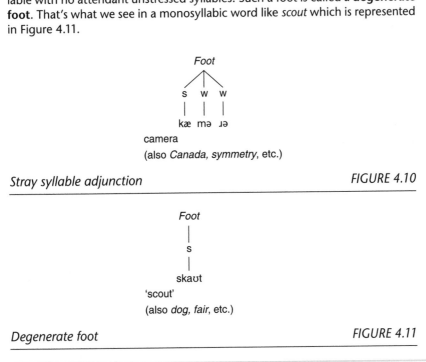

Stray syllable adjunction   FIGURE 4.10

Degenerate foot   FIGURE 4.11

which is more prominent, being the bearer of the primary stress of the word, is dominated by two s-nodes. This means that the second foot is stronger than the first in this word. In ˈscoutˌmaster, the reverse is true. The primary stress falls on the first foot ˈscout, which is dominated by two s-nodes and secondary stress is on the first syllable of the foot containing ˌmaster which is dominated by just one s-node.

Content words (i.e., nouns, adjectives, verbs and adverbs which are described in detail in Chapter 6, Section 6.2) must always have a syllable that is assigned primary stress. But unless they are being highlighted, monosyllabic function words like prepositions, pronouns, determiners are unstressed. So they cannot constitute a foot. Dynamic foot creation in speech takes advantage of this. When unstressed function words appear in connected speech next to

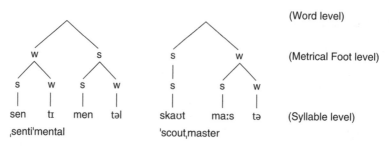

FIGURE 4.12   *Metrical trees showing stress*

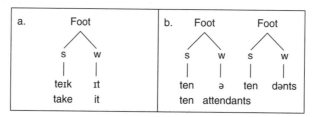

FIGURE 4.13   *Dynamic foot creation in connected speech*

a degenerate foot of a monosyllabic word, as in [4.13a], the two are joined together in a foot. Likewise, a stray weak syllable of a lexical word may form a foot with a preceding word which is a degenerate foot, as in [4.13b].

Word stress

In this subsection we look at the placement of primary stress in simple words as opposed to complex words with affixes and compound words (see Roach, 2000:93–103). Begin by observing stress in the trisyllabic words in [4.8]:

[4.8]	**Stress on 1st syllable**	**Stress on 2nd syllable**	**Stress on 3rd syllable**
	cinema	tomato	kangaroo
	elephant	potato	Tennessee
	liberty	aroma	refugee
	Canada	casino	clarinet

I don't know what you decided. But linguists think English word stress can be predicted, to some extent, using the principles set out below.

English is a **quantity sensitive** language, that is, a language in which syllable weight influences stress placement. In this regard, English differs from languages where no attention is paid to syllable weight and all syllables are treated in the same way by stress rules. For instance, in Finnish any word-initial syllable is stressed regardless of its internal structure. A heavy syllable like that at the start of *'palttina* 'linen cloth' is treated in the same way as the initial light syllables of *'tuolilla* 'on a chair' and *'halusi* 'wanted'. They are all stressed.

English stress interacts with syllable weight in a number of ways. We noted in the examples in [3.26] on page 53 that monosyllabic content words must have a heavy syllable (a long vowel, a diphthong or a coda consonant). Such syllables are the privileged sites for stress. In words of two or more syllables, only one syllable can receive primary stress. The decision is influenced by syllable weight and word class. Nouns are stressed following one set of rules and adjectives and verbs following another. But bear in mind that the rules are subject to numerous exceptions.

The interaction between stress and syllable weight is illustrated with the placement of stress in trisyllabic nouns which is governed by the rule in [4.9]. Normally, trisyllabic nouns are not stressed on the final syllable but rather on the penultimate (second from the end) or antepenultimate (third from the end) syllable:

[4.9]   **Trisyllabic noun stress rule**

> a.   **Penultimate**
>   Stress the penultimate syllable if it is heavy.
> b.   **Antepenultimate**
>   Stress the antepenultimate syllable if the penultimate syllable is light.

Examples showing the effect of this rule are listed in Table 4.4 which is based on Chomsky and Halle (1968).

There are many exceptions. There is penultimate stress in *confetti, Camilla, vanilla*, etc. and stress falls on a heavy final syllable in a very small group of words, most of which are borrowed, for example, *kangaroo, clarinet, magazine*.

Unlike nouns, verbs and adjectives frequently have final stress. Disyllabic verbs tend to be stressed on the second syllable, if it is heavy, as seen in Table 4.5.

However, stress falls on the first syllable, if the second is light as you can see in Table 4.6.

Stress placement in trisyllabic nouns   Table 4.4

Penultimate stress if the penultimate syllable is heavy with		*Antepenultimate stress if the penultimate syllable is light (i.e., has short vowel rhyme)*	
a) a long vowel or diphthong rhyme			
volcano	potato	cinema	avenue
aroma	arena	liberty	retina
catharsis	Karachi	Canada	calibre
		canopy	enema
b) A VC rhyme			
veranda	agenda		
surrender	disaster		
synopsis	department		
	(in rhotic accents)		

Table 4.5   *Disyllabic verbs and adjective with a heavy second syllable*

Verbs			Adjectives		
delay	*attract*	*decode*	*defunct*	*alive*	*sublime*
obey	*correct*	*elude*	*elite*	*correct*	*serene*
comply	*attend*	*abide*	*superb*	*rotund*	*robust*
review	*connect*	*connive*	*adroit*	*divine*	*supreme*

Table 4.6   *Disyllabic verbs and adjective with a light second syllable*

Verbs	Adjective
audit	*super*
open	*equal*
envy	*eager*
lever	*silly*

Table 4.7   *Noun-verb stress doublets*

Noun Initial stress			Verb Final stress		
'reject	'progress	'contract	re'ject	pro'gress	con'tract
'produce	'refuse	'digest	pro'duce	re'fuse	di'gest
'import	'insult	'escort	im'port	in'sult	es'cort

Linguists have noted a quirk in the system. When computing syllable weight, a single coda consonant in the final syllable of a verb or adjective is not counted. It is 'invisible'. Words like *audit* and *equal* are deemed to have a light second syllable and so stress falls on the first syllable. By contrast, in disyllabic nouns, the preference is for initial stress, for example, *England, jelly, petrol*, etc.

The difference between nouns on the one hand and verbs/adjectives on the other, with the former disfavouring final stress and the latter readily accepting it, results in disyllabic noun-verb doublets contrasted by stress. Examples of these are shown in Table 4.7.

4.5 Intonation

In the final section of this chapter we will look at **intonation**. 'Intonation' is pitch modulation used over an entire utterance. This must be distinguished from **tone** which is pitch modulation that serves to distinguish word meanings. For instance, Vietnamese has six tones, as seen in Table [4.8], which contrast word meanings.

Vietnamese tones (Đìn-Hoà, 2001: 795)   Table 4.8

Tone	Example	Gloss
Level	*ma*	ghost
Rising	*má*	cheek; mom
Falling	*mà*	but
Dipping-rising	*mǎ*	tomb; grave
Creaky	*mã*	horse
Constricted	*mạ*	rice-seedling

In English, pitch modulation is never used to distinguish word meaning. So, unlike Vietnamese, English is not a tone language.

So, how is intonation organized in English? Just as the largest unit of syntactic structure is the sentence, the largest unit in terms of which intonation patterns are analysed is the **tone-group** (also called the intonation phrase or tone unit). Major pitch changes up or down normally occur on stressed syllables. Unstressed syllables are not marked by significant pitch changes –unless they are at the end of an intonation group. (Gimson, 2001: 255–79). The structure of the intonation-group is as follows:

[4.10]   Pre-head | Head | Nucleus | Tail
          Ph   H   N   T

Note: 'l' marks the boundary between constituents of the tone group.

The structure of the intonation-group is exemplified in [4.11]:

[4.11] a. **Statement**
   She will | phone the patients when all the tests are | ＼COM|pleted.
   Ph   H   N   T

b. **Statement**
   She will | phone the patients when |＼ ALL | the tests are completed.
   Ph   H   N   T

c. **Statement**
   She will | phone the patients when all the tests | ＼ARE | completed.
   Ph   H   N   T

d. **Command**
   Tell Jane to | ＼ CHECK | in by noon.
   H   N   T

e. **Wh-question**
   ＼WHERE| are you going?
        N   T

f. **Wh-question**
   Where are you | ＼GOING?
        H   N

Note: Types of nucleus: Falling ＼; Rising ↗; Fall-rise ＼↗ or; Rise-fall ↗＼.

The **pre-head** consists of any unstressed syllables before the head. The **head** is the section from the first stressed syllable up to – but not including the nucleus. The **nucleus** (or **tonic syllable**) is the core of the intonation group. Of all constituents of a tone group, only the nucleus is obligatory, the rest may be omitted. The nucleus is the most salient syllable of the tone group. It gives its name to the intonation group – falling intonation, rising intonation, etc. The stretch before the nucleus often has fairly level pitch; the nucleus has significant pitch movement. The nucleus may have a significant fall in pitch (ˋ) or a pitch rise (ˊ), (or a fall-rise ˅ or rise-fall ˄ combination). The fall is the most common nucleus in most varieties of English. Typically, neutral statements, commands and wh-questions (i.e., questions introduced by *what, who, where, when*, etc.) have falling intonation. This is shown in [4.11]. The syllable with primary stress in the last content word of the utterance usually provides the nucleus in neutral utterances as in [4.11a]. But the placement of the tonic syllable can vary depending on which word the speaker intends to highlight as you can see in [4.11b] vs. [4.11c], and [4.11e] vs. [4.11f]. The pattern established on the nucleus is continued through the **tail**, that is, the nucleus. If the nucleus has falling pitch, pitch continues to fall through the tail and conversely, if it has rising pitch, the same pattern is continued through the tail.

Rising intonation is usually an indicator of incompleteness. It is often used in yes-no questions as the person asking the question expects the addressee to take up the next turn in the conversation (see [4.12a]). Non-terminal rising intonation is also found at the end of each item in a list, except the last one. For example, in [4.12b] each of the first two sports has rising non-terminal intonation; but the third and final one has a fall. Listing intonation is characterized by a low-rise (indicated by ˏ); the pitch does not go up quite as much as it does in a typical yes-no question. The utterance in [4.12b] contains three tone groups. Each stressed syllable with a significant change in pitch constitutes a nucleus and each nucleus heads a tone group of its own. Boundaries between them are marked with ' / '.

[4.12] a. **Yes-no questions**
Are you | enjoying the| ˊENG‖lish course?
  Ph   H   N   T

   b. **Listing intonation**
Chris plays| ˏ FOOT‖ball/ ˏ RUG|gby and/ ˋ BAS|ketball
  H   N   T   N   T   N   T

Intonation serves a variety of functions. We have already alluded to its discourse function. Placement of the tonic may be varied in order to highlight a key word (see [4.11]). Intonation is also used to mark certain syntactic distinctions such as that between restrictive and non-restrictive relative clauses. In writing, no commas are used to mark restrictive relative clauses but commas are used to separate a non-restrictive clause from the rest of the sentence. In speech, an utterance realizing a sentence containing a restrictive relative clause contains one tone group (see [4.13a]). But an utterance realizing a sentence with a non-restrictive relative clause has pauses corresponding to commas and, crucially, it contains two tone groups – the relative clause is a tone group which is inserted in the tone group associated with the main clause as you can see in [4.13.]:

[4.13] a. Restrictive relative clause (in italics): serves to identify the president. The head in which it is embedded is in bold type.

    The | **President** *who was born in a log cabin* **was a** | GREAT| hero.
    Ph   H   N   T

  b. Non-restrictive (in italics) supplies additional information not essential for identifying the president. The head in which it is embedded is in bold type.

$$\text{The} \mid \textbf{President,} \; / \begin{bmatrix} \text{Ph} & \text{H} & \text{N} & \text{T} \\ \textit{who was} \mid \textit{born in a} \mid \textit{LOG} \mid \textit{cabin,} \end{bmatrix} / \; \textbf{was a} \mid \text{GREAT} \mid \text{hero.}$$

  Ph   H   N   T

Intonation has a key role in conveying the speaker's intended meaning (see pragmatics chapter). Imagine a friend says to you: *Have you got a ⁄fiver?* You could answer ⌄*Yes*, and walk away. The friend would be disappointed as the most likely point of the question is not to interrogate you about your cash flow situation but to see if you can lend them some cash. The expected answer is ⌄⁄ *Yes*. The non-terminal fall-rise indicates to your friend that you are happy to explore what lies behind your question and may be lend them some money. So 'yes' can mean different things, depending on the intonation used.

4.6 Conclusion

A major finding of phonological investigations over the last few decades is that phonological structure consists of elements that are organized in inter-linked hierarchical patterns, with smaller units grouped together to form successively larger units. The phonological hierarchy in Table 4.9 summarizes the general structure of the English phonological system.

The focus has been on the part of the hierarchy going from the feature to the foot. We have seen that speakers have covert knowledge of this intricate phonological structure. At all levels there exist constraints on permissible combinations of units that form elements on the rank above in the hierarchy. For instance, feature combinations that yield sounds that represent phonemes are subject to various restrictions. Thus, an English vowel made in the front of the mouth must be produced with unrounded lips for example, [iː], [ɪ], [e] and [æ]. Front rounded vowels such as [y], [ø] and [œ] that are found in French [lyt] *lut* 'lute', [fø] *feu* 'fire' and [œf] *oeuf* 'egg' are normally disallowed in English. Likewise, allophones of phonemes are subject to many restrictions on where they can be deployed and these restrictions normally have a phonetic basis, for example, following an obstruent, an approximant has a voiceless allophone due to the assimilation of the voicelessness of the obstruent but elsewhere approximants are voiced. Again, when combining phonemes to form syllables, various constraints apply. Some combinations of phonemes are permitted in certain positions and others are forbidden, for example, /nd/ is a permissible cluster in codas but is prohibited in syllable onsets. We have also examined the role of syllable and foot structure in some

Table 4.9   *The phonological hierarchy*

Top of the hierarchy

Tone group (Intonation phrase)	e.g., *She missed the last train to Lancaster*
Phonological phrase	e.g., *the last train, to Lancaster*
Clitic group	e.g., *She'd, I've, Can't, won't*
Phonological word	e.g., *go, cucumber, broomstick*
Metrical Foot	e.g., Trochaic feet where a strong (stressed) syllable is followed by a weak (unstressed) syllable as in *better, Devon, top of* vs. iambic feet where a weak syllable precedes strong syllable as in *apart, prefer, to be, on high*
Syllable	e.g., *sig . ni . fi cant , Ma. til . da*
Phoneme	e.g., /θ/, /ɪ/, /n/ in /θɪn/ *thin*
Feature	e.g., [+voice], [−nasal], [+lateral]

Each level in the hierarchy contains constituents that consist of elements belonging to the rank below in the hierarchy

---

Bottom of the hierarchy

---

detail before providing a sketch of the phonology above the word. The chapter ended with a brief survey of word stress and intonation. Throughout, we have also seen that although there are many shared properties, variation is the norm. Different accents and dialects have somewhat different phonological systems, this is sometimes due to having different phonological inventories, and sometimes to having different rules and constraints, or having the same rules and constraints which are applied differently. This theme is going to be explored further in Chapter 18 and others.

Recommended readings

Carr (1999) and McMahon (2001) both contain straightforward introductions to many of the issues dealt with in this chapter. Roach (2001) is another very good, accessible textbook; it is aimed especially at those teaching or learning English as a second language. Gimson (2001) is a standard handbook on British English, especially Cruttenden (1997) is a sound, advanced survey of English intonation.

CHAPTER 5

Morphology: Word Structure

FRANCIS KATAMBA

5.1 Morphology: the study of word-structure

Morphology is the component of grammar that is devoted to the study of the internal structure of words. It is concerned not only with speakers' knowledge of the structure of existing, well-established words (e.g., *shopkeeper* is analysable as *shop-keep-er*) but also with the rules used to form or interpret new words. Look at the words below. I suspect some of them will be new to you; they are recent additions to the English lexicon. Explain how you might work out their meanings without resorting to a dictionary:

[5.1] earwitness   f.i.n.e.   McJob
        televangelist   wordrobe   disorient express

If you're unsure about some of these words, help is at hand in Table 5.1.

You know many things about word-formation, including the fact that words have internal structure. New compound words can be formed by combining two existing full words, for example, *ear-witness* (the analogy with *eyewitness* is obvious); and by combining chunks of words you can create a new blended word like *televangelist* (from *television-evangelist*). You know also that a new word can be formed by combining the first letters of words in a phrase as in *f.i.n.e.* or *imho*. In addition, you bring to the task of word-structure analysis considerable shared cultural knowledge. For instance, you have views about the classiness (or otherwise of) *McDonalds* that inform your interpretation of the likely meaning of *McJob*. The intended word play on *wardrobe* in *wordrobe* will not escape you; in the compound *disorient express* you see the allusion to the *Orient Express*, a train eponymous with luxury long-distance travel (with a touch of intrigue). Much of this knowledge is subconscious. The study of morphology aims to make it explicit.

Morphology is the study of word structure. The problem is that although everyone knows what a word is, it is very difficult to give a simple definition of the word and to provide reliable criteria for recognizing words. A standard definition of a word is this: 'a word is a minimum free form' (Bloomfield, 1935: 178). This means that a word can occur on its own as an utterance. For instance, you could say, *Boys!* (with a sigh in exasperation, on seeing boys behaving badly). In fact, the word not only is the smallest form that can occur

Table 5.1   *Some new words in English*

EARWITNESS, n. An individual who hears an incident occur, especially one who later gives a report on what he heard [blend of ear and eyewitness].
Context and source: 'I didn't see what happened, I just heard it. I guess I was an earwitness.' (Conversation)

IMHO, n. acronym (In My Humble Opinion)
Context: Acronym used on the internet

F.I.N.E., adj. acronym (F*cked up, Insecure, Neurotic, and Emotional). Usually derogatory; indicated by tone of voice.
Context: 'We all know he's F.I.N.E, just like those freaks he hangs out with.'

MCJOB, n. A job in a service related field with low pay, low prestige and little opportunity for advancement [analogous word formed from prefix Mc– and job].
Context and source: '... a message that I suppose irked Dag, who was bored and cranky after eight hours of working his McJob'. (Generation X, pg. 5)

TELEVANGELIST, n. An evangelist who conducts regular religious services on television. [Blend of television and evangelist]
Context and source: 'Ole Anthony and his merry band take on the televangelists.' (US News, 8 December 1997)

WORDROBE, n. a person's vocabulary. [blend of *word* and *wardrobe*]
Context and source: 'He has an extensive wordrobe'. (a web page on the Internet)

DISORIENT EXPRESS, n. A state of confusion. [novel formation]
Context and source: 'I felt like I was on the Disorient Express for good this time.' (*Newsweek*, 14 November 1996)

(Kemmer, 2004)

by itself as an utterance, it is also the smallest unit that can be manipulated by syntax. Consider the sentences below:

[5.2]   a.   The neighbour's dogs disturbed burglars.
         b.   Burglars were disturbed by the neighbour's dogs.
         c.   *s burglar weres disturb the ed by the neighbour's dog s.
         d.   *sdog the neighbour's disturbed s burglar.
         e.   The neighbour's *dog sdisturb burglar ed.
         f.   *Dog ed the s neighbour's disturb the s burglar.

Let us look more closely at some of these examples. We can say that *boys* and *disturbed* are words because they belong to the class of elements that are the smallest units that can be manipulated by syntactic rules. For instance, when passives sentences are formed, whole words (or phrases) are shunted around as you can see if you compare the active sentence in [5.2a] with its passive counterpart in [5.2b]. By contrast, the forms –s and –ed are not words. Neither of them can occur on its own, or be independently relocated in a new position in the sentence by a syntactic rule. Hence the ungrammaticality of the examples in [5.2c]–[5.2f] respectively. Of course, phrases like *the burglar* and *the neighbour's dog* are free forms capable of occurring in isolation, or being moved from one position to another in a sentence. But they are not words since they

ADVANCES BOX 5.1

Neologisms – *are you a shlumpadinka?*

Neologisms appear every day. Few of them become established words that the speech community broadly recognizes and which get listed in august dictionaries like Merriam-Webster or the Oxford English Dictionary. *Shlumpadinka* is one that seems to have made it. Slang words, especially those used by celebrities who are the high priests of popular culture, probably have a better chance of catching on than words like those listed in [5.1] that are created by anonymous speakers. Notice how this one introduces into English from Yiddish a consonant cluster in the *Shl* (/ʃl/) syllable onset that is not already found in the language (see also *Shm* – reduplication on page 89 below).

shlumpadinka • \shlum-puh-DINK-uh\ ◀•• noun
: a woman who dresses like she has completely given up on herself and it shows : a dowdy and unstylish woman

Example Sentence:
There you are running out to get the paper looking like a shlumpadinka. – Oprah Winfrey (27 April 2007)

Did you know?
'I have to practice not looking like a *shlumpadinka* on the air,' said Oprah Winfrey on her eponymous show, broadcast April 15, 1997. Oprah has occasionally separated *shlumpa* and *dinka*, the constituent parts of the word, for emphasis: 'You are watching right now in your sweats...the same sweats you had on yesterday and the day before...you are a shlumpa and a dinka and you know it!' Oprah has also used the word *shlumpadink* to refer to a masculine subject, although this form is somewhat less frequently heard. Oprah has often used *shlumpadinka* attributively to modify another noun, as in 'It's my *shlumpadinka* shoes!' or 'You're watching me right now in your *shlumpadinka* pajamas.'

By permission. From the *Merriam-Webster Online Dictionary*
© 2008 by Merriam-Webster, Incorporated (www.merriam-webster.com).

are not the smallest units that syntax manipulates. They can be broken down into smaller free forms, namely the words *the, neighbour's* and *boys*.

This is not the problem completely solved yet. We still need to clarify what we mean by **word**. The term 'word' is used in a variety of senses. These are summarized in Table 5.2.

5.2   Simple and complex words

Is a word the smallest unit of morphological structure? The answer has to be no. Take the word *boys*: it contains two meaningful structural units, *boy* and *–s* (plural). The minimal unit which has a meaning (e.g., *boy*) or a grammatical function (e.g., *–s* (plural)) is called a **morpheme**. Identify the morphemes found in each of the following words:

[5.3]   dog   childish   undeservedly   rewriting

| Table 5.2 | *Distinguishing between the senses of the term 'word'* |

What is a word?

Word-form

A word-form is a shape that represents a word in speech or writing. In the written language we call word-forms **orthographic words.** Thus, the last sentence has nine orthographic words. Normally, an orthographic word is preceded and followed by a space (or a punctuation mark). I say 'normally' because sometimes a compound word is written with white space surrounding each of its constituent words (see *disorient express* in Table 5.1). Conversely, Internet web-speak has produced a convention of writing web addresses 'as all one word' as in *http:// www.alloneword.org/* when clearly what we have are separate words.

The word-form in the spoken language is called the **phonological word.** It is subject to various phonological constraints. For instance, as we saw in Chapter 4 (Section 4.4), all content words must have a syllable that bears primary stress. Furthermore, in a compound word one word has a syllable that outranks the rest in prominence.

Lexeme

The term 'lexeme' (or **lexical item**) is used when by 'word' we mean **vocabulary item,** i.e., an item requiring a single dictionary entry. Thus we can say that the word-forms *speak, speaking, spoke* and *spoken* are all different manifestations of the lexeme *speak*.

Grammatical word

Words viewed as syntactic units are called **grammatical words.** In this case we consider a lexeme together with the morphological and syntactic properties (morpho-syntactic properties for short) associated with it. For example *speaking, spoke* and *spoken* are characterized as grammatical words in this way:

- *speaking* is the **progressive** form of the verb *speak*
- *spoke* is the is the **past tense** form of the verb *speak*
- *spoken* is the is the **past participle** form of the verb SPEAK (the past participle is the form of a verb that appears after the auxiliary verb *have*, as in *I have spoken, she has spoken, we had spoken*).

I expect that your solution is like the one in [5.4].

[5.4]	**Words**	**Constituent morphemes**
	dog	dog
	childish	child-ish
	undeservedly	un-deserv-ed-ly
	rewriting	re-writ-ing

We can distinguish between simple words which contain just one morpheme (e.g., *dog*) and complex words containing more than one morpheme, for example, *child-ish, un-deser-ed-ly* and *re-writ-ing*. The relationship between a linguistic sign and its meaning is arbitrary. There is no reason, for example, why *horse* means 🐎. In French the same animal is called *cheval,* in Italian *cavallo,* in Korean 말, in Dutch *paard,* in German *Pferd.* None of these is a better or worse way of symbolizing the concept 'horse'. There is no principle that can enable one to determine which linguistic sign will have a particular meaning. The meanings of all morphemes and of very many words therefore have to be listed in our mental lexicon, and memorized.

You might protest that in the case of **onomatopoeia**, where the word imitates some aspect of the meaning of the concept it represents, the linguistic sign is iconic and hence not arbitrary. You would be right, up to a point. But observe that the iconicity is heavily tinged with convention – and arbitrariness. Thus, for example, the sound imitative of a dog's bark is *woof* in English, but, in Romanian *ham ham,* in Russian *gaf gaf,* in Estonian *auh auh* and in Korean *meong meong.* And the differences do not reflect any discernible dialectal differences among canine populations found in the different countries where those languages are spoken.

Returning to morphemes, observe that they are classified as **free morphemes** or **bound morphemes**. A free morpheme can occur in isolation (as a word), for example, *dog, write, deserve* and *child.* But a bound morpheme cannot occur in isolation, for example, in [4.4] the forms *–ish, un–, –ed, –ly, re–, –ing* are bound morphemes.

Furthermore, any form that is used to represent a morpheme in called a **morph**. Thus the word *child-ish* has two morphs and *re-writ-ing* has three. Many morphemes are represented by more than one actual form. In other words, they have a number of variants that realize them in different contexts. Such variants are called **allomorphs**. (The parallelism between *morph, allomorph* and *morpheme* on the one hand, and *phone, allophone* and *phoneme* on the other (Chapter 3, Section 3.2) should be obvious.) Allomorphs are distinct with regard to form. But they have the same grammatical or semantic function. Allomorphs are always in complementary distribution, just like allophones. Each allomorph is restricted to appearing in its allotted contexts. For instance, the indefinite article in English has two allomorphs *a ~ an.* (The symbol ~ means 'alternates with' or plainly 'or'.) These two forms have exactly the same meaning. But they occur in different contexts (i.e., in complementary distribution):

[5.5] a. *a* is used if the next word starts with a consonant, e.g., *a leg, a mother, a tomato*

   b. *an* is used if the next word starts with a vowel, e.g., *an ear, an aunt, an egg*

5.3 Word structure: a closer look

In this section, we shall consider the various types of morpheme, on the basis of their location and role in the word.

Root, base and affix

A **base** is a unit to which elements can be added in word-formation. For instance, starting off with the base *write,* we can add the bound morpheme

–ing to form *writing*. Then *writing* can be used as a base to which we attach *re–* to form *rewriting*. An **affix** is a bound morpheme that must be attached to a base. If it precedes the base it is called a **prefix** and if it follows the base it is called a **suffix**. In [5.4] *re–* and *un– are* prefixes while *–ish, –ed, –ly* and *–ing* are suffixes. The base of a word may be a **root**. The root is the rump of a word that remains when all the affixes have been stripped away. *Write* is both a root and a base. But a base need not be a bare root. In many cases the base contains a root and one or more affixes; for example, we can take a root like *write* as the base, and add to it the prefix *re–* to obtain the word *rewrite*. This word, already containing a root and a prefix, can be used again as a base to which we add the suffix *–ing* to obtain the word *rewriting*. As mentioned above, at the start of this chapter, we can also form a compound word by combining two bases that are words in their own right, for example, *ear + witness* gives *earwitness*.

Another major dichotomy is between **lexical morphemes** (also known as 'content words') and **functional morphemes** (also called 'function words'). Lexical morphemes are nouns, adjectives, verbs and adverbs *(NAVA* words in Chapter 6, Section 6.2). Functional morphemes, so called because they mostly signal syntactic relationships, include prepositions, pronouns and determiners (see Chapter 6, Section 6.7). An obvious difference that has important consequences for morphology is that lexical morphemes belong to an open class which can expand. But functional morphemes belong to an essentially closed set that admits no new members. New nouns, verbs, adjectives (and to a lesser degree adverbs) are created all the time. However, new prepositions, pronouns, determiners and the like are very rarely created. It follows that the branch of morphology that examines the creation of new vocabulary items is primarily concerned with lexical morphemes (see Chapter 15).

5.4 Inflection versus derivation

This leads us to the two broad classes of word-formation processes: **inflection** and **derivation**. In general terms inflection is syntactically motivated word-formation. For a word to appear in certain syntactic contexts, the syntax requires that it must have certain morphological marking, otherwise the sentence is ungrammatical. For instance, in Standard English if you have a third-person singular subject of a present tense verb, you must suffix *–s* to it, or else your sentence will be ungrammatical:

[5.6] a. She sleeps.   b. *We sleeps.
           Othman sleeps   *They sleeps
           It sleeps   *You sleeps

Unlike inflection, **derivation** is not motivated by the syntax. Rather, its role is to create new lexical items. Derivation involves one or both of these two things: creating a new lexical item with a different meaning from that of the original word or changing the syntactic class of the input lexical item as seen in [5.7]:

[5.7] a. **Derivation changing meaning**
  Input   **Derived word**
  possible   impossible
  tell   retell
  do   undo
  b. **Derivation changing syntactic category**
  faith (noun)   faithful (adjective)
  fierce (adjective)   fiercely (adverb)
  sing (verb)   singer (noun)

In this section we will focus on the notion of inflection and the general morphological properties of inflectional morphemes, and return to derivation in Section 5.6.

English has a very small number of inflectional morphemes, and they are all suffixes. Inflectional suffixes form a closed set. The language no longer adds to its inventory of inflectional endings. But historically English used to have considerably more complex inflectional morphology (see Chapter 17). Inflectional suffixes are listed in Table 5.3. The next chapter provides an opportunity to see how these inflectional suffixes are used in grammar.

The fact that inflection is syntax driven has already been highlighted. Many inflectional processes involve **agreement.** This refers to cases where the head of a grammatical unit requires elements in construction with it to take on certain morpho-syntactic properties of the head. In [5.8], for example, the morpho-syntactic property number that is associated with the head of the noun phrase (NP) (see Chapter 7, Section 7.5) dictates the choice of inflection of the demonstrative. The demonstrative must agree in number with the head noun:

[5.8] **Singular**   **Plural**
  this boy (*these boy)   those boys (*this boys)
  that boy (*those boy)   those boys (*that boys)

Another example of inflection is subject-verb number agreement in Standard English as illustrated in [5.6] above.

Alternatively, inflectional processes may be due to what is called **government** in traditional grammar. The notion of government depicts situations where the head of a syntactic construction imposes certain morpho-syntactic properties on elements dependent on it. For example, English prepositions require NPs following them to be in the accusative (also called objective) case. This is overtly marked by case inflection if the NP is a pronoun as in *He ran **towards her** (*towards she*, etc.) The preposition itself is not in the accusative case – it has no case marking of any kind. But the pronoun that follows it (which it governs) must be in the accusative case.

Table 5.3   *Inflectional suffixes*

Inflectional suffixes of nouns		Orthographic form		Examples	
PLURAL					
Native regular plurals		–s		*toy*	*toys*
	Native irregular plurals	/f/ voicing		*leaf*	*leaves*
		internal vowel change		*mouse*	*mice*
		–en plural		*ox*	*oxen*
		zero	*sheep*	*sheep*	
		Sing.	**Pl.**		
	Borrowed (all) irregular plurals	–us	–i	*cactus*	*cacti*
		–a	–ae	*amoeba*	*amoebae*
		–ex/–ix	–ices	*matrix*	*matrices*
		–on	–a	*automaton*	*automata*
		–eau	–eaux	*bureau*	*bureaux*
		zero	zero	*chassis*	*chassis*
		–o	–i	*concerto*	*concerti*
		zero	–im	*seraph*	*seraphim*
GENITIVE		–s		*student's*	
Inflectional suffixes of verbs					
third-person, present, singular		–s		*cooks*	
	Progressive	–ing		*cooking*	
Past tense	Regular	–ed		*cooked*	
	Irregular	zero		*(let→) let*	
		(various) usually with internal vowel change		*(sing →) sang* *(take →) took,* etc.	
Past participle		–ed, –en		*cooked, driven*	
Inflectional suffixes of adjectives					
Comparative degree		–er		*longer*	
Superlative degree		–est		*longest*	

Finally, inflectional properties may be inherent. A morpheme is associated with those properties always regardless of context. For instance some nouns have the property [+count] and can be marked plural while others are not countable and lack a plural form, for example, *hammer* has the plural form *hammers* but *equipment* has no plural (**equipments*) (see Chapter 6, Section 6.5.1).

In forming a word, a lexical base to which inflectional morphemes are attached (e.g., *sleep* in *sleep-s*) is called a **stem**. In a complex word which contains a sequence of suffixes, the derivational suffix is normally part of the stem. So, derivational suffixes are nearer the root and inflectional ones are on the outside as in *sing-er-s* where *–er,* the suffix deriving an agentive noun (one who does X) is next to the root and the plural suffix is at the edge of the word.

Another difference, to be discussed in more detail below, is that inflectional morphology is for the most part regular, but derivational morphology tends to be sporadic. Almost all inflectional stems that are eligible to take an inflectional suffix do so. But rarely do a majority of bases eligible for a derivational process successfully undergo it. For instance, virtually all verbs have an *–ing* (e.g., *writing*). But in derivational morphology it is the norm for rules to apply patchily, for example, you can *whiten* or *darken* things but you cannot **greenen* or **yellowen* them. If a method of word-formation is actively used to form new words it is said to be 'productive'. So, we can say that, by and large, inflectional processes tend to be more productive than derivational ones. True, some of the irregular variants of the inflectional morphemes in Table 5.3 are virtually unproductive (e.g., zero plural). But all the regular variants are very productive. We can suffix *–ing*, *–ed –s*, etc. to new forms. If we tried to do the same with a derivational suffix, for example, *–fy*, we would produce acceptable words like *purify, glorify, terrify, gentrify*; but we must avoid getting carried away. Otherwise we would create words like **dilligentify*, **accountantify* and **joyify*, which are not allowed. The line between what is allowed and what isn't is fuzzy. What do you make of *complexify*?

5.5 Morphological processes

Let us now survey some common morphological processes used in word-building.

Conversion

When **conversion** (also called 'zero-derivation') is used, a new word is formed by assigning an existing word a new syntactic category without changing its form in any way. You can tell which word class the derived word belongs to by looking at the syntactic context in which it appears.

[5.9] a. Put it in the bin [noun]   b. Bin[verb] it!
           Take a fast[adjective] train   The train goes very fast[adverb]
           He has short legs [noun]   We legged [verb] it

Conversion is a very productive method of deriving words, especially verbs from nouns and nouns from verbs.

Affixation

Predictably, **affixation** is word-building involving the use of affixes. This is extremely common. Affixes can be classified as prefixes and suffixes depending on whether they precede or follow the root, as we have already seen in Section 5.3. Another type of affix is the **infix**. This is an affix inserted in the root itself. Thus in the Alabama language of east Texas the second-person singular is indicated by the infix *–chi–* as in *ho-chi-fna* 'you (singular) smell' (from *hofna* 'to smell') (Stump, 2001:131). In English, infixation is very marginal. Expletive infixation is used quite routinely for expressive purposes as in the examples in [5.10] from McCarthy (1982) but it has no grammatical role.

[5.10] Mononga-'fuckin-hela (Monongahela is a river in Pittsburgh, Pennsylvania)
        Ala-fuckin-'bama

fan-fuckin-'tastic
Dub-fuckin- 'rovnik
in-fucking-'stantiate

Other expletives such as *bloody* and *friggin* can also be infixed.

If one fancies a bit of colourful language, how does one decide when and where to deploy an expletive, you may ask. According to McCarthy (1982), the expletive infixation phenomenon is subject to a phonological constraint that is best stated in terms of metrical foot structure. The word in which the infix is inserted must be at least three syllables long and the infix must go inside the word after the syllable preceding a trochaic metrical foot (i.e., a foot with a stressed syllable followed by an unstressed syllable). Hence the unacceptability of **Glas-fuckin-gow* (from disyllabic *Glasgow*) and **Jo-friggin-hannesburg* (from four syllable *Johannesburg*). This is a good example of how phonological structure can play a key role in determining if and how a word-formation operation applies. It is a good example of how you cannot describe word-formation without taking into account phonological information.

Zero morph

In Table 5.3, under the list of allomorphs of the noun plural morpheme, I listed zero as one of the possibilities. This was to cover the case of the word *sheep* which, unlike other nouns, gets no overt marking of number even when its meaning is plural as in *Twenty sheep were stolen yesterday*. *Clearly twenty* indicates plurality. The auxiliary verb *were*, which is in the plural, indicates that English syntax recognizes the plurality of this noun which is in the subject noun phrase and requires the verb agreeing with it to be plural. Likewise many monosyllabic verbs, for example, *let, cut, hit*, are not marked overtly in any way when they occur in a context where the syntax requires past tense inflection on the verb, for example, *Yesterday I cut it* (**Yesterday I cutted it*). For this reason zero is listed as one of the allomorphs of the third-person singular present tense marker. Recognizing zeros, as we have done, makes sense because we have made the theoretical assumption that morphemes realize or represent the abstract concepts that lie behind morphemes. It wouldn't make much sense if we assumed rather that morphemes are actually made up of phonemes. (See the discussion of exponence below.)

Internal change

Sometimes inflection is done by changing a vowel in the root. This is called **internal change** (or 'apophony'):

[5.11] a.

Nouns		b.	Verbs		
Singular	**Plural**		**Present tense**	**Past tense**	**Past participle**
foot	feet		ride	rode	ridden
[fʊt]	/fiːt/		[ɹaɪd]	[ɹəʊd]	[ɹɪdən]
mouse	mice		sing	sang	sung
[maʊs]	[maɪs]		[sɪŋ]	[sæŋ]	[sʌŋ]

In some cases, apophony may be accompanied by affixation as in the case of *ridden.*

Exponence

The key point to note is that the relationship between morphs and morpho-syntactic features such as plural, past tense, present tense, etc. is one of realization (or representation) rather than composition. Morphs belonging to a given morpheme represent one or more morpho-syntactic features. Matthews, in a number of publications going back to the early 1970s, proposed characterizing this relationship using the notion of **exponence** (Matthews, 1991: 175). He distinguishes different types of exponence:

(i) **Simple exponence**
    Simple exponence occurs when one morph (form) realizes a single morpho-syntactic feature, for example, [s] in *sweets* realizes plural, and [t] (the actual pronunciation of *–ed*) in *parked* realizes past tense or past participle.
(ii) **Cumulative exponence**
    A single morph realizes more than one morpho-syntactic feature simultaneously. Take the example of [s] in *she thinks*. The [s] of the verb represents third person, present tense, and singular.

Suppletion

Normally allomorphs of a morpheme are phonologically related. Thus, the regular past tense ending in English is realized as [t] after a verb whose last sound is voiceless, and as [d] after a verb whose last sound is voiced (cf. *parked* [pɑːkt], *missed* [mɪst], *watched* [wɔːtʃt] vs. *lived* [lɪvd], *ruled* [ɹuːld] and *spied* [spaɪd]). The sounds [t] and [d] are quite similar, both being alveolar stops.

Occasionally we find allomorphs of the same morpheme whose phonological shapes are unrelated. If a phonological relationship is totally non-existent, we speak of **total suppletion**. The words *good* and *better, go* and *went* are examples of total suppletion. The term 'partial suppletion' is used to describe situations where residual phonetic similarity between allomorphs can be detected as in the case of the verb *seek ~ sought; bring ~ brought*, etc.

Syncretism

The term **syncretism** refers to a situation where morpho-syntactic categories that are represented by distinct forms elsewhere are mapped on to a single form in some contexts. This was obliquely noted in the discussion of exponence above. In many regular verbs, and some irregular ones, the morpho-syntactic properties past tense and past participle are mapped onto different forms as shown in [5.12a]:

[5.12] a. **No syncretism:**

Past	Past participle
ride	ridden
gave	given
sang	sung

 b. **Syncretism:**

Past	Past participle
cooked	cooked
listened	listened
brought	brought

ADVANCES BOX 5.2

Inflection vs. derivation – the importance of function

A matter related to the discussion of syncretism is the overlap in the realization of distinct inflectional and derivational morphemes. In Table 5.3, we noted that –*ing* is an inflectional suffix marking the progressive form of the verb. The use of –*ing* to represent the progressive is illustrated in [5.13a]. Contrast that with its use in [5.13b] where it is used to mark the gerund. (A gerund is a nominal form that comes out of a verb as a result of derivational operation.) *Taking cocaine* is a noun phrase headed by the gerund *taking*. We can use the standard syntactic test of substitution to confirm this. In syntax we can only replace like with like, without affecting grammaticality. We can replace *Taking cocaine* with a noun (noun phrase) like *Success*, so *taking cocaine* is also a noun phrase.

[5.13]	a.	*He is taking cocaine.*	Inflection : *taking* progressive form of verb formed by suffixing –*ing*
	b.	*Taking cocaine makes users feel on top of the world, allegedly.*	Derivation: *taking* gerund formed from verb by suffixing –*ing*

The moral of the story is that to determine whether a suffix is inflectional or derivational we need to examine how it is used in the syntax. Shape alone is insufficient.

Without syncretism there is internal change and suffixation of –*en*, or both, to signal past participle as seen in (4.14 a). With syncretism, exactly the same form, i.e., –*ed* is suffixed, only the context can help distinguish between past participle and past tense.

Haplology

Avoidance of sequences of identical linguistic forms is a phenomenon found in many languages. When two identical or very similar syllables or sounds occur next to each other it's not unusual for one to be deleted. This is called **haplology**. It can happen internally within a word or root morpheme of at least three syllables if a weakly stressed syllable is next to an adjacent syllable that is virtually identical as in *probably* [pɹɒbəbli] → *probly* [pɹɒbli]. Likewise, when a singular noun or a plural noun ending in [–s] or [–z] is put in the genitive, haplology occurs. Since the genitive suffix is spelled <s> and is phonologically realized as [s] ~ [z] (or [ɪz]), it is too similar to the final sound of the base for comfort. So, it is elided in many people's pronunciation and is normally omitted in the written form of the language (cf. *Jones's house* → *Jones' house*, *players's agents* → *players' agents*, etc.). The genitive in these situations is indicated merely by the presence of the apostrophe.

Noun-verb stress doublets   *Table 5.4*

| Noun | | | Verb | | |
Initial stress			Final stress		
'reject	'progress	'contract	re'ject	pro'gress	con'tract
'produce	'refuse	'digest	pro'duce	re'fuse	di'gest
'import	'insult	'escort	im'port	in'sult	es'cort

ADVANCES BOX 5.3

Shm-reduplication

None of the types of reduplication described above is very productive. By contrast **shm-reduplication**, a phenomenon that has attracted considerable interest among linguists of late, is quite productive. Shm-reduplication is not very new; it has been in the language for over half a century. According to Nevins and Vaux (2003), it came into English from Yiddish as a result of language contact. In Yiddish, many words beginning with *s(c)hm–* have negative connotations. The pejorative use of *Shm–* was extended to English by Jewish speakers in the northeast of the United States. Gradually it spread to other dialects.

Shm-reduplication derives its name from the fact that *shm–* is used as the onset of the first syllable of the reduplicated word. The meaning of the reduplicated word tends to have uncomplimentary connotations (e.g., *You call yourself a captain? Captain shmaptain, what leadership did you show? You just cried when we went a goal down*).

Shm-reduplication is subject to a variety of phonological constraints. They are enumerated as follows by Vaux and Nevin (2003):

(i) If the first syllable of a word contains a lone consonant, that consonant is replaced by *shm–*, e.g., *baby shmaby, plan shman* and *table shamble.*

(ii) If a word starts with a consonant cluster some speakers just replace the initial consonant of the cluster while retaining the rest, for example, *breakfast shmreakfast* while others replace the entire onset cluster with *shm–*, e.g., *plan shman, gravity schmavity.*

(iii) If a word starts with a vowel, *shm–* is put right at the beginning of the reduplicated form, which thereby acquires an onset to its first syllable, for example, *opinion shmopinion, apple shmapple, optician shmoptician* (see Vaux and Nevins (2003) for further discussion).

Observe that [ʃm]– is not a permissible onset in the native phonology. But language contact between Yiddish and English has resulted in the introduction of that syllable onset into English (see *shlumpadinka* on page 79). Also, observe that shm-reduplication illustrates another important general principle, namely the fact that certain morphological rules are very closely bound to morphological operations. We will return to this in the section below.

Stress placement

In a minority of cases, derivation is effected by changing stress placement. Nouns can be derived from verbs and verbs from nouns by the rule introduced above (Chapter 4, Section 4.4). The relevant data are in Table 4.7 which is repeated on page 89 as Table 5.4 for convenience.

Reduplication

Reduplication is the creation of a new word by repetition of an existing word in its entirety, or in part. Repetition of the entire word is called **full reduplication** to contrast it with **partial reduplication** where only part of a word is repeated. Full reduplication is exemplified by words like *bang bang, bye-bye, night-night* and *go-go.* Partial reduplication has traditionally involved rhyming, as in *airy-fairy, hoity-toity, razzle-dazzle, nitty-gritty* and *willy-nilly,* or ablaut as in *tip-top, shilly-shally, zigzag, pitter-patter.* The process affects a monosyllabic word. The vowel of the rhyme is changed, leaving the rest of the word intact. In addition, there is a highly productive 'shm– reduplication' pattern (see Advances Box 5.3 on p. 89).

5.6 Allomorphy

In Section 5.2 the concept of allomorphs was introduced. This is a central notion in morphology. We will revisit it now and look at it more closely. If a morpheme is represented by more than one form, on what basis is a particular allomorph selected to appear in a particular context? In a nutshell the factors that govern the selection of allomorphs can be one, or a combination, of the following: grammatical, lexical or phonological. We will consider the three in turn.

Occasionally, alternation in the representation of a morpheme is unique to a particular word. If the root of that word is associated with certain morpho-syntactic properties, a particular allomorph of the root morpheme or affix must be selected. A good example of this is the word *oxen,* the plural of *ox.* However, words like *box* and *fox* which rhyme with *ox* take the regular plural ending *–s* that is pronounced as [–ɪz] after a noun ending in a sibilant consonant (see [5.14], [5.15] below). Hence we say *foxes* [fɒksɪz] and boxes [bɒksɪz]. *Vixen,* the female *fox,* is another example. The root morpheme is changed in the formation of the feminine noun. We don't get the expected **foxess* or **she-fox.* Normally, to create a female noun referring to a person or animal, *she–* is prefixed, as in *she-goat* or *–ess* is suffixed as in *lion-ess, princ(e)-ess.*

Sometimes, the choice of allomorph is determined by the grammatical word of which the root is a part. For example, the verb root *speak* has two forms: [spəʊk] is the allomorph used when the grammatical word has morpho-syntactic properties, past tense (*spoke*) or past participle (*spoken*). In all other contexts, the allomorph [spi:k] is used. Likewise, verbs like *keep* [ki:p], *sleep* [sli:p] and *weep* [wi:p] have an allomorph with root vowel [e] in the past tense and past participle (*kept, slept* and *wept*), and an allomorph with [i] elsewhere. As what triggers the alternation is the association of the verb root with particular morpho-syntactic features, the phenomenon is called 'grammatical conditioning' of allomorphy.

However, by far the commonest reason for allomorphy is **phonological conditioning**. When morphology interfaces with phonology there is a strong tendency for allomorphs to accommodate to the sounds in their neighbours. To see this, before you read on, study the data in [5.14], paying special attention to the final sound of each stem without the suffix and then identify the allomorphs of the plural morphemes. Write a general rule stating the phonological factors responsible for the distribution of the allomorphs that you have identified:

Allomorphs of the regular noun plural morpheme

[5.14]	a.	bees	b.	buses	c.	socks
		dogs		judges		bits
		cribs		foxes		steps
		ways		badges		proofs
		buns		watches		paths
		bell		mazes		myths

I hope you have determined that the regular plural morpheme has the allomorphs [z] ~ [ɪz] ~ [s] and that their distribution is as follows:

[5.15]   a.   If a noun ends in a voiced sound (other than a sibilant) allomorph [z] is selected, as seen in [4.14a].
   b.   If a noun ends in a sibilant allomorph [ɪz] (or [–əz] for some speakers) is selected, as seen in [4.14b].
   c.   If a noun ends in a voiceless sound (other than a sibilant) allomorph [s] is selected, as seen in [4.14c].

Note: A sibilant is a hissing (strident) fricative or affricate – one of [s, z, ʃ, ʒ, tʃ, dʒ]).

You can see that there are systematic relationships between the allomorphs of this morpheme that can be stated in a general statement or rule. Let us assume that each morpheme has one **lexical representation** (or **underlying representation**) that is listed in the dictionary. The grammar provides a system of rules that enable us to map the underlying representation of a morpheme on to all the different allomorphs that represent that morpheme in different contexts. In this case, the best candidate to enter in the lexicon as the underlying representation of the plural morpheme is /z/, as it facilitates the simplest and most general statement of the regularities. The rules needed are given in [5.16]. They are written using the formalisms introduced in Chapter 3 (Section 3.1), please review that section before proceeding.

[5.16]   **Regular allomorphs of the plural morpheme**
   The underlying representation of plural is /z/.
   a.   **[ɪ] (or [ə]) insertion**
   Insert [ɪ] before /z/ if the noun ends in a sibilant (e.g., *bus → buses, judge → judges*).

$$\emptyset \rightarrow [\text{ɪ}] \; / \; [\text{+sibilant}]_\# \; \underline{\quad} \; \begin{bmatrix} \text{+alveolar} \\ \text{+fricative} \\ \text{+voice} \end{bmatrix}_\#$$

b. **/z/ devoicing**

In all other cases, if the noun ends in a voiceless consonant, remove voicing from /z/ so that it assimilates the voicelessness of the final voiceless consonant by becoming [s] (e.g., *sock* → *socks*).

$$\begin{bmatrix} +\text{alveolar} \\ +\text{fricative} \\ +\text{voice} \end{bmatrix} \rightarrow [-\text{voice}] \Big/ [-\text{voice}]]_{\#} \underline{\quad} {}_{\#}$$

c. Elsewhere (i.e., after voiced sounds (except voiced sibilants covered by [5.16a]), no rule is needed, just keep /z/ unchanged and pronounce it as [z] (e.g., *bee* → *bees*).

As seen in [5.17], what we have said about voice assimilation being the factor that motivates the selection of the allomorphs of the plural morpheme is true of other similar morphemes, namely the genitive suffix –*s* and the –*s* suffix of the third-person singular present tense:

[5.17]	**Allomorph of the genitive suffix**	**Examples**	**Allomorph of 3rd pers. pres. tense**	**Examples**
	[s] after voiceless sounds	*cook's, giraffe's, Jack's*	[s] after voiceless sounds	*packs, writes, laughs*
	[ɪz] after sibilants	*nurse's, witch's, judge's, Rose's*	[ɪz] after sibilants	*whinges, pushes, curses, advises*
	[z] elsewhere (i.e., after voiced sounds (excluding sibilants))	*Rita's, mum's, dog's, rogue's*	[z] elsewhere (i.e. after voiced sounds (excluding sibilants))	*spies, grabs, brags, wins*

Let us now consider the regular past tense spelled –*ed*:

[5.18]	**Allomorph of the regular past tense**	**Examples**
	[t] after voiceless sounds	*jumped, laughed, missed, pushed, cooked*
	[ɪd] (or [əd]) after alveolar stops (i.e., /t/ or /d/)	*sorted, granted, divided, branded*
	[d] elsewhere (i.e., after voiced sounds excluding /d/	*pursued, moaned, grabbed, paved, travelled*

The similarities among all these suffixes are obvious. Voice assimilation has a pivotal role in English inflectional morphology. The plural, the genitive and the third-person singular, present tense suffixes are each represented by an underlying /z/, which is a voiced alveolar obstruent. The past tense is also represented by a voiced alveolar obstruent, the plosive /d/. All of these suffixes must agree in voicing with the last sound of the stem to which they are attached. So, voiceless stem-final sounds are followed by [s] or [t] and voiced ones by [z] or [d]. In all cases, the insertion of [ɪ] before /z/ takes place to avert an alveolar stop standing next to [d] or [t] that precedes it in the stem. In the same vein, the insertion of /ɪ/ also prevents [s] or [z] from abutting with a sibilant that precedes it in the stem. It doesn't take a conspiracy theory *aficionado* to conclude that there is a conspiracy in English that prevents the sound of the suffix being too similar to the last sound of the stem before it.

A slight amendment of the rules in [5.16] is all that is needed to state the distribution of the allomorphs of the past tense morpheme:

[5.19]   **Regular allomorph of the past tense morpheme**
The underlying representation of plural is /d/

a.   [ɪ] (or [ə]) insertion
Insert [ɪ] before /d/ if the verb ends in an alveolar plosive (i.e., /t/ or /d/).

$$\emptyset \rightarrow /\,\text{ɪ}\,/ \; \left/ \; \begin{bmatrix} +\text{alveolar} \\ +\text{stop} \end{bmatrix} \right]_{\#} \underline{} \begin{bmatrix} +\text{alveolar} \\ +\text{stop} \\ +\text{voice} \end{bmatrix}_{\#}$$

b.   /d/ devoicing
In all other cases, if the verb ends in a voiceless consonant, remove voicing from /d/ so that it assimilates the voicelessness of the final voiceless consonant and becomes [t].

$$\begin{bmatrix} +\text{alveolar} \\ +\text{stop} \\ +\text{voice} \end{bmatrix} \rightarrow [-\text{voice}] \; \left/ \; [-\text{voice}]_{\#} \underline{} \# \right.$$

c.   Elsewhere (i.e., after voiced sounds), no rule is needed, just keep /d/ unchanged; pronounce it as [d].

Morphophonemic rules

Linguists have paid particular attention to those situations where, for a rule to apply, both phonological and morphological conditions have to be met. Rules implicated in such cases are called **morphophonemic rules**. A famous case is provided in [5.20]:

[5.20]

Plural		Genitive	
wives	[waɪvz]	wife's	[waɪfs]
lives	[laɪvz]	life's	[laɪfs]
thieves	[θiːvz]	thief's	[θiːfs]
leaves	[liːvz]	leaf's	[liːfs]

The alternation of the final consonant of the noun stem between [f] ~ [v] has a phonological basis. Only labio-dental fricatives are affected. But the rule voicing /f/ to make it [v] requires a morphological prompt. Although exactly the same phonological input is available in both the genitive and the plural, /f/ + /z/, only in the plural does the change of /f/ to [v] occur.

Morphophonemic rules are quite common. If you look back at the rule in [5.16] which accounts for the distribution of the allomorphs of the plural, genitive and a third-person singular present tense suffix, you will observe that this too is a morphophonemic rule. It is only sparked off where the /z/ in question represents one of the suffixes: plural, genitive or third-person singular. It does not apply where /z/ does not represent one of those suffixes (*cf. *prince* [pɹɪns] (*[pɹɪnz]), *abscond* [əbskɒnd] (*[əbzkɒnd]). Because morphophonemic rules require a morphological trigger, their application is never automatic. In this they differ from true phonological rules (like voiceless stop aspiration and /l/-velarization described in the last chapter), which are automatic and apply anywhere so long as their phonological prerequisites are met. Note also that morphophonemic rules tend to be exception ridden, unlike phonological rules (e.g., there are no subclasses of plosives that are exceptionally not aspirated when they occur in a context where aspiration is required). But, even when all the conditions for their application appear to be met, morphophonemic rules often fail to apply. For example, /f/ doesn't become [v] in the plural forms *chiefs*, *toughs* and *goofs*.

Recall the homorganic nasal assimilation rule governing *con–* that was presented in [3.16] and [3.17] in Chapter 3 (Section 3.1). It is reproduced in [5.21]:

[5.21] **Homorganic nasal assimilation**

$$\begin{bmatrix} +\text{nasal} \\ +\text{alveolar} \end{bmatrix} \rightarrow / \,[\alpha\text{place}] / \underline{\quad} [\alpha\text{place}]$$

This rule accounts also for the distribution of the allomorphs of the negative prefix /in–/ as shown in [5.22]:

[5.22]	[ɪm]	[ɪn]	[ɪŋ]	[ɪn]
	before a base starting with a labial consonant	before a base starting with an alveolar consonant	before a base starting with a velar consonant	if the base starts with a vowel
	imprudent	indirect	ingrate	inapplicable
	imbalance	intransitive	inconsiderate	inobtrusive
	impregnable	insolvent	incorporeal	inedible
	immaculate	insincere	inglorious	inimitable

The fact that [in] is used if a base starts with a vowel is clear evidence in favour of positing /in/ rather than any other allomorph as the underlying representation. Before a vowel there is no pressure to change the place of articulation of the nasal as vowels do not have places of articulation. So, the nasal that occurs in that position must be the nasal that is found in the underlying representation of the morpheme.

Finally, observe that, general though it is, homorganic nasal assimilation is not a purely phonological rule. It isn't automatically activated whenever its prerequisites are met. Accordingly, the negative prefix *in–* obeys it; but the negative prefix *un–* defies it (cf. *unbutton* [ʌnbʌtən], *uncap* [ʌnkæp], etc.). Since the circumstances where it applies must be expressly specified, homorganic nasal assimilation is a morphophonemic rule. Some nasals obey it, others don't. It depends on which morpheme they represent.

5.7 Derivation

As we noted in Section 5.3, derivation creates a new lexical item with a new meaning or grammatical category. In this section we will examine more closely the derivational morphology of English. The processes used are of three types: **affixation**, **conversion** and **compounding**.

5.7.1 Affixation

The most important method of derivation is affixation. Table 5.5 lists examples of English derivational affixes. Many well-established affixes are

Derivational affixes   *Table 5.5*

	Affix	Change	Examples
a.	**Suffix**		
	–able	V→Adj	likeable, lendable, teachable
	–acy	N→Adj	supremacy, conspiracy, celibacy
	–ant	V→N	celebrant, applicant
	–al	V→N	betrothal, denial
	–al	N→Adj	universal, educational
	–ee	V→N	payee, employee
	–er	V→N	driver, teacher
	–ful	N→Adj	pitiful, dreadful
	–ic	N→Adj	microscopic, philanthropic
	–ing	V→N	surfing, ironing
	–ing	V→Adj	sailing, travelling
	–ish	N→Adj	childish, boorish
	–ity	Adj→N	timidity, vanity
	–ment	V→N	government, amusement
	–less	N→Adj	shameless, joyless
	–ness	Adj→N	boldness, friendliness
	–ly	Adj→Adv	usually, quietly
b.	**Prefix**		
	a–	Adj→Adj	amoral, apolitical
	dis–	V→V	disagree, dislike
	ex–	N→N	ex-student, ex-chairman
	re–	V→V	re-write, re-sell
	un–	Adj→Adj	uncooked, unclean

productively used to create new words, for example, the word *retraditionalization* that I recently saw in an advertisement for a sociology conference at the university.

The set of derivational suffixes is large, and unlike the list of inflectional suffixes, it can have new members added to it (see Table 5.5). I will illustrate the open-endedness of the derivational affix inventory with the suffix *–lite*. The word *lite* (a play on 'light') entered the language as part of the compound word *Miller Lite*, the brand name of a beer launched on the US market in 1967. Soon *lite* was appropriated by many food and beverage manufacturers who used it to indicate that their products were low in calories and hence good for you. Subsequently, *lite*, which had been an independent word, was converted into a suffix and attached to bases as *–lite*. With regard to meaning, the favourable connotations of the suffix *–lite* were eventually eclipsed by ironic usage. I recently heard *marriage-lite* being used to refer to a marriage regarded by a speaker as a sham (see also *grief-lite, interview-lite, etc.*; Dent, 2004: 22).

The nature of word-formation rules

It is generally (but not universally) agreed that word-formation rules are the same as the 'phrase-structure rules' used in syntax (Selkirk, 1982). The next three chapters, which treat syntax, will explain the nature of phrase structure rules and their role in syntax. For now, suffice to say that a phrase-structure rule states the constituents of a syntactic phrase, or of a word in morphology. In other words, in the case of morphology, these rules list the different types of units that are allowed to form a word, and the order in which they occur. This can be seen in [5.23]:

[5.23]   Phrase-structure rule

	Word			Examples
a.	word	→	affix stem	exhale
b.	word	→	stem affix	sentiment
c.	word	→	word affix	amazement
d.	word	→	affix word	rewrite
e.	word	→	word word	motorway

Notes:
  (i)   Here 'stem' means a bound non-affix morpheme.
  (ii) The arrow means 'consists of'.
  (iii) The rule indicates the order of constituents, e.g., affix before stem vs. stem before affix.

A phrase structure rule is usually translated into a phrase structure tree diagram. It's easier to see the linguistic structure when information is presented in that form. The phrase structure rules in [5.23] can be re-written as phrase structure trees as shown in Figure 5.1 below.

Words have internal structure, as we saw in Section 5.3. Affixes and roots aren't piled together higgledy-piggledy. This structure includes having a head element which dominates everything else and determines the word class that

Phrase structure trees showing word structure   FIGURE 5.1

a word belongs to, and hence the slots it can occupy in sentences. Normally, in an English word the head is the right-hand-most element, be it a root or a suffix. This principle is known as the **right-hand head rule.** Its effects can be observed in Figure 5.2 where the word contains a category maintaining prefixes and a root:

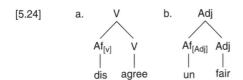

The right-hand head rule: derived words with category-maintaining prefixes   FIGURE 5.2

In the lexicon, each affix is assigned a syntactic category (N (noun), V (verb), Adj (adjective) and V (verb)) as you will recall from Table 5.5; this information is shown in square brackets in Figure 5.2 and other phrase structure tree diagrams depicting word structure. (Words and their syntactic categories are the subject of the next chapter.) The syntactic category of the affix percolates from it to the entire word if it turns out to be the last suffix in the word. This can be depicted using tree diagrams as shown in Figure 5.3 below.

Compositionality and its limits

If a linguistic structure is compositional, the meaning of the whole can be inferred from the meaning of the parts, taking into account the grammatical relations between them. In syntax, this principle lies behind the two different interpretations of these two sentences with the same words: *The big dog chased the black cat* vs. *The black cat chased the big dog*). **Compositionality** is an important concept in morphology also. Figure 5.3 shows that affixed words are composed of building blocks, each contributing its syntax and meaning. Often the meaning of a complex word containing affixes can be computed from the meaning of its parts. You can usually work out the meaning of a word that you may not have encountered before, if you know the meaning of its parts, as in the case of *retraditionalization* which I mentioned earlier in this chapter. But compositionality has its limits. Consider the interpretation of words containing the agentive nominalizing suffix *–er* as in *seeker* and *writer*. It derives a noun meaning 'somebody who does whatever the verb means'. However, if we applied the expected interpretation to *looker*, we would be wrong. A *looker* is not someone who looks, but a handsome person. The meaning of *looker* is noncompositional. So, this word has to be listed in the lexicon, and memorized.

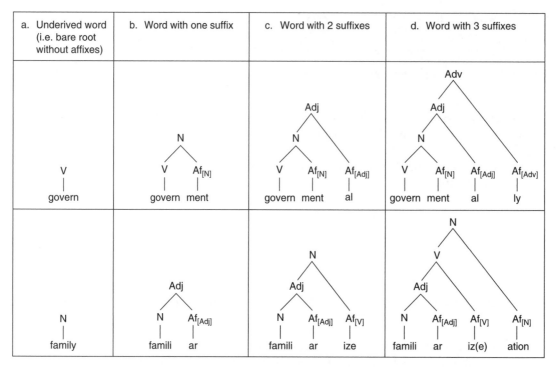

FIGURE 5.3   The right-hand head rule: derived words with category changing suffixes

Idioms are another type of complex lexical item that must be listed in the lexicon for the same reason. Normally, if we know the individual words found in a phrase or sentence, and the relationships between them, we can work out what the whole means (as in [5.25a]). But we can't do the same in the case of the idiomatic sentence in [5.25b] as in this instance *pull the plug on* means 'terminate':

[5.25]   a.   Ali pulled the plug out of the socket.
          b.   *The government has pulled the plug on prison privatization*
                plans.

Now, what do you make of [5.26]?

[5.26]   *In a Czechoslovakian tourist agency:* Take one of our horse-driven
          city tours – we guarantee no miscarriages.

(Lederer, 1987: 97)

You might have chuckled quietly when you read this. The prefix *mis–* meaning 'badly' or 'wrongly' is productive in English and we can interpret compositionally words containing it (cf. *misspell, mistranslate, miscarriage (of justice)*, etc.). The writer of the advertising slogan was right to think that *miscarriages* meant literally 'instances of being carried badly'. They expected the meaning of *miscarried* to follow automatically from the meanings of its parts. They were unaware that the more usual meaning of that particular word, and the only one that many speakers are aware of, and the one that would come up first in their minds is 'to give birth to a premature baby'. The existence of the established word *miscarriage* inhibits the creation of the word *miscarriage* with the meaning that compositionality leads one to expect.

What we have identified is part of a general pattern. The formation of words using derivational affixes tends to be patchy. Some possible derived words are simply not allowed. For instance, we have words like *horrible ~ horrid ~ horrific* but not *terrible ~ *terrid ~ terrific*, etc. In derivational affixation there are often unexplained gaps. In contrast, inflectional morphemes tend to be attachable to all eligible candidates, with very reliably predictable results. For instance, all verbs (apart from modal verbs, e.g., *can, may, shall* (to be described in the next chapter)) have a third-person singular present tense form, for example, *thinks, writes*, etc.

Affixes and the interplay between morphology and phonology

Word-formation has a grammar/meaning dimension as well as a phonological dimension. We have considered word-formation from the former perspective in the last section. Let us now turn to the latter perspective, with particular reference to affixes. English has two classes of suffixes and they are categorized as 'neutral' and 'non-neutral'. The neutral suffixes for the most part come from Old English while the non-neutral ones were directly borrowed from classical languages, in particular Latin or indirectly through its descendants, in particular French. This labelling of affixes captures the fact that when certain affixes are added, the base undergoes no change whereas the attachment of certain other suffixes causes either a change in the stress patterns of the base or some alterations in its segmental phonemes, or both. There is a very intimate interaction between phonology and morphology in this part of the grammar. The behaviour of some neutral suffixes is shown below in [5.27] and that of different types of non-neutral suffixes in [5.28] in Table 5.6.

As shown, the neutral suffixes in [5.25] (e.g., *–er* in *builder*) do not cause any changes in the phonological elements in the base. But non-neutral affixes cause stress to shift to the suffix itself if they are auto-stressed (i.e., attract stress to themselves, e.g., 'million ~ millio'naire) or to the syllable immediately preceding the suffix if they are of the strong mode pre-accenting type (e.g., 'morpheme ~ mor'phemic), or to shift variably to the immediately preceding syllable if it is heavy (e.g., 'adjective ~ adjec'tival) and to shift two syllables before the syllable realizing the suffix if the immediately preceding syllable is light (e.g., 'satire ~ sa'tirical). You will have noticed also that in some cases a non-neutral suffix may cause a change in the actual vowel and consonant segments, for example, a'nonymous loses its *–ous–* chunk when *–ity* is suffixed. In the case of *sanity*, stress doesn't shift but the vowel of the base changes [seɪn] → [sænɪti] ([eɪ] → [æ]).

The distinction between neutral and non-neutral (broadly Latinate) suffixes is also important for another reason. There are restrictions on which base can combine with which suffixes and depends crucially on the historical source of the suffixes. Normally, Germanic suffixes like *–ness* and *–hood* are attached to roots of Anglo-Saxon origin and Latinate ones like *–ity* and

Table 5.6   *Suffixes and the placement of English stress*

[5.27]	Neutral suffixes	input	output
	–er	'build	'builder
		re'mind	re'minder
	–ness	'serious	'seriousness
		pig'headed	pig'headedness
	–ly	'quiet	'quietly
		re'motely	re'motely
	–ism	'Calvin	'Calvinism
		'capital	'capitalism
	–hood	'king	'kinghood
		'sister	'sisterhood

[5.28]	Non-neutral suffixes		

Auto-stressed

	input	output
–aire	'doctrine	doctri'naire
	'million	millio'naire
–ee	em'ploy	emplo'yee
	'interview	intervie'wee
–eer	'auction	auction'eer
	co'mmand	comman'deer

Pre-accenting suffixes

a. **Strong mode**: always place stress on immediately preceding syllable

	input	output
–ous	'melody	me'lodious
	'efficacy	effi'catious
–ity	'timid	ti'midity
	'sane	'sanity
	a'nonymous	ano'nymity
–acy	a'ristocrat	aris'tocracy
	'diplomat	di'plomacy
–ic	'microscope	micro'scopic
	'morpheme	mor'phemic

b. **Weak mode**: place stress on immediately preceding syllable if it is heavy (see Chapter 4, Section 4.4)

	input	output
–al	'universe	uni'versal
	'adjective	adjec'tival
–ine	'elephant	ele'phantine
	'serpent	ser'pentine

place stress two syllables before the syllable with the suffix if the immediately preceding syllable is light

	input	output
–al	'politic	po'litical
	'satire	sa'tirical

Conversion
Table 5.7

V → N	N → V	Adj → V	Adj → N	Adj → Adv
walk	chair	sour	weekly	slow
throw	floor	cool	comic	fast
kick	plant	green	stiff	dead (as in dead slow)
dig	bottle	wet	wet	
kill	text	open		
cry	red card			
read	google			

–acy go with Latinate roots (cf. *kindness vs. magnanimity; kinghood vs. aristocracy*). But there is some fuzziness at the edges. Some Latinate loanwords, (e.g., *parent*) have been thoroughly nativized and may take a native suffix (cf. *parenthood*).

5.7.2 Conversion

Conversion is a very widely used method of forming words in English. When conversion occurs, the syntactic context is the only indicator that word class has changed. Conversion of N →V, and to a lesser extent V→N, is very productive. But that is not to say that anything goes. For example, deriving a verb from the noun *floor* works, but attempting the same with *ceiling* doesn't. Table 5.7 above gives some examples of conversion.

Sometimes, we are unsure which way the derivation went historically, for example, is *plan* a noun derived form a verb or a verb derived form a noun?

5.7.3 Compounding

Compounds are complex words containing at least two bases that are themselves words. It has always been a highly productive process in English (see Chapter 15). Normally compounds are classified on the basis of the word class of their constituents and the class of the entire resulting word. As we saw when we discussed affixes, the concept of head is important in morphology. Compounds always have a headword which assigns its syntactic properties to the entire word, and thanks to the right-hand head rule, it is normally the right-hand-most word. Examples of English compounds are given in Table 5.8.

It is very common for words formed by affixation to be part of a compound. Normally, the right-hand head rule applies and the last word in the compound assigns its class to the entire word as you can see in the tree in Figure 5.4 on page 102.

Compounds can also include other compounds, some of which may have affixes. This results in words of considerable complexity such as *armchair sportsman* (see Figure 5.5).

Table 5.8   *Examples of compound words*

a. **Noun compounds**
   N + N
   [school]_N [boy]_N → [schoolboy]_N
   [gun]_N [dog]_N → [gun dog]_N

b. **A + N**
   [wet]_A [lands]_N → [wetlands]_N
   [strong]_A [man]_N → [strongman]_N

b. **Verb compounds**
   N + V
   [house]_N [train]_V → [house train]_V
   [speed]_N [date]_V → [speed date]_V

   Prep + V
   [under]_{Prep} [sell]_V → [undersell]_V
   [over]_{Prep} [reach]_V → [overreach]_V

c. **Adjective compounds**
   Adj + Adj
   [yellow]_{Adj} [green]_{Adj} → [yellow green]_{Adj}
   [red]_{Adj} [hot]_{Adj} → [red-hot]_{Adj}

   N + A
   [razor]_N [sharp]_{Adj} → [razor-sharp]_{Adj}
   [war]_N [weary]_{Adj} → [war weary]_{Adj}

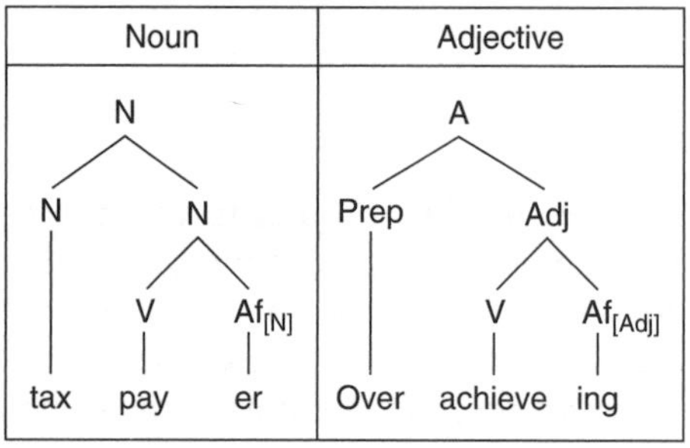

Noun		Adjective	
	N		A
N	N	Prep	Adj
	V Af_[N]		V Af_[Adj]
tax	pay er	Over	achieve ing

FIGURE 5.4   *Compounds including affixed words*

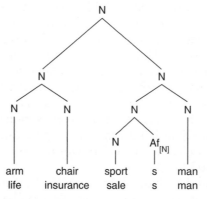

FIGURE 5.5   *Compounds containing an affixed compound*

Clearly, the right-hand head rule is very important in English word-formation. But it doesn't hold absolute sway. It is subverted in two major ways. First, as we have seen, English readily allows conversion. So a word's syntactic make-up may not reflect its syntactic category as indicated by the morphemes it contains, for example, *up market* (as in *an upmarket pub*) is an adjective not a noun, though the last word of the compound is a noun. Secondly, phrasal verbs (e.g., *look for, look up to, look into*, etc.) are a very large class of compound words with a head on the left.

Having said that, we still have to recognize the fact that many compounds are compositional. Their meaning can be inferred from the meaning of the words they contain. The word on the left serves as a modifier of the head-word that is on the right. So they needn't be listed as separate headwords in the dictionary; they don't need to be memorized. Such compounds are called **endocentric compounds,** for example:

[5.30] a. frying pan   b. can opener
       dancing shoes   candlestick maker

Endocentric compounds must be distinguished from compounds like those in [5.31] whose meaning is not compositional. Such words are called **exocentric compounds.** They must be listed in the lexicon; they must be memorized.

[5.31] green tax (N)   greenhouse (N)
        cold turkey (N)   bag lady (N)
        golden handcuffs (N)   stonewall (verb)
        cold shoulder (N,V)   carbon footprint (N)

Of course, there is the added complication that the same expression may be an exocentric or endocentric compound, depending on context. Take the adjective *knee-deep*. It can mean can literally 'sunk right up to the knees', in which case it is compositional and hence endocentric; or it can be figurative, meaning 'deeply involved with', in which case it is noncompositional and hence exocentric.

Now, here is another conundrum. Compound words are made by combining words. And so are syntactic phrases. So, how do we distinguish compound words from syntactic phrases? One of the clues we use is stress. English has a special rule for assigning stress to compounds which doesn't apply to syntactic phrases. Compare the words in [5.32]:

[5.32] **Compounds**   **Phrases**
        ' blue‚blood   ‚blue 'blood
        'green‚house   ‚green 'house
        'New‚house   ‚new 'house
        'old‚man   ‚old 'man

Various criteria for identifying compounds have been proposed. Some are phonological. For instance, in Adj + N compounds, the primary stress of the compound is on a syllable in the first word; the main stress of the second

ADVANCES BOX 5.4

Cranberry words

The impression that might have been given so far is that the difference between compounding and affixation is always clear-cut. Reality is more complex. The norm is to recognize affix morphemes as word-building elements that recur in many words for example, *re–, –er, –ing, non–*. This principle serves us well in most cases. But from time to time the evidence is indeterminate. If a form appears in only one word should we recognize it as a bound morpheme? Should we do so even if its meaning is totally obscure?

These questions arise when we consider the words in [5.33]:

[5.33]	a.	blackberry	b.	strawberry	c.	cranberry
		blueberry		raspberry		huckleberry
				gooseberry		mulberry

The words in [5.33a] are clearly compounds; they are made of the words *black, blue* and *berry*. The words in [5.33b] also appear to be compounds, for the same reason. But there is a problem here. Present-day speakers of English for the most part do not comprehend the meaning and relevance of *straw, rasp* and *goose* in these words and view them as simple, mono-morpheme words. The problem is even more severe in [5.33c]. The bound morphs *cran–, mul–* and *huckle–* occur only in these forms in the entire language. Their specific meaning is elusive. Nor is it clear whether they are root morphemes or prefixes. If they are root morphemes, the words in [5.33c] are compounds. Otherwise, in [5.33c] what we have is a prefix followed by a root. Should a form that is encountered just once in the language and which has no clear meaning be recognized as a morpheme? Those with a cautious disposition would and do argue for treating such forms as simple words with a single morpheme.

The knotty issues raised by cranberry words are of wider relevance. There are many other situations where the zeal with which the linguist identifies morphemes has to be tempered. It is uncontroversial to say that *dislike* and *disagree* contain two morphemes each. But what about *disgruntled, disturb* and *dismay*? If *dis–* is identified as a morpheme, the forms *–gruntled* (from *–gruntle*?) and *–may* cut unconvincing figures as morphemes since neither of them recurs nor has an independent meaning. For analogous reasons, *highfalutin* is problematic. Segmenting it into *high* and *falutin* gives a compound with a dubious second element.

There are many words borrowed from Latin or Greek with a root whose meaning classical scholars can identify but is hidden from the rest of us. For instance, the study of etymology shows that the root *–pol–* from a Greek word meaning 'city' or 'state' is found in words like *police, politic, policy, monopoly, metropolis*, etc. Should *–pol–* be recognized as a root morpheme in all those words in a description of present day English? I would suggest not. Since the task of the linguist is primarily to describe what current speakers of a language know about their language, there is no justification for identifying forms as morphemes if speakers in general are completely unaware of them and they have no relevance to their linguistic competence.

word is subordinated to it. But in phrases the reverse is true. In the written language a word has white space before and after it. Often this is true of compounds. They are written either without a space between them (e.g., *sunset*) or they are hyphenated (e.g., *double-sided*). But very many compounds are written as separate, unhyphenated words (e.g., *life insurance, Prime Minister*). (Revisit the discussion of word-forms in Table 5.2.) So, we need to rely on syntactic criteria in many cases. If two or more words are treated as a single unit for syntactic purposes, for example, if they can be moved, elided or substituted for as a single unit by the syntax, they constitute a compound. Another clue is inflection, normally, if a unit constitutes a word, any inflection it receives appears at its right edge (courtesy of the right-hand head rule.) Thus, the plural of *mousetrap* is *mousetraps (*micetrap); the* plural of *bean feast* is *bean feasts* (**beans* feast, etc.).

5.8 Further sources of English words

Derivation using affixation, conversion and compounding are the principal methods used to create vocabulary items. But there are also other methods. They are sketched out below.

Coinage

Word manufacture without recycling existing words and morphemes is called **coinage**. It is rare. It is mostly found in names of corporations and their commercial products; for example, according to the Oxford English Dictionary, *nylon* is an invented word. It was coined in 1938 by the DuPont pharmaceutical company by combining the fabricated stem *nyl* – with the pseudo-suffix *–on* found in other names of textile fibers (cf. *rayon, cotton*). *Likewise,* the New Yorkers Reuben and Rose Mattus fabricated the name *Häagen-Dazs* for their ice cream brand.

Eponyms

Eponyms are new words created by widening the meaning of a personal name to refer to a place, concept or product associated with that person, for example, *Kafkaesque* (from Franz Kafka); *lynching* (from Charles Lynch); *mesmerize* (from Franz Mesmer); *pasteurization* (from Louis Pasteur); *Seattle* (from Chief Seattle), *Victoria* (in Australia, British Columbia, etc. from Queen Victoria). Business people are normally no shrinking violets and often their big egos are projected in the names of their companies and their products. This makes eponymy a highly productive word-formation process as new companies and products come into existence all the time. Thus, *Boeing*, the aircraft manufacturer is named after its founder, William E. Boeing, whose name replaced the original name, Pacific Aero Products Co.; Michael Dell made sure that his computer company, and its products, were called *Dell*, and so on.

Backformation

Normally word-formation involves addition rather than subtraction. Affixes are added to a base, or two words are combined to form a word. The processes that we are going to be considering in this subsection, and in the subsection following it, all involve taking something away from the input. We will start with **backformation,** which arises from a reinterpretation of the structure of a word so that a chunk that is re-analysed as an affix is removed, leaving behind the assumed root. In the examples in [5.34], which are borrowed from Williams (1975), the schwa of the rhyme of the final syllable (spelled –er ~ –ar ~ –or) was re-analysed historically as the agentive suffix that forms nouns from verbs (as in sing > singer). It was removed yielding the words in [5.34b]:

[5.34] a. **Original word**   b. **Backformation**
            beggar   beg
            peddlar   peddle
            hawker   hawk
            scavenger   scavenge
            editor   edit

ADVANCES BOX 5.5

Back-formation on the march in current journalistic writing (after Neal, 2006)

There are interesting developments in the use of backformation in current journalistic writing, extending the process in an innovative way, as the excerpt below explains:

> ... The backformations that usually catch my eye (or ear) are those in which a noun or adjective form of a verb (i.e., a gerund or participle) is compounded by putting a noun or adjective in front of it, and then the –ing or –ed is stripped off to yield a new verb. For example, in *performance-enhancing drugs*, we have a noun+adjective compound (*performance* plus *enhancing*), and the whole thing functions as an adjective, modifying *drugs*. But in Ruben Bolling's *Tom the Dancing Bug* comic strip of Dec. 18, 2004, one character tells another:

> You've been performance-enhancing!

> Sure, it still sounds the same, but now *performance-enhancing* is the progressive form of a verb, not an adjective modifying something else. In the future, look out for finite verb forms, such as *He performance-enhanced illegally, None of our players performance-enhance*, or *Everyone performance-enhances!*
> Other examples of this kind of backformation where a noun glued to the beginning of the verb takes the place of a direct object after the verb:

- Adam's therapist mentioned that he 'emotion-shared' at some point.
- 'The decision puts Limbaugh back near square one and is likely to reinvigorate the criminal investigation into whether he "doctor-shopped"' ('Justices won't hear Limbaugh appeal', *Palm Beach Post*, 29 April 2005).
- From a Bionicle comic in a Lego magazine: 'We came, we scouted, we all-conquered.'

In the more recent past and in present-day English backformation has been used to derive *automate* from *automation*, *adulate* from *adulation*, *auto-destruct* from *auto-destruction*, *bulldoze* from *bulldozer*, *choreograph* from *choreography*, *babysit* from *babysitter*, *text*$_{(V)}$ from *text message*.

Blending

Chunks of words may be **blended** to form new words. Less commonly, and mainly in the realm of IT, it is the initial chunks of two words that are combined for example, *modulator + demodulator* gives modem; Wireless Fidelity gives *Wi Fi*. More commonly, the initial chunk of the first word is combined with the final part of the second word, for example, *brunch (breakfast lunch)*, *insania (insanity mania), chugger (charity mugger)*, etc.. *Adidas* was formed from a blend of the name of the company founder Adolf (*Adi*) + *Das*sler. Thus it exemplifies the use of both eponymy and blending.

Clipping

Shortening long words by dropping a part is called **clipping**. Some clipped forms like *fab* (from *fabulous*) and *brill* (from *brilliant*) are slang but others like *bus* (from *omnibus*) and *gym* from (*gymnasium*) are very much part of the standard language. We can distinguish between three types of clipping with regard to structure. First there is 'fore clipping', that is, deleting the first part and keeping the final part, for example, *varsity* (from *university)* and *phone* (from *telephone)* Second, there is 'middle clipping', that is, deleting both the first and last part and keeping the middle part, which is rare, for example, *jams* (from *pyjamas*) and *flu* (from *influenza*). Finally, there is 'back clipping', that is, deleting the second part and keeping the first part. for example, *exam* (from *examination*), *brill* (from *brilliant*), *ad* (from *advertisement*)). It is widely used with names, for example, Max (Maxmillian); Rich (Richard), etc.

Clipping may interact with compounding. Compounds can be clipped, for example, *pub* from *public house*; and compounds can be created from clipped words, for example, *hi-fi* (from *high fidelity*); *sci-fi* (from *science fiction*), *Britcom* (from *British comedy* on TV and film, e.g., *Blackadder*).

Hypocorisms

Hypocorism is used to refer to words formed by suffixing a vowel, usually *–y* or *–ie* [i] to a monosyllabic root or by suffixing *–y* or *–ie* [i] after clipping has reduced a longer simplex or compound word to one syllable. It is used to create the familiar forms of names, for example, *Johnnie* (from John*), Vicky* (Victoria), *Mandy* (Amanda), etc. It is also used for common nouns, for example, *chippy, movie, kiddy, bikkie, brownie, bookie*, etc. These contractions are usually referred to as **diminutives**. But this label is not always appropriate, especially in Australian English where this type of word-formation is most widely used. As well as being used in a diminutive sense, hypocorisms are used in Australian English for word play and for indicating empathy (Simpson, 2001). Examples include *baggie* (large school bag), *barrie* (as in 'give someone a barrie', i.e., give someone a ride on the bar of your bike), *Brizzie* (Brisbane), *Chrissy* (Christmas) and *Saffie* (a South African person). Another vowel commonly used in hypocoristics is –*o* (cf. *doco*– (documentary), *journo*– (journalist), *Nasho* (National Service)). Particularly interesting is the case of *hottie* (hot water bottle in Australian, and British slang). But in British slang *hottie* has been apparently re-analysd as a blend of *hot* + *(cu)tie* → *hottie*. Original *hotties* were all female. Subsequent widening of meaning made *hottie* a unisex adjective, applicable to women and men, prompting Safire to observe in *The New York Times Magazine*, '[R]arely do we come across a word that can be applied, with lust aforethought, to either sex.' This usage has spread to the other side of the Atlantic.

ADVANCES BOX 5.6

The privileged status of disyllabic forms

The fact that hypocoristics have two syllables is significant. We find the same pattern in numerous other languages that have hypocoristics, for example, German, as seen in [5.35]. This has led linguists to hypothesize that disyllabic words enjoy a privileged status in language, especially as many other unrelated phonological and morphological processes either require inputs two syllables long or deliver outputs two syllables long.

[5.35]			
Profi	Professioneller	'professional person'
Bundi	Bundesdeutscher	'citizen of the Federal Republic of Germany' (This tended to be used by people in former GDR to denote West Germans.)
Zoni	Zonenbewohner	'zone inhabitant' (The zone in question is the *Sowjetische Besatzungszone*, i.e., Soviet occupied zone and used by West Germans to denote inhabitants of the GDR – ironic or derogatory.)
Wessi	Westdeutscher	'person from former West Germany'
Fundi	Fundamentaler	'(environmental) fundamentalist'
Zivi	Zivildiensteilstender	' person who does Community National Service instead of Military National Service'
Nazi	*Nationalsozialist*	'National socialist'
Studi	*Student*	'student'

(Weise, 2000: 63)

The fact that hypocoristics are disyllabic gives strong support to the claim that words in both German and English are subject to a phonological 'minimality condition': a lexical word should not be less than two syllables.

Acronyms and Abbreviations

Word contraction is taken to its logical conclusion in **acronyms** and **abbreviations** (also called 'initialisms'). In this type of word-formation a group of words representing a concept or the name of an organization is reduced to their initial letters which are then treated as a word. In the case of an abbreviation, the reduced form does not result in well-formed syllables and so cannot be pronounced as a word. Rather, the letters are sounded out independently, for example, *EU* (European Union), *BBC* (British Broadcasting Corporation), *RBS* (Royal Bank of Scotland), etc.

In the case of acronyms, contraction delivers initial letters that constitute well-formed syllables and the string forms a perfectly normal word, for example, *NATO* (North Atlantic Treaty Organization), *NICE* (National Institute for Clinical Excellence), *laser* (light amplification by the stimulated emission of radiation); radar (radio detection and ranging), *sim (card)* (Subscriber Identity Module (card)), etc.

Borrowing

As well as using its own resources to enrich its lexicon, English very readily incorporates words from other languages into its vocabulary. Words like *resources, lexicon, incorporates, language*s and *vocabulary* are foreign imports. The role of borrowing is explored in chapter 15.

5.9   Summing up

This chapter has presented an overview of word-structure and patterns of word-formation. Defining a word is a knotty problem. It is best approached by distinguishing various senses in which the term 'word' is used (lexeme, grammatical word and word-form). With regard to structure, some words are simple and others complex. Normally, complex words can be decomposed into smaller structural and semantic units which are called morphemes. Many morphemes have variants which are called allomorphs that represent them in various contexts. Morphemes are classified as roots or affixes; free or bound.

Morphology has two broad types of affixes, namely inflectional affixes and derivational affixes. The former are there to ensure that the word has the right form if it occurs in a given syntactic slot while the latter serve to create new lexemes from bases. Various morphological operations are used in English derivational morphology, namely affixation, conversion and compounding. In inflectional morphology, too, there are a number of processes that can be identified, including affixation, internal vowel change and suppletion. There are also various additional ways of creating lexemes: coinage, eponymy, backformation, blending, clipping hypocorism, acronyms and abbreviations (and borrowing).

A thread that runs through the account of English word-formation presented here is the importance of seeing morphology in a wider context. Morphology interacts with meaning, syntax and phonology in intricate ways. So, word-formation can't be undertaken without considering the mutual relationship of morphology with phonology, with syntax, and with semantics. The next chapter investigates words from a syntactic perspective and the semantics chapter looks at words, from a meaning perspective. The study of words shows clearly the fact that there is no semi-detached component of grammar where life is lived by linguistic entities in total isolation from the rest of grammar.

Recommended readings

Accessible introductions to word-formation in English include Bauer (2003), Katamba (2005) and Stockwell and Minkova (2001) which includes a useful historical dimension. For more advanced general textbooks, see Matthews (1991), and Aronoff and Fudeman (2005). Marchand (1969) is the classic reference work on English word-formation.

Chapter 6

Grammar: Words (and Phrases)

Geoffrey Leech

6.1 Introducing word classes

Everyone knows that any piece of language, such as a written text or a spoken piece of dialogue, consists of **words**. But how many kinds of words are there? This is a matter for discussion and argument, but for the purposes of this chapter there will be 11 **word classes** (i.e., word classes which are not part of other word classes – commonly known as 'parts of speech'). By the end of this and the following chapter, you should be able to take a piece of language, such as a paragraph of text, and label each word as one of these 11 word classes and, even in uncertain cases, you will probably be able to make a good guess. Words are the main theme of this chapter – but we cannot talk seriously about words without talking about the 'word-chunks' that form larger units – **phrases** – a topic we look into more fully in the next chapter. Also, towards the end of this chapter, we will examine critically, in arriving at those 11 types, an assumption we have made about word classes.

Four of those 11 word classes – **nouns, adjectives, verbs** and **adverbs** – made their appearance in Chapter 5. Using the first letters of their names, we will call them 'NAVA' words for short (Table 6.1).

NAVA or 'content word' classes   Table 6.1

Word classes	Examples	Word classes	Examples
Noun	*girl, water, beauty*	Verb (=full verb)	*sing, walk, become*
Adjective	*good, watery, calm*	Adverb	*now, here, safely*

These four word classes stand out for three reasons:

- They are crucial for conveying information (in the broadest sense). For example, when you add together one word from each of the four classes to make a sentence, you get a rather precise picture of something going on in the real world, with each word making its own contribution to that picture: *Young cheetahs mature quickly*. This is why words of these classes are often called 'content words'.
- As we saw in Chapter 5, unlike other word classes, NAVA words have derivational morphology: we can form nouns, adjectives, verbs and adverbs

by adding suffixes, for example: *teach+er, wonder+ful, class+ify, sober+ly.*

- These classes have a very large number of members: English has many thousands of nouns, verbs, adjectives and adverbs. In comparison, other word classes have a very small membership, of 50 or less.

To show this last difference, you could try an interesting experiment. Take a normal desk dictionary of English, turn to a random page or two, and count the numbers of headwords (words printed in bold at the beginning of an entry) that are NAVA words that you find on these pages. You will find the large majority of headwords on these pages – probably close to 100 per cent – are NAVA words, labelled as *n, adj, v* or *adv.* Now, take a random paragraph or two of a text, say a novel, and count the number of running words that are NAVA words, and the number that are not: you will find that only about 35 per cent to 60 per cent of the words are NAVA words. The conclusion we can draw from this experiment is that the words which are **not** NAVA words, although small in number, tend to occur more frequently. Words like *the, of, it,* and tend to crop up on almost every line of text, whereas words like *young, cheetahs, mature* and *quickly* occur much more rarely.

Let's look for a minute at these other words, the 'non-content' words. They are often called **function words**, because their usefulness lies not so much in the information content they convey, as in their role of signalling grammatical function and grammatical structure. The other seven word classes, apart from the content classes I have mentioned, are given in Table 6.2:

Table 6.2   *'Function word' classes*

Word classes	Examples	Word classes	Examples
Determiner	*the, a, this, some, all*	Auxiliary (verb)	*can, will, may, be, do*
Pronoun	*I, she, all, him, anyone*	Numeral[†]	*one, two, 15, fifth, 10th*
Preposition	*of, in, on, at, from, to, as*	Discourse	*oh, well, yes, okay,*
Conjunction	*and, or, but, if, when, as*	marker[†]	*gee, right, heck, wow*

[†] In some ways numerals and discourse markers are like content classes, but for now we place them among the function classes.

Now we need to look more carefully at these word classes, starting with the NAVA or **content word** classes.

6.2   NAVA words – or 'content words'

First, here is a short test, which can be seen as an easy general-knowledge test about English grammar. Its purpose is simply to start you thinking on the right lines. For some of you, no doubt, this will be too easy; for others, it will mean remembering what you learned some years ago.

(a) From sentences [6.1]–[6.3] make a list, in four columns, of the italicised words which are (i) nouns, (ii) adjectives, (iii) verbs, and (iv) adverbs (ignore the other words):

[6.1]   *New cars are very expensive nowadays.*
[6.2]   *I understand* that even *Dracula hates werewolves.*
[6.3]   I have *won* more *rounds* of *golf* than you have *had hot dinners.*

(b)   Assuming you have made the list, say **why** you classified the words as you did. This will require a working definition of what a noun, a verb, an adjective or an adverb is.

If you remember something about these word classes, your lists will be something like the following:

Cars, Dracula, werewolves, rounds, golf, dinners are nouns;
New, expensive and *hot* are adjectives;
Are, understand, hates, won, had are verbs;
Very and *nowadays* are adverbs.

In order to explain your lists, you might rely on familiar schoolroom definitions like these:

(i)   'A noun is a naming word: it refers to a thing, person, substance, etc.'
(ii)   'An adjective is a word that describes something about a noun: it denotes a quality.'
(iii) 'A verb is a doing word: it refers to an action.'
(iv)   'An adverb is a word that says something about other types of words, such as verbs, adjectives and adverbs.'

These are largely **semantic** definitions, that is, definitions in terms of meaning. Such definitions are a useful starting-point, especially in the early days of learning about grammar, but they have two drawbacks: (a) they are often vague, and (b) they are sometimes wrong.

For example, *golf* and *dinners* in sentence (6.3) are nouns, but do not fit the definition given: *golf* names a type of game, and *dinners* a type of meal. This defect could be mended if we included games and meals under the 'etc.' of (i). But having widened the definition of nouns in this way, we would have to extend it in other ways, to include other words such as *rounds*. The fact is that it is difficult to see anything in common between all the 'things' nouns refer to, except the fact that nouns refer to them. On the other hand, it is true that the most typical or central members of the class of nouns, words like *Karen, cars* and *dog* refer to people, animals, things and substances that we can see and touch. (These are often called **concrete nouns**.)

Similarly with verbs, the definition of a 'doing word' applies naturally to *went, looked* and *won*, but does not so easily apply to *are, hates* and *understand*. We could improve the definition by saying that a verb can denote 'states' as well as 'actions', but the difficulty is partly that words like *state* and *action* are themselves vague in meaning. When we say *The girls seemed hungry*, for example, does *seemed* refer to a state? The adjective *hungry* fits the definition of 'state word' more easily than *seemed*. And what about *Two twos are four*? Saying that *are* refers to a 'state' here seems to be pushing the meaning of 'state' too far.

Another problem: such definitions fail to keep the word classes apart. Compare *hates* in *Dracula hates werewolves* with *hatred* in *Dracula's hatred of werewolves*. It is generally accepted that *hates* here is a verb, whereas *hatred* is a noun; but this cannot be due to the meaning of these words, for they both refer to the same 'thing' – that is, to an emotion which Dracula feels, and which is the opposite of love.

6.3   Defining word classes: form, function and meaning

We have just seen that we cannot rely on meaning when recognising word classes. In fact, instead of looking for a single-line definition like 'a verb is a doing word', it is best to see the definition of a word class as combining **three** elements: **form**, **function** and **meaning** (see Illustration Box 6.1).

ILLUSTRATION BOX 6.1

Defining word classes: form, function and meaning

(a)   **Form**: We can tell the class of a word partly from its form, made up of stems and affixes:

  (i)   We have seen that **derivational suffixes** (see Section 5.4) are characteristic of certain word classes: e.g., *electric-ity* (noun); *electr-ify* (verb); *electric-al* (adjectives).

  (ii)   We have also seen that **inflectional suffixes** (see Section 5.4) can be added to change the form of a word: *box* → *box-es* (noun); *work* → *work-ed* (verb); *tall* → *tall-er* (adjective). These purely grammatical endings can be simply called **inflections**, and compared to some other well-known European languages (e.g., Latin, German, Russian, French), English has only a few of them.

  (iii)   In some less regular cases, English words have inflections which involve some other change in the form of a word, e.g. a change of vowel (*man ~ men, sing ~ sang*), or in a few extreme cases a complete change in the word (*go ~ went*).

(b)   **Function**: We can tell the class of a word by the way it occurs in certain positions or structural contexts. Put differently, words have certain **functions** or roles in the structure of a sentence. For example, in *The cook does not actually cook the meal* we can recognise the first *cook* as a noun and the second as a verb because of their functions. Obviously there is no overt difference of form to help us, so it must be the position of the word in relation to other words that tells us its class.

(c)   **Meaning**: This is a less reliable criterion, as already pointed out. But if you learn to recognise certain semantic types of word (i.e., word types classified according to meaning), such as **action** verbs, **state** verbs, **abstract** nouns, etc., this will help you to check the purely structural criteria, those of form and function.

The three tests (a)–(c) in Illustrations Box 6.1 can be placed in the following order of importance:

- Function is most important
- Form is next most important
- Meaning is least important.

Why this order? First, we have already seen (Section 6.3) that meaning is not a reliable guide to word class; for example:

[6.4]   I *love*[verb] my country, but my *love*[noun] of humanity is greater.

In [6.4], *love* and *love* have the same meaning: they both refer to a particular emotion. But they differ in word class. Second, we cannot always rely on a word's form, because many words contain no suffix (*help, water, much, rather*), and many words (*the, of, too, quite*) are invariable – that is, they do not change their form by inflection at all. Also, just as with ambiguous word-forms like *love* and *love* in [6.4], we should also allow for ambiguous use of suffixes; for example, *–ing* marks three different word classes in:

[6.5]   It was very *amusing*[adjective] to watch the cops *trying*[verb] to break into the *building*[noun].

Even suffixes which seem to be thoroughly safe indicators of a word class are sometimes misleading, for example, *–ion* generally indicates a noun, but *mention* (as in *Don't mention it*) is a verb. The *–ly* ending is usually an adverb suffix, as in *quickly*, but there are also quite a number of adjectives that end in *–ly*: *likely, lively* and *lovely*, for example. So the form of a word in not an infallible guide.

But let's not be too hasty in downgrading the importance of form. Where we can use a test of inflection, it is often conclusive. For example, *question* as a verb has inflected forms *questions, questioned* and *questioning*. As a noun, however, *question* has only the plural inflected form *questions*. If we meet the word *question*, we can decide whether it is a verb by imagining similar sentences with the inflected forms:

[6.6]   We (always) *question* the usual suspects.
    a.   We *questioned* the usual suspects (yesterday).
    b.   We are *questioning* the usual suspects (tomorrow).

In [6.6] *question* is a verb because we can see that [6.6a] and [6.6b] are similar to [6.6] in structure and meaning. But English has few inflections: this inflection test applies mainly only to nouns and verbs.

Because of the limitations of form and meaning as criteria, we have to rely chiefly on a word's function as a criterion of its class. Later, in Section 6.5, we look again at the definitions of NAVA classes, using function, form and meaning. First, though, we need to examine this notion of function more carefully.

6.4 Recognising a word's function: a preview of phrases and clauses

It's all very fine saying that function (its position or role in the structure of the sentence) is the most important criterion for identifying a word's class. But how do we describe that function? Sentences vary in length and structure enormously, and the words in those sentences can occur in many different positions. We obviously need to have some notion of how words pattern in sentences, and for this we need to recognise units intermediate in size. Illustration Box 6.2 gives a brief preview of what we will be examining in more detail in the next two chapters.

ILLUSTRATION BOX 6.2

A hierarchy of units

The **sentence** is the largest unit of language that we are concerned with in grammar. Words, too, are little grammatical units, but to show how words pattern in sentences, we need to be able to recognise units that are intermediate in size between a word and a sentence. The terms most commonly used for these intermediate units are **phrase** and **clause**, and they will be the main topics of the next two chapters. Meanwhile, we'll think of a typical sentence as composed of a hierarchy of units, one inside another, like Chinese boxes or Russian dolls. This can be shown by bracketing: we will show phrases by enclosing them in round brackets ( ), and clauses by enclosing them in square brackets [ ]:

Each of the four NAVA word classes can be the main word of a phrase, which is called after the word. That is, there are **noun phrases, adjective phrases, verb phrases** and **adverb phrases**:

(my *hair*)	is a **noun phrase** because its main word (known as the head of the phrase) is a **noun**
(has been *growing*)	is a **verb phrase** because its main word (= head) is a **verb**
(very *untidy*)	is an **adjective phrase** because its main word (= head) is an **adjective**
(just *recently*)	is an **adverb phrase** because its main word (= head) is an **adverb**.

In fact, we can make these four phrases into a single **clause** by joining them in sequence:

[6.7] [(My hair)   (has been growing)   (very untidy)   (just recently)].
       noun phrase   verb phrase   adjective phrase   adverb phrase

A unit can consist of one or more than one unit of a lower 'rank'. For example, **a phrase can consist of one word or more than one word.** We see this when we compare example [6.4] above with a similar example, [6.4a]:

[6.7] a.   [(Beards)   (grow)   (untidy)   (quickly)].
       noun phrase   verb phrase   adjective phrase   adverb phrase

The whole of this sentence is a single clause (as signalled by the square brackets), and each phrase (in round brackets) consists of a single word. For that matter, a whole sentence can consist of a single word: *Shout!* is a **sentence** consisting of just **one clause** consisting of just **one phrase** consisting of just **one word**:

[6.8]   [(Shout)]!

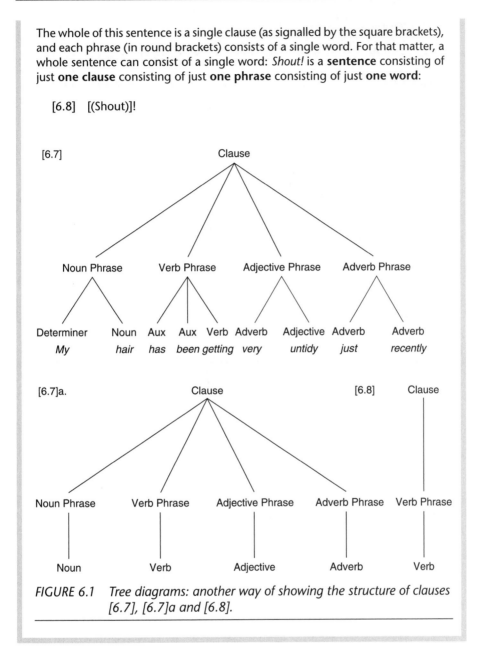

FIGURE 6.1   *Tree diagrams: another way of showing the structure of clauses [6.7], [6.7]a and [6.8].*

6.5   Defining 'content word' classes in terms of function, form and meaning

Now, let's define some word classes more carefully.

6.5.1 Nouns

The class of **nouns** is by far the most numerous word class:

(a) **Function**: Nouns can function as the **head** of a noun phrase (see Figure 6.1):

> (*donkeys*)
> (our *town*)
> (the worst *journey* ever)
> (Stanley's historic *meeting* with Livingstone).

A good way to recognise noun phrases is to see whether a word sequence will fit into a frame like *Have you heard about......?* or *How much do you know about......?* It is also generally possible for a noun phrase to begin with *the,* and so a useful test for a noun is whether it can fit the frame $\boxed{the \text{-----}}$. Try these tests on the four examples above: for instance, we can say:

> 'How much do you know about *donkeys*?'   and 'the *donkeys.*'
> 'How much do you know about *our town*?'   and 'the *town.*'

(b) **Form:**

   (i) Many nouns have characteristic suffixes: e.g. *–er* (*singer*), *–ism* (*fascism*), *–ion* or *–ation* (*caution*) *–ity* (*university*), *–ness* (*goodness*). There are many exceptions, of course, where these endings do not signal a noun: e.g., *longer* is an adjective, *linger* is a verb.

   (ii) Most nouns can change their form from **singular** to **plural** by adding *–s* or *–es* (*goal ~ goals*; *dress ~ dresses*) or by some other change of form (*woman ~ women*; *foot ~ feet*; *bacillus ~ bacilli*).

(c) **Meaning**: Nouns typically refer to physical things: people (*student*), objects (*book*), places (*city*), substances (*gold*), etc. These nouns are called **concrete** nouns; but there are also **abstract** nouns referring to events, states, times, etc.: *birth, happiness, revival, life.*

   Members of such a large class of words as nouns will obviously not all behave in the same way. We distinguish the various subclasses in terms of form, function and meaning:

   (i) **Count/non-count nouns**: Count nouns (e.g., *table, dog, idea, mile*) refer to things that can be counted, and so they can have a plural form (*tables*, etc.). Non-count nouns, on the other hand, refer to substances, qualities, etc., that we do not think of as coming in countable 'lumps': these nouns normally have no plural (**golds, *goodnesses*). Notice, however, that the same form can belong to both categories: in *Her hair is brown, hair* is a non-count noun, but in *I found two hairs in my soup,* it is a count noun.

   (ii) **Proper/common nouns**: Proper nouns denote an individual person, place, etc., whereas common nouns classify things into types. A proper noun normally begins with a capital letter: *John, Goldilocks, Africa, London.* It generally has no plural form

(*Johns, *Africas) and does not occur after *the* or *a/an*: (*a John, *the Africa*). Common nouns like *time, child* and *money*, though, can occur after *the*. So all the count and non-count nouns discussed in (i) are common nouns.

(iii) **Collective nouns:** These are generally count nouns, but even in the singular they refer to groups of people, animals or things: *family, government, team*. Grammatically, what we notice about collective nouns is this: they can sometimes go with a plural verb even when they themselves are singular: *Her family live/lives in Bangalore. The crowd was/were chanting loudly.*

6.5.2 Adjectives

(a) **Function:** Adjectives in general have two functions:

(i) as head (or main word) of an adjective phrase:

[6.9] [Dukes can be (*very rich*)].

(ii) as modifier in a noun phrase: (a *rich* duke).

If a word can fill both these positions we can feel confident that it is an adjective.

(b) **Form:** Most common adjectives can have comparative and superlative forms: *rich, richer, richest*. Thus we can often tell an adjective by its ability to take *−er* and *−est* as suffixes. However, longer adjectives do not take *−er* and *−est*, but combine with a separate comparative or superlative adverb: *more* or *most*. (We say *more beautiful*, not **beautifuller*; *more important*, not **importanter*.) There are also a few irregular adjectives which have special comparative and superlative forms, like *good, better, best*.

(c) **Meaning:** Adjectives typically describe some quality attributed to nouns. Most commonly they are used to narrow down, or specify more precisely, the reference of nouns, as *sympathetic* specifies what kind of *face* in:

[6.10]   a.   [(She) (had) (a *sympathetic* face)].
         b.   [(Her face) (was) (*sympathetic*)].

Adjectives have various types of meanings, for instance:

(i) physical qualities of colour, size, shape, etc.: *green, large, tall, round*
(ii) psychological qualities of emotion, etc.: *funny, brave, amazing, interested*
(iii) evaluative qualities: *good, wrong, beautiful, clever*.

It is a good test of adjectives that they can follow the so-called copula verb *to be*, in the frame Noun Phrase *be* --------, as in:

[6.11]   a.   [(Her eyes) (*were*) (*brown / blue / wary / intelligent / enormous*)].

(How many other adjectives can you think of, to fill the position of *sympathetic* in [6.10a] or [6.10b]?) It is also a good test of adjectives that they can occur between *the* and the head of a noun phrase, in the frame the ----- Noun :

[6.11] b. (the *new / large / old / tall / tumbledown / magnificent* building).

(Again, see how many additional adjectives you can fit into this position in [6.11b].) A further test is to insert the adverb *very* before the adjective, as a modifier in an adjective phrase:

[6.11] c. [(The building) (*is*) (*very* new / large / old / tall)].

This test, though, does not apply to all adjectives. Most adjectives describe qualities that vary along a scale of degree or extent, such as size, age, weight, etc.: *large/small*; *old/young*; *heavy/light*. But some adjectives, like *male*, refer to 'all-or-nothing' qualities, where *very* doesn't fit.

Table 6.3   *Comparison of adjectives*

	plain	comparative	superlative	+ degree adverb
Adjectives that can be compared	funny	funnier	funniest	very funny
	beautiful	more beautiful	most beautiful	rather beautiful
	good	better	best	quite good
	male	*maler	*malest	*somewhat male

Although we can talk of *a male wombat,* it is non-English to say **a maler wombat, *the malest wombat,* or **a very male wombat*. To be more precise, we **could** say *He's really a very male wombat*, but then *male* would take on a subtly different meaning, presumably referring to his macho qualities.

6.5.3 Verbs

(a) **Function:** Verbs as we discuss them now are **main verbs**; that is, they always function as the main element of a **verb phrase**. They can stand on their own as a verb phrase, or they can follow other verbs called auxiliaries (Section 6.5.2): [(Most wombats) (bite)], [(Every peach) (had been *eaten*)], [(The cat) (was *purring*)], [(You) (might *get*) (lucky)].

Because the verb phrase is the pivotal element of a clause, and because every verb phrase contains a main verb, it is always good to start analysing a sentence by **looking for the (main) verb** first. As a brief test, consider this example: which word is the main verb?

[6.12] One morning the little girl was hurrying along the street as usual.

Yes, the main verb in this case is *hurrying*.

Verb forms (inflections)   *Table 6.4*

	plain form	s-form	ed-form	ing-form	en-form
Regular	ask	asks	asked	asking	asked
	wash	washes	washed	washing	washed
Irregular	show	shows	showed	showing	shown
	write	writes	wrote	writing	written
	put	puts	put	putting	put
	give	gives	gave	giving	given

(b) **Form:**

(i) Some verbs, as we saw in Section 6.3, have derivational suffixes like *–ise, –ize* (*realise/realize*) and *–ify* (*clarify*), but these are not terribly important.

(ii) Much more important for verbs are inflections. Each verb has up to five different inflectional forms, which we can label **plain form**, *s*-**form**, *ed*-**form**, *ing*-**form** and *en*-**form**, as shown in Table 6.4. Notice that most verbs behave regularly, and have forms like those of *ask*. For these verbs, the *ed*-form and *en*-form are identical. For **irregular** verbs (there are about 200 of them in English), the *ed*-form and *en*-form can vary in a number of different ways: for example, we call the *en*-forms '*en*-forms' because they sometimes have the distinctive suffix *–en* (as in *eaten, written*), instead of *–ed*. The plain form of a verb is the form without any suffix.

(c) **Meaning:** Verbs can express actions, events, states, etc. Such 'goings on' can be physical (*eat*), mental (*think*), perceptual (*see*), social (*buy*), and so on.

An easy test for a verb is: Can the word vary its form from present tense to **past tense**? The plain form and the *s*-form are used for the present tense, while the *ed*-form is used for the regular past tense. For example, *happen* is a verb because we can contrast *Nothing happens* (present tense) with *Nothing happened* (past tense).

6.5.4 Adverbs

Adverbs are a particularly vague class of words to define. We can distinguish three major types of adverb, but there is considerable overlap between them.

1. Most adverbs add some kind of **circumstantial** information (of time, place, manner, etc.) to the state of affairs expressed in the main part of the clause:

[6.13] [(We) (sold) (the car) (*hurriedly*) (*yesterday*)].

2. Some adverbs modify adjectives and other adverbs in terms of **degree** (*fairly* new, *very* hurriedly, etc. – see Table 6.3).

3. **Sentence adverbs**, which apply semantically to the whole clause or sentence, express an attitude to it, or a connection between it and another clause or sentence:

> [6.14] [(*So*) (the whole thing) (was) (*frankly*) (too awful for words)].

In [6.14], the adverb *so* clearly connects what follows with what was said in an earlier sentence, while *frankly* tells us something about the speaker's attitude to what he/she is talking about.

All three types can be illustrated with the same adverb, *seriously*, which is a circumstantial adverb in [6.15a], a degree adverb in [6.15b] and a sentence adverb in [6.15c]:

> [6.15] a. They listened to her complaints *seriously*. (= 'in a serious manner')
> b. This cake is *seriously* scrumptious. (= 'to a serious degree')
> c. *Seriously*, do you mean that? (= 'I'm asking you seriously')

(a) **Function**: the primary function of an adverb is to be head (or main word) of an adverb phrase. It can stand alone as a minimal adverb phrase, or it can be preceded and/or followed by another word, which is often itself an adverb. Here the words in italics are all adverbs:

> [6.16] a. [She spoke (*softly*)].
> b. [She spoke (*very softly indeed*)].
> c. [She spoke (*too softly for me*)].

These examples show us a second function: an adverb can act as modifier in an adjective phrase (e.g., *very, rather, quite* and *somewhat* in Table 6.3) or in an adverb phrase (e.g., *very, indeed* and *too* in [6.16b] and [6.16c]).

(b) **Form:**

(i) Many adverbs are formed by adding *–ly* to an adjective.

(ii) In addition, a few adverbs resemble adjectives, in having comparative and superlative forms: *soon, sooner, soonest; well, better, best.*

(iii) Then there is a major group of adverbs that have no suffix and do not resemble adjectives. Among these adverbs are some of the most common: *now, then, so, too,* etc.

(c) **Meaning**: Adverbs can express many different types of meaning, especially as adjuncts in the clause. We can only give some important categories; and to distinguish them, it is useful to use a **question test**; for example, *home* answers the question *Where...?* in the following exchange (see also Table 6.5 opposite):

> [6.17] *Where* did Stefan go? He went *home.*

Some types of adverbs   Table 6.5

Adverb type	Eliciting question	Examples
Manner adverb	How?	well, nicely, cleverly
Place adverb	Where?	here, there, anywhere, home
Direction adverb	Where to? Where from?	up, down, away, ahead
Time-*when* adverb	When?	then, once, tonight, soon
Frequency adverb	How often?	always, weekly, often, usually
Degree adverb	To what degree? How much?	rather, quite, much, pretty

Unlike these, sentence adverbs, for example *fortunately, probably, actually* and *however,* do not answer questions. They can be divided into two main types:

Attitude (or stance) **adverbs:** *fortunately, actually, perhaps, surely*
Connecting adverbs: *so, moreover, however, therefore, though.*

For example, in [6.15] *fortunately* is an attitude adverb, while in [6.16] *however* is a connecting adverb:

[6.18]   ((*Fortunately*) (elephants) (can't fly)].
[6.19]   [(Some of them) (can run) (pretty fast), (*however*)].

6.6 'Function word' classes

We turn now to the seven **function word** classes. Luckily these do not need so much individual attention as the 'content word' classes. They have relatively few members, so we could, if we wanted, identify each of them by listing their members.

A thorough treatment of each class in terms of function, form and meaning would take up too much room here. But as the term 'function word' implies, it is their functional role that is most important, and on which we now focus. You will gradually grow familiar with these small but important word classes in the next two chapters, as we deal with phrases and clauses.

Here are brief definitions of the function classes, with listings of their most common members.

6.6.1 Determiners

Determiners begin noun phrases, and are sometimes obligatory. If the head of a noun phrase is a singular count noun, then some determiner has to be added. So [6.20a] is not acceptable in English, but [6.20b] is:

[6.20]   a.   *[(*Dog*) (bit) (*man*)].
         b.   [(The *dog*) (bit) (*a man*)].

The and *a/an* are the most common determiners, and are important enough to have their own unique names: they are called respectively the **definite article** and the **indefinite article**.

> Some common determiners:
>
> *the, a/an, this, that, these, all, some, any, no, every, each, many, which, what, his, our*

6.6.2 Pronouns

Pronouns are words which are in a sense 'dummy' nouns or noun phrases, because they have a generalised or unspecific meaning. For example, the pronoun *she* can refer to any female person. Because they usually stand alone in noun phrases, we consider pronouns to be the head of such phrases, though they are limited as to what words can be added to them. For example, we cannot say **a strange it* or **the old everybody*.

> Some common pronouns:
>
> *I, me, mine, myself, we, he, she, it, they, this, that, these, everything; some, many, who, which, what.* (See further Chapter 7, Section 7.5.2.)

You can see that there is a large overlap between determiners and pronouns: *this, that, some, which,* for instance, can belong to either category. Take *this* is an example:

[6.21 a. [(*This* wine) (is) (much too sweet)]. (*This* is a determiner)
       b. [(*This*) (is) (an excellent Chablis)]. (*This* is a pronoun)

6.6.3 Numerals

Numerals include **cardinal numbers** (*one, two, three, ... ten, ... 29*); and **ordinal numbers** (*first, second, third, ... tenth, ... 134th*). We will say no more about them here, except that they are exceptional as a function word class: there is an infinite number of numerals. However, the vast majority of these numerals are compounds made up from a few basic number words. For example, *two hundred and twenty* (or *220*) is composed of the basic numerals *two, hundred* and *twenty*.

> Some basic numerals:
>
> *one, two, three, four, five, ten, eleven, twenty, eighty, hundred, thousand, million*
> *first, second, third, fourth, fifth, tenth, eleventh, twentieth, hundredth, thousandth*

6.6.4 Prepositions

Prepositions introduce prepositional phrases, and express relations of possession, place, time, and many other meanings: (*of the world*), (*by it*), (*on the* *coldest night of the year*). What follows the preposition in the prepositional phrase is typically a noun phrase.

Some common prepositions (in order of frequency):

of, in, to, for, with, on, by, at, from, as, into, about, like, after, between, through, over

---

There is large overlap between prepositions and adverbs, particularly adverbs of place or direction:

[6.22] [(I) (looked) (*up* the chimney)].
[6.23] [(I) (looked) (*up*)].

In [6.22] *up* is a preposition, while in [6.23] *up* is an adverb.

6.6.5 Conjunctions

Conjunctions, like prepositions, are introductory linking words; but they often introduce clauses rather than phrases. In fact they subdivide into two different classes, **subordinating** conjunctions and **coordinating** conjunctions:

Some common subordinating conjunctions (in order of frequency) (see Chapter 8, Section 8.3):

that, as, if, when, than, because, while, where, although, whether, before, since, so.

Coordinating conjunctions (in order of frequency): *and, but, or, nor* (see 8.4.1).

6.6.6 Auxiliaries

Auxiliaries are a small class of verbs which precede the main verb in the verb phrase (see Chapter 7, Section 7.6). They fall into two main categories:

The **modal auxiliaries** are best considered invariable words, though for some purposes *could, would, might* and *should* can be regarded as *ed*-forms (past tense forms) of *can, will, may* and *shall*. The **primary verbs** are the three most important verbs in English, and we will refer to them by their plain forms: <u>be</u>, <u>have</u> and <u>do</u>. They are very irregular, and are the only English verbs that have an irregular *s*-form (*is, has, does*). Another important thing

---

Auxiliaries   *Table 6.6*

modal auxiliaries: can, will, may, shall, could, would, might, should, must					
primary auxiliaries:	plain form	s-form	ed-form	ing-form	en-form
	<u>be</u>, am, are	is	was, were	being	been
	<u>have</u>	has	had	having	had
	<u>do</u>	does	did	doing	done

about them is that they can each function **either** as auxiliaries, **or** as main verbs (see Section 6.5).

6.6.7 Discourse markers

Discourse markers are peripheral to grammar: we can add them (particularly in speech) at the beginning, middle or end of utterances, without obvious constraints on position. Their role is to signal feelings and interactive meanings between speakers in dialogue, and also to indicate how the discourse is developing. They include exclamatory words like *ugh, um, oh, ouch*, only loosely integrated into the language system. We can include here, too, swear words (*heck, bullshit*, etc.), greetings (*hello*), response words (*yes, no*) and other signalling words like *goodbye, right, okay, hey*. They can occur in combination:

[6.24] *Oh heck well* you'll have to go on the bus.

6.7 Summary

We have now said something about all the 11 word classes used in this book. One last thing: some words are unique in function, and cannot be readily classed with any other words – for example, the *to* which precedes a verb (*to work, to have*) and the negative word *not*. For these words the time-honoured word 'particle' can be used, meaning 'a little part of speech'.

The word classes we have distinguished are:

| 'Content word' classes: | noun, adjective, verb (i.e., full-verb) and adverb. |
| 'Function word' classes: | determiner, pronoun, numeral, preposition, conjunction, auxiliary and discourse marker. |

6.8 The fuzzy boundaries of grammatical classes: prototypes

We have implied that classifying words in word classes is a clear-cut business. But in fact, most grammatical categories have fuzzy boundaries.

Defining grammatical terms like *noun* and *verb* is like defining many other concepts of the language, such as *cup, chair, bird, mountain* (see Chapters 10 and 16). We can easily identify the features of the most typical members of the class: for example, a 'prototype' chair – the typical chair you might see in your mind's eye when asked to imagine a chair – has four legs, a back and a seat, is made of wood, and is used for sitting on. But there are other objects that we would be less inclined to call chairs, though they are marginally so; for example, a sofa, a settle, a pew, a deckchair, a park bench. In such cases, we cannot easily give a yes-or-no answer to the question 'Is this a chair?'. Similarly with birds: the typical bird has two legs, two wings, feathers, a

ADVANCES BOX 6.1

Word classes and frequency – comparing nouns and pronouns

If we count the **tokens** (individual instances) of word classes in texts, we find that the use of word classes varies greatly in frequency. Perhaps the most noticeable difference is in nouns and pronouns: nouns are very common in typical written texts – especially in newspapers – while pronouns are very common in speech. Here are typical examples from a written text and a spoken dialogue illustrating this. All the underlined words are nouns:

[6.25] The <u>aviation</u> and <u>casino</u> <u>kingpin</u> <u>Kirk</u> <u>Kerkorian</u> finally sold <u>MGM's</u> <u>film</u> <u>entertainment</u> <u>division</u> to <u>Pathe</u> <u>boss</u> <u>Giancarlo</u> <u>Parretti</u> in <u>November</u> ...
(Example from the Freiburg-Brown Corpus: US newspaper reporting)

[6.26] *I* think *you*'ll find *it* counts towards your <u>income</u>.
(Example from the British National Corpus: British conversation)

Compared with the 14 nouns in example [6.25], example [6.26] has only one noun, but it has three pronouns (in italics). A reason for this kind of difference is that serious writing tends to convey a lot of densely packed information, while conversation is less dense, and relies a lot on shared contextual information. For example, only context can tell us whom or what *I*, *you* and *it* refer to in [6.25].

Surprisingly, in view of such differences, Hudson (1994) wrote an article 'About 37% of word-tokens are nouns', based on a study of a wide range of written English, where he claimed that the magic 37 per cent was more or less constant in all text types. But – an important 'But' – Hudson here was using 'noun' to include pronouns as well as common nouns and proper nouns. Actually, within this magic percentage figure, the proportion of pronouns to nouns varies greatly. Nevertheless, Hudson's finding was interesting in showing that there is a precise trade-off between frequency of nouns and of pronouns.

Leech and colleagues (forthcoming: Chapter 10) show that frequency of word classes also varies over time. For example, the frequency of nouns (especially when combined in sequences such as *film entertainment division* in [6.22]) was increasing significantly in written texts over the later part of the twentieth century. Although in other respects written English has been becoming more colloquial (i.e., more like speech), it has also been getting more informationally dense, which is an 'anti-colloquial' trend. In general, then, content word classes have become more frequent, and function words less frequent.

---

beak and a tail; it flies, perches on branches, lays eggs in a nest, and sings. In these respects, sparrows and robins are typical, whereas eagles, ducks and penguins are to varying degrees less 'birdy'.

Prototype theory was developed by Eleanor Rosch and her team of psycholinguists in the 1970s (see Chapters 10 and 16 which also refer to prototype theory; see also Ungerer and Schmid, 2006: ch. 1).

The same idea of prototype categories with degrees of membership applies to grammar. Just as some birds are less 'birdy' than others, so some nouns are

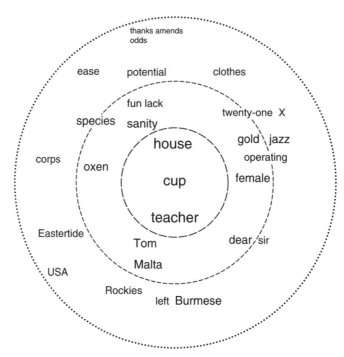

FIGURE 6.2   *An impressionistic picture of the NOUN word class, showing by their size of print and centrality that some nouns are more 'nouny' than others*

less 'nouny' than others, and some verbs less 'verby' than others. The typical or **prototype** nouns are those which refer to people, animals and things – and among these, incidentally, are the nouns which children learn first, when they start to use language to identify the phenomena around them. Similarly, the prototype verb is a 'doing word' such as *walk* or *carry* – although the most common verb of all, *be*, is far from typical in this respect.

In what follows, then, we will often, when defining grammatical terms, use words such as 'typical' or 'generally', rather than 'every' and 'always'. We do not see this as a weakness – it is a reflection of the fuzzy boundaries of grammatical classes, especially in the area of meaning.

But this concept of a 'fuzzy' category does not just apply to meaning: it applies also to formal aspects of definition. For example, a **typical** noun has a plural in *–s* and a **typical** verb has a past tense in *–ed*; but there are less typical nouns that have a plural in *–en* (e.g., *oxen*), and way-out nouns that have no plural at all (e.g., *sunshine*). There are also less typical verbs which have an irregular past tense, such as *win/won* or *eat/ate*. And the most way-out verb is *go*, which has an unrelated past tense *went*.

Hence grammar is not a precise logical or mathematical system, but has much in common with systems or organisms in the natural world, in that it involves typical and atypical membership. There are plenty of linguistic parallels to the duck-billed platypus.

6.8 A last word on terminology: morphology and syntax

This chapter, like the preceding one, has been mainly about words. But, unlike Chapter 5, it has looked ahead to the **function** of words in larger units such as phrases, clauses and sentences. Words, that is, are at the boundary between two major subdivisions of grammar: **morphology** and **syntax**. Morphology (more particularly inflexional morphology) deals with grammar **within** the scope of words. **Syntax**, on the other hand, deals with grammar **outside** the word: that is, with how words behave in larger units (phrases, clauses and sentences). The next two chapter present an outline of English syntax.

Recommended readings

For more detail on English grammar, using essentially the same framework as in this and the following chapters, see Ballard (2001), Chapters 4–7 and Leech et al. (2006) Chapters 3–8. (The present chapter is modelled closely on parts of Chapters 2 and 3 of the latter book.) Other introductory books dealing with grammar, going into greater detail, are Börjars and Burridge (2001) and Biber, Conrad and Leech (2002) – with an accompanying workbook (Conrad, Biber and Leech, 2002) – and Collins and Hollo (2000). Another good textbook is Miller (2002), which takes a somewhat more theoretical stance, and uses data from other languages as well as English. Miller's Chapter 4 deals with word classes.

On the prototype theory of categories, originating in the work of Eleanor Rosch and associates in the 1970s, see Ungerer and Schmid (2006), Chapter 1.

CHAPTER 7

Grammar: Phrases (and Clauses)

GEOFFREY LEECH

Now that we have investigated word classes in English, it is not too difficult to explain **phrase classes**. First we take a further look at the closed classes of words (such as determiners) which play an important role in phrases, and become familiar with the classes of phrase already introduced in Chapter 6, Section 6.4. But we cannot deal with phrases without paying some attention to the clauses they function in, which is the reason for the second part of the chapter title above.

7.1 Classes of phrase

We will need to look at five classes of phrase. Of these, **noun phrases, adjective phrases** and **adverb phrases** all have the same basic structure:

(Modifier(s)) Head (Modifier(s)) ...   where the brackets indicate optional elements

This means that the main word in the phrase, the **head**, is the only word that **has** to occur in the phrase. The modifiers, occurring either before or after the head, are optional (although this is a statement that will have to be reconsidered later in Section 7.5, for noun phrases). So some of the possible structures are:

Head	**Modifier + Modifier + Head**
Modifier + Head	**Modifier + Head + Modifier**
Head + Modifier	**Modifier + Modifier + Head + Modifier**

and so on. In Section 6.4 we showed modifiers only in front of the head, but now we have two positions for modifiers: before the head, and after the head. **(From now on in this chapter, heads are marked by underlining).**

[7.1]	*awful weather*	(This is a noun phrase with *awful* as the modifier and *weather* as head.)
[7.2]	*awful drizzly weather*	(...a noun phrase with two modifiers, both before the head *weather*.)
[7.3]	*awful weather outside*	(...a noun phrase with two modifiers, one before and one after the head.)
[7.4]	*very noisy*	(...an adjective phrase, with *very* as the modifier and *noisy* as the head.)

[7.5] *very <u>noisily</u> indeed*   (an adverb phrase, with two modifiers, one
                                           before and one after the head.)

For these types of phrase, the head usually belongs to the class of words we
see in the name of the phrase type. Thus:

a **noun phrase**   has   a **noun** as its head
an **adjective phrase** has   an **adjective** head
an **adverb phrase**   has   an **adverb** as head

> **Note:** We will use these abbreviations for the three most common types of
> phrases:
>
>   NP = noun phrase   PP = prepositional phrase   VP = verb phrase

Of the remaining two types of phrase, **prepositional phrases** (PP) begin with
a preposition (such as *of, in, at, with, on*), which is followed by a noun phrase
(NP) – remember that in the examples, round brackets enclose phrases:

[7.6] *(on (<u>Friday</u>))* (In this prepositional phrase, *on* is the preposition and
        Friday is a single-word noun phrase)

(Although prepositions can be considered the heads of prepositional
phrases, we will not underline them in examples.) In the following examples,
the outer brackets enclose the prepositional phrase, and the inner brackets
enclose the noun phrase inside it:

[7.6] a. (with (incredible <u>force</u>))   b. (off (the <u>wall</u>))
       c. (at (our <u>meeting</u> yesterday))   d. (in (a colourful new <u>outfit</u>))
       e. (on (a bright, cold, winter <u>afternoon</u>))

Finally, the **verb phrase** (VP) is special to itself: it is rather different from the
other phrases, and has a special pivotal role in the clause. We will discuss it
last, as this will lead on to the further treatment of clauses in Chapter 8.

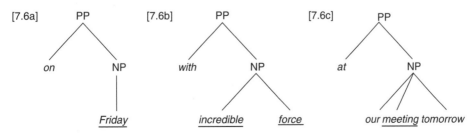

Simplified tree diagrams of prepositional phrases   FIGURE 7.1

7.2 Phrases inside phrases

The distinction between main and embedded (or **subordinate**) **clauses** is probably familiar to many of you: Chapter 8 (Section 3) of this book deals with embedded clauses. But here we introduce the same idea for phrases. A **main phrase** is one which is a direct part of a clause, that is, which is not part of another phrase, while an **embedded phrase** is one that **is** part of another phrase. Now this idea must be explored. So, returning to examples [7.6a]–[7.6e], we notice that each example has two pairs of brackets (( )). The inside pair of brackets in each case encloses a phrase which is part of another phrase. The outer phrase is a prepositional phrase, while the inner phrases is a noun phrase. Another way to represent this is by a tree diagram, as in Figure 7.1.

7.2.1 Embedded phrases

In Chapter 6, Section 6.4 (Illustrations Box 6.2) we presented the hierarchy of units (clause – phrase – word) such that a unit (e.g., a clause) higher in the scale consists of one or more examples of the next lower unit (e.g., a phrase). This idea was correct, but we could have misled you by what it did not say. Now we have to add to it: we have to allow for the possibility that units are not merely divisible into units of the next lower rank, but can contain units of the same, or even of a higher rank. This is the phenomenon of **embedding** – and it is important because it allows us to make sentences as complex as we like.

Consider, for example, examples [7.6a]–[7.6e] above. As the round brackets show, these are structures where one type of phrase – a PP – has another type of phrase – an NP – embedded inside it. Consider, now, a more complex example: the sequence of words *the bride of the heir apparent*: it is a phrase (actually an NP), and contains another phrase (a PP) as a modifier within it: *of the heir apparent*. And now, we go one step further, and observe that this PP itself contains a further phrase inside it – an NP. We can represent these cases of subordination as brackets within brackets as follows:

[7.7]   (the <u>bride</u> (of (the <u>heir</u> apparent)))

Wherever we have two or more sets of round brackets like these, one within the other, the inner brackets enclose an embedded phrase. We can also represent the same structure of 'embedding' by Chinese boxes or by a tree diagram:
Consider now:

[7.8]   [(The <u>heir</u> apparent) (<u>nearly</u>) (<u>became</u>) (an Olympic <u>champion</u>)].

FIGURE 7.2   *Embedding of phrases: NP in PP in NP*

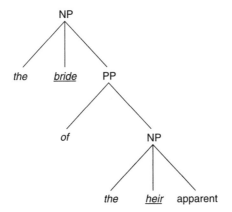

A simplified tree diagram of the same structure   FIGURE 7.3

Here *The heir apparent* is functioning as part of clause structure, that is, as Subject (see Section 7.4). It is not an embedded phrase – it's a main phrase. We can tell this at a glance, because the round brackets are immediately within the square brackets of the clause. In simple bracketing notation, then, the following are indicators of main and embedded phrases:

Main phrase   **Embedded phrase**
[(Phrase)]   ((Phrase))

In terms of tree diagrams, the following configurations indicate main and embedded phrases respectively:

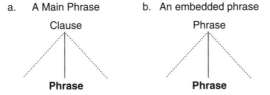

A phrase in a clause, and a phrase in a phrase   FIGURE 7.4

Where there is an embedded phrase, it will always be directly or indirectly a part of a main phrase:

[7.9]   [(The <u>bride</u> (of (the <u>heir</u> apparent))) (<u>nearly</u>) (<u>had</u>) (a <u>fit</u>)].

Here, *the heir apparent* is an embedded noun phrase, *of the heir apparent* is an embedded prepositional phrase and *the bride of the heir apparent* is the main noun phrase which includes them both.

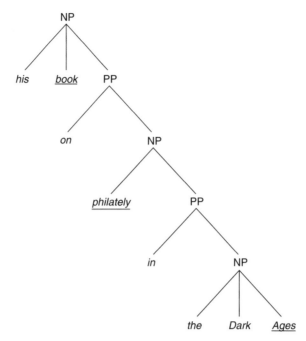

FIGURE 7.5   *Simplified tree diagram: prepositional phrase*

Once we have got used to the idea of phrases within phrases, there is nothing to stop embedded phrases themselves containing further embedded phrases, and so on indefinitely:

[7.10]   (his <u>book</u> (on (<u>philately</u> (in (the Dark <u>Ages</u>)))))
[7.11]   (my <u>review</u> (of (his <u>book</u> (on (<u>philately</u> (in (the Dark <u>Ages</u>))))))))
[7.12]   (his boisterous <u>reply</u> (to (my <u>review</u> (of (his <u>book</u> (on (<u>philately</u> (in (the Dark <u>Ages</u>))))))))).

Embedding of phrases is one of the chief sources of complexity in grammar, particularly in NPs (see pp. 132, 161). As tree diagrams, example [7.10] translates into Figure 7.5 and example [7.8] translates into Figure 7.6.

7.2.2   A preview of embedded (=subordinate) clauses

While on the subject of embedding, we should mention that **embedded clauses** work on the same principle, as we will see more fully in 8.3. This time we will indicate subordination by a nesting of square brackets:

[7.13]   [Joel thinks [that Ann loves him]].
[7.14]   [Ann thinks [that Joel thinks [that she loves him]]].

Figure 7.7 shows [7.13] as a simplified tree diagram:

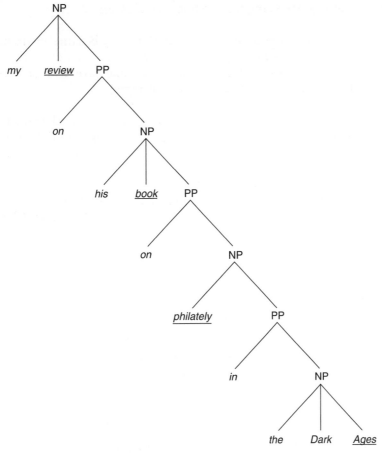

Simplified tree diagram: prepositional phrase with embedding   FIGURE 7.6

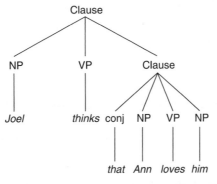

Simplified tree diagram: a main clause containing a complement clause   FIGURE 7.7

Here are four more examples of embedded clauses:

[7.15]   [[That this was a tactical decision] quickly became apparent].
[7.16]   [[If you go to a bank], they'll rip you off].
[7.17]   [Most ions are colourless, [although some have distinct colours]].
[7.18]   [The conclusion, [it seems], is intolerable].

Taking the matter just one stage further, we have to allow for the possibility of the embedding of one unit (a clause) within a unit of **lower** rank (a phrase). In such a case the bracketing will show square brackets inside round brackets:

[7.19]   (the <u>house</u> [that Jack built])
[7.20]   (the <u>malt</u> [that lay (in the house [that Jack built])])
[7.21]   (the <u>rat</u> [that ate (the malt [that lay (in the house [that Jack built])])])

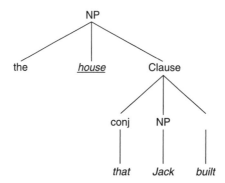

FIGURE 7.8   *Simplified tree diagram: clause embedded in a noun phrase*

The clause *that Jack built* here is called a **relative clause**, and is part of an NP. Again there is the possibility of repeated embedding in the same structure. Thus [7.20] shows us one relative clause indirectly inside another relative clause, and [7.21] shows a further repetition of the same structure. Relative clauses are taken up later in Chapter 8, Illustrations Box 8.3. Meanwhile, here are three more examples, using round brackets just for the NPs containing the relative clauses. The underlined word is the head of the NP, the word whose referent the relative clause tells us more about:

[7.22]   [He warned the public about (the <u>men</u>, [*who are armed and dangerous*])].
[7.23]   [(The <u>person</u> [*who rents this apartment next year*]) might have trouble.]
[7.24]   [We followed (a <u>footpath</u> [*which disappeared in a landscape of fields and trees*])].

If you find the notion of embedding puzzling at this stage, there will be plenty of chance in the next chapter to become more familiar with it.

7.3 Noun phrases (NP) and related types of phrases

We saw in Chapter 6 that words can be classified into various word classes. But when we examined how these words behave in phrases, we found ourselves using terms like **head** and **modifier**. These are not labels for word classes as such, but for the kinds of role they have in relation to other words, that is, to the **function** they perform in a phrase. Hence there are two labels for each point on the tree-diagram in Figure 7.9:

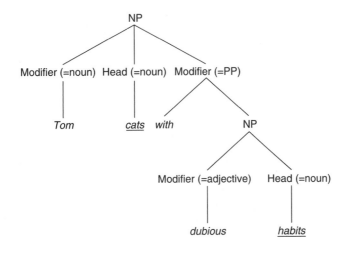

FIGURE 7.9

(For simplicity, though, we will use only one kind of label in tree diagrams in this chapter and the next – either form or function labels.)

Like words, phrases can be classified partly by their external function and partly by their internal form. By 'form', with phrases as with words, we mean the way the structure of the unit is made up of other, smaller constituents. Typically, as we have seen, a phrase is composed of head and modifiers.

As noted in Chapter 6, the meaning words convey is another factor in classifying them. The same can be said about phrases. When we ask 'What are phrases useful for?' the natural answer is that they enable us to elaborate on the meaning of the word which is their head.

Let's take noun phrases as an example. In a simple NP like *the book*, the head noun *book* has a fairly general meaning, and might refer to any book you can think of. If I tell you to go to a library bookcase and to *Bring me (the book)*, most likely you will not know which book to bring. But if I add an adjective *Bring me (the green book)*, you will have a better idea which book to choose, especially if I combine more than one adjective in the single phrase: *Bring me (the large thick green book)*. In an NP, adjectives function as modifiers, adding more information about the head, telling us **what book** or **which book** is intended. A similar information-adding role is performed by modifiers (especially PPs) following the head: *Bring me (the large thick green book (on the top shelf))*. And, as we noted above, a relative clause can also be added as a modifier: *Bring me (the book [that you were reading yesterday])*.

A relative clause will be useful when we want to add information about the book's involvement in actions or events or states of affairs. Here's another example combining different kinds of modifiers: *Bring me (the large picture book (about caterpillars)[that Marie gave me for my birthday]).* This NP contains 15 words, and NPs much longer than this can also be constructed! No wonder NPs are often complex in varieties of written English – such as news reporting and academic writing – where information-giving is at a premium.

Later in this chapter, we will spend time looking in more detail at the two most important types of phrase in English: the noun phrase (NP) and the verb phrase (VP). But first, to say more about the function of these phrase types, we will need to introduce the main structures in the English clause.

7.4   A preview of clauses

Many sentences consist of a single clause, for example:

[7.25]   Subject = NP   VP   Object = NP
          [(Some greedy <u>person</u>)   (<u>ate</u>)   (my cucumber <u>sandwiches</u>)].

This clause contains three phrases, an NP + VP + NP. (The NPs both contain three words, and the VP just one word, but here we are not interested in their make-up in terms of words, but in the function each phrase has in the clause.) The first NP is known as the Subject, and the NP at the end is known as the Object (we write these words with a capital, to avoid confusion with other, everyday meanings of 'subject' and 'object'.)

7.4.1   Subjects and Objects

Most clauses have a Subject which is an NP and which precedes the VP. Here we regard the VP as the pivotal element in the clause, and as there is only one VP in the structure of a clause, we do not need to bother about a second label for its function. In contrast, as we have just seen, there can be more than one NP in a clause. However, not all clauses have an Object. In the following clause, there is just a Subject NP and a VP:

[7.26]   Subject = NP   VP
          [(Lazy <u>Mary</u>)   (was <u>yawning</u>)].

Notice again that the same phrase, the same piece of language, can have two labels. The phrase *Lazy Mary* here is labelled both as a noun phrase (NP) and as a Subject. NP is the 'form' label, and Subject is the 'function' label. We found this dual labelling was also useful at the word level. In a similar way, *Lazy Mary* can be called a noun phrase (because it has a noun as head), but it can also be called a Subject, referring to its function in the clause.

Can meaning help us to distinguish Subjects and Objects? The Subject of a clause is often said to refer to as the 'doer' of an action represented by the verb. So, in [7.25] and [7.26], 'some greedy person' did the eating, and 'lazy Mary' did the yawning. But in other cases, it is difficult to interpret the

VP as representing the action and the Subject as representing the actor. For example, in:

[7.27]   Subject = NP   VP   Object = NP   Adjunct = AdvP
         [(Sam)   (admires)   (Kylie)   (very much)]

Sam is not the doer of any action, but (for reasons we will return to in Chapter 8, Section 8.1.1) we will still say that *Sam* is the Subject. A similar thing can be said about the Object, which is often described as referring to something or somebody affected by the action represented by the verb phrase: what we may call the 'doee'. This notion is all right for examples like [7.25], but not for examples like [7.27], where nothing (necessarily) happens to Kylie as a result of Sam's admiring her. So, as we have found before in word classes, semantics will often account for typical cases, but not for all cases.

7.4.2 Adjuncts

Example [7.27] contains another type element of clause structure: here we will call phrases like *very much* Adjuncts – that is, phrases which are not intimately connected with the verb in describing an event or state of affairs, like the Subject and Object, but which rather describe incidental circumstances such as the time, place or manner (the 'when', 'where' and 'how') of an action, event or state. In [7.27], *very much* is an adverb phrase, telling us about the degree or extent of Sam's admiration. Like most Adjuncts, it is optional: that is, we could omit the Adjunct and simply say *Sam admires Kylie,* and the sentence would still make good sense.

Two other points to notice about Adjuncts is that (a) they can occur in various positions in the clause, and (b) more than one or two of them can occur in the same clause. These points are illustrated in 7.28 and 7.29:

[7.28] Subject = NP   VP   Adjunct = AdvP Adjunct = PP   Adjunct = PP
       [(The committee)   (is meeting) (promptly)   (at our house) (at seven o'clock)].

[7.29] Adjunct = PP   Subject = NP   Adjunct = AdvP VP   Object = NP   Adjunct = AdvP
       [(On Saturday) (the Doe family)   (usually)   (ate)   (their dinner)   (early)].

Example [7.28] has three Adjuncts: all placed at the end, after the VP. In example [7.29], the first adjunct is in front position, before the Subject; the second is in a medial position; and the third is at the end, after the Object. (We will leave you to work out what meaning each Adjunct has – does it indicates time, place or manner, for example?) Also, there is one Adjunct which deals with frequency (time 'how often'), rather than time 'when'. (Which one is it?)

We have said enough about Adjuncts for now. In terms of form, note that the Adjuncts in [7.27[, [7.28], and [7.29] are either adverbial phrases (AdvP) or prepositional phrases (PP). These are the types of phrase most commonly acting as Adjuncts. But time-when can also be indicated by NPs (e.g., 'this week'), which can act as adjuncts, as in *The committee is meeting this week*.

> **Note:** Incidentally, the term 'Adverbial' is sometimes used instead of 'Adjunct'. Here, we use the term 'adjunct' in a very wide sense. We use it also for the sentence adverbs (strictly speaking, these are minimal, i.e., one-word adverb phrases) discussed in Chapter 6, Section 6.5.4, which have an attitudinal or connective meaning:

[7.30] Adjunct = PP   Adjunct = AdvP Subject = NP Head = VP Object = NP
     [(<u>To</u> our surprise), (<u>however</u>),   (the <u>mouse</u>) (<u>attacked</u>) (the <u>aardvark</u>)].

There is more to be said about phrases in clause structure, but we will leave the topic now and return to it in the next chapter. Meanwhile, here is a summary of the relation between phrases and their functions (i.e., the slots they fill in clause structure):

- Noun phrases can be Subjects or Objects (and occasionally Adjuncts) in the clause.
- Prepositional phrases can be Adjuncts
- Adverb phrases can also be Adjuncts
- Verb phrases are the central or pivotal elements of clauses, and, by analogy with head words in phrases, we can think of them as the head phrase in a clause.

The next two sections, 7.5 and 7.6, look more carefully at the structure of NPs and VPs.

7.5 More on the structure of the noun phrase (NP)

> **ILLUSTRATION BOX 7.1**
>
> **Noun phrase structure**
>
> The structures of NPs are very diverse, but the chief elements are these:
>
> (a) **The head of an NP can be:**
>
>   (i)   most often, a **noun**: (the <u>doll</u>), (dear <u>Margaret</u>), etc.
>   (ii) a **pronoun**: (<u>it</u>), (<u>herself</u>), (<u>everyone</u> (in (the street))), etc.
>   (iii) less usually, an **adjective** (the <u>absurd</u>), a **numeral** (all <u>fifteen</u>), or a **genitive** (<u>Joan's</u>).
>
> The first two possibilities in (iii) are shown in:
>
>   [7.31] [[If you offer them three types of ice cream,] (the <u>greedy</u>) (will take) (all <u>three</u>)].

But in such cases there is usually a noun which, semantically, is understood to be the head: e.g., the last part of [7.31] means: [(*The greedy people) (will take) (all three types (of ice cream))*].

(b) **The words preceding the head of an NP can be:**

(i) **Determiners,** including the articles *the* and *a*: (*the* <u>morning</u>), (*a* <u>girl</u>), (*some* <u>water</u>)

(ii) **Numerals:** (*two* <u>eggs</u>), (the *third* <u>man</u>), (my *last* <u>throw</u>)

(iii) **Adjectives:** (*red* <u>shoes</u>), (*older* <u>children</u>), (the *strangest* <u>coincidence</u>)

(iv) **Nouns:** (a *garden* <u>fence</u>), (this *gold* <u>ring</u>), (*London* <u>pubs</u>), etc.

(v) **Genitives:** (*Gina's* pet <u>marmoset</u>), (*Tokyo's* <u>skyline</u>), etc.

(vi) **Adverbs** in initial position: (*quite* a <u>noise</u>).

(vii) An assortment of other categories, such as adjective phrases ((*awfully bad*) <u>weather</u>); other phrases ((*round the clock*) <u>service</u>); compound words of various kinds (the *kind-hearted* <u>vampire</u>); *–en* and *–ing* forms of verbs (*grated* <u>cheese</u>), (a *working* <u>mother</u>).

This last set of modifiers is so miscellaneous that we can only give a small sample.

(c) **The modifiers following the head of an NP can be:**

(i) **Prepositional phrases:** (the best <u>day</u> (*of my life*)).

(ii) **Relative clauses:** (a <u>quality</u> [*that I admire*]).

(iii) Various other types of modifier, including **adverbs** (the <u>girl</u> *upstairs*), **adjectives** (<u>something</u> *nasty* (in the woodshed)), and embedded **noun phrases** (the <u>bandicoot</u>, (*a tiny marsupial*)).

Because of these various kinds of modifier, you can imagine that an NP can reach considerable complexity. With modifiers both before the head and after, such phrases as [7.32] are not unusual:

[7.32] (the brassy, boobsome, bawdy bar <u>owner</u> (in (the British soap *Eastenders*)))

In modification following the head, there is in principle no limit to the length of NPs. We can get an idea of this from examples like 7.12 and 7.21 above.

7.5.1 Determiners: are they modifiers?

Earlier we said that the basic formula

(Modifier(s)) <u>Head</u> (Modifier(s))

fitted NPs, as well as other kinds of phrases. This needs to be rethought a little. Most NPs with a common noun as their head need to begin with a determiner (see Chapter 6, Section 6.6.1), especially *the* and *a*, whose semantic role is not so much to add more detail of information to the head, as to specify *how* it refers to something: whether it has definite or indefinite reference. So determiners are somewhat different from modifiers: they are like anchors anchoring the NP to some kind of reality, rather than adding more content. Some other determiners (e.g., *all, some, no, every, many, few*) are known as 'quantifiers', as they specify the amount or quantity the NP refers to. Numerals like *two, three, five, fifty* can also be considered quantifiers, and behave much like determiners. So a more complete formula for NPs would be this:

(Determiner) (Modifier(s)) <u>Head</u> (Modifier(s))

> **Note**: There is an alternative account of NPs which treats them as determiner phrases (DPs) – with the determiner as head.

7.5.2 Pronouns and determiners

Pronouns and determiners are two function word classes in the NP which have similar subdivisions:

ILLUSTRATION BOX 7.2

Pronouns and determiners

- **Pronouns** function as head of an NP. Some examples:

  Personal pronouns: *I, you, she, it, we, they, myself, him,her*
  Possessive pronouns: *mine, ours, yours, his, hers, theirs*
  Demonstrative pronouns: *this, that, these, those.*
  Quantifier pronouns: *all, some, any, one, another; everybody, someone; many, much, little, less*
  Wh– pronouns: *who, whom, whose, what, which, whatever*

- **Determiners** function as words at the beginning of the NP, preceding heads and modifiers, and specifying mode of reference:

  Articles: *the, a/an*
  Possessive determiners: *my, our, your, his, her, its, their*
  Demonstrative determiners: *this, that, these, those* (**the same as pronouns**)
  Quantifier determiners: *all, some, any, one, another; everybody, someone; many, much, little, less* (**the same as pronouns**)
  Wh– determiners: *what, which, whose, whatever, whichever*

Notice that the demonstratives and the quantifiers are the same word as both pronouns and determiners. The other classes are also very similar, except that personal pronouns are always pronouns, and articles are always determiners. Nevertheless, function being more important than form, we treat these as separate word classes. The simple rule is that words from these classes which function as **heads** of the NP are **pronouns,** and those which precede the head are **determiners**. This rule applies even to POSSESSIVE words:

possessive pronouns	possessive determiners
mine, ours, yours, his, hers, theirs	*my, our, your, his, her, its, their*

Possessive pronouns can stand alone as the head of an NP: (This) (is) (*mine*). Possessive determiners need a head to follow them: (This) (is) (*my* mouse).

Similarly *your sister, her book,* etc. In meaning, words like *my* and *your* are the 'pronoun' equivalent of genitives like *Gina's,* but as they are single words filling the determiner 'slot', we treat them as determiners like *the* and *a.* Compare:

[7.33]   [(Those) (are) (your books)]. – where *your* is a determiner
[7.34]   [(Those books) (are) (yours)]. – where *yours* is a pronoun

Or, equivalently, in these tree diagrams:

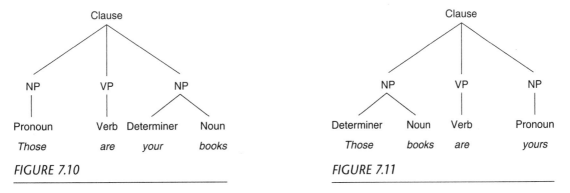

FIGURE 7.10   FIGURE 7.11

(These sentences also show the difference between *those* as a pronoun and *those* as a determiner.)

7.6   The verb phrase (VP)

The verb phrase, of course, it central to the clause and it is now time to examine VPs in detail. We will need to distinguish in Chapter 8, Section 8.4 between **finite** and **non-finite clauses,** but at present we limit ourselves to finite clauses, which means that we concentrate on the fullest kind of VP, the **finite verb phrase** (the kind of VP that has present or past tense).

Structure: We have already outlined (in Chapter 6, Section 6.5.3) the structure of the VP in terms of two kinds of element: the **main verb** and **auxiliaries.** The auxiliaries are optional, and precede the main verb. At the most general level the structure of the VP is:

(Auxiliary/Auxiliaries) Main Verb

with any number of auxiliaries from zero up to four. Most commonly, the VP consists of one verb, the **main verb,** which expresses the general idea of what is happening in the clause: what action, event or state of affairs is being described. The auxiliaries are rather like modifiers, but they add not so much information as a perspective or viewpoint on the action or state expressed by the verb. This includes **modality** (viewing the action as filtered through concepts such as possibility and necessity), **aspect** (how we view the action or event in temporal terms – as in progress, or as completed, etc.), and **active** versus **passive** (see Chapter 8, Section 8.1.2).

In Table 7.1, we have replaced the general 'Auxiliary' label by some more specific optional 'slots' or function labels: **Modal, Perfect, Progressive** and **Passive**. The Modal slot is filled by one of the modal auxiliaries such as *will, can, could* (Chapter 6, Section 6.6.6). The Perfect slot is always filled by the auxiliary *have*, and the Progressive slot is always filled by the auxiliary *be*; similarly, the Passive slot is always filled by *be*, and the main verb slot can be filled by any full verb, including one of the primary verbs (*be, have, do*), which can be either auxiliaries or main verbs. We can now enlarge on the structure of the VP:

(Mod) (Perf) (Prog) (Pass) Main Verb

(Remember that ( ) means optional.) The terms 'modal', 'perfect', 'progressive' and 'passive' describe the kinds of meaning expressed by an auxiliary, when it is combined with a following verb. For example:

ILLUSTRATION BOX 7.3

Auxiliary verb constructions

can swim	is an example of a **modal** construction:	modal auxiliary + infinitive
has eaten	is an example of a **perfect** construction:	*have* + past participle (an *en*-form)
is eating	is an example of a **progressive** construction:	*be* + –*ing* participle (*ing*-form)
was eaten	is an example of a **passive** construction:	*be* + past participle (*en*-form)

These types of constructions can be combined, as shown in Table 7.1. However, the more complex verb phrases combining three or four of these constructions (e.g., examples 12–16 in the Table) are extremely rare.

Where there is no passive auxiliary (e.g., in examples 1–4, 6–7, 9, and 12–13 in the Table), the verb phrase is said to be in the **active voice**. We will return to passive VPs later (Chapter 8, Section 8.1.2).

7.6.1 Verb forms

We make a distinction here between **finite** and **non-finite** forms of verbs. In this chapter we are dealing only with **finite verb phrases**, where the first word is always a **finite verb form** (marked by being placed in a box in Table 7.1)

Patterns of the Verb Phrase   *Table 7.1*

Subject Noun phrase	Verb Phrase					Adjunct Adverb Phrase
	modal	*perfect aspect*	*progressive aspect*	*passive voice*	*main verb*	
the tree					shook	violently 1
the tree	might				shake	violently 2
the tree		had			shaken	violently 3
the tree			was		shaking	violently 4
the tree				was	shaken	violently 5
the tree	might	have			shaken	violently 6
the tree	might		be		shaking	violently 7
the tree	might			be	shaken	violently 8
the tree		had	been		shaking	violently 9
the tree		had		been	shaken	violently 10
the tree			was	being	shaken	violently 11
the tree	might	have	been		shaking	violently 12
the tree	might	have	been		shaken	violently 13
the tree	might		be	being	shaken	violently 14
the tree		had	been	being	shaken	violently 15
the tree	might	have	been	being	shaken	violently 16

Finite verbs vary for present and past tense (using an *ed*-form for the past tense). For example:

Present tense	*look, looks*	*am, is, are*	*has, have*	*do, does*	*come, comes*
Past tense	*looked*	*was, were*	*had*	*did*	*came*

In Illustrations Box 7.3, we have also mentioned an extra verb form, in addition to the plain form, *s*-form, *ed*-form, *ing*-form and *en*-form listed in Table 6.4. This new form is the **infinitive** form of the verb, but it is identical to the plain present-tense form dealt with in Table 6.4 except for the verb *be* (where *be* is the infinitive, and *am* and *are* the plain finite forms). In general, then, the infinitive is the form of the verb which has no ending, the **plain** form, just like the present tense plural.

Important! – The initial word (usually the *only* word) of finite VPs is finite, whereas non-initial words of *any* VP are always non-finite.

7.7 Grammar wars?

This chapter, like the last chapter, has presented terms and definitions as if they are the 'gospel truth'. But it might not be a surprise to learn that there are basic differences about terminology and definitions in the study of grammar. When you read grammar books, you may find they are all preaching a slightly different 'gospel'!

To illustrate this, consider the type of phrase called a verb phrase (VP). We have introduced it as a construction consisting of a main verb and preceding (optional) auxiliaries. In some grammar books, though, you will find that the VP is a bigger part of the clause, consisting of not only the main verb, but the elements that follow the verb, such as Objects and Adjuncts. Using round brackets for boundaries of phrases, as before, here are two different analyses of the same clause:

```
          NP      VP      NP        PP
[7.35]   [(Lisa) (bought) (her clothes) (in (Paris))]
                        (where her clothes is Object, and in Paris an Adjunct)
          NP                         VP
         _____
[7.36]              NP         PP
         [(Lisa) (bought (her clothes) (in (Paris)))]
```

(where, again, *her clothes* is Object and *in Paris* an Adjunct; but where both are included in the larger constituent, the VP which extends the length of the horizontal line.)

For convenience, we can call the VP in [7.35] the 'small VP', and the VP in [7.36] the 'large VP'. (In some analyses, the term **predicate** is used for the large VP and **predicator** – as a functional label – for the small VP.) The relation between the two analyses can be seen more clearly if we use tree diagrams as in Figures 7.12 and 7.13:

In the large VP analysis, auxiliaries are often treated as heads of VPs, and the sequence of auxiliary/auxiliaries and main verb is shown by embedding one VP in another. Hence Figure 7.14 would be the tree-diagram analysis of the perfect progressive equivalent of [7.35]:

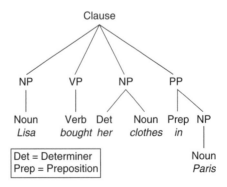

FIGURE 7.12   *A clause analysed with a 'short verb phrase'*

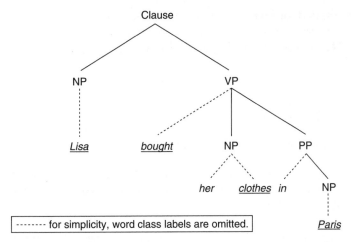

The same clause analysed with a 'long verb phrase' one possible analysis only)   *FIGURE 7.13*

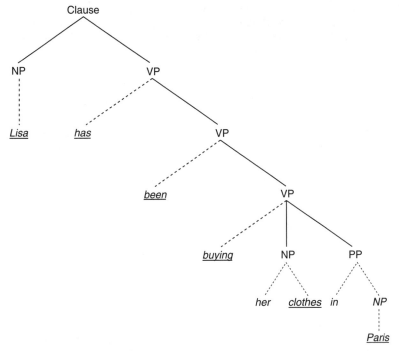

'Long verb phrase' analysis with embedding of VPs: one possible analysis   *FIGURE 7.14*

To explain in detail why one analysis can be considered better than another would take us too far, in this 'foundation' chapter, into the argumentation of linguists. We simply have to live with differences of opinion!

ADVANCES BOX 7.1

Comparing the 'small VP' and 'large VP' analyses

Nevertheless, to give a glimpse of the kinds of argumentation you will find in advanced grammar publications, the following are a couple of arguments in favour of each analysis:

In favour of the 'small VP' analysis are mainly arguments from meaning and the ease of teaching grammar:

- The elements which contribute to the meaning of the clause can be displayed in one line: for example, S V O is the traditional and convenient way of spelling out the structure of a clause as Subject, Verb Phrase, Object. Adjuncts can be placed before or after the main part of the clause, as in A S V O and S V O A. The difference of structure, and the sameness of meaning (though difference of emphasis), between [7.37a] and [7.37b] can thus be captured in a simple and intuitive way:

[7.37]   a.   [(On Friday) (we) (reached) (our final destination)].   A S V O
         b.   [(We) (reached) (our final destination) (on Friday)].   S V O A

  With the large VP analysis, on the other hand, the Subject and Object and the different adjuncts are on different 'layers' of the tree structure.
- The relation between different clause structures, such as the criss-cross relation between active and passive (see Chapter 8, Section 8.1.2) can also be easily captured with the small VP:

[(The dog owner) (found) (little Nancy) (yesterday morning)].   S V O A

[(Little Nancy) (was found) (by the dog owner) (yesterday morning)].   S V A A

  Here the Object of the active sentence corresponds to the Subject of the passive sentence, while the Subject of the active sentence corresponds to the agent *by the dog owner*, here represented as an adjunct (A).
- A third reason is a practical one: it is simpler to draw the tree diagrams with a small VP than with a large VP, because the large-VP diagrams tend to have considerably more 'layers' of structure. This we see to some extent in Figure 7.14, where there are a number of VPs, one embedded inside the other, for a single clause.

In favour of 'the large VP' analysis are more theoretical arguments, some of which have to do with the representation of sentences containing coordination, and the use of 'pro-forms' such as *one* and *do* in examples [7.39] and [7.40] below:

- The parts of a sentence yoked together by a coordinating conjunction like *and* rarely correspond to a 'small VP', but often correspond to a large VP, as in:

  [7.38] [The dog owner has (found little Nancy) and (phoned the police)].

  (Here the underlined round brackets do not correspond to phrases such as NPs and small VPs as introduced in this chapter, but they do correspond to large VPs.)
- In English we often omit the part of a clause following an auxiliary verb, when this part corresponds to a large VP that has already occurred in a preceding clause:

  [7.39] [She can dance the samba better [than I can].]

  To get the meaning of this sentence, we have to imagine the words *dance the samba* repeated at the end: ... *than I can dance the samba*. This phenomenon, where we omit some words that can be understood from a previous occurrence, is known as ellipsis, and again we see that the omitted part corresponds to a large VP *dance the samba*.
- A similar argument is that we can use the 'pro-verb' (dummy verb) *do* to avoid repetition of a sequence of words that has just occurred:

  [7.40] [Merga got to the finishing line [just before Lel did]].

  The last word of [7.40], *did*, in this case stands for *got to the finishing line*, which again corresponds to a large VP. So *did* could reasonably be described, here and in similar cases, as a 'dummy large VP'. How to analyse such cases using a small VP is by no means clear.

No doubt the heading 'grammar wars' for Section 7.7 was too dramatic. But we hope that this box has given some insight into the arguments grammarians might have about the English language. In the next chapter, where we concentrate on clauses and sentences, we will continue to use the 'small' rather than the 'large' definition of VP – but it is worth remembering that this is far from a universally accepted analysis.

Recommended readings

The topics of this chapter are handled in more detail in the books recommended for Chapter 6. Phrases are dealt with in Chapter 5 of Ballard (2001: 85–110), in Chapter 5 of Leech, Deuchar and Hoogenraad (2006: 66–84), and in Chapters 3–5 of Collins and Hollo (2000). In these books you may also find it useful to take a 'preview' of the following chapter, Chapter 8, on clauses. Biber, Conrad and Leech (2002: chs 3–6), with the corresponding chapters of Conrad, Biber and Leech (2002), cover much the same ground at a higher level. See also Chapters 4, 6 and 7 of Börjars and Burridge (2001). They adopt the large VP analysis discussed in Section 7.7 above, and refer to the 'small VP' as a 'verb string'.

The two most detailed and authoritative grammars of contemporary English, Quirk et al. (1985) and Huddleston and Pullum (2002), take opposite sides in the 'small VP vs. large VP' dispute. But interestingly, they both give some credit to the other side of the argument. Quirk et al., although firmly in favour of small VPs, allow the large VP (called predicate or predication) as an alternative analysis (1985: 80, 90). Huddleston and Pullum, while espousing the large VP, also allow some practical advantage in the small VP (which they call 'verb group') (2002: 1213–14). The two small sections referred to here may be read by those who want to dip their toes into a massive ocean of grammar. These tomes, each of more than 1700 pages, should not be read in their entirety!

CHAPTER 8

Grammar:Clauses (and Sentences)

GEOFFREY LEECH

8.1 Another look at clause structure

We are now embarking on the third and final part of our exploration of the grammar of English, focusing on the **clause** as the major unit of grammar. Like words (in Chapter 6) and phrases (in Chapter 7), clauses can be viewed either from 'inside', in terms of their form or structure; or from 'outside', in terms of their function in **sentences**.

We start with an 'inside' view of the clause. In Chapter 7, Section 7.4.1, we introduced the following elements, or 'slots', in clause structure: the Subject (usually an NP), the VP (verb phrase) and the Object (usually an NP). These three elements are often abbreviated to S, V and O; and English is often said to be an **SVO language**, because unlike many other languages, these three elements usually occur in that fixed order. In *(The cat) (chased) (the rat)*, *the cat* is the Subject, *chased* the VP, and *the rat* the Object, and it would be hard to put them in any other order.

In Section 7.4.2 we also introduced another kind of element in clause structure: the Adjunct (A), which adds to a clause an extra piece of information (usually optional) about time, place, manner, etc. So we can specify the structure of a clause in terms of symbols such as 'SVO', 'ASAVA', like this:

[8.1] [(An <u>expression</u> of extreme annoyance) (<u>crossed</u>) (her <u>face</u>)]. SVO
[8.2] [(<u>Actually</u>) (<u>we</u>) (quite <u>often</u>) (<u>breakfast</u>) (<u>at</u> Tiffany's)]. ASAVA

There is a fifth clause element that should be illustrated at this point, although we will not have room to explore it very far. After certain verbs, especially the verb *to be*, an NP is not an Object. Instead, it is often called a **Complement** (or Predicative Complement), and is represented by the symbol C:

[8.3] [(Fawlty <u>Towers</u>) (must <u>be</u>) (the best-loved bad <u>hotel</u> in the world)]. SVC

Here the final phrase is an NP, but it does not refer to the 'doee' (the thing or person affected by the action of the VP). Instead, it tells us something more about the Subject. This is the job of a Complement, rather than an Object.

Also, it is important to note that a C does not have to be an NP: it can be an adjective phrase (AdjP) instead:

[8.4] [(The <u>steak</u> tartare) (<u>was</u>) (*totally <u>inedible</u>*)].   SVC
[8.5] [(<u>In</u> a moment) (his <u>face</u>) (had <u>turned</u>) (*bright <u>red</u>*)].   ASVC

But now let's focus again on the Subject and Object (S and O).

8.1.1 Defining Subjects

ADVANCES BOX 8.1

On the definition of subjects

By now you will be used to the idea that grammatical definitions involve a lot of use of words like 'usually', 'often' and 'normally'. As explained in Chapter 6, Section 6.8, grammatical concepts have prototype characteristics, which means that they cannot be defined in 100 per cent true statements, but must be seen as bundles of qualities of varying 'typicality', none of which apply to every case. This is also true of elements like Subjects and Objects. Almost all statements we can make about them have exceptions. For example:

(a) '**Subjects precede the verb phrase**.' This is generally true, but: [(*Here*) (*comes*) (*the bus*)] has the structure AVS, with the Subject at the end.

(b) '**Subjects are noun phrases**.' This is generally true, but in [(*Carefully*) (*does*) (*it*)] the Subject (*carefully*) is an adverb.

(c) Another thing to notice is that if the Subject is a pronoun, it has to be in the correct form: *I, he, we* and *they* are used as Subject pronouns, while *me, him, us* and *them* are used as Object pronouns. So can we definitely say...:

   '**Subjects are marked by Subject pronoun forms**'? *He saw her* is correct, not **Him saw she*. Similarly, *She saw him* is grammatical, not **Her saw he*.

   Yet, again, this pronoun test doesn't always work, as other pronouns like *you* and *it* have no distinction between Subject and Object forms: *You carry it* and *It carries you* are both grammatical.

(d) '**Subjects "agree" with the VP**': for example, a singular subject requires a singular verb phrase, and a plural subject requires a plural verb phrase. The two words that 'agree' are underlined in:

[8.6] a. (The <u>policewoman</u>) (<u>has</u> spotted) (the thugs). <u>SV</u>O (singular + singular)
        b. (The <u>thugs</u>) (<u>have</u> spotted) (the policewoman). <u>SV</u>O (plural + plural)

   However, this agreement is not absolutely necessary. As we saw in 6.5.1, some nouns, called collective nouns, can break the agreement:

   (*Liverpool's A <u>team</u>*) (<u>have</u> beaten) (*Spurs*).   <u>SV</u>O (singular + plural)

> (e) **Subjects refer to the doer of an action, while Objects refer to the 'doee'.** As we already saw in Chapter 7, Section 7.4.1, this semantic statement is not always true.

As the five criteria (a)–(e) in the box show, there is no one 100 per cent test that can identify Subjects, although the Subject is a key element in the structure of the clause. A similar case is the Object of a clause, as the next sections will show.

8.1.2 Defining Objects – and a glance at the passive

We will not go into such detail with Objects, but they are also in the prototype category. We have already seen:

- that, like Subjects, Objects are typically NPs;
- that, unlike Subjects, they typically refer to the 'doee' rather than the 'doer';
- that, unlike Subjects, they are realised by the Object form of the pronoun, not the Subject form (*him*, not *he*; *me*, not *I*, etc.).

But as with Subjects, there are sometimes exceptions to these rules. In addition to these, there is an important test that applies to Objects, but not to Subjects. This is the **Passive Test**. In Section 7.6 and the Advances Box at the end of Chapter 7, we briefly introduced the passive verb construction, consisting of a form of the auxiliary *be* followed by the *en*-form (past participle) of the main verb. Here are pairs of VPs, with the non-passive (or **active**) on the left, and **passive** on the right:

	active	**passive**	**active**	**passive**	**active**	**passive**	**active**	**passive**
(present)	*eats*	*is eaten*	*take*	*are taken*	*writes*	*is written*	*use*	*are used*
(past)	*ate*	*was eaten*	*took*	*were taken*	*wrote*	*was written*	*used*	*were used*

If we take a clause with the structure SVO (where the V is an active VP), it is possible to turn this into a **passive clause** – a clause with a passive VP – like this:

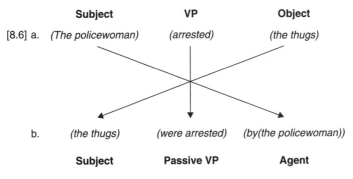

Changing active into passive

FIGURE 8.1

As this example shows, the passive clause differs from the active one in three ways:

(i)   The Object of the active clause becomes the Subject of the passive one.
(ii)   The Subject of the active clause becomes the **agent** of the passive one.
(iii) And of course, the active VP is replaced by the passive VP.

Statements (i)–(iii) give us the rules for forming a passive sentence from an active sentence with an Object. The phrase *by the policewoman* in 6b, corresponding to the Subject of 6a, is called the **agent phrase.** It is actually an Adjunct, as we realise when we notice that the *by*-phrase can be omitted: *The thugs were arrested* is a passive clause without the agent, and in fact this kind of 'agentless passive' is far more common than the passive with an agent. Users of English generally find it easier to use active rather than passive clauses – for example, 6a is preferred to 6b. But in the box at the end of this chapter, we will illustrate how people find it useful to use passive clauses in certain types of writing.

8.1.3   Direct and Indirect Objects

One more thing about Objects. There can be two, one or zero of them in a clause. Suppose someone asks you: 'What have you been doing?' You could answer in three slightly different ways:

[8.7]   a.   [(<u>I</u>) (have been <u>writing</u>)].   SV
        b.   [(<u>I</u>) (have been <u>writing</u>) (a thank-you <u>letter</u>)].   SVO
        c.   [(<u>I</u>) (have been <u>writing</u>) (Auntie <u>Becky</u>) (a thank-you   SVOO
             <u>letter</u>)].

Example [8.7a] has no Object NP after the VP. Example [8.7b] has one Object, and [8.7c] has two. In [8.7c], the two Objects are given different names: *a thank-you letter* is called a Direct Object, and *Auntie Becky* is called an Indirect Object. These labels go back to the semantic notion that the Object refers to the 'doee'. *A thank-you letter* refers to the thing affected most closely by my action of writing. *Auntie Becky*, on the other hand, refers to someone who is **indirectly** affected by the writing action: she is not the thing that is written, but the person who is written **to.** Indirect Objects typically identify people who benefit as a result of the action. How do we know that both *Auntie Becky* and *a thank-you letter* in [8.7c] are Objects? Because they can both be turned into the Subject of a passive clause: *Auntie Becky has been written to*... and *A thank-you letter has been written* ....

In the next section we leave Objects behind, and focus on the Subject and verb phrase (VP) as key clause elements.

8.2   Making statements, asking questions, giving orders, and uttering exclamations

We come now to some important distinctions in the communicative role of clauses. All the clauses we have presented so far have been statements (about things going on in the world). This is no doubt the most common use we make of clauses, but it is certainly not the only use. We can use clauses also for questions, directives and exclamations. According to its communicative role, a clause can be classified into four types.

There are many ways of forming statements, questions, directives and exclamations. For instance, we often rely on question marks <?> (in writing) or intonation (in speech) to signal that we are asking a question. But here, we are interested particularly in the way grammatical structure signals these communicative roles. In their most general form, the rules are as follows.

ILLUSTRATION BOX 8.1

Clause types

- **Declarative** – i.e., the clause acts as a statement, or assertion, claiming to tell us something about the world of reality: e.g., *His girlfriend has left him. Life is like that. I didn't believe it.*
- **Interrogative** – i.e., the clause acts as a question: e.g., *Has his girlfriend left him? When did she leave him? How should I know?*
- **Imperative** – i.e., the clause acts as a directive – e.g., a request, instruction or suggestion: *Pass me that drink please. Put oil in a pan over a low heat. Look out!! Just hurry!*
- **Exclamatory** – i.e., the clause acts as an expression of emotion. *What a weekend I've had! How that kid squealed! How ghastly you look!*

8.2.1 Declarative clauses

These have a Subject and a VP in that order: SV: <u>*Sophie watered* the budgerigar</u>. Almost all the clauses illustrated in Chapters 6 and 7 belong to this type.

8.2.2. Interrogative clauses

These have two main grammatical signals, neither of which always occurs:

(a) They begin with one of the question words (or *wh*-words) *Who, What, Which, When, Where, How, Why, Whom, Whose*. These words occur in phrases which may act as Subject, Object, Adjunct, or Predicative Complement. Except when they function as Subject (as in *Who said that?*), they are moved out of their normal position, and placed before the VP. For example, in <u>*How many Maltesers* have you eaten?</u>, the first three words *How many Maltesers* form an NP functioning as Object, although being an Object it would normally occur after the VP *have eaten*. Someone asked this question would answer in a statement with the normal order: *(I)(have eaten)(seven Maltesers)* SVO.

(b) They have an inversion (i.e., reversal) of the normal ordering, so that the (first) auxiliary precedes the Subject:

> *How many Maltesers have you eaten? Who are you meeting? Where can we meet?*

8.2.3 Imperative clauses

These generally have no Subject, and the verb is in the plain form, just like the infinitive (7.6.1): *Have fun; Get a life; Mark your calendars now.* The VP very rarely contains an auxiliary, except when *do* or *don't* precede the main verb: *Do be careful; Don't worry; Don't rinse it under the water.* Although there is no visible Subject, the implied Subject of imperatives is 'you'.

8.2.4 Exclamatory clauses

English has a special kind of exclamatory clause, beginning with *What* or *How*. As in questions, the phrase containing *What* or *How* comes at the beginning of the clause, even though it may be an Object or Adjunct which normally comes after the VP. But unlike questions beginning with these words, the exclamations do not have inversion of the Subject and auxiliary: *What a mess they've made. What big teeth you have, Grandma.* So there is an interesting contrast between these two clauses, [8.8a] with inversion and [8.8b] without. Note that [8.8a] is interrogative, and [8.8b] is exclamatory:

[8.8] a.   C   V   S   b.   C   S   V

      How tall   are   you?   How tall   you   are!

Incidentally, [8.8a] illustrates an important point about inversion: the verb *be* behaves like an auxiliary and inverts, even when it is a main verb, as in this example.

A last point about exclamatory clauses. Very often the phrase beginning *What* or *How* stands alone, without the VP or any other element. *How wonderful! What a mess!* In the context in which they occur, the meaning of the omitted elements will be clear (e.g., *What a mess!* might mean 'What a mess you've made!').

8.2.5 More about questions

There are two main classes of interrogative clauses: (a) *wh-*questions; and (b) *yes-no* questions.

(a) **Wh– questions,** as the name suggests, begin with a *wh-*word. (In a rather formal style, the *wh-*word sometimes comes after a preposition, as in: *In which building are the T-shirts kept?*)

> Notice that *wh-*words do not all belong to the same word class. For example, *who* is a pronoun, *what* and *which* are pronouns or determiners, and *when*, *where* and *how* are adverbs.

Although it begins the clause, the following examples show the *wh*-phrase or *wh*-word can occur in various 'slots' in the clause structure:

[8.9]   a.   *Who has been eating my porridge?* [*Who* is the Subject; no inversion occurs.]

b.   *What excitement have I missed?* [*What* is the Object; compare the declarative: *I have missed some excitement*.]

c.   *When will we know the result?* [*When* is an Adjunct of time; compare the declarative: *We will know the result on Friday*.]

d.   *In which town are you staying?* [*In which town* is an Adjunct of place. In form, it is also a PP, which means that we can use a more informal type of interrogative clause where the preposition comes at the end: *Which town are you staying in?*]

(b) **Yes-no questions**, as their name suggests, are interrogative clauses which can be answered 'Yes' or 'No'. They do not have any *wh*-word at the front, but they have inversion of Subject and auxiliary. The following examples are followed by the corresponding declarative, for comparison:

[8.10]   a.   *Is she really going to Oslo?*   [compare: *She is really going to Oslo*.]

b.   *Could you pass me that drink?*   [compare: *You could pass me that drink*.]

c.   *Are you kidding?*   [compare: *You are kidding*.]

d.   *Have you tried my monster cookies?*   [compare: *You have tried my monster cookies*.]

8.2.6 The 'dummy' auxiliary *do*

The rules of language sometimes produce strange results. English puts its users in a 'Catch 22' situation with two rules which seem to conflict.

One structural rule (see Section 8.6) says: 'Auxiliaries are optional'. A verb phrase does not have to have any auxiliary verbs. In fact, most VPs have no auxiliary:

[8.11]   [(Great Uncle Silas) (<u>drinks</u>) (several screwdrivers a day)].

Here the VP has a main verb *drinks*, but no auxiliary.

Another structural rule, this time for forming questions, says 'Reverse the order of the Subject and the auxiliary' (see Section 8.2.1).

But if (auxiliaries being optional) there is no auxiliary, how can we obey the second rule and form a question? You will discover the answer soon enough if you turn [8.11] into a yes-no question as in [8.12]:

[8.12]   <u>Does</u> Great Uncle Silas drink several screwdrivers a day?

Yes, the 'magic auxiliary' *do* fills the gap, acting as the missing auxiliary which is not found in the declarative sentence. Whenever we need an auxiliary, and there is no auxiliary available from the declarative form, *do* (or *does* or *did*) comes to the rescue. Further examples of yes-no questions with *do* are:

[8.13]   <u>Did</u> *you make your own coleslaw?*   [Answer: *No, I didn't make my own coleslaw.*]

[8.14]   <u>Do</u> *the people next-door breed dogs?*   [Answer: *No, they don't breed dogs.*]

Notice that the answers to *yes-no* questions on the right also have an auxiliary *do*. Why? Because there is another simple rule, a rule for negation in English: 'To negate a main clause, add the word *not* (or its short form *n't*) after the auxiliary', as in *We haven't eaten yet*. But, as before, the Catch 22 situation arises. What happens if there is no auxiliary in the corresponding positive clause? Once again, the 'dummy' auxiliary *do* comes to the rescue:

[8.15]   a.   **positive:**   b.   **negative:**
         The taxi arrived late.   The taxi <u>did not</u> arrive late.

[8.16]   a.   **positive:**   b.   **negative:**
         She knows the answer.   She <u>does not</u> know the answer.

[8.17]   a.   **positive:**   b.   **negative:**
         Some kids like rugby.   Some kids <u>don't</u> like rugby.

8.3 Subordination: embedded clauses

Now that we have examined the structure of main clauses in some detail, it is time to turn to how clauses behave in larger units. Let's call these larger units 'sentences'. As a first step, though, we consider only how clauses can be parts of other clauses. This has already been the topic of one section in Chapter 7 – Section 7.2.2 – when we introduced **embedded clauses** as parts of larger clauses called **main clauses**. Here are two examples of embedded (or **subordinate**) clauses as part of a tree diagram:

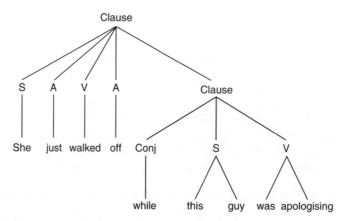

FIGURE 8.2   *Tree diagram: main clause and embedded (subordinate) clause*

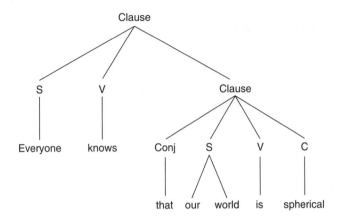

Another tree diagram: main clause and embedded (subordinate) clause   FIGURE 8.3

We can also show embedding (as in Section 7.2.2) by using square brackets to enclose the clauses, and round brackets to enclose the phrases:

[8.18]   S   A   V   A   A
        [(She) (just) (walked) (off) [while (this guy) (was apologising)]].
                                      Conj.   S   V

[8.19]   S   V   O
        [Everyone knows [that our world is spherical]].
                          Conj.   S   V   C

We can tell that [8.16] and [8.17] contain two clauses, because the word-strings in square brackets have a clause-like structure SVO, SAVA, etc. 'Conj.' is the abbreviation here for 'conjunction', which is the term usually used for the little word that introduces a subordinate clause. More precisely, it can be called a **subordinating conjunction**. We can now see that the structures of the two clauses in [8.18] and [8.19] are as follows:

[8.18]   Main clause: SAVA<u>A</u>   Embedded clause: Conj.SV
[8.19]   Main clause: SV<u>O</u>   Embedded clause: Conj.SVC

The underlined element of the main clause shows where the embedded clause is located: it is an Adjunct of time in [8.18], and the Object in [8.19]. So embedded clauses can have functions similar to those of phrases in the main clause. Compare [8.18] with *She just walked off in the middle of his apology* and [8.19] with *Everyone knows that joke*, where phrases (a PP and an NP respectively) fill the corresponding Adjunct and Object 'slots'.

ILLUSTRATION BOX 8.2

Three key types of embedded (or subordinate) clause

The most important types of embedded clause are **adverbial**, **complement** and **relative** clauses.

Adverbial clauses typically begin with a conjunction such as *if*, *when*, *because*, *while*. They fill the function of Adjuncts in the main clause, and can take different positions:

[8.20]   [[If you buy the food], I'll do the cooking].
[8.21]   [I am very excited [because this is my first podcast]].
[8.22]   [You will find, [when you get older], [that the mind often wanders]].

The term 'adverbial clause' recalls that adverbs and adverb phrases often function as adjuncts, and can have a similar role of elaborating time, manner, reason, etc. with respect to the main clause. The adverbial clauses above are similar in function to adverbs like *then, therefore* and *later*.

Complement clauses are so called because they are typically required to complete the meaning of the rest of the main clause. They can also be called 'noun clauses' or 'nominal clauses', because their function is similar to that of noun phrases, filling Subject and Object slots, for instance. In [8.23] and [8.24], they fill the slot of Object and (Predicative) Complement respectively:

[8.23]   [Angie asked herself [what the problem was]].
[8.24]   [The funny thing is [that the dog didn't bark in the night]].

The embedded clause is introduced by a *wh*-word in [8.23] and the conjunction *that* in [8.24]. These are two important types of complement clause, and they correspond to declarative and interrogative main clauses as discussed in Section 8.2, except that they **report** what someone said or thought, rather than representing the utterance directly. For this reason, such constructions are often called **reported speech**, as contrasted with **direct speech** (see Chapter 24):

	Direct speech	Reported speech
[8.25]	'[It is all a mistake.]'	[Jamie maintained [that it was all a mistake].]
[8.26]	'[What is the problem?]'	[Angie asked [what the problem was].]

Complement clauses are very useful devices for representing what people say and what goes on in people's minds.

Relative clauses (see Chapter 7, p. 136) resemble another major word class – adjectives – in that they modify a noun (known as the **antecedent**) in an NP, and tell us more about what the noun denotes. The modifying role makes it possible to compare relative clauses which follow the noun with adjectives which precede it, in examples such as these:

An *old* house = a house *which was built long ago*.
A *wealthy* man = a man *who has lots of money or property*.
An *edible* fungus = a fungus *that can be eaten* OR a fungus *that you can eat*.

House, man and *fungus* here are the antecedents of the relative clauses.

As these examples show, relative clauses, like complement clauses, are introduced either by a *wh*-word (especially *who* and *which*) or by *that*.

The zero option

However, there is also often the further possibility, in both complement and relative clauses, to omit the word *that*. We can call these clauses 'zero complement clauses' or 'zero relative clauses', illustrated with:

complement clause	→ **zero complement clause**
Gus felt [that nobody loved him].	→ *Gus felt [nobody loved him].*
I think [that she was on TV].	→ *I think [she was on TV].*

relative clause	→ **zero relative clause**
a book [that everyone hates].	→ *a book [everyone hates].*
the people [that I stayed with].	→ *the people [I stayed with].*

8.4   Embedding and coordination

We have now met embedding of phrases and embedding of clauses (or subordination). Embedding is a very powerful means of elaborating the content of what we want to say, particularly because it is iterative. This means that not only can one clause (call it 'Clause b') be embedded in another clause ('Clause a'), but a third clause can be embedded in 'Clause b' (call it 'Clause c') and this process can be repeated indefinitely, as is shown in this rough sketch of a tree diagram:

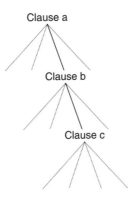

A tree diagram sketch: repeated embedding of clauses   *FIGURE 8.4*

Here is an example of the embedding involving three steps of iteration:

[8.27]   [I was wondering [when you would finally admit [that you're only sticking with me [because you want all my money]]]].

8.4.1 Coordination

Coordination is another powerful elaborating device, like embedding. But it is different in that the elements coordinated occur side by side in the sentence, rather than one inside the other. The three most common coordinating words (called **coordinating conjunctions**) are *and, or* and *but*, and the most common combination involves simply joining two similar units of language together like this: X and Y: for example, *(my sister) and (her boyfriend)*.

However, coordination has a similar potential for elaborating meaning by iteration. Consider this sentence with three coordinated clauses:

[8.28]   [Words are great] and [falling in love is wonderful], but [only money pays the rent].

Like embedding, coordination can be iterated any number of times, as in:

[8.29]   The wall was painted in <u>red and green and blue and black and white</u> ...

It's easy to imagine this list extended beyond the five items coordinated in [8.29]. But, to avoid repeating the word *and*, you are more likely to omit it between all items except the last:

[8.29]   a.   The wall was painted in <u>red, green, blue, black and white</u>.

Yet another option is to omit *all* the coordinating conjunctions:

[8.29]   b.   The wall was painted in <u>red, green, blue, black, white</u>.

The difference between [8.29], [8.29a] and [8.29b] is a matter of stylistic preference, rather than meaning. Notice, finally, that coordination can take place between units of various sizes: in Figure 7.5 the units coordinated were phrases; in [8.28] they were clauses, and in [8.29] they were words. The example *((my sister) and (her husband))* shows coordination of phrases – to be more precise, of NPs. The main requirement is that the items coordinated be equivalent in their grammatical function.

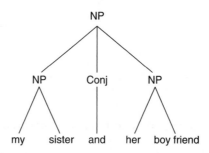

FIGURE 8.5   *Coordination of noun phrases*

8.5 Non-finite clauses

This chapter has already introduced a lot of grammatical concepts, but we should deal briefly with yet another common type of structure that adds to the expressive possibilities of English grammar: **non-finite clauses**. The three main types of non-finite clause are italicised in these examples:

[8.30] They advised the minister [to leave the building immediately].
[8.31] [Opening her eyes suddenly], Meg caught a glimpse of a retreating figure.
[8.32] The information [given to the press] was totally and deliberately false.

Notice that, unlike the types of subordinate clauses discussed up to now, these begin with a non-finite verb (see Section 7.6.1). The three kinds of non-finite verb illustrated here are:

(a) **infinitive** (normally preceded by *to*): e.g., *to leave, to open, to give*
(b) **–ing form** (also called 'present participle'): e.g., *leaving, opening, giving*
(c) **–en form** (also called 'past participle'): e.g., *left, opened, given*

Non-finite clauses obviously have no finite verb, and generally have no Subject. Consequently, they tend to be shorter, more compact than finite clauses, and are useful for simplifying sentences that would otherwise be complex and unwieldy, especially in writing. For example, [8.32] could be alternatively expressed using a relative clause (see Section 8.3):

[8.32] a. The information [*that was given to the press*]....

But the non-finite clause in [8.31] takes fewer words. Similarly, the non-finite clauses in [8.30] and [8.31] could be replaced by finite clauses of roughly the same meaning. How could this be done? The answer is in [8.30a] and [8.31a] below.

Like the finite embedded clauses discussed in Section 8.3, non-finite clauses can have various functions in the main clause they are part of. For example:

• In [8.30], the infinitive clause is a complement clause. Compare the finite complement clause:

[8.30] a. They advised the minister *that she should leave the building immediately.*

• In [8.31], the *ing*-clause is an adverbial clause, filling the slot of Adjunct of time:

[8.31] a. *As she suddenly opened her eyes*, Meg caught a glimpse of a retreating figure.

- And as we have already seen (in [8.32a]), the past participle clause in [8.32] is like a relative clause: it modifies the noun *information* which is head of an NP.

8.5 Simple, compound and complex sentences

This chapter has already briefly described the major building blocks that go to make up a sentence. But what is a sentence? One way to describe it is as the unit that defines the upper limit of grammatical structure. If we start with clauses as major structures, and consider how larger structures can be built out of clauses, we will make progress towards giving an account of sentence structure. But this is a rather controversial subject we will return to in Section 8.6.

Traditionally, a distinction is drawn between four patterns of sentence construction.

In practice, this classification, although popular, is not particularly useful, because of the many variations that are possible. The main thing is that there are two important devices for combining clauses: coordination and subordination (embedding). It is also worth remembering that sentence complexity is not just a matter of combining clauses: sometimes a more important element of complexity is found in complex phrases, particularly noun phrases.

ILLUSTRATION BOX 8.3

A traditional classification of sentences

(a) **Simple sentences** consisting of just one clause:

[8.33] [They gave me access to the site].
[8.34] [Muriel was brought up by her grandma].
[8.35] [Have you seen my trainers?]

(b) **Compound sentences** consisting of two or more coordinated clauses:

[8.36] [Use it] or [lose it].
[8.37] [I didn't buy you a pint] but [I did link you to my website].
[8.38] [It's my birthday], and [I enjoy making other people happy].

Example [8.28] earlier showed another compound sentence.

(c) **Complex sentences** consisting of one main clause with one or more embedded clauses inside it:

[8.39] [[If it's hurting [it's working]].
[8.40] [I'm starting tomorrow, [although I don't have an on-line name yet]].
[8.41] [An artist has constructed a 5ft tower [using junk mail [that she has received since January 1st]]].

(d) **Compound-complex sentences** combining both these types of clausal relationship – coordination and embedding:

> [8.42] [[Just as he had plucked up courage [to talk to her]] [the train stopped] and [he lost her in the crowd]].
>
> [8.43] [I actually didn't know [she was pregnant]], but [I just assumed [she was]].

Here is the opening of a children's story (slightly adapted) where you are invited to insert the square brackets we have used to delimit clauses. After inserting the brackets, you should have no difficulty in deciding which of the sentences types (a)–(d) above are represented by the sentences numbered [1], [2], [3] and [4].

> [8.44] [1]Once upon a time there was a little girl who didn't like going to school. [2]She always set off late, then she had to hurry, but she never hurried fast enough. [3]One morning she was hurrying along as usual, when she turned a corner, and there stood a lion blocking her way. [4]He glared at her fiercely.

Answers: Sentence 1: (c). Sentence 2: (b). Sentence 3: (d). Sentence 4: (a).

8.6   Spoken language and the sentence

Does spoken language have grammatical structure? Of course it does. But grammar has been so closely associated with written language that the question has seemed problematic (for a more general discussion of the differences between speech and writing, see Chapter 23). On the one hand, people sometimes tie themselves in knots when they are trying to explain something 'off the cuff':

> [8.45]   No. Do you know erm you know where the erm go over erm where the fire station is not the one that white white

But in other circumstances – for example, when improvising a story, people produce quite lengthy sentence-like units made up of grammatically well-formed clauses. In this case, the story is presumably about the narrator's dog (the square brackets, as ever, showing clause boundaries):

> [8.46]   [The trouble is [[if you're if you're the only one in the house] [he follows you] and [you're looking for him] and [every time [you're moving around] he's moving around behind you <laughter> [so you can't find him]]]]$_{(\cdot)}$ [I thought [I wonder [where the hell he's gone]]]$_{(\cdot)}$ <laughter> [I mean [he was immediately behind me]]$_{(\cdot)}$

(Both [8.45] and [8.46] are from the conversational data in the British National Corpus [BNC].) Although naturally there are no full stops in speech, if we wanted to divide [8.45] into written sentences, we would probably place full stops where the bracketed full stops have been placed in the example. But often when we transcribe speech, the boundaries between sentences are not clear, and linguists sensibly prefer to avoid using ordinary punctuation for a spoken transcription (for further issues relating to spoken transcription, see Chapter 21, Section 21.6).

Another difficulty about spoken grammar is that many of the units we find in speech do not have a sentence structure or even a clause structure. This piece of dialogue (also from the BNC – and punctuated according to the BNC transcription) is not untypical:

[8.47]   A: Oh just as easy to um
         B: What go by car?
         A: Go by car.
         B: Oh
         A: It takes about...well
         B: About two ticks, ya. Alright.

None of the speaker-turns in this dialogue contains a complete clause or sentence, and yet (strangely enough) the speakers seem to be communicating effectively![1] It has been calculated (Biber et al., 1999: 1071) that over a third of all units functioning independently (i.e., not as part of a larger grammatical structure) in conversation cannot be analysed as clauses or sentences – usually because they are too fragmentary, like the elements of the dialogue in [8.44]. This means that the classification of sentence types given above in Illustrations Box 8.3 is pretty useless when applied to ordinary spontaneous speech.

Faced with this kind of data, some linguists (e.g., Brazil, 1995; Carter and McCarthy, 1995) have argued that the grammar of speech needs to be analysed in quite a different way from the mainstream way of analysing grammar in written texts, as presented in this and the preceding two chapters. Another approach, less radical, is to say that although the same grammar in broad terms is found in writing and in speech, the unit known as the 'sentence' is an artefact of the written language – that, indeed, it is defined by punctuation (initial capital, final . ? or !) rather than by grammatical structure. The structures described in Illustrations Box 8.3 can then be described as **clause complexes**, rather than sentences. It happens that in written texts, most sentences – in punctuation terms – are also clausal structures, but not always. There have been, in this chapter, a number of sentences which are not clausal structures. (Examples: *One more thing about Objects* in Section 8.1.3, and *Why?* in Section 8.2.6.) I wonder if you noticed that a chapter on grammar does not always consist of 'grammatical sentences'!

Conclusion. You can define a sentence in grammatical terms, as a clause complex, or you can define it in punctuation terms, as something that happens between a capital letter and a full stop. The thing is that these definitions do not always match. Quite a few people have reached the conclusion that the most important unit of grammar is the clause – and that the sentence has no place in grammatical description.

ILLUSTRATION BOX 8.4

Applying grammar to different genres of text

It is not enough just to 'learn grammar': it is also important to make use of this grammatical know-how by applying it to the characterisation of spoken discourse or to textual data. To anticipate the topic of the next chapter (Chapter 9 and in particular Chapter 23), in this last box we examine some brief specimens of discourse and text, noting some ways in which grammar functions differently in different genres of speech and writing.

(a)   **A transcribed extract from a spoken discourse**

[8.48]   Well, em...those that come from agricultural families will work on the land, others will probably just help the family. Quite a lot of them, especially at university. They will have to study to get through the exams in order to get a good job. Em...the people themselves don't actually get many more days than six a year. They just get......

Given that this is an excerpt from some unscripted dialogue, our question is: in what ways does this piece illustrate the difficulties of applying the typology of sentences in Illustrations Box 8.3 to spoken language? Look particularly for examples of 'sentences' without a verb (and therefore without a clause structure), and of discourse markers (Chapter 6, Section 6.6.7), which tend to stand alone without being integrated into clauses or sentences. There is no doubt that this extract is structured in a 'grammatical way', but at the same time we have to admit that the well-behaved picture of grammar built on the traditional categories of Illustration Box 8.3 above is something of an idealisation. This is especially the case with spoken language.

(b)   **Passives in academic writing**
Passive verb phrases like *was eaten* (see Section 8.1.2) are rare in spoken English, but they are common in some kinds of writing, especially academic writing. It is argued that the agentless passive (the passive without the *by*-phase following the verb) is well suited, for example, to the impersonal ethos of scientific writing. This is because the focus of interest in science is on the domain of inquiry, such as biology or physics, and it arguably does not matter which people did the experiments or wrote up the results. That is, the human doer or agent is irrelevant, and does not have to be mentioned. Here is a passage of academic writing that illustrates this point:

[8.49]   Having defined the quantities that are normally measured in a nuclear reaction we here outline the typical experimental procedures which are followed for studying the symbolic reaction A(a, b)B. No details are given of the apparatus other than to mention very briefly the underlying physical principles. Details of low energy nuclear physics apparatus are given, for example, in Burcham (1988) and of high energy elementary particle apparatus in a book in this series by Kenyon (1988).

How many examples of passive verb phrases can you find in this passage? (Notice that the verb *to be* can be separated from the past participle by an adverb or one or more other words, as in *is often used*.) Could the examples of the passive be replaced by active equivalents, and if so, what other word changes would have to be made, and how would this change the style of scientific writing?

(c) **The grammar of headlines (or 'headlinese')**
We conclude our three chapters on grammar with a glance at the peculiar grammar of newspaper headlines (or the equivalent 'news footlines' that nowadays occur at the bottom of the screen on some TV channels):

[8.50]   OJ ON THE RUN FROM DAILY MIRROR (*Daily Mirror* 13/5/96)
[8.51]   Cops grab psycho as 32 die in shooting rampage (*Daily Star* 29/4/96)
[8.52]   MIRACLE OF MOSES BABY (*Daily Star* 29/4/96)
[8.53]   52 die in bus blast. (*Daily Star* 29/4/96)

The goals of the headline writer include conveying as much of an interesting story as possible while reducing the number and the length of words. Saving space is imperative. In [8.50] we see this in the use of just two letters (*OJ*) to name the person concerned, and the omission of the verb *to be* and the definite article *the*. Hence to render [8.50] in 'normal' English we would have to write something like this:

[8.50]   a.   O J Simpson is on the run from the Daily Mirror.

What changes would have to be made to make similar 'decompressed' versions of [8.51] and [8.52]? One clue is the tendency of headlines to rely on juxtaposed nouns in the NP, as in *MOSES BABY* in [8.52]. (Another example is *bus blast* in [8.53].) Such noun sequences are a favourite device for compressing meaning, and as readers we have to reconstruct what, for brevity, is not stated: the meaning relation between one noun and the other. Here we may get help from the Biblical story of Moses (who was saved from death by being hidden in a basket of bullrushes). But for full understanding, we will probably have to read the whole news article.

This topic brings us back to the one which began our exploration of grammar in Chapter 6 (Sections 6.1–2): the distinction between **content words** (or NAVA words) and **function words**. Headlines reduce the number of function words as far as possible, relying on content words, which convey most information, to communicate a story to the reader. Hence the words omitted are mostly function words such as articles, the verb *to be* and prepositions.

(a)–(c) above have provided three examples of how grammar is tailored to the particular uses it has to serve in different types of text. In the next chapter, we turn to the study of texts as the main theme.

Recommended readings

The topics of this chapter are again handled in greater detail in the books recommended for Chapters 6 and 7 (see Recommended readings, Chapter 6). See especially Ballard (2001), Chapters 6 and 7, and Leech, Deuchar and Hoogenraad (2006), Chapters 6 and 7. There are some minor variations of terminology: for example, Ballard uses 'adverbial' for my 'adjunct', and 'nominal clause' for my 'complement clause'. Unfortunately it is difficult to get grammarians to agree on terminology!

On grammar in spoken English, see Biber, Conrad and Leech (2002), Chapter 13. You may find Chapter 14 of Biber et al. (1999) an easier read, though longer and more advanced. Another excellent treatment of spoken English grammar (though again, more advanced) is found in Carter and McCarthy (2006: 164–236). My own position on this topic is found in an introductory form on the web (Leech, 1998).

Note

1 The third turn of [8.47], *Go by car*, could be analysed as a complete imperative clause (see Section 8.2.3) but here it is clearly not intended to be an imperative.

CHAPTER 9

Text Linguistics

PAUL CHILTON

9.1 What is text?

Like phrases, clauses and sentences, texts have what we might call meaning, 'text meaning'. But just as not all combinations of words in a sentence make grammatical sense, so it is with a text and its constituent sentences. Consider:

> *A teacher was awarded some money. Ms Ball's conduct was to blame. I don't want a new car.*

Though the individual sentences are grammatical, you have to work quite hard to give this short text a meaning. The point is that the words in it do not give much help to the text interpreter. By contrast, in Illustrations Box 9.1 we have a text that makes sense. The task of the linguist is to understand how we make sense of texts, what it is that makes the parts of a text 'hang together'.

The etymology of the term gives us some help. The word *text* is from the Latin word *texere*, meaning weave. We can think of texts as woven together from different strands or threads. Texts, like textiles, come in different shapes and sizes and have different functions in human life. In general, the parts of texts have an analogous kind of **coherence** or **cohesion** – technical terms, about which more later.

The term **text** is not to be confused with **discourse**. When we focus on text we are freezing in time one moment of the ongoing dynamic use of language in the speech community, that is, discourse (see Chapter 35, Advances Box 35.2, for further discussion of the term 'discourse'). In fact, texts cannot usually be understood fully without understanding their **context** in that discourse, but it is important to focus on the text itself, in order to understand how the linguistic elements that make up texts interact with discourse and with processes in the human mind in general. Texts, as objects of linguistic inquiry, are in some sense whole in themselves, as are sentences. They may be either written or spoken, despite the fact that the term is strongly biased towards the written form. An unscripted speech or conversation, for instance, is a text in this sense, even before linguists transcribe it for analysis. Texts do many jobs in society, although for some people the notion of literary texts may come especially to mind. It is true that societies build up a

ILLUSTRATION BOX 9.1

The *Bully Text*

Guardian
Saturday 5 October 2002

Bullied teacher wins £230,000 damages

Rebecca Smithers
Education correspondent

(1) A bullied teacher has been awarded a £230,000 payout for personal injury and loss of earnings after being forced out of his job by his head.

(2) A judge ruled that the sacking from Coedffranc junior school in Skewen, South Wales, was unlawful, and had already awarded Alan Powis, 53, £80,000 in interim payments pending a full settlement scheduled for yesterday.

(3) But Mr Powis was given the payment in an out-of-court settlement on Thursday to end a lengthy legal battle.

(4) He lost his job after the head, Sheena Ball, questioned his ability and accused him of incompetence. (5) When he won the support of the parents, Ms Ball claimed he was undermining her authority and he was sacked for gross misconduct. (6) Mr Powis, a father of two, suffered a nervous breakdown but found work as a £2.50-an-hour security guard and a door-to-door salesman to make ends meet.

(7) Judge Gary Hickinbottom, sitting at Swansea's civil courts of justice, said that the sacking in 1997 was unlawful and that it was Ms Ball's conduct that was to blame.

(8) The settlement against Neath and Port Talbot county borough council's education authority was settled by its insurers.

(9) Yesterday Mr Powis said he was pleased with the ruling. (10) 'I'm not the least bit interested in having a flash new car. (11) What I did want when I began this claim was the return of my good name, the return of my dignity, and the return of my peace of mind. (12) I'm starting to get that now.'

culture of 'texts' in this sense, to include sacred texts or great authors; this is an important fact about the sociology of texts that we shall not address here. A text may be long like the Bible or short like a 'No Smoking' notice. Finally, from the analytic point of view, we can focus on either the production (speaking or writing) of texts or the interpretation (understanding or processing) of texts. In the end, however, these two aspects complement one another, to a certain extent, for text producers do not produce text (usually) without making assumptions about the way hearers or readers normally interpret texts. But the qualification 'to a certain extent' should be noted carefully, since different text processors bring their own experiences and tacit knowledge to bear and these may vary in many ways.

9.2 Is there a grammar of texts?

When linguists first started to ask what exactly makes a text hang together, they attempted to do so by using the methods of analysis that had been used for sentences (as well as other levels of language).

Zellig S. Harris outlined a formal method of text analysis in the 1950s that was less influential in the English-speaking world than in continental Europe, especially France. Harris's approach was rooted in the American **structuralist** approach to language and attempted to describe the structure of a text in the same way as he described the phonology, morphology and grammar of a whole language (Harris, 1951). This approach involved defining phonemes and grammatical categories in terms of their **distribution**. Essentially, Harris tried to apply a similar approach to whole texts which involves the following steps. First, analyse the grammatical structure of each sentence in the text to reveal constituent sentences coded in relative clauses, nominalizations (i.e., the use of nouns instead of verbs to refer to actions or events), adjectival phrases, prepositional phrases and so forth. Second, examine the lexical content of subjects, verbs and objects to see if there are any regularities of distribution. That is to say, ask the question: does the same sort of lexical content in the subject position always occur before the same sort of lexical content in the verb? If the answer is 'yes', then Harris says that we have an **equivalence class** for that text. The set of equivalence classes for a text gives us a kind of **grammar** for that text: it tells us the sort of combinations that are 'grammatical' for that text.

In general, it seems highly unlikely that we can come up with a rich and convincing theory of texts without including meaning in our analysis. Other linguists tried to develop 'grammars' for texts. Van Dijk, for example, attempted in his early work (van Dijk, 1972) to set up a text grammar on the basis of meaning rather than wholly on the basis of syntactic form, later moving wholly toward an explanation of text production and text understanding which took into account not only internal text structure but also what people know about the world in which texts are embedded.

9.3 Cohesion and Coherence

Attempts to write generative grammars for texts constantly came up against detailed questions concerning how the words and constructions in texts link up with one another. In this section and the following ones we turn to the descriptive study of the linguistic elements that link sentences, or create **cohesion**. It turns out, however, that this is not enough, since texts seem to get their 'hanging-togetherness' from outside the text as well, in particular from what text interpreters know about the world in general – this is what is called **coherence**. Simplifying somewhat, coherence is a relation between conceptual structures (things, people, activities, etc.) which may be expressed by words in the text but which, and more usually, may be present in the mind of the text producer or processor. These two dimensions are not entirely independent of one another, as will be pointed out. Cohesion devices frequently depend on coherence.

Substitution and ellipsis

Texts appear to avoid the repetition of the same word, at least in close proximity to one another. We can see this in the use of **substitution**, that is, 'dummy' words like *one(s)*, *do*, *it*:

These towels are dirty; we need some clean <u>ones</u>.
Have you written that essay yet? I've not <u>done</u> it yet but I'll <u>do</u> it tomorrow
Is the meeting still going on? Sounds like <u>it</u>.

The underlined words in the second clause of each example are cohesive with a noun or a verb in the preceding clause.

Ellipsis is the leaving out of some element of the grammatical structure of a sentence:

John won a clock and Mary <u>won</u> a TV set.

The books on the table are from the library but <u>those [books]</u> are mine.
Jane went to the lecture but Harry <u>didn't [go]</u>.

In the *Bully Text* in Illustrations Box 9.1 we find:

(7) The sacking was unlawful and it was Ms Ball's conduct that was to blame [for the sacking].

While there is no problem in understanding what is referred to by 'was to blame', it is still true that there is no overt expression that tells us what Ms Ball's conduct is to be blamed **for**. We know of course from the co-text. In this example, what are the mechanisms that account for the fact that a reader can fill in the gap? First there is the meaning of the word *blame* itself, including its 'semantic frame': *X blames Y for Z*. The reader knows that the meaning of blame involves a blamer, a blamed person and some situation caused by the behaviour of the blamed person. So if the sentence does not specify the 'for Z' part of *blame*, the reader will look for something to fill it in. This is where the second mechanism comes in, the general principle of ellipsis, which says, roughly, that some element can be left out if the surrounding text provides the relevent meaning. This meaning may sometimes be within the same sentence or it may be distant, either before or after the sentence in question. In the present text, we can say that the missing part, what Mrs Ball was to blame **for**, can be found in sentence (1) and perhaps other parts of the text.

9.4 Reference

A general introduction to the idea of **reference** and a more detailed discussion of some specifics can be found in the following chapter, Section 10.2. Here, I will focus on two areas particularly pertinent to the discussion in hand.

Third-person pronouns

Third-person pronouns are used to refer to entities, situations or events that may be denoted by lexical material in the co-text, or sometimes to entities, situations or events that are outside the text. Those that link up with co-text are of two types: **anaphora** (a Greek word meaning roughly 'carrying back') and **cataphora** (roughly meaning 'carrying forward').

An example of anaphora is:

(i) *The Judge said the sacking of Mr Powis was unlawful. Yesterday, he said he was pleased with the ruling.*

Here, you probably automatically related *he* back to *Mr Powis*; this proper name is usually called the antecedent of the anaphoric pronoun *he*. As for cataphoric pronouns, we can construct an example such as the following:

(ii) *After he heard the Judge's ruling, Mr Powis said he was pleased.*

In this case, the first *he* refers forwards to *Mr Powis*. A text processor has to put the linkage on hold until he or she comes across a suitable noun phrase.

Reference to entities outside a text is called **exophoric**. Consider the second occurrence of *he* in the last example. The most likely reading is that *Mr Powis* is the antecedent. However, it all depends on context. Suppose that this sentence occurred in a different text and situation. Maybe the speaker of the sentence is reporting that Mr Powis is telling a story, perhaps in a conversation. Then the speaker of this sentence could be using *he* to refer to somebody not referred to by any noun phrase in the co-text at all; he could be referring outside the text to some male person known to the hearer of this sentence.

The interesting question is: how do we know what the 'phoric' words in a text relate to? Number, person and gender are clues in the English pronoun system, but things are by no means that simple. Take the special case of anaphora. One might suppose that the antecedent of the anaphoric word is always the last noun that was mentioned. This is, however, obviously not the case.

Consider (i) again. It is perfectly possible, taking these two sentences in isolation to think that *The Judge* is the antecedent – that it is the judge who is pleased with his own ruling. But if you did not arrive at that interpretation, it is probably because you were primed by having read the co-text, which makes Mr Powis, not the Judge, the main focus of interest, as well perhaps as your background expectation that judges do not conventionally express self-satisfaction in this fashion. Here are two more examples of how co-text changes antecedent assignment:

(iii) *The Judge said the sacking of Mr Powis was unlawful. Yesterday, he said he was pleased.*

(iv) *The Judge said the sacking of Mr Powis was unlawful. Yesterday, he said he had changed his mind.*

The difference in wording is slight but leads to different assignment of antecedents for *he*. In (iii) the first *he* can refer to the judge, Mr Powis or to someone outside the text and the second *he* can similarly refer to one of these three, at least in principle. In (iv), the preferred reading is probably that *he* refers to the judge, however. In addition to background knowledge, a further principle may be involved – that a second sentence is expected to say something 'about' the preceding one. In (iv) it is hard to see, given our background knowledge, how 'he said he had changed his mind' can be saying anything about Mr Powis, but it could conceivably be saying something about the judge, given that we know the judge has expressed an opinion.

Indefinite and definite articles

Indefinite and definite articles play several roles in English, but one of their functions is to indicate whether something has been referred to before or is assumed to be known to the text interpreter. For example:

A man in a dark suit sidled up to the bar. Mary watched him warily. After a few seconds, the man said, 'Hello, darling.'

Here *a* introduces a new referent, while *the* mentions a referent already introduced. Creative writers do of course play tricks with this tendency for special effects. Suppose a short story began like this:

The street was dark. The curtains were drawn across the windows. Mary walked cautiously along the pavement.

Here, there is no prior introduction by way of an indefinite article but the text is still coherent. This can be explained by the general semantic fact that definite articles **presuppose existence**. In reading the first sentence, the reader simply adds to his or her mental model of the text that a certain street exists in the fictional world of the story. The fact that *the* is also used with other nouns (*curtains, windows, pavement*) in this little text is explained in a slightly different way – we expect a street to have pavements, be lined by houses, houses to have windows, windows to have curtains. This again shows that the words in texts do not entirely depend on the co-text but on stored background knowledge.

ADVANCES BOX 9.1

Models and frames

In the theory of language known as cognitive linguistics, a **frame** can be (a) a semantic frame, specifying, e.g., the complements associated with a particular verb (Fillmore, 1982), or (b) a non-linguistic knowledge structure for a particular domain of human experience, e.g., school, law court, or bullying (Minsky, 1975). A related term is **script** (Schank and Abelson. 1977), background knowledge about sequences of events; these are often components of frames. Frames and scripts are held in long-term memory and are activated by the meanings of words when you process texts. A text **model** (van Dijk and Kintsch, 1983) is not already available to the text processor: rather, it is built up in working memory to represent the global text meaning. People construct a mental model justified by the text; if they can do this, then the text is coherent. As van Dijk puts it: 'Understanding a text means that people are able to construct a mental model for the text' (2004: 10).

Examples

A frame is structured knowledge. For example, your conceptual frame for legal procedures might include: judge, jury, defence, prosecution, jury, court room, etc., and associated sequential scripts, e.g. accuse–charge–trial–verdict–sentence, etc.

We have noted that definite pronouns frequently serve to refer back to an item already introduced in the text or understood to be in the context. In S5 in Illustration Box 9.1 we see *the parents* but there is no previous mention of parents in the text. How do we explain the occurrence of *the* here? In fact we can use its occurrence as evidence that a frame has been activated, the school frame. Thus *the* occurs because the school frame has been activated by the word *teacher* in S1, and associated elements in the frame, like *parents, pupils, headmistress* can be picked out by the definite article or by other words presupposing existence in the text world such as possessive pronouns (cf. *his head* in S1).

9.5 Junctions

The term **junction** (see de Beaugrande and Dressler, 1972) is used to refer to a set of words that relate propositions to one another in a variety of ways. This term includes 'conjunctions' in the grammatical sense of the term. Halliday and Hasan (1976) use the term **conjunction** rather than **junction**. Often these junctive relations are not like relations between propositions in formal logic, but are peculiar to texts in human language. We shall not list all the different types of junction that have been identified (for more, see the sources just mentioned).

The word *and* is interpretable in many different ways in texts (e.g., as expressing causation) but one of its jobs is simply the addition of information:

(2) A judge ruled that the sacking from Coedffranc junior school in Skewen, South Wales, was unlawful, *and* had already awarded Alan Powis, 53,

£80,000 in interim payments pending a full settlement scheduled for yesterday.

Here the text's use of *and* does not seem to be implying any extra unspoken meaning. Statements about facts can, however, be conjoined also by *but* in English, with the implication that there is a relation of incongruity, unexpectedness or contradiction between two statements, for example:

(6) Mr Powis, a father of two, suffered a nervous breakdown *but* found work as a £2.50-an-hour security guard and a door-to-door salesman to make ends meet.

Another example is the *But* between sentences (2) and (3) in our text. In fact *but* is but one of a set of related words and phrases that could be used:

(6') Mr Powis, a father of two, suffered a nervous breakdown. *But/yet/ however/nevertheless/even so/in spite of this* he found work as a £2.50-an-hour security guard and a door-to-door salesman to make ends meet.

The important point here is that the two main clauses are about separate events (suffering a nervous breakdown and finding work). It is in the human conceptualization of the world that there is a contrast, and it is this contrast that the text enables readers to construct in their minds. The contrastive (or contrajunctive) expressions impose a contrastive relation but also depend on background knowledge – for example, that if you are suffering from a nervous breakdown, you are not normally fit enough to work. Once again we see that texts take the form they do not simply because of their internal structure, but because they interact with our (non-linguistic) knowledge about the world.

Junctive expressions also relate events within a time frame:

(1) A bullied teacher has been awarded a £230,000 payout for personal injury and loss of earnings *after* being forced out of his job by his head.

Between sentences we might have:

(1') A bullied teacher was forced out of his job by his head. *Afterwards/ some time later* he was awarded a £23,000 payout for personal injury.

As can be seen from this adapted sentence, temporal conjunctions may imply different amounts of time lapse: *afterwards* seems to imply close temporal proximity to the preceding event. There may be a sequence relationship (*then, next, subsequently*...), between a past event and the present time of writing or reading *(since, since then...)*. Certain junctive words (*meanwhile, in the meantime, while, during*...) imply a 'parallel' event, that is, an event taking place in the same time interval as a previously mentioned event. Since two events cannot occur in the same space, this kind of junctive produces a shift of scene: 'Meanwhile, back at the ranch...'. It is important to note that temporal junctives interact with the tense system of verbs, which itself pays a crucial role in the cohesion of texts.

ADVANCES BOX 9.2

Text worlds

Junctive words can have a radical effect on text processing, creating several 'worlds' that are related in the overall 'world' constructed by the text. The term **text(ual) worlds** was introduced by de Beaugrande (1972): text interpreters build conceptual 'models' that can be diagrammed as networks of concepts. A further advance was Werth's theory of conceptual space in discourse (1999; also Gavins, 2007). Werth introduced the idea of 'sub-worlds' triggered by 'world building elements'. Fauconnier (1985) had already developed the related idea of **mental spaces** in cognitive linguistics. In this Illustrations Box we look at some distinct 'worlds' triggered in the Bully Text. What we are calling 'junctives' can perform world-building functions.

Example

When combined with tense forms *if* sets up in the text processor's mind a 'world' that is conceived as possible, probable or not true at all (counterfactual) (see also the discussion of presuppositions in Chapter 11). This is similar to what modal verbs (*may, might, must, should*, etc.) do. For example:

(a) If Ms Ball apologizes, Mr Powis will be content.
(b) If Ms Ball were to apologize, Mr Powis would be content.
(c) If Ms Ball had apologized, Mr Powis would be content.

In (a) and (b) there is a future possible world in which Ms Ball might yet apologize and the text could continue to add events and situations within that possible text world. In (c) Ms Ball has definitely not apologized, but the text creates an imaginary world in which she has done so, and goes on to mention what possible things could have happened in that particular 'world'. Notice that the imaginary world is still linked to, i.e. cohesive with, the 'base world' of the text as a whole.

A different type of 'parallel universe' is set up by verbs of saying, believing etc., which 'distance' their complement clauses from the commitments of the writer or speaker. An example in the *Bully Text* is:

(5)...Ms Ball claimed he was undermining her authority.

The statement *he was undermining her authority* is not taken on board by the writer/speaker. It is only in Ms Ball's world that *he*, Mr Powis, is *undermining her authority*. Similarly, in S9 the verb *say* creates a separate world for Mr Powis. Texts thus require readers to carefully separate different kinds of reality and also to 'tag' claims about the truth of events and situations.

9.6   A method for analysing cohesion and coherence

When we summarized Harris's version of text linguistics we noted his concern with the reappearance of the same, similar or related expression in the same grammatical environments. This phenomenon can be viewed as a crucial aspect of text cohesion. In the *Bully Text*, it can be seen very clearly if we analyse the text as in Table 9.1.

What this table does is analyse the sentences of the text into their clauses and their clauses' grammatical constituents (subject, verb, complements of the verb, adjunct, and conjunctions). This includes clauses in which the subject is not overtly expressed, although, for simplicity, some of these are not shown in the table. Grammatical subjects that are not overtly expressed in certain kinds of embedded clauses are in brackets. Main clauses are S1, S2, etc., where S stands for 'sentence', because each clause is analysed out into a full sentence form. You read the table across the rows, giving you the original word order; each column you cross tells you what is in each grammatical category that makes up the sentence.

In each column we can see (a) which sorts of expressions hang together and (b) which sorts of lexical relationships obtain between them. In the rows we can see which kinds of grammatical subjects and complements are combined with which kinds of verbs. While adjuncts can also display certain kinds of cohesion, we will not discuss them here – we leave it to you to consider them further.

In the Subject column we can identify the **actors** in the little 'world' constructed by the text. In sentence (1) an indefinite article is used, in the way discussed above, to introduce an individual: *a teacher*. Looking down the Subject column and the Complements column, we can see other items that the text processor relates anaphorically to this individual: *Alan Powis, 53* (S2.2), *Mr Powis* (S2.3), *he, his, him* (S4), *he* (S5), *Mr Powis, a father of two* (S6), *Mr Powis, he* (S9). In S10 the pronoun *I* appears and the text processor has to determine its referent. In this instance it is related not to the producer of the text, but to *Mr Powis*. This is done by the text's use of the verb *say*, which introduces a separate 'world' (see Advances Box 9.2), and by the typographical convention of quotation marks for direct speech. There is thus a chain of anaphoric reference for this actor. Much of this is in the mind of the text interpreter. In particular, consider:

S1 *A bullied teacher has been awarded a £230,000...*
S2 *A judge [...] had already awarded Alan Powis, 53, £80,000 in interim payments.*

There is no overt indication that the teacher is Mr Powis, but we 'instinctively' know that it is on reading the text. How do we know this? One explanation is that there is a kind of repetition at work in S1 and S2 that is not only a mater of the repeated word *awarded*. The two sentences quoted in the above form have different grammatical structures: S1 is the passive construction, S2 active. What counts here is not the grammatical subjects (*a bullied teacher* in S1, and *a judge* in S2), but the **roles** that they play. In S2 *a bullied teacher* is the grammatical subject and plays the recipient role. In S2, he is the grammatical object but still plays the recipient role. The inference that *Mr Powis* refers to the same person as *a teacher* is probably based largely on this type of repetition, the repetition of the role played, as well as on lexical

Table 9.1 Lexical and grammatical cohesion in the Bully Text

Sentence (clause)	Subject noun phrase	Verb	Complement(s): direct object, indirect object, prepositional phrases	Adjunct: Adverb, prepositional phrases	Conjunction
S1	A bullied teacher	has been awarded	a £230,000 payout	for personal injury and loss of earnings after S1.1	
S1.1	(a bullied teacher)	being forced out	of his job S2.1	by his head	
S2	A judge	ruled	that S2.1		
S2.1	the sacking from Coedffranc junior school in Skewen, South Wales,	was	unlawful,	and S2.2	
S2.2	(a judge)	had awarded	Alan Powis, 53, £80,000 in interim payments	already, pending a full settlement scheduled for yesterday.	
S3	Mr Powis	was given	the payment	in an out-of-court settlement, on Thursday, to end a lengthy battle.	But
S4	He	lost	his job		after S4.1
S4.1	the head, Sheena Ball,	questioned	his ability		and S4.2
S4.2	(the head, Sheena Ball)	accused	him of incompetence.		When
S5.1	he	won	the support of the parents S5.2		
S5	Ms Ball	claimed	S5.2		
S5.2	he	was undermining	her authority		and S5.3
S5.3	he	was sacked	for gross misconduct.		
S6	Mr Powis, a father of two,	suffered	a nervous breakdown		but S6.1

S6.1	(Mr Powis)	found	work as a £2.50-an-hour security guard and a door-to-door salesman		to make ends meet.
S7	Judge Gary Hickinbottom, sitting at at Swansea's civil courts of justice,	said	that S7.1		
S7.1	the sacking in 1997	was	unlawful		and S7.2
S7.2	(Judge Gary Hickinbottom)	(said)	that S7.3		
S7.3	it	was	Ms Ball's conduct that 7.3'		
S7.3'	(Ms Ball's conduct)	was	to blame		
S8	The settlement against Neath and Port Talbot county borough council's education authority	was settled		by its insurers	Yesterday
S9	Mr Powis	said	S9.1		
S9.1	he	was	pleased with the ruling.		
S10	I	'm not the least bit	interested in S10.1		
S10.1	(I)	having	What a flash new car.		
S11.1	I	did want	this claim		
S11.1'	I	began	the return of my good name, the return of my dignity, and the return of my peace of mind		
S11	S11.1	was			when S11.1'
S12	I	'm starting to get	that		now

repetition. The chain of references that this contributes to is structured in such a way that generalization is filled in with increasing detail. First, there is a general categorization as a teacher, then his name, then his age, then his family status.

Table 9.1 also clearly reveals the other actors: a judge and Ms Ball. We can see the same pattern of progressive specification of the social category of these actors.

The cohesion device in these cases is generally called **reiteration**, since some words or related words are repeated. A case of repetition in this text is the word *unlawful* (S2.1 and S7.1), another is *pay(out)*in S1, *pay(ment)* in S2.2 and S3, and another is *settle(ment/ed)* in S2, S3 and S8. In some texts we find that reiteration involves **sense relations** such as synonymy, antonymy, meronymy and hyponymy (these are discussed in more detail in Chapter 10, Section 10.3.3). An example of hyponymy contributing to textual cohesion would be:

Ms Ball is in education. She teaches in a primary school,

where *education* is the superordinate term and *primary school* is the hyponym.

By comparing expressions in the Verb column in Table 9.1 we can see an example of antonymic cohesion between S4 and S5:

S4　*He lost his job*
S5　*He won the support of the parents.*

Table 9.1 also enables us to see which roles the actors play and how they relate to one another. As we have seen, Mr Powis plays the role of recipient (S1, S2, S3), to which we might add S4 and S6: the verbs *lose* and *suffer* have an interesting semantic specification that makes their grammatical subject some sort of 'undergoer' or 'patient'. Mr Powis, then, is cast in the role of someone who is in a conceptual sense 'passive'. The verb *find* in S6.1 has ambiguous semantics: the grammatical subject may be an agent in the finding or a more passive recipient or beneficiary. Aside from these examples, the only other verb we find linked with Mr Powis is *say*, but this verb is also combined with the various expressions referring to the judge.

The frequency of reference to Mr Powis, and his appearance as the subject in passive constructions leads to the feeling a reader may have concerning the 'aboutness' of the text: it is primarily about Mr Powis and what happened to him. His relationship to the other actors can be seen by examining the rows where he is referred to in the Complement column, as well as the Subject column where he (Mr Powis) occurs as the grammatical subject of a passive construction but has the semantic role of undergoer. The Complement column includes direct objects (e.g., Powis is the 'object' of *accusations* in S4.1) and indirect objects (e.g., S2.2, *Alan Powis, 53*). He thus emerges as undergoer of actions whose agent is Ms Ball, and the beneficiary of assertions made by the judge. As for the role of the judge, and the way in which he is repeatedly referred to, these can be clearly read off from the table.

Sometimes this kind of linkage between words is called **collocation**, usually defined as the co-occurrence of lexical items in the same environment. 'In the same environment' can be defined in different ways: two or more items can be close together or relatively far apart, grammatically combined (as noun and verb, for example) or found in different sentences. However, we need to distinguish collocations that occur in the language at large (e.g., *pretty* has a statistical tendency to collocate with *girl* or *woman* not with *boy* or *man*) and those that occur in specific texts, such as the *Bully Text*. Furthermore, we need to realize that lexical collocation is a reflex of mental organization of the world – that is, frames. Thus, for example, *a judge ruled* (S1) is cohesive with *out-of-court* (S2), *sitting at ... civil courts of* justice (S7), and *ruling* (S9). These words create a cohesive effect across sentences. However, cohesion (a lexical and grammatical relationship) cannot easily be distinguished from coherence (a conceptual phenomenon). In other such cases, the reason for the co-occurrence of such terms in the same text is due to their role in the conceptual frame for legal proceedings.

9.7 Superstructure and sequence

Texts not only depend on the weaving together of lexical and grammatical strands, they have a level of organization sometimes called **superstructure** (van Dijk, 1980). This term refers to the fact that texts have recognizable parts that are organized according to conventional patterns. The *Bully Text* has the typical superstructure of a newspaper report, with easily recognizable sections: a headline, a by-line and the named journalist's specialism, then the body of the text. Sometimes the body of the text will have a 'lead', the first sentence or two printed in bold. What is less obvious is the internal organization of the report itself.

Reports are essentially narratives or stories. In reading the text, you will have had little difficulty in building a mental model of the sequence of events being reported. However, closer inspection shows that these events are not reported in the order they occurred chronologically: they are scrambled. It is therefore important to distinguish between **story** (the chronological sequence of episodes) and **plot** (the order in which the text presents them). The effects of such 'story scrambling' are various: they may, for instance, create dramatic suspense or they may highlight some facts or events. Even when stories are scrambled, texts retain their cohesion and coherence by means of the tense system and other markers that indicate the time at which events take place relative (a) to one another and (b) to the time of writing or speaking.

In the *Bully Text* we can see how this works by listing the episodes in what must be their chronological order, alongside the number of the sentence in which they are expressed:

S4   Ms Ball questions Mr Powis's ability
S5.1   Mr Powis wins parents' support

S5	Ms Ball claims Mr Powis is undermining her authority	
S5.2	Ms Ball sacks Mr Powis	
S6	Mr Powis suffers nervous breakdown	
S6.1	Mr Powis finds work as guard and salesman	
S2, S7	Judge says sacking is unlawful and blames Ms Ball	
S2	Judge awards £80,000 interim payment to Mr Powis	
S1	out-of-court settlement of £230,000	[Thursday]
S8	settlement is settled by insurers	
S2	full payment scheduled to be paid	[yesterday (Friday)]
S9	Mr Powis says he is pleased.	

Clearly, the sentences are not in the 'natural' order. How does the reader establish the probable real-world order of events? In addition to the background knowledge frames concerning legal procedure employment and causation (losing one's job causes certain effects), the use of tenses and other temporal indicators help the reader to sequence the episodes. Since this text occurs in a newspaper, there is an explicit **deictic centre** (or 'anchor') for temporal coordinates (Saturday, 5 October 2002). Hence, the deictic words *yesterday* and *Thursday* can be given a precise meaning (deixis is more fully introduced in Chapter 11, Section 11.2). The fixed present-time-of-writing also explains the use of the present perfect in S1, referring to a recent event. In S1, *after* relates the monetary award to an event before it, the sacking, and strongly implies a causal link (via background knowledge, as well as the informal principle of *post hoc ergo propter hoc*). In S2, the simple past points to a more remote event. There is insufficient information in the text to locate it precisely. If the reader takes the trouble to locate it in the text model he or she is building up in working memory, either in processing S2 or at a later point, then the reader has to rely on his or her own inferencing. In S2 we also have a past perfect tense, whose job is to locate an event before the time of some other past event, known as the reference time. Here, the reader has to decide which is the relevant reference time.

The tense in S3 is the simple past, even though the event is recent, because of the precise time indicator *Thursday*. In S4, however, the reader must infer that the simple past (*lost his job*) refers to an episode considerably earlier than *Thursday*. In S5 and S6 the simple past tense (*won, claimed, was sacked, suffered, found*) relates to remote events. There are no words to indicate explicitly which event followed or preceded which; even the temporal subordinating conjunction *when* does not do this job. What we have is an **iconic** sequence in which the sequence of the clauses corresponds to the natural sequence of events – a sequence which is of course already expected on the basis of non-linguistic knowledge. Sentences S4 to S6 constitute a 'flashback'.

S7 takes us back to a different scene and time scale (or 'sub-world' in terms of text world theory), though here again it is up to the reader to infer the exact time point in his or her model at which the judge said what he said. In S8 the same is true: the reader has to use S3, aided by the lexical repetition and conceptual frames, to locate the event in the text model he or she is building. The relevant frame is the world of law, local government, the world already called up in S2.

S9 represents yet another scene or text world, triggered by the temporal deictic *yesterday*, the verb *say* and the quotation marks. The time is past relative to the utterance time but 'now' – hence the present tense – for Mr Powis in S10 and S11.

We have seen that there is some indeterminacy in the sequencing but on the whole the text enables the reader to construct a model of the sequence of events. The analysis may seem complicated and unnecessary but the fascinating thing for linguists is that the human brain appears to be able to do all these complex things rapidly and unconsciously.

9.8 To conclude

We should not assume that because this chapter has been illustrated by means of a written text that the principles and methods we have outlined do not also apply to the spoken word. Indeed we can, and some linguists do, use the term 'text' to refer also to spoken utterances. After all, there have to be principles of cohesion and coherence that hold spoken words together too, and principles and practices by means of which hearers make sense out of what they hear. Whether a 'text' is written or spoken, the process of 'making sense' is not a mechanical affair. Many people assume that using language is simply a matter of putting ideas into words and transmitting them to a hearer or reader, who will then decode them. Perhaps even the early text grammars suffered from this misapprehension. Things turn out to be not so simple, as this chapter has tried to suggest. Texts are perhaps more like structured sets of 'cues' that 'prompt' the hearer to bring all manner of knowledge to bear in the search for intelligible coherence. This chapter has aimed merely to introduce some of the ways in which linguists are beginning to understand what it means to understand a text.

Recommended readings

A useful survey is G. Brown and G. Yule, *Discourse Analysis*, Cambridge: Cambridge University Press (1983). The more recent cognitive approach is summarized in a readable introduction by J. Gavins, *Text World Theory: An Introduction*, Edinburgh: Edinburgh University Press (2007). A more detailed approach, on which Gavins draws, is P. Werth (1999).

CHAPTER 10

Semantics

ANNA SIEWIERSKA

10.1 Defining semantics

Semantics is the branch of linguistics devoted to the study of linguistic meaning. I stress that it is only linguistic meaning that semantics is concerned with since the verb *mean* and noun *meaning* in English may be used to indicate a range of non-linguistic notions, namely intentions, values, significance, signs or symbols, respectively as suggested by the examples in [10.1]:

[10.1] a. I did not mean to do it.
  b. Life without love has no meaning.
  c. What is the meaning of that cheeky smile on your face?
  d. A red light means stop.
  e. A red flower behind the right ear means that the person is engaged.

The type of linguistic meaning which falls within the scope of semantics is not conceived of in the same way by all. Traditionally semantics is seen to be restricted to the investigation of so-called **descriptive meaning**. Such meaning (also termed referential, ideational, representational or propositional) is concerned with objective, factual information, that is, information that seeks to describe some situation or event, as in, for example, *On the 17th of December 2007 the British moved out of Basra*, and can be explicitly asserted or denied and sometimes objectively verified. Under this traditional approach to semantics, the investigation of other types of linguistic meaning, such as the meaning conveyed by the use of the word *fascist* in [10.2a] or the word *fell* rather than *hill* in [10.2b] or the clause *I have a headache* in [10.2c], fall within the domain of branches of linguistics such as **pragmatics** (see the following chapter):

[10.2] a. I really hate the man. He never allows anyone to present their own point of view. He's simply a fascist.
  b. When someone says fell instead of hill, I can't help feeling an instant bond with them.
  c. A: We're going to the pub. Do you want to come along?
    B: I have a headache.
    A: OK then, another time then.

The use of the word *fascist* in [10.2a] reflects the emotional state of the speaker rather than the actual political affiliation of the person being talked about. This is an example of so called expressive meaning. In [10.2b] we have an instance of evoked meaning which taps into the dialectal (regional, social or professional) associations of particular words (see Chapters 18–22), while [10.2c] illustrates what is known as conversational meaning which surfaces only in a particular conversational context (see Chapter 11). Note that while the descriptive meaning of *I have a headache* is that of the speaker having a pain in the upper-most reaches of his or her body, in the context specified its pragmatic meaning is quite different, namely it means 'No, I don't want to' or 'No, I'd rather not'. Nowadays many scholars reject the distinction between meaning as studied within semantics as opposed to pragmatics and argue that all linguistic meaning must be studied in context and relative to how speakers use language. There are also scholars who argue that there is no autonomous level of purely linguistic meaning which can be studied, in its own right, in isolation from other cognitive capabilities such as those illustrated in the examples in [10.1] given earlier. Nonetheless, I will restrict this chapter to the traditional view of semantics, according to which there is a distinction between linguistic meaning and other types of meaning, and within linguistic meaning, a distinction between semantic meaning and pragmatic meaning.

The discussion will focus on meaning as reflected in the examples in [10.3], each of which illustrates a different facet of linguistic meaning, namely reference [10.3a], sense [10.3b) and propositional meaning [10.3c], respectively:

[10.3] a. By 'my best friend' I meant Sue Carter and not Sally Brown.
        b. What is the meaning of 'axiology'?
        c. The sentence *James murdered Max* means that 'someone called James deliberately killed someone called Max'.

In Section 10.2 we will present the notion of reference, exemplify the different types of reference distinguished in languages, and consider the attempts to define meaning based on reference. Section 10.3 will explore the notion of sense and the different attempts to characterize it based on the nature of the referents of words and on the relationships between words. And finally, in Section 10.4, we will briefly look at sentence meaning and the propositional content that sentences are used to express.

10.2 Reference and referential relations

In the previous chapter, Section 9.4, we saw some specific aspects of reference in operation. **Reference**, as traditionally conceived of by philosophers of language and linguists, is the relationship between linguistic elements and the non-linguistic world of experience, that is, entities (persons, things, places) or situations external to the language system. It is the relationship between, for example, the linguistic expression *the car* in [10.4] and the vehicle which I am currently driving (I only have one car):

[10.4] I was late because I couldn't park the car.

The entity identified by the linguistic expression *the car*, that is, the vehicle which I drive, is called the **referent** and the linguistic expression which identifies the referent, that is, *the car*, is called a **referring expression**. When reading about reference you are likely to come across statements that a given referential expression X refers to a particular referent Y. You need to be aware of the fact that, strictly speaking, such statements are not correct and are used just as convenient shorthand. Reference does not reside in linguistic expressions. It is an act. Therefore linguistic expressions cannot of themselves refer. They can only be used by speakers to refer. In other words, linguistic expressions only have the potential of reference. Accordingly, *the car* in [10.4] does not refer to the vehicle that I drive, but rather I am using it to refer to the relevant vehicle.

If reference is an act, it follows that the real world entity identified by the act of reference is tied to a particular occasion of use. Thus the referent of *the car* when [10.4] is produced by me now, in the last days of 2007, is quite different from what it would have been early in the year because my husband and I bought a new car in March. And if [10.4] were to be produced by my next door neighbour, the referent of *the car* would be different yet again.

Reference is traditionally associated with existence. This is due to the fact that when speakers use referential expressions, they present the referents of these expressions as existing in the non-linguistic world. Originally the non-linguistic world in which referents exist was assumed to be our real world, our reality. This very reasonable assumption, however, had to be subsequently modified. You can appreciate why a modification was necessary when you consider how often you speak about entities and situations which exist not in reality, but only in fictional worlds, books, films, computer games, your dreams, etc. Under the traditional approach to reference, linguistic expressions such as *a goblin*, *the trolls*, *three unicorns*, *Harry Potter*, *Dr Who*, etc. would all have to be considered as non-referential by virtue of not having a referent in the real world. Yet neither English, nor any other language that linguists are aware of, distinguishes in any way between language expressions which refer to real world entities as opposed to fictional or imaginary entities. Observe, for example, that in [10.5] there is no difference between *an old man* and *an old elf*; the same referring expressions, *he* and *himself* are used to refer subsequently to either:

[10.5]   There was once an old man/an old elf who lived in the forest. He lived all by himself and was very lonely. One day he met a frog near a pond.

In light of the above, nowadays reference is treated as relating to existence not in the real world, but rather in the world of discourse created between the speaker and hearer or alternatively in the mind(s) of the speaker and/or hearer (see Advances Box 9.2 in Chapter 9). Not all linguistic expressions have the potential of being used as referring expressions. Many do not identify entities, situations or events, but rather are used as predicates (which define properties of entities or relations between entities) or as modifiers (which qualify entities or events). Other non-referring expressions fulfil various grammatical functions to do with determination (e.g., articles or demonstratives) or modality (e.g., auxiliary verbs). Non-referring expressions are often called **designating**. It is important to remember that the same linguistic expression may be used as referring and as non-referring (designating) on different occasions of use. Two cases in point are illustrated in [10.6] and [10.7].

[10.6]   a.   The Prime Minister made a statement to the press.
          b.   Gordon Brown is the prime minister.
[10.7]   a.   A man was looking for you.
          b.   Be a man.

The expression *The Prime Minister* in [10.6a] is used to identify a specific individual who at a particular time and place made a certain statement to the media. It is thus used referentially. In [10.6b], by contrast, *the prime minister* is used to express a role or property, not to identify an individual. It is thus a designating expression. The same distinction can be observed in the use of *a man* in [10.7a] as compared to [10.7b].

10.2.1   Different types of reference.

Within reference a number of distinctions need to be drawn. The most important of these is that between **definite** and **indefinite** reference. A linguistic expression is used definitely or (using the short cut mentioned earlier) is definite, if the speaker assumes that the referent of the linguistic expression can be identified by the addressee. By contrast, the referents of indefinite expressions are assumed by the speaker not to be identifiable by the addressee. Speakers' assumptions with respect to the identifiability of referents by addressees are based on a range of factors including: general mutual knowledge (knowledge that we have in common by virtue of living on the same planet or in the same country or in the same town) as in [10.8a], shared past experiences as in [10.8b], the situational context of the discourse as in [10.8c] and, crucially, mention in the preceding discourse as in [10.8d]:

[10.8]   a.   The moon was beautiful last night.
          b.   The girl who used to give us a lift to uni turns out to be our new next door neighbour.
          c.   Can you put the vases on the tables please?.
          d.   A woman came in with a child. I didn't recognize the woman but the child was my cousin.

As suggested by the above examples, in English the definite vs. indefinite distinction with common nouns is indicated explicitly by articles placed in the initial position of a noun phrase; *the* is used with definite singular and plural nouns (e.g., *the moon*, *the vases*) and *a(n)* is used with indefinite singular, countable ones (e.g., *a woman*, *a book* vs. *wine*, *sand*). Indefinite plural nouns, both countable (e.g., *women*, *books*) and uncountable (e.g., *wine*, *sand*), are typically seen as occurring with a zero-article (an article with no

ADVANCES BOX 10.1

The status of the indefinite articles

Not all scholars agree that English marks indefiniteness by the articles *a(n)* and zero, as sketched above. Lyons (1999: 33–5), for example, argues that indefiniteness in English is indicated by the absence of the definite article. According to him, there is no zero indefinite article with plural indefinites while *a(n)* is an article marking cardinality, i.e., singular number rather than indefiniteness. Lyons' main argument for considering *a(n)* as a marker of cardinality rather than indefiniteness is that it is restricted to singular countable entities, which is a strange restriction for an indefinite article. Notice that the definite article is not restricted in a similar way; it can occur with any type of noun, irrespective of its cardinality and countability. Moreover, even with indefinite singular count nouns, *a(n)* does not occur when another indicator of singularity, namely the numeral *one* is present, e.g., *one orange* not **a one orange*. Lyons also considers *some* to be an article of cardinality analogous to a(n) marking a vague quantity (e.g., some milk) and, with count nouns, more than one (e.g., *some books*).

phonetic form), as in the case of *books* in *The table was covered with books* or *wine* in *There is wine on the table*.

While the English article system allows us to indicate fairly clearly the definiteness status of a referent, this does not mean that definiteness should be equated with the use of the articles. Definiteness may be marked by demonstrative pronouns (e.g *that book*, *those photographs*) or possessive pronouns (e.g., *my mother*). And some linguistic expressions are inherently definite, namely personal pronouns (*I, you, he*, etc.) and proper names (e.g., *Emma, Mr Jones, Professor Blake*).

Indefinite reference can be further subdivided into specific and non-specific. Whereas definiteness relates to the speaker's assumptions about the state of mind of the addressee, specificity has to do with the mind of the speaker. A linguistic expression is used with **specific** reference if the speaker has a particular entity in mind. If the speaker has no entity in mind, but rather is thinking only of an arbitrary member of a class, the linguistic expression is used **non-specifically**. Unlike in the case of definiteness, English does not require that the distinction between specific and non-specific referents be overtly encoded. The noun phrase *a painting by Frieda Kahlo* in *The curator wants to buy a painting by Frieda Kahlo* is thus open to both a specific reading and a non-specific one. Under the specific interpretation, there is a particular work by Frieda Kahlo that the curator wants to buy, under the non-specific interpretation all that the curator wants to have is a painting by Frieda, he doesn't really care which painting it is. The two readings may be distinguished from each other by looking at the following discourse; if the non-specific reading was intended the pro-form *one* can be used for the non-specific entity (e.g., *But he doesn't have the money to buy one*); if a specific reading was intended, the pro-form *one* cannot be used, only the pronoun *it* can be used (*But it is not clear whether he will be able to buy it*). Another means of distinguishing between specific and non-specific readings of indefinite noun phrases is via the modifiers *a certain* or *a particular*. Needless to say, such modifiers can only be used with specific NPs.

A third type of referential usage, closely related to the non-specific use, is so-called **generic** reference. Generic reference involves not individual entities, but rather kinds. Generic NPs are used in timeless statements, in statements expressing law-like properties or rule-like behaviour, as in [10.9]:

[10.9] a. The boa constrictor is very dangerous.
        b. A dog is more loyal than a cat.
        c. Cigarettes cause lung cancer.

ADVANCES BOX 10.2

Use of different types of generics

Of the three types of generics that occur in English, the definite generics are the most restricted in use (they are typically used with nouns denoting nationality, animals and plants) as they are often ambiguous between a generic reading and a definite one. Observe that [10.9a] could very well be used to refer to a definite boa constrictor identifiable by the addressee, as in [10.10], for example:

[10.10] Don't worry about all those reptiles over there. They're sedated. But even when sedated, the boa constrictor is very dangerous.

Of the other two ways of expressing generic reference in English, the use of bare plurals is more common than that of indefinite singulars. A particularly good discussion of the different uses of the two is presented by Cohen (2001). For example, an indefinite singular as opposed to a bare plural cannot be used for defining a class as a unit, or for specifying an incidental as opposed to an essential property (the term essential will be explained in Section 10.3.1), as reflected in the contrasts in [10.11]:

[10.11] a. *A dodo is extinct.
         b. Dodos are extinct.
         c. *A madrigal is popular.
         d. Madrigals are popular.

Note also that indefinite singular generics have a normative force which makes them more likely to be used as admonishments than bare plurals. Compare [10.12a] with [10.12b], for instance:

[10.12] a. In that scene when you're walking alongside a lady, you must remember that gentlemen walk on the roadside of the pavement.
         b. In that scene when you're walking alongside a lady, you must remember that, a gentleman walks on the roadside of the pavement.

English has more ways of expressing generic NPs than many other languages. As shown in [10.9], in the case of countable entities, a definite noun may be used [10.9a], an indefinite singular noun [10.9b] and a bare plural [10.9c].

10.2.2 Reference and meaning

Reference is clearly a very important component of linguistic meaning. In order to understand what people are saying you must be able to identify the correct referents of the linguistic expressions that they are using. Otherwise, you won't know who is doing what to whom, where and when or why. However, can semantic meaning be equated with reference? Equally clearly it cannot.

First of all, as I have already mentioned, many linguistic expressions (e.g., predicates such as *write* or *sing*, modifiers such as *very* or *terribly,* and grammatical markers such as determiners (e.g., *the*) or auxiliary verbs (e.g., *may*) do not refer, but rather designate, yet no one would like to suggest that they have no meaning. Consequently, any theory of meaning based on reference would only cater for some subset of linguistic expressions. Secondly, since reference implies existence (in some world) and lack of existence is associated with non-referentiality, under a reference-based approach to meaning all expressions of non-existent entities (e.g., *no paper, no nuts, no one, nowhere*) would have to be considered as having the same meaning or no meaning. Consider, for instance, the expressions *no one, no fridge, no food* in [10.13]:

[10.13]   a.   There is no one in the kitchen.
           b.   There is no fridge in the kitchen.
           c.   There is no light in the kitchen.

Since there is no entity that can be described as *no one* or *no fridge* or *no food*, and the three clauses differ from each other only with respect to these expressions, under a reference-based approach to meaning, there could be no difference in meaning between the three clauses. Again this would be far from satisfactory. And thirdly, identity of reference is not the same as identity of meaning. The expression *the man over there* does not have the same meaning as *my father,* while the two can quite easily identify the same referent, as in [10.14] compared to [10.15]:

[10.14]   Who is the man over there?
          He's my father.
[10.15]   Who is the man over there?
          He's the new president of the student union.

In fact, all of us are frequently referred to by a variety of expressions in addition to our names, in particular by relational terms (*the son/daughter of X* or *sister/brother of Z*) and by our various social and professional roles (*student of English Language, member of university, participant of excursion Y, competitor of contest Z*). Each of these terms has its own meaning and is used in preference to other terms precisely because of this meaning. The aspect of meaning which differentiates all the expressions in question from each other is called sense and we will take a closer look at it now.

10.3 Sense and sense relations

Sense is typically understood as the mental representation of a linguistic expression. Unlike reference, which is dependent on context of use, sense is intended to capture the aspect of meaning which is invariant across contexts. For example, the sense of *prime minister* could be something like 'chief minister within the national parliament'. This invariant aspect of meaning comprising sense has proved to be very difficult to characterize. There are two broad approaches to sense. The first of these sees sense as a relation between a language expression, on the one hand, and certain characteristics of the set of potential referents of that language expression, on the other hand. Following Lyons (1977) and Cruse (2004), I will use the term **denotata** for the set of potential referents to avoid confusion between individual referents and the class of potential ones. This type of approach (it comes in many guises) involves decomposing lexical items into a set of features or semantic components which reflect the properties of their denotata. For example, the sense of *man* is seen to correspond to some combination of the features that men have, such as: human, adult, male, tall, muscular, heavy-boned, etc. The second approach to sense is language internal and is based on the relationship between the words of a given language to each other. It views the sense of a language expression as corresponding to the totality of all the possible relations it enters into with all the other words of the same language system. Thus, within the context of this approach, the sense of *man* is determined by its relationship to *woman, boy, child, animal, ram, breadwinner, father, mother,* etc. In Section 10.3.1 we will first consider the denotationally-based attempts to characterize sense, then in Section 10.3.2 we will take a brief look at the language internal approaches to establishing sense. In Section 10.3.3 we will review the major sense relations that lexical items enter into and see how these relations permeate the whole of the vocabulary of English.

10.3.1 Sense and the characteristics of denotata

The denotationally-based view of sense has in the last thirty years or so undergone significant changes. What is now considered to be the classical (and for many outdated) approach is based on two fundamental assumptions, namely (a) that all the denotata of a given language expression X share a set of essential common features and properties and (b) that these essential features and properties are 'knowable'. Given these two assumptions, sense is seen to correspond to the **essential** characteristics of the denotata of X. In the case of *man*, for example, the essential characteristics are taken to be adult, human, male. Other features often borne by males but not by all males, such as strength, bigger body weight than females, good spatial sense, problems with multi-tasking, etc, are considered to be not essential. In more formal approaches to semantics, instead of the term 'essential characteristics', the notion of **necessary and sufficient conditions** is used. The sense of X is thus seen to correspond to the necessary and sufficient conditions which need to be met in order for an entity to qualify as an instance of X. **Necessary** conditions are conditions that must be met in order for the entity to qualify as a denotatum of X while **sufficient** conditions are conditions which, if they are met, are enough in themselves to guarantee that a given entity is a denotatum of X. Accordingly, each of the above essential features of *man*, that is, human, adult, male, are necessary conditions, and together all three are sufficient.

The determination of the essential properties of the denotata of most lexical items has proved to be highly problematic. One reason for this is that contrary to assumption (a) above, often not all denota of X share a common set of properties. As famously argued by Wittgenstein (1953), on the basis of the denotata of the lexical item *game*, some may lack even a single common property. Note that the word *game* in English is typically associated with competitive sports such as football or other type of competitive activities involving several or at least two participants, as in the case of monopoly or chess. However, the term may also be used for activities involving a single individual, such as in the case of the card game patience, and even when no element of winning is involved, as when a child bounces a ball against the wall, or someone makes up new words. Nor is short or a specified duration a common factor as some games may last a lifetime, as in the case of the games that siblings sometimes play with each other. The second reason why the determination of the essential properties of denotata has proved to be problematic is that counter to assumption (b) there is often a discrepancy between what ordinary speakers think the common properties of the denotata of X are and the actual common properties of the given denotata. Thus, for example, while most speakers of English would list, as the common features of fish, living in water, moving via swimming, slippery streamlined body, presence of fins and scales, breathing through gills, the only features common to all fish identified by ichthyologists is that they are cold-blooded, aquatic vertebrates. This suggests that not all features of properties of denotata are equally important and specifically some are more of relevance to speakers (who are the ones who count as opposed to specialists) than others.

In light of the above, over the last thirty years an alternative approach to sense has been developed which relies crucially on the notion of **prototype**, a notion which was introduced in Chapter 6, Section 6.7 (see also the discussion in Chapter 16, Section 16.2). Under this now widely accepted view, sense is seen as corresponding to the perceived salient characteristics of the prototypical denotata of X. The major modification here, relative to the classical approach to sense, is that now, in the determination of the sense of X, not all denotata of X are considered but only the prototypical ones. Thus, for example, penguins, emus and ostriches are disregarded as non-prototypical birds and consequently the ability to fly is viewed as belonging to the sense of *bird*. The second crucial modification is that the properties which are seen as relevant to the determination of sense are not the 'essential ones', known only by specialists, but those that are perceived by speakers to be salient to them, that they have noted and observed and consider to be important. For example, although strictly speaking a *bride* is a female who has just married, irrespective of age, many speakers would include in the sense of bride, the feature young. This approach to sense thus places the ordinary human speaker at the centre of the determination of sense rather than at its periphery. While the use of prototypes and salient rather than essential features does not solve all the problems surrounding the determination of sense – it begs the question of what is the prototype and which are the salient features – it is widely considered to be a step in the right direction and to hold the promise of a more convincing theory of sense than the classical view.

10.3.2 Sense as a relation between language expressions

Unlike the denotational approach to sense which attempts to provide a full account of our understanding of the meaning of words, most attempts to characterize sense in terms of the relationships between words in a language system aim to capture merely how words differ from every other within a given semantic field. Thus they do not actually consider the totality of the language system but merely circumscribed bits of it, for example, the words in the semantic field of kinship terms or football or cooking utensils, etc. This makes the task of establishing the similarities and contrasts between words more manageable. The best know method of carrying out such a systematic comparison of the words within a given semantic field, introduced by Hjelmslev (1961), is known as componential analysis.

Classical **componential analysis** involves comparing a set of words in a semantic field in pairs and distinguishing between them in terms of a set of **binary features**. A very simple example is shown in [10.16]:

[10.16] man: + male, + mature
         woman: – male, + mature
         boy: + male, – mature
         girl: – male, – mature

We see that the four lexical items in this small semantic field of humans contrast with each other in terms of just two features [+/-male] and [+/-mature]. The contrasts between lexical items in most semantic fields, however, cannot be so succinctly captured by just two features. Consider, for instance, another four lexical items, namely *chair, armchair, stool* and *sofa*. To capture the contrasts between the French equivalents of these words, Pottier (1963) showed that as many as five features are required, namely (a) with back support; (b) with legs; (c) for one person; (d) for sitting on; and (e) with arms. My own allocation of these five features to the four English words is shown in [10.17]:

	a	b	c	d	e
[10.17] chair;	+	+	+	+	–
armchair	+	+	+	+	+
stool	–	+	+	–	–
sofa	+	–	–	+	+

For semantic fields involving a greater number of lexical items even more features are necessary. The types of features used must also be more complex.

ILLUSTRATION BOX 10.1

How to deal with relational notions

Consider the type of features that are necessary to deal with expressions such as *mother, father, brother, son, teacher* or *pupil*. These lexical items express relational notions, i.e., between entities. Thus a *mother* can only be of someone and a *pupil* must have a *teacher*, etc. If you try to distinguish between, say, *father* and *son* by binary features, say, [+/− parent], you will not be able to capture the full difference between the two because a father is also someone's son, and a son may also be someone's father. What you need therefore are directional features, e.g.:

[10.18]   a.   X is father of Y; X + male, X is parent of Y
              b.   X is son of Y; X + male; Y is parent of X

And in order to deal with kin terms within the same generation, you need a relation of sameness of reference (=), as in [10.19]:

[10.19]   X is brother of Y; X + male, parent of X = parent of Y

Further, to avoid unnecessary proliferation of features, multi-valued features rather than just binary features need to be employed. Over the years these and other modifications have been introduced into componential analyses which have enabled successively larger sets of lexical items to be dealt with, and even allowed the procedure to be extended to cover the whole vocabulary of a language rather than just restricted semantic domains.

It needs to be pointed out that the language internal approaches to determining sense are not in fact completely distinct from the denotational approaches discussed in the previous section. Though the internal approaches seek to determine sense in terms of the relationships between words rather than the relationship between a word and its denotata, the systematic contrasting of words with each other cannot be achieved without considering their denotata. In short, the determination of the most salient characteristics of the denotata of lexical items is of paramount importance to either approach.

10.3.3   Sense relations

Of the many **sense relations** which lexical items enter into with each other, the ones that are of chief interest to linguists are those which are: (a) recurrent, that is, recur frequently in the vocabulary of a language and (b) discriminatory, that is, embrace some pairs of lexical items but not others. The major sense relations which meet these criteria are: hyponymy, meronymy, synonymy and oppositeness.

Hyponymy is the sense relation holding between, for example, *rose* and *flower, stallion* and *horse, scarlet* and *red*. The relation of hyponym corresponds to what we would in everyday language call the type of relation, that is, X is a type/kind/sort of Y. The X, for example, *rose*, is called the hyponym and the Y, for example, *flower*, is called the **superordinate**. Knowing which lexical items are in a relation of hyponymy allows us to understand the logic of sentences containing them, as in the case of the examples in [10.20a] and [10.20b]:

[10.20]   a.   I'll bring Mary some roses because she told me she wants some flowers.
          b.   Jane was disappointed to get the flowers since she had been hoping for roses.

Normally a sentence containing a hyponym implies (more formally entails) the superordinate, but not vice versa. Therefore we may well expect Mary to be pleased with the roses in the case of [10.20a] and also understand why Jane was disappointed with her flowers in [10.20b].

Meronymy is the part/whole relation, which holds between, for example, *hand* and *finger*, *book* and *cover*, *tree* and *branch*. The details of how the part and whole are related to each other vary considerably. For instance, in the case of *finger* and *hand*, the finger is a necessary part of the hand, but this is not so in relations to *hair* and *head*. A handle is a much more integral part of a spoon than it is of a door as you can see by the oddity of *the handle is attached to the spoon* as compared to *the handle is attached to the door*. And a leg is evidently a much more distinct part of the body than a tip is of a tongue. Because of these differences, there is no single logical relationship between the lexical items related by meronymy corresponding to that found in hyponymy. Nonetheless, with expressions of locations, the location of the meronym (part), implies that of the **holonym** (whole) but not vice versa, as exemplified in [10.21]:

[10.21]   a.   Is Bob in the house? Yes, he's in the dining room.
          b.   Is Bob in the dining room. No, but he is in the house.

Synonymy is arguably the best known of the sense relations. It is typically described as reflecting the identity of senses, but in fact there are always some differences between synonymous items. A better characterization of synonymy is that it reflects a relationship in which the similarities outweigh or eclipse the differences. A good test for whether two expressions are indeed synonymous is to see whether they have the same truth conditions, that is, whether sentences differing from each other only with respect to the expressions in questions are both necessarily true or necessarily false. As shown in [10.22], the expressions *father* and *daddy* are clearly synonymous since if [10.22a] is true so is [10.22b], and if [10.22a] is false, so is [10.22b]. This is underscored by the oddity of [10.22c], which involves a contradiction:

[10.22]   a.   He is your father.
          b.   He is your daddy.
          c.   He is not my father, he is my daddy.

By way of comparison, *laugh* and *giggle* emerge in terms of the truth conditional test as non-synonymous as [10.23a] and [10.23b] do not involve a contradiction, though there are contexts where the two expressions may be used interchangeably, as in [10.23c] for example:

[10.23] a. She laughed. No, she didn't. It was more of a giggle.
         b. Did I hear a giggle? No, not really. It was more of a laugh.
         c. We always have a good giggle/laugh together over how unsophisticated we used to be when we were still at school.

It is rare to find pairs of words which can be used as substitutes for each other in all contexts, perfect or absolute synonyms, as words develop semantic associations, commonly called connotations, from the contexts in which they are typically used. Thus while *fiddle* and *violin* are truth conditionally synonymous, it would be strange for anyone to say *I am going to a fiddle concerto* rather than a *violin concerto*.

Oppositeness involves some form of conflict of senses along a given dimension. One type of opposites are **complementaries** (e.g., *alive/dead, open/shut, hit/miss)* which exhaustively divide some conceptual domain into two mutually exclusive compartments with no no-man's land in-between. If two lexical items are complementaries, the denial of one entails the applicability of the other. Thus if something is alive, it is not dead, and if it is open then it is not shut, etc. Further, you cannot deny both without anomaly as evidenced by the oddity of [10.24a] as compared to [10.24b] which features two non-complementaries *happy* and *sad*:

[10.24] a. She was neither alive nor dead.
         b. She was neither happy nor sad.

Another type of opposites are **antonyms** which, in contrast to complementaries, are gradable as they represent a range of values of a variable property such as beauty, height, heat, length, light, size, etc. There are various types of antonyms: polar such as *large/small* and *long/short*, equipollent such as *hot/cold* and *happy/sad,* and overlapping such as *good/bad* and *polite/rude*. Their gradability is reflected in their ability to occur with degree modifiers (e.g., *very long, awfully rude*), in the comparative and superlative degrees (e.g., *large, larger, largest*), and in *How X is it?* questions (e.g., *How long is it?*). The third major type of opposites are directional opposites which involve motion or change in opposite direction (e.g., *rise/fall, ascend/descend, enter/ leave*) or the direction of one element relative to another along some axis (e.g., A *is above* B, B *is below* A; A *is before* B, B *is after* A).

In considering how lexical items relate to each other in terms of the above type of sense relations, we must take note of the fact that a lexical item may have more than one sense. It is traditional to distinguish between two types of multiplicity of senses, polysemy and homonymy. We speak of **polysemy** when the senses that a lexical item displays are related to each other, and of **homonymy** when they are not. Whether the multiple senses of a lexical item are related to each other is not always clear or even easy to determine. For example, the lexical item *queen* has two senses 'the consort of a king/female monarch' and a 'gay male'. These are homonyms, though I dare say you could think of a way in which the two could be related. Conversely, although the noun *bachelor* is polysemous, the relationship between some of its senses, namely that of 'an unmarried man of any age' and 'a person who has taken the first or lowest degree at a university' is no longer as obvious as it once might have been (only men went to university and the men who did go were typically young). The various senses of a polysemous item are often related metaphorically or metonymically. A **metaphor** is the structuring of one concept in terms of another, for example, the conceptualizing of love as a journey, as when someone, instead of saying *We are going to separate*, says, *We have come to the end of the road*. **Metonymy**, in turn, is the use of some part or feature associated with a concept for the concept as a whole. For instance, the use of a place for an institution as in *Downing Street has not responded* instead of *The Government has not responded* or using a sub-event for the whole event as in *What shall I pour for you?* instead of *What would you like to drink?* (For further discussion of both metaphor and metonymy, see Chapter 16, Section 16.3) The workings of both metaphor and metonymy can be observed in some of the senses of *crawl* illustrated in [10.25]:

[10.25] a. He crawled on the ground like a snake.
         b. The traffic crawled to a halt.
         c. Dark clouds were crawling across the sky.
         d   The way you crawl to them makes me sick.
         e. Hilary's share of the vote is crawling up to slowly for her to win.
         f. The morning crawled past.

The basic sense of *crawl* is typically taken to be 'to move slowly on the hands and knees, or by dragging the body along the ground' as reflected in [10.25a]. The sense of 'to advance slowly, feebly, or with frequent stops' illustrated in]10.25b, c] is seen to be a metonymic extension which focuses on the 'slow' element of the basic sense. The sense illustrated in [10.25d], 'to proceed or act in a servile manner', is also a metonymic extension which centres on the spatial aspects of the basic sense, namely it being an activity taking place close to the ground and our negative associations with humans adopting a position at ground level particularly vis-à-vis other humans. The extension of the sense of crawl from motion to any kind of activity as in [10.25e], and even a process such as the passing of time in [10.25f], on the other hand, is considered to be due to metaphor.

10.4 Propositional meaning

So far we have been looking at the meaning of individual lexical items. Now we must devote at least a few words to the meaning of larger units, namely sentences and the propositions that they are used to convey.

Sentences are fairly abstract entities. In order to understand the meaning of sentences, we need to compare sentences with utterances on the one hand, and propositions on the other. Sentences consist of words and morphemes arranged according to the grammatical rules of a language. Their meaning is invariant across contexts, that is, independent of what was said before or after and who produced them, when, where and to whom. Thus the meaning of [10.26] is that 'An adult human male stroked gently with the palm of his hand a canine':

[10.26]   The man patted the dog.

However, people do not normally produce sentences, unless they are playing linguistic games or participating in a grammar class. What they produce are instantiations of sentences, which are called **utterances**. Once a sentence is written or said, it becomes an utterance, since it acquires a context, a speaker, addressee, etc. Accordingly, *the man* in [10.26] acquires reference and is transformed from any adult human male to a concrete individual who the speaker assumes that the addressee can identify. And analogously with *the dog* in [10.26]. Furthermore, the speaker in producing [10.26] says something about something or, to put it slightly more technically, expresses a **proposition**. The propositions that sentences are used to express have a truth value, that is, they can be considered true or false. Sentences, by contrast, have no truth value. You cannot say whether [10.26] is true or false until you know which individuals it is being said about and where and when.

A very important difference between sentences and propositions is that whereas sentences are purely linguistic entities, propositions are not. What exactly propositions are is a controversial matter, but let's just say that they are an item of thought. As linguistic entities, sentences are tied to a specific language but propositions are language independent. So [10.26] is a sentence of English and the Polish equivalent, *Mężczyzna pogłaskał psa*, is a sentence of Polish. Yet both can express the same proposition, for example, that my friend Neil patted his black Labrador Tess. Moreover, as linguistic objects, sentences are dependent on the words used and their arrangement. Therefore each of the examples in [10.27] constitutes a different sentence:

[10.27]   a.   The man patted the dog.
          b.   The dog was patted by the man.
          c.   The dog, the man patted him.
          d.   My friend Neil patted Tess.
          e.   Neil patted his black Labrador.

By contrast, provided the referents of each of the referential expressions in [10.27] are the same, all the examples in [10.27] may be used to express the same proposition, that is, may have the same propositional content or meaning. Thus, in sum, whereas sentences are used to express propositions, sentence meaning is not the same as propositional meaning. Propositional meaning is more abstract than sentence meaning.

Given that different sentences may express the same proposition, as in [10.27], it follows that there may be aspects of sentence meaning that are not propositional. These include any elements of a sentence which cannot contribute to the truth or falsity of the proposition expressed by the sentence. Take, for example, the words *still, yet, already* or *just*. There is no difference in the truth value of a proposition underlying a sentence with or without one of these words. Thus if [10.28a] is true, so is [10.28b], and if [10.28a] is false, so is [10.28b].

[10.28]   a.   Adam is waiting for Roz.
          b.   Adam is still waiting for Roz.

The difference in meaning resulting from the use of dialectal terms such as *fell* rather than *hill* mentioned in the introduction, Section 10.1, is another example of non-propositional meaning. For yet other examples, see Chapter 11 on pragmatics. Here I would just like to mention a related point, namely that not all sentences can be considered with respect to their truth or falsity. For instance, non-declarative sentences, that is, questions or commands, do not have truth values. It does not make sense to ask about the truth or falsity of *Who is Adam waiting for?* or *Wait for Roz!* In the past, this led some scholars to claim that only declarative sentences may be considered to have propositional content (and therefore to fall within the domain of semantics as opposed to pragmatics). Nowadays, however, questions and commands, with their accompanying responses, are viewed as having propositional content, and equivalents of truth values; namely so called answer values in the case of questions, and compliance values in the case of commands. Non-declarative sentences are thus treated on a par with declarative ones.

Recommended readings

There are many introductory books on semantics which deal extensively with the issues that this chapter has focused on, namely reference, sense and propositional meaning. You will find a very good and clear discussion of all of these in Cruse (2004) and especially Allan (2001). Both offer good exercises. Another good introductory textbook which offers some interesting comparisons of English with other languages is Goddard (1998). If you are especially interested in reference and definiteness, you should have a look at the introductory chapters of Lyons (1999). Sense and sense relations, in turn, receive an excellent extensive treatment in Croft and Cruse (2004). And for an elementary but very good introduction to propositional semantics, I suggest Hurford and Heasley (1983). If you would like to consider the more formal aspects of semantics, Cann (1993) is a good choice.

CHAPTER 11

Pragmatics

JONATHAN CULPEPER AND GILA SCHAUER

11.1   What is Pragmatics?

Consider this example:

[11.1]   [Travelling in a car, past a field with cows in it]
    Jonathan: They're lying down...means it's going to rain.
    Emily: Well, what if it doesn't.
    Natalie: They'd be lying.

The word *lying* has two senses, either telling untruths or the opposite of standing/sitting. What determines which sense or, indeed, whether both senses should be understood? The word *well* clearly has nothing to do with being healthy. What is it doing here? The pronoun *they* would be difficult to understand without the situational context. What is it referring to? And what is *it* referring to? These, and other aspects of this short dialogue, illustrate the *indeterminate* nature of language: meanings are not simply matched to language forms on a one-to-one basis. Pragmatics accepts the existence of indeterminacy – unlike traditional syntactic and semantics theories – and offers principled ways in which it can be handled. It focuses on language use in context, not language in the abstract.

Views about what the field of Pragmatics encompasses and what its main thrust should be are controversial. Two principal camps can be identified, one involving a relatively narrow view and the other a relatively broad view.

The narrow view: syntax, semantics and pragmatics

Many notions in pragmatics can be seen in the work of the American philosopher Charles Sanders Peirce (1839–1914) and his work on **pragmatism**, or even earlier writers – Immanuel Kant or Plato, for example. However, it was another American philosopher, Charles Morris (1901–1979), drawing on Peirce's work along with that of Rudolph Carnap, who provided a point of departure for the field of pragmatics. In his *Foundations of the Theory of Signs* (1938: 6–7), Morris argues for the following three-way distinction:

- Syntax (or syntactics) = mono relationship (relationships between linguistic signs)

- Semantics = dyadic relationship (relationships between linguistic signs and the things in the world that they designate)
- Pragmatics = triadic relationship (relationships between linguistic signs, things they designate and their users/interpreters)

This has provided linguists with a way of understanding how pragmatics relates to other key areas of linguistics.[1] Specifically, it distinguishes pragmatics as the area that deals with context, but also makes clear that it has some aspects in common with syntax and semantics. Pragmatics is seen as another component in a theory of language, adding to the usual phonetics, phonology, morphology, grammar/syntax and semantics. Moreover, the objective, in this view, is usually to get pragmatics to 'rescue' other more formal areas of linguistic theory. This view of Pragmatics is often identified as the Anglo-American view. The topics typically discussed within it include: reference (also discussed in Chapters 9 and 10), deixis and presupposition, speech acts and implicature – all of which will be treated in this chapter.

The broad view: pragmatic functions

What is often identified as the Continental European view of pragmatics does not exclude the kind of topic areas discussed in the Anglo-American view, but it encompasses much beyond them and has a rather different perspective. In this view pragmatics is the superordinate field, with disciplines such as linguistics, sociology and psychology as sub-fields. Thus, the range of topic areas is potentially huge. Moreover, pragmatics is not simply about adding a contextual dimension to a theory of language, but a 'general cognitive, social, and cultural perspective on linguistic phenomena in relation to their usage in forms of behaviour' (Verschueren, 1999: 7). The first part of this quotation indicates that pragmatics is not simply sited within linguistics, but could equally be within cognitive, social or cultural fields of study. The middle part of this quotation indicates that pragmatics does not look at linguistic phenomena *per se*, but only at linguistic phenomena in actual usage (the abstract patterns that characterize many areas of linguistic theory are not to be found here). And finally note that the last part of the quotation broadens the object of analysis to behaviour, which is to say, what people **do**, whether with language or something else, in social contexts. In practice, this view of pragmatics emphasizes a socio-cultural perspective on the functioning of language. Our section on cross-cultural pragmatics at the end of this chapter, for example, is more typical of this pragmatic view. Also, the topics that appear in Part 5 of this book, English: Communication and Interaction, could sit easily within this view. Regarding example [11.1] above, this pragmatic view would not ignore the indeterminacies noted earlier and how they might be resolved, but considerably more discussion would be devoted to the fact that it is a joke. How does the joke work? Why is it being told here (what are its social functions)?

It is important, however, that one should not overemphasize differences between the Anglo-American and the Continental European views. A topic such as politeness, as discussed in Chapter 31, has a foothold in both, as it both seeks to explain some aspects of linguistic structure and some aspects of social function. Moreover, one could argue that any comprehensive analysis of linguistic data should do both, as indeed this chapter attempts to do.

11.2   On the semantic-pragmatic interface: A glance at deixis and presuppositions

Deixis

Regarding example [11.1], people present during this interaction would have had less difficulty interpreting the referents of *they* if they had seen that I was looking at the cows when I said it. Just as my head and eyes pointed towards the cows, certain expressions can point towards aspects of the context. These are deictic expressions. Consider these definitions of deixis:

> By deixis is meant the location and identification of persons, objects, events, processes and activities being talked about, or referred to, in relation to the spatio-temporal context created and sustained by the act of utterance and the participation in it, typically, of a single speaker and at least one addressee.
>
> (Lyons, 1977: 37)

> Deixis concerns the ways in which languages encode or grammaticalize features of the context of utterance or speech event, and thus also concerns ways in which the interpretation of utterances depends on the analysis of that context of utterance.
>
> (Levinson, 1983: 54)

The first quotation is in fact from a semantics book, and the second, from a pragmatics book, talks about grammaticalized features. Deictic expressions are part of systems that contribute to the formal structure of languages. But they are clearly also pragmatic in that they specify a particular relationship with the context which is not encoded, but needs to be inferred. Consider these words written on a post-it note found on the floor of the corridor of my department: 'I'll be back in five minutes.' One's understanding of this would be rather limited, because one doesn't know the context. In fact, *I* referred to the first author of this chapter, *be back* referred to his return to his office (on whose door the post-it note had been attached), and *in five minutes* referred to a point of time 5 minutes ahead of when he left the note. The reason it was difficult to understand this note is that it is not anchored to a particular point regarding person (who will be back?), time (5 minutes from when?) and space (back to where?) – it has no clear deictic centre. The default deictic centre of an expression is usually assumed to be the person who produced it, and the time and place in which they produced it. However, there are occasions when we project the deictic centre, as when you tell your friend that you are *coming over* to their house (*coming* suggests movement towards a deictic centre, thus you have projected the deictic centre from yourself to the person you are addressing).

There are different kinds of relationship involved in deixis. The big three are:

Person: Typically personal pronouns, e.g., *I*, *you*, *we*, etc.

Spatial: Typically demonstratives, and certain adverbs, verbs of motion and prepositions, e.g., *this*, *that*, *here*, *there*, *come*, *go*, *opposite*, *away*, etc.

Temporal: Typically adverbs and names for units of time, and, e.g., *now*, *then*, *recently*, *soon*, *today*, *tomorrow*, *yesterday*, *next week*, etc.

Other types of deixis include **social deixis**, distinguished by the fact that it captures a social relationship. It is often achieved via terms of address (e.g., *Jonny*, *Jonathan*, *Mr Culpeper*, *Dr Culpeper*), but also – particularly in languages other than English – certain pronouns (see Advances Box 11.1, for an example

ADVANCES BOX 11.1

Grammaticalized deictic expressions in the history of English

English used to have somewhat different systems of grammaticalized expressions available for deictic purposes. Regarding personal pronouns, whilst today we can use most personal pronouns to distinguish number insofar as the referent is singular or plural (e.g., *I* versus *we*), in Old English there were also the remnants of the 'dual' forms of the first- and second-person pronouns. Thus, *wit* meant we-both, and *yit* meant you-both. Moreover, there have been radical changes in second-person pronouns. Elizabethan English, for example, offered a choice between two sets of pronominal forms for the second person: the forms *ye*, *you*, *your*, *yours* and *yourself* (the *you*-forms), and the forms *thou*, *thee*, *thy*, *thine* and *thyself* (the *thou*-forms). In Old English, you simply used the first set for a plural referent and the second for a singular. But by Middle English times, the variant chosen could have significant social implications. One might say that these items had taken on a stronger social deictic role, rather than just personal. The usage of these sets is a matter of great controversy. Brown and Gilman (1960) predict that high social status equals use of *you*-forms to each other, low social status equals use of *thou*-forms to each other, high-status individuals use *thou*-forms to those of lower status, and low-status individuals use *you*-forms to those of higher status. These predictions, however, frequently do not match the facts; meanings have to be inferred from the specifics of context. Nevertheless, one can see a certain similarity in the way *you*-forms and *thou*-forms were used in earlier periods of English with the way, for example, *tu* and *vous* is used in today's French or *du* and *sie* in German. More recently, of course, except for in some areas of Yorkshire and Lancashire, *thou*-forms have become obsolete. The fact that English second-person pronouns have been reduced to a single set of forms based on *you*, without any encoded meanings regarding number or social position, marks English out as distinct from many languages, especially European.

of this), affixes and particles. Note that the examples of deictic expressions given in this section cannot be assumed to be *always* acting deictically. For example, in the utterance *you just can't get decent service these days*, the item *you* does not point to anybody in particular but refers impersonally to anybody (it could be replaced by the pronoun *one*) – it is not used deictically.

Presupposition

Presupposition is a notion that inhabits semantics and pragmatics books in equal measure. It has its roots in logic and philosophy (notably in the work of Gottlob Frege), where it has been much discussed. It has something to do with linguistic form, yet it also requires a pragmatic inference to be made; that is, for a full understanding, it requires the target to work out aspects of meaning beyond what is specified by the linguistic form (much as the referring expressions in example [11.1] require pragmatic inferencing for full understanding). It should not be confused with the everyday usage of this term, where it is taken as near enough synonymous with the term *assumption*, meaning that something is taken as being true without any explicit evidence (e.g., *by the 1980s many of its presuppositions/assumptions were being questioned*). The technical sense of presupposition is more restricted, referring to: 'certain pragmatic inferences or assumptions [which] seem at least to be built into linguistic expressions and which can be isolated using specific linguistic tests' (Levinson, 1983: 168).

You are reading this chapter. In fact, you cannot see that the chapter exists. Yet the expression *this chapter* invites you to infer that it does: it is an **existential presupposition**. Consider another example: *We are glad to write this chapter.* Being truly *glad* about something presupposes that that something truly happened (i.e., that we wrote the chapter is a fact). This is a **factive presupposition**. Note the presupposition is not what is asserted by the sentence (essentially, what is being claimed about the subject of the sentence); it is a background assumption taken for granted. It is largely for this reason that what is presupposed generally survives when the sentence is negated. Thus, the sentence *We are not glad to write this chapter* still contains exactly the same presupposition about the fact that we wrote it (as well as the embedded presupposition that the chapter exists) (the assertion about our not being glad is, of course, untrue!). Hence, we have the classic presupposition test of **constancy under negation**. Note in our example that the presupposition is conventionally associated with particular linguistic forms – a definite noun phrase (*this chapter*), a particular emotive verb expression (*are glad*). Such linguistic forms are called **presuppositional triggers**. Table 11.1 summarizes the types of presupposition and presuppositional trigger that are generally discussed in the literature (see, in particular, Levinson, 1983: 181–4, for further references). It should be noted that there is disagreement in the literature about types of presupposition and whether particular items are presuppositions at all.

Table 11.1 captures conventional ways in which presuppositions are embedded in English. Other languages will have their own sets of presuppositional triggers, which will overlap to varying degrees. Presuppositional triggers do not determine presuppositions, but rather have the potential to trigger an inference

Table 11.1   Types of presupposition and presuppositional triggers[2]

Type	Presuppositional trigger	Example	Presupposition
Specific existential	A definite noun phrase (a definite article, demonstrative, possessive pronoun or *s*-genitive followed by a noun phrase, or a proper noun)	*My car is red*	≫There is a car which is mine
Non-specific existential	*Wh*-questions (i.e., questions beginning *who, what, when, why, where* or *how*)	*Who drove fast?*	≫There is somebody who drove fast
	Cleft (or pseudo-cleft) sentences	*It wasn't me that drove fast*	≫There is somebody who drove fast
Factive[3]	Factive emotive verbs (e.g., *regret, be sorry, be glad*)	*I regret driving fast*	≫I drove fast
	Factive epistemic verbs (e.g., *realize, know, be obvious*)	*I realize that I was driving fast*	≫I drove fast
Counterfactive	Counterfactual verbs (e.g., *imagined, dreamed*)	*I pretended to drive fast*	≫I was not driving fast
	Counterfactual conditionals	*If I had been driving fast, I might have crashed*	≫I had not been driving fast
Other	Implicative verbs (e.g., *manage, forget, be aware, know, be obvious*)	*I managed to drive fast*	≫I tried to drive fast
	Change-of-state (inchoative) verbs (e.g., *stop, begin, enter, come, go*)	*I stopped driving fast*	≫I had been driving fast
	Iteratives (adverbs and verbs) (e.g., *again, returned, repeat*)	*I drove fast again*	≫I had been driving fast
	Temporal clauses (subordinate clauses beginning *when, before, while, since, after,* etc.)	*When I drove fast, I skidded*	≫I had been driving fast

about what is presupposed. Importantly, what is presupposed is defeasible, which means that what is inferred can be cancelled or at least suspended. Thus, when you read the sentence *We are glad to write this chapter* above, if you knew that we were accepting an invitation to write it, you would cancel the presupposition that we had written it or were currently writing it (i.e., that all or some of it existed). Similarly, in the sentence *We are glad to write this chapter, if nobody else can be found who will write it*, the content of the if-clause blocks the presuppositions that we had written it and that it existed. Note here that the presupposition was cancelled when we created a complex sentence. The ability, or otherwise, of presuppositions to survive in complex sentences is a tricky issue, frequently referred to as the **projection problem**.

ADVANCES BOX 11.2

Presuppositions and assumed common ground

Is presupposed information assumed to be true by *both* the speaker and hearer, and the speaker assumes that both assume this, and so on? Some researchers (e.g., Karttunen and Peters, 1979; Stalnaker, 1972) think that presuppositions relate to assumed common ground between speaker and hearer. The reality, however, is more complex. Presuppositions can be used to trick people into accepting background assumptions which they have not and would not have. Consider this courtroom discourse. Izola Curry, on trial for the attempted murder of Dr Martin Luther King in a restaurant in 1958, was asked:

> Q: When did you find out that Dr King was going to be at Bloomstein's this afternoon?
> A: Well, I didn't find out I didn't find out. I'll answer that I didn't find out...

Clearly, Curry inferred the presupposition embedded in the *Wh*-structure (i.e., that she had found out), despite the fact that it was not common ground. Blocking this kind of presupposition is difficult, as one has pointedly to avoid answering the question; to do so would mean accepting what is presupposed.

11.3 Speech act theory

Traditionally, semanticists, influenced by writings in the philosophy of language, have focused on the *truth value* of sentences, that is, whether a sentence is a true or false representation in the light of real-world facts or conditions. Semanticists have been particularly interested in linguistic manipulations of the truth value of sentences. Compare:

(a) *Jonathan and Gila wrote the pragmatics chapter.*
(b) *Jonathan and Gila did not write the pragmatics chapter.*

If (a) is true, then (b) is false; if (b) is true, then (a) is false. Wittgenstein, however, took an entirely different tack, arguing that language was a social activity and that 'the meaning of a word is its use in the language' (1953: §43, 20, cited in Bach, 2004: 463). Both this section and the next describe aspects of meaning and use.

The language philosopher J. L. Austin ([1962] 1975) – who apparently once lived in Lancaster – observed that some declarative sentences seemed not to concern matters of truth (i.e., they are not truth conditional). He focused in particular on a special class of verbs, **performative verbs**, whose purpose is to 'do things', for example:

- I *pronounce* you man and wife.
- I *sentence* you to six months' imprisonment.
- I *apologize* for the noise.

Performative verbs name the action they perform, and can often be identified by the 'hereby test'. All of the above examples could accept the word *hereby* before the performative verb (though the formality of the word would make it sound odd for an everyday apology). Moreover, performative verbs, as above, typically co-occur with the first-person singular pronoun, and in sentences which are present tense, active and indicative. Such sentences are **performative utterances**. The use of the term 'utterances', rather than sentences, captures the fact that we are talking about a concrete performance of language, an act, rather than an abstract category. Such acts are not dependent on truth conditions, but instead are dependent on a set of contextual factors, which Austin termed **felicity conditions**. Note, for example, that if a judge sentenced somebody in a courtroom according to established procedure, one could not dismiss the sentencing as false (untrue), as the judge would have acted appropriately (felicitously) in performing the **act** of sentencing. If, however, it turned out that the judge was in fact the court-cleaner or that the judge had sentenced the defendant at the beginning of the trial instead of at the end, then the act of sentencing would not be felicitous. The felicity conditions associated with particular speech acts overlap with what subsequent researchers have referred to as 'pragmatic presuppositions'.

Austin further observed that utterances do not need a performative verb to perform an act. Compare:

(a)   *I promise to give you the money back tomorrow.*
(b)   *I'll give you the money tomorrow.*

Both involve an act of promising: (a) is usually referred to as an explicit performative, and (b) an implicit performative. Towards the end of his book, Austin shifted position, concluding that all utterances, not just explicit performative utterances, involve an act. Even declarative sentences, like *We are glad to write this chapter*, perform an act: they **assert** that a particular state of affairs applies. So, in this view, performative utterances are just a particular kind of **speech act**. In fact, it was just as well that Austin made this shift, as hitherto his scheme was better suited to English, which is richer in performative verbs compared to many other languages.

Austin suggested that there were three aspects to every speech act, which we can simplify thus (for more detailed definitions, see Austin (1975: 94–132):

- **Locutionary** – the production of a meaningful expression
- **Illocutionary** – the action intended by the expression
- **Perlocutionary** – the effect of the expression on the hearer

For example, in a hot classroom, I might articulate to the student sitting next to the window the words *It's hot in here* (locutionary act), intending that they open the window (illocutionary act of request), with the effect that they open the window (perlocutionary act). Although speech act theory encompasses all three aspects, in subsequent work the notion of a speech act is virtually synonymous with **illocutionary act or force**. Speech acts include, for example, assertions, requests, commands, apologies, threats, compliments, warnings and advice. They are what the speaker intends to do in saying something.

Austin's notion of felicity conditions was developed and formalized by his student J. R. Searle (1969). Searle tried to devise **constitutive rules** for speech acts; that is, rules that create the activity itself, just as is the case with a game of football or chess. Consider his felicity conditions for a speech act of promising (adapted from Searle, 1969: 63):

Table 11.2   *Felicity conditions and promising*

Felicity condition	*Clarification*	*Exemplification: Conditions for promising*
Propositional content	What the utterance is about (what the utterance predicates)	Future A (act) of S (the speaker)
Preparatory	Real-world pre-requisites (the interlocutors' beliefs about ability to perform the act, the act's costs or benefits, its norms of occurrence, etc.)	1. H (the hearer) wants S to perform A 2. It is not obvious that S will do A in the normal course of events
Sincerity	The beliefs, feelings and intentions of the speaker	S intends to do A
Essential	What is needed for the act to be performed (i.e., the mutual recognition that the speaker intends an utterance to count as a certain act)	Counts as an undertaking by S of an obligation to do A

This scheme seems to have the potential to distinguish one speech act from another, and thereby to offer a robust and comprehensive description of speech acts. For example, in order to achieve a description of the speech act of threat, we simply need to tweak one felicity condition of promising: changing the first preparatory condition to 'H does not want S to perform A'. In practice, however, such descriptions are of limited use, notably because speech acts do not lend themselves to neat to categorization (see Advances Box 11.3).

Searle called the formal devices of an utterance used to express illocutionary force **illocutionary force indicating devices** (IFIDs). We have already met a very explicit IFID, namely, performative verbs. IFIDs need not be lexical or grammatical: a rising intonation contour has some kind of conventional association with speech acts that question or inquire. It is crucial, however, to remember that even with IFIDs there is no guarantee of a particular illocutionary force – that depends on the rest of the discourse and the context (e.g., *I promise I'll withhold your pocket-money* is a threat not a promise, despite the IFID). The issue of form and whether it matches a particular illocutionary force is pertinent to the apparent correspondence between grammatical sentence type (or form) and speech act (or illocutionary force). In English, there are three major

Sentence type and speech act correspondences   *Table 11.3*

Sentence type	Example	Speech act
Imperative	*Finish your homework!*	Command
Interrogative	*Have you finished your homework?*	Question/inquiry
Declarative	*My homework is finished.*	Assertion

Sentence type and speech act mismatches   *Table 11.4*

Sentence type	Example	Speech act
Imperative	*Give me a hand*	Request
Interrogative	*Can you give me a hand?*	Request
Declarative	*I can't do this on my own*	Request

sentence types which are associated with three speech acts, as displayed in Table 11.3. The problem is that in present-day English there is frequently a mismatch between sentence type and speech act. Consider Table 11.4.

Despite the mismatches between requests and the interrogative and declarative sentence types, it is not difficult to imagine contexts where these would count as requests. Note that they differ in terms of how directly the speech act is performed. *Give me a hand* is direct; *Can you give me a hand?* is conventionally indirect; and *I can't do this on my own* is non-conventionally indirect or off-record (i.e., a hint). The second and third examples here fit Searle's classic definition of indirect speech acts: 'cases in which one illocutionary act is performed indirectly by way of performing another' (1975: 60). With respect to our second example, Searle's idea is that you first understand that it is a question, but then work out that it is actually a request. In fact, it is rather doubtful whether people actually do this in their heads for all cases, particularly for conventionalized indirect requests, like the *can/could you X* type here. Nevertheless, the idea that speech acts vary according to directness has had a huge impact on scholarship, particularly on (1) politeness research, where being more indirect is often correlated with being more polite, at least in British English culture (see Chapter 31, and in particular Section 31.3.2), and (2) cross-cultural pragmatics, where the amount of directness, as well as how it is perceived, has been shown to vary from culture to culture (British culture is usually assumed to favour much indirectness).

11.5 Grice's conversational implicature

H. P. Grice (e.g., 1989), another language philosopher, produced work on meaning and communication that has had a huge impact on pragmatics. His key insight was that meaning in communication is more than the face value (or conventional) meaning of the words that are said. This point was echoed in our discussion of speech acts. Take our earlier example *It's hot in here*. At

---

ADVANCES BOX 11.3

Problems with speech act theory

Much work has detailed problems with classical speech act theory and/or suggested revised schemes or improvements (Bach and Harnish, 1979; Leech, 1983: ch. 9; Thomas, 1995: 94–107 – to mention but a few). Let us briefly consider two issues: (1) the indeterminacy of the concept, and (2) its status in discourse.

Speech acts have fuzzy edges. Consider the following sets:

- suggestion / advice / warning / threat
- apologizing / informing
- ordering / requesting / inviting

It is difficult to specify where one speech act ends and the next begins. Moreover, speakers may intend speech acts to be indeterminate (resistant to classification). As Leech puts it:

> The indeterminacy of conversational utterances...shows itself in the NEGOTIABILITY of pragmatic factors; that is, by leaving the force unclear, S may leave H the opportunity to choose between one force and another, and thus leaves part of the responsibility of the meaning to H. For instance,
>
> 'If I were you I'd leave town straight away'
>
> can be interpreted according to the context as a piece of advice, a warning, or a threat. Here H, knowing something about S's likely intentions, may interpret it as a threat, and act on it as such; but S will always be able to claim that it was a piece of advice, given from the friendliest of motives. In this way, the 'rhetoric of conversation' may show itself in S's ability to have his cake and eat it.
>
> (1983: 23–4)

Speech acts are often played out over a number of turns. Consider the conversation below, in which A pursues a goal of changing the TV channel:

A: Are you watching this?
B: No
A: Do you mind if I change the channel?
B: No

A's first utterance seems to be a question, but it is also a pre-request of some kind. Thus, speech acts are not simply couched in the single sentences that you see discussed so often in the literature, but form sequences.

---

face value, it is about the temperature in the room, but the speaker clearly meant more by it than this. The communicative meaning, so Grice argued, is what the speaker intended those words to mean (i.e., a request to open the window). In fact, Grice went further and argued that communicative meaning is reflexive; that is to say, when you intend to communicate something,

ADVANCES BOX 11.4

Pragmatic meaning

Speaker-meaning might be summarized by the formula: S [= speaker] meant M by utterance U. However, other researchers have emphasized the role of the hearer in interpreting both the utterance and the context in which it appears. Regarding context, we have the particular difficulty that the speaker and hearer cannot know for sure that they know exactly the same context; they can only assume that they share aspects of the context. All this means that the formula should be extended to something like: S in context C^1 meant M^1 by utterance U, which was interpreted as M^2 by H [= hearer] in context C^2. Thus, *It's hot in here* might be interpreted as intending to mean *Please open the window* if the hearer makes the same contextual assumptions about the hot state of the room, the possibility of opening the window for cool air, etc.. On the other hand, the hearer might make different contextual assumptions and assume it is intended as a comment on, for example, the heated argument that has just taken place in that room. Grice's work is not well equipped to deal with these issues, not least of all because it provides limited treatment of context. A more promising framework in this respect is **Relevance theory** (Sperber and Wilson 1995). The reason for this is that Relevance theory encompasses not just communication but also cognition, and it is cognition that can help explain how people construct contexts in their heads in order to account for what something means.

you intend the target to recognize your intention to communicate that something. This may seem like a bit of philosophical nonsense, but expressing an intention without the target recognizing that you have done so would mean that you have not **communicated** your meaning. Note here the focus on **speaker-meaning** – what the speaker intends to communicate and how they communicate it.

In the remainder of this section we will consider key aspects of Grice's theory of **conversational implicature**, first detailed in 1967, but only officially published in 1975 (and reprinted in 1989).[4] This theory offers an account of the relation between what someone says and what they mean. As a preliminary, let us untangle some terminology which is somewhat muddled in everyday English usage:

- **Imply** – The speaker generates some meaning beyond what is said (i.e., the conventional or semantic meaning of the words).
- **Implicature** (a technical term devised by Grice) – The implied meaning generated intentionally by the speaker (see also below).
- **Infer** – The hearer derives new meaning from available evidence (e.g., what is said, the context).
- **Inference** The inferred meaning derived by the hearer, which may or may not be the same as the speaker's intended implicature.

Grice proposed that contributions to conversation are not random, irrational or disconnected, but follow a general principle: the Cooperative Principle. He states this as follows: 'Make your contribution such as is required, at the stage at which it occurs, by the accepted purpose or direction of the talk exchange in which you are engaged' (1989: 26). In subsequent research, some debate has emerged as to what this cooperation consists of. Is it social cooperation (i.e., interlocutors help each other achieve their real-world desires motivating the conversation)? Is it informational cooperation (i.e., interlocutors help each other achieve understanding within the conversation)? The first interpretation is unrealistic as a principle underpinning all communication, as any communication that is at all antisocial falls by the wayside. The second interpretation is possible as a general principle. Even antisocial utterances, such as 'you're stupid' or 'piss off', still cooperate, and are assumed to abide by the Cooperative Principle, in providing enough information for the target to be able to understand the speaker's antisocial intentions.

The Cooperative Principle includes the following four maxims (simplified from Grice, 1989: 26–7):

(i) **Maxim of Quantity:** (1) Make your contribution as informative as is required (for the current purpose of the exchange); (2) Do not make your contribution more informative than is required.
(ii) **Maxim of Quality:** (1) Do not say what you believe to be false; (2) Do not say that for which you lack evidence.
(iii) **Maxim of Relation:** Be relevant
(iv) **Maxim of Manner:** (1) Avoid obscurity of expression; (2) Avoid ambiguity; (3) Be brief; (4) Be orderly.

Grice argues that we make an assumption that generally people proceed in accordance with the Cooperative Principle. Certainly it is difficult to see how conversation could proceed if we regularly nattered on about irrelevancies, and expressed it all in an unclear fashion. However, importantly, he describes some of the ways in which the interlocutors may fail to fulfil a maxim (1989: 30). One can 'quietly and unostentatiously *violate* a maxim', sometimes misleading the hearer. A lie, for example, is an example of a violation of the maxim of quality. One can 'opt out' from both a maxim and the Cooperative Principle. A politician saying 'no comment' would be explicitly opting out. One might have a clash. For example, in academic writing, one is often faced with balancing saying as much as possible about something (maxim of quantity) with saying only as much as you really have evidence for (maxim of quality). Finally, Grice describes the particularly important category of **flouts**, where the speaker 'blatantly' fails to fulfil a maxim. It is important because this is when implicatures are generated. For example, saying to somebody *you are a rock* is blatantly untrue in a literal sense; it flouts the maxim of quality. But Grice's point is that if you assume the Cooperative Principle does in fact apply, then the exploitation of the maxim can be taken as a signal for you to work out how it applies. Thus, in an appropriate context (e.g., you have supported your friend during a difficult period), the utterance *you are a rock* might be taken to implicate that the hearer has positive rock-like qualities – they are loyal and steadfast. The implicature maintains consistency between what is being said and the Cooperative Principle.

ILLUSTRATION BOX 11.1

Flouts of Grice's maxims

The following are examples of flouts of maxims and their possible implicatures.

Relation

[A is working at a computer in library when she experiences a problem.]

> A: Can you help me?
> B: Try the librarian.

Implicature: I mean no (but the librarian might be able to).

Quantity

[A, sensitive about his lack of progress in Italian, has just returned from an Italian evening class. B is his wife.]

> B: What did you do?
> A: This and that.

Implicature: I mean this is not a topic I wish to discuss.

Quality

[Victor has been buried up to his neck in the back garden by an irate builder. His wife, Margaret, comes out and sees him.]

> M: What are you doing?
> V: I'm wallpapering the spare bedroom...
>
> (One Foot in the Grave, BBC 12/11/1996)

Implicature: I mean it is obvious that I'm not doing anything, I am stuck.

Manner

[E adores strawberries, and would willingly base her diet entirely on them. A and B, her parents, aim to restrict how frequently she eats them. A addresses B, with E in earshot.]

> A: Shall I get the you-know-whats out of the fridge?

Implicature: I mean the food she will go crazy about if I mention it.

Grice (1989: 39) proposed that implicatures have a number of specific characteristics. Perhaps the most important is that, like presuppositions, they are defeasible (can be cancelled). And, if they are defeasible, this means that (1) they are not simply a part of the conventional meaning of what is said, and (2) they are sensitive to context. For instance, in the final example of the

---

ADVANCES BOX 11.5

More on the non-observance of maxims

There are other ways of not observing the maxims. Grice (1989: 39) mentions that implicatures can be 'contextually cancelled', and hints at contextual sensitivity in various places. There are contexts in which there is no expectation that all the maxims will be observed, and so no implicatures can be derived. Compare an interrogation with a confessional. In the former, it is assumed that the person being interrogated is likely to opt out of the maxims of quantity (and/or quality); in the latter, it is assumed that the person 'confessing' will strongly uphold the maxim of quality. If we accept the idea that maxims can be *suspended* to some degree, then cross-cultural differences in communication, such as those found in Malagasy culture by Keenan (1976), can more easily be accommodated by the Cooperative Principle.

Thomas (1995: 74) mentions the possibility of *infringing* a maxim, where 'a speaker who, with no intention of generating an implicature and with no intention of deceiving, fails to observe a maxim'. She adds that such non-observance could occur because:

> the speaker has an imperfect command of the language (a young child or a foreign learner), because the speaker's performance is impaired in some way (nervousness, drunkenness, excitement), because of some cognitive impairment, or simply because the speaker is constitutionally incapable of speaking clearly, to the point, etc'

There is an interesting connection with people's personalities here. Consider this Snoopy cartoon:

Peanuts © 1971 United Syndication Inc.

Illustrations Box above, A could have added *Oh, I forgot, she doesn't like strawberries any more*. In fact, defeasibility is one of the most important general characteristics of pragmatics, and one that ties in with the indeterminacy mentioned at various points in this chapter.

11.6.1 Pragmatics across languages and cultures

How would you react if someone were to say to you *Greet God!* instead of *Hello* or *Good morning*? Would you think that that person was very religious in apparently asking you to greet God? Would you think the person is trying to be humorous? Or would you just categorize it as 'odd behaviour'?

Your reaction would probably depend on a number of contextual variables, such as the cultural norms that you were brought up with, your own native language, the number of foreign languages you speak and how familiar you are with different cultures and the way people from different cultures express themselves in either their first or foreign language.

How you perceive and evaluate utterances such as the above is very closely related to the pragmatic norms and conventions of your first language (Gudykunst and Kim, 2003; Schauer, 2006; Wierzbicka, 2003). Each language has its own pragmatic norms, which may be similar to that of another language or not. If the pragmatic norms of two languages differ very much, native speakers of these two languages may find it difficult to understand what their interlocutor is really trying to say. Researchers investigating how greetings and other speech acts are performed in different cultures work in a subfield of pragmatics called **cross-cultural** or **intercultural pragmatics**. Yule (1996: 87) defines cross-cultural pragmatics as 'the study of differences in expectations based on cultural schemata' whereby an individual's cultural schemata are 'culturally determined' and 'developed … in the contexts of our basic experiences'. Wierzbicka argues that four fundamental points form the basis of cross-cultural pragmatics:

1. In different societies, and different communities, people speak differently.
2. These differences in ways of speaking are profound and systematic.
3. These differences reflect different cultural values, or at least different hierarchies of values.
4. Different ways of speaking, different communicative styles, can be explained and made sense of, in terms of independently established different cultural values and cultural priorities.

(2003: 69)

One of the seminal research projects in the field of cross-cultural pragmatics is the *Cross-Cultural Speech Act Realization Project* (Blum-Kulka, House and Kasper, 1989), to which scholars from a variety of countries contributed. The data for the project were collected with Discourse Completion Tasks (DCTs), which are pragmatic production questionnaires that provide a description of a specific scenario followed by a blank space for participants to fill in their response. The findings of the project suggested that when making requests, native speakers of Argentinean Spanish and Hebrew were considerably more direct than Australian English native speakers, while native speakers of Canadian French and German were located in the middle of the scale (Blum-Kulka and House 1989: 149).

In addition to its cross-cultural focus, the project also contrasted how native speakers (British English, Danish, German) and learners of a foreign language (Danish learners of German and Danish learners of English) perform requests (Faerch and Kasper, 1989). The researchers found that learners had a tendency to be more verbose than native speakers, which was later termed the 'waffle phenomenon' (Edmondson and House, 1991), thus giving 'the conversational principle of clarity priority over the principle of quantity' (Faerch and Kasper, 1989: 245).

Pragmatic investigations that compare how learners and native speakers communicate in a specific language belong to the subfield of **interlanguage pragmatics**. Interlanguage pragmatics is concerned with learners' use and awareness of the rules and conventions of their second or foreign language and has been defined in more detail as

> the study of second language use, interlanguage pragmatics examines how nonnative speakers comprehend and produce action in a target language. As the study of second language learning, interlanguage pragmatics investigates how L2 learners develop the ability to understand and perform action in a target language.
>
> (Kasper and Rose, 2002: 5)

Our example of *Greet God* at the beginning of this section is a direct translation of *Grüss Gott!* a frequently used greeting in southern Germany, which is employed by nearly all members of society irrespective of whether they are Christian or not. From a cross-cultural pragmatics perspective it is interesting that today there does not appear to be a commonly used British English (originally religious) counterpart with the same pragmatic function (i.e., a greeting). If a German native speaker were to use this greeting in English, it would be regarded as negative pragmatic transfer (Kasper, 1992; Thomas, 1983) from their native language, because it would not be understood as an unmarked (i.e., typical, frequently used), appropriate greeting by speakers of English. This also shows that cross-cultural pragmatics and interlanguage pragmatics can be closely linked, as learners of a foreign language may translate expressions that are pragmatically appropriate in their first language into their second language, such as the following examples reported by Bodman and Eisenstein (1988):

(i)   Response to a friend who brought along a gift from a Punjabi native speaker in English:
Why did you bother to bring a gift? Your presence is a big gift for me. (p. 13)

(ii) Response to colleague offering a farewell from a Punjabi native speaker in English:
Oh, really, indeed, there is no need for a party. You are making a big deal out of nothing. Moreover, I am not going far away, and I will stop by to see you. (p. 13)

(iii) Response to boss offering a pay rise from a Chinese native speaker in English:
Thank you very much. But I think I have not done so well to get such a raise. Anyway, I'd try to do better. (p. 14)

The examples above indicate that the Punjabi and Chinese native speakers consider stating the lack of necessity for the positive act directed at them (scenario 1) or refusing to accept the positive act directed at them (scenario 2 and 3) to be the appropriate response in English. While mentioning the interlocutor's non-existent obligation to perform a positive act towards the recipient is a strategy also employed by English native speakers in expressions of gratitude, native speakers tend to use formulaic expressions for scenario 1, such as *Oh, you didn't have to get me anything* (Eisenstein and Bodman, 1986: 172) or *Thank you, but you shouldn't have* (Schauer and Adolphs, 2006: 129). The following case study explores expressions of gratitude when receiving gifts in more detail.

11.6.2   Case study on expressions of gratitude

Fourteen British English native speakers and twelve German native speakers, who were also advanced learners of English, filled in a DCT that included the following situation based on one of Eisenstein and Bodman's (1986) scenarios:

> It is your birthday. You and one of your friends have just sat down at a small table in a coffee shop near the university to have a quick snack before another lecture. Your friend says 'Happy birthday!' and gives you a nicely wrapped present.

The English native speakers completed the DCT in English, while the German native speakers' completed the DCT in English and German – their DCT also contained a translation of the scenario above. Figure 11.1 illustrates how frequently expressions that (1) address the gift-givers' non-existent obligation (e.g., *You shouldn't have* or *Das waere doch nicht noetig gewesen*); (2) compliment the gift-giver (e.g., *How lovely of you!* or *Danke, das ist total lieb von dir*); or (3) are exclamations of surprise and joy (e.g., *Oh wow!* or *Oah*) were employed in English and German.

The findings show that more than 50 per cent of the English native speakers who completed the DCT used an exclamation that indicated their positive feelings, whereas this was only used by 25 per cent of the Germans in their native language. Interestingly, even though some of the Germans did not use an exclamation in their L1, they employed it in English (41.66 per cent). There do not appear to be considerable differences concerning participants' thanking strategies that focus on complimenting the interlocutor or stating their non-existent obligation to give the recipient a present. The data

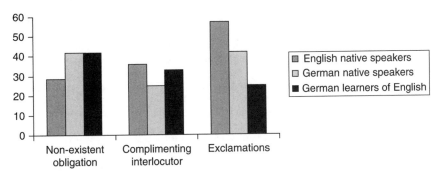

Expressions of gratitude to gift-giver in per cent

FIGURE 11.1

do show, however, that for the latter there appear to be particular formulaic expressions in English (*You shouldn't have* used in three of the four instances) and German (*Das waere [doch/aber] nicht noetig gewesen* used in four of the five instances). Surprisingly, not many of the learners were aware of the formulaic expression in English, which leads to them using expressions that could possibly be perceived as somewhat curt in this context such as *You needn't do this*. This shows that even though two languages may share the same pragmatic conventions for certain speech acts, language learners may not always be aware of the routinized formulaic expressions with which they are performed, which could result in them not doing the things with words that they had intended to do. Of course, the numbers of speakers involved in this study are rather small, but it exposes some similarities/differences that could easily be further explored with a more widely distributed DCT.

Recommended readings

A gentle and clear introduction is Yule (1996), or a somewhat more extensive introduction, with activities, is Grundy (2000). If your interests are more geared to the pragmatics of real language use, as opposed to abstract philosophical thinking, try Thomas (1995); or, if you are in interested in cognitive issues, try Green (1996). Both are accessible. An excellent stepping-stone to the more advanced literature is Huang (2007). The *Concise Encyclopedia of Pragmatics* (1998) (edited by J. Mey) contains very useful overviews of most topic areas, and similar overviews of many topics can be found in Horn and Ward (2004).

One of the earliest and most frequently quoted articles in cross-cultural pragmatics is Thomas's (1983) description of cross-cultural pragmatic failure. Another classic is the *Cross-Cultural Speech Act Realization Project* (Blum-Kulka, House and Kasper, 1989), which compared requests and apologies in a variety of L1s and L2s. A valuable, accessible, wide-ranging and up-to-date collection of papers is Spencer-Oatey (2008). If you are interested in how interlanguage pragmatics and grammar are linked, try Bardovi-Harlig and Dörnyei (1998) and Schauer (2006). Finally, on the question of whether pragmatics can be taught, Kasper (1997) and Bardovi-Harlig (2001) provide very useful overviews.

Notes

1 Morris himself was not in fact articulating a theory of language. He did not see these divisions as a matter of dividing up language, but of dividing up semiotics – the science of signs (e.g., words, gestures, pictures) and how they are organized, used to signify things and understood.

2 We thank Noel Burton-Roberts for his advice on this table. Of course, remaining errors and infelicities are ours.

3 The classic work on factivity, Kiparsky and Kiparsky (1970), discusses verbs that presuppose the **truth** of their complements, and subsequent scholars have largely restricted their discussions to such verbs. The notion of factivity is not generally taken to involve the existence of facts – a state of actuality.

4 Grice also proposed the category **conventional implicature**, suggesting the words *but* and *therefore* as examples. *But*, for instance, conventionally implicates a contrast between what comes before and after it (i.e., its conjuncts). Since few items are discussed in the literature under this heading, and, moreover, since the notion of conventional implicature overlaps with some scholars' views of presupposition, we will not discuss it here.

PART 2

English: History

EDITED BY JONATHAN CULPEPER

CHAPTER 12

Standard English and Standardization

PAUL KERSWILL AND JONATHAN CULPEPER

12.1 Introduction: what do we mean by a 'standard language'?

The other chapters in this section will to some extent focus on the history of English with **Standard English** as the endpoint. What exactly is Standard English? Where did it come from? And why does it often have such a privileged status, both generally and in histories of English? Actually, the notion of Standard English is a decidedly recent development: English had been around for about a thousand years before the development of standard written English. But our previous sentence begs another question: what exactly is English? This chapter addresses these questions. It also picks up on some of the issues, including historical ones, raised in Chapter 18 on variation in **dialects** and **accents**.

English, like most languages, exists in many forms, and is used for a vast array of purposes. As competent users of English we can immediately spot the difference between formal and informal language (for instance, in official documents vs. cartoons), and we can tell, say, an American from a British person by their accent alone. The chapter headings in this book bear witness to this diversity of uses and forms. We might then wonder how it is that, given this variation, users of English still manage to communicate effectively, making sure that what they say or write doesn't diverge too much from what is either **intelligible** or **acceptable** to the person they are addressing. So we can simultaneously send a formal email to somebody in Canada and another to somebody in Ghana, and the import of the message will be well understood in both places. The same goes for a text message, even though we might use conventions like 'u r' for *you are*, because these conventions, like the 'normal' English of the email, are valid across continents. Sharing conventions of this sort is part of a wider human tendency to share **norms of behaviour** with other members of the same community, which may be a village, or among a group defined by a common interest, such as adolescent skaters. We see these norms in styles of clothing and shared tastes, and also in characteristic ways of speaking, including accent, dialect and slang.

For most of the European languages, and many others too, this conventionalization is taken to a further stage through the existence of a **standard** form of the language. Often this form is known simply as the **standard** language – perhaps misleadingly so, because this suggests that it is an entity entirely separate from other varieties of the language. For now, we can adopt the following fairly comprehensive definition:

> A standard language is usually identified as a relatively uniform variety of a language which does not show **regional variation,** and which is used in a wide range of communicative functions (e.g., official language, medium of instruction, literary language, scientific language, etc.). Standard varieties tend to observe prescriptive, written norms, which are codified in grammars and dictionaries. They are thus different from non-standard varieties, whose norms are generally uncodified and unwritten.
>
> (Swann, Deumert, Lillis and Mesthrie, 2004: 295)

The possession of a standard language is often seen as advantageous to a society, because it allows people right across its territory, and in different walks of life, to communicate more easily than if only regional dialects were available. This is most obviously so in the written medium, where **standardization** is usually much more complete than in speech. Standardization is the process leading to the emergence of a standard language, and involves the reduction in variability in terms of the grammatical and vocabulary choices that can be made. For example, in earlier forms of English multiple negatives were frequent, but not universal, even in the written language. Today, Standard English insists on a single negation of the type *I don't want any* as opposed to **I don't want none.* The written Standard English of the United Kingdom and that of the United States are grammatically very similar. On the other hand, educated people within the **same** country differ in the way they speak, even if we disregard accent differences. They are often not aware that their usages are not adopted everywhere. Even so, in the course of a conversation, there are relatively few points at which Standard English speakers could differ one from another. Illustration Box 12.1 shows a few of these differences.

A consequence of seeing a standard language as being essentially uniform is the idea that it functions as a true 'standard' in the way that kilograms and metres do. Trade relies on a standardized set of weights and measures, and buyers and sellers need to trust the value of the money they use. Standard English is regarded as a kind of 'gold standard' against which other types of English are measured – and all too often found wanting, as we shall see shortly. Far from being a neutral standard (like the metre), Standard English is in many ways a social class dialect used by middle-class speakers. Studies have repeatedly shown that it is difficult for some children from working-class backgrounds to acquire written Standard English (Williams, 2007). Moreover, as we saw from the examples in Illustration Box 12.1, it is only in the written medium that it is possible to talk about a fully standardized language (or nearly so in the case of English).

So far, we have assumed that, despite some variability and clear differences between speech and writing, we are in no doubt as to what constitutes 'Standard English' – we know it when we see it. A more fundamental assumption still is that we can actually recognize 'English' (indeed, Chapter 1

ILLUSTRATION BOX 12.1

Standard English in writing and speech in the United States, Scotland, Northern England and Southern England

1 Writing

The usages we have listed are also characteristic of educated speech.

USA vs. UK

USA	UK	Comment
The government was unable to agree…	*The government were…*	USA singular vs. UK plural agreement for collective noun
He had never gotten anything from her…	*He had never got…*	Different participle form of *get* in the meaning 'acquire'
I dreamed, I learned, I leaped	*I dreamt, I learnt, I leapt*	USA has regular –ed past tense suffix in verbs where UK has –t suffix (and vowel change when spoken)
They just ate	*They have just eaten*	USA use of simple past for events in recent past, UK use of present perfect
She appealed the decision	*She appealed against the decision*	Different constructions required with the same word
sidewalk	*pavement*	Different word – same referent

Scotland vs. England

Scotland	England	Comment
It has been proven that…	*It has been proved that…*	Different form of the past participle of *prove*. USA mainly as England
This remains outwith the remit of the committee	*This remains outside/beyond…*	Use of *outwith* more common in Scotland. Unknown in USA
Had they a good day?	*Did they have a good day?*	*Have* as main verb can be inverted in questions in Scotland. In England and the USA, it requires the auxiliary *do*

2 Speech

In speech, more differences exist. Mostly, this is because of greater differences in informal vocabulary and differences in the way auxiliaries are used. All of the examples below could be used by people who would be considered Standard English speakers.

USA vs. UK

USA	UK	Comment
I travel for a whole bunch of reasons	*I travel for a whole lot of reasons (also USA)*	Difference in informal intensifier
Do you have any apples? Yes, I do	*Do you have any apples? Yes, I have*	Different auxiliary used in reply

Northern vs. Southern England

Northern England	Southern England	Comment
Have you not got it?	*Haven't you got it?*	Contraction less common in North
I'll not go	*I won't go*	Auxiliary contracted in North, negator in South
He's great is John	*John's great*	Different way of commenting on something already mentioned
lass	*girl*	different word – same referent

broached this very issue). Starting with English itself, let us see if both of these assumptions hold true.

12.2 What is 'English'?

Consider the statements in Illustration Box 12.2. Each of the statements in the box raises an issue related to the question, 'What is English?'. (1) suggests that British and American English are different, while there are some people who are too ignorant to speak either; (2) suggests that African American English either doesn't measure up to the standards set by English, or else that it is a different language – the question of whether or not this language variety is a form of English is in fact a politically charged debate (see Wolfram and Schilling-Estes, 1998: 169–84); (3) is Churchill's humorous riposte to an editor who tried to 'correct' a preposition placed at the end of one of the former

ILLUSTRATION BOX 12.2

Pushing at the boundaries of English

1. Americans say 'Scuba-diving is different from snorkeling,' the British often say 'different to' (though most UK style guides disapprove), and those who don't know any better say 'different than.'

   (Paul Brians: *Common Errors in English Usage*, http://www.wsu.edu/-brians/errors/different.html accessed 4 March 2008)

2. No. Ebonics [African American English] is poor grammar or another language entirely. You can't substitute 'I be' for 'I am'. It just isn't English.

   (Posting on City-Data.com poll: 'Which is your least favorite English-language accent?', http://www.city data.com/forum/general u s/217862 least favorite english language accents 9.html, accessed 4 March 2008)

3. Ending a sentence with a preposition is something up with which I will not put.

   (Winston Churchill)

4. 'It is I'

   (teacher, on entering a primary school classroom in which the first author was a pupil)

5. Me and him went shopping

6. Sometimes the past participle of a strong verb such as 'do' is used in place of the past tense. For example, 'I done it already' instead of 'I did it already' or in the case of the verb 'see,' 'I seen' instead of 'I saw.'

   (Wikipedia: Appalachian English, http://en.wikipedia.org/wiki/Appalachian English, accessed 4 March 2008)

7. Walcum tae the Scots Language Centre on line. Come awa in an hae a look roon. The site haes aa kin o information aboot Scots, the language spoken aa ower Scotland fae Shetland to Gallowa an Aiberdeen tae Glesga.

   (Scots Language Centre home page: http://www.scotslanguage.com/, accessed 13 March 2008)

8. Language in the lower class ... consists more of a relatively small repertoire of stereotyped phrases and expressions which are used rather loosely without much effort to achieve a subtle correspondence between perception and verbal expression. Much of lower-class language consists of incidental 'emotional' accompaniment to action here and now. ... [M]iddle-class language is more abstract and necessarily somewhat more flexible ...

   (Jensen, 1968: 118–19, cited in Bailey, 1991: 280–1)

prime minister's sentences – an indication that constructions like *that's the chair I was sitting on* might be considered ungrammatical by some, while the 'corrected' version is rather stilted; (4) represents the speech of a teacher who was a stickler for 'correctness', insisting on the use of this construction instead of the normal *It's me*; (5) is probably used by the majority of English speakers either habitually or occasionally: a study showed that many people will accept it as normal 'usage', possibly finding the 'correct' *he and I went shopping* rather awkward (Kerswill, 2007b); (6) claims that the participles *done* and *seen* are being wrongly used, when a moment's reflection reveals that these are actually the forms of the past tense used by many speakers; (7) demonstrates that Scots, which is closely related to English, nevertheless has a visible presence as a separate language; and finally, (8) suggests that working-class language is inflexible and inexpressive, and hence inadequate – a view which is not held by linguists.

Where does all this lead us? **Descriptive linguists** would see all of the linguistic forms cited above as, in one way or another, 'belonging to' English: for them, there is no 'good' or 'bad' English, and they prefer instead to take what is apparently a dispassionate stance in describing (as opposed to **prescribing**) standard and non-standard, formal and informal language. However, being dispassionate, or objective, is not the only answer. It seems that what is as important as linguistic description is to establish the point of view of the language user in determining what is 'English'. We'll have a look at the evidence now.

12.2.1 The boundaries of English and the observer's viewpoint

To refer to 'English' implies that we know what comes under the umbrella of English (and what doesn't). This is not as straightforward as it seems, as we have already seen. Consider the following questions: is there just one 'English', or are there two, or perhaps more (the most obvious divide being between the English of Great Britain and that of the United States of America, as noted in the box)? Is English the sum of all and only the words and phrases contained in a dictionary, together with a grammar, or does it also include all the accents and dialects of the English-speaking world? Can we say that only 'correct' English should be included in our definition, with 'incorrect' forms excluded? (We are used to hearing complaints about 'bad English' or 'bad grammar'.) What about the language of people in the Caribbean and elsewhere who speak a creole (see Chapter 21)? And we might also wonder about the 'English' of the more than one billion people who have learnt it **after** acquiring their first language, far outnumbering the 350 million or so native speakers (Crystal, 2003: 1–10; 2004: 13). Turning to the example of Scots above, we can note that, since March 2001, this has been recognized alongside Gaelic as a minority language of Scotland under the European Charter for Regional and Minority Languages. Scots is the 'vernacular' speech of much of Scotland, and exists as a range of local dialects in the same way as dialects exist in England or North America. Does this official recognition mean that Scots suddenly ceased to be a kind of English, becoming its own language overnight? The answer is complicated by the fact that Scots functioned as a written language in Scotland from the late fourteenth to the mid-sixteenth centuries (Knowles, 1997: 130–1), and that it has enjoyed a considerable literary revival since the time of Robert Burns (1759–1796). In other words, it already enjoys some aspects of what might be termed **languagehood**.

The answers to these questions are in each case not at all clear. The reason for posing them in the first place is to emphasize that what we are used to thinking of as a unified object, 'English', seemingly easy to define, in fact has fuzzy boundaries. What is more, those boundaries depend crucially on whose perspectives we take. Thus, we can view English from the point of view of the educationist, who might want to inculcate 'standards' or at least 'correctness' in written English, or the politician, who perhaps wants to promote nationhood by establishing independence for local varieties of the language (such as Scots), or the linguist, who claims to be a dispassionate observer. Or else we could take the perspective of ordinary people with no professional investment in the English language. In this case we would find an array of views, some consciously expressed and with a degree of rational thought behind them, others much more subjective and in the nature of gut reactions. We will be exploring the perspectives of both the 'language professionals' and the 'lay' language users.

12.2.2 The 'standard ideology'

Until relatively recently, the history of the English language was presented as if it was a single, and unbroken, line of development from the Anglo-Saxon settlers' language to today's highly developed Standard English (L. Milroy, 2002; Crystal, 2004: 1–14). The consequence of this is that Standard English takes on the role of a target towards which English had been striving, and which it eventually achieved some time during the eighteenth century, having begun in earnest the fifteenth century. Crystal (2005: 5) sees Wyld's *A Short History of English* (1914) as the chief culprit, citing the following passages to illustrate his point:

> After the end of the fourteenth century, the other dialects, excepting always those of Lowland Scotch, gradually cease to be the vehicle of literary expression, and are no longer of importance to us as independent forms of English.
>
> (Wyld, 1927: 17)

> Fortunately at the present time, the great majority of the English Dialects are of very little importance as representations of English speech, and for our present purpose we can afford to let them go, except in so far as they throw light upon the growth of those forms of our language which are the main objects of our solicitude, namely the language of literature and Received Standard Spoken English.
>
> (Wyld, 1927: 16)

Wyld is the clearest representative of what Crystal calls the 'standard story' (2004: 3). Crystal also mentions Baugh's *A History of the English Language*

(1935), and it is not until the fifth edition (Baugh and Cable, 2002) that we find coverage of African American English and English in Singapore, for instance. Apart from Baugh and Cable, it is only with books such as Leith (1983), Fennell (2001), and Watts and Trudgill (2002) that we find any treatment of the diversity and complexity of the history of English. We return to the history of English in Section 12.2.3, below.

If we deem Wyld's approach to be outdated (or just plain wrong-headed), then we must replace it with something better. Essentially, this means taking both a **sociolinguistic** and a **critical** approach. A sociolinguistic approach takes account of the variability that exists in English, as in any language. At the very least, there will be variation by social group (e.g., class; see Chapter 19), gender (Chapter 32), region (Chapter 18) and ethnicity (Chapter 20) – to varying degrees, depending on the time and place. A critical approach would see the variability against the background of **power relations** in the society (Chapters 30 and 35) and, with them, the prevailing **ideologies**, that is, the ways of thinking about the social world that are usual in the society, for instance, people's attitudes towards social class and gender differentiation. Crucially for us, language itself is subject to **ideology**. Currently, according to J. Milroy (1999), in Great Britain, the United States and most developed countries, a **standard ideology** prevails, meaning that we see it as a matter of common sense, even morality, that the standard language is intrinsically both correct and therefore better than other forms of English. We shall now examine these points through the extended example in Illustration Box 12.3.

How does this short newspaper article relate to the idea of a standard ideology? We can analyse the comments under four headings:

Accent and dialect. Throughout the article, there appears to be a conflation of 'received pronunciation' (1 and 3) and 'standard English' (5, 6 and 7). Given that what is being talked about are matters of pronunciation (accent and diction) and not vocabulary and grammar (after all, actors speak scripted lines), it is clear that the journalist and his interviewees see 'standard English' as covering pronunciation as well. As we shall see, many linguists keep the grammar and phonology 'components' of language separate when discussing varieties of English (see Chapter 18 and Kerswill, 2007b, c on the 'accent' vs. 'dialect' distinction).

Standard English and class. In (2), Atkins talks about the benefits of social mobility ('Does that mean I always have to have lino on the floor?'), and indicates that part of social mobility is changing one's accent. In (4), Scales seems to both accept that there are accents associated with a higher social status (she refers to 'posh English'), while also maintaining that these accents are classless ('... classical English which does not say anything about a person's background'). This is a contradictory statement which reflects a commonly held set of beliefs about language. This is that the standard language exists outside both time and place ('classical English', as she calls it) and as such is an unchanging yardstick against which to measure particular instances of the use of language. At the same time, it is openly admitted that it is closely connected with high social status, as paragraphs (2), (3) and (4) show.

ILLUSTRATION BOX 12.3

The standard ideology in action

Actors say they are alarmed by obsession with regional accents, reports Chris Hastings (*Daily Telegraph*, 31 October 2004)

1. Dame Eileen Atkins, Prunella Scales, and the Oscar-winning screenwriters Ronald Harwood and Julian Fellowes argue that greater emphasis should be given to received pronunciation rather than encouraging regional accents.
   [...]

2. 'My [Dame Eileen Atkins's] argument is that I was brought up with lino on the floor. Does that mean I always have to have lino on the floor? I was brought up in a council house. Does that mean I have always got to live in a council house? Can we not change our minds about something? Have we got to stay – for the sake of political correctness – in the same mindset as our childhood? Of course we don't. So why shouldn't people change their voice?'

3. Dame Eileen said that received pronunciation was vital for bringing energy to a performance. The fashion for 'Estuary English', which meant 'dropping all the vowels', was 'ruinous' to Shakespeare. 'If you cannot speak proper received English you end up with working-class parts. ...

4. Prunella Scales ... said: 'There is an inverted snobbery about posh English which we have to get away from ... There is no social snobbery here, it is about the accuracy of playing a part. Anthony Hopkins was born with a Welsh accent, but he did not have a Welsh accent when he played King Lear. He used classical English which does not say anything about a person's background.'
   [...]

5. Ronald Harwood, the Oscar-winning writer of *The Pianist*, said that the declining emphasis on standard English was 'terrible'. 'If you have standard English you can work on any dialect that exists. If you only have the dialect you can hardly do anything,' he said.
   [...]

6. The schools had failed to realize that those same stars were successful precisely because they were capable of speaking standard English. The problem of poor language skills is particularly acute among child stars, many of whom have limited vocabulary and grammar.

7. Julian Fellowes, the Oscar-winning writer and director ... said that falling education standards meant that casting children could be very difficult. 'I remember when we were casting *The Prince and the Pauper* a few years ago, we searched for stars in drama schools throughout the country. We ended up going to Dulwich Prep School [a well known fee-paying school – PK] where we found our star,' he said.

8. 'I think the worry is not regional accents, it is clarity of speech. There is a kind of sloppiness of speech, with children unable to understand anything they have not seen on television or a video game. There is a tremendous paucity of grammar because children have not been taught any basic vocabulary skills.

NB: For ease of reference, the paragraphs have been numbered.

Sloppy speech and class. In (3), Atkins adds an explicit evaluative dimension: according to her, only 'proper received English' is pronounced correctly, while other varieties such as 'Estuary English' is sloppy ('dropping all the vowels'). She goes on to say that the use of this kind of speech would only secure actors 'working-class parts'. In so doing, she unwittingly fails to recognize that **Received Pronunciation (RP)** can also be spoken in a phonetically reduced manner, while dialect can be spoken with great clarity – a fact that Fellows actually recognizes in (8). From Atkins's stated view, it is only a short step to suggesting that working-class people are 'sloppy' in other areas of their lives, an obviously discriminatory claim that can give rise, at the very least, to social stigma.

'Grammar' equals standard grammar. Both Harwood (in 6) and Fellows (in 8) suggest that children today have limited 'grammar'. This echoes two of what Leith (1997: 87–8) has labelled 'misconceptions about grammar'. One of these states: 'Some people are supposed to "know" the grammar of the language, while others do not', and another: 'grammar is something that can be either "good" or "bad"'. It is not clear what either commentator means by 'grammar', but it is plainly something that can be taught at school – and which is taught so badly today that people have less of it ('falling educational standards' in (7)). Linguists claim that a grammar is a complex system residing in the human mind, the product of a genetic propensity to acquire such a system. Hence, the idea that any normally developing child's grammar is 'limited' makes little sense, as does the idea that 'grammar' is the preserve of a standard language. The conclusion must be that 'limited grammar' here refers to 'non-standard grammar'.

12.2.3 The standard ideology and writing the history of English

Even when tracing the history of the language, there are problems with the definition of 'English'. English has a history dating back some 1500 years, if we take as its starting point a date given by the Venerable Bede, a monk at Jarrow in Northumberland. Bede claims that AD 449 saw the arrival of several waves of invading Germanic tribes (Angles, Saxons and Jutes) from the Continent, the Romans having withdrawn in AD 410. By the eighth century, the descendents of the settlers had adopted the term 'englisc' (which survives in the modern form 'English') for their language and people (*Oxford English Dictionary*), suggesting that a commonality was perceived, at least by those who held power, between the various forms of the language which had developed from the imported Germanic varieties. It is uncontroversial to say that these Germanic dialects, which are usually labelled **Old English**, gradually transformed themselves into the modern language over the ensuing centuries. But precise dates are more controversial, and much 'spin' is put on the historical 'facts'. Bede was actually writing his account 400 years after the events. At that point it suited his purposes to create a precise, unified Anglo-Saxon history, with clear dates and identifiable tribes acting in a warrior-like manner, not least because Bede was writing around the time of real threats to the Anglo-Saxons from the Vikings. In fact, contact with continental Europe had been taking place for centuries prior to AD 449, largely through trading. The terms 'Angle', 'Saxon' and 'Jute' were not used consistently by contemporaries, suggesting that they were not distinct tribes. Moreover, archaeological evidence does not support the idea of dramatic 'invasion' with attendant evidence of destruction. Instead, we have evidence of inter-marriage and adoption of the new Germanic culture, particularly in the east of Britain. Above all, it should be remembered that these Germanic tribes never made it to the western or northern extremes of Britain: Celtic languages continued to be spoken in Cornwall, Wales, Ireland and Scotland, as they do today, except in Cornwall (Cornish having died out in the eighteenth century). From the beginning of English, then, Britain was a multilingual country, though this is played down in the standard histories.

It is conventional to divide this history into periods, roughly as follows:

Old English (OE): 449–1100
Middle English (ME): 1100–1500
Early Modern English (EModE): 1500–1750
(Late) Modern English (LModE): 1750–present
Present-day English (PDE)

This, too, is uncontroversial, as long as we realize that the divisions are to some extent arbitrary – scholars do not agree on the exact dates. However, there are at least some cultural and linguistic reasons supporting them. The date 449 is not arbitrary, assuming that indeed was the date that saw a significant influx of Germanic tribes, but it goes without saying that the language of the invaders and settlers didn't suddenly become 'English' the moment they came ashore – it would be three centuries before the label 'English' appears. Moreover, it is not until around AD 700 that written records appear in any quantity beyond fragments and inscriptions (see Chapter 13). Not surprisingly, some historians of English date Old English from 700. The start of **Middle English** clearly tallies with the Norman Conquest of 1066, though the date is usually placed somewhat after because the effects of that conquest were not immediately reflected in the language. The transition to **Early Modern English** tallies with William Caxton setting up his printing press in 1476, something which was to have a standardizing influence (see below and Chapter 13, Section 13.5), and the beginning of the Renaissance. The beginning of **Late Modern English** tallies with the North American Declaration of Independence in 1776, something which marks the fact that English had gone global. There are linguistic differences too. Lass (2000) examined ten linguistic features that might diagnose how archaic language was (e.g., whether an infinitive ending such as *singen* was present). The presence or absence of these features in texts representing the various periods of English revealed that there were clear differences between the periods in general. But the study also revealed that there are no clear transition points between the periods, and that there was much variation for individual texts (Chaucer, in fact, represents the norm for ME fairly well).

The general problem is that, as L. Milroy (2000) and Crystal (2004: 3–4) point out, the history of English is conceived as the history of **Standard English** – as we saw earlier. This is true particularly of accounts of the period after 1500, when standardization is regarded as the major 'achievement'. The labels for the periods themselves came to the fore in the nineteenth century when there was a surge of interest in the history of English. They perhaps suggest that a single entity, 'English', meaning Standard English, changed over time, and not the linguistic reality: a bunch of various dialects developing over time at various rates (cf. Knowles, 1997: 32). But the idea of triumphal continuity better suited the imperial political aspirations of the nineteenth century, much as it had Bede a thousand or so years before. This perspective reflects the standard ideology. The argument is that an excessive focus on Standard English leads language historians to look for signs of earlier standardization. In fact, West Saxon, the dialect of Old English covering the south of England except Kent and cultivated at the court of King Alfred (849–99) in Winchester, served as a scribal standard throughout much of England until some time after the arrival of the Normans in 1066 (Crystal, 2004: 54–6). But it is false to argue for West Saxon as any kind of ancestor of modern Standard English, because the latter is very much based on fifteenth-century London speech (and writing) – and London itself had a strongly East Midlands character, as we shall see.

Fifteenth-century London English illustrates a further point about the operation of the standard ideology. Until recently in histories of English, regional dialects have been sidelined, except when they are known to feed into the standard language. An example of this is the influence of the East Midlands dialect on the speech of the capital, something that is regularly acknowledged in the histories. London was sited on the boundary of three dialects: south-eastern (Kentish), southern and East Midlands. Through the prism of knowledge about today's dialects (e.g., which dialects are prestigious, have the greatest number of users), we might expect influence to come from the south. Actually, in the fifteenth and sixteenth centuries it came from the north, from the East Midlands dialect and also from dialects in the north of England. London attracted a large number of merchants and migrants from these wealthy regions, and their speech rapidly became prestigious. In fact, it is East Midlands speech, mixed with central Midlands and Northern elements which had been transplanted to London and influenced by other forms of language, including the written language of administration – '**Chancery English**' (Chancery being roughly equivalent to today's Civil Service in the UK), which became the basis of Standard English. (The nature of so-called Chancery English and the degree of influence it had on the eventual standard

ILLUSTRATION BOX 12.4

Northern linguistic forms arriving in London by the end of the fifteenth century

	London English c.1390 (e.g., Chaucer)	London English c.1550
1. Third-person singular suffix:	*giveth*	*gives*
2. Third-person plural pronouns:	*they* (earlier *hei*)	*they*
	hem	*them*
	hir	*their*
3. Forms of the verb *be*:	*he beeth*	*he is*
	they been	*they are*

Commentary: What strikes us today is that the forms on the right are part of Standard English, which evolved in London. The northern forms *they, them, their* and *are* (but not *is*) are all words originally borrowed from the Old Norse of the Danish and Norwegian Vikings who invaded and settled in the north of England and parts of Scotland in the ninth and tenth centuries. All the forms entered London directly or via the East Midlands dialect of the fourteenth and fifteenth centuries.

English is controversial; see also Chapter 13, Section 13.2.5.) We have given three examples in Illustration Box 12.4.

These are just three examples of regional features ending up in early London English, and, from there, being adopted into the standard. Wyld, as we saw, claimed that regional varieties of English after this period had no particular influence on the standard. As a consequence, the regional varieties themselves were viewed as having little merit as objects of academic study. Even after the first flowering of English **dialectology** in the late nineteenth century, accessible to us today in Ellis (1889) and Wright (1898–1905), the phonetician and linguist Henry Sweet (1845–1912), the model for Bernard Shaw's Henry Higgins in *Pygmalion*, could write:

> Most of the present English dialects are so isolated in their development and so given over to disintegrating influences as to be, on the whole, less conservative than and generally inferior to the standard dialect. They throw little light on the development of English...
>
> (Sweet, 1971, cited in L. Milroy, 2000: 17)

Much later, Wales (2002, 2006) has argued that the language of Northern England has far greater importance, both historically and in contemporary society, than has been assumed: for example, this is the region in which the Industrial Revolution flourished, and where the writing of literature in dialect has continued for over 150 years.

ADVANCES BOX 12.1

Northern influence on standard English

The leading researchers in historical sociolinguistics are Terttu Nevalainen and Helena Raumolin-Brunberg. Using their Corpus of Early English Correspondence (CEEC), a large electronic collection of transcribed letters from late ME and early ModE, they have investigated how dialects have changed over time. Figure 12.1 illustrates the change presented as the first feature in Illustration Box 12.4, namely the shift from a third-person present tense *–eth* inflection to the 'standard' *–s* (e.g., *giveth* > *gives*). Three dialects are presented, London, Northern and East Anglia.

Drawing on comments in Nevalainen and Raumolin-Brunberg (2000, and also 2003), one can make the following observations:

* There clearly is **dialectal variation**.
* *–s* predominated in the north in the fifteenth century. The statistics for the period prior to the earliest represented in the Figure 12.1, i.e., 1420–1500, are: 1 per cent East Midlands, Southern 17 per cent, Northern 80 per cent. This is not perhaps surprising as the *–s* form seems to have originated in the North (it is first recorded in the Northumbrian dialect in the tenth century); some historians think that it might be borrowed from Old Norse, the language of the Vikings, who settled predominantly in the North and East (though a problem for this view is that the grammatically equivalent item is not in fact *–s* in Old Norse).
* Why the decline of *–s* in the first part of the sixteenth century and a shift towards *–th*, even in the north? This may be the influence of Chancery English where *–s* is rare (there are no instances in Henry V's signet letters).

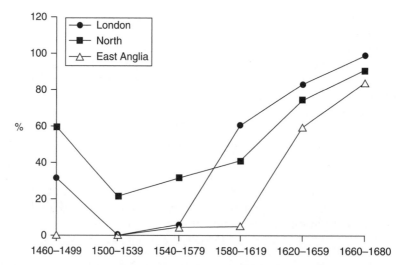

FIGURE 12.1   *The replacement of the third-person singular suffix –th by –s in three dialect areas (excluding have and do). Percentages of –s (CEEC, 1998) (Nevalainen and Raumolin-Brunberg, 2000: 305)*

The *-th* inflection was favoured by higher social ranks; in contrast, *-s* was favoured by lower ranks. So, *-th* was prestigious and *-s* probably stigmatized and seen as colloquial. Nevalainen and Raumolin-Brunberg make the following intriguing observation: 'If standard English had been codified in the first half of the sixteenth century, it would have included *-th* in the third person singular present indicative' (2003: 311). So, we might all now be saying *taketh, drinketh, knoweth*, etc.!

- *-s* appeared in London but not East Anglia. How did it get there? The most likely cause is immigration from the north into the capital.
- Why the revival of *-s* around the middle of the sixteenth century? Nevalainen and Raumolin-Brunberg (2000, 2003) suggest it spread out from the colloquial language and lower social ranks. (There may be a phonological motivation: *-s* was probably considered the contracted form of *-eth*).
- London follows in the direction of the north and eventually overtakes it; East Anglia is slower to change, despite being geographically closer.

12.3 Where did Standard English come from?

We can now draw together some of the threads of the story of Standard English. The American linguist Einar Haugen (1972) outlined four stages in the development of a standard language: **selection, elaboration, codification** and **implementation**. We have already seen that it was a London-based variety of English that was selected, with its strong Midlands basis. London had the prestige of being the capital – it was the centre for the Court, administration, trade, etc. It was the largest population centre by far (it surpassed all Western European capitals by 1700). In 1476, Caxton had established the first printing press in England at Westminster, near the Chancery itself, and not surprisingly he modelled what he printed on the language produced there. Printed books from London became available throughout the country, with the result that this form of the language became familiar everywhere. The first English Bible to be printed was William Tyndale's New Testament translation (in 1525–6; Crystal, 2004: 271), followed by others during the century. These were widely read, and influenced written English in vocabulary and style. (Crystal, 2004: 222–48; Fennell, 2001: 122–5; Leith, Graddol and Jackson, 2007: 83–110 provide further information on the emergence of a standard during this period.)

Elaboration means ensuring that the language is capable of being put to all the uses required of it. Up to about 1380, English had been in competition with French for official affairs of state (the 1362 Statute of Pleading ensured that court proceedings would be conducted in English (Baugh and Cable, 1993: 145)). And it was not English, but Latin which was the main language of science (as in the rest of Europe). Scientific writing in English only really began to appear in English during the seventeenth century. Now that English was no longer competing with other languages, there was a need for a great expansion of the vocabulary, largely achieved by the adoption of Latin and Greek words, and an expansion in the range of styles, especially written, which were available (see Chapter 15).

Codification refers to the writing down, in grammars and dictionaries, of the 'rules' and vocabulary of the language – which in virtually all cases means the standard variety. In the seventeenth century, there were discussions about the establishment of an English Academy, to regulate the language as the *Académie Française* was doing for French, but nothing came of it (Fennell, 2001: 149–52). English did not receive a dictionary in the sense in which we understand the term until 1755, when Samuel Johnson published his *A Dictionary of the English Language* (although it should be acknowledged that there were some lesser-known, shorter precursors to Johnson's dictionary). Words and their usages appeared according to their occurrence in what he considered the 'best' authors – thereby confirming the standard as a language of literacy and 'high' culture. Descriptive grammars were more limited in scope: with the exception of Joseph Priestley's 1761 *The Rudiments of English Grammar*, grammars were **prescriptive** (stating what should and should not be said or written). These grammars used Latin as a model, and this led to some of their recommendations being inappropriate for English. Most notable among the prescriptive grammars are Bishop Robert Lowth's 1762 *Short Introduction to English Grammar* and Lindley Murray's *English Grammar* of 1795 (which sold 20 million copies). The latter, particularly, is the source of many of the **prescriptive rules** which bedevil writers today. Between them, the two grammars state, for example, that:

- double negatives should not be used, as in *Nor* let *no comforter approach me*
- in the future tense, *shall* should be used with *I* and *we*, and *will* with *you* and *he/she/it/they*
- sentences should not end with prepositions, as in *Generosity is a showy virtue, which many persons are very fond of*

– despite the fact that the forms being criticized were widely used at the time, even by the prescriptivists themselves!

Finally, implementation involves making available sufficient samples of the language and ensuring its general acceptance. We have already seen how the emerging standard was both stabilized and disseminated through print, and how influential eighteenth-century writers stated with the authority of their social and cultural standing what should and should not be used. The status of Standard English, together with its eighteenth-century prescriptive additions, remained unchallenged during the nineteenth century, with the 1870 Education Act promoting the teaching of Standard English, as did official educational policy in England throughout the twentieth century and up until today (Williams, 2007: 402–9 expands on these policies).

12.4 Defining Standard English

We argued earlier that a definition of Standard English is subject to how the observer views the matter – something of a **social judgement**. So far, we have not looked at specific linguistic features which might rule a piece of speech or writing in or out. Advances Box 12.2 examines this.

ADVANCES BOX 12.2

Can we define Standard English purely linguistically?

A number of linguists have argued strongly that Standard English is easily defined and delimited: it is largely uniform throughout the world with a few grammatical differences. Its vocabulary is less fixed, though it avoids regional, traditional words. While it is the only form of English used in writing, it is also used in speech, and has native speakers throughout the world. Trudgill (1999) gives perhaps the clearest statement of this position. He argues that Standard English is not a style, a register or an accent, noting that its speakers have access to a full range of informal styles, and can produce it with different accents, while non-standard speakers can discuss technical subjects without switching to Standard English. Standard English is a dialect, defined by its grammar. Hence the name should be spelt with a capital <S>, as I have chosen to do, on the grounds that a small <s> suggests a benchmark or yardstick and implies 'good' usage. However, because it is standardized and codified, Standard English is not part of a continuum of dialects: either a feature is standard, or it is not (Trudgill, 1999c: 124) – for example, *I didn't want any* is standard, while *I didn't want none* is non-standard. It also does not have a particular pronunciation associated with it – in principle it can be pronounced with any accent, though in England there is one accent which can only go with Standard English – RP. Trudgill lists eight 'idiosyncrasies' of Standard English grammar, four of which are the following:

1. Standard English does not distinguish between the forms of the auxiliary *do* and its main verb forms. Non-standard varieties normally include the forms *I done it* (main verb), *but did he?* (auxiliary): Standard English has *did* for both functions.
2. Standard English does not permit double negation (negative concord), as in *I don't want none.*
3. Standard English has an irregular formation of the reflexive, with *myself* based on the possessive *my*, and *himself* based on the object form *him*. Non-standard dialects generalize the possessive form, as in *hisself.*
4. Standard English distinguishes between the preterite and past participle forms of many verbs, as in *I saw – I have seen*, or *I did – I have done,* where dialects have forms like *seen* or *done* for both.

(adapted from Trudgill, 1999c: 125)

Trudgill gives a sociolinguistic characterization of Standard English. For him it is a 'purely social dialect' (1999c: 124). He estimates that it is spoken natively by 12–15 per cent of the British population, concentrated at the top of the social class scale. It was selected in the first place because it was the variety of the most influential social groups (as we have seen). Subsequently, according to Trudgill, its 'social character' was reinforced through its use in an 'education to which pupils...have had differential access depending on their social-class background' (199c9: 124). Hudson (2000) takes a slightly different approach, focusing more on the written form and literacy. He states that Standard English is '(1) written in published work, (2) spoken in situations where published writing is influential, especially in education..., [and] (3) spoken natively by people who are most influenced by published writing ...'.

> Trudgill and Hudson take an uncomplicated approach to Standard English. While this is reasonable, it does not reflect the views of both 'professional' (but non-linguist) and 'lay' people, who, as we have seen earlier in this chapter, both conflate Standard English and an RP accent and remain unable to describe its defining features.
>
> Kerswill (2007b) discusses in detail the problems posed by the idea of **spoken** Standard English.

12.5   Received Pronunciation

In England, and to a lesser extent in Scotland and Wales, RP is an accent which traditionally serves as a phonetic counterpart to Standard English. This means that RP is only spoken using Standard English, even though the latter can be, and is, spoken in virtually any accent. As we saw in Illustration Box 12.3, this pronunciation is held by many to be a neutral standard, even though it is easy to demonstrate that it is an upper-middle and upper-class accent. People's reactions to RP strongly reveal their admiration for it, as well as their ambivalence towards it – the latter being especially true of younger people and people outside the south-east of England (Coupland and Bishop, 2007: 83).

Defining RP is more difficult than defining Standard English, because speakers vary their pronunciation for stylistic purposes, and because differences between speakers' pronunciations are more subtle than differences in their grammatical usage. While Standard English has barely changed grammatically in 200 years, pronunciation has changed greatly in that time. In any case, RP is recent compared to Standard English, arising in the last part of the nineteenth century, most probably in Oxford and Cambridge universities, among officers in the army and navy and in the public (i.e., private) boarding schools. It was spread as a result of the considerable mobility of wealthier people, including postings in the colonial administrations overseas. From the 1920s onwards, it was deliberately promoted by the BBC (Crystal, 2004: 270). However, it seems that RP has always been somewhat variable and hard to pin down – the phonetician Ellis admitted as much (Ellis, 1875, quoted in Mugglestone, 2007: 165).

RP can be defined sociolinguistically or linguistically. A sociolinguistic approach is to define a population, in this case the products of the more prestigious fee-paying schools and typically Oxford or Cambridge universities, and examine their speech. This is what Fabricius (2002) has done, and her findings suggest that RP is still a native variety for some people (it isn't 'put on' in any sense). Since it is a spoken variety with native speakers, it is subject to change. In particular, younger RP speakers glottalize /t/ much more than older people at the ends of words before a pause, as in *I live in London Street*, and across word boundaries, for instance the /t/ in *sort of*. Trudgill (1999c, 2002) makes the point that the principal defining feature of RP is that the place of origin of an RP speaker cannot be determined from their accent. This means that if a change, such as the increasing use of the glottal stop for

/t/, turns out not to be uniform throughout the country, then the speakers who use the new feature are no longer speaking RP. So far, to our knowledge, there have been no studies of Northern RP speakers, so we cannot judge this point with certainty.

There have been a number of phonetic descriptions of RP; these are reviewed in Kerswill (2007b).

12.6   RP subverted

RP has not always had its way. As early as the 1940s, the BBC experimented with having Wilfred Pickles, an actor who maintained his Yorkshire accent, read the news. Complaints prevented this from continuing, but Pickles warned:

> While I have the greatest respect for the many achievements of the B.B.C., I believe that they are guilty of the offence of trying to teach Great Britain to talk standard English. How terrible it is to think that we may some day lose that lovely soft Devonshire accent...
>
> (Pickles, 1949: 146–7, quoted in Crystal, 2004: 473)

By the 1960s, BBC policy on the strict use of RP had relaxed, and more and more (admittedly mild) regional accents could be heard, but always with Standard English grammar. In 1984, David Rosewarne wrote a newspaper article in which he claimed to identify a new accent, which he labelled **Estuary English** (see also Rosewarne, 1994). This accent lay 'between Cockney and the Queen', as the *Sunday Times* later put it, and it was intended to capture the middle ground of accents in the south-east which, according to Rosewarne, were about to replace RP as the new prestige variety. Evidence for this is that some RP speakers show **downward** mobility by adopting elements of Estuary English. What commentators such as Trudgill (2002) have claimed, with some truth, is that this is not a new accent, but that it represents the increased audibility of upwardly mobile, but non-RP accents in occupations where RP had been expected, such as in the Civil Service, government, the law and (as we have seen) broadcasting. On the other hand, there is now a great deal of dialect levelling (erosion of accent and dialect differences; Chapter 18), especially in the south-east, and the resulting 'levelled' accents share the middle ground with Estuary English. Research in Milton Keynes, a new city with a mobile population, demonstrates this point (Kerswill, 1996; Kerswill and Williams, 2005).

12.7   The standard ideology strikes back

Even so, there is huge resistance to Estuary English among quite large sections of society, as revealed in the persistent complaints in the media. In the 1990s in particular, there were a number of editorials, articles and readers' letters deploring the state of the language – and these continue today, if with less vehemence. Estuary English – together with, briefly in 1994, Milton Keynes English (as later reported in Kerswill and Williams, 2005) – was seen as the root of the evil. This is what the late playwright John Osborne wrote about the Milton Keynes accent on 7 August 1994 in the *Daily Mail*:

> It was announced last week that Essex girl has been supplanted by the children of Milton Keynes, who uniformly speak with a previously unidentified and hideously glottal accent... Nothing is more depressing than [Milton Keynes], this gleaming gum-boil plonked in the middle of England. And now there is a home-grown accent to match.

All the accents vilified in this and other letters and articles are characteristic of working-class speech in Britain. These pronouncements can be regarded not as 'racist' but as 'classist', even though the features – such as saying *Chewsday* for *Tuesday* (reader's letter, *Daily Telegraph*, 17 June 2000) – are mostly also used by middle-class speakers as well – a fact which the correspondents don't seem to realize.

So what is happening? Even though RP is receding from view to some extent, it is still visible and still, according to Fabricius, the major reference point for accent and dialect variation and language ideology in Britain. This stability in the face of what appears to be social change (particularly through globalization and the development of new urban youth varieties) is surprising, but is corroborated by Coupland and Bishop's (2007) survey, which revealed that the prestige hierarchy of British English accents remains much as it was in the 1960s (Giles, 1970).

Recommended readings

Further discussion of many of the points raised in this chapter can be found in Graddol, Leith, Swann, Rhys and Gillen (eds, 2007). Mugglestone (2003) is a fascinating account of attitudes to accent in the nineteenth century, as is her chapter in Graddol et al. (2007). Britain (ed., 2007) is a wide-ranging scholarly account of English and other languages spoken in the British Isles, as is Kortmann and Upton (eds, 2008), which focuses on English. Trudgill and Hannah (2002) discuss the different forms of Standard English throughout the world.

Regarding the history of English specifically, Crystal (2004) is the most comprehensive – yet accessible, portable and single-authored – account of the history of English to date. For something briefer, try Culpeper (2005a), which is also designed to be a workbook. Hogg and Denison (2006) is a good, authoritative complement to the chapters in this section of the book, as it contains chapters organized according to particular topics, just as is the case with our chapters, rather than chronologically. Mugglestone (2006) is a fresh, wide-ranging single volume of illuminating papers on the history of English with a sociolinguistic emphasis. For a largely descriptive account of the linguistic characteristics of each period, we recommend Smith (1996); or, for something much more detailed there is Richard Hogg's (the series editor) *The Cambridge History of the English Language,* particularly, volumes I (1992), 11 (1992) and III (1999), covering the Old, Middle and Early Modern

English periods. Of the many 'standard' works on the history of the English language, there are Barber (1993), Baugh and Cable (2002) and Pyles and Algeo (2004).

There are a number of very useful websites covering seemingly all aspects of the history of English. The following are particularly good: http://www.uni-essen.de/SHE/ and http://ebbs.english.vt.edu/hel/hel.html.

CHAPTER 13

The History of English Spelling

JONATHAN CULPEPER AND DAWN ARCHER[1]

13.1 Is English spelling a problem? Can it easily be fixed?

The English spelling system is often considered to be not merely complex but also chaotic. An often-cited example of the apparent chaos relates to the following differently pronounced words, all of which have the same final spelling, <ough>: *cough, tough, bough, through* and *though*. Actually, English spelling is not truly chaotic. For instance, the classic example above ignores the fact that the earlier words in the list have sound-letter correspondences which are extremely rare; the default is that <ough> corresponds with /əʊ/, as illustrated by *though* at the end of the list. More fundamentally, claims about the apparent chaos almost always ignore how English spelling actually works, and, instead, focus solely on (the lack of) sound–letter correspondences.

The vast majority of spelling mistakes present no problem whatsoever for comprehension: whether you spell the word *accommodation* with a double <c> and a double <m> or not is hardly going to impede your ability to understand the word. What is important, however, is the social impression created when words are 'misspelt', and this is why it looms large. Consider these comments taken from Weblogs:

> People b*tched at me all the time that my spelling was inferior, juvinel, like a retard wrote it, I heard these things every time some one tried to read my handwriting,
>
> http://www.43things.com/things/view/16802

> I am one of the worst spellers in the world or at least I feel that way....I applied for work at one of the temporary employment services. I tested so badly that they never called me, and I never called them back. I was more than embarrassed.
>
> http://www.ldresources.org/?p=970

Notice that bad spelling is assumed to be an indicator of one's lack of intelligence, and that assumption has real social consequences, as illustrated by the second comment above. In fact, as we will show, 'bad' spelling as a social problem is a modern invention: there used not to be a limited number of 'correct' ways of spelling words.

In parallel with the development of 'bad' spelling as a social problem, we see the idea that the problem can be solved, either through regularization of the spelling system or through educational policy (or both). The Simplified Spelling Society, founded in 1908, has been a strong advocate of the former position (see: http://www.spellingsociety.org). The latter position is often taken by self-appointed individuals, who sometimes have a political agenda. Let us consider the position of the commentator Minette Marrin (*The Sunday Times*, 23 October 2005, summarized in *The Week*, 28 October 2005).

How the trendies made us illiterate

Minette Marrin

The Sunday Times

Teaching people to read should be the first job of any education system, says Minette Marrin, but it is one we're still getting wrong. Last week a Unicef study of 24 countries called the UK's adult illiteracy rate of 10% a "statistic of shame". A separate Ofsted report found that a quarter of all 11-year-olds cannot read or write well enough to follow the secondary school syllabus. What makes these figures all the more disgraceful is that they are so unnecessary. Learning to read is "very easy". Almost everyone can use the old-fashioned system of "synthetic phonics" (teaching the sounds and shapes of letters – C-A-T – and putting them together into words). In the Sixties, alas, this winning formula was replaced with a mix of trendy new approaches that encouraged children to guess a word's meaning by context or total word shape. Today, the national literacy scheme still employs many of these discredited methods at the expense of pure phonics. Tony Blair is threatening to scrap this failed strategy in a year if there's no improvement. "Wh-y n-o-t d-o i-t n-ow? It's that simple really."

The 'easy' solution that Marrin advocates seems to be learning how 'sounds' correspond to 'shapes of letters', and then 'putting them together into words'. The assumption, then, is that there is a simple system – it's just a matter of teaching it. Yet, we have already seen from the beginning of this chapter, as well as from Chapters 2 and 3, that the correspondence between spelling and pronunciation is neither simple nor straightforward. Consider, for example, some of the difficulties by examining the first letter of Marrin's own example, namely *cat*, drawing examples from her article. The first letter of *cat*, <c>, corresponds to the sound /k/, and this correspondence seems to hold in quite a number of words within the article, including *education*, *countries*, *statistic*, *cannot*, *secondary* and so on. But then we see words such as *Unicef*, *disgraceful*, *unnecessary* and *literacy*. Here <c> corresponds with /s/. Then there are occasions where <c> clearly does not operate on its own but in conjunction with <h> to form the digraph <ch>, which corresponds with /tʃ/. Thus we have, for example, *teaching* and *children*. However, there are also words in our text where the <ch>–/tʃ/ correspondence does not work; specifically, *school* and *scheme*. (Outside this text, we could also fret about words like *cello*). Looking at things in reverse, that is, how the sound /k/ might correspond with letters, one might also note *week* and *makes*, where /k/ corresponds with <k>. We also discover that the sound /k/ can operate with other sounds, which together correspond to a letter or letters. Consider the words *Sixties, mix* and *expense*. Here, /ks/ corresponds to a single letter <x>. Then there is *quarter* which is similar to a group of English words – *queen, quid, quite* and so on – that show a correspondence between /kw/ and <qu>. That said, the correspondence between <qu> and /kw/ has weakened in the case of *quarter*, so that we hear pronunciations such as [kɔːtə]. (For further discussion of such correspondences, see Chapter 3, examples in [3.3] and the commentary relating to them).

Marrin might argue that, whilst there are complications, it is generally the case that <c> corresponds with /k/. The issue, then, is how strong that generalization is. In fact, for someone who hears a /k/ and wishes to write it down, the generalization is not at all robust. Carney's (1994: 216) corpus-based study suggests that only 59 per cent of the time does /k/ correspond with <c>. Put another way, this means that every ten times this sound is written down four of them are likely to be wrong if the speller is following this one 'rule' – that's quite a lot of mistakes!

What this discussion illustrates is that English spelling is not based on simple sound–letter correspondences as far as today's English is concerned: it is not a simple phonemic system. We can say this about today's English, but not about the English of a thousand or more years ago. Then it actually was a relatively simple system based largely on sound–letter correspondences (see Section 13.2.2). As our survey will reveal, subsequent historical events have not only made those sound-letter correspondences more complex, or in some cases seen them unravel, but have also made the basis of English spelling itself

---

ILLUSTRATION BOX 13.1

A system of systems?

Common misspellings concern words like: *gallary, succesful, exibition, definate, politition, extasy* and *morgage*. History can help account for their standard 'correct' spellings, which follow the conventions of the languages that gave them to English. Thus: *gallery* (Old French *galerie*), *successful* (Latin *successus* + *ful*), *exhibition* (Old French *exhibition* from Latin *exhibition*), *definite* (Latin *definitus*), *politician* (Old French *politique* from Latin *politicus* + *ian*), *ecstasy* (Old French *extasie*, but the <c> is in the Greek ἔκστασις), *mortgage* (Old French *mort* + *gage*, literally 'dead pledge'). Obviously, learners of English are unlikely to be familiar with the etymology of these words, so they will get no help from this quarter. Instead, they will fall foul of English pronunciations of words which have spellings more suited to pronunciations in the original language. Thus, unlike in French, the second vowel of *gallery* is reduced to schwa /ə/, which could match various English vowel letters; the doubled consonants of *successful* make no difference to the pronunciation compared with single consonants, unlike the Latin original; the <h> of *exhibition* is silent, which was not the case in Latin; and so on. Note that these examples illustrate the general and important point that English has incorporated other spelling systems within it. This is partly why it is so complex.

more complex. Rather than attempting a complete description of the English spelling systems of particular periods, we will focus on aspects that help explain the nature of spelling today.

13.2 Historical explanations for apparent chaos in spelling

13.2.1 The development of the English stock of letters

One of the basic problems for English spelling is that it inherited a stock of letters designed for other languages. Amazingly, Egyptian hieroglyphs seem to provide a starting point for at least some letters, but notably <K N O A>. For example, if you rotate the symbol <A> 180 degrees, one can see that it vaguely resembles the horned head of an ox. Egyptian hieroglyphs are not an alphabetic system, that is, a system of symbols representing sounds. Rather, they are a complex system involving pictograms (symbols representing meanings, rather like written Chinese), as well as some symbols representing sounds. The earliest alphabetic system that English can trace a line to is a Semitic alphabet, remnants of which have been found in the area of Sinai. This system seems to have been adopted, adapted and passed on by various peoples, often as part of military conquest or cultural influence. In brief, the history is thus:

> Egyptian hieroglyphs (at least for some letters) (*c*.2000 BC) → A semitic alphabet (in Sinai) (*c*.1750 BC) → Phoenician alphabet (based initially in today's Middle East) (*c*.1000–800 BC) → Greek alphabet (based initially in today's Greece) (after 800 BC) → Etruscan alphabet (based initially in today's Italy) (*c*.650 BC) → Roman alphabet (based initially in today's Rome) (after 550 BC)

It's worth noting that the Roman alphabet was not the only alphabet to appear in early Britain, as we also find the **Runic alphabet**. This has a rather mysterious history, probably being derived from the Etruscan alphabet and developed in Northern Europe. Its spiky appearance is thought to be due to the fact that it was designed for wood carving. It consists of 24 letters (see: http://www.omniglot.com/writing/runic.htm), and was traditionally called **futhorc,** after its first six letters. Very few of the Anglo-Saxons were literate and the amount of writing that was done was limited, so Anglo-Saxon Runic examples are restricted to a few engravings and inscriptions on stone, wood or horn, most of which do not pre-date, as far as scholars can ascertain, the early seventh century and most of which are found in northern England. An example of Anglo-Saxon Runic writing can be seen in Figure 13.1. This is the front panel of the Franks Casket (named after the archaeologist who donated it to the British Museum), the edges of which contain Runic script. It is thought to date from the early seventh century, and is perhaps the earliest example of English poetry. However, the Runic alphabet did not catch on and very soon died out.

Two events helped bring Britons into contact with the **Roman alphabet:** trading contact with continental Europe, and the arrival of Christian

FIGURE 13.1   The Franks Casket. Photo by © Jo St Mart/British Museum

missionaries in Britain in AD 597 (the latter also helped to spread literacy). The Roman alphabet donated 23 letters to English: <A B C D E F G H I K L M N O P Q R S T V X Y Z> (lower-case variants were later developments). However, even at this early stage, this system was less than ideal for English from the perspective of sound–letter correspondences, as some sounds of Old English (OE) had no letter counterpart:

- [w], the first sound of *wet*, generally utilized the Runic symbol <ρ> (called 'wynn'). It was rarely used after 1300, and was replaced by 'double-u' <uu> or <vv>.[2]
- [θ] and [ð], as in *thin* and *the*, were represented by the Runic symbol <þ> (called 'thorn'), and later by <ð> (called 'eth') (possibly an Irish development of <d> with a line through it). Both were used interchangeably, and eventually replaced by <th> in Middle English (ME). Thorn survives in the first letter of: *Ye Olde Tea Shoppe* (this letter is often pronounced as if it were the letter <y>, whereas in fact that is a printer's substitute for a thorn).
- [æ], somewhat like the vowel of *mat*, was represented by two letters <a> and <e>, 'ligatured' to form <æ> (called 'ash', after the Runic symbol that represented the same sound). It ceased to be generally used during the ME period.

There were a few other issues, including: the use of an open <g>, giving <ʒ> (so-called 'yogh'), which was used for various sounds including [g], three variant letter forms for [s], and the lack of a dot on <i>.

Of course, today we have 26 letters in the alphabet. We mentioned <w> above. The other two later developments are as follows:

- Today's <j> is a development of <i>, and began to be established in the seventeenth century.

- Originally, <f> did service for the first sounds of both *vat* and *fat*. If <f> occurred in the context of vowels, then it would be realized as [v] not [f] (consider today's *of*). <v> used to be a letter variant of <u>, but eventually took over the representation of the sound [v].

It is worth mentioning that not all Roman letters were immediately deployed in English: <q> and <z> were little used until the Norman French conquest, whilst the use of <k> has always remained fairly rare.

13.2.2   Spelling in the OE period

Despite the inadequacies of the Roman alphabet as far as English is concerned, sound-letter correspondences capture much about OE spelling. For example, the following sets of words all contain silent letters that would have been pronounced by contemporaries:

- *two, sword, answer*
- *walk, half, folk*
- *wreck, write, wring*
- *gnat, gnarl, gnaw*
- *knee, know, knight*
- *might, daughter, plough*
- *will, bliss, hill*
- *life, name, broke*

These words had very similar spellings in OE (though most words would have included a grammatical inflection at the end). For the purposes of illustrating spelling and pronunciation, let us ignore the precise OE spelling of the word and predict what an OE pronunciation of some of the above words would have been. The pronunciation of a form like *wring* would have been [wrɪŋg] (or possibly [vrɪŋg]). Today, it is generally [rɪŋ], the area of exception being Western central and northern areas in England where one can still find the <g> articulated, as in [rɪŋg]. The pronunciation of *knight* would have been [knɪçt] (rhyming with German *nicht*). The set consisting of words with double consonants is there to illustrate the fact that, in OE, double consonants were distinguished from singular consonants in pronunciation (and the difference had phonemic significance). This is not as bizarre as it sounds: Modern Italian has 'geminate consonants'. Thus the spelling of *broccoli* can clearly be heard in Italian pronunciation, but cannot in English, and hence it is frequently misspelt. (To get a sense of the Italian pronunciation, try saying the word as if it had the following syllables *broc-co-li*). We will return to the final set of words – *life, name, broke* – in Section 13.2.4. One other point we should briefly note is that letters were not the only way in which pronunciation was represented in OE writing. OE had phonemic vowel length that was indicated by a macron (short line above a vowel), for example, *sōna* 'immediately'.

ILLUSTRATION BOX 13.2

Spellings before standardization

Spellings often reflected different accents prior to the sixteenth century. For example, the *Oxford English Dictionary* cites the following variant spellings for the word *sword*:

> *sweord, sueord, swurd, suord, swyrd, suerd, swerd, swærd, swuerd, swerde, sworde, surd, squorde, zuord, swerid, swert, sward, swirde, swhirde, squrd, sqwerd, swearde, swyrde, swurde, shorde, showrde, swoord, swoorde, swrd, sourd, sword*

Zuord offers the clearest evidence in the above list of a spelling reflecting an accent. This is the only variant to begin with <z> instead of <s>, and it seems to be the only example from a Kentish text; that text is *Ayenbite of Inwyt* ('the remorse of conscience') and was written in 1340 by Michael of Northgate, a monk from St Augustine's, Canterbury. Spellings such as the <z> in *zuord* are not one-offs that can be dismissed as a mistake, for we also find *zuo* ('so'), *zen* ('sin'), *zaule* ('soul'), and so on, in this text. Such examples enable us to infer that, in the Kentish of that time, [s] was pronounced [z] if it occurred at the beginning of a word (or root syllable). Similarly, [f] was pronounced [v] if it occurred at the beginning of a word (or root syllable), and gave us spellings such as *uram* ('from'; remember that <u> also did the work of modern <v>), *uor* ('for'), *uader* (the 'father') and so on. A general feature of the Kentish accent, then, was that – like many southern England accents – fricatives were voiced in initial position. Today, this can still be heard in the speech of some speakers from the southwest of England.

13.2.3 French influence and developments in ME

Another significant historical event to impact on English spelling was the arrival of the Norman French in 1066 (not least because they took over the administrative system, and thus the powerhouse of the country). Norman French, a dialect of Old French, had a different sound system and a different spelling system from English. Let us consider some consequences of French influence on English, specifically, some place names. Turville was originally spelt with initial <th> (or, more accurately, a thorn). However, as neither of the sounds that <th> (or thorn) represented in English are part, or were part, of French, the spelling changed to fit the French sound system. Similarly, initial consonant clusters consisting of <s> followed by a consonant were not a feature of the French system. Thus, place names such as Tutbury and Nottingham lost the initial <s> that they used to have (probably a fortunate change for the latter place name, given the unpleasant meaning of the first syllable if it had retained <s>!).

Norman and other scribes in the ME period promoted the digraphs <th>, <uu> (or <vv>) and <sh>, and, consequently, the distinctive – from today's point of view – letters of the OE period (thorn, eth and wynn) begin to disappear. Note that more digraphs resulted in a loosening of strict sound–letter correspondences. Norman scribes also introduced a number of Old French spelling conventions (some specific to Norman French) into English, notably:

<cw>	(as in O.E. *cwen* 'queen')	→ <qu>	(cf. Mod. French *quatre*)
<c>	(as in O.E. *cild* 'child')	→ <ch>	([tʃ] has weakened to [ʃ] in Mod. French words like *chef*)[3]
<s>	(as in O.E. *is* 'ice')	→ <c>	(cf. Mod. French *Citroën*)
<u>	(as in O.E. *hus* 'house')	→ <ou>	(cf. Mod. French *vous*)

To be fair, not all of these changes were negative. In particular, <c> had two correspondences in OE; [tʃ] (as in O.E. *cild*) and [k] (as in O.E. *clif*). The adoption of the digraph <ch> thus helped to simplify things.

In the ME period we also see words such as *love, come, some, son, monk* and *wolf* regularly spelt with an <o> for the vowel sound rather than the original <u>, as in OE *lufu, cuman, sum, sunu, munuc* and *wulf*. Why did this happen, given that <u> had a much better correspondence with pronunciation then, as it does now? The answer is to do with legibility. In some early writing styles, some letters, notably <ɩ n u m>, were made with one or more down strokes of the pen (these are 'minim' letters) (<i> did not in its early history have the dot). Once stacked together, it could be tricky to distinguish individual letters. This was particularly the case for words written in the writing style known as 'text hand', 'textura' or 'Gothic', which spanned the ME period and dominated formal book writing. It gave rise to an early print style known as 'black letter' (this was used in, for example, Germany, up to the middle of the twentieth century). Some sense of the difficulty can be seen by rendering our examples in that script: 𝔩𝔲𝔣𝔲, 𝔠𝔲𝔪𝔞𝔫, 𝔰𝔲𝔪, 𝔰𝔲𝔫𝔲, 𝔪𝔲𝔫𝔲𝔠 and 𝔴𝔲𝔩𝔣.

13.2.4 Developments in the Early Modern period

We will mention three specific developments for the Early Modern period, ordered according to the degree of impact on the spelling system, from least to most. This is also the period in which the standardization of English took place, but we will deal with that in the following two sections.

The Early Modern period, overlapping as it does with the Renaissance, saw huge interest in, and admiration for, classical Greek and Roman culture. Ancient Greek and Latin were extolled as perfect languages (see, for example, Swift's words in the following section), whilst English was considered to be in a bad state. One consequence of this is that some individuals promoted etymological re-spellings. For example:

langage	>	language (Latin *lingua*)
dette	>	debt (Latin *debitum*)
receite	>	receipt (Latin *receptum*)

| samon | > | salmon (Latin *salmo*) |
| sisoures | > | scissors (Latin *scindere*) |

The spellings on the left, which were current in ME, were altered to the Latin spelling, and, in the process, helped to further weaken sound-letter correspondences.[4]

During this period, English phonology underwent the greatest change in its history. This change is referred to as the Great Vowel Shift, and you will hear more about it in Chapter 14 on sound change. In a nutshell, the long vowels of ME underwent a related set of changes. For example, in ME, the first vowel of the word *life* used to be [i:] – a pronunciation which better matches its spelling. Also, the final <e>, a remnant of a grammatical noun inflection (see Chapter 17), was not silent but pronounced as something like a schwa [ə]. Thus, the pronunciation in ME was [li:fə] – quite a good match in terms of sound-letter correspondences. During the Early Modern English (EModE) period, the long vowel first shifted to [əɪ], and later to what many English speakers have today, namely, [aɪ]. In parallel, the final <e> ceased to be pronounced. The problem is that these changes were taking place in a period when spelling was being standardized. Put simply, spelling ceased to change to any great degree, but changes in pronunciation have never stopped; hence the erosion of sound-letter correspondences.

Borrowing words from other languages has always been a feature of the history of English, but it gathered pace in the ME period, and peaked in the EModE period (see Chapter 15, for more detail on loanwords). The important point for this chapter is that we borrowed the spelling systems of other languages when we borrowed words from them. Thus, for example, we have the French convention representing a word-final [k] (e.g., *grotesque*), the Latin convention for representing geminate (double) consonants (e.g., *accommodation*), the Greek convention for representing [f] (e.g., *philosophy*), and so on (see Illustration Box 13.1).

13.2.5 The impetus for Early Modern spelling standardization

In this section we will focus on three factors of particular importance in galvanizing the standardization of spelling, namely printing, dictionaries and spelling reformers. Readers may wish to note the more general discussion of the standardization of English in Chapter 12. Remember that, prior to the Early Modern period, there was huge variability in the way words were spelt. Whilst commentators, such as the monk Orm writing in the twelfth century, might not have considered the spelling system optimal for particular purposes (such as reading a text out in church), there was no sense in which spelling a word one way as opposed to another would be taken as a reflection of something about the speller (e.g., their (lack of) intelligence). Variability was normal, not socially proscribed.

William Caxton set up a printing press at Westminster in 1476, thought to be the first in England. The whole point of printing is the mass reproduction of written material. This means one way of spelling a word replicated many times, obviously contributing to creating a uniform spelling system. But which way of spelling a word would be replicated? Caxton was located close to the government offices, and there is a certain logic in supposing that he gravitated towards the English of official circles, a variety of English dubbed by Samuels (1963) **Chancery standard** (mentioned briefly in Chapter 12). However, the key role of the Chancery standard in the standardization of spelling or other aspects of English, or indeed in Caxton's printed texts, may be an over-simplification. For one thing, as Benskin (1992) argues, the Chancery standard was not a neat, homogenous variety. Most so called Chancery documents did not actually emanate from the Chancery (there were in fact four important offices: Chancery, Privy Seal, Signet and the Parliament). Also, there is the small matter that Chancery English contains features that are not part of the eventual standard. Clearly, things are more complex.

We should briefly note that the contribution of printing to spelling included some counter-movements to uniformity. In particular, printers had no easy way of producing a neat right-hand edge to a text, as one can do with a computer by clicking a line justification button. Instead, to get a particular line to spread out so that it was level with the right-hand edge, they would add superfluous letters (often an extra <e>, or a doubling of the consonants of some words). They would also use <y> instead of <i>, because <y> took up more space on a given line.

The printing of written material of various kinds in ever-larger quantities paralleled increasing education amongst the middle ranks. There is general consensus amongst historians that literacy, however it is defined, was expanding during the Early Modern period. Social groups outside the aristocracy needed assistance in coping with reading and writing. Enter the dictionary. The first monolingual dictionary of English was published by Robert Cawdrey, in 1604, and covered approximately 2500 words. As Cawdrey's preface indicates, the point of the dictionary was not just to help people understand words but to teach them the 'true writing' (i.e., 'correct' spelling) of them. From the beginning, then, dictionaries propagated particular spellings of words, and acted as authorities on what 'correct' spellings should be.

These developments were part of an increasing focus on a **national standard** of written English, as we saw in Chapter 12. From the sixteenth century onwards, the standard was codified in language books – not just dictionaries, but also grammars – that were then widely used in schools. Moreover, all this was underpinned by a prescriptive movement, constituted by self-appointed individuals concerned with the social evaluation of English in general and the standardization of English in particular. Perhaps the most famous statement on the matter is that made by Jonathan Swift (1712) in his *A Proposal for Correcting, Improving, and Ascertaining the English Tongue*, in which he says for example:

The Roman Language arrived at great Perfection before it began to decay: And the French for these last Fifty Years hath been polishing as much as it will bear, and appears to be declining by the natural Inconstancy of that people…But the English Tongue is not arrived to such a degree of Perfection, as to make us apprehend any Thoughts of its Decay; and if it were once refined to a certain Standard, perhaps there may be Ways found out to fix it fore ever.

Similar attitudes can be seen in the statements of spelling reformers. Perhaps the most famous of the spelling reformers is John Hart. In his *An Orthographie* (1569), he wrote:

Which is uppon the consideration of the seuerall voices of the speech, and the use of their seuerall markes for them, which we cal letters. But in the moderne & present maner of writing (as well of certaine other languages as of our English) there is such confusion and disorder, as it may be accounted rather a kinde of ciphering, or such a darke kinde of writing, as the best and readiest wit that euer hath bene, could, or that is or shalbe, can or may, by the only gift of reason, attaine to the ready and perfite reading thereof, without a long and tedious labour, for that it is unfit and wrong shapen for the proportion of the voice.

Hart argued that letters should match speech sounds, but bewailed the fact that they did not. He also noted that learners were in for a 'long and tedious labour', as is true today. Later, he pointed to spelling reform as the solution that would 'bring our whole nation to one certain, perfet and general speaking'. Here we have the old dream of one perfect language matched to one perfect nation.

ADVANCES BOX 13.1

Variability in English spelling across time

Until recently, studies that have explored spelling from a diachronic (i.e., historical) perspective have tended to be qualitative in focus, that is, they have attended to the most obvious spelling patterns for a given period. By way of illustration, Smith (2005: 222) comments on the following patterns for Shakespearean English: the interchangeability of <u> / <v> (depending on their initial/medial positioning), the use of <i> to represent <j> and the use of <vv> for <w> (see also Blake, 1996; Scragg, 1974). This focus is not surprising, given that these are the patterns that will strike the consciousness of the researcher as they read through texts. Patterns below the level of consciousness – patterns that, for example, might be more subtle or only emerge across many texts – go unnoticed. However, the advent of computers and computer software means that researchers are beginning to explore spelling variability more subtly and systematically.

Computers can overcome the difficulties occasioned by attempting to identify a large number of variants across many texts, genres and centuries. Archer and Rayson (2004) used their VARD tool to identify, from a number of historical texts, 3823 English words whose spelling differed from the modern written standard, and manually mapped those spelling variants to their normalized equivalent (i.e., to the modern standardized spelling of that particular word).

They then undertook a study to determine the frequency of the 3823 spelling variants in historical texts of the seventeenth, eighteenth and nineteenth centuries. These texts represented a number of genres, including seventeenth-century newsbooks taken from the *Newsbook Corpus*, 'economy', 'religious', 'political', 'sciences' and 'law' texts taken from the *Lampeter Corpus* (1640–1760), fictional texts such as *Gulliver* (1726) and *Tristram Shandy* (1757–67) and play texts (for example, the works of Shakespeare). They were particularly interested in determining whether we are right to assume that:

(i)   the more standardized written English is the fewer spelling variants there will be,
(ii) genre plays a part in which variants are used as well as the extent to which they are used, and – importantly –
(iii) the standardization of English spelling was largely completed by 1700 (see, e.g., Howard-Hill, 2006).

Archer and Rayson found that the 3823 'non-standard' spellings (from the perspective of standard written English) did decline quite markedly in frequency from the seventeenth to the eighteenth century (i.e., from 10,252 occurrences per million words in the seventeenth century to 5661 occurrences per million words in the eighteenth century), but they also found evidence of the same spelling variants being utilized well into the nineteenth century, albeit to a lesser degree (i.e., 1063 occurrences per million words). This result simultaneously confirms a **move towards** standardization and suggests that variation has remained – and will probably remain – a feature of the English spelling system for the foreseeable future (consider, for example, the impact of texting/computer mediated communication (CMC) on our spelling system today).

A number of the 3823 spelling variants occurred in (texts representative of) all three centuries – but they were not always utilized most frequently in the seventeenth century, as we might expect given the differences in frequency highlighted above. For example, words ending with <'d> were most frequent in the eighteenth-century texts (with forms such as *look'd*, *answer'd*, *ask'd* and *offer'd* accounting for just a few of the 1287 occurrences per million words). In contrast, words ending in <'d> were only found 498 times per million words in the seventeenth-century data and 177 times per million words in the nineteenth-century data. Other forms of spelling variation common to all three centuries include consonant doubling (e.g., <tt> for <t>) and the omission (from the perspective of standard written English) of letters (e.g., <o> for <ou>).

Archer and Rayson opted to explore the seventeenth century (i.e., the century that displayed the highest level of spelling variation) in order to assess whether genres within particular periods demonstrated differences in variant patterning (in terms of type and frequency). Interestingly, their findings with respect to the same 3823 forms suggest that spelling variation was not a prominent feature of all of the seventeenth century genres. For example, the *Newsbook Corpus* effectively contained 296 occurrences per million words (of the 3823 forms identified by Archer and Rayson) – a frequency that seems very low, when compared to the 2247 occurrences (per million words) found in the *Lampeter* dataset. It is worth highlighting once again that the *Lampeter* dataset contained genres such as 'science', 'religion', 'politics', 'law' and 'economy', for these are genres which are regarded as having some of the very factors, namely prestige and power, that are meant to provide a motivating force for standardization. Yet, Archer and Rayson's study suggests that the more broad-based, popular genre of newsbooks was in the vanguard instead (at least in the seventeenth century). The *Lampeter* and *Newsbook* corpora are also interesting for the number of spelling variants that were indicative of a particular genre in this period. Thus, several of the most frequent variant forms within the *Newsbook Corpus* were shortened versions of temporal nouns – for example, *Decemb*, *Decem*, *Novemb* and *Wedneseve*.[5] Similarly, *Sinne* was the second most frequent variant form in 'Religion' (with 82 occurrences per million words), whilst *Countrey*, *Expence* and certain types of commodity, such as *Wooll* and *Linnen* were all frequently utilized in the 'Economy' dataset (with 85, 60, 53 and 45 occurrences per million words respectively). These and similar results seem to confirm that the process of standardization did not proceed evenly across genres. However, more work is required to determine exactly which of the genres standardized first (and in which century).

13.4 Order in chaos

Earlier in the chapter, we touched on the universally acknowledged 'truth' that English spelling is chaotic. 'Let me spell it out – our language is chaotic', declares the title of Guy Keleny's article in the *Independent* newspaper (19 November 2004). Unfortunately, this is wrong. Chaos means that there is no regularity or system, but this is not true of English spelling. There are indeed regularities such as: <b> corresponds to [b]. According to Carney's (1994: 212) study, the sound [b] is represented as < b> 98 per cent of the time when we write it down. The **impression** of chaos is caused by the fact that English is not an alphabetic system with strict one-to-one letter–phoneme correspondences. In fact, the basis of English spelling is not solely a matter of matching pronunciation – something which commentators invariably ignore. Consider the following generalizations.

Marking sound correspondences of other letters

Well-known (at least in UK schools) are two complementary generalizations:

- A doubled consonant indicates that the preceding vowel is short (e.g., *navy* versus *navvy*)
- A final <e> indicates that the proceeding vowel is long (e.g., *mat* versus *mate*)

These generalizations account for spellings like: *bite/bitter*, *lobe/lobby*, *nape/nappy*, and so on. The point is that, although the double consonant or final <e> are not now pronounced (as they would have been in earlier periods of English), they do have a role to play in marking how other letters are pronounced. Neither generalization is completely watertight (consider the very frequent word *have*).

Sound correspondences and word position

As we saw in Chapter 2, according to George Bernard Shaw's somewhat tongue-in-cheek account, the word *ghoti* could be pronounced the same as the word *fish*. In fact, any competent reader would pronounce *ghoti* as either [gəuti:] or [gəutɪ]. The main feature of English spelling that Shaw ignores is the position of the letters in the word. Consider these generalizations:

- word-initial <gh> corresponds to [g]
- word-final <ti> corresponds to [ti:] or [tɪ]

Word-final <ti> is in fact very rare, applying to a handful of borrowed words like *graffiti*.

Letter distribution

Some generalizations are possible with respect to letter distribution in words. A fairly robust generalization is as follows:

- Words do not end in <i>, <j>, <q>, <u>, <v> or single <z>

Exceptions to this generalization tend to be obviously foreign. Note that the word *graffiti*, mentioned above, would be such an exception.

Grammatical part of speech

English spelling takes account of grammatical parts of speech. The best-known generalization is the so called 'three letter rule':

- Open class words will not be spelled with less than three letters

This helps account for pairs like *be/bee, in/inn, I/eye, no/know, or/oar*, and *so/sew*.

Lexical sets

English spelling better preserves relations between words than does English pronunciation in the main (and thereby creates lexical sets). In the following sets of words, the letters of the first word are all represented in the second, but there is no corresponding identity of pronunciation: *sign/signature, paradigm/paradigmatic*, and *solemn/solemnity*.

Etymological sets

English spelling often preserves etymological relations between words, thereby creating sub-systems within English spelling. As an illustration, let's return to the discussion in our first section: the first letter of *cat*, <c>, corresponds with /k/, a correspondence that existed in OE (although not unambiguously), and, for that matter, in classical Latin. As noted in Section 13.2.3, the correspondence of <c> with /s/ generally reflects a different set of words that were borrowed from French (or from Latin via French), as in the case of, for example, *literacy*. Also in that section, we noted the arrival in English of the French digraph <ch> corresponding with /tʃ/, which was then deployed in native English words like *children*. The fact that <ch> corresponds with [k] in words like *scheme*, reflects a Greek convention (consider also words like *chorus*, *chrysanthemum* and *chiropodist*). Of course, there is no suggestion that users of English are aware of etymologies, but it seems likely that they are aware of different sub-systems.

Recommended readings

For a fairly detailed, authoritative and yet highly accessible introduction to spelling, including its history, and indeed the English writing system generally, Cook (2004a) is highly recommended. The same author also has an amusing, lightweight, miscellany on spelling (Cook, 2004b), as well as useful material that can be accessed from his personal web page. The standard historical treatment of spelling is Scragg (1974). Carney (1994), a monumental survey of present-day spelling, is a goldmine of information. A good entry point for the history of English letters is Sacks (2004).

Notes

1 Now based at the University of Central Lancashire.
2 In fact, <u> or <uu> (or <v> variants) were used in the earliest OE texts, but then wynn took over.
3 English borrowed this word twice at two different stages in the evolution of French. The first time resulted in the English word *chief*, in which we can hear the older pronunciation of <ch>, the second time resulted in the English word *chef*, in which we can hear the newer pronunciation.
4 The spelling of *ecstasy*, mentioned in Illustration Box 13.1, is most likely an etymological re-spelling, moving the word closer towards ancient Greek.
5 The use of such abbreviations is an important reminder that the standardization of spelling will have been (and, to some extent, still is) subject to differing methods of production: consider the role of compositors and editors, and the presence of a house style, for example.

CHAPTER **14**

Phonological Change

Francis Katamba and Paul Kerswill

14.1 Introducing phonological change

All aspects of language change with the passage of time. The previous chapter treated changes in the spelling and following chapters will describe changes in vocabulary, meaning and grammar. The present chapter introduces the study of **sound change** (**phonological change** and **phonetic change** to be exact) and then proceeds to trace the major sound changes that have taken place from Old English to the present. It also acts as a springboard for the remaining chapters in this section (see in particular Section 14.2 on language change in general).

14.1.1 What is sound change?

It is for the most part impossible to establish the minutiae of pronunciation in ancient times (e.g., allophonic variation in the realization of phonemes) because we don't really know what English sounded like until a relatively short time ago when sound recordings became available. All that can be reconstructed are the broad outlines of phonological systems, for example, phoneme inventories, major phonotactic constraints and silhouettes of stress systems.

Despite the problems involved in establishing what the pronunciation of English might have been like many centuries ago, you don't need to be persuaded of the reality of sound change. You know, for example, that your pronunciation of certain words is not identical to that of your parents, let alone grandparents. What would have been fairly minor changes in the pronunciation of successive generations got cumulatively magnified down the ages. The English spoken today is very different from the English spoken by King Alfred the Great in the ninth century.

14.1.2 Evidence of earlier pronunciation

How can scholars tell what the sound system of Old English (OE) was like? Of course, they cannot piece together a picture of the phonological system of OE by analysing audio recordings of, say, conversations at Alfred the Great's Court in Winchester. Before the 1870s it was not possible to make audio recordings. Before 1950, although recordings of speech could be made, the technology was cumbersome and the sound quality poor. So, we have had to rely on other means to reconstruct the pronunciation of English until quite recently. The principal sources of information about pronunciation are sketched below.

Written records provide most of the evidence that scholars rely on when reconstructing the pronunciation of the language before audio recordings became possible – or readily available. When deciphering written records, being able to interpret reliably the relationship between spelling and pronunciation is of paramount importance. So, gaining an understanding of the relationship between orthographic symbols and speech sounds is a necessary first step (see Chapter 13).

As we saw in the previous chapter, OE spelling was largely phonemic, but that is not to say that there was always clear-cut correspondences between phonemes and graphemes across the board. We noted earlier (Chapter 12) that standardization had not yet happened. So, there was plenty of scope to reflect dialectal and idiolectal variation. This lack of standardization isn't necessarily a curse. In fact, there are many cases where it is a boon. Because there was quite a lot of spelling variation there was more scope for comparing and contrasting spellings and drawing conclusions on that basis. Particularly helpful are **naive** or **inverse spellings** whereby writers attempting to mirror the actual pronunciation go against conventional practice. A good example of this is the use of *nought* in stead of *naught* and *abought* for *about*.

Rhymes and **rhyming dictionaries** are an even more readily available source of phonological evidence. Rhyme has always been a prominent feature of English verse and poetic texts are among the most significant body of texts preserved from the earliest period of the history of English. For instance, following Crystal (2005: 53) we can use evidence from rhyme to establish that in Shakespeare *haste* had the /æ/ vowel that was found in *fast*:

> *Romeo*: O, let us hence! I stand on sudden haste.
> *Friar*:   Wisely and slow. They stumble that run fast.
> (*Romeo and Juliet, Act II , Scene 3*)

Crystal confirms this by showing that *haste* was also alternatively spelt *hast* and rhymed with *last* in *Venus and Adonis*, lines 575–6. Note that when considering rhymes, care must be taken to include only words which phonologically rhyme and to exclude eye-rhymes, where the spelling is the same but the pronunciation is known to be different (e.g., *steak* and *weak*; *mow* and *cow*).

Puns are an additional, but less reliable source of evidence: it is not always clear what counts as a pun, let alone a good pun. Bad puns, like the one in the cartoon in Figure 14.1, are a poor guide to pronunciation (though they may have a high groan factor, as intended).

Good puns, like the one below, can provide useful information about pronunciation:

> *Samson*:   Gregory, on my word, we'll not carry <u>coals</u>.
> *Gregory*: No, for then we should be <u>colliers</u>.

Bad pun   *FIGURE 14.1*

Source: 'Fire Hydrant and Mailbox' © Word Sell Inc/Brad Shorr.

> *Sampson*: I mean, an we be in choler, we'll draw.
> *Gregory*: Ay, while you live, draw your neck out of <u>collar</u>.
> *(Romeo and Juliet,* Act I, Scene 1)

Notes: *collier* = coal miner or merchant; *choler* = anger; *collar* = hangman's noose

The underlined words that had a (long) /oː/ in Shakespeare's English do not work as puns in most current varieties English because the vowels have changed (cf. RP *coals* /kəʊlz/, colliers /kɒlɪəz/ and collars /kɒləz/).

Commentaries on pronunciation by **orthoepists** (pronunciation and diction experts), **grammarians** and **spelling reformers** are another source of evidence. Such commentaries are available mainly from the sixteenth century onwards. The pre-eminent orthoepist during the early Modern English period was the courtier and scholar John Hart (1551–1579). Hart distinguished five pairs of long and short vowels. He represented them with the vowels *i e a o u*. He provided a sophisticated description of the various sounds. For instance, he observed that *a* was articulated 'with a wyde opening of the mouth as when a man yauneth'. This can be translated in modern parlance as 'the sound represented by <a> was a very low open vowel'.

Clues from other languages can also help linguists discern patterns. For example, from a comparison with other West Germanic languages (e.g., Dutch, High German (ancestor of Modern Standard German and Yiddish)), we can be fairly certain that in OE the main stress generally fell on the first syllable of words.

The **nativization of loanwords** is another source of pronunciation clues. It may give an indication of the phonological rules that were available at different historical points. When words are borrowed from other languages, their pronunciation is adapted to fit in with the norms of the importing language. This is done, in part, by subjecting them to the phonological rules in force at the time when the word entered the language (see Chapter 15, Advances Box 15.1). Consequently, phonologically similar words imported at different times may show different modifications. That can be seen in the treatment of Latin loanwords that entered English at different times. For instance, Pyles and Algeo (1982: 294) citing Serjeantson (1935: 271–7) give an account of various imports including scrīn 'shrine' (Latin *scrīnium*). This word was borrowed quite early on during the period of Roman rule. At that time English had a rule converting /sk/ in syllable onsets into [ʃ] . Consequently, the word was pronounced with an initial [ʃ] (eventually the spelling <sh> was adopted to reflect this). Later on, Old English borrowed scōl 'school' from Latin *scōla*, which also had a /sk/ syllable onset that was realized as [sk]. In this case, however, [sk] <sc> remained unchanged. This is a good indication that the rule that yielded [ʃ] from /sk/ was no longer in use at this time.

14.2   Language change: why does pronunciation change?

All living languages are in a constant state of flux. That has been true of the English language at all times in its history. To understand language change, it is helpful to distinguish the causes of language change from the mechanisms that enable innovations to spread. These will be treated summarily here, and the reader is referred to sociolinguistics textbooks such as those by Holmes (2008) and Mesthrie and colleagues (2000).

There are competing views of the nature of language change. Very broadly speaking, the causes of language change can be divided into five categories, namely, **imperfect learning of grammar, social, functional, structural** and **contact.**

In the Chomskyan tradition, where knowledge of language is above all else seen as knowledge of a tacit system of principles and rules, language change is viewed as grammar change. It is attributed to the **imperfect learning** of rules that results in the modification of the grammar by the younger generation. For instance, at some point a new generation of English speakers would have added to their grammar a rule deleting coda-r in words like *for* and *form*. This rule was absent from the original grammar.

Linguists like Labov (1963) focus on the **social** nature of language. The attitudes, identities and interaction of members of a speech community are regarded as the principal motivators of language change (see, for example, the factors discussed in the formation of Standard English in Chapter 12). A speech community may be stratified by age, gender, geographical provenance, class, ethnicity, etc. and all these parameters may be reflected in the linguistic patterns used by different subgroups, and crucially, such linguistic features may serve as markers of identity. Language is used in a speech community, not only to communicate, but also to express and assert who we are and how we wish to be identified. The pronunciation of *bus* as [bʊs], for example, may be a useful way of telling the world that one is from the north of England. Prevalent usage in social networks that one belongs to will promote the diffusion and maintenance of the group norms (Milroy, 1980) (see also Section 14.6).

If a language has variant forms in competition with each other, there are normally winners and losers, eventually. Innovation involves the introduction of a novel linguistic feature which results in new variants. Consider the way in which in Cockney [f] has replaced [θ] in *teeth* [ti:θ] > [ti:f], *think* [θɪŋk] > [fɪŋk], etc. At first, this may have been in just one person's speech in one word, and it may have been regarded as a speech error. However, gradually, more words would have been pronounced in this way, not just by one or two speakers but by a growing number of speakers. The new pronunciation would have begun to be viewed as an alternative pronunciation. As such, it would have been positively evaluated by some, and stigmatized by others. Gradually the innovation diffused through the lexicon, affecting more and more words and eventually won and became the norm in Cockney – and is spreading to other dialects. But sometimes there is no clear winner; two variant forms coexist as near equals (cf. *eclectic* [ɪkˈlektɪk] ~ [ekˈlektɪk]). Alternatively, one variant may win but without delivering a knock-out blow. For instance, in most dialects, /h/ deletion removed all [h] sounds in /hw/ clusters(spelt <wh>) as in *why* [waɪ], *which* [wɪtʃ], *whale* [weɪl]). But this didn't happen in Scottish dialects that retained [hw] (cf. [hwaɪ], [hwɪtʃ] and [hweɪl]). Why does a variant spread not only from word to word in a single speaker's lexicon but also across the speech community? The desire on the part of some people to use a new variant as a badge of linguistic identity is a major factor. Many of the points made in the discussion of social factors were discussed and illustrated in Chapter 12 (see, for example, Advances Box 12.1).

Functional factors such as **iconicity** are also seen as being important by cognitive linguists like Croft who explains that 'The intuition behind iconicity is that the structure of language reflects in some way the structure of experience' (Croft, 2003:102). In phonetics, iconicity is seen in the onomatopoeic expressions found in language for example, *whine, meow, bang,* etc. In telling a story, normally grammar requires the structure of clauses and sentences to mirror the sequence in which events happened, for example, *He scored a goal and celebrated* vs. *He celebrated and scored a goal.* **Frequency** of usage matters. It leads to phonological fusion for example, *going to > gonna* and *I do not know > I don't know > don't know > dunno.* Likewise, suppletive stems are more likely to be learned, and remembered, and to resist change if they are in high frequency forms like the verbs *be, go, bring,* etc. It might be noted here that the cognitive approach underpins parts of both Chapter 16 on semantic approach and Chapter 17 on grammatical change.

Others offer **structural explanations**. They focus on formal relationships between linguistic elements. For instance, there is a strong tendency for phonological inventories to be symmetrical. Where there is a hole in the pattern, language change may (but doesn't have to) take place to fill it. Thus, if a language has obstruents phonemes that normally come in pairs, with each voiceless stop, fricative or affricate having a voiced counterpart, there will be structural pressure to fill any gaps in the pattern. That was the situation in OE where there were no voiced /v/ and /z/ phonemes corresponding to the voiceless fricatives /f/ and /s/. Change took place and these fricatives split into two phonemes /f/ and /v/ on the one hand, and /s/ and /z/ on the other.

Finally, change may be induced by languages coming into **contact** and as a result linguistic properties passing on from one language to another. Chapter 15 on lexical change will provide much illustration. Sounds are also among the linguistic features than may be borrowed, for example, English acquired /ɔɪ/ from French following the importation of words like *coin, boil*, etc. We are now ready to look at the evolution of English phonology.

14.3 Old English Phonology (450–1150)

As seen above, the largely phonemic orthography and surviving texts between them provide many useful clues about the phonemic system of Old English. Nonetheless, following Lass (2006), we advise you to read what we have to say about OE phonology in particular, and pre-twentieth century English historical phonology in general, bearing a number of caveats in mind.

The challenge of reconstructing in detail the OE phonological system is immense. The first problem is that the notion of Old English is an idealization of great magnitude. Then as now, there was considerable dialectal variation. (The map in Figure 14.2 shows the principal dialects.) Moreover,

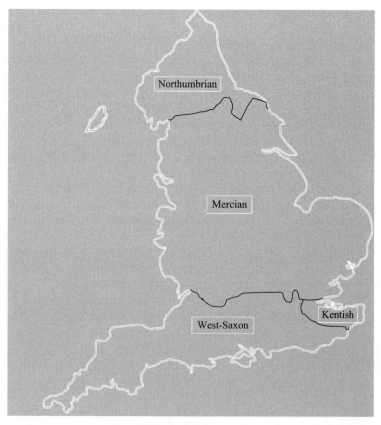

FIGURE 14.2   *Map of England showing Old English dialects*

over the six centuries spanned by the OE period, there were many changes in pronunciation. Early OE differed significantly from late OE. Furthermore, scribal practice, on which we mostly rely, was not always consistent as we have already noted. As well, the set of records that survive are not always complete. At best what we have is a rather blurred picture of what the phonological system of OE was like – and an even hazier picture of what it may have actually sounded like.

Let's start with an examination of the vowels system. Much has changed, but much has also remained broadly constant. The OE vowel inventory is presented in Table 14.1.

Words exemplifying OE vowels are listed below in Table 14.2.

OE vowel phonemes *Table 14.1*

	Front			Back	
Monophthongs		Short	Short	Short	Long
	High	i, y	iː, yː	u	uː
	Mid	e	eː	o	oː
	Low	æ	æː	ɑ	ɑː
Diphthongs	Short eo, æɑ			Long eːo, æːɑ	

Words illustrating OE vowel phonemes *Table 14.2*

Short vowels	Example	Gloss	Long vowels	Example	gloss
i	*riht*	'correct'	iː	*fīf*	'five'
y	*cynn*	'kin'	yː	*brȳd*	'bride'
e	*feld*	'open country'	eː	*brēda*	'breed'
æ	*glæd*	'glad, happy'	æː	*ǣg*	'egg'
u	*duru*	'door'	uː	*hūs*	'house'
o	*lof*	'praise'	oː	*fōt*	'foot'
ɑ	*nɑmɑ*	'name'	ɑː	*bāt*	'boat'
		Diphthongs			

Short			Long		Gloss
eo	*sweord*	'sword'	eːo	*dēop*	'deep'
æɑ	*æarm*	'arm'	æːɑ	*lēaf*	'leaf'
(ie)	*giefan*	'to give'			

There are a number of features that stand out. Three degrees of vowel height were distinguished, namely high, mid and low; and the vowel system was symmetrical. At each level of vowel height, a front vowel was matched with a back vowel. By contrast, present-day English contrasts 4 degrees of vowel height (see Figure 3.3 on page 49). The distinction between long and short vowels was important – and remains so to this day as we saw in Chapter 3. OE also had diphthongs. But their number was limited, and one of them, /ie/, was restricted to the early West-Saxon dialect. Interestingly, there were also two high front rounded vowels /y/ and /yː/.These front rounded vowels were lost by the end of the OE period.

Turning to the consonants, we observe that much has changed. But again, much has remained broadly constant. The consonants of OE are listed in Table 14.3 below and words exemplifying OE consonants are listed in Table 14.4 on page 267, with the relevant phoneme underlined.

When taking a bird's-eye view of the consonant system the first thing to observe is that OE contrasted short consonants (such as /n/, as in *spanan* 'entice, seduce' with **geminate** (double) consonants (such as /nn/, as in *spannan* 'span, link') (see also Chapter 13, Section 13.2.2). At first, geminate consonants were restricted to intervocalic position. In later OE, when word-final unstressed vowels and syllable rhymes were lost, geminate consonants could also now contrast with singleton consonants as in *mann* 'man, person' vs. *man* 'one, someone' (indefinite pronoun). Degemination of word-final consonants started occurring in later OE (giving *man* from *mann*) and the process was extended to intervocalic position in Middle English (giving *spanan* from *spannan*).

Table 14.3   *OE consonant phonemes*

	Stops	Affricate	Fricative	Nasal	Liquids	Glides
Bilabial	p pː b bː		m mː			w
Labiodental			f fː			
Dental			θ θː	n nː		
Alveolar	t tː d dː		s sː		l lː; r rː	
Palato-alveolar		tʃ tʃː dʒ dʒː	ʃ			
Palatal						j
Velar	k kː g gː		x xː			

Notes:

(i)   /w/ was labio-velar rather than bilabial, to be precise.

(ii) Consonant length was phonemic; geminate consonants contrasted with singleton consonants except in the case of /ʃ/ and the glides /j/ and /w/.

Table 14.4   Words illustrating OE consonant phonemes

Phoneme		Gloss		Phoneme		Orthographic form	
p	/preːost/	*prēost*	'priest	pː	/upːe/	uppe	'above'
b	/beran/	*beran*	'to bear, carry'	bː	/nabːan/	nabban	'to have not'
m	/morgen/	*morgen*	'morning	mː	/temːan/	temman	'to tame'
w	/wriːtan/	*wrītan*	'to write'	—			
f	/faran/	*faran*	'to go, travel'	fː	/ofːrian/	offrian	'to offer'
θ	/soːθ/	*sōþ*	'truth'	θː	/moθːe/	moþþe/	'moth'
n	/niːwe/	*nīwe*	'new'	nː	/benː/	benn	'wound'
t	/toːdæg/	*tōdæg*	'today	tː	/sitːan/	sittan	'to sit'
d	/dæg/	*dæg*	'day'	dː	/ θridːa/	ðridda	'third'
s	/sunu/	*sunu*	'son'	sː	/masːepreost/	massepreost	'mass-priest'
l	/leːof/	*lēof*	'precious, dear'	lː	/wilːan/	willan	'to wish'
r	/riːdan/	*rīdan*	'to ride'	rː	/steorːa/	steorra	'star'
tʃ	/ tʃild/	*cild*	'child'	tʃː	/wi tʃːekræft/	wiccecræft	'witchcraft'
dʒ	/swindʒere/	*swingere*	'scourge	dʒː	/edʒːe/	ecg	'edge'
ʃ	/ʃiːeran/	*scīeran*	'shear, cut'	—			
j	/jeong/	*geong*	'young'	—			
k	/kuː/	*cū*	'cow'	kː	/lekːan/	leccan	'to moisten'
g	/goːs/	*gōs*	'goose'	gː	/hogː/	hogg	'hog'
x	/xund/	*hund*	'dog'	xː	/hlæxːan/	hlæhhan	'to laugh'

14.3.1   Major developments in OE segmental phonology

Nasals

There were only two nasal phonemes /m/ and /n/. The velar nasal [ŋ] was merely the allophone of /n/ found before the velar consonants /k/ and /g/ as in *drincan* 'drink' and *hōring* 'adulterer'.

Fricatives: phonemic split

Whereas today voicing is contrastive for fricatives, in early OE, voiced fricatives were allophones of the voiceless fricative phonemes. For instance, /f/ had a voiced allophone [v] that occurred in between vowels inside a metrical foot (e.g., *ofer* 'over', *ǣfen* 'evening', and as [f] elsewhere, that is, syllable-initially as in *findan* 'find' and word-finally as in *hrōf* 'roof'. Allophone [f] also occurred in geminate clusters, e.g., *hrōffæst* 'well-roofed' as well as before another consonant as in *fifta* 'fifth'). Likewise, the velar fricative phoneme /x/ had an interesting set of allophones. It was realized as [ç], a palatal fricative (the sound in German *ich* 'I') before the sonorant consonants /n r l w/ in words like *hnutu* 'nut', *hring* 'ring', *hlæder* 'ladder' and *hwīl* 'period of time'. Elsewhere, it was realized as [x] as in *hand* 'hand', *leoht* 'light' and *eahte* 'eight'. It wasn't until the sixteenth century that /x/ started being realized by the glottal fricative [h] used in present-day English. To begin with, this happened in syllable-initial position. Meanwhile, a long process of attrition (that is still ongoing as we saw in Chapter 3) that curtailed the appearance of /x/ in speech had already started in the early thirteenth century when, in the south of England, a rule deleting coda /x/ sandwiched between a back vowel and a consonant had been introduced. As a result, words like *dohter* 'daughter' and *sohte* 'sought' were pronounced without [x]. Deletion was widened to include word-final /x/ (<h>) as in *frēoh* 'free', *fāh* 'hostile'. In this case /x/ could be deleted. But deletion was not always invoked. The constraint barring /x/ from word-final position could be satisfied by changing the sound realizing it from [x] to [f]. This is what happened in words like *rough* and *tough*.

We saw above that OE fricatives phonemes /f θ s/ had no voiced counterparts. Rather, these phonemes had voiceless and voiced allophones, with the latter occurring intervocalically in foot-medial position as in *ofer* [over] and voiceless allophones elsewhere. By the end of the OE period this had changed. A phonemic split had taken place and now voiced and voiceless allophones had become separate phonemes. A number of factors conspired to bring this about. The loss of word-final schwa that started in the twelfth century meant that an allophone of a fricative that had been between vowels, and hence voiced, would now find itself in word-final position and still voiced although the environment responsible for its voicing had disappeared. As a result, voicing of word-final fricatives became unpredictable–and hence phonemic as shown in [14.1].

[14.1]   a. *nosu* 'nose': [nosu] > [nozə] > [nɔːzə] > [nɔːz]
        b. *lufu* 'love': [luvu] >[luvə] > [luv]
                        (Lass, 1992: 59)

The borrowing of many French words such as *vois* 'voice', *veel* 'veal', *virgine* 'virgin'; *zele* 'zeal', *zani* 'zany', *zéphr* 'zephyr', etc. which had word-initial voiced fricatives [v] and [z] was another factor that facilitated the phonemic split.

This discussion of changes affecting fricatives has illustrated two key principles. First, sound change tends to be regular. It is subject to '**sound laws**', as it were. Normally, the same sound changes in the same way when it appears in the same phonological environment. Second, phonological systems may change not only with regard to their inventories of phonemes and their allophones but also in terms of their phonotactic constraints. We have seen that some consonant clusters in syllable onsets that were allowed in early OE became illegal subsequently, and disappeared. A constraint was introduced that banned /x/ from appearing in onset clusters with sonorants /n r l w/. The same prohibition also affected /w/ in ME. So, words like *wlite* 'beauty' and *wrītan* 'write' lost their initial /w/.

As we said earlier, all living languages constantly change. That was true of OE, as well. The picture painted above is static, for convenience. The reality was that the phonology of OE mutated continually. Below, we will highlight some of the most salient developments. The account presented is based mainly on Lass (2006) and (Jones 1989).

Palatalization and assibilation

Velar consonants were palatalized (velar /k/ > palatal [c]) when followed by a front vowel as in *cild* 'child', *cempa* 'warrior', *cæster* 'city'. Likewise, velar /g/ > palatal [ɟ] as in *gyst* 'stranger', *gyrdan* 'to gird', *hālgian* 'to consecrate', etc. Palatalization was especially prevalent in word initial velars (Hogg, 1992b: 257–73). Palatalization also affected /sk/ <sc> when next to a front vowel, for example, /skip/ *scip*, /skeːap/ *scēap* and /skieppan/ *scieppan* which became *ship*, *sheep* and *to shape* respectively. The name for this process whereby an original stop, here /k/, becomes a fricative (i.e., sibilant /s/) is called **assibilation**. Predictably, there was no assibilation before back vowels (cf. *scūfan* 'to push', *scand* 'shame, disgrace' where [sk] was retained.)

I-umlaut

In Pre-Old English, as in the other Germanic languages, there existed a phonological process called **I-umlaut** or **mutation**. A back vowel was fronted in anticipation of a front vowel [i] or the (front) palatal glide [j] in the following syllable.

[14.2] **i-umlaut rule**

$$[+\text{vowel} \rightarrow [-\text{back} \ /\_\_ \ C_o \begin{bmatrix} +\text{sonorantl} \\ -\text{back} \\ +\text{high} \end{bmatrix}$$

This phonological process was fully automatic. As a result of umlaut, long [ɑː] became [æː]; [oː] became [eː]; [uː] became [yː]; etc. and their short counterparts changed in a similar way [ɑː] > [æ]; [o] > [e]; [u]> [yː]; etc. The effect of the rule can be seen in [14.3]:

[14.3]

Nominative (subject) case, singular	**Nominative (subject) case, plural**	**Accusative (object) case, plural**	
/foːt/	/feːt-iz/	/foːt-unz/	'foot'
/goːs/	/geːs-iz/	/goːs-unz/	'geese'

Later the /i/ in the suffix was dropped and as a result, the conditioning environment for umlaut was lost. /oː/ and /eː/ became separate phonemes in this environment since [foːt] ~ [feːt] , [goːs] ~ [geːs] were minimal pairs. What happened next is a case of rule morphologization: what had been an automatic allophonic alternation took on the morphological role of marking the grammatical difference between singular and plural. The umlaut rule applied to other words with different vowels where the plural suffix was originally /-iz/. For instance, it applied to /muːs/ 'mouse', to yield the plural /myːs/ 'mice' and to /luːs/ 'louse' to give the plural /lyːs/ 'lice'.

Ablaut

OE also had **ablaut** or **vowel gradation** (i.e., a pattern of root vowel alternation) signalling various morphosyntactic properties. Ablaut occurs in so

Table 14.5   OE ablaut

	Infinitive		Simple past tense singular	Simple past tense plural	Past participle
Class I	drīfan	'to drive'	drāf	drifon	gedrifen
	rīdan	'to ride'	rād	ridon	geriden
Class II	crēopan	'to creep'	crēap	crupon	gecropen
	sprūtan	'to sprout'	sprēat	spruton	gesproten
Class III	drincan	'to drink'	dranc	druncon	gedruncen
	findan	'to find'	fand	fundon	gefunden
Class IV	beran	'to bear'	bær	bǣron	geboren
	stealan	'to steal'	stæl	stǣlon	gestolen
Class V	sprecan	'to speak'	spræc	sprǣcon	gesprecen
	gifan	'to give'	gæf	gǣfon	gegifen
Class VI	faran	'to fare, go'	fōr	fōron	gefaren
	standan	'to stand'	stōd	stōdon	gestanden
Class VI	cnāwan	'to know'	cnēow	cnēowon	gecnāwen
	slǣpan	'to sleep'	slēp	slēpon	geslǣpen

called **strong verbs** which instead of signalling certain verbal morphosyntactic properties by adding affixes did so by just changing the root vowel or by changing the root vowel and attaching affixes. See Table 14.5 (borrowed from Pyles and Algeo 1982: 126-7, and simplified).

Pre-homorganic consonant lengthening

If a short vowel (and especially a high one) was followed by a consonant cluster with either a nasal or liquid that shared the place of articulation of a following voiced obstruent (i.e., stop, fricative or affricate) normally the vowel would be lengthened. See the rule in [14.4]:

[14.4]   **OE pre-homorganic lengthening**

$$
\begin{bmatrix} +\text{vowel} \\ +\text{high} \\ -\text{long} \end{bmatrix} \rightarrow [+\text{long} \; /\_\_ \; \left\{ \begin{bmatrix} +\text{nasal} \\ \alpha\text{place} \end{bmatrix} \atop \begin{bmatrix} +\text{consonant} \\ +\text{liquid} \\ \alpha\text{place} \end{bmatrix} \right\}
$$

The effects of this rule can be seen in the following examples (where v̄ indicates a long vowel and v̆ a short vowel):

[14.5]

		Short vowel	Long vowel
a.	**Vowel lengthening before a nasal plus a homorganic consonant**	climb 'climb' >	clīmb
		hand 'hand' >	hānd
		hund 'dog' >	hūnd

b. **Vowel lengthening before a liquid plus a homorganic consonant**

cild 'child' >   cīld

folde 'earth, ground' >   fōlde

ford 'ford' >   fōrd

Note, however, that the presence of a third consonant following the vowel inhibited this rule. There is no lengthening in *cĭldru* (plural) 'children' and *fŏldweg* 'path, way'.

Pre- cluster shortening

A long vowel would be shortened if it occurred before any geminate consonant or consonant cluster – unless the cluster in question met the conditions for vowel lengthening that are shown in [14.4] and exemplified in [14.5] above.

[14.6] **Pre- cluster shortening**

$$\begin{bmatrix} +\text{vowel} \\ +\text{long} \end{bmatrix} \rightarrow [-\text{long} \; / \underline{\quad} \left\{ \begin{bmatrix} +\text{consonant} \\ \alpha\text{features} \\ C_1 \end{bmatrix} \begin{bmatrix} +\text{consonant} \\ \alpha\text{features} \\ C_2 \end{bmatrix} \right\}$$

Notes:

(i) $\begin{bmatrix} +\text{consonant} \\ \alpha\text{features} \end{bmatrix} \begin{bmatrix} +\text{consonant} \\ \alpha\text{features} \end{bmatrix}$ = Geminate (identical) consonants.

(ii) $C_1 \neq C_2$. consonants that are not geminate and which don't satisfy the requirements of homorganic clusters in [14.4] and [14.5].

Pre-cluster shortening is illustrated in [14.7]:

[14.7]

Long vowel		**Pre-cluster shortening**	
fīf	'five'	fĭfta	'fifth'
cēpan	' keep'	cĕpte	'kept
wēpan	'weep'	wĕpte	'wept'
wīse	'wise'	wĭsdom	'wisdom'

Trisyllabic shortening

In a word of at least three syllables, a long vowel occurring in antepenultimate position (i.e., three syllables from the end) would be shortened if the syllable in penultimate position (second from the end) was unstressed. This process is called **trisyllabic shortening** or **trisyllabic laxing** (because short vowels are also called lax vowels):

[14.8] **Trisyllabic shortening**

$$\begin{bmatrix} +\text{vowel} \\ +\text{long} \end{bmatrix} \rightarrow [-\text{long} \; / \underline{\quad} C_o \begin{bmatrix} +\text{vowel} \\ -\text{stress} \end{bmatrix} C_o \, V$$

Trisyllabic shortening came into force around the eleventh century, applying not only in native words like OE *'wīlde* 'wild' ~ *'wĭldēornes* 'wilderness' (from earlier 'wīlde 'wild' ~ 'wīldēornes; 'sūþ 'south'~ 'sǔþerne 'southern' (from earlier 'sūþ ~ 'sūþerne'). Post-Norman conquest, trisyllabic shortening was applied vigorously to French loanwords, for example, Old French divīn ~ divīnité was modified to divīn ~ divĭnite.

Old English breaking (diphthongization)

Breaking (i.e., diphthongization) is depicted in [14.9] and illustrated in [14.10] where OE is compared with other West Germanic languages. Breaking turned both long and short front vowels into diphthongs when they appeared either before a liquid (/l/ or /r/) that was followed by a consonant or before a consonant followed by /x/ (in the spelling <h>) (Jones, 1989: 33–58):

[14.9]
i	→	io	Before
ī	→	īo	l (+ Consonant)
e	→	eo	or
ē	→	ēo	r (+ Consonant)
æ	→	æɑ <ea>	or
ǣ	→	ǣɑ	h (+ Consonant)

[14.10] **OHG**   **WS**

a. **Breaking before r/ (+consonant)**

barn	bearn	'child'
hirti	hiorþe	'shepherd'
erda	eorþe	'earth'

b. **Breaking before /l/ (+consonant)**

wal	weall	'wall'
kalt	ceald	'cold'
melkan	meolcan	'to milk'

c. **Breaking before /x/ (+consonant)**

līhti	lēoht	light
līh	lēoh	lie
fehtan	feohtan	'to fight'

Note:
OHG = Old High German
WS = West Saxon dialect of OE

Vowel mergers and the rise and rise of schwa

There were a number of other processes affecting vowels that significantly altered the vowel system of OE. They are treated summarily below. For detailed accounts see (Campbell, 1959; Jones, 1989; Hogg, 1992b; Lass 2006).

• The most striking changes involved the development, and eventual loss of word-final **schwa**. In many cases vowels in unstressed word-final syllables gradually weakened and became schwa, which was spelt as <e>. Thus, earlier OE *guma* 'man' > ME *gume*; OE *whalas* 'whales' > ME *whales*, *lufu* 'love' > ME *luve*, etc. With the passage of time, this schwa tended to become less and less distinct and eventually dropped off the ends of words in the pronunciation although it may have been retained in the spelling (cf. *love*). This process was carried out with great vigour especially from the tenth to the thirteenth centuries and was complete by the end of the fourteenth century. The loss of final schwa had a serious impact on grammar since many of the final vowels that disappeared represented inflectional morphemes. It was a major factor in the morphological developments that followed in Middle English. OE was a richly inflected language; from the ME period onwards English became a language with very little inflection (see Chapter 17).

- The **unrounding** of the high front vowels /y/ and /yː/ started in late OE. In many dialects /y/ and /yː/ became /i/ and /iː/ respectively. But for the most part this change was no completed till the ME period.

- From the eleventh century, various vowels underwent **smoothing** (monophthongization) and **mergers**. The low diphthong /æːa/ became /æː/. This resulted in its merger with the original long /æː/; the diphthong /eːo/ became /øː/ (a front rounded vowel); short /æ/ and /a/ also merged and became a low central vowel /a/ (see similar changes in contemporary English (Chapter 3, Section 3.3.2).

Stress

Turning to the stress system of OE briefly, we note that, like other Germanic languages, OE normally placed primary stress on the first syllable of content words as shown in [14.11a]. Normally prefixes were discounted when assigning stress. So stress fell on the first stem syllable, overlooking the prefix, as you can see in [14.11b]. In all the examples, primary stress is marked by ' '' before the syllable that gets primary stress and ',' marks secondary stress:

[14. 11] a **Stress falls on first syllable of a content word**
'wilsum	'enjoyable'
'lemphealt	'lame'

b. **Prefixes are unstressed; stress falls on first syllable of a content word**
ge'hātan	'to promise'
on'bindan	'to unbind'

However, a few prefixes occurring with both nouns and verbs had stress induced allomorphs: they were stressable when attached to nouns but not when they were attached to verbs. This resulted in the allomorphy shown in the examples in [14.12]:

[14.12]

	Nouns		**verbs**	
a.	'æˌwyrp	'what is cast away'	ˌaˈweorpan	'to throw away'
b.	'biˌgeng	'worship'	beˈgan	'to go over, worship'
	'biˌgenga	'worshipper'		
c.	'andˌsæc	'denial'	ˌonˈsacan	'to contest
	andˌsaca	'adversary'		

The pattern of having primary stress on the first syllable in nouns, and primary stress on the second syllable in verbs is something that has survived to some extent to the present day cf. ˈproject (noun) vs. proˈject (verb) (see Table 4.7 in Chapter 4, Section 4.4).

Another stress rule that has remained unchanged is the **Compound Stress Rule**. In OE compound nouns, the first syllable of the first word was stressed and secondary stress was assigned to the syllable of the second element of the compound that is stressed when that word occurs on its own. Thus, from ˈleorning 'learning' and ˈcniht 'knight' we get ˈleorningˌcniht 'disciple'. This is analogous to present-day English ˈbasketˌball (from ˈbasket and ˈball).

14.4 Middle English (1150–1450)

Many more developments took place in the transition from OE to ME. We will first consider what happened to the vowels. The changes and the resulting vowel phoneme system are summarized in Table 14.6 and Table 14.7.

A major change was an increase in the phonologically distinctive degrees on opening from 3 to 4, in the case of long vowels (see Table 14.1).

Words exemplifying these vowel sounds are listed in [14.13]:

[14.13]	iː	*wile*	'formerly'
	eː	*grete*	'weep'
	ɛː	*death*	'death'
	aː	*name*	'name'
	ɔː	*holy*	'holly'
	oː	*loke*	'look'
	uː	*dun*	'down'

Table 14.6   *Short vowels (Southeast Midland dialect)*

	Front	Central	Back
High	i		u
Mid	e		o
Low		a	

Table 14.7   *Long vowels (Southeast Midland*

	Front	Central	Back
High	iː		uː
Mid-high	eː		oː
Mid-low	ɛː		ɔː
Low		aː	

ME had an elaborate system of diphthongs, including the following:

[14.14] /ei/~/ai/   ðei 'they'; *bait, eight*
/au/   author, cause
/ɛu/   ewe, shrewd
/iu/   brewe 'brew'
/ɔu/   rowm ' roam'
/oi/   (borrowed from French though loanwords like *coin, point*

14.4.1   ME stress: competing stress rules

Early loanwords like Old French *ani'mal* 'animal', *ar'me* 'army' and *pui'son* 'poison' were assigned word-initial stress following the Germanic Stress Rule (cf. ME *'animal, 'army* and *'puison*). During and especially after the age of Chaucer (1343–1400) there was massive borrowing of French words (see Chapter 15). This resulted, briefly, in the adoption of the French Stress Rule.

[14.15]   **French Stress Rule**
Stress the final syllable (unless it contains a schwa).

Following the French Stress Rule, in the opening lines of the *General Prologue* in *The Cantebury Tales*, Chaucer allowed stress to go on the final heavy syllable in *li'cour* (which rhymed with *'flour*), and on the penultimate syllable of *co'rages* which rhymed with *pilgri'mages* (Blake, 1996:164–5). The flirting with French stress patterns had no lasting impact. The words *'liquor, 'courage* and, *'pilgrimages* did fall in line and eventually followed the Germanic Stress Rule that put stress on the initial syllable. What was of lasting importance, however, was the adoption of the Latin Stress Rule for the learned latinate vocabulary that was swelled by Latin and Greek borrowings in late ME and Early Modern English (see Chapter 15).

[14.16]   **The Latin Stress Rule**
a.   A syllable is heavy if its rhyme contains a long vowel or is closed by a consonant; a syllable is light if it only has a short vowel in the rhyme.
b.   When determining syllable weight ignore the final syllable; it is unstressable (except in monosyllabic words).
c.   Stress the penultimate syllable if it is heavy (e.g., *mo'ne:bat* 'he was advising', otherwise stress the antepenultimate syllable (e.g., *'regitis* 'you rule').

As we observed in Chapter 4, predicting English stress is not an exact science. In modern English as well as words being stressed at the beginning following the Germanic stress rule (e.g., *'secretary, 'cellulose, 'animal*, etc.), they may alternatively be stressed following the Latin Stress Rule, especially if they are borrowed from Latin or French. Weight considerations analogous to those in Latin apply in this case. A syllable is heavy if its rhyme contains either a non-reduced vowel plus at least one consonant, or a long vowel or diphthong, optionally followed by one or more consonants; it is light if its rhyme contains a lone short vowel or a reduced vowel plus one or more consonants. The Latin Stress Rule gives the forms in [14.17].

[14.17] a. **Stress the penultimate syllable if it is heavy (final syllables are ignored)**

Scandinavia	[skændɪˈneɪvɪə]
cathedral	[kəˈθiːdɹəl]
agenda	[əˈdʒendə]

b. **Stress the antepenultimate syllable if the antepenultimate syllable is light (final syllable ignored)**

acclimatize	[əˈklaɪmətaɪz]
asparagus	[əsˈpæɹəgəs]
testify	[ˈtestɪfaɪ]

As mentioned above, in Middle English there were two rival stress systems, the Germanic pattern coming down from OE and the newer borrowed Latin Stress Rule system. The matter is not fully resolved yet. There are some words that have variable stress, with some speakers applying the Germanic stress rule and placing stress at the beginning while other speakers appear to follow the Latin Stress Rule which gives non-initial stress:

[14.18] ˈcontroversy   conˈtroversy
         ˈcoronal   coˈronal
         ˈapplicable   aˈpplicable

14.5 Early Modern English (1450–1800)

The treatment of Early Modern English (EModE) will start with vowels.

14.5.1 The Great Vowel Shift

The biggest phonological change during this period affected vowels. It is referred to as **The Great Vowel Shift** (GVS). Whereas EModE short vowels correspond quite systematically to the phonemes and letters of OE (cf. *sittan* 'to sit', *helpan* 'to help', *spannan* 'to span, link', etc.) the same isn't true of long vowels. The lack of a one-to-one correspondence between letters and sounds of English in general, and vowel sounds in particular, has already been highlighted. The discrepancy is especially noticeable in the case of the long vowels (cf. *name, mouse, fool, nose*). This is due to the fact that English spelling became fossilized following standardization (see Chapter 13, Section 13.2.5). Today's spelling reflects fairly well Middle English pronunciation, ignoring the changes since then. The letters for long vowels typically represent a vowel sound one degree of opening lower than the actual sound. A change that started around the early fourteenth century and continued until after Shakespeare's time in the early seventeenth century (and beyond in some dialects as we will see) is to blame.

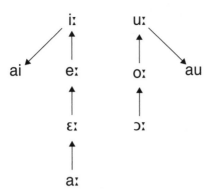

The Great Vowel Shift   *FIGURE 14.3*

We owe to Jespersen (1909) the diagrammatic representation in Figure 14.3 of the massive changes affecting vowels that stated in the Middle English period and continued in the Early Modern English period and beyond.

But why did the speakers of Middle English decide to shunt all their long vowels around vowel space? Good question. No doubt there were social forces that militated in favour of the spread of these changes. But why did they start in the first place? Opinion is divided on this. According to Jespersen (1909) and many other scholars, the GVS was a **drag chain**. It was kicked off with the diphthongization of the two highest long vowels: initially /iː/ became /əɪ/ and /uː/ became /əʊ/ before eventually becoming /ai/ and /au/ respectively. Having moved sideways, as it were, the highest vowels left a void at the top of vowel space and in this void were sucked /eː/ and /oː/. This in turn created a new void into which were sucked /ɛː/ and /ɔː/. The drift upward of /ɛː/ in turn left an empty space into which /aː/ was subsequently sucked. In other words there was a chain reaction caused by the general preference for symmetrical vowel systems. The change resulted in new realizations of the original phonemes, but the original relationships between vowels were in the main unaltered. Except for the lowest long vowel, all front long vowels still had a corresponding back vowel of the same height.

While also espousing an internal phonological explanation for the origins of the GVS. Luick (1921/1941) has a different story concerning the driving force behind it. He suggests that the GVS was a **push chain.** On this view, the raising of each long vowel, starting with the lowest, so that it occupied the vowel space that was previously the territory of the vowel above, progressed predictably till the highest vowel were reached. At that stage there was no higher vowel space to colonize. The problem was solved by turning the highest vowels into diphthongs.

As we saw in Table 14.1, the OE vowel system was symmetrical (like most vowel systems in the world's languages). Restoring symmetry was the motivation behind both the push chain and drag chain hypotheses, they say. But as Wari' testifies, vowel systems don't have to be symmetrical. For instance, Everett and Kern (1997) show that this language of western Brazil lives happily with a skewed vowel system, with five front vowels and only two back

Table 14.8   The Phases of the GVS (Lass, 2006: 83)

	ME	1569	1653	1687	C19th	
bite	iː___	ɛi___	əi___	ʌi___	ai:	bite
meet	eː___	iː___	iː___	iː _____	iː	meet, meat
break, meat	ɛː___	ɛː___	eː___	eː ___		
name	aː___	aː___	ɛː___	e ː___	eː	name, break
house	uː___	ɔuː___	əu ː___	ʌu ː___	au:	house
food	oː___	uː___	uː___	uː___	u:	food
bone	ɔː___	ɔː___	o ː___	o ː___	o ː	bone

vowels. This suggests that establishing and maintaining symmetry is not mandatory. So, reasonable doubt remains as to whether restoring symmetry was the factor that led to the GVS.

What do we make of all this? I think we should take our lead from Smith (1996: 88–92) and Lass (2006: 82) who argue that the thinking behind the GVS illustrated in Figure 14.3 and the account of the vowel change it depicts (regardless of whether it is interpreted in terms of push chains or drag chains) is a useful snapshot of where the change started and where it ended (more or less). But what it is not, is an account of the actual triggering and implementation of changes. The triggering and propagation of the GVS had strong sociolinguistic drivers, notably the ascendancy of London and its socially stratified speech community that spearheaded these phonological developments (Smith, 1999: 90–2) (see Chapter 12). The GVS is nothing more than convenient shorthand for summarizing a set of complex, broadly related changes affecting long vowels, that started in late ME and continued into Early Modern English (see Table 14.8 and Advances Box 14.1 on p. 279). Just as historians find it useful to talk about the Industrial Revolution, as a convenient label for many relatively small-scale technological, cultural and social developments with no clear starting point and finishing line, which resulted in significant cultural change, the historical phonologist too may find it useful to talk about the GVS. But the claim that it was a single chain-like event is unwarranted (Lass, 1988: 396; Lass, 2006: 81–3).

14.5.2   Early Modern English consonants (based on Dobson, 1968; Görlach, 1991: 74–6)

Let's turn to the consonants. Most consonant phonemes remained very roughly unchanged from late OE until the Early Modern period, but in some cases their realization then changed. We will focus on /r/. This seems to have been a trill word-initially and alveolar fricatives elsewhere, but gradually an approximant articulation ([ɹ]) prevalent today became more common. The major phonological change affecting /r/ was its gradual elimination from coda position which was discussed in detail in Chapter 3 (Section 3.3.1).

Another development was the rise of the phoneme /ʒ/ resulting allophonic variation and borrowing. Originally [ʒ] was a palatalized allophone of /z/

ADVANCES BOX 14.1

Phases of the GVS

According to Lass (1988, 2006), the GVS happened in two broad phases and was not a single event.

Phase 1 (see in Table 14.8)
(i)   First round of raising: The high-mid vowels were raised /eː/ > /iː/; /oː/ > /uː/; (see *meet* and *food*).
(ii) The highest vowels were diphthongized /iː/ > /ɛiː/; /uː/ > /ɔu/; (see *bite* and *house*). Subsequently (mid-seventeenth century) low-mid vowels were raised /ɛː/ > /eː/ (see *break*); /ɔː/ > /oː/ (see *bone*).
(iii) At about the same time, low vowel /aː/ was raised to /ɛː/ (see *name*).

Phase 2 (see Table 14.8)
(i)   Second round of raising: ME /ɛː/ raised; this resulted in a merger with /eː/. Later /eː/ developed into ME /iː/ (cf. *meet* and *meat*, which rhyme in Modern English, but were different in ME).
      To understand the GVS changes it is important to realize that **phonological change diffuses gradually** through the vocabulary. The slow spread of change across the lexicon means that change can go on for many generations before it affects all eligible words in one dialect, let alone all dialects. For instance, the most conservative Geordie and Scottish dialects still have a vowel that is very close to the pre-GVS vowel in /huːs/ *house*, /duːn/ *down*, etc. (but there is a tendency to centralize it (cf. [hʉs], [dʉn]) etc. (see p. 282)). Meanwhile, other changes affecting the same candidate words may get underway and compete with a change already in progress. Or, the change might just peter out prematurely.
(ii) In either case, many candidate words may escape the change. The result may be a **phonemic split**. Thus, some words with ME /ɛː/ underwent raising and today have the /iː/ phoneme (e.g., *meat, leaf, clean*, etc.) while others didn't and have retained the unraised vowel /ɛː/ (~/eː/) (cf. *head, bread*). Because the raising /ɛː/ and its merger with /eː/ stalled before all eligible candidates had been affected, a side-effect of this change was to split ME /ɛː/. Some cases of /ɛː/ were raised to /iː/ as shown above but those words with the /ɛː/ phoneme that stayed unchanged merged with words that contained a raised /aː/ by the end of the seventeenth century (cf. *name* and *break*).

arising from /zj/ sequences in words like *erosion, provision, collision*, etc. The frequency of phonetic [ʒ] was bolstered by the introduction of French loanwords containing [ʒ] (e.g., *measure, leisure, treasure*, etc.) This encouraged the split of the new phoneme /ʒ/from /ʃ/, which had been inherited from OE as /ʒ/, now contrasted with its voiceless counterpart /ʃ/ which had been inherited from OE. Note that although the phonemic status of /ʒ/ is beyond doubt, it retains a whiff of foreignness as many of the words that it appears in are not fully nativized (cf. *rouge, gigolo, bijou*) (Gimson, 2001: 190).

ADVANCES BOX 14.2

Persistent trends: syllable structure constrains and conspiracies

When phonologists see apparently independent rules acting in unison, as it were, they speak of a **conspiracy**. In Chapter 4 (Section 4.2) we saw that English has rich and complex syllable structure. It might therefore come as a surprise to learn that a recurrent theme in the history of English phonology has been consonant cluster simplification. Deep down, English prefers simple to complex syllable onsets and codas. Many changes that have taken place have been motivated by the desire to satisfy the injunction to avoid complexity. Below we sketch some of the major simplification processes that have taken place over the centuries.

Let us consider syllable onset cluster simplification first.

Onset simplification

- The loss [w] from [wr] syllable onsets in *write, wring, wrath, wren*, etc. had started in the fifteenth century and was completed in the EModE period in the seventeenth century.
- Onset [kn] and [gn] clusters as in *knavish, knocked, kneed, knight's, knife* and *gnarl, gnaw, gnats*, etc. had all lost their velars by the late seventeenth century.
- OE had [hw, hn, hl, hr] onsets as in *hwǣt* 'what', *hnutu* 'nut', *hlæf* ' loaf', *hrēod* 'reed'. None of these clusters survived into modern English, with the exception of [hw] (Hogg, 1992b: 94). See also the discussion of [hw] in Scottish dialects on page 45 in Chapter 3.

Coda simplification

- Recall that word-finally, [b] was usually deleted from [mb] clusters as in *lamb, thumb, climb, dumb, comb*, etc. in OE.
- Also famously subject to deletion was coda [r] (post-vocalic r) (see Chapter 3, Section 3.3.1). The deletion of coda-r, which started in late ME, gradually became established as the norm in the London standard. This fact is shown by the end of the seventeenth century by r-less spellings that mirrored the pronunciation of words like *passel* 'parcel', *posshene* 'portion', *Dasset* 'Dorset', *passons* 'parsons' and *Wosseter* for 'Worcester', which became increasingly common. In Shakespeare there were spellings like *accust* 'accurst', *depature* 'departure' and *gater* 'garter', etc. Loss of coda-r resulted in rhymes like *forsworn: John, earth: death* (McLaughlin, 1970: 113). A very few such r-less pronunciations have survived in mainstream English, creating doublets (with different but related meanings) such as *bust/burst* and *cuss/curse*, as well as the dialectal *hoss* for *horse* and East Anglian [ʧeʧ] for *church* (Trudgill, 2008: 184). In Section 14.7 we will look at today's distribution of post-vocalic r.
- Often a disappearing coda-r leaves behind a trace. It is vocalized, becoming a schwa and this gives rise to centring diphthongs in certain contexts (cf. *tear* [teə], *beard* [bɪəd], *roar* [rɔə], etc. (see Chapter 3, Section 3.3.2).

14.6 Present-day English: phonological change from 1800 to today

The previous section brought us up to a time which is just prior to what we feel is 'our' English: the English we can hear all around us, stretching back to the speech of those we still have memories of – our immediate ancestors, going back, say, three or four generations. There are a number of reasons for taking a special interest in this contemporary period. The first is that, from the end of the nineteenth century, there is simply vastly more scientifically produced material, not only on the speech of the educated, who might be expected to speak something not too distant from today's Received Pronunciation, but also regional, dialectal speech. Much of this is contained in the work of Alexander Ellis (1889) and Joseph Wright (1898, 1905), both linguists who produced work on a grand scale and with great powers of phonetic observation. The second reason for taking an interest in the contemporary period is that we now have a reasonable number of recordings of speakers from about 1930 onwards, but with a great increase since the late 1960s. The third reason is that the sociolinguistic methods of William Labov (1927–), first on the Massachusetts island of Martha's Vineyard (1963) and then in New York City (1966), demonstrated that it is in fact possible to observe sound changes in some detail, as they are actually happening. Labov found, not surprisingly, that older people use older forms, or variants, of a particular sound, while younger people use newer ones. Not only that, but these particular variants are not used by everybody of the same age: there are marked differences according to social class, gender and ethnicity, and this enabled Labov to suggest that most phonetic changes seem to be female-led, and also to emanate from people occupying the middle strata in a social class hierarchy. (Chapters 18, 19, 20 and 32 contain further details on how class, gender and ethnicity are related to language use.) As we indicated in Section 14.1.2, people may adopt a new sound as a sort of badge of identity. From the point of view of the investigation of sound change as such, we can now state in much more precise terms whether or not a change is gradual, or abrupt, and whether all words are affected at the same time, or only some.

The remainder of this section will focus on phonological changes which have happened more or less in living memory; many are still ongoing. The focus will be on British English, but we will mention other 'inner circle' varieties as well (see Chapter 22).

14.6.1 The aftermath of the Great Vowel Shift

We left English vowels shortly after they had undergone the GVS. How did the Shift progress? The first thing to note is that, in the far north of England (roughly north of a line from the River Lune to the River Humber) and in Scotland, it took a very different path. Here, people can be heard saying [tɛɪm] for *time*, instead of more southerly [taɪm] or [tɑɪm]. Many Scots say [sten] for *stone*, and until recently, pronunciations like [stɪən] could be heard in the far north of England instead of the more usual [stʊən], [stoːn] or [stɔːn] in Newcastle, Cumbria and Lancashire/Yorkshire, respectively. A remnant of this pronunciation is the north-east English [jɛm] for *home*, corresponding to [hoːm] further south. Most strikingly, the pronunciations [tʉn], [ʉt] and [nʉ] for *town*, *out* and *now* are common in local accents in Scotland, matched by [tuːn], [uːt] and [nuː] in Cumbria and Northumberland, though the latter have all but disappeared except in fixed expressions like *The Toon*, referring to Newcastle Football Club. These pronunciations are being replaced by diphthongs similar to [aʊ], which are found south of the Lune–Humber line. The details are complex, but all the traditional dialect pronunciations mentioned here are the outcome of a different set of GVS changes in the far north.

Of course, not everybody uses these pronunciations any more, especially in England. Does this mean that the southern version of the GVS has 'hit' the North? No, it does not, since what seems to have happened is that the southern pronunciations have simply supplanted the northern ones by a process of **borrowing** (Kerswill, 2002) – speakers have taken on these pronunciations for socially motivated reasons. Since the southern pattern is the majority one in England, and includes the great population centres of Merseyside, Manchester and the Yorkshire cities, it is not surprising that this is so. This is an example where detailed knowledge of contemporary speech helps us to understand how a linguistic change progresses.

Turning to the southern half of England, we find that accents in the region from the Midlands and East Anglia down to the Channel coast, though not including the south-west, have relatively extreme versions of the GVS. Wells (1982: 308–10) shows this for London's 'Cockney' in Figure 14.4, where he places the broadest, most local Cockney variants on a diagram showing more mainstream London ('Popular London') and also RP. As Wells's figure shows, Cockney has what are termed wide diphthongs, where the articulators travel a relatively great distance from the beginning to the end of the vowel. In terms of the GVS, it is as if the process has continued, and indeed started afresh with the diphthongization of the monophthongs /iː/ to [əi] (as in *fleece*) and /uː/ to [əʉ] (as in *goose*). Wells refers to these vowels as 'diphthong shifted'.

What does the future hold for diphthong shifted vowels? Will they shift any further? Recent research has shown a dramatic and rapid *reversal* of the

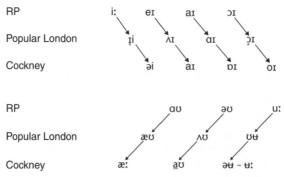

FIGURE 14.4   *Vowels in Received Pronunciation, Popular London and Cockney, showing Diphthong Shift in Cockney (from Wells 2002: 308; 310)*

process, centred on the speech of young inner-city minority ethnic Londoners and spreading from them to other groups of young people in the south-east, via their social networks (Kerswill, Torgersen and Fox 2008). Typical variants found in this 'Multiethnic London English' are the following:

fleece[1]	[iː]
face	[eɪ] or [e̝ɪ] (the latter representing a 'raised', more [i]-like version of [eɪ])
price	[aː]
mouth	[aː] (similar to [aː], but with a more back pronunciation, approaching [ɑ])
goat	[oʊ] (a back vowel, resembling northern variants)
goose	[yː] (a front pronunciation)

Research suggests that some of these vowels are in conflict with other developments in the south-east of England. This is especially true of the *goat* vowel (RP /əʊ/), where accents similar to Popular London now have a considerably 'fronter' diphthong than the [ʌʊ] Wells gives. In Milton Keynes, for instance, pronunciations as front as [əʏ] can be heard (Kerswill and Williams, 2005), giving rise to potential confusion between 'cake' and 'Coke' (as witnessed by the second author!). Careful sociolinguistic research shows us that, unlike the abrupt replacement of [uː] by [aʊ] in the north, the changes in the London vowels are phonetically gradual. Further to that, we can see that a particular social group leads and other follow – an essential sociolinguistic finding.

14.6.2 Other vowels

If you ask a person from England about differences between accents, they are most likely to mention the presence of the vowel /ʌ/ in words like *strut* and its absence in northern varieties, where the vowel of *foot* is used instead – in fact, the 'north' includes most of the Midlands. We have already discussed the linguistic details of this change. The second feature is the use of the vowel of *palm* in words like *bath*, *past* and *dance* in the south of England (though not the south-west), and the use of the short *trap* vowel in these words in the north (see Chapter 18, Section 18.4.2). Both features are the result of sound changes in the south in the sixteenth to the eighteenth centuries. Given that both are stereotypes symbolizing a linguistic north–south divide, how stable are they today? Britain (2002) shows, first, that both boundaries are geographically extremely stable, at least in their rural, eastern portions. Secondly, he shows that there is a transition zone where people use either phonetically intermediate pronunciations, or they use varying percentages of the one form or the other. Thirdly, he finds that, whereas older people are generally more variable, younger people are actually 'homing in' on the one or the other, or in the case of *strut* a phonetic half-way house, [ɤ]. Thus, detailed sociolinguistic work again shows us how a sound is changing, or rather, how a sound behaves in a dialectal border area.

Despite the vowel changes we have discussed, it is nevertheless the case that the vowel system of British English (in all its varieties) has remained relatively stable since around 1700. There is little to measure up to the far-reaching consequences of the GVS, taking place as it did over a relatively short time-span of 200–300 years, depending on how one defines the endpoint.

14.6.3 Consonants

Of all regional accent features, the one which is contracting in the most geographically systematic way is the use of post-vocalic r. Trudgill (1999: 27, 55) has shown that, around the middle of the last century, older rural people used post-vocalic r in much of England, except East Anglia, the north-east Midlands and Yorkshire. By the latter part of the century, the 'r' pronouncing areas had contracted to the central south and south-west and a pocket in east and central Lancashire. More recent observations show that it is now being lost in Lancashire, remaining only in Blackburn and its immediate hinterland. It remains strong in Bristol and in parts of the south-western counties, though, even in Exeter, the feature is being lost (Sullivan, 1992). At the same time, the feature remains solid in Scotland (where the linguistic border with England is apparently getting sharper), Ireland and North America.

One of the most vilified phonological changes in British English is the use of the glottal stop [ʔ] for /t/ after a vowel, as in *Gatwick, let me, sort of, street, city*. This feature is treated in Chapter 3 (Section 3.3.1) and Chapter 18 (see Table 18.7 and surrounding discussion). This change is now extremely firmly established, especially before consonants (as in the first two examples). Almost equally vilified is the use of /f/ for /θ/, representing a loss of a phoneme (Chapter 18, Table 18.8). This feature is now the norm in working-class speech in southern England and much of the Midlands, as well as in some northern cities, including Manchester and Hull. However, it is only beginning to permeate cities farther north, such as Newcastle and Glasgow, via young children, particularly boys (Kerswill, 2003; Stuart-Smith, Timmins and Tweedie, 2007). A parallel change is the replacement of /ð/ by /v/ (see Chapter 18): what is interesting is that, in London, this rarely takes place in word-initial position, where the favoured form is /ð/ (with no change) or /d/. However, many northern English young people produce /v/ initially, giving pronunciations like [vat] for *that*. This can be interpreted as the over-generalization of a phonological rule borrowed from the south, or simply as a different rule from the southern one.

A very noticeable feature of southern English English and many Scottish accents is l-vocalization (see Chapter 18, Table 18.8 and following text for details). By this is meant that, for such speakers, /l/ does not involve any contact between the tongue-tip and the alveolar ridge, the consonant being produced instead as a vowel in the region of [o] or [ɤ]. This gives rise to pronunciations such as [fio] for *feel*. This is clearly a 'natural' change, in that it increases the ease of pronunciation. And yet, beyond the regions mentioned, vocalization is still relatively rare.

Finally, we look at what was a shibboleth of 'bad' speech all through the nineteenth and twentieth centuries (Mugglestone, 2003): so called 'h-dropping', giving rise to pronunciations such as [amə] for *hammer*. h-dropping is a feature of all English dialects in England and Wales except Northumberland

and Tyneside, and among older people in parts of Norfolk and Somerset. /h/ is not dropped in Scotland, Ireland or the 'inner circle' English speaking countries of the United States, Canada, South Africa, Australia and New Zealand. It is relatively rare among middle-class speakers generally. However, in recent years /h/ has been gradually reinstated in working-class accents in the south, with young females in the Home Counties (surrounding London) and, unexpectedly, inner-city minority ethnic speakers in the lead (Williams and Kerswill, 1999; Cheshire et al., 2008a, b).

We have sketched the main phonological changes that took place in English from Old English times to the present. We have seen that the causes of these changes have been a mixture of contact with other languages and dialects, social factors within a speech community, functional factors and structural factors. We have seen that phoneme inventories and stress patterns have changed over the centuries and across dialects, and that so have phonological rules and constraints. However, amidst all this flux, much has remained constant, for example, the OE Compound Stress Rule remains unchanged; nasal consonants have resisted mutation for the most part; and the liquids [l] and [r] have often coloured vowels and induced diphthongization of preceding vowels in different centuries and in different dialects. Many of the changes are driven by syllable structure considerations that don't change (e.g., deletion of consonants in order to simplifying syllable codas). But it is uncanny sometimes to see analogous innovations, in the absence of contact, in dialects far removed in space or time. For instance, the replacement of /θ/ with /f/ (e.g., <with> > <wif>) and /ð/ with /v/ (e.g., <brother> > <brover>) in British English is also found in African American Vernacular English. Perhaps most striking of all, is the persistent restlessness of vowels which has made them go on a walk-about in vowel space resulting in vowel shifts great, small and otherwise (Lass, 1988). This happened not only in Early Modern English but is again happening in the contemporary diphthong shift in Cockney noted above and also in the United States in the Northern Cities Shift and the Southern Shift (Labov, Ash and Boberg, 2005). Though much has changed since OE, there is much that has remained constant.

Recommended readings

For a more comprehensive description of the sound systems of each period of English, try Jeremy Smith's *Essentials of Early English* ([1999] 2005). Lass (2006) offers an excellent, concise scholarly overview of the history of English phonology and morphology. Dobson (1968), in two volumes, is the classic source on the early modern period. Melinda Menzer's website http://alpha.furman.edu/~mmenzer/gvs/ will make the task of understanding the GVS much easier, and, more generally for the history of the English sound system, we highly recommend William E. Roger's comprehensive website http://alpha.furman.edu/~wrogers/phonemes/.

Note

1   See Chapter 11 for an explanation of the use of this word and the words below as mnemonics.

CHAPTER 15

Lexical Change

SEBASTIAN HOFFMANN

15.1 Introduction

Let us start by having a look at the two short extracts shown in [15.1] and [15.2] :

[15.1]   Soðlice wæs geworden þa he wæs on sumere stowe hine gebiddende: þa þa he geswac. him to cwæð an his leorningcnihta; Drihten. lær us. us gebiddan. swa iohannes his leorningcnihtas lærde;

[15.2]   And it came to pass, that, as he was praying in a certain place, when he ceased, one of his disciples said to him, Lord, teach us to pray, as John also taught his disciples.

You will no doubt agree that these two extracts are strikingly different – so different in fact that you may not have immediately noticed that they are versions of the same text; both extracts are verse 11:1 from the *Gospel According to Luke*. It might therefore come as an even bigger surprise that both texts are written in English: while extract [15.2] is from the *Revised King James New Testament* (2000 edition), extract [15.1] is taken from a late tenth-century manuscript known as the *Wessex Gospels* (or *West Saxon Gospels*), the first full translation of all four gospels from a Latin source into Old English (OE).

Although the two extracts show differences at various levels (e.g., spelling and grammar), a particularly striking aspect of [15.1] is its vocabulary. While it is possible to find a small number of items that look and appear to function the same as in Present-day English (*he, on, him, to, his* and *us*), the large majority of words in [15.1] clearly do not belong to the stock of lexical items that a modern-day speaker of standard English would be able to use. For example, instead of the verb *teach*, we find *læran* (the form *lær* is the imperative), *Drihten* is used where the modern text has *Lord*, and *leorningcniht* is the Old English equivalent of today's *disciple*.[1] Nevertheless, there are good reasons to claim that the two extracts are indeed both samples of one and the same language – albeit at very different stages of its development. By directly comparing its oldest with its most modern form, I have of course highlighted the differences between the two versions of English. However, once the intermediate stages in the development are considered, it becomes clear that extracts [15.1] and [15.2] are in fact linked by a long succession of changes that have affected the English language in its eventful history.

In the present chapter, I will discuss in some detail how English could change its vocabulary so drastically within a time-span of about 1000 years. As the following section shows, it will be necessary for this purpose to relate the lexical developments that can be observed in the English language to important historical events as well as major changes in society.

15.2   Why does a language acquire new words?

Before we have a closer look at what happened to English vocabulary over time, it may be worth thinking about the question why a language – or rather: its speakers – should change and expand the existing stock of words in the first place. There are at least two main reasons. First, it is clear that people who lived a thousand years ago led very different lives from what we know today. An inhabitant of the British Isles during the time of Old English would have had little or no use for the words *television*, *cash*, *network*, *unemployment*, *aircraft* or *newspaper* – for the simple reason that these items and concepts did not yet exist. Today, however, these words belong to the 1000 most frequently used nouns in British English. Language – and its vocabulary – is tightly linked to the circumstances in which its speakers find themselves; new forms of government, new inventions, new social structures, etc. all require new words for people to be able to talk about them. One way of adding new words to a language is to use the existing inventory of lexical items and to create new ones by means of a set of regular **word-formation processes**. For example, the words *air* and *craft* both existed in English prior to the invention of airplanes (*craft* is a native Anglo-Saxon word; from the seventeenth century onwards, it was used to refer to 'a small vessel or boat'), and it is easy to see how (and why) the new word was created as a combination of the two older words. This type of change is thus language-internal in the sense that no resources from other languages are involved.

The second major reason for changes in the vocabulary of a language is language contact. If two groups of people who speak different languages come in direct contact with each other (e.g., through trade, migration or because one group invades the territory of the other), they will of course eventually need to communicate with each other, and this is highly likely to influence their respective languages. Various scenarios are possible when this happens, ranging from the extinction of one language to a complete merger of the two. Because situations of language contact often go along with drastic changes in the living circumstances of the people involved, it is no surprise that this typically also has an impact on the vocabulary of their language. Rather than trying to express newly available concepts with the help of existing words (as in the case of internal word-formation mentioned above), speakers of a language may choose to adopt – or **borrow** – existing words from the other language and integrate them as loanwords into their own.

However, there is often more at stake than simply the introduction of new concepts, for example, as a result of contact with an invading people or settlers with a different culture and different structures of society. The key word here is prestige: even though the word for a thing or a concept may already be present in a language (or could otherwise easily be expressed with the help of the existing inventory of the language), its speakers may nevertheless choose to adopt the corresponding word of the other language because it carries more prestige than the native word. If this happens, the old word may disappear completely. Alternatively, the two words may coexist in the language, expressing roughly the same concept, but typically with somewhat different meanings or connotations.

For the rest of the chapter, I will show how these two major types of lexical change have shaped the English lexicon from Old English to today. I will begin by looking at borrowing from different languages and discuss how English has become an etymologically highly diverse language. This will be followed by a short discussion of the different internal processes of regular word-formation that have been at work at various stages in the history of English. The chapter then closes with a brief look at evidence of very recent lexical change in the age of the Internet.

15.3   Old English – the Germanic basis of English

When according to the traditional account, the Angles, Saxons and Jutes invaded Celtic-speaking Britain in the fifth century, they brought with them an almost entirely Germanic vocabulary. This is surprising because its speakers must have been in contact with Latin-speaking Romans for several centuries. However, only a small number of Latin borrowings remain today that were integrated into the language before it became English. For example, *wall* was borrowed by Germanic speakers on the continent from Latin *vallum*, and *wine* goes back to Latin *vinum*. This Germanic language spoken in Britain from around the fifth century onwards was thus very closely related to what became German or Dutch. In fact, if you know some German, you might have noticed that two of the words in extract [15.1] are very familiar to you: *geworden* and *læran*. While the former has the exact same form in present-day German, the latter corresponds to *lehren*, which means 'to teach'.

Only a relatively small proportion of the roughly 23,000 to 24,000 words of Old English vocabulary have survived to the present day (Scheler, 1977: 14). However, what is left is typically both frequent and basic. As a case in point, consider again the words in extract [15.1] which are still in the English language today: they are personal pronouns (*he, him, us*) and prepositions (*on, to*), and they therefore form part of the highly frequent grammatical building blocks of modern English. Of the ten most frequent nouns in Present-day English (as represented in the 100-million word British National Corpus), six are of Germanic origin: *time, year, way, man, day* and *thing*,[2] and frequent Old English verbs that have survived until today are *go, have, think, find* and *come*.

15.4   Borrowing I: early influences on English

Surprisingly, only a very small number of words were borrowed from Celtic into Old English and even these are virtually restricted to place names like

Kent, Avon, Esk, Ouse, Thames and probably even *London*.[3] Various attempts at explaining this lack of borrowings exist, but none of them is truly convincing. For example, genetic tests of men in a selection of towns in northern Wales and England have revealed major differences in Y-chromosome markers between the two areas, but English men and their counterparts on the European side of the channel display a remarkable similarity in their genetic make-up (cf. Weale et al. 2002). This finding suggests that speakers of Celtic may have been either ruthlessly killed or very quickly driven out of their areas by the Germanic invaders. Historical evidence indicates, however, that such a radical view may not be fully accurate. For example, the fact that some members of the Anglo-Saxon nobility had Celtic personal names (e.g., Caedwalla, king of Wessex, 685) suggests intermarriage – and therefore at least some degree of integration of Celtic and Anglo-Saxon cultures.

A far greater influence was exerted on Old English from a different source: Latin. By the end of the seventh century, all of England had been converted to Christianity, and as the influence of the church gradually increased, Latin words made their way from the monasteries into everyday English language. Not surprisingly, the bulk of these new words have to do with religion. Typical examples are *angel, altar, nun, monastery, priest* and *temple*. But these borrowed words also include expressions referring to other areas, for example those of education, household, clothing and medicine (e.g., *school, chest, sock, plant, fennel* and *fever*). These words quite nicely exemplify the mechanism outlined in Section 15.2: contact with speakers of another language leads to the integration of words for new concepts that are being introduced to the native population by these speakers.

During much of the ninth and tenth centuries, and particularly in the first part of the eleventh century, many parts of England were either under constant assault or under direct rule by Scandinavian Vikings. Large numbers of Scandinavian migrants came to England to settle for good, and although the initial phases of Viking occupancy were certainly characterized by violence, conquerors and conquered eventually came to live peacefully in adjacent communities, and intermarriage must have been quite common. Astonishingly, however, many Scandinavian loanwords only entered the language after the Viking rule came to an end; in fact, this process really only started after a gap of more than 100 years when, suddenly, considerable numbers of Scandinavian borrowings can be found. Perhaps even more surprising than the delay in borrowing is the nature of the borrowed words: many of them constitute very basic vocabulary referring to aspects of everyday life. As Table 15.1 shows, these words not only include nouns, verbs and adjectives but also an astonishing number of function words – that is, grammatical or closed-class items – such as pronouns and conjunctions, some of which belong to the most frequent words in the language today.

It is difficult to find a convincing explanation for this pattern of borrowing. One interesting hypothesis put forward by Crystal (2004: 82–5) is that a considerable level of linguistic mixing would in fact have occurred in areas where Scandinavian settlers were most frequent (the so-called 'Danelaw', that is, the north-eastern areas of England). Anglo-Saxon speakers would have been likely to adopt lexical items of the language of their conquerors and,

Table 15.1   *A selection of words that were borrowed from Scandinavian settlers*

Nouns	bank, birth, bull, egg, leg, root, seat, sister, skin, sky, window
Verbs	call, die, get, give, raise, scare, take
Adjectives	flat, ill, low, odd, tight, weak
Function words	they, their, them, both, though, are

more importantly, bilingualism must have been the norm among children. In a situation like this, the more prestigious language – in this case clearly Scandinavian – typically wins out, with speakers of the third generation opting to drop the language of their ancestors.[4] However, the Scandinavians never ruled long enough for this process to go full circle. Furthermore, since the area of the Danelaw had no great literary tradition, little of its presumably highly mixed language made it into writing.

Crystal further speculates that people in the rest of England will not have wanted to use words that they associated with the Scandinavian aggressor or invader. In other words, the Scandinavian language very likely had low prestige in those areas of England which had greater literary output. But after the Vikings relinquished power, these negative connotations gradually disappeared. This made it possible for previously borrowed lexical features that had already been fully integrated into the English dialect spoken in the Danelaw to spread to all parts of the country, and thereby crucially also into writing. This kind of interpretation relies on the assumption that prestige indeed plays an important role in lexical change – in this case, it would explain why words were **not** borrowed for quite some time, at least not by all speakers of English. Yet, more linguistic detective-work is necessary to uncover the full story of Scandinavian borrowing in English.

15.5   Borrowing II: French influence on English vocabulary

After England's defeat by William the Conqueror in 1066 at Hastings, England became a country where three languages were spoken – but by different people for very different purposes. While the native English population continued to speak English, French was the language of the new ruling elite. In addition, Latin continued to be used in religious contexts, and it was also the language of science and learning. By the time this clear-cut division between languages gradually broke down, two centuries of French rule had dramatically changed society: it had brought new ways of governing the country, new laws, new food (and new ways to prepare food), and new fashions, to name just a few aspects. And the Old English of the Anglo-Saxons did not have the words to express all these new concepts. As a result, French words were borrowed into English on a large scale. This process was helped by the fact that many of the concepts that required new names carried prestige – they were things that had to do with such areas as administration, warfare and arts. In other words, the same mechanism that may have prevented Scandinavian words from being integrated a few centuries earlier was at work – just the other way round. This may also explain why many native

Some English words that were borrowed from French during Middle English   Table 15.2

Nouns	beauty, beef, button, complaint, fashion, forest, government, marriage, paper, prince, punishment, toast, volume
Verbs	advise, arrest, compile, furnish, marry, pay, rejoice, reply, roast, seize, stew, summon, wait
Adjectives	courteous, foreign, honest, innocent, large, luxurious, natural, perfect, poor, pure, safe, tender, usual

Old English words were replaced by their French counterparts – for example, the *stowe* of extract [15.1] was substituted by *place*. In even more cases, however, English ended up with two words for related concepts. If this happened, the native word typically carries more common, basic connotations while the French word belongs to a more elevated style. Table 15.2 lists some of the words that entered the English language during this period. However, given that the total number of borrowed words is estimated to be as high as 10,000 (cf. Baugh and Cable, 2002: 178; Crystal, 2004: 154), this table can only give a weak impression of the full scale of lexical change that occurred during this period.

As mentioned above, Latin continued to be an influential language – and it also continued to be a source for new English words. However, since it was the language of religion, education and science, and manuscripts were typically written in Latin, many of the borrowed words entered English through contact with the written language. As a result, these words tend to carry even more formal and stylistically elevated connotations than the French borrowings. This is nicely shown in Table 15.3, which lists a number of related words from all three languages. On some level, the three words mean the same thing – they are synonyms – but they clearly carry very different connotations.

Three levels of synonymy   Table 15.3

Germanic	French	Latin
ask	question	interrogate
fire	flame	conflagration
kingly	royal	regal
rise	mount	ascend

At the end of the Middle English period, that is, towards the end of the fifteenth century, the lexical stock of English was thus dramatically different from Old English. Not only was it much larger and more stylistically flexible than before, it was also much more varied in terms of its linguistic background.

15.6 Borrowing III: from Early Modern to Present-Day English

The Early Modern English period – that is, roughly the time from 1500 to 1700 – presents a highly complex picture to the historical linguist, and it is impossible to summarize all aspects that relate to the development of the English lexicon here. Perhaps the most important point to mention, though, is that the later decades of the seventeenth century saw a general decline of Latin as the language of learned discourse. Yet at the same time, an enormous increase in specialist knowledge in the sciences took place. As a result, thousands of new words were required to express this new knowledge in a suitable way. Many speakers of English felt, however, that their language was inadequate for this purpose – and they therefore called for 'enrichment' of their language. In doing so, they turned to Latin (and to some extent also Greek) to expand the vocabulary of English. The result was a massive influx of borrowings that were added at an unprecedented speed, even though native words already existed for some of these concepts. There was great disagreement among contemporaries about the usefulness and value of these additions, and the expression 'inkhorn term' was coined by its critics to refer to such – as they felt – useless and artificial additions. Eventually, many of the new words again disappeared (e.g., *adminiculation* 'aid', *accersited* 'summoned, sent for' or *deruncinate* 'to weed'). However, many others remained in use and form an essential part of the English lexicon today. Typical examples are the nouns *atmosphere, dexterity, disrespect* and *expectation*, the adjectives *conspicuous, habitual* and *malignant*, and the verbs *assassinate, excavate, extinguish* and *meditate* (cf. Baugh and Cable 2002: 224). As in the case of the Latin and French borrowings that were added during Middle English, if both the new addition and a native equivalent survive, the borrowed word tends to belong to a more elevated and formal style.

The Early Modern English period also marks the beginning of an era that sees the introduction of words from many languages other than Latin (and

Table 15.4   *The composition of the English lexicon (cf. Scheler 1977: 72)*

Language	Percentage	
Anglo-Saxon		**22%**
Other Germanic Languages		4.1%
a. Scandinavian	2.2%	
b. German	1.9%	
Romance Languages		30.2%
a. **French**	**28.4%**	
b. others	1.8%	
Latin		**28.3%**
Greek		5.3%
Celtic languages		0.4%
Other European languages		0.1%
Non-Indo-European Languages		2%
Of unknown origin		4.2%
Proper names		3.3%

ADVANCES BOX 15.1

Quantifying the extent of borrowing

The overview presented in Table 15.4 above shows very precise proportions for the different languages that have contributed to Present-day English vocabulary. But how exactly do you measure the amount of foreign lexis that is in use today – or in fact at any time in the history of English? For this type of exercise, the *Oxford English Dictionary (OED)* no doubt represents the most suitable source of data: it not only attempts to cover any word ever used in English after the year 1150 (in addition to all Anglo-Saxon words that are still in use today), but it also puts a date on the first known use of any of its entries in (written) English. Furthermore, many of its entries contain extensive etymological information, including an indication of the immediate donor language for borrowed words. Since the *OED* is nowadays available in electronic format (on CD-ROM or via an online Web interface), this wealth of data can be searched and analysed in a very efficient manner.

However, as Culpeper and Clapham (1996) have explained, even such an extensive source of information as the *OED* has its limitations. For example, it is sometimes unclear whether a word was directly borrowed from Latin or whether it entered the language via an intermediate French stage instead. Also, it is well known that some of the first citation dates in the *OED* are fairly inaccurate – Schäfer (1980: 67) estimates that about 7 per cent of all headwords can be antedated by at least a century. Furthermore, there is uneven coverage of different time periods in the OED. As a result, the chances of the first citation for a headword being 'missed' are higher for some underrepresented periods (e.g., the eighteenth century) than, for example, for the Elizabethan period. This, in turn, may mean that a drop in the number of newly borrowed words in any given period could simply be an artefact of uneven coverage, rather than evidence that foreign languages had less influence on English in that period.

Finally, it may be worth noting that studies such as Culpeper and Clapham's (1996), which chart the overall proportions of loanwords from different languages in earlier periods of English, do not take into account the actual frequency of the borrowed words. In other words, they count the number of different types rather than the number of individual tokens. As a result, a very rare – and nowadays obsolete – loanword such as *evigilation* (with a single citation from the year 1720 in the *OED*) 'weighs' the same in their statistics as the French borrowing *government* (first used in 1483), which is one of the most frequent nouns in English today. This may have important implications for the interpretation of findings extracted from the *OED*. For example, while the sixteenth and seventeenth centuries certainly saw the introduction of many new loanwords (cf. the 'inkhorn controversy' mentioned above), a large number of them clearly did not acquire general currency and have indeed since gone out of use.

ILLUSTRATION BOX 15.1

An extract from *Harry Potter*

Let's test the degree to which English is made up from borrowed words by taking a look at a quite randomly chosen extract from the first *Harry Potter* book – this is the beginning of Chapter 12. Before you read the brief explanations below the text, try to guess which of these words are not native (i.e., Anglo-Saxon) words.

> Christmas was coming. One morning in mid-December, Hogwarts woke to find itself covered in several feet of snow. The lake froze solid and the Weasley twins were punished for bewitching several snowballs so that they followed Quirrell around, bouncing off the back of his turban. The few owls that managed to battle their way through the stormy sky to deliver mail had to be nursed back to health by Hagrid before they could fly off again.

Discussion: This extract has much less Latinate vocabulary than many other modern English texts would have. This is not surprising, as *Harry Potter* is a book aimed at young audiences, and Latinate vocabulary often creates a formal and elevated style, even today. Only the word *mass* in *Christmas* (= *Christ* + *mass*) is borrowed directly from Latin. In fact, *mass* is one of the words that were borrowed during the early Old English period. There are, however, quite a few other loanwords in this short passage. For example, the noun *sky* and the pronoun *they* are from Scandinavian. The largest batch of borrowings comes from French: *December, covered, several, lake, solid* (although this might also be a direct loan from Latin *solidus*), *punished, around, battle, deliver, mail* and *nurse*. The verb *manage* is Italian and the noun *turban* is from Turkish (which originally took it from Persian). Finally the word *bouncing* is of unknown origin.

Greek) into the English lexicon. Partly through written sources, but increasingly also via direct contact with other cultures during an age of exploration and the expansion of the British Empire, words such as *balcony* and *opera* (from Italian), *banana* and *maize* (from Spanish/Portuguese), *coffee* and *kiosk* (from Turkish), *harem* and *sheikh* (from Arabic), *bungalow* and *guru* (from Hindi), and *ginseng, ketchup* and *kimono* (from Chinese and Japanese, respectively) were added to the inventory of English.

Today, the vocabulary of the English language is a conglomerate of many different origins. The exact proportions are difficult to assess – they partly depend on what you count as a distinct word. Table 15.4, which is an attempt at capturing this diversity, shows that Anglo-Saxon, French and Latin together make up more than 80 per cent of today's English lexicon. However, this still leaves almost 20 per cent for other languages, including many non-European ones!

ADVANCES BOX 15.2

Nativization

If you have been surprised at the extent to which foreign words make up the vocabulary of the English language, then this may be partly so because many of these words feel 'perfectly English'. Thus, there is really nothing in the way that they are pronounced – or spelled – which singles them out as borrowings. In fact, as part of their integration into the language, loanwords often undergo a process of nativization, i.e., an adaptation of the foreign word to the linguistic system (e.g., the phonological rules) of English (cf. McMahon, 1994: 204–8). As a case in point, consider the word *cul-de-sac*, which is a French borrowing meaning 'street, lane, or passage closed at one end, a blind alley'. In Present-day English, most speakers of RP would pronounce this as /kʌldəsæk/, which is quite different from its original French /kydsak/. This change can be partly explained by the absence of the vowel sound /y/ in the phonological system of RP – and its ensuing substitution with an appropriate (i.e., typically closely related) native sound. In addition, the elision of the sounds for the letters *l* and *e* in French appears unmotivated to a speaker of English. As a result, the word is pronounced as it would be according to the rules of English.

As part of the nativization process, speakers of English also sometimes reanalyse the internal structure of borrowed words or phrases to make them appear more 'logical', or similar to existing English lexical items. This is typically referred to as folk etymology. For example, the word *alligator* comes from Spanish *el* or *al lagarto*, meaning 'lizard'. Since the Spanish (or possibly Arabic derived) determiner does not exist in English, it is (re-)interpreted to be part of the lexical item which it precedes. The resulting *allargato* is then further adapted – e.g., by analogy with existing words ending in *-or* – to become today's *alligator*.

15.7 Internal lexical change

As mentioned in Section 15.2 above, borrowing is not the only way for speakers of a language to extend the lexicon. Instead, they can use language-internal mechanisms to form new words. Since these mechanisms were already discussed in detail in the chapter on 'Morphology: Word Structure' (Chapter 5), this section will only be a brief reminder of the major types. In addition, I will point out which of the different processes were particularly prominent during the various periods of the English language.

A brief typology of word formation processes

- **Compounding:** Combining of two or more existing words to form a new word. This type of process is the most common in English today – about 40 per cent of new words today are compounds (cf. Algeo, 1991: 14) – and it was also highly frequent in Old English. An example taken from extract [15.1] is *leorningcniht*, where the two separate lexical items *leorning* and *cniht* – literally 'learning' + 'boy/attendant'[5] – are combined to form the meaning 'disciple'. While earlier compounds tended to combine two nouns, Present-day English allows a whole range of combinations (e.g., adjective + verb, as is *shortcut*; noun + adjective, as in *knee-deep*).

- **Derivation** (also **Affixation**): Creating new words by adding affixes (i.e., prefixes and suffixes) to existing words. This mechanism of forming new words was very common in Old English, and many of the affixes used back then are still frequent today (e.g., *–ness*, *–ful* or *–ish*). But some of the very common Old English prefixes (e.g., *for–* as in *forgo* and *forsake*; *with–* as in *withdraw* and *withhold*) and suffixes (e.g., *–ship* as in *friendship* or *-lock* as in *wedlock*) fell out of use in the transition to Middle English as Latinate suffixes such as *counter–*, *dis–*, *re–* and *trans–* became available (cf. Baugh and Cable, 2002: 181–3).

- **Conversion** (also **Zero-Derivation**): Changing the word class of a lexical item without changing its form. Typical examples are *to drink* ⇒ *have a drink* (from verb to noun), or *access* ⇒ *to access a database* (from noun to verb). This process is common in Present-day English, where it accounts for about 20 per cent of new words. However, it was impossible in Old English due to its system of inflections, which meant that different word classes were marked by differences in their morphological features.

- **Shortening (clipping, back formation, acronyms, initialisms)**: Shortening of an existing word by dropping part of it (e.g., the clipping of *influenza* to *flu*; the back-formation of *edit*, from *editor*), or by reducing a long phrase to a few letters (e.g., the acronyms *NATO* or *RADAR*, which are

---

ADVANCES BOX 15.3

Lexicalization/grammaticalization

There are additional mechanisms of language-internal lexical change which, however, have to remain beyond the scope of this chapter. Consider, for example, the complex prepositions *because of* and *instead of*. Although they consist of two orthographic words – they are separated by a white-space – it makes sense to regard them as a single lexical item, functioning in the same way as simple prepositions like *with* or *by*. However, if you look at their history, you will see that these complex prepositions originally developed from three separate words: *by cause of* and *in stede of* (with *stede* meaning 'place' in older periods of English). In other words, already existing, autonomous lexical items were fused together, so to speak, to form new words in English – in this case new members of the grammatical word-class of prepositions (hence the term 'grammaticalization'; cf. Hopper and Traugott, 2005). There are many other examples of this type of change in the English language – e.g., OE *hlaf* + *weard* ('loaf' + 'keeper') > *hlaford* > *loverd* > *lord*, or OE *bere* 'barley' + *ærn* 'house' > *barn*. In these cases, the resulting new words are members of the open word-class of nouns, and the process is typically referred to as 'lexicalization'. The exact mechanisms of how these kinds of change happen (and even what to call them) are a matter of intense debate in current linguistics (cf. Brinton and Traugott, 2003).

pronounced as single whole words; the initialisms *BBC* or *FBI*, which are pronounced as separate letters). Shortening is a common process in more recent periods of English (and particularly today), although it is of course much less frequent overall than compounding or derivation: only 8 per cent of all newly added words nowadays are shortenings (cf. Tottie, 2002: 106). In Old and Middle English, many words were consistently shortened in order to save expensive manuscript material. However, this is a convention of written English and should not be confused with the actual process of forming new words.

- **Blending** (sometimes called **Portmanteaux**): Combining parts of existing words to form new ones (e.g., *smoke* + *fog* ⇒ *smog*, or *breakfast* + *lunch* ⇒ *brunch*). This process was invented – and in fact also given its name – by Lewis Carroll in *Through the Looking Glass* (cf. Hughes, 2000: 351–2). The popularity of blending has risen considerably in recent decades. Today, this process accounts for about 5 per cent of all new additions to the lexicon.

15.8 Very recent lexical change

The development of English – and its vocabulary – has of course not stopped. In fact, the opposite is the case. The enormous expansion of the Internet over the past 15 years has revolutionized our communication patterns in a number of ways. Everybody who feels like it can create their own web page and make it available to the rest of the world at the click of a mouse, and various other modes of computer-mediated communication (e.g., chat-rooms, blogs, etc.) are widely used by an increasing part of the population. In other words, today a much larger proportion of English speakers than ever before write for audiences other than their immediate family and friends – but much of what they write does not undergo the rigid editing process that is typical for publications that are printed on paper. In a sense, the production of (parts of) written language has become more speech-like: more spontaneous, less controlled and more informal.

This type of situation invites change. Writers can be innovative and creative, easily replacing worn-out words and phrases with more expressive alternatives.[6] Many of these new creations will of course not catch on and will therefore never acquire sufficient currency among language users to be counted as 'new words'. Others, however, will spread and eventually make it into general usage.

For today's linguist, this is a fascinating research area for two reasons: not only is language changing fast and in interesting ways, but it is also possible to chart these changes (and failures to change) more easily than ever before since the relevant data is readily available in electronic format on the Internet. In fact, the very medium that is (at least partly) driving the change also offers the basis for establishing a thorough linguistic description of what is going on.

Let us therefore finish this section by looking at one such recent innovation in a little bit more detail, viz. the use of the German prefix *über–* in English (typically realized as *uber–*, without the umlaut mark). In German, this prefix can be used in a number of ways, but its use in English probably goes back to the term *Übermensch* (literally 'over' + 'human being'), which was used by the philosopher Friedrich Nietzsche in the nineteenth century to refer to a superior human being. In fact, the straight translation of this term gave English *superman*. Other related uses of the prefix *über–* in German are *übergross* ('oversized') and *übersättigt* ('oversaturated') – both uses suggest that *über–* can also mean 'too much of something'. The *OED* online edition does not list this prefix. Also, there is not a single use of a word starting with *uber–* in the 100 million words of the British National Corpus, which contains texts (both spoken and written) that were produced up to the year 1993. This suggests that it must be a very recent borrowing.

In order to test its currency in English, I therefore searched over 2.6 million messages that were posted in a number of Usenet discussion boards; one example of such a group is rec.equestrian, which deals with everything related to the topic of horses (cf. also Hoffmann, 2007, for a description of Usenet and the compilation of the corpus). My search retrieved 232 instances – a small number indeed, given that the corpus of texts is rather large. However, the instances were quite evenly distributed over different discussion groups, which suggests that we are not dealing with a highly specialized, topic-specific language feature. Examples [15.3] to [15.7] are typical uses of *uber-* in my corpus:

[15.3]   Who appointed you the Uber Arbiter of dressage, anyway. (rec. equestrian)

[15.4]   Reminds me a bit of that woman who presented 'Home Front' – she had the same sort of *uber*-chuffed tone as if she was about to start giggling, combined with a permanent rictus grin. (uk.media. tv.misc)

[15.5]   Fads I understand, but not the designer label *uber* pricey thing. (misc.kids.moderated)

[15.6]   She's *uber*-cute and likes to be scritched and begs for treats (loudly) when I come in the room. (rec.equestrian)

[15.7]   They do more or less what it says on the tin, although I had an *uber*-stain which required three coats of the Aquaseal product to kill it. (uk.d-i-y)

The five instances given here show that *uber-* is used in English in a variety of ways. Example [15.3] is closest to the meaning suggested by Nietzsche's *Übermensch*: the *uber arbiter* is presumably an arbiter with a special moral right or qualification to set him or her apart from (i.e., above) the other arbiters. In both [15.4] and [15.5], the meaning is 'too much'; the presenter of 'Home Front' in [15.4] is portrayed as being overly chuffed ('pleased, satisfied'), and the designer label goods in [15.5] are too expensive. In [15.6], however, the animal (in this case actually not a horse but a pig) is extremely cute – not too cute. And in [15.7], the *uber-stain* presumably refers to a very strong stain. Notice that in contrast to [15.3], *uber–* is here affixed to an inanimate entity.

A lot more can be found out about the use of *uber–* in English on the basis of the complete set of 232 instances. For example, one could ask the question whether it actually is a prefix in English or not. Thus, the use of *uber pricey* in [15.5] suggests that it functions as an adverb-like intensifier (similar to *very* or *extremely*) rather than as a prefix. This is interesting since it presumably started out as a prefix, and prefixes do not usually turn into adverbs. It is also noteworthy that 152 out of the 232 instances (66 per cent) contain a hyphen – like in examples [15.5], [15.6] and [15.7] – and all remaining uses are written as two separate orthographic words. In other words, not a single instance is found where *uber–* behaves like a fully established prefix would do, that is, as a morpheme that forms a single orthographic unit together with the base.

Nevertheless, this mini-investigation has clearly shown that *uber–* has become a productive prefix in English, which has developed additional uses to its suggested original meaning. However, it is certainly an infrequent prefix; only time will tell whether it will become fully established among the common prefixes of English.

15.9   What if...?

To close this chapter on lexical change, it may be a useful – and I hope amusing – exercise to ask a hypothetical question: What would we say today if English hadn't been exposed to the influence of all those foreign languages and if the more recently established word formation processes had never been introduced? Table 15.5 gives a few suggestions.

These constructed alternative words clearly show that the same concepts could, at least to some extent, also be expressed using a completely native Anglo-Saxon word stock. The fact, however, that these words sound in a way more foreign to present-day speakers than their real counterparts, which are – like tens of thousands of other English words – made up of (originally) foreign lexical material is a telling testimony to the varied history of the language as well as to the flexibility of its speakers to adapt to new communicative environments.

Recommended readings

An excellent – and much more complete – overview of the history of English words is given in Hughes (2000). For a shorter treatment of the main issues, you might also want to consult Chapters 7 and 8 in Katamba (2005: 135–96).

Alternative words – the Old English way　　　　　　　　　　　　　　　　*Table 15.5*

Current word	Alternative	Current word	Alternative
the past	the forgonehood	astronomy	starnaming
the present	the gainwait	astrology	starlore
the future	the tocome	geography	earthwrit
return	backgive	science	knowcraft
simplicity	onceliness	linguistics	speechlore

Furthermore, Baugh and Cable's *History of the English Language* (2002) offers extensive lists of words that were added to the lexical inventory of English at various stages in its development. Also, Crystal's (2004) *The Stories of English* is a very good and easy read that includes many interesting examples relating the development of the English lexicon. Finally, the *OED* provides detailed etymologies (word histories) and first datings (i.e., the first known uses of a word or a word meaning) for its entries.

Notes

1 Notice, however, that in some dialects *learn* is still used to mean 'teach'. This nicely illustrates that change may proceed at a different pace for different communities of speakers – and for some perhaps not at all.
2 The other four are *people*, *child*, *government*, and *part*.
3 Most of the words of Celtic origin listed in the *Oxford English Dictionary* – e.g., *bard*, *clan*, *slogan* – were borrowed at a much later stage in the history of English.
4 This kind of argumentation relies on the assumption that Scandinavian and Anglo-Saxon speakers would not have been able to understand each other easily. However, this view is debated by other scholars. After all, they argue, the Old Norse spoken by the Vikings was a direct descendant from the very language that the Anglo-Saxons brought to England.
5 The modern-day form of *cniht* is *knight* – the development of this English word is an example of semantic change (cf. Chapter 16).
6 The web site http://www.urbandictionary.com is a fascinating collection of thousands of recent coinages, many of which are decidedly politically incorrect. Interestingly, even though many of the words listed are highly unconventional, they are usually formed by completely regular word-formation processes.

Semantic Change

WILLEM B. HOLLMANN

16.1 Preliminaries

This chapter discusses how linguistic expressions may change their meaning over time. Actually the scope is a bit more limited than that, in the sense that here we will only see examples of how words – for example, *silly, very* – change their meaning.

The term 'linguistic expressions' includes words, but also larger grammatical constructions. Grammatical constructions – for example, what in Present-day English (PDE) are the *BE going to* + infinitive and *WILL* + infinitive future tense constructions, as in *It's going to/will rain tomorrow* – may also change their meaning. Indeed, these two future tense constructions started out with the verbs *GO* and *WILL* used in their primitive sense. In the case of *GO* this was the motion meaning, which it still often has in PDE. The old sense of *WILL* has almost completely disappeared: it used to mean something like 'want, desire'. One may wonder why the developments that gave rise to these two future tense constructions are seen as semantic changes in constructions, as opposed to meaning changes in the single words *go* and *will*. To see that what is involved is actually a change in grammatical construction, consider that originally both these verbs would not be combined with infinitives, see *I am going to London, I will* ('want') *more silver*). Over time, it became possible to combine them with infinitives. Now in order to account for these grammatical facts, it is not sufficient to think of the changes as having affected only the verbs *go* and *will*. (Another reason why we treat these developments as examples of grammatical change is that many linguists consider future tense marking as part of the grammar of a language.) The exact way in which both of these constructions developed into future tense constructions will be discussed in Chapter 17, on grammatical change. In other words, while here we are concerned with **lexical semantic change**, one of the topics of the next chapter will be **grammatical semantic change**.

The fact that we discuss these two levels of change in different chapters should not be taken to mean that the causes and mechanisms involved are completely different: there is actually a lot of overlap. We will see, for instance, that the development of *very* (from an adjective meaning 'true' to the intensifying meaning it carries today) and the trajectory that led to (especially certain uses of) *WILL* + infinitive both involve a mechanism called **subjecti-fication**—which will be explained in detail in Section 16.4, below.

The overlap in this case goes even further: just as a lot of linguists consider future tense marking to be part of the grammar of a language, so too would many see intensifiers as grammatical items. This means that the development of *very* could have legitimately ended up in the chapter on grammatical change as well (as an example of **grammaticalization**, see Section 16.4, below, and particularly Section 17.3 of Chapter 17). For these reasons, readers may find it useful to treat this chapter and the subsequent one on grammatical change as companions, and to study them together. Indeed, many linguists nowadays argue that it is impossible to say where the lexicon ends, and syntax begins.

16.2   Semantic change and semantic theory

Studying semantic change presupposes a more general understanding of semantics. In order to grasp what it means for a meaning to change, we need to know what meanings are in the first place. What do we mean when we say that a word (or larger construction) means something? Chapter 10 on semantics contains an elaborate discussion of this and related issues.

For our purposes, we may divide the history of the study of semantics in linguistics, as well as in cognate disciplines such as philosophy and psychology, into roughly two stages. Traditionally, linguistic expressions have been said to be meaningful because they are connected to aspects of the real world **in some objective way**. That is to say, the connections in question are either there, or they are not. Let us consider a simple example. If we describe the differences in meaning between the words *man, woman, boy* and *girl* in terms of the properties [+/− male] and [+/− adult], we can take a human being, and use those properties (often called **semantic components**) to decide objectively whether to refer to them as a *man, woman, boy* or *girl*. This is the basis of the so-called **objectivist** or **truth-conditional** theory of semantics (see e.g., Cann, 1993) (see also Chapter 11, Section 11.3).

Among a multitude of other problems, one of the things that critics of the objectivist view of linguistic meaning have pointed out is that it would fail to explain how we are able to produce and – quite literally – **make sense of** examples such as the following:

[16.1]   I agree that maybe Robben is a girl...More suited to ballet than football...

(http://www.theflyingshuttle.com/weyosc.html, accessed 25 November 2007)

Football fans will easily recognize the problem that is posed by this (real!) example, but the reader who is less knowledgeable in this area should know that Robben is a male, adult football player. We see here that the two semantic components identified above clash with the word used to describe him, that is, *girl*. What this example shows is that assigning meanings to words may be a much more subjective process than the traditional view suggests. Opponents of traditional, objectivist semantics add that creative examples such as the sentence in example [16.1] are in no way exceptional but actually extremely common in our everyday use of language. Therefore, we need a theory of meaning that is able to accommodate this kind of subjectivity and flexibility.

Taking their cue from some pioneering research in the 1970s, by cognitive psychologist Eleanor Rosch and her colleagues (e.g., Rosch, 1973, 1978; Rosch et al., 1976), critics of the objectivist approach look to **prototype-theoretical semantics** as the solution to problems caused by examples such as [16.1] (and many other issues, see Chapter 6, Section 6.7, for an introduction to this theory and application to grammatical word-class, as well as Chapter 10, Section 10.3.1 on semantics; also see, for example, Croft and Cruse, 2004: ch. 4; or Taylor, 2003). Very briefly, the prototype-based alternative takes as its starting point the realization that, for almost every aspect of the real world, it is impossible to devise adequate definitions in terms of a delimited list of semantic components. Instead, we have some idea of what a 'perfect' category member is or would be like (the **prototype**[1]). On the basis of how similar some other person or object (or whatever) is to that prototype, we may consider them to be anything from a very good member of the category, via being a not-so-good member or a marginal member, to not being a member at all.

With reference to the words *man, woman, boy* and *girl*, the idea is that we all have some image of a prototypical man, a prototypical woman, and so on. Each time we encounter a putative member of any of these categories, we judge how much they resemble this prototype; the closer the resemblance, the more likely we are to assign them to the category in question, and therefore label them with the corresponding word. Moreover, again based on important research from the 1970s (e.g., Labov, 1973), followers of prototype semantics argue that category boundaries may shift depending on the (linguistic/situational) context.

We are now in a position to understand how we make sense of example 16.1: in the context of football players our category of girls may shift its boundaries a bit, so that it may include adult males if, perhaps, they move in a certain way and so on.

Given the failure of the objectivist approach to semantics to account for examples such as [16.1], compared to the apparent success of the prototype-based view, it should not be surprising that most historical semanticists favour using the latter over the former (see Illustration Box 16.1 in the section below, and also for example, Geeraerts, 1997; or Györi, 2002 for elaborate scholarly discussions and many concrete examples).

16.3 Semantic change: traditional classifications

Semantic change has traditionally been looked at from a variety of angles. Before we discuss the various classifications of **meaning change** corresponding to these angles, it is important to realize two things:

(i)   The traditional classifications cannot be applied to all changes.
(ii) The classifications are not mutually exclusive: sometimes we can apply two or even more labels to a single change, depending on which aspect of the change we choose to use as the basis of our classification.

Some of the examples given below will illustrate the second point. Later, we will also see that some examples of meaning changes are not easily accommodated by the traditional types – we have already mentioned one such example: the development of *very* from an adjective meaning 'true/real' into an intensifier. We come back to this in Section 16.4.

The first traditional typology of semantic changes is the division into changes whose result is a more positive meaning – so-called **melioration** – and those which give a more negative meaning – known as **pejoration**. A recent case of melioration in British English is illustrated in the following two lines taken from *Fit but you know it*, a song by The Streets:

[16.2]   I didn't wanna bowl over all geezer and *rude*,
         Not rude as in good but just rude like uncouth

These lines illustrate that the word *rude*, whose original meaning of 'unmannered' (or indeed 'uncouth') is obviously rather negative, can nowadays be used in a more positive sense. Discussions with my undergraduate students at Lancaster University suggest that the exact meaning is something like 'physically attractive (often in a slightly vulgar way)'. It actually seems to be applied especially to females, as in *She's rude* or – using the currently fashionable intensifier *well* – *She's well rude*.

In order to understand the development of this more positive meaning, we may need to look to the dancehall and hiphop subcultures. In 1960s Jamaican English, expressions such as *rude boy* or *rude girl* were used to refer to 'cool' members of the dancehall scene. From there it may have spread (due to migration and the popular media) to the United Kingdom. The sexual connotations of the new use of the word may be related to the fact that, in Jamaican English, *rudeness* was used to mean 'sexual intercourse'. (For some of these points see, for instance, the interesting discussion at http://www.knkmusic.net/2006/07/rude-boy-mix_20.html [accessed 6 February 2008].) As an example of pejoration, consider that English *sinister* was derived from Latin, where the word did not carry any negative meaning but simply meant 'left'. (It may well be relevant, though, that most of you would refer to your left hand as your 'bad hand'.)

The second traditional classification of changes in meaning is in terms of whether it becomes broader or narrower. *Dog* used to refer not to any old dog, but to some specific large and strong breeds. It is interesting in this connection to compare English to Dutch, where this is still the case: to a Dutchman the word *dog* summons up an image of a Great Dane or perhaps the kind of dog featured in the film Turner and Hooch (Dogue de Bordeaux); to talk about dogs in general he would use the word *hond*. (The English cognate *hound* has gone in the opposite direction: it now describes some particular breeds used in hunting.) The development the English word *dog* has undergone is known as **generalization**, **widening** or **broadening**. (As is so often the case in linguistics and other sciences, several different terms are around for what is essentially the same thing.) The opposite of generalization is **specialization** (also known as **narrowing**). In Middle English any young person could be called a *girl*; the restriction to female young persons is a development that occurred in the early Modern period.

The third dimension on which certain semantic changes may be classified is whether they result from **metaphor** or **metonymy**. In metaphorical meaning changes, speakers perceive some sort of similarity between one concept (the source concept S) and another concept (the target concept T), and press the word for S into service to talk about T. The famous TV-chef Gordon Ramsay regularly calls participants in his cooking contests *doughnuts* if they fail to perform well. This is clearly not intended literally but figuratively. The basis of this metaphor is some sort of similarity between doughnuts and the contestants in question, probably including the fact that they are not very sophisticated or do not display any intelligence. This example demonstrates two characteristics of metaphor. First, the comparison between the source (here: doughnuts) and target (here: the contestants) is only partial: Ramsay is not implying, for instance, that the contestant could be filled with jam then eaten. Second, the source is more 'concrete' than the target. To see that this is the case, consider that all of us can easily point to doughnuts. Sub-par contestants, on the other hand (or people who display a lack of some skill more generally), are much harder to identify objectively.

Metonymy, like metaphor, involves some sort of connection between concepts, but in this case there is no similarity between them but they are closely linked in some other way; for example, because one is part of, or contains, the other. If we ask someone if they watched *Gordon Ramsay* last night, we actually want to know whether they watched the TV-show that the cook was in. This type of metonymy is sometimes known as **pars pro toto** ('part for whole'). Another example of this would be where we use the phrase *Number 10* to refer to the British Prime Minister (and possibly his government), who lives at 10, Downing Street.

The development of the word *rude*, which we described above, could also be seen as a case of pars pro toto. A *rude person* used to refer to someone who was bad-mannered or vulgar. By applying the term to persons whose vulgarity is part of their attractiveness, young speakers of British English are using it metonymically. This example, then, shows that semantic changes may sometimes be of more than just one type: in this case melioration and metonymy, specifically **pars pro toto**.

The reverse, so-called **totum pro parte** ('whole for part') is also possible. When I discuss the expansion plans of *Lancaster University* I do not mean that, for example, the students have taken part in devising this policy: only a relatively small number of university administrators have done that. Likewise, by saying that *Liverpool* should attract José Mourinho as its trainer, one does not refer to the city as a whole, or even the whole Liverpool Football Club, but only the part of it that is made up of the people in charge of the club.

The fourth way in which semantic changes have traditionally been classified depends on whether they are driven by factors within the language itself, or by language-external factors. The main language-internal factor that is relevant to meaning changes is other changes in the lexicon, and in the meanings of lexical items. Consider the word *gay*, a classic example. Until a number of decades ago, this was commonly used to mean 'cheerful'. Nowadays, however, the term *gay* conjures up a homosexual person; the older meaning has virtually disappeared.

ILLUSTRATION BOX 16.1

Another use of the term metonymy

The introductory section to this chapter mentioned that the word *silly* has changed its meaning. This case of semantic change is rather remarkable, having gone from something like 'blissful' or 'blessed' all the way to 'foolish'. The contrast between these two meanings is so pronounced that it is clear that there must have been some intermediate stages.

Using the *Oxford English Dictionary* or any other dictionary that contains etymological information we may piece together the various steps. Our earliest recorded examples of the word occur around 1200, and in the first 100 years or so the meaning was quite clearly 'blissful' or 'blessed'. The following example (taken from the *OED*) illustrates this: *A Jhesu, blyssede [es] þat abbaye and* cely *es þat religione* (*Abbey of Holy Ghost* in *Hampole's Wks*) 'Oh Jesus, blessed is that abbey and silly [i.e., blessed] is that religion'. (This example is actually from the first half of the fourteenth century but is convenient as it does not require a lot of context to make the meaning of the word *silly* clear.)

The next stage is the rise, towards the end of the thirteenth century, of the meaning 'innocent' or 'harmless'. Consider for instance: *'Alas', he seide, 'þis seli best: þat no-þing ne doth a-mis!'* (*S. Eng. Leg.*) ' "Alas", he said, "this silly [i.e., harmless] animal, that does not do anything amiss!" '. The following step is the development, soon thereafter, of the meaning 'deserving of pity or sympathy', as in *Sely Scotland, that of helpe has gret neide* (Henry, *Wallace*, ii) 'Silly [i.e., pitiable] Scotland, which is in great need of help'.

The next meaning is 'weak/feeble', first in relation to physical strength or fitness (e.g., *Here we see that a smal sillie Bird knoweth how to match with so great a Beast* (J. Maplet, *Gr. Forest*)), then also of intellectual capacities, i.e., 'ignorant' (e.g., *The silly herdman all astonnied stands* (Surrey, *Æneid*, ii)).

Finally, in the sixteenth century we arrive at the meaning of 'foolish', as in *In pride wee speake it, or at least inwardlie thinke it, wee are not as those seely Idiotes are* (Babington, *Commandm.*).

Having worked out the different stages of this development we are now in a much better position to understand how the word *silly* could have developed from 'blessed' or 'blissful', which were very positive (especially in the Middle Ages), into something as negative as its present-day meaning of 'foolish'. The key is to realize that while the development as a whole is very drastic, the individual steps are not. Thus, 'blissful/blessed' is not that far removed from 'innocent/harmless'. More precisely, blissful or blessed people and things are often also innocent and harmless, and (again particularly in a medieval mindset) vice versa. As there was thus some overlap between the categories of blessed/blissful people and things and innocent/harmless people and things, speakers may have reinterpreted utterances about, for example, a blessed religion as statements about a harmless religion. The same reinterpretation may have driven the next step: innocent/harmless people/things often deserve our pity/sympathy. Moving on, we can say that if people/things are deserving of our pity/sympathy this will often be because they are too weak to stand up or maintain themselves, either physically or through the use of their intellectual abilities. And people who are ignorant may of course display behaviour that others consider foolish.

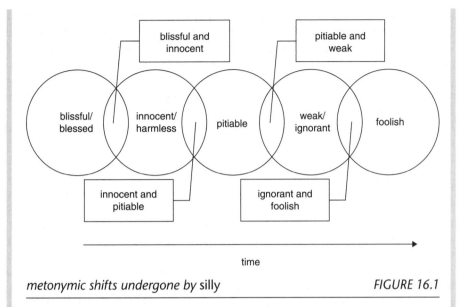

metonymic shifts undergone by silly FIGURE 16.1

What we have here, then, is a chain of semantic developments where a word starts out by referring to one category of things, then moves on to an adjacent, partly overlapping, category, then to another, and so on, as in Figure 16.1, above. Note, incidentally, that in terms of the semantic theories discussed in Section 16.2 of this chapter (and also in Chapter 10 on semantics), the proto-type-based approach does, but the objectivist theory does not, offer the kind of flexibility we would need to account for this gradual change.

This kind of development is also known as metonymy, though it is clearly not the same as **pars pro toto** or **totum pro parte**. It would of course be useful if we had a separate term for it, but we do not, unless we said that this third type of metonymy is 'metonymy in the narrow sense', metonymy in the broader sense being the label that subsumes all three subtypes.

There are many cases where older meanings happily coexist with newer ones. While the word *screen*, for example, nowadays often means 'television or computer screen' its older meaning of a large wooden panel, used for example to shield off one part of a room from the rest, has by no means disappeared. In order to understand what has happened to the word *gay* we must realize that its new meaning is a socially loaded concept, and speakers will thus be inclined to try and avoid confusion between the new meaning and 'cheerful'.

This example, then, shows that a distinction between language-internal and language-external factors in semantic change is often hard to draw. Language-external factors are broadly cultural-social. The development of the word *screen*, sketched above, is a suitable example: with the development in our society of television and computer technology we needed a new term to refer to that part of the technologies that we now call screens. Above, we saw that the semantic change undergone by *rude* is melioration and metonymy (**pars pro toto**) at the same time. We may wish to add that it is partly caused by social-cultural factors. Proper social-cultural history is best left to social and cultural historians, but on the basis of, for example, women in classical paintings from masters such as Rembrandt or Rubens, or in the work by the pre-Raphaelite Rossetti, it seems clear that our ideas of beauty and attractiveness have not always been the same as they are today. It is tempting to speculate that to many, an element of vulgarity is becoming a more acceptable and desirable part of attractiveness. To the extent that this is correct, it would help us understand why *rude* has developed an alternative meaning of 'attractive'.

Yet many other semantic changes that are related to social factors can be found in taboo areas. It is easy enough to think of examples of euphemistic expressions that came to be used to refer to sexual acts, excrement, and so on, but here let us consider an area that is, at least to us, a bit less immediately obvious, namely dangerous animals. The English word *bear* originally meant 'the brown one'. Rather than referring to these dangerous animals directly, speakers apparently preferred a euphemistic term. If this strikes you as odd, consider that it is actually a common process across languages. The Russian word for bear, *medvedev*, originally meant honey-eater. Nowadays, in Western countries, the threat of dangerous animals has of course decreased considerably, but it is still possible to find euphemisms. Following the release of the film *Wallace & Gromit: The Curse of the Were Rabbit* in 2005, the newspaper *The Times* reported that on Portland, an island in the county of Dorset in the south of England, local authorities strongly objected to posters being put up with the official film title. The island's stone quarry industry has experienced many problems caused by rabbits' burrowing habits; a land slip even led to the death of a worker around a century ago. As a result of all this, rabbits are considered bad luck, and the animals are usually referred to euphemistically as *underground muttons* or *furry things*. (The film's production company decided to heed the locals' warnings, and instead of using the full title, put up alternative posters bearing the tagline *Something bunny is going on.*)

16.4   Recent developments: regularities in semantic change

We have seen that the traditional ways of classifying meaning changes involves various oppositions or contrasts, and that the meaning of linguistic items may develop in either direction. Meanings may become more positive or negative, broader or narrower, may involve metaphor or (different kinds of) metonymy, and may be caused by factors within or outside language.

This impression that, at first blush, in semantic change 'anything goes' was a problem for the status of the study of this level of language change as a serious scientific endeavour. After all, in science we are interested in finding patterns that, if not strictly predictable (as in for instance physics), are at least to some extent regular. Scientists, in other words, are not primarily interested in just cataloguing every phenomenon that is possible, but in constraints on those phenomena. Now, in a field where anything and everything is possible, we can really only offer descriptions of individual cases of historical semantic change, which are more like mere anecdotes as opposed to rigorous scientific analyses of what constrains what is possible, what isn't, and why that should be so. These anecdotes may be interesting and entertaining enough to read, but they are not conducive to a general understanding of the phenomena in question.

Indeed, a review of conferences and publications in historical linguistics in the previous century reveals that for a considerable period of time semantic change was not seen as worthy of many historical linguists' attention. Fortunately some scholars, such as Elizabeth Traugott, persisted in the study of the phenomenon, and since about the 1980s some regularities have come to light. These regularities mainly fall under the umbrella term **subjectification**. Although many questions still remain in connection with subjectification, the discovery of this pattern (or **set** of patterns, see e.g., Traugott's pioneering 1989 paper) has meant that linguists now take semantic change as an area that does merit serious scholarly attention.

In order to understand what we mean by subjectification it is important to note that the term is not connected to what, in grammatical analysis, we call the subject of a clause. Instead, it is related to the notion of subjective judgments (as opposed to objective statements): subjectification is the change from relatively objective meanings into increasingly subjective ones.

The development of *very* is a clear case of this. When the word was borrowed from French, following the Normal Conquest, its meaning of 'true' or 'real' was borrowed along with it. (The French adjective *vrai* still means precisely that, and if you suspect a historical connection with the English words *verify, veracity* and *veritable* – all of which have an element of 'truth' in their meanings – you're absolutely right.) Thus, when a speaker of Middle English described a man as a *very knight* they meant that he was a true or real knight. Whether or not someone was or not could be established objectively: one would have been born as one or have been knighted by another knight. Nowadays if we say that language change is *a very interesting area*, we use the word *very* in a much more subjective sense: someone else may well disagree with our personal evaluation.

The interesting thing about subjectification, from a scientific point of view, is that it is claimed to be unidirectional. That is to say, over time meanings may gradually become more subjective, but they do not become more objective. This is therefore a clear constraint on what is possible and what is not. Whether or not this **unidirectionality** is truly without exception is controversial: there are some debates over certain cases. The word *gay* could be a possible exception. Deciding whether or not someone is cheerful would, if anything, appear to be more subjective than saying whether or not they prefer partners of the same sex. But exceptions such as these do not detract much from the value of the notion of subjectification: the overwhelming evidence from English and other languages is that there are many more changes that go in the expected direction than in the opposite one.

Coming back to our example of *very*, this is by no means the only case of an intensifier developing out of an adjective meaning 'true' or 'real'. There are many other languages where we observe this, and in fact English itself provides other examples of this development as well. *Right* and *really* (and

ADVANCES BOX 16.1

Subjectification and egocentricity in cognition and language

Important though the discovery of subjectification is, a great deal of what goes on in semantic change still seems rather haphazard. Whilst we are now in a position to say something about the development of *very*, *real* and many other expressions in English and other languages, some of the changes we mentioned above do not fit our notion of subjectification.

The change in meaning of *dog*, from a particular breed of dogs to dogs in general, for instance, is not a move towards a more subjective meaning (though, significantly, it is not a development in the opposite direction either). Nor could we say such a thing about *girl* changing its meaning from 'young person' to 'young female person', or about the semantics of *silly* going from 'blessed/blissful' to 'foolish'.

Although subjectification admittedly seems a pretty robust concept, another question that remains as yet unanswered is why meanings develop in the direction stipulated, and not (or hardly ever) the other way around. In fact, not only is this question unanswered, it has generally been simply avoided in studies on subjectification.

We may start finding the answer by drawing a parallel with certain aspects of the grammar of the world's languages. It is a well-known fact that in terms of making grammatical distinctions in and around nouns and pronouns, most distinctions are usually available for first- and second-person personal pronouns, followed by third-person pronouns, human or at any rate animate nouns, and finally inanimate and abstract nouns. Consider, for example, that in English we have a subject form *I* that is separate from an object form *me*, and a possessive form *my*. For the second person we only have two forms: *you* (subject and object) and *your* (possessive). The third person has three distinctions again, at least in the masculine (*he, him* and *his*) and is, in this respect, a notorious oddity in the eyes of language typologists. (Standard English has quite a few more oddities like this that lead typologists to warn students of language against relying on it too much if they want to find out what is universal to human language. The reason why the language is so deviant should be sought, at least partly, in its unnaturally high degree of standardization and codification.) The feminine forms are better behaved (*she, her*), and for human/animate nouns we have two forms as well; e.g., *man* for subject/object vs. possessive *man's*. However, for many inanimate and abstract nouns in most contexts we feel uncomfortable using a separate morphological form if we want to indicate 'possession', preferring the **of**-construction instead; e.g., *the thrill of a live concert* rather than ??*a live concert's thrill*. The **of**-construction does not count as a separate form of the noun as it clearly involves other elements and the noun itself remains the same, so we only have a single form (here: *concert*). Croft (2003: 137) suggests that the reason why the hierarchy from first- and second-person personal pronouns to inanimate/abstract nouns is ordered the way it is, is that the more similar persons and things are to ourselves, the more distinctions we are likely to recognize.

Moving on now to subjectification, as a very tentative suggestion, one wonders whether a similar egocentric tendency may underlie this phenomenon as well. Perhaps we are inclined to reinterpret situations, and linguistic expressions describing those situations, in our own subjective terms.[3] Györi's interesting (2002) study (which is not restricted to changes which we would normally classify as displaying subjectification) discusses this possibility, but there is still plenty of scope for further research in this area.

increasingly *real*, especially in American English) were not always used as an intensifier almost synonymous with *very*.[2] The fact that we see word meanings travelling down this historical path again and again, and in languages that we do not consider to be related, is clear evidence that we have discovered something about the human mind, whose architecture and mechanisms are after all what language users around the globe have in common.

16.5 Semantic change: diachronic or synchronic?

Some of the examples of semantic change discussed in this chapter happened quite a while ago (such as the change involving the word *girl*) and/or correspond to considerable intervals in the history of English (e.g., the change in meaning of *silly*, which we have seen spans several centuries). They are therefore all clear cases of **diachronic** change: changes that happen through time.

A few other changes, on the other hand, are happening as we speak. *Rude* has only acquired its meaning of 'attractive' very recently. While my undergraduate students readily accept and report using it, colleagues in their thirties and forties would generally not use it, and sometimes do not even recognize the newly acquired meaning. As such, this change has not been adopted by the whole British English speech community. Likewise, not all native speakers will use or perhaps even recognize *doughnut* as a term for 'inadequate person'. The question arises as to when we can legitimately speak of a semantic change (or a language more generally): when the whole speech community has implemented it? when a number of language users have? or perhaps when only a single speaker has created a new usage? The latter situation is sometimes dismissed as a case of language change, but consider that a semantic or other type of change always starts in some speaker's here and now. The phenomenon is, in that sense, **synchronic**.

In addressing this issue, we follow Croft (2000) in distinguishing between two stages in a given change: the **innovation** (first new usage) and the **propagation** (spread to other members of the speech community). Thus, we see semantic change and language change in general as both synchronic and diachronic. It is important to point out that the propagation/spread of a new variant in many cases does not go all the way to completion – indeed, in many cases it does not. In relation to *rude,* for example, one could hazard the reasonable guess that it will never be adopted by all speakers of (British) English. Words for 'attractive' replace each other fairly rapidly, and it is therefore likely that the next generation will not copy the present teenagers and 20-somethings, but recruit a different word to convey the meaning in question. In fact new usages may never spread beyond their innovators. Historical linguists terms these unique usages **nonce-formations**.

Semantic nonce-formations and changes that do spread to some or all members of the speech community all start out the same: a speaker makes some sort of creative association or connection between some idea s/he wants to express and (the meaning of) some existing word or expression. The mechanisms by which these connections are made are clearly **psychological** in nature. They were touched upon above – see, for example, the Advances Box 16.1 on subjectification.

One may wonder why nonce-formations do not spread to other speakers, why some changes only spread to a few speakers, and others, to most or all of them. Croft explains the different outcomes of innovations in **social** terms. Roughly speaking, if a new usage has prestige – that is, is used by a speaker whom other speakers would like to be associated with; see the work by Labov (e.g., 1972) and his followers – then the innovation is likely to catch on and spread. If we recall the development of *rude*, it is possible that (some) British English speakers ascribed some form of prestige to certain members of music-related subcultures, and that this led them to adopt novel expressions such as *rude boy/girl*. More information about the role of social factors in language change is given in various parts of Chapters 12 and 19, and also 33, Section 33.2.

16.6 Conclusions

Let us wrap up this whistle-stop tour of the study of semantic change offered by this chapter by offering a few conclusions.

Semantic change does not only concern words. Grammatical constructions also have meanings. These do not remain constant over time and the ways in which they change often overlap with certain types of lexical semantic change, see especially subjectification – more about this in Chapter 17.

Traditional, objectivist or truth-conditional semantic theory has a hard time accounting for the minutiae of meaning change; we saw that the more recent prototype-based view of meaning allows more flexibility and as such is a more convincing candidate.

Moving on to ways of classifying semantic change, traditional typologies give us terms that we can use to describe many different kinds. Unfortunately, these classifications give the impression that semantic change is far from predictable in that several opposite directions are possible. However, recent research, especially on subjectification, shows that there **is** some regularity – and this regularity may be related to what we may call certain egocentric tendencies of human cognition.

Finally, we saw that meaning change always starts in some creative speaker's here and now and is, in that sense, a synchronic phenomenon. From there it may or may not spread to other speakers. This process of propagation inevitably takes time, and meaning change is therefore also manifested diachronically. While the innovation is a cognitive process and as such requires a psychological explanation, propagation depends on social factors, and must therefore be explained in terms of sociolinguistic theory.

While semantic change was, due to its apparently complete unpredictability, for a long time the black sheep of the family in areas of language change, as a result of recent developments it is now very well respected, and as such is likely to attract a lot more research in the future.

Recommended readings

Historical descriptions of English (e.g., Smith, 1996; Crystal, 2004) traditionally include some examples of meaning changes, but generally do not offer very much in the way of systematic explanation. As we have seen above, explaining semantic change has become a serious enterprise only since the discovery and subsequent study of subjectification, especially by Elizabeth Traugott. For more information on this you will have to consult some relatively advanced work, for example, Traugott's milestone (1989) paper. For her more up-to-date ideas see, for example, the relevant sections in Hopper and Traugott (2003), or (even more advanced but also more complete) Traugott and Dasher (2001). In relation to the notion of egocentricity in language change, Györi's (2002) article offers the most comprehensive discussion. For the important distinction between innovation and propagation in language change (including semantic change) the best reference is Croft (2000). His thought-provoking evolutionary approach to linguistic change also includes a useful summary of the importance of social factors.

Notes

1 Note that the term 'prototype' as used here is not the same as in examples like *Motorola has built a working prototype of a new colour display that uses tiny filaments called carbon nanotubes* (adapted from an article on cnet.co.uk), where it means something like 'an exploratory model'.
2 Intensifiers such as *dead* and *bloody* also arose in a process of subjectification, though the source meaning is obviously different here than in the case of *very, right* and *real(ly)*.
3 This line of reasoning fits in with the suggestion, made above, that *sinister* developed its negative meaning because, from the point of view of most of us, our left hand is our 'bad hand'.

CHAPTER 17

Grammatical Change

WILLEM B. HOLLMANN

17.1 Preliminaries

Grammatical change is an extremely interesting area but does presuppose some knowledge of grammar. For this reason, if you do not have this knowledge yet, this chapter will work best if you have first familiarized yourself with the terminology discussed in the chapters on morphology and grammar, that is, especially, Chapter 5 and Chapters 6–8, respectively.

Chapters on grammatical change in traditional textbooks on the history of English or historical linguistics by and large focus on change in morphology (the structure of words) and/or syntax (the structure of phrases and clauses). Some of the most important changes in the history of English can indeed be described in more or less purely structural terms, that is, without considering meaning very much.

The sentences in examples [17.1–2], below, illustrate object-verb (or OV) constituent order,[1] which was quite frequent in Old English but became less and less common during Middle English, until it was completely lost in the sixteenth century:

[17.1]   Gregorius [hine object] [afligde verb]. (*Homilies of Ælfric*, 22.624)
Gregory him put-to-flight
'Gregory made him flee'

[17.2]   Ne sceal he [naht unaliefedes object] [don verb]. (*Pastoral Care*, 10.61.14)
not shall he nothing unlawful do
'He will do nothing unlawful'

Example [17.2] shows that we must be careful when discussing OV order in Old and Middle English: the finite verb (here: *sceal*) actually often occurred before the object, taking up the second position in the clause (the initial position here being occupied by the negator *ne*). Thus, it is often only the lexical verb (here: *don*) that follows the object. Further complicating matters, the writer of example [17.1], the monk Ælfric, who lived around the turn of the first millennium, would almost certainly have positioned the object after the verb *afligde* if, instead of the pronoun *hine*, it had been a full noun phrase such as *the man* in OE. This would then have yielded something like [17.3], below:

[17.3] Gregorius [afligde ᵥₑᵣᵦ] [þone guman ₒᵦⱼₑ𝒸ₜ]
Gregorius put-to-flight the man
'Gregorius made the man flee.'

We shall discuss the loss of OV order in more detail in Section 17.2.1, where we will show, in particular, how it is related to a change in the English morphological system – which, in its turn, was partly brought about by a change in stress (which happened before the start of the Old English period). The point here is that these interrelated changes are all of a structural (phonetic, morphological and syntactic) nature.

In the last few decades, however, there has been a significant move in the study of grammatical change in English, and other languages, towards looking at developments that also involve meaning (i.e., semantics-pragmatics). Most of these studies rely on and/or contribute to what has become known as **grammaticalization theory** – named after the phenomenon of **grammaticalization**, which may be defined as the development of grammatical constructions out of more lexical expressions. The reverse (i.e., grammatical constructions developing into more lexical expressions) does not, or hardly ever, appear to happen.

From a scientific point of view, this **unidirectionality** renders grammaticalization extremely interesting, as it allows us to make certain predictions as to what changes are likely to happen, and what changes would be unexpected. Some examples of grammaticalization were introduced in Chapter 16, on semantic change; for example, the future tense constructions based on *BE going to* and on *WILL*. Examples [17.4a–b] illustrate these constructions, while [17.5a–b] show how the verbs were used before the future tense uses became available. (Example [17.5b] is taken from the *Oxford English Dictionary* entry for the verb *WILL*, and dates from *c.*1205.) These uses are more lexical than grammatical in the sense that their meanings, motion and desire, are more concrete than future tense. Note also that in many languages future tense marking is part of verbal morphology (e.g., Spanish *como* 'I eat/am eating', *comeré* 'I will eat'). Motion and desire, on the other hand, do not develop into inflections on verbs quite so regularly (though it is not impossible).

[17.4] a It's going to rain tomorrow.
b It will rain tomorrow.
[17.5] a I am going to London.
b Wenne þu wult more suluer, sæche hit at me suluen.
'When you want more silver, say it to me'.

In the case of *BE going to* the older (motion) construction still coexists today with the newer, more grammatical use; in the case of *WILL* the original (volitional) use is now almost obsolete – **almost** because while examples such as [17.5b] are no longer acceptable, if you ask someone if they *will* marry you, you're not asking them to make a prediction about the future but whether they **want** to marry you. In other words, when lexical expressions develop into grammatical constructions the older meanings may, but need not, continue to exist. If they gradually die out, there are often some remnants that persist for quite some time. (In an important (1991) article on grammaticalization, the American linguist Paul Hopper calls this the **principle of persistence**. Hopper and others have identified several other principles, or typical characteristics of grammaticalization, some of which we will see below.)

The point of giving these examples here is that they clearly illustrate that grammatical change is often not just about linguistic structure, but frequently also involves changes in meaning. In addition to grammatical structure and meaning, grammaticalization typically involves a **third** level, namely phonetics. Consider, for instance, that it is possible to say [17.6a], where *going* and *to* have been phonetically reduced and fused into a single form, but not [17.6b]:

[17.6] a It's gonna rain tomorrow.
        b *I'm gonna London tomorrow.

This phonetic reduction – labelled **attrition** by the German historical linguist Christian Lehmann (1985) – illustrates a second characteristic of processes of grammaticalization.

Many historical linguists working on grammaticalization have suggested that there is also reduction on the level of meaning in that the richer, more lexical meanings (in the case of the future tense constructions at hand, motion and desire) are stripped off, while more grammatical meanings (here: future tense) come to the fore. In a study published in 1912, the French linguist Antoine Meillet, generally considered to be the founding father of grammaticalization studies, called this *affaiblissement* ('weakening'), but it is nowadays more commonly known as **semantic bleaching**. Having already mentioned persistence and attrition, we now have semantic bleaching as the third property of grammaticalization. We return to grammaticalization in Section 17.3.

17.2 Structural changes in the history of English

17.2.1 Changes in constituent order and changes in (pro)nouns

In Section 17.1 we saw that one of the major structural changes in the history of English was the disappearance of OV order. The 'new' constituent order was VO, where 'new' is in scare quotes because it was already common in Old English as well (especially in main clauses with subjects in the initial position; remember that the reason why [17.1] is an exception is that the object is a pronoun; [17.2] displays OV order because, instead of the subject, we find the negator in the initial position).

In some historical descriptions OE constituent order is characterized as SOV. This is a considerable oversimplification in two respects. First, the position of subjects depended heavily on whether or not the sentence started with an adverb (such as *þa* 'then', *forþon* 'therefore', or *nævere* 'never'). In clauses with such an initial adverb, we tend to find the subject later in the sentence (as in [17.7a–b]), unless it is a pronoun, in which case it usually is found before the verb and the object (see [17.7c]):

[17.7]   a   Forþon [afligde ᵥₑᵣᵦ] [Gregorius ₛᵤᵦⱼₑ꜀ₜ] [þone guman ₒᵦⱼₑ꜀ₜ].
         b   Forþon [afligde ᵥₑᵣᵦ] [þone guman ₒᵦⱼₑ꜀ₜ] [Gregorius ₛᵤᵦⱼₑ꜀ₜ].
             'Therefore Gregorius made the man flee.'
         c   Forþon [he ₛᵤᵦⱼₑ꜀ₜ] [afligde ᵥₑᵣᵦ] [þone guman ₒᵦⱼₑ꜀ₜ].
             'Therefore he made the man flee.'

There is a remnant in Present-day English (PDE) of this effect of sentence-initial adverbials: if they have what we may describe as some kind of negative meaning (*never, no sooner*, etc.) the (finite) verb is also found in the second position, while the subject comes later:

[17.8]   a   Never had Gregory seen so much rain.
         b   No sooner did he see the rain than he decided to leave London.

Note that in PDE, contrary to OE, it no longer matters whether the subject is a full NP (e.g., *Gregory*) or a pronoun (e.g., *he*).

The second reason why it is misguided to characterize the normal constituent order of OE as SOV is that the degree of variation is so high that it may not make sense to talk about OE in terms of having one single basic constituent order. In this connection, we must make it clear whether we are referring to main clauses, subordinate clauses or coordinate clauses (see Chapter 8). In addition, when discussing the position of the verb in OE (and to a lesser extent ME), it is important to distinguish between finite and non-finite verb forms (see, for instance, the discussion of example [17.2], above). We will not go into the differences in any great detail here, but thorough discussions of the OE facts may be found in Mitchell (1985) and Traugott (1992); for the ME situation, see especially Fischer (1992). Denison (1993) conveniently summarizes much of the literature for both periods.

Having discussed some basic facts of constituent order from Old through Present-day English, we now move on to asking the question as to why these changes should have happened. Specifically, we will discuss the gradual shift, from OE (or actually the Germanic ancestral languages of OE) to PDE, of a relatively free constituent order to a much more rigid (SVO) one. First, we will show that the increasing rigidity in word order was caused to a large extent by a change in inflectional morphology. Then we will push the question back even further, and reveal how, in its turn, this morphological change had come about.

We have already seen some examples of constituent order variation in OE. Sentences [17.7a–b] showed that in OE it was possible for the subject to precede or follow the object. In PDE the latter order (*Forþon [afligde ᵥₑᵣᵦ] [þone guman ₒᵦⱼₑ꜀ₜ] [Gregorius ₛᵤᵦⱼₑ꜀ₜ]* 'Therefore Gregorius made the man flee') is clearly unacceptable (with the exception of special cases such as *Peas I like*, as

ADVANCES BOX 17.1

The structure of OE and ME and Chomsky's view of language

We saw in the main text that it may not be possible to characterize OE as having a single basic constituent order. A lot of research on OE and ME in the so-called Generative tradition (named after Chomsky's theory of language, known as Generative Grammar) does try to argue that there is a basic order. Fischer and colleagues (2000) offer an excellent overview of this work. It is important to note that Fischer et al. explicitly avoid the basic mistake of typifying OE as SOV (see 2000: 49 and *passim*). Instead, they attempt to weigh up the evidence in favour of basic OV or VO order.

This is not the place to discuss all the pros and cons of these two suggestions in detail. What is important to note here is that Generative historical linguistics makes the assumption that speakers, as they acquire their language, have a kind of switch (a **parameter**, in Chomsky's terms) in their minds which they set to either OV or VO, the setting depending on the language they hear around them. To Generative scholars who assume that the basic order in OE is OV, examples with VO order like [17.3] would clearly be a problem. They approach this kind of problem by suggesting that in producing a sentence like [17.3] speakers would start with OV order, but then (for some reason) shift the position of one of the constituents such that the object ends up in the 'exceptional' position. Similarly, if the basic constituent order is supposed to be VO, then examples like [17.1–17.2] are said to be the result of the speaker moving the verb to a position following the object.

We will not be adopting the Chomskian idea of a necessarily fixed constituent order – one of the reasons being that the evidence for the idea that constituents are moved around in sentence production is not overwhelming. In other words, speakers may have a variety of orders available straight 'off the shelf', so to speak. Also, even if we allowed for the movement of constituents, the presence of a basic order in a language would seem to make sense only if that basic order is at least (considerably) more frequent than other orders. For PDE this can be shown quite easily: almost every sentence is SVO. The rare exceptions include cases such as *Peas I like*, where the object occurs sentence-initially, usually to emphasize it for some reason or other. For OE it is harder but not impossible to establish a basic order that reflects speakers' statistical preferences (in this case, the so called verb-second order, see the discussion above). For many other languages in the world, however, it is. In those languages, different word orders are constantly used to suit speakers' communicative purposes of drawing more or less attention to certain parts of the sentence, much like in the English example [*Peas* object] [*I* subject] [*like* verb] (following, for instance, a sentence like *I hate sprouts*).

Chomsky and his followers have established their theory of grammar by working mainly on (Present-day) English. One suspects that there is a link between the idea that languages have a single basic order, and the fact that almost all data these scholars have looked at is from a language where word order indeed happens to be relatively fixed.

discussed in Advances Box 17.1, above): we need to mention *Gregory* before we can mention *the man*. We can admittedly switch the order around, but we then get a very different interpretation:

[17.8] a Gregory made the man flee.
        b The man made Gregory flee.

The question arises as to how OE speakers could hear sentence [17.7b] and still decide that Gregory made the man flee rather than vice versa. The answer lies in the endings of the nouns in question (as well as the determiners and adjectives they may occur with). Thus, if an OE speaker heard the form *þone guman*, s/he knew that this was the direct object of the clause, that is, roughly speaking, the person undergoing the action carried out by the subject rather than the person carrying out the action themselves. In order to get the reverse interpretation, as in [17.8b], the form used would be *se guma*. To show what would happen if an adjective entered the picture as well, the subject form of 'the good man' would be *se goda guma*, and the direct object form, *þone godan guman*.

The subject form is often called the **nominative** case; the (direct) object form, **accusative**. There were two additional case forms: the **dative** (used for indirect objects) and the **genitive** (used to signal a possessor). In OE the dative and genitive singular of *guma* were the same as the accusative, that is, *guman*. In PDE the genitive is still available (see, for example, *the man's name*), but common nouns do not distinguish between nominative, accusative and dative. This information is captured in Illustration Box 17. 1 (Tables 17.1–2b), below, which also includes pronouns. (Note: Sg = singular; Pl = plural; 1 = first person; 2 = second person; 3 = third person; M = masculine; F = feminine; N = neuter).

Illustration Box 17.1 shows that, interestingly, in personal pronouns the case system is still more intact than in common nouns: in addition to a distinction between nominative and genitive (e.g., *he* vs. *his*) there is also a case form for objects (*him*). Since we now use the same pronoun forms to refer to direct and indirect objects, grammarians tend to label the form *him* the **object** or **objective case** (i.e., instead of accusative or dative). Parallel to this the term **subject(ive) case** is now often preferred to nominative. (By contrast, in languages such as German, where the case system has not collapsed to nearly the same extent as in English, it does still make sense to refer to nominative, accusative, dative and genitive, namely *er* 'he', *ihn* 'him (direct object)', *ihm* 'him (indirect object)', *sein* 'his'.)

Not all nouns declined in the same way (we have not discussed the proper noun *Gregorius*); there were a number of different classes, the exact number depending a bit on the way one counts. Moreover, much like German, there were three genders: **masculine**, **feminine** and **neuter**, each with its own sets of forms. We will not go into the details of the different **declensions** and genders here (but see, for example, Hogg, 1992, 2002) – the main point is simply that OE signalled grammatical functions such as subject, direct object, etc. largely by using distinct morphological endings. Over the course of the history of the language these endings gradually disappeared, leading to a situation (in the

ILLUSTRATION BOX 17.1

Simplification of noun and pronoun inflections from OE to PDE

Table 17.1 The word guma *'man' in Old English vs.* man *in Present-day English*

	Old English	Present-day English
nominative Sg	*guma*	*man*
accusative Sg	*guman*	*man*
dative Sg	*guman*	*man*
genitive Sg	*guman*	*man's*
nominative Pl	*guman*	*men*
accusative Pl	*guman*	*men*
dative Pl	*gumum*	*men*
genitive Pl	*gumena*	*men's*

Table 17.2a The OE pronoun system

	Nominative	Accusative	Dative	Genitive
1Sg	*ic*	*me*	*me*	*min*
2Sg	*þu*	*þe*	*þe*	*þin*
3SgM	*he*	*hine*	*him*	*his*
3SgF	*heo*	*hi(e)*	*hi(e)re*	*hi(e)re*
3SgN	*hit*	*hit*	*him*	*his*
1Dual[2]	*wit*	*unc*	*unc*	*uncer*
2Dual	*git*	*inc*	*inc*	*incer*
1Pl	*we*	*us*	*us*	*ure*
2Pl	*ge*	*eow*	*eow*	*eower*
3Pl	*hi(e)*	*hi(e)*	*him*	*hira*

Table 17.2b The PDE pronoun system

	subject	object	possessive
1Sg	*I*	*me*	*my/mine*
2Sg	*you*	*you*	*your(s)*
3SgMasc	*he*	*him*	*his*
3SgFem	*she*	*her*	*her*
3SgNeut	*it*	*it*	*its*
1Pl	*we*	*us*	*our(s)*
2Pl	*you*	*you*	*your(s)*
3Pl	*they*	*them*	*their(s)*

late Middle English period) when there was so little left that speakers had to rely primarily on a different strategy to do the job: designated positions in the clause (see again the contrast between [17.8a] and [17.8b]).

An additional strategy is the use of prepositions – consider, for example, the use of the preposition *to* to signal indirect object status of *him* in sentence [17.9], below:

[17.9]   Gregory gave the book to him.

The OE dative form *him* for the masculine third person singular personal pronoun was different from the accusative form (used for direct objects) *hine* (familiar from example [17.1], above) so prepositions were not used as much to perform this function.

When studying the history of a language such as English it is easy to fall into the trap of treating the earliest attested stage – in this case OE – as the starting point of developments one is interested in. But OE did not emerge out of the blue, and although we have no direct documentary evidence of its ancestral language, by using evidence from related Germanic languages as well as our knowledge of how languages tend to change over time, we can piece together a fairly good picture of what the **proto-language**[3] would have looked like.

The oldest Germanic language for which we have documentary evidence is Gothic. Gothic is in many respects very similar to OE but it retains even more inflectional morphology. The word for 'man', also *guma*, for instance, had separate forms for the accusative and the dative singular (*guman* and *gumin*, respectively). We may infer that Proto-Germanic, the common ancestor of OE and Gothic (as well as of some other languages such as Old Norse, the language of the Vikings who started to invade the British Isles from the eighth century) had a system at least as rich as Gothic, and that in OE we already see the first indications of morphological simplification. Connected with this, we may also assume that constituent order in Proto-Germanic was even freer than it was in OE. In other words, rather than being the starting point of the development towards simplified inflectional morphology and more rigid constituent order, OE should actually be seen as a system that was very much in transition.

Having shown that the development in constituent order was linked with morphological simplification, we now turn to the question as to why the various distinctions that were made in Proto-Germanic, and to a large extent still persist in OE, came to be lost.

In older handbooks English historical linguists would sometimes argue that the case forms were lost because they were, in a way, redundant. Strang, for instance, suggests for one class of noun forms that in early ME it 'incorporates a good deal [i.e.,of different case inflections] that serves no purpose ... and ... is ripe for further development' (1970: 260). The view underlying Strang's claim is thus that the language made distinctions – such as between nominative and accusative – that speakers could actually perfectly well do without (see also 1970: 281); in this case because they could use different positions in the clause to distinguish between subject and object.

This fits in with the notion that the English language has become more and more efficient, a view which goes back to at least the nineteenth century when, under the influence of Darwin's ideas of evolution, some scholars believed that languages evolved into increasingly efficient tools for communication. Nowadays, many historical linguists disagree with this general view, and with Strang's (and others') implicit or explicit application of this view to English. By positioning a subject early in the clause and an object later, and by using different case markings for the two, it is certainly true that English speakers signalled the subject–object distinction in two simultaneous ways. But it does not simply follow that one of them is therefore redundant, and inevitably lost over time. There are many languages in which certain functions are marked twice, three or even more times. PDE itself provides many examples. The sentence in [17.10] below illustrates this point in two different ways:

[17.10]   Three boats sank yesterday.

First, consider the noun *boats*, which is marked by *–s* for plural number. Strictly speaking this is redundant, as the idea that there was more than one is already indicated by the quantifier *Three*.

Second, while the verb *sank* is marked for past tense (by a vowel change from *sink*), the fact that the event took place in the past is also signalled by *yesterday*. Now would we want to say that plural marking on nouns and past tense marking on verbs is redundant, and that the system 'is ripe for further development'? The resultant, 'more efficient', system would be exemplified by the sentence in [17.11], below:

[17.11]   Three boat sink yesterday.

If this might seem an implausible way for speakers to communicate with each other, bear in mind that this is exactly how one expresses oneself in a language such as Mandarin Chinese. Clearly there are many speakers for whom it works absolutely fine! Nonetheless, our current understanding of grammatical change suggests that languages need not go on simplifying their morphology until there is nothing left. Quite the contrary, we know of many cases of languages developing more elaborate morphology rather than simplifying it. For examples we do not need to look any further than English itself.

In standard English there is no longer a distinction between singular and plural *you* (see Table 17.2b above, and compare with 17.2a). In many dialects, however, this distinction has been reintroduced. One especially frequent form of a 2Pl form is *yous* (sometimes spelt *youse*), which we find in, for example, Liverpool, Glasgow and Irish English.

It is clear, then, that languages do not simply lose morphology over time: they also develop it. (Indeed it would be a logical impossibility to assume that morphology can only be lost: after all, where, then, in the evolution of human language, would it have come from in the first place?)

The approach taken here departs significantly from the idea of Strang (and others), that once English had developed alternative strategies to perform the role that in OE and earlier had been fulfilled by inflectional morphology, the remnants of those inflections were redundant and therefore lost. Instead, it seems that we must interpret the historical facts such that as the inflections were getting lost, a more fixed word order (and the use of certain prepositions to signal grammatical function) was gradually developed to compensate for this (i.e., what historical linguists sometimes call a **therapeutic** change).

So if inflectional morphology was not lost because other mechanisms of signalling grammatical functions had become available, then why did it happen? The answer is a complex one, and is still being debated by English historical linguists. Despite certain disagreements that still exist, there is some kind of a consensus about at least two factors: the effect of the Viking invasions from around the eighth century, and a stress shift that took place considerably earlier, namely in Proto-Germanic (so early because we can observe the results of this stress shift in a number of related Germanic languages, and it is more likely that the change happened only once, in the ancestral language, than several times, more or less independently, in OE, Gothic, Old Norse, etc.).

Regarding the effect of Viking invasions, we must remember that Old Norse was very similar to OE. Many words were virtually identical, and so was the grammar. It would thus have been possible for speakers of the two languages to communicate rather well. And indeed we know that this happened on quite a large scale: archaeological evidence of intermarriage, for instance, suggests that after an initial period of violent raids (in the eighth century), the Viking settlers came to coexist with the Anglo-Saxons relatively peacefully (although there was again a tumultuous period in the tenth century).

Interestingly, we also have some linguistic evidence for this. The OE word for *they* was *hi* or *hie*; the PDE form is a borrowing from Old Norse – in ME texts we see it slowly spreading from northern and Midland areas (where the Viking settlers had occupied the area often referred to as the Danelaw) to the south. Borrowing in language contact situations is in itself far from uncommon, but the borrowing of a **grammatical** term such as a personal pronoun is not that frequent – if it happens it suggests that the two speech communities are on rather good terms with each other (for borrowing in general, see Chapter 15).

When we said above that the grammar of OE and Old Norse were similar, we should add that there were of course differences in some details. Importantly for our discussion, the inflectional endings were often a bit different (see, for example, Chapter 12, Advances Box 12.1). Now in a situation where speakers of OE and Old Norse speakers talked to each other, historical linguists think that these different endings would perhaps be pronounced a bit less clearly, in order for communication to be smoother.

Let us now turn to the second, earlier, factor that contributed to the disappearance of the many distinct morphological endings. Simply put, at some stage in the history of Proto-Germanic the endings were often (though not always) stressed. A change then took place which resulted in a stress pattern which was fixed in such a way that the endings were no longer stressed.[4] Now if syllables are not stressed, it is much harder for speakers to distinguish between different sounds that may make up those syllables. Consider the word *chocolate*, for instance. The first syllable is stressed, and its vowel is easily recognizable as [o]. But the vowels in the remaining, unstressed, part of the word are either not pronounced at all (the second <o> and final <e>) or in the case of <a> as the neutral vowel sound schwa, that is, [ə] or perhaps [ɪ]. (One of my students once suggested that the spelling should be reformed to *choklit*.) Originally, however, the second <o> would have been pronounced [o] as well, the <a> as [a], and <e> as [ə]. (See also Chapter 13, Section 13.3.2, on spelling) Because of the lack of stress, speakers found these three sounds more and more difficult to perceive as such, and increasingly reduced them phonetically or omitted them altogether. The stress shift in Proto-Germanic had similar effects: the endings gradually came to be pronounced less and less distinctly.

This clearly set up a situation in which, centuries later, when the Vikings arrived, speakers of OE and Old Norse would have found it easy to reduce the endings even more – until they disappeared completely (with the exception, in common nouns, of the genitive and plural endings, which we still have in PDE). (Further information on the rise of schwa and stress patterns can be found in Chapter 14).

17.2.2   Changes in verbal morphology

As we have seen in Section 17.2.1, the decline of inflections in nouns and pronouns is interesting from the point of view of explaining changes in constituents. The system of verbal inflections was also much richer in OE than it is in PDE, but because it is less related to major syntactic changes we will only discuss the developments very briefly here. More detailed descriptions are referred to in the list of recommended readings at the end of this chapter.

Just like in PDE, verbs in OE and ME may be divided up roughly into three classes. We traditionally call these the **weak**, **strong** and **irregular** classes. Weak verbs are nowadays most common: they are the ones that take *–ed* endings in the simple past and past participle forms (e.g., *love, loved, loved*). Strong verbs signal past tense by a change in their stressed vowel (e.g., *bind, bound, bound*). Irregular verbs, finally, display all sorts of anomalies, not necessarily just in the way they form their past tense and past participle, but sometimes also elsewhere, for example, in the simple present. The most typical irregular verb in English (and in other languages) is *be*: consider that the past forms *was/were* and the past participle *been* do not look in the least related to, for example, present tense *is* – which, in its turn, is very different from *am* and *are*.

These three classes are often divided by scholars into certain subclasses, but we will not concern ourselves with these details. The main point, instead, is to show that this is another area of English grammar that has undergone simplification.

It is traditional in language textbooks to present the inflections of the verb *love* and here we see no reason to be different. Illustration Box 17.2, below, displays the inflections of the verb in OE, ME and PDE. Bear in mind that there was considerable dialectal variation in OE and ME; to give one or two variants for each verb form is therefore actually a bit of a simplification. The term **indicative** is used to describe the verb forms that are used in ordinary declarative and interrogative sentences. The **imperative** is used for giving people orders, commands, etc. The **subjunctive**, finally, is used to express various situations that we may describe as somehow 'unreal', for example, because they are a wish or desire. PDE does not have many distinct subjunctive forms left any more, but if (using a somewhat formal register) you tell someone who is always late for their appointments that it is desirable that next time they *be* (instead of *are*) on time, you are using a form that is essentially unchanged from the OE subjunctive.

It is clear from Table 17.3 that the simplification goes much beyond the disappearance of the distinct subjunctive forms. Some changes are related, once again, to unstressed endings becoming harder to distinguish and eventually disappearing. But another important change (not obvious from the table) is the enormous growth of the class of weak verbs, at the expense of the strong ones. This growth has been so considerable that we nowadays often refer to the former as **regular** verbs.

A full explanation would take us too far afield, but one important factor was the huge influx of French verbs following the Norman Conquest, for example, *crye(n)* 'cry', *obeie(n)* 'obey', and *servi(n)* 'serve'. These verbs fit in most easily in the weak class, as this meant that to make a past tense speakers could leave the verb intact, and just add the relevant past ending, giving for example, *cryed, obeyed, served* (see for example, Brunner 1963: 81). As the

---

ILLUSTRATION BOX 17.2

Simplification of verbal morphology from OE to PDE

Table 17.3   The verb love *in OE, ME and PDE*

	OE		ME		PDE	
	Present	*Past*	*Present*	*Past*	*Present*	*Past*
Indicative						
1Sg	lufie	lufode	loue	louede	love	loved
2Sg	lufast	lufodest	louest	louedest	love	loved
3Sg	lufað	lufode	loueth	louede	loves	loved
1,2,3Pl	lufiað	lufodon	loue(n)	louede(n)	love	loved
Imperative						
Sg	lufa	—	loue	—	love	
Pl	lufiað	—	loueth	—	love	
Subjunctive						
Sg	lufie	lufode	loue	louede	love	loved
Pl	lufien	lufoden	loue(n)	louede(n)	love	loved
Participle	lufiende	gelufod	louying(e)	(y)loued(e)	loving	loved

class of weak verbs was growing, it even started 'attracting' verbs that originally did not belong there (see, for example, Strang, 1970: 276). One example is *help*: while its past tense is nowadays *helped*, it used to be – up until some point in the ME period – *holp*.

17.3 Recent trends in the study of grammatical change in English: grammaticalization

17.3.1 From a changing language to changing constructions

Section 17.2.1 discussed a set of interconnected changes that affected large parts of the grammar of English: inflectional morphology and constituent order. In the light of these developments, the English language has often been characterized as having moved from a **synthetic** type to an **analytic** type. It is true that grammatical function in a clause used to be signalled to a large extent synthetically, that is, by using inflectional morphology, whereas it is now signalled by means of word order and prepositions (i.e., independent grammatical markers) which are associated with more analytic languages. In the development of Latin into Spanish, French, Italian, etc., the Romance languages are often said to have undergone a parallel development.

There are, however, serious problems with the suggestion that languages as a whole undergo such typological shifts, or indeed with the notion that languages can straightforwardly be classified as belonging to either the synthetic or the analytic type. The latter problem we may illustrate with an example from Romance. Consider the contrast in Spanish – supposedly now an analytic language – between *voy a Londres* 'I'm going to London' and *vas a Londres* 'you're going to London'. The verb forms show that a lot of grammatical information, in this case person, number and tense, is still signalled synthetically, that is, by different inflections. The moral is that it is dangerous to characterize a language as a whole as belonging to either the analytic or the synthetic type.

In relation to the idea that English has undergone a typological shift from analytic to synthetic, Kytö and Romaine (1997) have shown that in the area of comparison (e.g., *big-bigger-biggest, pretty-prettier-prettiest, beautiful-more beautiful-most beautiful*) the synthetic method (A-*er*, A-*est*) lost ground for a while to the analytic (sometimes also known as **periphrastic**) strategy (*more* A, *most* A) – as we would expect if the synthetic>analytic suggestion is correct – but then started gaining territory again.

Contrary to the traditional view, many linguists working on English, Romance and other languages and language families now suggest that it does not make sense to characterize entire languages as falling into the synthetic or analytic categories. Instead, we must examine **individual constructions** (or families of related constructions; for example, the constructions used for comparison, future tense constructions, causative constructions), and we should not expect that over time they will all necessarily develop towards the analytic type (see, for example, Schwegler, 1994; Vincent, 1997).

The evidence actually suggests that in terms of analysis and synthesis, grammatical change is cyclic. The Romance languages, for which we have

ADVANCES BOX 17.2

More problems for the synthetic-to-analytic claim: developments in causative constructions after Middle English

In the main text we problematized the idea that the English language is becoming more analytic by referring to research on comparison, which suggests that the synthetic method (A-*er*, A-*est*), rather than being pushed out by the newer analytic/periphrastic strategy (*more* A, *most* A), is actually 'fighting back'. Thus in this area English is not obviously becoming more analytic. We can find another example of this in constructions such as *cause, force, get, have* or *make someone/something (to) do something*, e.g., *By giving them too much food, I once **caused my parents' goldfish to die*** (a true event, sadly!). These are known as **periphrastic causatives**. They are called causative because they describe acts of someone or something causing something to happen, and they are periphrastic (or analytic) because the cause and effect are described by separate words (here: *cause* and *die*) instead of by a single one. Compare *I killed my parents' goldfish*, where cause and effect are both described by the single verb *kill*. In relation to the synthetic-to-analytic claim, things are a little complicated, in that the ME developments seem to support the claim, but if we assume that an increasingly analytic language should develop more periphrastic constructions rather than lose them, then later changes contradict it.

Compared to PDE, OE had rather few periphrastic causatives. Two were especially frequent. The first of these is *don* 'do'; see, e.g., *Aswindan þu didest … sæwle his* (*Vesp. Psalter*, xxxviii. 12 [*OED*, do, *v.*, s.v. 22.a]) 'You made [lit. did] his soul perish'. In PDE *do* can of course no longer be used in this manner. The second common periphrastic causative involved the now obsolete verb *gar*, e.g., *Oft þu geris mi wondis blede* (*Cursor M.* 17160 (Gött.) [*OED*, gar, *v.*, s.v. 2.b]), 'Often you make my wounds bleed'. *Gar* is mainly found in northern texts, which is unsurprising given that it was borrowed from Old Norse. In this language one of its meanings was 'make (something)'. Its development into a causative verb is thus parallel to *make*, which developed its causative use later (sometime in the twelfth century – for details, see Hollmann, 2003: 111).

In ME we see many of these constructions developing. Some scholars point to French as a possible influence. French had a causative construction consisting of *faire* 'do, make' with an infinitive, and the idea is that some time after the Norman Conquest in 1066 this construction would be translated into English and used as a model for other constructions, e.g., periphrastic causative *have* (Baron, 1977: 86), the first example of which dates from c.1440: *And when Alexander saw that þay walde one na wyse speke wit hym, he hadd a certane of his knyghtes nakne þam & swyme ouer þe water to þe castell* (*Prose life of Alexander* [also, with less context, *MED*, s.v. haven, v. 10.(a)]), 'And when A. saw that they would in no way speak to him, he had one of his knights strip naked and swim over the water to the castle'. However, one should be wary of invoking language contact as a very significant factor too readily, since English itself already had a number of such constructions (including, as we have seen, *do* and *gar*), which may have served as a model.

At any rate, the rapid increase in the number of periphrastic causatives in ME (for details, see Bock, 1931: 156, Visser, 1973: 2255ff; and Hollmann, 2003: 109ff) might support the claim that the English language was in transition from a synthetic to an analytic type. But the trouble is that quite a few of them disappeared again later on. The following example from the thirteenth century, for instance, features *give* used causatively, but in the translation we must now resort to a verb such as *make*: *Seinte Marie … ʒif me deien mid him & arisen* (*c.*1225 *Ancr. R.* (EETS 1952) 17, 4 [Visser, 1973: 2260]) 'Saint Mary … make me dye with him and arise'. Note also that the OE periphrastic causatives *do* and *gar* have both died out. This decrease in the number of periphrastic causatives seems to be at odds with the idea that English as a whole is moving in a more analytic direction.

a long recorded history, show what we mean by this. In Classical Latin the future 'we will sing' was expressed synthetically as *cantabimus*. This later became *cantare habemus*, an analytic expression which originally meant something like 'we have to sing'; 'have' verbs often develop into markers of future tense in the languages of the world. In Spanish the normal future tense is *cantaremos* – a contracted and now synthetic form of *cantare habemus*, that is, a case of attrition, see Section 17.1 above. (To understand this development just try saying *cantare habemos* very fast ten times in a row; you will very likely end up saying something like *cantaremos*). This means that in a sense we are back where we started. But the development does not end there: nowadays more and more speakers use the periphrastic construction *vamos a cantar*, lit. 'we go to sing' ('go' verbs are another common source of future tense markers across languages, cf. the English *BE going to* + Infinitive future). We cannot be completely sure what will happen in the future, but it would not be surprising if the elements of the current analytic construction somehow fuse again, at which point Romance will have gone full circle towards a synthetic future once more.

Grammaticalization theory, of which we have discussed some important aspects before in this chapter, fits in with this growing conviction that the object of study in grammatical change is often individual (groups of) constructions, rather than entire languages. But grammaticalization theory has also partly grown out of a different set of concerns, which we turn to in Section 17.3.2.

17.3.2 Who changes the grammar? Grammaticalization vs. the child-based theory

In this section we assess the merits of grammaticalization theory in relation to the very important question of who is responsible for grammatical change. Many non-linguists, including journalists, seek the source of change in grammar in modern technology and the media. Consider, for instance, the following statement, which I found while surfing the Internet looking for folk beliefs concerning language change: '[People] use text messaging in everyday life in a very conversational, informal manner. Traditional rules of grammar … go straight out of the window when you're typing a quick note using a phone keypad' (http://www.tomhume.org/archives/000017.

html [accessed 29 February 2008]). However, most journalists and people who post messages on the Internet are not trained linguists, and it is to their (rather different) views that we must turn.[5]

Until recently, the dominant idea in historical linguistics was that grammatical change is possible when children acquire a language and, in the acquisition process, come up with a different set of rules from their parents' generation. The most prominent historical linguist associated with this idea is David Lightfoot, who published a very influential reconstruction of the rise in English of modal verbs (*will, may, can, must,* etc. (see Lightfoot, 1979)). He later revised aspects of his theory (see, for example, 1991, 1997, 1999), but the fundamental claim that child language learners are responsible for grammatical change still stands.

Lightfoot's claim is intimately tied up with Chomsky's view of language acquisition, which suggests that acquisition is complete by the end of the so-called critical period (which has not been defined precisely but is supposed to be around the age of 13 or 14). If this is indeed one's view of the acquisition process, it follows that grammatical change must take place in young language learners, since in more mature speakers grammatical knowledge is completely fixed.

Very briefly, Lightfoot's reconstruction of the rise of English modal verbs runs as follows. OE had a set of verbs which would later develop into modals, including *wile* 'wish', *mæg* 'have power', *cann* 'can, know', and *mot* 'can, must'. These verbs – labelled the 'pre-modals' by Lightfoot – were almost identical to ordinary lexical verbs. For example, while PDE modals do not have non-finite forms (such as infinitives), the pre-modals did – all the way into and just beyond the ME period:

[17.12]   who this book shall <u>wylle</u> lerne (Caxton)
          'who this book shall will learn'

They could also take nominal direct objects as in example [17.5b], above, repeated below as [17.13]:

[17.14]   Wenne þu <u>wult</u> more suluer sæche hit at me suluen. (*Laȝamon,*
          1786)
          'When you want more silver, say it to me.'

There was one respect in which the pre-modals were already a little bit different from ordinary lexical verbs: their inability to take an ending in the third-person singular present tense, and the unavailability of regular past tenses. Both of these peculiarities can be explained if we consider that the present-tense verbs forms had originally been *past* tenses. (An old-fashioned term for past tense is **preterite**, which is why these verbs are sometimes called **preterite-present** verbs.) In the past tense the third-person singular did not have a distinct ending from the first person. Also, because the forms were already etymologically past tenses, different ways of forming the past had to be devised once they started to be used as present tense verb forms. We thus see that while the pre-modals were for the most part pretty normal and as such part of the category of verbs, they were already a little bit out of line with the rest of the verbs.

Lightfoot suggests that in the early or mid-sixteenth century, child language learners drastically restructured their grammar in such a way that the pre-modals became a truly separate category, the category of modals. He argues that the data show that this happened fairly instantaneously: non-finite forms, the ability to take noun phrase direct objects and other properties associated with normal lexical verbs were lost very rapidly and simultaneously – so much so that Lightfoot uses the term **catastrophic change** in this context.

Aspects of Lightfoot's account of the rise of English modal verbs, and his theory of grammatical change, have been criticized strongly by many scholars (see, for example, Fischer and van der Leek, 1981; Plank, 1984; Warner, 1983; Denison, 1993 summarizes the discussion).

One of the most serious criticisms is that a close examination of the data shows that far from being catastrophic, the changes actually took place over a long period of time, were not simultaneous, and happened at different points in time for the different verbs involved. Denison (1993) suggests that the future tense meaning of *will* may have already been attested as early as OE, when according to Lightfoot the verb only meant 'wish':

[17.14] Gif me seo godcunde geofu in ðære stowe forgifen beon wile…, ic ðær luctlice wunige
'If the divine gift is granted to me in that place…, I will happily remain there'

(Denison 1993: 304)

This and other facts suggest that the development of English modals may have taken many centuries. From the point of view of our theory of grammatical change, it is important to note that grammaticalization theory suggests that change is normally slow and gradual. The data, therefore, are much more in line with this theory than with Lightfoot's suggestion of a drastic restructuring of the grammatical rules in one generation of child language learners.[6]

Another bit of evidence in favour of grammaticalization theory is the emergence of reduced and fused forms such as those in [17.15]–[17.16], below. Remember that attrition is an important aspect of grammaticalization. In Lightfoot's theory, by contrast, this is not really accounted for.

[17.15] Next time weele haue some prettie Gentle-women with vs to walke. (1591, LYLY Endym., I. iii)
[17.16] Sister you'l [Qo. 2 youle; Folio you'le] goe with vs? (1608 SHAKES. Lear, V. i. 34 (Qo. 1))

Grammaticalization theorists often reject Lightfoot's idea that grammatical change happens in child language acquisition. Croft (2000) offers some outspoken criticism in this relation. He observes that the changes (or errors) that children typically make are of a very different kind from what we tend to see in grammatical change in English and other languages. Furthermore, referring to important work in sociohistorical linguistics on the role of prestige, he points out that children do not normally enjoy the kind of prestige in the speech community that would stimulate other members to copy them. The picture that emerges in the grammaticalization theory alternative to Lightfoot's child-based theory is one in which adults (and/or adolescents) make the innovations.

Some linguists have suggested that they make these innovations (e.g., using *going to* + Inf. for the future tense where previously speakers used *will*) in order to stand out from the crowd, so to speak, and be noticed by others. Croft (to appear), however, has argued that the innovations are simply slightly different ways of describing some situation. These different verbalizations are produced naturally by all of us, all the time – not just if we want to be noticed. They may subsequently spread to others if the speaker has enough prestige, be it overt or covert; see also Chapter 19 on language and social class, and Chapter 12). The likelihood, or indeed very possibility, of this scenario obviously depends on a rejection of Chomsky's idea that our grammatical knowledge is essentially fixed after early puberty. In the area of language acquisition there is indeed increasing evidence that the critical period does not end abruptly: while there are certain undeniable changes in the brain's plasticity and so on after childhood, the evolutionary psychologist Michael Tomasello (e.g., 2003) and others have suggested that learning continues our entire lives (see further also Chapter 37).

17.4   Concluding remarks

In the course of this chapter we have discovered that the grammar of the English language has undergone many changes over time.

As a descendent from Proto-Germanic, it started out as a language that relied heavily on inflectional morphology to signal grammatical distinctions. As the result of a stress shift, however, the seeds had already been sown, in a manner of speaking, for the collapse of this system. The arrival of the Vikings, and the language contact situation that OE speakers found themselves in as a result, contributed greatly to this collapse. (It is important to realize that the stress shift alone would not necessarily have led to this: compare present-day German, where the system of inflectional morphology is still intact to a relatively high degree.)

The morphological changes impacted on constituent order, and we have seen how with the disappearance of the OV pattern, the order gradually became more rigid. The increased reliance on prepositions has also helped make up for the almost complete loss of inflections. Verbal inflections have also been simplified over the course of time, not only in terms of the number of distinct endings, but also in the sense that the vast majority of verbs now belong to one class, that of regular verbs (formerly known as weak verbs). By way of explanation we pointed to especially the influx of French verbs. These were accommodated into the weak class, which as a result became so large that even originally strong verbs started gravitating towards it.

Section 17.3 brought us up to speed with more recent developments in the study of English historical syntax (and of grammatical change in general). We problematized the custom of classifying English (or indeed any language) as belonging to the synthetic or analytic type, and the idea that English has undergone a clear shift from synthetic to analytic. In addition we pinpointed some of the flaws in the traditional view that grammatical change is effected by child language learners. The solutions to both problems, we argued, can be found in grammaticalization theory.

Grammaticalization theory directs the historical linguist's attention to individual (sets of) constructions, that is, away from languages as a whole. We showed that by combining grammaticalization theory with a view of language acquisition in which learning does not necessarily end at puberty, we can offer a more convincing reconstruction of the rise of English modal verbs than was afforded by Lightfoot's more traditional child-based approach.

While we thus stressed the merits of grammaticalization theory in relation to the creation (innovation) of new grammatical constructions such as modal verbs, we must add that it has nothing to say about their spread (propagation) from one speaker to other members of the speech community. In this connection we must turn to lessons learnt in sociohistorical linguistics, especially concerning the notion of prestige (for the sharp distinction between innovation and propagation see also Section 16.3 in Chapter 16, on semantic change).

Recommended readings

The most comprehensive and authoritative treatment of many aspects of grammatical change in the history of English is to be found in the six-volume *Cambridge History of the English Language* (listed as Hogg (1992–2001) in the References section, below). A useful, more compact version of this work is Hogg and Denison (2006). For verbal constructions the best reference is Denison (1993), which combines a very impressive and accurate overview of previous scholarship with novel data and insights. On a more basic level, Hogg (2002), Horobin and Smith (2002) and Nevalainen (2006) provide excellent, concise overviews of Old, Middle and Early Modern English, respectively – including grammar. However, given the focus of these volumes on individual periods, the reader should expect description rather than explanation.

More general books on grammatical change are plentiful as well. One of the most stimulating treatments to have appeared recently is Croft (2000). For readers who have a particular interest in grammaticalization, the first port of call should be Hopper and Traugott (2003).

Notes

1   A **constituent** is a word or group of words that functions as a unit on some level of our analysis of a sentence. Other textbooks sometimes use the term **word order** instead of constituent order. We avoid this here because what matters is really the sequence of constituents such as subjects and objects – and constituents of course need not be restricted to one word; see, e.g., example [17.2], where the object *naht unaliefedes* is made up of two words. Yet another synonymous term we sometimes find is **element order**, but the term element is much less well established in the grammatical literature than the term constituent.

2   **Dual** was a number that we find in some, though not all, Old English texts. It is in between Sg and Pl in that it refers to two people, i.e., 'I and another' (*wit*) or 'you and another' (*git*) – the other person could be the addressee or not. If it seems strange to you that Old English had these

pronoun forms, consider that many languages of the world do. Some have even more forms, such as a **trial** (to refer to three persons) and/or a **paucal** (to refer to 'a few' persons).

3 By proto-language we mean the ancestral language, of which we have no direct written evidence.

4 For more details and the interesting hypothesis that the stress shift may have been due to language contact with the non-Indo-European language Old European, which had initial stress, see Vennemann (1994).

5 The reason why I comment on the difference between linguists' and non-linguists' ideas about the causes – and causers – of language change is not to deprecate the non-specialists. If there is any implicit criticism, it is rather directed in the opposite way: we, the historical linguistic community, are clearly not doing enough to inform the public about our findings.

6 For a more detailed reconstruction of the rise of the English modals from the perspective of grammaticalization theory, see Hopper and Traugott (2003: 55–8) and especially Fischer (2006), who also explicitly compares it with Lightfoot's story (159–209).

PART 3

English Speech:
Regional and Social Variation

EDITED BY PAUL KERSWILL

CHAPTER 18

Regional Variation in English Accents and Dialects[1]

Kevin Watson

18.1   What are regional varieties and how do they vary?

This chapter focuses on geographical or regional variation in English. A **regional variety** is a form of language which conveys information about a speaker's geographical origin via words, grammatical constructions or features of pronunciation which are present in some regions but absent in others. Take, as an example, the conversation represented in example [18.1], between an American and an Englishman.

[18.1]   *JOHN:*   Excuse me, do you know where [weə] the nearest bus stop [bʊs stɒp] is?

      ANDY: Yeah, cross the street and you'll see it right around [ɹaɪɾ əɹaʊnd] the corner [kɔɹnəɹ].

Even though John or Andy do not say anything specific about where they come from, it is possible to identify who is American and who is English. How? There are several clues. First, John does not pronounce word-final /r/ (in *where*), but Andy does (in *corner*). The lack of /r/ here is more common in England than America. Second, Andy pronounces the /t/ in *right around* as a tap, [ɾ], rather than as [t]. The tap as a realization of /t/ is more common in America than in England. Third, John pronounces *bus* as [bʊs], which is not a pronunciation that is typically found in American Englishes. So, Andy is the American, and John is English. However, we can be even more specific than that. John's pronunciation of *bus* says more about him than simply 'I am a speaker of English English'. It tells us he is from somewhere in the north of England, rather than the south.

The pronunciation features recorded in [18.1], then, not only tell us about the speakers' country of origin, but also provide more localized regional information. Of course, sometimes local cues are not recognized by listeners, because their recognition depends to an extent on a listener's familiarity with the variety of English in question. We only know that a pronunciation such as [bʊs] can cue 'a northern English speaker' if we know that such pronunciations are typically found in the north of England. It can be very difficult for listeners to distinguish between varieties of English with which they are unfamiliar: British people typically struggle to tell the difference between

American and Canadian Englishes, for example, or between Australian and New Zealand Englishes, even though the linguistic differences between these countries can be very noticeable to the people who live there. Of course, a variety of English need not belong to another country in order for listeners to be unfamiliar with it. Someone from the south of England might struggle to distinguish between the accents of Lancashire and Yorkshire, even if they were able to recognize that these varieties are 'from the north'.

Whether the regional features present in speakers' utterances are recognized or not, they are always there. Everybody comes from somewhere, and everybody has a variety of language. In this chapter, we will explore the connections between the two. Our focus will mostly be the English of England, but we also will explore some other Englishes. A number of questions will be addressed, namely: Why do regional varieties exist? How does pronunciation and grammar differ across varieties of Present-day English? Are regional dialects 'incorrect' or 'grammarless'? Are regional accents in England in danger of disappearing? In the remainder of this introductory section we will set the scene broadly by asking: What *is* a regional variety?

18.1.1   *What* varies?

What do we mean when we say language **varies**? What is it, exactly, that varies between regional varieties? Linguists often say that variation in language is pervasive at every linguistic level. This means that as well as variation in pronunciation (the levels of phonetics and phonology), variation can be found in grammatical structure (the levels of syntax and morphology), vocabulary and meaning (semantics), and discourse (pragmatics). Each level is of interest in the study of regional variation because each level can provide clues about where a speaker is from. Linguists studying variation typically group these levels into two categories: those relating to **dialect** and those relating to **accent**. Differences between varieties that are related to vocabulary or grammar, including discourse features, are classified as differences in dialect. We explore dialectal variation in Section 18.3. Differences related to pronunciation, such as those in [18.1] above, are classified as differences in accent. We explore accent variation in Section 18.4. Most of the time, the linguistic features that vary across varieties of English do not vary in an absolute way. A speaker might say *I ain't got none* one minute and *I haven't got none* or *I haven't got any* the next. Because linguistic features vary, within and across speakers, they are called **linguistic variables** (Labov, 1972; Watt, 2007). A linguistic variable is a set of linguistic features which 'mean the same thing', but which vary according to some regional or social parameter. Thus, the study of regional variation, called **dialectology** or, more recently, 'geolinguistics' (Britain, 2002), is the study of the geographical distribution of linguistic variables.

18.1.2   *Who* varies?

In Section 18.1 we saw that Americans and English people speak differently, and that English in the north of England differs from that in the south. Of course, variation in English, or most other languages, does not stop with very general regional distinctions. In England, there is more than one 'northern English' and 'southern English'. Liverpool English, Manchester English and Newcastle English, although all 'northern', are very different from each other. Furthermore, variation is frequent even within the same geographical location. Two people speaking London English, for example, would not sound exactly alike. Someone could have what is popularly called a 'broad' variety (referred to as a **basilect** or a **local vernacular** by linguists), and someone else could have a less broad variety, which is more standardized (see Chapter 12). Indeed, even two speakers who speak with basilectal varieties will not sound exactly alike, because no two speakers of any language have exactly the same set of linguistic features which they use in exactly the same way all the time. Instead, everyone speaks using their own, individual linguistic system, called their **idiolect**. Variation, then, is pervasive not only across every linguistic level, but in every single speaker.

This section began with a question: who varies? The answer, clearly, is **everybody**. If everybody is different from everybody else, how can we say 'New York English' or 'London English' or any other kind of English exists at all? The reason, of course, is that whilst two speakers from London may not sound exactly alike, they will sound more similar to each other than they do to someone from Liverpool or New York. Labels for regional varieties such as 'London English' or 'New York English' denote abstract categories into which speakers' idiolects can be grouped and classified as 'the same', even if they are subtly, or not so subtly, different. Such labels also suggest that varieties of English exist in some definite geographical area. Of course, it is not always easy to agree the exact place where one variety of English ends and another begins. This is because, as Hughes and Trudgill (1996: 7) wrote, '[i]n Britain, from the south-west of England to the north of Scotland we do not have a succession of distinct accents, but a continuum, a gradual changing of pronunciation.' Consider the following example. In Britain, people would probably be quite confident that they could distinguish between a Scottish English speaker and an English English speaker. These varieties of English can indeed be rather different, and are separated by a political boundary, the border between England and Scotland. However, there is no sudden and complete change from English English to Scottish English when you cross the border from England into Scotland. Instead, linguistic features blend into each other, and speakers living near to the border may use features attested on both sides (see, for example, Watt and Ingham, 2000, for a study of Berwick-upon-Tweed, England's northernmost town).

However, as long as this is kept in mind, it is often helpful to speak of regional varieties as though they can be found within certain geographical limits. In doing this, linguists have created maps delimiting accent regions, as in Figure 18.1.

Maps like the one in Figure 18.1 show broad similarities and differences between varieties of English. That is, we can infer that varieties in any given region are similar to each other in some way. However, it is impossible to work out just how similar the varieties are, or which linguistic features contribute to the similarities. For this information, we can employ the notion of the **isogloss**. An isogloss is a line on a map which denotes the boundary

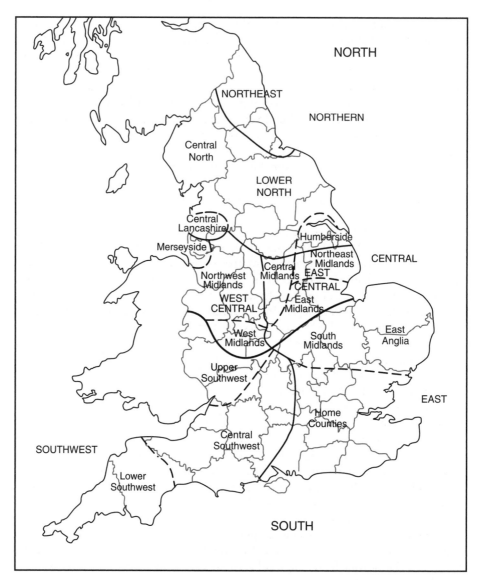

FIGURE 18.1   *Regional varieties of English (Trudgill, 1999a: 65)*

between linguistic features (of vocabulary, grammar or pronunciation). We can best see how isoglosses work by considering linguistic variation amongst a number of accents. Figure 18.2 shows the location of four English cities: London (1 on the map on the left), Bristol (2), Liverpool (3) and Manchester (4), and the location of three isoglosses (the map on the right).

The accents of London and Bristol, in the south of England, differ from the accents of Liverpool and Manchester, in the north, in a number of ways. For example, the word *bath* has the vowel of *father* in London and Bristol but the vowel of *cat* in Liverpool and Manchester. The dotted isogloss, beginning at the Wash in the East Midlands and running westward to the border

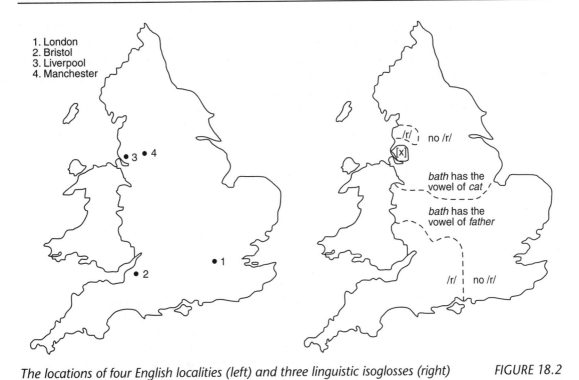

1. London
2. Bristol
3. Liverpool
4. Manchester

/r/ no /r/

[x]

bath has the vowel of *cat*

bath has the vowel of *father*

/r/ no /r/

The locations of four English localities (left) and three linguistic isoglosses (right)   FIGURE 18.2

with Wales, represents the boundary for this feature. Whilst the accents of London and Bristol are more similar to each other than they are to Liverpool or Manchester, there are differences between them. For example, the word *car* in London lacks /r/, but in Bristol /r/ is maintained. The dashed line, in the south-west, represents the boundary for this feature. Likewise, there are differences between Liverpool and Manchester. For example, in Liverpool, /k/ at the end of a syllable can be pronounced as a fricative, as in *back* [bax], but this is not found in Manchester (Watson, 2007). The solid boundary, in the north-west, delimits the boundary of this feature. Using isoglosses in this way can help shed light on the similarities and differences between varieties of English.

18.2 Why do regional varieties exist?

We have seen that large geographical regions can be divided up into smaller localities according to the presence or absence of linguistic features. But how do the boundaries that differentiate them get there? The answer to this question is complex, but perhaps the overarching reason is the fact that language is inextricably linked with the communities in which it operates. The contact and conflict between these communities, both hundreds of years ago and in the present day, can weaken or strengthen boundaries, with the result that language change can be promoted or inhibited. In this section we will briefly explore why some of the boundaries between regional varieties of English exist, in England and elsewhere.

During the early development of English, as discussed in Chapters 12 and 15, England was invaded and reinvaded, and boundaries between settlers were drawn and redrawn. For example, according to the traditional account, the invasion of the Angles, Saxons and Jutes in the fifth century pushed Celtic speakers to the western edges of Britain (where they would later form a people known to the Anglo-Saxons as the 'welisc', or Welsh, meaning 'foreigner'), creating new boundaries which, of course, still exist today. By the ninth century, the Danish and Norwegian Vikings had invaded and successfully settled in the north and east of Britain. This led to the division of the country into two parts: to the north and east of a line running roughly from Chester to London was the area of Viking settlement called the Danelaw (i.e., the area administered according to Danish law); to the south and west was the Anglo-Saxon area, which included the kingdom of Wessex. The dialects of the localities in the Danelaw, such as present day Yorkshire and Norfolk, continue to have a large number of words of Scandinavian origin, introduced by the Vikings, which are not present elsewhere: examples are *laik* 'play' and *beck* 'stream'. Moving forward a few hundred years, the boundaries between the north and the south were to be important in influencing the spread of sound changes, particularly in the Early Modern English period (roughly 1500–1750) (see Chapters 12 and 14). For example, prior to the seventeenth century, the words *cut, son, run, put, pull* and *wolf* had the vowel [ʊ] across England. However, in Early Modern English [ʊ] began to change into [ʌ]. This occurred gradually, and only in certain phonetic contexts, so that a distinction eventually developed between words like *cut, son, run* on the one hand, which had the new vowel, [ʌ], and *put, pull, wolf* on the other, which kept [ʊ]. This change did not spread into the north of England, where all words retained [ʊ], leading to what is now one of the major phonological differences between northern and southern English.

England was not just the recipient of invaders. The migration of people from England to places like North America and Australia is responsible for English spreading beyond the British Isles. In the early seventeenth century, for example, English settlers arrived in America, colonizing present-day New England, to the north, and Virginia, to the south. Just as the invasions of England had linguistic consequences, so did the English invasion of America. The settlers arriving in Virginia came from the west of England, for example, from Somerset and Gloucestershire, and so would have maintained /r/ in words like *farm*, whereas those arriving in New England came mostly from the east, for example, from Lincolnshire, Nottinghamshire and London, and so would have lacked /r/ in this position (Crystal, 2003: 92–3). This is a situation still found in today's American English, where Virginia has /r/ in words like *farm*, but New England lacks it.

Because travel across the Atlantic was relatively arduous, contact between English speakers in North America and the British Isles was much more limited than it is now. This meant that the two varieties began to develop in their own way. For example, in the seventeenth century English English accents had the same vowel in *bath* as in *cat*, [æ]. In many modern English English varieties, as we saw in Section 18.1.2, the vowel of *bath*, [ɑː], is different from the vowel of *cat*, [æ]. However, because settlers arrived in America before this change had occurred in England, modern American Englishes have [æ] in *bath* and *cat*, as in seventeenth century English English. In all of North America the [æ] in *bath* was later lengthened to [æː] and sometimes 'raised' to [ɛː], which is a pronunciation similar to Received Pronunciation *air*.

Boundaries continue to be important in the present day, but are not always of the same kind as those we have just seen. Because of increased mobility and contact between speakers, regional varieties are not as isolated as they once were. However, boundaries can exist for social as well as geographical reasons (see, for example, Britain, 2002). An example of this is to be found in Martha's Vineyard, an island off the east coast of the United States (Labov, 1963). Martha's Vineyard is an attractive summer destination for thousands of tourists, much to the annoyance of the residents. Labov discovered that younger Vineyarders used local phonological features very frequently, sub-consciously identifying with the island, and differentiating themselves lin-guistically from the invading tourists. Thus, regional phonological features were maintained in spite of, indeed *because* of, contact with other varieties. (Also see Chapters 21 and 22.)

Differences between regional varieties, then, exist for historical, geograph-ical and social reasons. In the next two sections, we will examine some of those differences.

18.3 Examining contemporary dialects

18.3.1 Dialects and correctness

Research on geographical variation in English has tended to focus on accent rather than dialect. The map of regional varieties in Figure 18.1 above, for example, as Beal (2004) notes, was created entirely from phonological rather than syntactic variables. There are a number of reasons for this. Firstly, syn-tactic variables are usually spread across much wider geographical spaces than phonological ones, and so are not quite as 'regional' (Hollmann and Siewierska, 2006). Secondly, much more data is usually necessary for dialect work because whilst recording an hour or so of conversation will probably yield enough data to allow a basic analysis of a speaker's accent, there will be many dialectal features missing because particular syntactic construc-tions occur less frequently than phonemes. However, technological advances and developments in corpus linguistics have made it possible to analyse vast amounts of data suitable for dialect analysis, and this has helped facilitate a surge of recent work in regional dialect syntax (Tagliamonte and Lawrence, 2000; Kortmann et al., 2005; Cheshire, 2007; Trousdale and Adger, 2007).

The general dearth of linguistic research on dialect grammar is not mir-rored in the amount of commentary amongst the general public or the media. People like to talk about dialects, and if speakers speak or write in a way which is perceived to be 'incorrect', it does not often go unnoticed. So high is the level of interest that an Internet movement called The Society for the Promotion of Good Grammar (see http://www.nationalgrammarday.com/), proclaimed that 4 March 2008 was 'National Grammar Day', which aimed to encourage people to 'Speak well!' and 'Write well!' But, in all debates

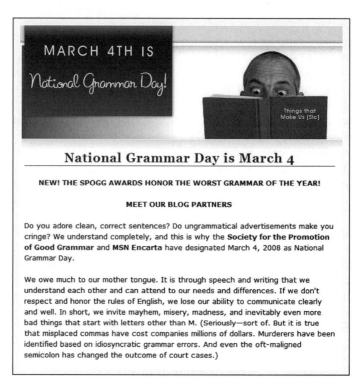

about 'speaking well', it is rarely clear what 'well' means. Usually, to use English 'well' means to use Standard English, and in advertising National Grammar Day, on the Society's website (see Figure 18.3), that appears to be the implication. By equating 'the rules of English' and 'clean, correct sentences' with Standard English, it is implied that dialects of English, because they are non-standard, are unclean and ungrammatical. Because Standard English is seen to be the benchmark of educated English, indeed a benchmark for English **grammar**, as far as prescriptivists are concerned (see Chapter 12), non-standard dialects are often thought of as incorrect or, even, grammar-**less**. In the next section, we explore some examples of regional variation in dialect syntax, and question whether it is valid to see to see the dialects of English as being unstructured or grammarless.

18.3.2   Exploring dialect variation in English

There are far more syntactic and morphological differences between dialects than we can examine in detail here. Instead, we will explore a selection of grammatical features with the aim of showing not only that English dialects are as structured and grammatical as Standard English, but also how, for some features, dialects arguably do 'a better job' than the standard.

Verb inflection for speak *in four language varieties*   *Table 18.1*

Person and number	Standard Italian	Standard English	Norwich English	Bristol English
First-person singular (e.g., 'I VERB')	*parlo*	*speak*	*speak*	*speaks*
Second-person singular (e.g., 'You VERB')	*parli*	*speak*	*speak*	*speaks*
Third-person singular (e.g., 'Sarah VERB')	*parla*	*speaks*	*speak*	*speaks*
First-person plural (e.g., 'We VERB')	*parliamo*	*speak*	*speak*	*speaks*
Second-person plural (e.g., 'You VERB')	*parlate*	*speak*	*speak*	*speaks*
Third-person plural (e.g., 'Sarah and Leanne VERB'	*parlano*	*speak*	*speak*	*speaks*

First, we will examine dialectal variation relating to verbs. In many languages, verbs receive a particular inflection according to their grammatical person, number or tense. In Standard English, for example, singular third-person present tense verbs are inflected with –s. Standard English is simpler than some other languages in this respect, as the data in Table 18.1 shows for the verb *speak* which, in Standard Italian, receives a different inflection for each person and number.

Some regional dialects of English have an even simpler system than Standard English, either having an –s inflection for all persons (such as Bristol English: *I likes you. You likes me. Dave likes me*), or not having –s for any person (such as Norwich English *I like you. You like me. Dave like me*). In Italian, information about the subject of the sentence is provided by the inflection (as a consequence Italian can, and usually does, drop the pronoun altogether), but in Standard English it is provided by the subject. If we were to say Norwich and Bristol had 'less grammar' than Standard English, and so were inferior, it would follow that Standard English has 'less grammar' than Standard Italian. Of course, Standard English is generally not considered to be grammatically inferior to Standard Italian, or any other language which marks grammatical person differently, and so it is unnecessary to see dialects as inferior to Standard English for the same reason.

The next feature we will consider is often referred to as an example of 'syntactic doubling', because it involves the duplication of a particular syntactic element. Indeed, this particular non-standard feature has probably attracted more popular commentary than any other: the 'double negative'. If you have ever been told any 'rules' of English, it is likely that you will have been told not to use a double negative because 'two negatives make a positive'. Of course, whilst this is true in mathematics, it is not true in language as Illustration Box 18.1 shows (see Cheshire, 1998, for a well-argued stance relating to this point).

ILLUSTRATION BOX 18.1

Negatives

Sentences such as those below are usually frowned upon in modern English because they contain multiple negations:

> *I didn't see nothing*
> *I didn't get nothing from nobody*
> *John won't do nothing*

In many other languages (e.g., French), having two markers for negation is perfectly acceptable and, indeed, the double negative used to be considered acceptable in English. Beal (2006: 71) points out, for example, that such constructions can be found in Shakespeare's writing:

> *I have one heart, one bosom and one truth*
> *And that no woman has, nor never none*
> *Shall mistress be of it, save I alone*
> (Twelfth Night)

And similar constructions can be found in Chaucer's Canterbury Tales:

> *...Curteis he was and lowely of servyse.*
> *Ther nas no man nowher so virtuous*
> (The Friar's Portrait)

It should be clear that Chaucer and Shakespeare were not using double negatives in order 'to make a positive'. Chaucer is actually using three negative elements, as *nas* is a contraction of *ne* and *was*. They add emphasis here; certainly, there is no sense in which this usage is considered 'bad' or 'nonstandard' (the notion of standard had not yet developed; see Chapter 12). In fact, a fairly regular way of forming negative statements in Old English (roughly 450–1100; see Chapter 12) was to use two negative elements: *ne* and *noht* (modern 'not'; e.g., *Ne con ic noht singan* 'I know not [how] to sing'). But today, because double negatives are not part of Standard English and are typically used most often by working-class speakers, they are stigmatized and frowned upon by prescriptivists. Their stigma exists for social, not grammatical reasons (see also Chapter 19 for a discussion of this point).

The double negative is not really a 'regional' dialect feature because it can be found in many non-standard dialects of English from around the world. However, another manifestation of negation is more regionally restricted, whilst still having a fairly wide geographical distribution: the use of *ain't*. In some varieties of English (e.g., Reading, see Cheshire, 1991), *ain't* neutralizes the contrast between persons and between the verbs *have* and *be*, as shown in Table 18.2.

However, whilst the neutralization between auxiliary *be* and *have* is frequently attested, sentences such as *I ain't a swimming lesson tomorrow*,

The use of ain't for auxiliary verbs be *and* have *(from Trudgill and Chambers, 1991: 51)*

Table 18.2

Person	Standard English		Non-standard dialect	
	be	have	be	have
1st	I'm not	I haven't	I ain't	I ain't
2nd	You aren't	You haven't	You ain't	You ain't
3rd	He isn't	He hasn't	He ain't	He ain't

Plural second person pronouns in English

Table 18.3

	Standard English	Liverpool, & the north-east of England	Southern US English	Pittsburgh
Second-person singular	Are you coming?	Are you coming?	Are you coming?	Are you coming?
Second-person plural	Are you coming?	Are youse coming?	Are yall coming?	Are yinz coming?

meaning 'I don't have a swimming lesson tomorrow' are not found. This is because *Ain't* can only replace *have* when it functions as an auxiliary verb, and not when it functions as a lexical verb. *Ain't* must be governed by the grammatical system to behave in this way.

Next, we will consider dialectal variation in the noun phrase. Table 18.3 shows how plurality can be marked on pronouns in the second person. In Standard English, the personal pronoun *you* is used for both singular and plural subjects. Speakers of Standard English may include an additional word such as *all* or *guys* to signal plurality, but in many other dialects there is a particular form of the second-person pronoun which performs this function. In the British Isles, *youse* is found in the dialects of Dublin, Belfast, Liverpool, Glasgow, Edinburgh, Newcastle and other north-east dialects. In the United States, *youse* is found in, for example, New York and New Jersey, as well as in non-standard Australian and New Zealand English. The pronoun *yall* is typical of Southern US English dialects, and *yinz* is used in Pittsburgh, Philadelphia. It is thought that both *yinz* and *youse* found their way into their respective dialects via contact with Irish varieties (Knowles, 1973; Crozier, 1984; Beal, 2004).

According to the *Urban Dictionary* (http://www.urbandictionary.com, accessed 12 February 2008), *youse* is 'the pinnacle of ignorant grammar'. However, the non-standard dialects are actually doing a 'better job' here than the standard variety because they can make a contrast, like many other European languages, which Standard English cannot without adding a phrase like *you guys*. As Beal (2006: 68) writes, 'Who can say [*youse* is] wrong when [it] makes a grammatical distinction (singular versus plural) that Standard English can only make through circumlocution?'

Table 18.4   Examples of singular objective us in Middlesbrough English (from Snell, 2007)

Example
Let us see
Give us it
Pass us that book
Show us yours
Turn it off for us
Give us my shoe back

ADVANCES BOX 18.1

Exploring dialect features

Asking questions such as the following about any dialect of English will help build up a picture of its grammatical system. Not all of the features mentioned below have been covered in this section, but more information about them can be found in the further reading at the end of this chapter. For a more comprehensive list of grammatical features, see Beal (2006: 78–9):

- Are multiple negations used?
- How are verbs inflected for person?
- How is verb tense marked? Are irregular verbs regularized (e.g., what is the past tense of come? Came or come)?
- Are both was and were used, or just one of them (e.g., I was tired, they were tired, I were tired, they was tired)?
- Is there a plural second-person pronoun?
- Can us be used as both a singular and plural pronoun?
- Can definite articles be omitted (e.g., I was at park)?
- What relative pronouns are most common (e.g., is The car what I bought possible)?
- What intensifiers are used?
- What is the typical pattern of direct and indirect objects (e.g., is it give it me, give me it, give it to me, give me the book, give the book me)

Another difference relating to pronouns is the use of *us* for the first-person singular object, where Standard English would have *me* (e.g., *pass it to us* vs. *pass it to me*). This is found in many dialects of English, but in certain regions, such as the north-east of England, it is used more frequently than elsewhere. Examples can be found in Table 18.4, from the north-eastern city of Middlesbrough (Snell, 2007).

Speakers of Middlesbrough English do not replace *me* with *us* all the time. However, using one or the other does not appear to be random. Instead, Snell (2007) argues that the use of *me* or *us* is governed by politeness principles (see Chapter 31). Using interactions between young schoolchildren as evidence, Snell shows, for example, that speakers use *us*, not *me*, in imperatives (e.g., *give it us*) as an attempt to soften a potentially fact-threatening act. Because speakers use *us* for a particular communicative purpose, it cannot be a feature of sloppy grammar or, indeed, be grammarless. It is performing a specific communicative function.

In this section we have seen that regional dialects, although sometimes frowned upon by prescriptivists, have an intricate grammatical structure, just as Standard English does. Sometimes dialect grammar is simpler than Standard English (in the case of –s regularization and the neutralization of *be* and *have* with *ain't*), and sometimes it is more complex (e.g., by having a second-person plural pronoun). We have also seen that some features of grammar which came to be attacked by prescriptivists have often been around for a very long time, and have not always attracted negative comments, but do so when associated with working-class speech (e.g., double negatives). Finally, we have seen non-standard dialects employ all their grammatical resources as an aid to communication. Regional dialects cannot be grammarless. If they were, successful communication would be impossible.

18.4 Examining contemporary accents

18.4.1 Phonological variation, variables, and lexical sets

An investigation of an accent is an investigation of its phonological variables. So, before we can begin to analyse accent variation, we need some way of denoting those variables. For consonantal features, the standard practice is to use round brackets to distinguish variables from phonemes or allophones (e.g., the phoneme /t/ but the variable (t)). A different method of referring to vocalic variables is now widely used, particularly in Britain: the **lexical set** (Wells, 1982). A lexical set is a group of words which share a similar phonetic feature. For example, the words *cat*, *back* and *ham* belong in the TRAP lexical set, and the words *stop*, *swan* and *rob* belong in the LOT lexical set (lexical sets are usually written in SMALL CAPITALS). The name of the set provides no information about the way a vowel is pronounced (e.g., words in the LOT set have /ɒ/ in English English and /ɑ/ in American English), but does provide a way of grouping together words that behave in the same way phonologically. So, whilst we might not know how the LOT lexical set is realized in any given variety, we can assume that if a speaker has /ɒ/ in *stop* they will also have /ɒ/ in *swan*, *rob* and, indeed, *lot*, because these words belong to the same lexical set. The standard lexical sets are presented in Table 18.5, along with the typical realizations in some general regional varieties. (Of course, you should not assume the varieties listed are homogenous entities, because of the variation described in Section 18.1. Here, I have listed some vowels that are widely used in these varieties.)

Because Received Pronunciation and General American were used as the model for lexical sets, some contrasts that occur in non-standard varieties cannot be represented easily. For example, in most varieties of English, words like *look* and *book* belong in the FOOT lexical set, along with other words like *full* or *could,* and have the vowel /ʊ/. In parts of the north of England, however, such as Merseyside and Tyneside, the vowel in *look* and *book*, and other

Table 18.5   *Wells's (1982) lexical sets*

Lexical Set	Example words	Southern English English	Northern English English	General American
KIT	*kit, build, pretty*	ɪ	ɪ	ɪ
DRESS	*dress, any, bread*	ɛ	ɛ	ɛ
TRAP	*trap, cab, ham*	a	a	æ
LOT	*lot, stop, swan*	ɒ	ɒ	ɑ
STRUT	*strut, done, touch*	ʌ	ʊ	ʌ
FOOT	*foot, put, good*	ʊ	ʊ	ʊ
BATH	*bath, dance, grass*	ɑː	a	æ
CLOTH	*cloth, off, soft*	ɒ	ɒ	ɔ
NURSE	*nurse, burn, work*	ɜː	ɜː	ɜɹ
FLEECE	*fleece, these, brief*	iː	iː	i
FACE	*face, name, change*	eɪ	eː	eɪ
PALM	*palm, calm, father*	ɑː	ɑː	ɑ
THOUGHT	*thought, chalk, taught*	ɔː	ɔː	ɔ
GOAT	*goat, soap, sew*	əʊ	oː	o
GOOSE	*goose, loop, fruit*	uː	uː	u
PRICE	*price, time, height*	aɪ	aɪ	aɪ
CHOICE	*choice, noise, boy*	ɔɪ	ɔɪ	ɔɪ
MOUTH	*mouth, out, loud*	aʊ	aʊ	aʊ
NEAR	*near, beer, here*	ɪə	ɪə	ɪɹ
SQUARE	*square, care, their*	ɛə	ɛə	eɪɹ
START	*start, part, farm*	ɑː	ɑː	ɑɹ
NORTH	*north, or, war*	ɔː	ɔː	ɔɹ
FORCE	*force, store, court*	ɔː	ɔː	oɹ
CURE	*cure, pure, poor*	ʊə	ʊə	uɹ
happY	*happy, crazy, city*	ɪ	ɪ	i
lettER	*letter, paper, whisker*	ə	ə	ɚ
commA	*comma, quota, vodka*	ə	ə	ə

words spelled with <ook>, have a longer vowel, /uː/, but other words in the set, such as *full* and *could*, have /ʊ/. This is a problem because there is no lexical set which distinguishes '<ook> words' from the others belonging to FOOT. So, to deal with these words, we would need another set, such as BOOK.

In the next section, we will explore how to use these lexical sets in exploring some of the phonological variation between English accents.

18.4.2   Exploring accent variation in English

The sounds of English can vary dramatically, even over quite small distances. We cannot consider every aspect of this variation here. Instead, we will see that, just like the grammars of regional dialects, the phonologies of regional accents are highly structured and not, as is sometimes thought, the result of speakers being 'sloppy' or 'lazy'.

Some systemic differences related to vowels   *Table 18.6*

LEXICAL SET	Example word	Variety of English	
Dataset (a)		**Southern English English**	**Northern English English**
FOOT	*put*	/ʊ/	/ʊ/
FOOT	*book*	/ʊ/	/ʊ/
FOOT	*look*	/ʊ/	/ʊ/
STRUT	*putt*	/ʌ/	/ʊ/
STRUT	*buck*	/ʌ/	/ʊ/
STRUT	*luck*	/ʌ/	/ʊ/
Dataset (b)		**Manchester English**	**Liverpool English**
NURSE	*her*	/ɜː/	/ɛː/
NURSE	*fur*	/ɜː/	/ɛː/
SQUARE	*hair*	/ɛː/	/ɛː/
SQUARE	*fair*	/ɛː/	/ɛː/
Dataset (c)		**English English**	**American English**
LOT	*stop*	/ɒ/	/ɑ/
LOT	*swan*	/ɒ/	/ɑ/
PALM	*calm*	/ɑː/	/ɑ/
PALM	*drama*	/ɑː/	/ɑ/

When exploring accents of English, differences between varieties can be categorized into three types. These are (i) systemic differences; (ii) realizational differences; and (iii) distributional differences. We will examine each type in turn below. First, we will explore **systemic differences**, so called because they relate to the number of phonemes in a phonological system. Consider the data in Table 18.6.

In each dataset, one variety of English can make a phonological contrast that the other cannot, because one variety has a phoneme that the other lacks: (a) Southern English English contrasts *put* and *putt* (or, in terms of lexical sets contrasts FOOT and STRUT), but northern English does not, (b) Manchester English, and many other Englishes, contrast *hair* and *her* (NURSE and SQUARE), but Liverpool English does not, and (c) American English has the same vowel in *stop* as in *calm* (it merges LOT with PALM) but English English does not. A systemic difference, then, occurs when one variety makes a contrast between words that is impossible in another variety.

Next we will consider **realizational differences**, so called because varieties may share the same phonemes but realize them differently. Consider the data in Table 18.7, illustrating typical realizations of /t/ in a number of varieties of English. A well known pronunciation of /t/ across the British Isles is the **glottal stop**, [ʔ], found in Newcastle, Sheffield, Wirral, Norwich, Reading, Milton Keynes, Hull, Cardiff, Glasgow, Edinburgh, Dublin and many other places (see chapters in Foulkes and Docherty, 1999). However, accents differ in terms of the position in a word in which the glottal stop is likely. Very few accents use a glottal stop for /t/ if it occurs word-initially (e.g., *top* is usually [tɒp] not [ʔɒp]), but the

Table 18.7   Some realizations of /t/ in English

	Received Pronunciation	London English	Liverpool English	New York English
top	[t]	[t]	[t]	[t]
talk	[t]	[t]	[t]	[t]
atlas	[ʔ]	[ʔ]	[ʔ]	[t]
football	[ʔ]	[ʔ]	[ʔ]	[t]
water	[t]	[ʔ]	[s]	[ɾ]
better	[t]	[ʔ]	[s]	[ɾ]
cat	[t]	[ʔ]	[s]	[t]
what	[t]	[ʔ]	[s]/[h]	[t]
get off	[t]	[ʔ]	[ɹ]	[ɾ]

great majority of accents, including Received Pronunciation (Cruttenden, 1994; Fabricius, 2000), have [ʔ] if the /t/ occurs before a consonant (e.g., _atlas_ [ʔ]). In some accents (e.g., London English), but not others (e.g., Liverpool English) the glottal stop is likely intervocalically (e.g., _better_ [bɛʔə]). In each case, though, the glottal stop is a realization of /t/.

The glottal stop is not the only possible realization of /t/. In Liverpool English, for example, /t/ can be realized as [s] (Honeybone, 2001; Watson, 2007), or, in a restricted set of words when a pause follows, such as _what_ and _that_, [h] (see Section 18.5). Also in Liverpool, and elsewhere in the north of England (Wells, 1982: 370; Broadbent, 2008), /t/ can be realized as [ɹ] when word-final and followed by a word beginning with a vowel (e.g., the /t/ in _get off, lot of, shut up_). Finally, /t/ can be realized as a tap, [ɾ], in New York, and other American Englishes. These accents all have the phoneme /t/ in their system. These are realizational differences, because we are not dealing with the introduction of a new phonological contrast, but a number of different ways of realizing the same phoneme. Some other realizational differences are presented in Table 18.8.

In dataset (a), we see that London English has three different realizations of the phoneme /l/: [l], occurring in syllable onsets, and either the velarized variant, [ł], or the vocalized variant, [o], occurring in syllable codas. Welsh English, on the other hand, just has one realization in the onset and coda, [l]. In dataset (b), we see that the phonemes /θ/ and /ð/ are [θ] and [ð] respectively in RP, but that London English has other possibilities, [f] for /θ/ and [v] or [d] for /ð/. The realization of /θ/ and /ð/ as [f] and [v] is known as TH-fronting. In dataset (c), we see that Liverpool English has a number of ways of realizing /k/, such as [k], found in all varieties, or the fricatives [x] or [χ], not found with the same frequency elsewhere (Watson, 2007).

Finally, we will consider **distributional differences** between accents, so called because they relate to how phonemes are distributed into lexical sets, and also the position in a word in which phonemes appear. Examine the data in Table 18.9.

In Table 18.9(a) we see that while both northern Englishes and southern Englishes have the phonemes /a/ and /ɑː/, they appear in different words. In

Some realizational differences between English varieties   *Table 18.8*

Example word	Variety of English	
Dataset (a) /l/ velariation and vocalization		
	London English	**Welsh English**
leap	[l]	[l]
well	[ɫ] or [o]	[l]
milk	[ɫ] or [o]	[l]
Dataset (b) TH-fronting		
	London English	**Received Pronunciation**
the	[ð] or [d]	[ð]
brother	[v]	[ð]
bath	[f]	[θ]
think	[f]	[θ]
three	[f]	[θ]
Dataset (c) /k/ fricativization		
	Liverpool English	**Other English Englishes**
case	[k]	[k]
back	[x] or [χ]	[k]
chicken	[x] or [χ]	[k]

Some distributional differences between varieties of English   *Table 18.9*

Example word	Variety of English	
Dataset (a) The vowel in BATH		
	Northern English English	**Southern English English**
cat	/a/	/a/
calm	/ɑ:/	/ɑ:/
bath	/a/	/ɑ:/
laugh	/a/	/ɑ:/
Dataset (b) /r/ in rhotic and non-rhotic accents		
	American English	**Received Pronunciation**
rat	/r/	/r/
parrot	/r/	/r/
car	/r/	No /r/
farm	/r/	No /r/

both the north and the south, words like *cat, mat* and *trap* have /a/ and words like *palm, calm, barn* have /ɑ:/. However, words like *glass, laugh,* and *path* have /a/ in the north and /ɑ:/ in the south. This is because in the eighteenth century, /a/ began to change to /ɑ:/ in southern England in words which had [s, f, θ]. However, this change was incomplete, meaning that /ɑ:/ does not occur in all words that are eligible: *bath* is [bɑ:θ], but *maths* is [maθs], and *mast* is [mɑːst] but *mass* is [mas]. This type of difference, because it results from phonemes appearing in different sets of words, is a difference in **lexical distribution**. The examples in (b) are also related to the distribution of phonemes. In (most varieties of) American English, as we saw earlier in this chapter, /r/ can occur in all positions: word-initially in *rat*, intervocalically in *parrot*, word-finally in *car* and pre-consonantally in *farm*. For this reason, American English is said to be **rhotic**. In Received Pronunciation, and many other English English accents, /r/ can only occur if a vowel follows it (i.e., /r/ is present in *rat* and *parrot* but absent in *car* and *farm*). RP is **non-rhotic**. Thus, while both American English and Received Pronunciation have /r/, it is distributed differently in terms of the positions it can occur in a word. For this reason, these are differences in **phonotactic distribution** (see Chapter 4, for further discussion of phonotactics).

In this section we have seen that far from being 'sloppy', regional accents of English are highly structured. Northern English speakers do not say [bʊs] for *bus* because they are too lazy to say [bʌs], but rather because their phonological system has not developed in the same way as the phonologies of southern Englishes. Likewise, speakers who use the glottal stop do not do so because they are too lazy to pronounce [t]. If laziness was the issue, why not have a glottal stop at the beginning of words, too? Or, in fact, why not just remove the glottal stop altogether? The answer is because the glottal stop, just like every other accent feature, is governed by the intricacies of the speakers' phonological systems.

ADVANCES BOX 18.2

Exploring accent features

Asking questions such as those below about any accent of English will help build up a picture of its phonological system. Not all of the features mentioned have been covered in this section, but more information about them can be found in the further reading at the end of this chapter.

- What vowels occur in FOOT and STRUT?
- What vowel is in BOOK?
- Does BATH have PALM or TRAP?
- Do GOAT, FACE and PRICE have a monophthong or a diphthong?
- Is there a distinction between NURSE and SQUARE?
- Is /r/ pronounced at the end of a word or only before a vowel?
- Is a glottal stop used for /t/? If so, in which positions in a word can [ʔ] occur?
- Are there other realizations of /t/? [ɹ], [ɾ], [s]?
- Is /h/ dropped or maintained?
- How is /l/ realized?
- Can /r/ be a tap? Or a labiodental approximant?
- Do all 'ng clusters' (e.g., *sing*) have /ŋ/ or /ŋg/?
- Are /θ/ and /ð/ pronounced as [f] and [v]?

ILLUSTRATION BOX 18.2

How to compliment a Kiwi

Overheard in Wellington, New Zealand:

> British tourist to New Zealander: *Excuse me, could you tell me how I can I get to Courtenay Place?*
> New Zealander: *Well, you go straight on and then you turn to the* [lɪft].
> British tourist: *The lift?*

The tourist heard *lift*, while the New Zealander actually said *left*. How could this misunderstanding have taken place? The answer lies in what has been called the New Zealand Short Front Vowel Shift (Hay, Maclagan and Gordon, 2008: 41–2). During the twentieth century, the vowels of TRAP, DRESS and KIT have moved in a clockwise direction in both NZE and Australian English. However, the two varieties have done this is different ways. This will become clear if we examine the vowel diagrams below:

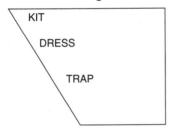

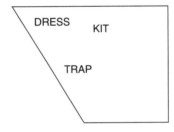

(a) Australian English front vowels vowels

(b) New Zealand English (NZE) front

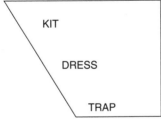

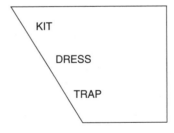

c) London English, early 21st century

(d) London English, *c.*1900

Diagrams (a) and (b) represent the two Southern Hemisphere varieties. Diagram (d) shows the approximate position of the vowels in late nineteenth-century London, and this can be considered the ancestor of the Australian, New Zealand and contemporary London vowels (diagram (c)). As we can see, the Southern Hemisphere varieties and London have *diverged* by shifting their vowels in opposite directions from a probable common origin. What strikes Australians about New Zealanders, however, is that they appear to say 'fush and chups', while New Zealanders accuse Australians of saying 'feesh and cheeps' – all because of the huge difference in the KIT vowel. Meanwhile, British listeners hear NZE DRESS as KIT or FLEECE, giving rise to the *left–lift* confusion. So, if you spot the NZE DRESS and KIT vowels in a stranger's speech, you can confidently enquire if they are from New Zealand, rather than from Australia!

The phonological variation we have seen in this chapter must be taken into account by listeners when talking to each other. If it were not, communication between speakers with different accents would be very difficult, because they would not understand each other. It is very rare that confusion or miscomprehension occurs, but it is not impossible. Illustration Box 18.2 demonstrates how misunderstandings could occur.

18.5   Are regional accents disappearing?

In Section 18.3 we saw that contact between speakers has linguistic consequences. To conclude our exploration of regional variation, I will consider briefly the implications of increased contact on modern day varieties and ask: are regional accents in England disappearing?

A frequent observation amongst the general public and the UK media is that English accents are indeed becoming more alike. In the UK press, there have been comments like 'England's most distinctive dialects may be doomed to disappear' (Martin Wainwright, The *Guardian*, 6 June 2001). The phenomena highlighted in reports like this are actually also frequently attested in the linguistic literature. In fact, this convergence, referred to as accent or **dialect levelling** by linguists, has been one of the most widely considered concepts in British sociolinguistics. Williams and Kerswill (1999: 149) provide a definition of levelling as 'a process whereby differences between regional varieties are reduced, features which make varieties distinctive disappear, and new features emerge and are adopted over a wide geographical area'. Levelling has been noted in Newcastle (Watt, 2002), Hull, Reading, Milton Keynes (Williams and Kerswill, 1999), Middlesbrough (Llamas, 2007), Northamptonshire (Dyer, 2002), Norwich (Trudgill, 1999b), and elsewhere – see also Kerswill (2003). Two examples are considered below.

First, regional features have been abandoned in favour of features which are found over a larger geographical area. For example, in the north-east of England, the traditional FACE vowel is [ɪə]. However, younger speakers have been found to be abandoning this vowel in favour of [eː], which is found across the north, for example, in Lancashire and Yorkshire. For this variable, although younger speakers still sound 'northern', they no longer sound 'north-eastern'. They have replaced a very local feature with a less local one (Watt, 2002).

Second, new features are introduced into varieties and spread, or diffuse, from place to place, making the accents of those places sound more similar to each other. Indeed, we saw in Section 18.4.2 that a frequent realization of /t/ is the glottal stop, [ʔ]. The glottal stop is often considered to be the classic diffusing variable. As Kerswill writes:

According to Andrésen (1968), the first evidence of glottal replacement in the London area is from around the beginning of the twentieth century. By the middle of the twentieth century, glottal replacement and glottal reinforcement of intervocalic /t/ was a feature of rural dialects in most of eastern England, but not the southwest, the Midlands or northern English, including Yorkshire (Trudgill, 1974: 81). The feature seems to have diffused to urban centres outside the southeast within the last 30–40 years.

(2003: 232)

This diffusion has meant that many varieties now have the glottal stop as a realization of /t/, and so sound similar to each other in this respect.

However, despite instances of levelling like these, it is unlikely that accents of English will disappear completely. As we saw in Section 18.2, boundaries of a range of types can help block the diffusion of linguistic features into particular regions. Furthermore, there is evidence of phonological divergence in England, as we will see below.

In Liverpool, as we saw in Section 18.4.2, there are a number of possibilities for the realization of /t/, including one which is rarely found elsewhere, [h]. This occurs, according to Knowles (1973: 234) in a 'small class of words including *get got bit what that it not* in absolute final position [i.e., before a pause]'. So, in Liverpool, when Knowles collected his data in the 1960s, [h] for /t/ was common in phrases like *which one did you get?* [gɛh], or *is this it?* [ɪh]. In Watson (2006), however, I show that the environment in which /t/ can be [h] has extended to polysyllabic words like *climate, maggot, chocolate* and *aggregate*. This is only found in the speech of younger speakers. Crucially, this cannot be a feature that has diffused from elsewhere, because no other variety of English English has [h] for /t/ as regularly as Liverpool. Instead, in relation to this variable, Liverpool English is becoming more regionally distinctive.

So, whilst convergence, rather than divergence, has been more regularly recorded in accents of English over recent decades, we know that divergence is also occurring. We can predict that although English will continue to evolve, just as it always has, it will also continue to vary.

Recommended reading

Detailed general works about accent variation are Wells (1982), Hughes, Trudgill and Watt (2005) and Foulkes and Docherty (1999). A good resource for dialect syntax is Kortmann et al. (2005). Excellent volumes which deal with both grammatical and phonological variation are Britain (2007) and Kortmann and Upton (2008). For further information about the development of dialectology as a discipline, see Chambers and Trudgill (1998). One aspect of dialectology missing from this chapter because of space constraints is that of lexical variation. Two good, succinct summaries of work in this area can be found in Trudgill (1999a, ch. 5) and Beal (2006, ch. 5). Two very good websites about accent and dialect variation are *Collect Britain* (http://www.collectbritain.co.uk/) and *BBC Voices* (http://www.bbc.co.uk/voices/). On both of these sites you can listen to audio clips of a wide range of English varieties.

Note

1 Thanks are due to Paul Kerswill for providing Illustration Box 18.2.

CHAPTER 19

Language and Social Class[1]

PAUL KERSWILL

19.1 Introduction

In the Preface to *Pygmalion* (1913), George Bernard Shaw wrote: 'It is impossible for an Englishman to open his mouth without making some other Englishman hate or despise him.' This was stated in the context of the famous play, in which a phonetics professor, Henry Higgins, trains Eliza Doolittle, a young Cockney (or working-class Londoner), to use what would today be known as **Received Pronunciation** (**RP**). Under some protest, Eliza acquiesces to this because she sees the tremendous social advantage of a middle- or upper-class accent. But the play is about more than accent. Eliza has to use 'correct' grammar and she mustn't swear. And she has to dress and comport herself in a way befitting a lady.

What underlies all the changes Eliza undertakes is the notion that society is stratified (layered) and, moreover, that there is a direct correspondence between this **stratification** and all levels of language and language use (grammar, pronunciation, pragmatics, even which language is used). Stratification is not neutral: it implies inequality, and Eliza reluctantly sacrifices her social identity as a working-class Londoner in order to gain what she perceives as the advantages of a higher social class.

All human societies – not just London's – are internally differentiated, whether by gender, age, ethnicity, caste or class. These are all at a 'macro' level, that is, broad groups into which people can be categorized. Categorization may appear straightforward, as with gender and age, which correspond to a biological distinction (sex) or to something inexorable (time). Yet even these divisions turn out to vary between societies and across different eras: gender roles change rapidly, gay identities are accepted as alternatives, and 'adolescence' as a distinct life-stage is recent in Western societies and is not shared across the globe. As we shall see, for class there is no single obvious external measure, like sex or time, which can be used as a defining principle. Even so, social stratification based on some concept of 'class' is pervasive, and a great deal of sociolinguistic research has been focused on it.

19.2 Feudalism, caste and class: the importance of mobility

Historically, **social class** is recent: in the Middle Ages in Europe, notions of rank were paramount (aristocracy, free men and serfs). Property, but not

ILLUSTRATION BOX 19.1

Social class differences in English pronunciation

English pronunciation varies strongly between and within English-speaking countries. Some of this variation tells us which territory a person comes from – Canada, Scotland, etc. – as well as the location within the territory – e.g., Newfoundland, Glasgow. It turns out that the features which are most diagnostic of location are also those which are associated with a low social status. Thus, people with strong Glaswegian or Cockney accents are very easy to identify, and very likely to be 'working class'. (Later, we will consider Trudgill's model summarizing this insight.) The same holds true for grammatical differences, but these are far fewer in number, both within and across countries, so it is more difficult to be particularly precise about where somebody comes from. As a consequence, the link between grammar and class is less subtle, and may in fact be gross (see Section 19.5).

Consonants
/t/ between vowels, as in *butter*:
/bʌtə/ vs. /bʌʔə/ (Britain)
/bʌtə/ vs. /bʌɾə/ (Australia and New Zealand)

Comment: In all three countries the right-hand pronunciation is increasingly regarded simply as informal, losing its class connotations. In Australia and New Zealand, the left-hand pronunciation is nowadays regarded as rather stilted.

Initial /h/

In most of the English-speaking world, initial /h/ is pronounced by members of all social classes in words like *hospital*, *house* and *hedge*. However, in England and Wales, with the exception of much of the north-east and parts of Norfolk and Somerset, word-initial /h/ is missing in most working-class speech – a feature known as *h*-dropping – but present in middle-class speech. Thus, people typically pronounce *home* as /əʊm/. Note that /h/ in unstressed pronouns, such as *his*, is often absent in all accents. Interestingly, there has been a dramatic change in this feature in the south of England, where /h/ has largely been reinstated by younger people. Among broadly working-class young speakers, those with the highest use of /h/ are Londoners with an inner-city and ethnic minority background, as well as people living in areas of generally high mobility, such as new towns (See Kerswill and Williams, 1999; Cheshire et al., 2008a,b). By contrast, the north of England remains solidly h-dropping.

Vowels

As in all languages, the vowel phonemes of English are subject to a vast range of nuances. Much of this variation is linked to class differences; for example, in the south-east of England, we can observe the following variations:

Vowel of FACE: [feɪs] vs. [fæɪs]
Vowel of GOAT: [gəʊt] vs. [gɛʊt]

Comment: The left-hand pronunciations approximate to RP, the right-hand ones traditional Cockney. For both of these phonemes, RP has a *narrow* diphthong, Cockney a *wide* diphthong, with a greater difference between the beginning and end of the vowel. It is a fact that most RP speakers are middle or upper middle class, while Cockney speakers are likely to be working class. However, as with the loss of *h*-dropping, recent changes have blurred the class dimension: many young working-class Londoners are now producing narrow diphthongs, or even monophthongs, such as [fe:s] and [go:t]. The people who do this the most have a minority ethnic background, but it is spreading to other groups and other locations. (See Cheshire et al., 2008a,b and Kerswill et al., 2008 on London, and Foulkes and Docherty, 2007 for details of phonetic variation more generally.)

ILLUSTRATION BOX 19.2

Social class differences in English grammar

In a Great Britain-wide survey conducted in the 1980s, Jenny Cheshire and her colleagues found that the following non-standard grammatical features were reported by at least 80 per cent of schools participating in the study:

- *them* as demonstrative adjective, e.g., *Look at them big spiders*
- Absence of plural marking in words expressing measurements, e.g., *Two pound of flour*
- *what* as a relative pronoun, e.g., *The film what was on last night was good*
- *never* as past tense negator, e.g., *No, I never broke that*
- Participle *sat*, e.g., *She was sat over there looking at her car*
- Adverbial *quick*, e.g., *I like pasta. It cooks really quick*
- *ain't/in't* for *haven't, hasn't, aren't, isn't*, e.g., *That ain't working*
- Participle *stood*, e.g., *And he was stood in the corner looking at it*
- Non-standard *was*, e.g., *We was singing*
                    (adapted from Cheshire, Edwards and Whittle, 1993: 64–5)

The authors add multiple negation, as in *I don't want none*, to this list of geographically widespread features. Unlike pronunciation features, there are relatively few grammatical features which are only found in working-class speech in a single region. A good example is the present tense –*s* in the verb, e.g., *I likes, you likes, she likes, we likes, they likes*, in the south and south-west of England. There are virtually no grammatical features used only in a small area.

(financial) capital, was strongly tied to rank. Political power was vested in royal and aristocratic lineages. Linguistically, this was reflected most obviously in the rise of pronoun systems in Europe where unequal rank was explicitly signalled; thus, in English, the second-person plural pronoun *you* was enlisted as the 'polite' pronoun, used by a socially inferior person when addressing a higher ranking individual, who in turn would address the lower ranking person with the singular *thou* (see Trudgill, 2000: 92 on how this pattern emerged in other European languages). In Hindu society, caste is an organizing principle affecting what types of occupation are permitted and who can speak to whom (Coulmas, 2005: 25). In some places, this is even reflected in the maintenance of separate languages by members of different castes (Gumperz and Wilson, 1971).

Neither caste nor rank systems permit social mobility: you are born into your social position, and only radical social change – or your own migration – can allow you to step outside it. On the other hand, social mobility is a defining characteristic of class systems. This means that your social position can rapidly change upwards or downwards during your lifetime, or between generations of the same family. The fact that mobility is possible means that people strive to improve themselves, or their children's prospects, through their own actions. Acquiring new ways of speaking is one such action.

19.3   Social class

As we have seen, there is no 'natural' way of defining social class. Scholars who have investigated class agree that a hierarchy exists, but disagree on the relative emphasis that should be placed on economic factors and more broadly cultural factors in defining it. The first class theorist was Karl Marx (1818–1883), who related social structure to the position of individuals in relation to the means of production. *Capitalists* own the means of production, while the *proletariat* sell their labour to the capitalists (Giddens, 2006: 301). This theory is grounded in the circumstances of mid-Victorian industrial Britain, with its extremes of exploitation and control by capitalists. Growing class segregation in Britain led to a divergence in speech at the level of dialect and accent. The new urban vernaculars which emerged in places like Manchester and Leeds had powerful working-class connotations. Alongside them, there was the increasingly uniform 'Received Pronunciation' of the elite, which consisted not only of the capitalists, but also traditional landowners, senior managers and civil servants, and the aristocracy. (See Chapter 12. Mugglestone (2003) is an excellent account of this process; see also Kerswill (2007b).) Nineteenth-century British English was therefore not only split up into regional dialects, but also **social dialects** or **sociolects**.

19.3.1   Social status and functionalism: Weber and Parsons

The Marxian approach is the classic 'conflict' model, with class struggle at its core. However, it quickly acquired critics, not least because, by the beginning of the twentieth century, Western society was changing: there were increasing numbers of people in the 'middle classes', including managers and bureaucrats, whose wealth was not linked to capital or property. Max Weber (1864–1920) took an approach which allowed for greater complexity in modern societies. According to Giddens, Weber agreed with Marx in seeing class as 'founded on objectively given economic conditions', though class divisions 'derive not only from control or lack of control of the means of production, but from economic differences which have nothing directly to do with property' (Giddens, 2006: 302). Weber saw people as having differing 'life chances' because of differences in skills, education and qualifications. In a capitalist society, it is necessary to recognize that social **status**, independent of Marxian 'class', might in fact be relevant to stratification in society. Status differences lead to differences in 'styles of life' (Weber; Giddens, 2006: 303), marked by such things as 'housing, dress, manner of speech, and occupation' (Giddens, 2006: 303). This is, of course, very close to what we nowadays label 'lifestyle' (see Section 19.4.1).

Weber's work is very much the precursor of contemporary, composite models combining a number of criteria – and we return to these below (Section 19.4.1). However, we need to consider a third scholar, whose work turned out directly to influence sociolinguists of the 1960s and 1970s: Talcott Parsons (1902–1979). Parsons focused on the idea of status, and transformed this into a hierarchy in which all elements interlocked. This is the theory of functionalism, which Holborn and Haralambos summarize as follows:

> To understand any part of society, such as family or religion, the part must be seen in relation to society as a whole … The functionalist will examine a part of society, such as the family, in terms of its contribution to the maintenance of the social system.

> (2000: 9)

'Class' is a major factor in this jigsaw. It is a hierarchy of esteem or status – a doctor is higher on the scale than a nurse – and is only indirectly connected to a person's income or whether or not they are themselves capitalists. A perceived occupational ranking is central to this functional approach, and in some countries surveys have been carried out to find out what precisely the 'pecking order' of occupations is (we mention an example below).

In the 1960s and 1970s, sociolinguists such as William Labov (1966), Walt Wolfram and Peter Trudgill adopted just such a hierarchical model in their early studies of language and class in US and British cities. It is easy to see the appeal of this approach: it is possible to look for a relationship between people's level of use of certain linguistic features, such as the ones listed in Illustration Box 19.2 above, and their position in the social class hierarchy.

19.4 Class and stratification in contemporary Western societies

19.4.1 Integrated models

Since the 1970s, purely functionalist models have largely been replaced by models which combine status (i.e., hierarchy), income, wealth, a person's prospects, security and autonomy at work, and cultural elements (such as choice of newspapers or decisions about children's education). Arguably, this is a return to a Weberian view, but it also adds a strong element of lifestyle choice. That is, in our affluent, consumer society, we are now faced with a menu of possible lifestyles and are (relatively) free to select from it. An example is many young people's enjoyment of particular styles of popular music, along with the clothing fashions and modes of behaviour associated with them. These alignments are to some extent correlated with the parents' social class (measured, for instance, by occupation), but often the correlation is far from categorical and the issue seems to be as much a matter of personal choice. This is what the anthropologist and sociolinguist, Penelope Eckert, found in her study of a Detroit high school (1989; 2000). (See Giddens, 2006: 321–4 for further discussion.)

A view which extends the Marxian idea of capital to both culture and language is that of the French sociologist, Pierre Bourdieu (1988). **Cultural capital** gives us advantages over other people: we may 'inherit' wealth and tastes, and we 'invest' in education and in lifestyle choices. Bourdieu sees this investment as favouring the dominant class. He in fact sees language as central to this form of capital: linguistic capital is embodied by socially highly valued language forms, such as (in Great Britain) Standard English and Received Pronunciation (see Chapter 12). Milroy and Gordon (2003: 97) have put it this way: 'language constitutes symbolic capital which is potentially convertible into economic capital, and some kinds of job (such as a business executive's personal assistant) require more than others (such as a chemical engineer) the employee's control of a widely marketable standard language variety'. In addition to cultural capital, Bourdieu refers to social capital, which is the network of long-term social contacts an individual has, and symbolic capital, which concerns the standing, reputation and status of an individual (see Giddens, 2006: 322 for a further explanation of 'capital' in Bourdieu's sense).

19.4.2 How many classes?

Before we look at a particular scheme of social stratification, I will consider the subjective side of social class – the perception of class that we share as members of our society.

In many parts of the Western world, there is only a weak 'discourse' of class. In the Scandinavian countries, a viewpoint held by the majority of the population is that their societies are not divided by 'class', and hence do not exhibit sharp differences in wealth and lifestyle. As early as the 1950s, the British sociologist John Barnes discovered an 'egalitarian dogma' in Norway which meant that people regarded almost everybody else as being of the same class, despite differences in 'income, upbringing, interests and occupation' (Barnes, 1954: 47). In Canada, a study argued that '[m]ore than 85 per cent of the population is…middle-class, sharing to a greater or lesser extent their values, aspirations, living standards, and…speech standards' (Chambers, 1991: 90), and, according to Chambers, this is made possible by 'social egalitarianism and freedom of movement and social mobility on a scale unknown in the colonizing nations' (Chambers, 1991: 90). In the United States, the main cleavage is felt to be race, and not class (Milroy, 1997; 2000), no doubt reflecting the fact that African Americans and other minority ethnic groups are over-represented among the less privileged.

By contrast, in Britain, a survey found that 36 per cent of adults considered themselves 'middle class', while 46 per cent viewed themselves as 'working class', reflecting a relatively polarized view (Argyle, 1994: 4, citing Reid,

ADVANCES BOX 19.1

Gender and class

Until the 1980s, research on stratification was 'gender blind' (Giddens, 2006: 324), i.e., 'it was written as though women did not exist, or...for the purposes of analysing divisions of power, wealth and prestige...were unimportant ...' (Giddens, 2006: 324). This was because they were simply seen as economically dependent on their husbands (ibid.). With the huge increase in women's participation in the economy, Giddens sees this position as untenable, and modern stratification schemes now include the main breadwinner in a household or a combination of both breadwinners. I would add that the position also fails to take into account how women and men may evaluate prestige and hierarchy in different ways – a point which chimes with Marshall's comment at the bottom of this page, and which is not addressed by any purely socio-economic classification scheme. This issue is crucial to the discussion of language and class, because it affects how we interpret the fact that men and women within a single class grouping differ in their language use (see Milroy and Gordon, 2003: 101–3).

A possible explanation for these linguistic differences lies in differences in cultural, social and symbolic capital between working-class women and men (see Section 19.4.1 for an explanation of these forms of capital). Skeggs (1997; cited in Giddens, 2006: 323) describes how women from this class find they have less of these non-economic forms of capital, as well as less economic capital, than men. This led them to be reluctant to label themselves as working class, because of a fear of jibes about 'white stilettos', 'Sharons' and 'Traceys'. Working-class men, on the other hand, can, according to Skeggs, achieve positive identities by, for example, being active in the trade union movement. The women in Skeggs's study claimed they were not working class, and that class was marginal in their lives. Yet the way they distanced themselves from 'class' was, she writes, central to their lives, and this actually ensured that class was important. As we shall see below, women use slightly more 'standard' or 'prestige' features than men in their own social class grouping. It seems probable that part of working-class women's striving to dissociate themselves from the working class lies in their adoption of language features characteristic of a higher class. Gender and language are discussed further in Chapter 26.

1989; cited in Macaulay, 2005: 36). Thus, it is not surprising that these terms ('middle class' and 'working class') are routinely used without explanation by the media. Their ability to do so is doubtless grounded in what Cannadine (1998: 161) calls 'the language of class', which is employed by lay people, politicians and social commentators alike. It is doubtless this which gives rise to the survey statistics, rather than any objective socio-economic differences between Britain and other Western countries. It is arguably a matter of perception, an ideology – an interpretation supported by the fact that 'the "class consciousness" of the majority of people is characterized by its complexity, ambivalence and occasional contradictions. It does not reflect a rigorously consistent interpretation of the world' (Cannadine, quoting Marshall et al. 1988: 187).

19.4.3   Inequality and mobility

Giddens states that, '[a]lthough the traditional hold of class is most certainly weakening in some ways, particularly in terms of people's identities, class divisions remain at the heart of core economic inequalities in modern societies' (2006: 333). Although class-based culture exists, in terms of values, tastes and 'ways of doing things', it is misleading to say that these are simply 'different' without recognizing the inequality which gives rise to them. Similarly, a functional model of society, where the classes slot into their pre-allocated places, cannot easily accommodate the potential for conflict which exists wherever there is inequality. Sociolinguists have been able to use these insights in their interpretation of linguistic differences, as we shall see.

It follows from both the notion of 'hierarchy' (with a 'top' and a 'bottom'), as well as from the more conflictual view of class, that individuals will strive to 'better' themselves by moving 'up' the class ladder. This is known as (upward) social mobility, which is a feature of all class societies. Such mobility can be **intergenerational**, where a second generation is of a higher class than the first. **Intragenerational** mobility refers to mobility within an individual's lifetime. (See Giddens, 2006: 327–31 for further discussion.) Social mobility potentially leads to a sense of conflict or 'dissonance' within the individual, who sees a contradiction between her former lifestyle and culture and her present one, or senses this between her parents and herself. Linguistically, the effect is obvious and sometimes uncomfortable: with social mobility, many English speakers, particularly in the United Kingdom, feel the need to change their accent, and in doing so they may feel they are betraying their roots. Yet, for many, other people's negative attitudes are too high a price to pay for keeping their working-class accent, and the effort of acquiring another accent reaps sufficient rewards.

19.4.4   A hierarchical model of class: The 2001 UK Socio-Economic Classification

Since the beginning of the last century, governments have published lists of occupations ranked according to either assumed status or position within the socio-economic system – or a combination. In the United Kingdom, the first was the Registrar General's Social Classes (1913). In Canada, a system has been developed combining a subjective ranking of 320 occupations with the income and educational level of typical people in that occupation (see Chambers, 2003: 47–8). In 2001, the UK government introduced the scheme in Table 19.1. The scheme combines 'different labour market situations and work situations' (Office for National Statistics, 2001) in terms of income and security. Unlike the Canadian scheme, it does not include a subjective evaluation element, although it probably corresponds quite closely to British people's perceptions of the matter.

Sociolinguists investigating social class differences use schemes similar to this, though usually with the addition of education and 'status' factors such as housing type or neighbourhood.

ILLUSTRATION BOX 19.3

Attitudes to working-class accents

Former British Home Secretary John Reid, who speaks with a Glasgow accent, once said in an interview: 'If you're a PhD with a middle-class accent, you're an intellectual; and if you're a PhD from Glasgow with a working-class accent, then you're a thug' (http://www.guardian.co.uk/politics/2006/sep/23/labour. uk, accessed 12/2/08). Here, Reid, as a 'powerful' figure, is using the supposed perception of Glaswegians with working-class accents as 'thugs' to his own advantage, by creating a 'tough' image for himself.

However, for the less powerful, this is often not an option. A 2007 survey by the insurance company Combined Insurance found a high proportion of British parents believing that children should be discouraged from speaking with regional accents:

- 'One in two British parents (51 per cent) discourage their children to speak [*sic*] with their regional accent because they fear it will go against them in later life…
- In fact, one in three British parents (33 per cent) are actually encouraging their children to speak the Queen's English in favour of their local dialect.
- Over one in four (27 per cent) parents living in the West Country are worried that their child might be teased and bullied in their future job for having a local accent. They also thought that by having a local accent their child may be considered to be not very bright (26 per cent).'

There were strong regional variations:

- 'In contrast, only 3 per cent of people living in Lancashire think their child might be bullied or teased by workmates due to their accent, and only one in 20 (5 per cent) of East Anglian parents think their child would be viewed as not very bright because of their local accent.'

(quotes taken from http://www.combinedinsurance.co.uk/
regional_accents.html, accessed 12/2/08)

This survey shows the persistence of negative attitudes to working-class accents and people's anxiety that they might inhibit social mobility. The regional differences may reflect a stronger sense of local identity in northern England than in the south. The northern identity tends to be constructed in opposition to the south, and also as a working-class identity. This is shown by Joan Beal's analysis of 'Word for Northerners' (Beal, 2006: 16–26), a spoof advertisement for a supposed new version of the popular word-processing package. Commands are 'translated' into Yorkshire dialect and peppered with obscenities, while the surrounding text makes much of the putative working-class culture of the north.

The National Statistics Socio-Economic Classification Analytic Classes (Office for National Statistics, 2001)

Table 19.1

1   Higher managerial and professional occupations
    1.1   Large employers and higher managerial occupations
    1.2   Higher professional occupations
2   Lower managerial and professional occupations
3   Intermediate occupations
4   Small employers and own account workers
5   Lower supervisory and technical occupations
6   Semi-routine occupations
7   Routine occupations
8   Never worked and long-term unemployed

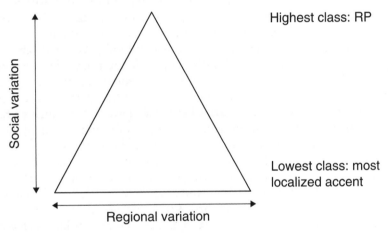

Social and regional accent variation (Trudgill 2000: 32)

FIGURE 19.1

19.4.5   Trudgill's model of social class and language variation in Great Britain

An influential conceptualization of the relationship between regional and social variation in British English is that of Peter Trudgill (2000, but first proposed in the first, 1974 edition). It is shown in Figure 19.1, which represents variation in phonetics (a similar diagram exists for grammatical variation).

It recognizes the fact that the amount of regional variation in English is much greater among people of lower social status than higher. This means that it is possible to tell more precisely where someone comes from if they are working class rather than middle class. It also shows that people in the middle of the hierarchy sound more alike across the country than do people at the bottom. Turning to people at the very top, we see that many of them speak a variety which, by definition, shows no regional variation at all: Received Pronunciation (RP). In Chapter 12, we look more closely at RP and Standard English.

Trudgill's model works poorly in other English-speaking countries, notably Australia and New Zealand where there is little regional differentiation, class differentiation being relatively more prominent (Gramley and Pätzold 1992: 396, 405). This is true also of those parts of Canada and the United States where European settlement has been relatively recent, say, from the middle of the nineteenth century. Areas along the eastern and southern seaboard, from Newfoundland to Texas, were settled earlier and show much more regional variation in working-class speech, partly reflecting differences among the original English-speaking settlers, but also differences which have arisen in the mean time (see, for example, Wolfram and Schilling-Estes, 1998: 105).

19.5   Language and the social class hierarchy

The founder of systematic studies of language and class is William Labov (1927–). Here I present an example from the work of the first British linguist to adopt Labov's methods, Peter Trudgill (1943–). Trudgill (1974) obtained a random sample of 60 inhabitants of Norwich, dividing them up into social class groups based on a composite score combining occupational status, income, education, locality and housing type. He interviewed these people in different **styles**, from formal to informal, and calculated frequency indexes for the particular features he was investigating. One of these is /t/ between vowels, which as we have seen varies between [t] and [ʔ] in much of Britain. In Norwich, there is an intermediate form, combining [t] and [ʔ], which Trudgill gives an intermediate score. Figure 19.2 shows the score for this feature, where 0 = full use of [t] and 200 = full use of [ʔ]. The classes are: Lower Working Class (LWC), Middle Working Class (MWC), Upper Working Class (UWC), Lower Middle Class (LMC) and Middle Middle Class (MMC), while the styles (along the bottom axis) are Word List, Reading Passage, Formal and Casual Styles. As can clearly be seen, the classes are ranked perfectly, and each class also increases its use of [ʔ] with increasing informality. This is an extremely strong vindication of the decision to use this hierarchical model.

However, many sociolinguists see social class differentiation from the perspective of a conflict model. Milroy and Gordon (2003: 96) point to

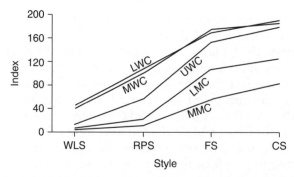

FIGURE 19.2   *The variable (t) by class and style in Norwich (Trudgill, 1974: 96; see text for explanation)*

studies which show **bipolar variation**, for example, in the speech of villagers on a plantation in Guyana, where a social divide is reflected linguistically (Rickford, 1986). It is apparent, too, that a gradient (gradual) scale of variation in one part of the language – typically phonetics, at least in English – is not matched by gradience in another, say, the grammar. This turned out to be the case in a comparative study of two medium-sized towns in the south of England, Reading (an old, well-established town) and Milton Keynes (a new town dating from 1967) (Cheshire, Kerswill and Williams, 2005; Kerswill and Williams, 2000a, b, 2005). Adolescents were selected from schools whose catchments were either mostly working class or mostly middle class. Figure 19.3 shows the scores for the use of the glottal stop [ʔ] for /t/ between vowels as in *letter*, the use of [f] for 'th' as in *thin*, and [v] for 'th' as in *brother*.

The 'middle class' use considerably less of the non-standard forms than do the 'working class'. This effect is much stronger in the old town of Reading, where polarization exists in a way not found in the socially fluid new town: the two classes show extreme divergence. However, even in Milton Keynes it turns out that there is an almost categorical class divide in the use of non-

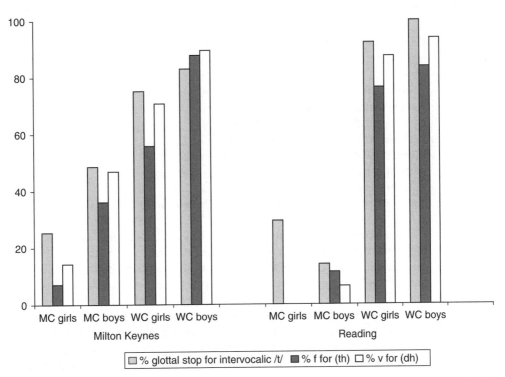

FIGURE 19.3   Percent use of non-standard forms of three consonantal variables among adolescents in Milton Keynes and Reading (adapted from Cheshire et al. 2005: 146)

Key: MC = middle class, WC = working class

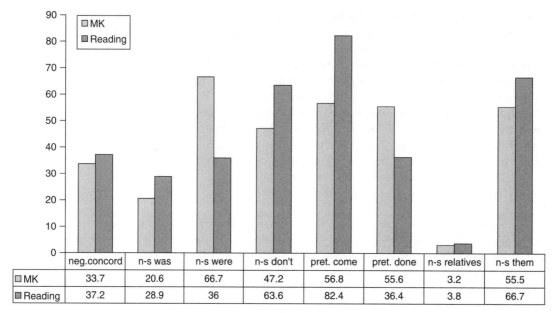

	neg.concord	n-s was	n-s were	n-s don't	pret. come	pret. done	n-s relatives	n-s them
☐ MK	33.7	20.6	66.7	47.2	56.8	55.6	3.2	55.5
■ Reading	37.2	28.9	36	63.6	82.4	36.4	3.8	66.7

FIGURE 19.4   Non-standard grammatical features used by working-class adolescents in Milton Keynes and Reading (per cent) (from Kerswill and Williams, 2005: 1041)

standard grammatical features. Figure 19.4 shows the use of the following eight variables:

negative concord – e.g., *I don't want none*
non-standard *was* – e.g., *we was*
non-standard *were* – e.g., *she weren't*
non-standard *don't* – e.g., *he don't*
preterite *come* – e.g., *he come here yesterday*
preterite *done* – e.g., *we done that yesterday*
non-standard relatives – e.g., *the man what we saw*
non-standard *them* – e.g., *look at them houses*

The figure shows that neither town has the 'advantage' over the other, and that working-class speakers in both use the features frequently. However, in the middle-class speakers the usage was so rare as to be negligible. We interpreted this result as showing that, despite the more 'standard' phonologies of the Milton Keynes working-class adolescents and the highly mobile society in which they lived, there was still a powerful class awareness, with strongly negative views expressed about 'posh' people (Kerswill and Williams, 1997, 2000b: 11). Polarization, and with it a Marxian social analysis, can apparently live alongside what appears to be a more hierarchical structure.

19.6   Social class differences in discourse

Since the late 1950s, a parallel track within sociolinguistics has investigated social differences in the way talk is organized. The most prominent figure is

Basil Bernstein (1924–2000), who in 1958 suggested that educational failure among working-class (WC) children may be due to their use of what Bernstein later called a 'restricted code'. Bernstein's main contention is that, because of supposedly 'relational' family structures where roles are implicit rather than negotiated, WC children use a much more implicit type of language, lacking in adjectives and adverbs, using stereotyped phrases, not clearly differentiating cause and effect, using commands and questions, and using 'sympathetic circularity' shown by phrases like 'It's only natural, isn't it?' (Bernstein, 1971, cited in Macaulay, 2005: 41). Middle-class (MC) children can use an 'elaborated code', which does not contain the implied deficiencies of the restricted code. (The characteristics of the codes are cited in full in Macaulay, 2005: 41 and usefully paraphrased in Stockwell, 2002: 56.) Bernstein has been roundly criticized, not least because of the 'deficit' that his theory implies, but also because of the weak empirical basis for it (Macaulay, 2005: 40–4; Montgomery, 1995: 134–46).

Is there any evidence for Bernstein's contention? Wodak (1996: 116–20) used the technique of oral retelling of news stories as a means to find out. She found that MC people would focus on accuracy, backgrounding their own stance, while WC people often incorporated the news report into their own world-view, with comments like 'You can't do anything about it anyway'. Wodak (1996: 119) found statistically significant class effects, but no sex or age effects. She attributes this to the MC speakers' years of socialization, through schooling, into producing 'oversophisticated', fact-orientated summaries, rather than the more 'natural' mode of telling narratives used by the working-class respondents. These differences are consistent with Bernstein's view, and have the potential to lead to discrimination.

While some experimental studies (e.g., Bedisti 2004) have supported some of Bernstein's claims, other studies have tended to disconfirm them, and the trend now is to look beyond them and focus instead on class differences in how conversations are managed, doing away with any 'deficit' notion, while focusing also on the way gender interacts with class. Macaulay (2002) indeed finds a much greater use of adverbs by MC speakers – as Bernstein predicts – but fails to find any evidence that they are being used to make reference more explicit. Instead, they use them 'to make emphatic statements, making quite clear their opinions and their attitudes' (Macaulay, 2002: 415). This appears to contradict Wodak's finding that it is WC speakers who relate events to their own world-view. However, Macaulay's MC subjects are being speaker- (i.e., self-) oriented, wanting to make their opinions clear. Wodak's WC speakers appear, from the transcripts, to be struggling to reconstruct the gist of what they have heard by relating it to their own experience, rather than reproducing the story in a disinterested way in a manner they are not trained to do.

19.7 Conclusion

Western societies are characterized by structured inequality expressed through a class system which is both hierarchical (functional) and potentially conflictual. In language use, we find both grading by social class and also a tendency for differences to be polarized. Class interacts with gender, and men's and women's usages differ in systematic ways even within a class. Language use, both in terms of features (like consonants) which we can count and those (especially discourse features) which we cannot, proves to be extremely sensitive to class differences. Language use therefore has the power to tell us about social structures themselves.

Recommended readings

Certainly the most accessible and up to date account of social class is to be found in Giddens (2006). Although he makes no mention of language, a great deal of what he writes can be related to it. So far, the only single-chapter account of social class in sociolinguistics is by Ash (2002), though this is limited to the so-called **variationist** work of Labov and others, mainly in the United States. Chapter 2 of Chambers (2003) covers similar ground. Pages 40–8 and 95–103 in Milroy and Gordon (2003) provide a more advanced discussion. Wolfram and Schilling-Estes (1998) have a good section on language and class in the United States.

Note

1 This chapter is substantially modified from Kerswill (2007a).

CHAPTER 20

Language and Ethnicity

ARFAAN KHAN[1]

20.1 Ethnicity: definitions and perspectives

Both language and ethnicity play a central role in society, as well as in individual lives. As we can see from almost every chapter in this book, language is a crucial factor in the way societies are organized, relating as it does to almost all our everyday activities. As with both gender and social class, ethnicity influences the way people behave. It, too, just like gender and social class, serves as something around which we can form our own identities. When both language and ethnicity play such central roles in our social lives and the ways in which we interact with others, it is no surprise that language and ethnicity should be related in some way. As will become clear in this chapter, language and ethnicity certainly are related; as a matter of fact, they are so closely related for some people that language does not simply reflect their ethnic identity, but is that ethnic identity. It is therefore inevitable that the subject of the relationship between language and ethnicity should on occasion generate heated debate, and that it will continue to do so.

Before we go on to explore this relationship, let us define what is meant by **ethnicity**. Firstly, ethnicity is not the same as race: two white men, although sharing the same race, can have different ethnic identities, as can two black women or any other pairing that may share similar phenotype (physiological) features. So it is not simply a question of biology, although biology may play an important part in our understanding of our own ethnic identity. Ethnicity has proved difficult to define because people (both lay and academic) tend to give different factors greater importance in its definition; this can result in a rather broad, all-encompassing conceptualization of ethnicity: physiology, psychology, geography, religion, culture and language have all been listed as factors defining an **ethnic group**. In his survey of 27 definitions of ethnic group, Isajiw (1974: 117) found that they made reference to the following common features:

(a)   a common national or geographical origin or common ancestors;
(b)   similar culture or customs;
(c)   shared religion;
(d)   similar race or physical features;
(e)   language;

(f) consciousness of kind or 'we feeling', a sense of loyalty to the peoplehood;
(g) a sense of community;
(h) common values or 'ethos';
(i) involvement in a set of institutions separate from the larger political society;
(j) minority status, subordinate status, or dominant status;
(k) ethnic group often cited as an immigrant group.

It is generally agreed that an ethnic group is a collection of individuals who have in common one or more of the above listed factors (e.g., Barth, 1969: 10–11; Rampton 2005: 285). However – and this is where it becomes controversial – which of the listed factors is indispensable to one's ethnic identity and which are incidental? This question gives rise to another equally contentious question: is one's ethnicity inherited and unchanging, or is it a particular type of response to certain situations in which we find ourselves? Of course, there is no single answer to either of these questions, which is why they are so contentious and continue to give rise to passionate debate. Whereas some will feel language is indispensable to one's ethnic identity, others will see it as incidental and claim religion is **the** defining factor. In response to the second question, some believe that one's ethnic identity is inherited from one's parents; thus, one has an ethnic identity prior to coming into the world, before acquiring a specific language or adopting certain socio-cultural behavioural norms. These social norms, or ways of doing things, are seen as simply reflecting one's ethnicity, which is not only unchanging, but has always been there. So, therefore, even in the absence of these outward manifestations, one's ethnicity will always be there and it will remain the same. The inheritance of an ethnic identity need not be biological, but simply

---

ILLUSTRATION BOX 20.1

Essentialism

Hewitt (1986) found that at a time when Caribbean identity was being promoted and celebrated among black Britons of Caribbean descent, black British teenagers made considerable use of symbolic resources to signal their ethnic identity, and language was one such resource. However, they also vigorously objected to the use of these ethnic symbols by their white peers, as illustrated in the quotation below. These teenagers had an idea of ethnicity which was **essentialist** in its conceptualization, as something that **is inherited** and **not adopted**. This was expressed by one of the young people Hewitt recorded as follows:

> But the point is no matter if they speak fluent Jamaican and they dress as well as us, they're never gonna be what they wanna be. No way.
> (Hewitt, 1986: 208–9)

ILLUSTRATION BOX 20.2

Constructivism

The incident described below illustrates how on the basis of an individual's linguistic and non-linguistic behaviour he is categorized into a contrasting ethnic group by others with similar phenotype features and ancestry as his own. It provides an extreme example of the constructivists' argument that ethnic identity is the result of behaviour in relation to other actors in particular contexts:

> One Afro-American Peace Corps volunteer was quite hurt to learn that the Sierra Leoneans referred to him as *oyimbo*, 'white man', not because of his appearance but because of his language and behaviour.
>
> (Hancock, 1974, cited in Giles, 1977: 2)

---

the belief that there is a timeless link between you and your (imagined) ancestors (Geertz, 1996: 41–2). This particular view of ethnicity is referred to as **essentialism** (Joseph, 2004: 83–4).

In an opposing view, it is argued that ethnic identity is neither innate nor unchanging (Giddens, 2001: 247). Instead, it is argued that individuals acquire their ethnic identities through their participation in society. So, from this perspective, and unlike from the **essentialist** viewpoint, an individual does not have an ethnic identity prior to his/her coming into the world. Rather, depending on the circumstances, individuals may adopt or construct their ethnic identities through the use of particular ethnic symbols, such as the use of certain types of accents or clothing. The central tenet of this view, which is referred to as **constructivism** (Joseph, 2004: 83–4), is that individuals will construct, emphasize, adjust and erase ethnic group boundaries in response to their needs and the particular social circumstances in which they find themselves. Harris and Rampton refer to this as the 'roUtes' as opposed to the 'roOts' conception of ethnicity:

> Instead, in this 'strategic' view, ethnicity is viewed more as a relatively flexible resource that individuals and groups use in the negotiation of social boundaries, aligning themselves with some people and institutions, dissociating from others, and this is sometimes described as the 'roUtes' rather than a 'roOts' conception of ethnicity.
>
> (2003: 5)

However, there is a paradox: cultural globalization and greater inter-cultural contact can not only give rise to the opportunity to construct new identities, but they can, as was shown in Illustration Box 20.1, also encourage the resurgence of traditional identities, and thus **ethnic essentialism**:

> The globalization of late modernity is destabilizing traditions and bringing people into greater contact with cultural differences. The meeting of

---

ADVANCES BOX 20.1

A post-modern perspective

A number of sociologists (Hall, 1988; Back, 1996, 2003; Bilton et al., 2002; Harris and Rampton, 2003) have noted the emergence of what they refer to as **hybrid identities** or **new ethnicities**. These are multi-dimensional identities that have as their reference local and global groups/cultures. They are the result of the extensive contact, cultural diffusion and shared experiences characteristic of the modern world. A post-modernist view of the world is one that is characterized by instability and diversity. However, rather than lament the uncertainty of our condition in the modern world, post-modern theorists argue that humans should celebrate the freedom of choice and 'the triumph of style' this offers, which extends to social identity:

> According to this view the pace of change in the (post) modern world, together with an ever-expanding array of choices and possibilities, creates conditions in which individuals are increasingly freed to make multiple identity choices which match the purpose (or even the whims) of the moment.
>
> (Mason, 2000: 144)

A number of writers are critical of such post-modern theories of identity, particularly when applied to ethnicity (Modood, Beishon and Virdee, 1994; Mason, 2000; Nazroo and Karlsen, 2003). They argue that ethnic identities are not 'simply clothes on a shop peg that can be tried on by the same person one after the other, or mixed and matched with varied accessories' (Modood, Beishon and Virdee, 1994: 6–7). As ethnic identity is felt to be 'grounded' in shared social histories, material relations and cultural experiences (Fenton, 2003: 194–5), this places constraints on the ethnic identities one can lay claim to.

---

ethnicities is generating hybrid cultural forms, but, paradoxically, it is also lending urgency to the reassertion of absolute, unchanging ethnic identities.

(Bilton et al., 2002: 189)

20.2 Ethnolinguistic differences and language variation

Language played a central role in one of the earliest records of human genocide; it was the primary criterion for a group's identity and ultimately each individual's fate. In the Old Testament, *Judges* (12: 6) tells of the conflict between the Semitic tribes of Gilead and Ephraim and how the pronunciation of a single word decided each man's fate:

4 Then Jephthah gathered together all the men of Gilead, and fought with Ephraim: and the men of Gilead smote Ephraim, because they said, Ye Gileadites are fugitives of Ephraim among the Ephraimites, and among the Manassites.

5 And the Gileadites took the passages of the Jordan before the Ephraimites: and it was so, that when those Ephraimites which were escaped said, Let me go over; that the men of Gilead said unto him, Art thou an Ephraimite? If he said, Nay;

6 Then said they unto him, Say now Shibboleth: and he said Sibboleth: for he could not frame to pronounce it right. Then they took him, and slew him at the passages of Jordan: and there fell at that time of the Ephraimites forty and two thousand.

Language is a particularly effective marker, or a way of signalling, social identity. A language can be used to construct, demarcate and maintain ethnic boundaries. The maintenance of linguistic differences is a means of maintaining and signalling ethnic distinctiveness. If speakers do not have a specific language by which to signal their ethnic distinctiveness, then a dialect or a particular variety of a language can just as successfully signal ethnic identity. Where more than one language is spoken, or there are dialects which differ considerably from the standard form of the language, choosing a particular language or dialect can be a very effective means of self-representation (Bucholtz, 1995: 357). The use of linguistic features (e.g., a particular pronunciation) can successfully signal the level of differentiation from and integration with other ethnic groups (Giles, 1979: 267). It is no surprise therefore that, during periods of inter-ethnic tension or conflict, language is given greater importance in the social life of the group. The fact that stigmatized languages and dialects are maintained by particular ethnic groups is indicative of their importance as symbols of group identity, solidarity and shared values (Giles, 1979: 261; Milroy, 1982: 210). For example, despite the fact that it has been disparaged by certain groups, African-American English has played a central role in the African-American community's struggle for civil rights and the promotion of their ethnic identity (see Smitherman, 1986).

Why is language so central to ethnic identity, or felt to be so? Nash (1996: 26) notes that language has far more 'social and psychological weight' than other symbolic phenomena, such as the way people dress. He goes on to explain that one reason for this is that 'Successful mastery of language implies learning it from birth, in the context of the kinship or primary group.' Clearly, the idea that a language is something associated with a kinship group, with all the obligations and shared values this entails, would explain some of the reasons why language can be such an emotive topic. However, for many people language does not simply **signal an association** with a particular group, but it actually **is** that group. As Fishman (1977: 19) notes, it is because language is viewed as a 'biological inheritance', acquired along with the parents' genes, that its association with ethnic inheritance can be so compelling. A language can provide a link with one's ancestors and therefore a sense of belonging. This is one of the reasons why once dead languages such as Hebrew or those languages that have been in decline such as Welsh have been successfully reintroduced or revitalized. It is also the reason why, despite the suppression of their cultures, such as the use of their language, music and dress in public, certain ethnic minority groups have taken considerable risks to preserve these symbols of their identities.

Ethnolinguistic variation, whereby linguistic differences correspond to speakers' ethnic differences, can take a number of forms, including the use of different languages, different linguistic forms and/or different frequencies of the same feature in the same language (see Fought, 2002). Ethnic differences in discourse structure have also been the focus of research (e.g., Reisigl and Wodak, 2001). The most obvious difference is when the ethnic boundary corresponds with a language boundary, in other words, the ethnic groups speak different languages. For example, at a very general level the Russians speak Russian and the Japanese speak Japanese. But within a particular country, one also finds different ethnic groups speaking different languages. This situation is common in many parts of the world. In Western countries, it is most evident in cities (e.g., London) where various immigrant communities have settled. Within these multi-ethnic cities, as well as speaking the dominant language, for example, English in England and Swahili in East Africa, the minority groups may have also preserved the ethnic minority language for practical and/or cultural reasons (e.g., Fishman, 1977; Romaine, 1989).

Code-switching, which occurs when speakers switch from one language to another in the same conversation, is one way in which languages can be effectively used to signal ethnic identity, reaffirm social bonds and even

---

ILLUSTRATION BOX 20.3

Code-switching

In the following extract, the female speakers, who are British Pakistanis, are talking about relations between the sexes. Speaker A switches from English to Urdu for the word 'honour' (*izut*). The concept of 'honour' is of considerable importance within the ethnic group to which the speakers belongs. The purpose of the switch is to signal the common ethnic identity she, speaker B and the interviewer share and therefore their (assumed) shared social values. It is of interest to note that the interviewer gave no indication that he and speaker A spoke the same language; this was inferred by the speaker from the interviewer's ethnicity.

(Participants: Interviewer, male, 28; Speaker A, female, 16; Speaker B, female 16)
A: She didn't want to go
B: I don't understand why she [ ]
A: Guess what I heard her mom
B: That she was gonna mess up with guys and like
A: yeah yeah yeah
INTERVIEWER: Really?
B: Because I heard that she used to talk about guys and that as well, but it's like we're not that stupid, us girls we all talk about guys...but come on like us girls like we know the limit to it we know how far to go
A: And we know not to mess with our *izut* (/ɪzʌt/)

appeal to ethnic group obligations. As illustrated above, language can be such an efficient marker of ethnic group identity that in some cases a single word from the relevant language can communicate a shared history, moral code and a set of cultural norms.

It may also be the case that where the different ethnic groups speak the same language, one of the groups may use linguistic features not used by the other group. This situation may or may not be due to the influence of an additional language (usually the language used by that ethnic group as a home language, or used by the group at an earlier time or else, in the case of a migrant group, in their place of origin). Where an additional language is involved, the unique features may be traced to that language. There are many examples of this: the influence of South Asian languages on the English spoken by certain British Asians (Khan, 2006), the influence of Spanish on the Chicano English spoken by Latinos in the United States (e.g., Wald, 1984) and the influence of African languages on the development of African-American Vernacular English (Mufwene et al., 1998; Rickford, 1999). It is also possible for an ethnic group to distinguish itself from other ethnic groups with which it shares certain linguistic features by the frequency with which they are used. A study of a tri-ethnic community in the United States (Wolfram and Dannenberg, 1999), consisting of Lumbee Indians (Native Americans), African Americans and European Americans, found that not only were the Lumbee Indians using linguistic features not used by the other two ethnic groups (e.g., the use of *were* where *was* occurs in Standard English), but the features they shared with the African Americans, such as the lack of post-vocalic *r* (e.g., in *card*), were being used with significantly different frequencies (Schilling-Estes, 2004).

It is possible for an ethnic group to exhibit all the ethnolinguistic variation types mentioned above, or to switch between these. If a community is undergoing language shift, whereby a community drops one language in favour of another as the primary means of communication (Mesthrie et al., 2000: 253), one type of ethnolinguistic variation may be replaced with another. Individuals from the Cajun community of Louisiana (Dubois and Horvath, 1998), which is undergoing language shift from French to English, have switched from signalling their ethnic identity by using their ancestral language (Cajun French) to signalling it with the use of ethnic forms (in this case, pronunciations) in their spoken English.

When discussing ethnolinguistic variation, a distinction must be made between influence and interference, as the former, unlike the latter, may be intentional. Giles (1979: 260) warns that the use of non-standard linguistic features in the dominant language should not be mistaken for language interference as they may be deliberately employed to signal ethnic identity. Joseph (2004: 192) makes a similar point, arguing that accented speech or minority features may not necessarily be due to a failure to assimilate or acquire a language, but a form of linguistic resistance to dominant groups in society. In many cases the use of Jamaican Creole features by certain British Black adolescents can be seen as the intentional projection and celebration of a Black identity (Edwards, 1986: 55; 1997: 411), thus highlighting the socially purposeful nature of language use and language variation in particular.

20.3 Ethnolects: emergence, maintenance, variation and change

An **ethnolect** is a variety of a language which is associated with a particular ethnic group, such as African-American Vernacular English. An ethnolect may differ from other varieties of the language in one or more ways (in phonetics, grammar and vocabulary). Like other language varieties, the emergence, change and use of an ethnolect have identifiable underlying social causes. In this section, I will outline a number of these social factors.

20.3.1 The Labovian framework

William Labov is an American linguist who has demonstrated that there are highly systematic links between social factors such as class, ethnicity and gender and what he terms **language variation**: the way in which a single language, such as English, varies (particularly) in its phonetics and grammar (Labov, 1966, 1972a). He has focused very strongly on language change, showing how particular social groups initiate a change before it spreads to other social groups. He also points out that individuals reflect in their speech those social categories that have been particularly formative in their social development and hence their linguistic behaviour (Labov, 2001: 34). For a better understanding of linguistic variation within a particular community, one must therefore look closely at its social structure.

A number of studies have examined ethnicity-based linguistic variation (e.g., Labov, 1966, 2001; Laferriere, 1979; Wolfram and Dannenberg, 1999; McCafferty, 2001; Kerswill, Torgersen and Fox, 2008; Cheshire et al., 2008a, b). Khan (2006) is a study of language variation among three ethnic groups in Birmingham, England – those of Pakistani, West Indian and white British descent. The study explored, from a linguistic aspect, the interaction of ethnicity with other social factors such as age, sex, social network and attitude towards identity. It attempted to show how the interaction between these social factors influenced adolescents' use of language and accounted for linguistic variation in the city. I will use data from this study to illustrate the types of relationships between language and ethnicity.

20.3.2 Social network framework

The concept of **social network**, which has its origins in social anthropology (see Haralambos and Holborn, 1995: 359–60), has been employed by sociolinguists in their analyses of linguistic variation (e.g., Labov, 1972b; Milroy, 1987; Lippi-Green, 1989; Edwards, 1992). An individual's social network is 'the aggregate of relationships contracted with others ...' (Milroy, 2002: 549). The social network framework in sociolinguistics postulates a close correspondence between a speaker's social network structure and his/her linguistic behaviour. The type of people in one's social network and the strength of the ties with these people can have an influence on an individual's language. Close-knit networks, where the individuals in the network know each other, and a network containing individuals of similar social background,

ILLUSTRATION BOX 20.4

Ethnolinguistic variation among adolescents in Birmingham

Figure 20.1 shows the different realizations of the PRICE vowel by male and female adolescents from three ethnic groups in Birmingham – 'Pakistani', 'Caribbean' and 'English'. The chart shows a number of differences among the groups in their pronunciation of the PRICE vowel. Firstly, only the English informants make any noticeable use of the traditional Birmingham pronunciation [ɔɪ] (similar to the vowel sound in RP *boy*). This suggests that this is a pronunciation which, though not specific to the English group, is far more prevalent among the local English population than among the other ethnic groups. Secondly, although all the ethnic groups and both sexes make use of the local form [ɑɪ] (a sound between RP *buy* and RP *boy*), the Pakistani and Caribbean groups show a stronger preference for [aɪ] (similar to the vowel sound in RP *buy*).

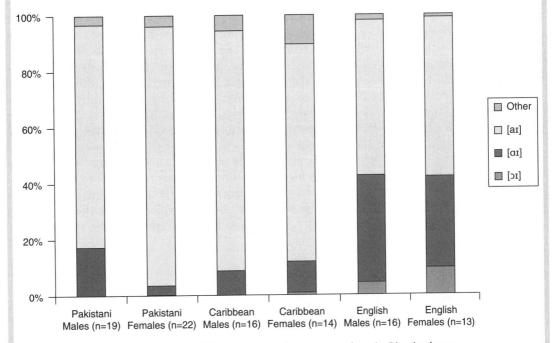

FIGURE 20.1 *Percentage of PRICE forms for adolescent speakers in Birmingham*

help maintain the group's language (Milroy, 2002: 550). Conversely, a weakening of the ties and an increase in the social diversity of the network will facilitate language change. Individuals with weak ties are able to introduce linguistic innovations from one group to another (Milroy, 2002: 563; also see Milroy and Milroy, 1997).

One of the reasons why African American Vernacular English has remained a distinct variety of American English is because of the residential segregation of the African-American and European-American communities (Graff, Labov and Harris, 1986; Labov and Harris, 1986; Bailey and Maynor, 1987, 1989). As residential segregation prevents extensive face-to-face interaction between groups, this may not only maintain the existing linguistic differences, but also encourage the tendency for two language varieties whose speakers are not in contact with each other to become more different. McCafferty (2001) found a pattern of sociolinguistic variation in the city of (London)Derry, Northern Ireland, which resembles that of some American cities. Past and more recent hostilities between the Protestant and Catholic communities have resulted in the residential segregation of these two ethnic groups in many Northern Irish cities. The residential segregation of the two communities in (London)Derry is exacerbated by the 'avoidance strategies' employed by the communities, such as avoiding leisure venues frequented by the other group; such behaviour reduces even further the likelihood of face-to-face interaction (McCafferty, 2001: 85). The maintenance of segregated communities, and thus separate social networks, has repercussions for the diffusion of linguistic features between the groups. Whereas the Protestant inhabitants are introducing linguistic innovations (particularly vowels) into (London)Derry English from elsewhere in Northern Ireland, the diffusion of these features into the Catholic community is being hindered by the residential segregation of the two groups (McCafferty, 2001: 202–3). For example, the (London)Derry Protestant community is introducing a change in the pronunciation of the FACE vowel that is similar to the vowel sound in RP *pier*; the Catholic community makes little use of this innovation, instead showing a stronger preference for the local pronunciation (similar to RP *pit*). The fact that the (London)Derry Protestant community is introducing linguistic innovations from other parts of the country, which unlike (London)Derry have majority Protestant populations, further highlights the role of social networks in language change.

20.3.3 Social psychology framework

Theories of the **social psychology of language** postulate that an individual's social psychological orientation, that is, his/her self-identification in relation to the interlocutor and/or wider community, is an important factor underlying linguistic behaviour, and thus language change/maintenance. A strong orientation towards a local/ethnic identity may encourage the maintenance of a distinctive accent, dialect or language: '… a strong sense of ethnicity or of local identity often creates and maintains localized cultural and linguistic norms and value systems that are presented and perceived as sharply opposed to the mainstream values of outsiders' (Milroy and Milroy, 1992: 6). The degree to which one identifies with a particular ethnic group will have a manifest influence on one's linguistic behaviour.

Le Page and Tabouret-Keller's (1985) concept of **acts of identity** explicitly relates the linguistic and the social psychological domains in that 'the individual creates for himself the patterns of his linguistic behaviour so as to resemble those of the group or groups with which from time to time he wishes to be identified, or so as to be unlike those from whom he wishes to

ILLUSTRATION BOX 20.5

Social network and accent maintenance in Birmingham

Figure 20.2 shows the correlation between the percentages of British White Friends (BWF) and the use of the traditional Birmingham PRICE form [ɔɪ] for the English adolescents. The graph shows that the more British White friends a speaker has, the greater his/her use of the traditional form. The results suggest that whereas a network that contains individuals who are socially similar will maintain group specific linguistic forms, for example, a certain pronunciation, a network that is socially diverse will encourage the spread of linguistic features among the groups and possibly language change in the long-term. The results suggest that a social network underlies the maintenance of the Birmingham accent and therefore it is also the driving force behind language change in the city, for the English community at least.

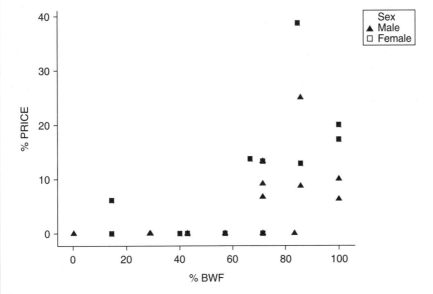

FIGURE 20.2   *Percentage of [ɔɪ] in the PRICE vowel and British white friends (BWF) for English adolescents in Birmingham*

be distinguished' and that 'we can only behave according to the behavioural patterns of groups we find it desirable to identify with to the extent that:

(i)   we can identify the groups
(ii)   we have both adequate access to the groups and ability to analyse their behavioural patterns

(iii)   the motivation to join the groups is sufficiently powerful, and is either reinforced or reversed by feedback from the groups

(iv)   we have the ability to modify our behaviour'.

(Le Page and Tabouret-Keller, 1985: 181–2)

Speakers will manifest their positive attitude towards a particular group, be it present or imagined, by sounding like members of that group (or what they imagine the group sounds like). By doing this, they can identify themselves with that group. Dubois and Horvath's (1998) study of linguistic variation in a Cajun French-English bilingual community in Louisiana, USA, is a case in point. They found that, relative to older speakers, young speakers made greater use of [t] and [d] for /θ/ and /ð/ in words such as *think* and *that* respectively. Whereas the middle-aged speakers had 14 per cent for the [t] form and 22 per cent for the [d] form, the younger speakers had 34 per cent and 43 per cent for the same forms (Dubois and Horvath, 1998: 252). If the use of these ethnic forms was simply due to the level of proficiency in the English language, then one would have expected a decrease in their frequency over the three generations investigated – not an increase, as was actually the case. Dubois and Horvath explain the young speakers' increased use of the ethnic forms as the corollary of a heightened sense of ethnic pride within the context of language shift, so that young speakers signal their social identity by employing the ethnic forms:

> For the younger generation, being Cajun has become socially and economically advantageous, and so they take pride in their Cajun identity. But because the functional load of the ancestral language has been significantly reduced to speaking French only to the people in their extended family domain, they signal their Cajun identity through English. The stops in the speech of the young group are identity markers, not accented English.
>
> (1998: 258)

Not only did the young Cajun males most frequently use the ethnic forms, but, unexpectedly, young males with open networks (i.e., comprised of individuals who are socially diverse) made greater use of the ethnic forms than young males with closed networks (i.e., comprised of individuals who are socially similar). Whereas young males with closed networks had 47 per cent for [t] and 55 per cent for [d], those with open networks had as many as 56 per cent and 87 per cent for the same forms (Dubois and Horvath, 1998: 254–6). This suggests that the males' orientation towards a Cajun ethnic identity had a far stronger influence on their linguistic behaviour than their social networks. The use of the ethnic forms seems to have been a conscious decision by the young Cajuns to signal their ethnic identity and attitude towards the local community.

20.4   Ethnic and ethnolinguistic differences in a multi-ethnic community

Throughout this chapter I have not only tried to show how and why ethnolinguistic differences persist, but have on occasion mentioned the breakdown

ILLUSTRATION BOX 20.6

Ethnic orientation and linguistic variation among British Caribbean adolescents in Birmingham

Figure 20.3 shows the relationship between the British Caribbean adolescents' choice of ethnic self-ascription labels and their realizations of the GOAT vowel. Ethnic self-ascription refers to the participants' own choice of ethnic identity, which may be expressed as a simple (e.g., Jamaican) or hybrid (e.g., Jamaican-English) identity.

The ethnic form [o:] (similar to the vowel sound in RP *gore*) is most frequently used by Caribbean informants who describe themselves as 'Jamaican' and 'Black Caribbean', while avoided or least frequently used by the 'British Black' group and the 'English' speaker. The monophthong [o:] is a pronunciation found in many Caribbean varieties of English. This suggests that the ethnic form may be avoided by speakers not strongly oriented towards a **Caribbean** identity. The 'English' speaker's greater use of the traditional Birmingham [ʌʊ] pronunciation (similar to the vowel sound in RP *gout*) suggests it functions as a marker of an **English** identity for the Caribbean informants. This can be accounted for by the fact that the traditional [ʌʊ] form is associated with the White English community in Birmingham. Furthermore, the 'British Black' group's and the 'English' speaker's relatively greater use of [əɣ] (with an offset similar to the vowel sound in RP *too*) may be indicative of an orientation towards a more inclusive **British** identity; this form has no strong association with any local ethnic group but is also found among adolescents in other British cities. Interestingly, the ethnic composition of the young Caribbean speakers' social networks had little influence on their choice of vowel pronunciation. (For a more extensive discussion of Jamaican Creole, including its role in London, see Chapter 21, Section 21.8, and Chapter 22, Section 22.5).

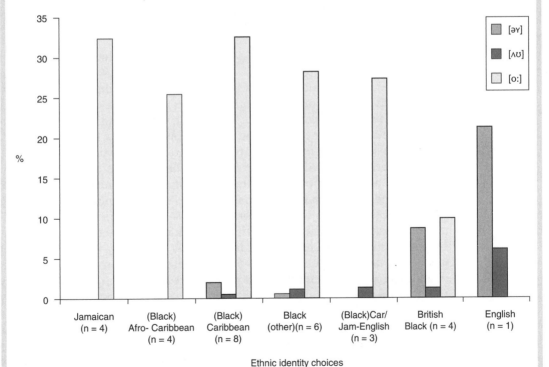

FIGURE 20.3   Percentage of forms of the GOAT vowel and Caribbean adolescents' ethnic identity choices in Birmingham

of such linguistic differences between groups. The data from the Birmingham study clearly show evidence of inter-ethnic linguistic diffusion – the passing of linguistic forms from one group to another. Whether this is temporary or permanent, it shows that the link between language and ethnicity is not static, but constantly being reinterpreted. A number of researchers have identified a variety of British English they refer to as **local multi-ethnic vernacular** (Hewitt, 1986, 2003; Back, 2003; Rampton, 2005; Cheshire et al., 2008a in press; Kerswill, Torgersen and Fox, 2008). Despite the fact that this variety draws its componential parts from a number of ethnic varieties of English, the multi-ethnic vernacular does not function as a marker of any particular ethnic group, but a certain type of British urban community:

> I have called it a 'local multi-ethnic vernacular' and also a 'community English'. The point about it is that it is the primary medium of communication in the adolescent peer group in multi-ethnic areas [in London]. It is the language of white as well as minority youth and it is the language which is switched from and back into when its users choose to move into Creole or Punjabi or whatever other minority language, yet it is itself an 'impure', mixed form. Nevertheless, there is no evidence of it having any symbolic status on its own territory. Its transparency is what actually allows its permeability by diverse communicative (i.e., including but not restricted to purely linguistic) features. Thus in being unselfconsciously the language of the streets between adolescents of all ethnicities, it strips its contributory ethnic components of any capacity for symbolic stress whilst reassembling these diverse elements, on an ad hoc day to day basis, into a truly mixed, truly 'impure' form.
>
> (Hewitt, 2003: 1923)

There is a question which is as interesting as any regarding the local multi-ethnic vernacular: why do the speakers of the local multi-ethnic vernacular still 'choose to move into Creole or Punjabi or whatever other minority language'? We can answer the question quite simply: ethnicity has been and will continue to be of great importance to humans, and linguistic means of marking it will remain. It will continue to matter because it is an aspect of people's everyday experiences. An ethnic group offers one a history and a sense of belonging in the world. This may go some way to explaining the strong attachment we have to our ancestors and the sometimes fierce response elicited by the appropriation of a group's ethnic identity. It is true that the saliency of ethnic identity for a particular group is relational, which means that it will vary depending on the types of social relationships and groupings individuals feel are important within a particular society. That said, it is equally true that there are certain constraints on the extent to which ethnic identity is negotiable.

As long as ethnicity continues to be of importance to human experience, so too will language continue to be the symbolic manifestation of ethnicity par excellence; it more than any other symbolic resource provides a sense of continuity and link with one's ancestors. Language is infused with the history of a people and keeping the memory alive requires keeping the language alive. It is no surprise, then, that even in multi-ethnic, cosmopolitan British cities a Black British teenager should object to a White British teenager's use of Creole by claiming 'It seems they are stealing our language' (Hewitt, 1986: 161). It is precisely because language is so central to the existence of humans as social beings, that it is the primary symbolic resource employed in the signalling of ethnic identity.

Recommended readings

Fought (2006) is a comprehensive introduction to the topic of language and ethnicity, with a particular focus on the ethnolinguistic situation in the United States. Rickford (1999) and other texts on African-American Vernacular English are also useful due to the amount of sociolinguistic research on this variety of English. Harris and Rampton (2003) is a useful collection of articles, including contributions from contemporary British writers, which provides an up-to-date introduction to the debates and controversies. Also relevant to the British context are Hewitt (1986), Rampton (2005) and Sebba (1993). Journals such as *Language in Society* and the *Journal of Sociolinguistics* are essential reading for current research in the field of sociolinguistics and do occasionally contain articles on language and ethnicity. Fishman (1991) may come across as esoteric and therefore a challenging read, but will ultimately be rewarding. A rather more personal, but also scholarly discussion of the relationship between language and ethnicity is provided by Joseph (2004).

Note

1 Now based at Queen Mary, University of London.

CHAPTER 21

Pidgins and Creole Englishes

MARK SEBBA

21.1 What are pidgins and creoles?

Pidgins and **creoles** (P/Cs) are new languages which come into being in situations of **language contact**, where speakers of two or more different languages need to communicate with each other on a regular or prolonged basis. Pidgins and creoles usually draw most of their common vocabulary from one specific language (called the **lexifier**), which often leads to them being named after that language; 'Pidgin English', 'Creole French' and so on. This is misleading for two reasons: firstly, there is not just one 'Pidgin English' – there are several different pidgins in different parts of the world which have English as their lexifier. Secondly, the similarity between the pidgin or creole and its lexifier is very superficial, being largely the result of shared vocabulary. In terms of their linguistic structure, both pidgins and creoles show **simplification** and **reduction** compared with their lexifiers. Thus the grammar of an English-lexicon pidgin or creole can be shown to be simpler in various ways than the grammar of English. At the same time, the pidgin or creole will have a reduced lexicon, or vocabulary, in comparison with English.

Pidgins, by definition, are languages without native speakers; in other words, they are learnt (often in adult life) by people who already have a first language. Creoles, on the other hand, are first languages for a community of speakers; of course, they can also be learnt as second languages as well.

Pidgins and creoles always come about as a result of language contact, but not all language contacts result in a pidgin or creole. There are many possible outcomes of language contact – for example, people may become bilingual, using both languages regularly and even mixing them in their speech, or one language may be influenced by another and incorporate large amounts of vocabulary from the other (as happened with English and French in medieval times). It is also possible for the grammar of a language to become simplified over time. This is also the case with English, which had far more complex morphology (verb and noun forms) in Anglo-Saxon times (see Chapter 17). These outcomes are not pidgins or creoles, however. Pidgins and creoles are particular kinds of product of language contact, and arise in a fairly limited set of situations as a result of certain social conditions which arise from time to time in human history.

ILLUSTRATION BOX 21.1

Tok Pisin

Papua Niugini em i wanpela kantri long rijen Melanesia long Pasifik. Giraun bilong kantri i stap long isten hap bilong Niugini Ailan na tu long ol narapela ailan olsem Niu Briten, Niu Ailan, Bogenvil, Manus, na planti moa. Kapitol na nambawan taun bilong em i Pot Mosbi.

Papua Niugini igat antap long 800 tokples...i no gat narapela kantri long wol i winim dispela namba bilong ol tokples.

'Papua New Guinea is a country in the region of Melanesia in the Pacific. Its territory lies in the eastern half of New Guinea Island and also in other islands such as New Britain, New Ireland, Bougainville, Manus and many more. Its capital and main town is Port Moresby.

PNG has more than 800 local languages...there is no other country in the world which surpasses this number of languages.'

(Wikipedia entry for Papua New Guinea in Tok Pisin /
New Guinea Pidgin version: http://tpi.wikipedia.org/wiki/Papua_Niugini)

ILLUSTRATION BOX 21.2

Sranan

Sranankondre, diri kondre
Yu wi lobi nomru wan
Eri libi te na dede
Wi sa singi fu Sranan

Sranan country, dear country
You we love number one (= the most)
Whole life until death (= all our lives, until we die)
We shall sing of Surinam

(National anthem of Surinam, South America)

To summarize, then:

- Pidgins and creoles are new languages which result from **language contact**.
- Pidgins and creoles (usually) have a **lexifier** language which provides most of the vocabulary.
- Pidgins and creoles show **simplification** and **reduction** in their grammar and vocabulary, when compared with the lexifier language.

- Pidgins are languages which are learnt as second languages, i.e., they lack native speakers.
- Creoles are native languages for a community of speakers.

21.2   English-lexicon pidgins and creoles around the world

Most pidgins and creoles result from people moving from one place to another, either as **traders** or as **labourers**. In South China, for example, an English-based pidgin developed as the result of trading contacts between locally-based speakers of Chinese and English-speaking traders, who were allowed to live locally but were socially segregated from the Chinese. This pidgin was a language with limited vocabulary, suited to its limited functions. In the South Pacific, a trading jargon was widely spread by English seafarers in the eighteenth century through the trade with the indigenous inhabitants of some islands. Later, this language became much more widespread through the development of a plantation labour system, where speakers of many different languages were brought together to work on plantations owned by colonists. In New Guinea, the language was known as New Guinea Pidgin; nowadays it is called Tok Pisin and is an official language of Papua New Guinea (see Illustration Box 21.1).

Many of the English-lexicon creoles in the world today owe their existence to the system of slavery and slave plantation labour which was practised by European countries in their American colonies. It was probably the slave trade which led to the development of a number of pidgins on the coast of West Africa, where the European slavers collected their cargoes at fortresses along the coast. In West Africa, West African Pidgin English is a generic term for varieties of a language which are spoken, sometimes as a pidgin and sometimes as a creole (i.e., as a first language), in Nigeria, Ghana, Gambia, Cameroon and some other coastal countries of West Africa. In Sierra Leone, Krio is a first language for most people in the capital, Freetown.

In the former English colonies of the Caribbean, to which the Africans were shipped as slaves to provide labour on the plantations, creole languages which developed during the slavery period remain the first language for the majority of the population. English-lexicon creoles are the vernacular language in Jamaica, Trinidad, Grenada and some smaller islands. Creoles related to these are spoken in Belize on the Central American mainland, and on the Caribbean coast of Costa Rica and Nicaragua, as well as on some offshore islands which are part of Colombia. On the South American mainland, an English-lexicon creole similar to that of Trinidad is spoken in Guyana, but a number of very different English-lexicon creoles are spoken in the adjacent country, Surinam, which was a Dutch colony: these are Sranan Tongo, Saramaccan, Djuka and Boni.

In the Pacific region, some English-lexicon creoles are spoken by Aboriginal communities in the Northern Territory of Australia, for example, Roper River Creole. These have similarities to the pidgins of the South Pacific islands. Two more creoles in this region are Hawaiian Creole English, widely spoken by the population of Hawaii (not to be confused with the indigenous Hawaiian language, which is a Polynesian language and not a creole), and the creole of Pitcairn and Norfolk Islands. This creole was the outcome of the famous mutiny on the English ship the *Bounty*, which led to the mutineers eventually settling on the island of Pitcairn, where some of their descendents still live. The creole resulted from contact between the sailors and the Polynesian women who became their wives. Part of the population was later moved to less inaccessible Norfolk island, where a somewhat different version of the creole continues to be used.

Though there are currently no known pidgins or creoles spoken in Europe which originated there, migration from former colonies of European countries has brought creoles to many European cities. You may hear Jamaican or other Caribbean creoles spoken in London, Birmingham and several other cities in England, while Sranan (see Illustration Box 21.2), the creole of Surinam, has many speakers in the Netherlands. Jamaican Creole, more than any other, has 'gone global' – as the language of Reggae lyrics and strongly connected with other music styles such as hip-hop, it is familiar to people in many countries even if they would not use it in their everyday speech styles.

21.2.1   Stages of pidgin and creole development

Pidgins and creoles can be thought of as evolving through a number of developmental stages, depending on the historical circumstances in which they exist and how long they continue to be used. Stages which have been hypothesized by researchers are shown in Table 21.1 below.

Two 'transitional stages' need a special explanation. The first of these is the 'tertiary hybridization' stage, so named in a biological analogy by the creolist Keith Whinnom (1971). The early pidgin involves attempts by speakers of different indigenous languages to speak a version of the lexifier language with native speakers of the lexifier, that is, it is a medium for native speaker–non-native speaker communication. If the speakers of the indigenous languages begin to use the pidgin to communicate among themselves rather than with speakers of the lexifier – that is, to use the pidgin as a lingua franca – then a crucial change has taken place. Speakers of the lexifier are no longer involved, and the lexifier is no longer serving as a model for the speakers of the pidgin. This 'freedom' from the dominance of the lexifier allows the pidgin to develop in its own way, independently of the lexifier, and to develop its own stable **norms** of grammar and vocabulary.

The process of **creolization** is the transition whereby a pidgin becomes a creole. This is a much disputed area in the study of pidgins and creoles. We can say definitely that **some** pidgins turn into creoles by a gradual or 'natural' process: a community forms in which the pidgin is the common language or main language of everyday use, and children born within that community become first-language speakers of the pidgin – which is now said to have become a creole. This process has happened for Tok Pisin in the last 40 years or so, and has been documented by linguists.

Unfortunately the emergence of most creoles happened some centuries ago, and has never been fully documented. We do know that it can take place very rapidly – for example, an English-lexicon creole emerged in Surinam despite the fact that English planters were settled there only from 1651 to 1667, when

Table 21.1   *Stages of pidgin and creole development*

Stage	Characteristics	Example
Rudimentary pidgin	Unstable grammar and vocabulary, very limited functions, used in occasional or casual contacts between two groups; no native speakers	Russenorsk (extinct Russian-Norwegian seasonal fisherman's pidgin)
Tertiary Hybridization		
Stable pidgin	Regularized, stable grammar and vocabulary, somewhat larger range of functions, in widespread use; no native speakers	Early New Guinea Pidgin
Extended/ expanded pidgin	Regularized, stable grammar and vocabulary, wide range of functions, possibly used for literature, education and administration, may be main language (but usually not **only** language) in a community; may have some native speakers; may be developing different stylistic registers for different functions	Tok Pisin, West African Pidgin English
Creolization		
Creole	Has grammar which is stable and has stylistic registers like any other language; wide range of functions; vocabulary sufficient for all the functions for which the language is used; has a community of speakers for whom it is a first (possibly only) language	Jamaican Creole, Krio, Sranan Tongo, many others

they were replaced by the Dutch. However, by 1730 the plantation slaves were recorded as speaking Sranan – very definitely an English rather than a Dutch-lexicon creole – and their descendants continue to speak it. One generation was apparently enough for the genesis of this creole. So it is not clear that all creoles come into being through a gradual process similar to that of Tok Pisin: for example, it has been pointed out (Mufwene, 2001) that there is no evidence for a pidgin stage preceding many of the existing creoles. An alternative has been proposed called **abrupt creolization** (Thomason and Kaufman, 1988). This is where a creole-speaking community arises before a stable pidgin has had time to emerge; the creole would have the typical pidgin/creole characteristics, but the pidgin stage would have been short-circuited to a large extent. Something like this may have happened in the upheaval of slavery times, but as there are no records, we rely on circumstantial evidence.

21.2.2   Linguistic characteristics of pidgins and creoles

A number of linguistic features of pidgins and creoles have already been mentioned. Two key characteristics are **simplification** and **reduction** compared to the lexifier and, usually, the substrate languages. What does this mean in practice?

Phonological simplification

Typical forms of simplification in the sound system would be:

- Avoidance of multi-syllable words (preference for words of three syllables or less).
- Avoidance of consonant clusters by dropping consonants or inserting vowels (e.g., *tan* 'stand' in Sranan, *siton* 'stone' in Cameroonian Pidgin).
- Avoidance of sounds which are 'difficult', i.e., those which are found in relatively few languages and/or are acquired late by children (e.g., English <th> (=/ð/, /θ/) often becomes /d/, /t/.

Grammatical simplification

This typically takes the form of some or all of the following:

- Lack of inflections, e.g., the past tense marker *–ed* and plural marker *–s*.
- Use of separate words to indicate tenses, e.g., *baimbai* in Tok Pisin for the future, *bin* (from English *been*) in many P/Cs to mark past tense, *don* as a marker of completed action in some Creoles.
- Lack of some 'less essential' word classes, e.g., indefinite article *a* and (sometimes) definite article *the*, absence of the copula (*to be*) in some circumstances.
- Lack of some 'less essential' grammatical constructions, for example, passives.
- Just one word order, so the word order does not change in questions as it does in English. Tok Pisin *Yu kukim wanem?* 'What are you cooking?'

Lexical simplification and reduction

The fact that the vocabulary of pidgins and creoles is reduced compared to the lexifier has already been mentioned. One way of achieving this is simply to have few synonyms: for example, in Tok Pisin *stret* has the meanings 'straight, flat, exactly, honest, correct'. However, there are some other ways as well, which have to do with **semantic simplicity and transparency**. For example, the number of basic prepositions is reduced to a small number, each with a wide range of meanings, for example, Tok Pisin *long* ('in, on, at, ...'), *bilong* (most often translated 'of', but can be used to indicate almost any kind of connection between two things).

Derivational morphology, that is, the building of more complex nouns and verbs from basic parts, is very limited and more transparent in terms of its meaning than in English. Compare Tok Pisin *wokman* and Sranan *wrokoman* with their English meaning '(male) worker'. In both the pidgin and the creole the word is made up of two morphemes, both words in their own right, and the meaning is immediately derivable from the component parts. The same is not true of *work+er*, where *er* is not an independent word and does not have a meaning except when it is attached to a stem.

ILLUSTRATION BOX 21.3

A pidgin and its lexifier

As an example of how a pidgin may be both like and very different from its lexifier, here is a single sentence spoken by a man in a 1984 documentary film, *The Shark Callers of Kontu*.

New Guinea Pidgin	*sapos*	*mi*	*stat*	*long*	*kisim*	*devol*	*bilong*	*sak*
English source	suppose	me	start	along	catch-him	devil	belong	shark
Translation	'if I start to get the spirit of the shark'							

Here we can see multiple differences between Tok Pisin and English.
Phonological: simplification, e.g., *kisim*, *sak*
Grammatical: the suffix *–im* is required on the verb when it has an object
Semantic: *belong* is reinterpreted as a preposition meaning 'of'. *Devil*, which in Western theology is a very specific kind of (evil) spirit, is reinterpreted with a more general meaning, which is not necessarily negative.

21.2.3   The origins of pidgin and creole characteristics

The processes which give pidgins and creoles their special character is the subject of a great deal of research, and are much discussed and disputed. A number of different theories have been put forward, and have prevailed at different periods. For all of these, a fundamental problem is that the processes have never been observed as they happen; researchers have to make educated guesses based on the known historical facts, and the linguistic structures of the pidgins and creoles about which they have information.

Imperfect second language learning

Almost all the pidgins and creoles which we know about derive most of their vocabulary from just one language, the lexifier. Most commonly this is the language of a people who colonized or dominated the indigenous people of a region – for example, the English who were the plantation owners in the Caribbean islands and the slave traders in parts of West Africa. What this suggests is that the indigenous people were attempting to learn the language of the colonizers, in circumstances where they were unlikely to be able to learn to speak it perfectly. For the limited communication which was needed – trading or receiving instructions as servants, for example – perfect knowledge of the language was not required anyway. A limited vocabulary and a vague idea of grammar would suffice. Thus **imperfect** or **incomplete second language learning** is likely to be one factor in the development of pidgins.

Foreigner Talk

When confronted with the need to communicate with a person who has a limited command of their language, most people are able to draw on a 'foreigner talk' register. **Foreigner Talk** is talk designed for a 'foreign' hearer – it is not a term for the way that foreigners talk, which might be better described 'imperfect second language learning' as above. Characteristics of Foreigner Talk are:

- Use of a limited vocabulary; replacing 'hard' words with simpler ones
- Use of simple grammar, e.g., omitting tense markers, the verb *to be* and other 'dispensable' items
- Using short phrases and doing frequent understanding checks

The following exchange, which I quote from memory from a conversation I had in Brazil with a landlady who had just served me breakfast, shows some of these characteristics:

NS:	*è saboroso?*	'Is it tasty?'
NNS:	[silence]	
NS:	*è bom?*	'Is it good?'

NS here is the landlady, a native speaker of Brazilian Portuguese, while NNS is myself, a non-native speaker of the language with a very low competence in it. NS took my silence to indicate lack of understanding; she therefore rephrased her question (which was already fairly simple) using a very common word with a much more general meaning.

Since Foreigner Talk is apparently a natural response of native speakers when trying to communicate with people who have little knowledge of their language, and since several of the characteristics of Foreigner Talk are found in pidgins and creoles, it is reasonable to conclude that Foreigner Talk is another factor in the development of pidgins.

Linguistic universals

Since the 1960s it has been widely accepted within linguistics that all languages have certain common properties which make it possible for human children to learn any language they are exposed to, on fairly short (and similar) time scales. There is rather less agreement about exactly what these common properties are, and how they are manifested in language. Another way of looking at this is to say that some features of language – whether phonological, morphological or syntactic – are easier to learn than others. This could be demonstrated, for example, by the fact that they are learnt earlier by children, and that they occur in more languages. These 'easier', 'simpler' or 'more basic' sounds or constructions are the ones which we would expect to find in pidgin languages, where the driving force is the need to communicate successfully without any need for elaborate stylistic variants.

Layers of lexical development

Many pidgins and creoles have fairly complex histories involving, for example, several different periods and types of contact with different colonizers. This history is often reflected in the lexicon of the contact language. Although the majority of the everyday vocabulary is typically from just one language, the one we have called 'the lexifier', there are often contributions from other languages as well, which can be linked to specific historical periods. For example, in Tok Pisin we find:

Portuguese: A few common words are of Portuguese origin, e.g., *save* 'know', *pikinini* 'child'. It has been observed that many creoles around the world have these words or similar ones, no doubt due to the prevalence of the Portuguese mariners in the early days of European expansion.

German: *blaistik* 'pencil', *raus* 'get out'. New Guinea was a German colony 1884–1914.

Tolai: The indigenous language Tolai has contributed some words, e.g., *lapun* 'old', *kiau* 'egg'.

English I: The 'older' layer of English words in Tok Pisin tend to be short, common and have been adapted to the sound patterns of indigenous languages, e.g., *han* 'hand', *het*, 'head', *kis(im)* 'get' (from English *catch*).

English II: More recent words of English origin are similar to loan words in other languages, having less adaptation and usually having meaning related to new concepts or technology: *teprikoda* 'tape recorder', *autbotmota* 'outboard motor', *edukeit(im)* 'educate'.

21.2.4   A 'layered' model of pidgin and creole development

Substrate and superstrate

The terms 'substrate' and 'superstrate' used in pidgin and creole studies involve a metaphor in which a pidgin or creole language is seen as a series of layers or 'strata' as in geology (cf. the definition of stratification in Chapter 19, Section 19.1). The bottom layer, or **substrate**, refers to the indigenous language or languages which are spoken by the dominated group who usually make up the majority of the speakers. The **superstrate**, or top layer, is the same as the lexifier, the language of the colonizers or dominant group. The role played by the superstrate and the substrate has at various times been controversial in pidgin and creole studies.

The superstrate contribution

The superstrate, by definition, is the source of most of the vocabulary, but also of some of the grammar. It is important to remember that when talking of the superstrate or lexifier of the English-lexicon creoles, we are not talking about contemporary Standard English. Most currently spoken pidgins and creoles are creations of the period between 1600 and 1800, and the English which formed their superstrate is different from modern Standard English in at least three important ways:

(i) **Historical:** the forms of English date from an earlier period of the language.
(ii) **Social:** the speakers of English who are most likely to have influenced a developing pidgin were sailors or labourers, who would not have had access to 'educated' vocabulary and prescribed forms of grammar. Evidence of non-standard (stigmatized) forms is common.
(iii) **Regional:** the said sailors or labourers would have been speakers of local varieties of English, especially from coastal parts of southern and western England (and possibly Ireland). There is evidence of dialectal forms appearing in particular pidgins or creoles.

To take an example, Table 21.2 shows some vocabulary items from Tok Pisin (New Guinea Pidgin), their meanings and English sources.

The first four of these words in Table 21.2 have English sources which would probably be marked in an English dictionary as 'vulgar' or 'obscene' – certainly too rude to feature in a polite conversation or an essay. It is important to understand that these are 'normal' words in Tok Pisin, and have no connotations of rudeness or vulgarity and no stigma attached to them. *Pispis* and *kok* could be used appropriately in a medical article, though they could be used in 'crude talk' as well. This is also a good example of how a pidgin offers a **reduced stylistic range** – Standard English, for example, has a whole range of words for these body parts and functions, with different ones appropriate for talking to children, vulgar use, polite use and medical or scientific use, while Tok Pisin has just one for all purposes. This has not prevented Tok Pisin from expanding its stylistic range recently, however (for example, it is quite possible to 'talk dirty' in Tok Pisin).

The word *baimbai* (sometimes shortened to *bai*) is an example of an English expression which is preserved in the pidgin although it sounds distinctly old-fashioned to modern speakers. It also illustrates how the function of pidgin words can be very different from that in the lexifier: baimbai is a grammatical marker of the future, not an adverb as in English.

Stap is an example of a word which has derived from localized or non-standard meanings of a word in English. English *stop* in the sense in which it has entered Tok Pisin has the meaning 'stay, remain,' (e.g., 'the match was

Tok Pisin vocabulary and English sources   *Table 21.2*

Tok pisin word	Meaning	Source
bagarap	spoil, ruin	bugger up
as	buttock, base, cause, origin	arse
kok	penis	cock
pispis	urinate	piss
baimbai	future tense marker (grammatical)	by and by
stap	stay, continue to do something	stop

called off so I stopped at home') which it has in many regional varieties of English but not in the standard language.

The substrate contribution

The substrate languages are the languages other than the lexifier, and are usually the indigenous languages which are spoken in the region where the pidgin originates or becomes a lingua franca. For example, languages of West Africa (particularly a group of languages known as Kwa) form the substrate for some of the Caribbean creoles because these languages were the native languages of many of the people taken in slavery to the Caribbean. (We have independent historical evidence for this fact.) In the case of New Guinea Pidgin (Tok Pisin) the substrate is formed by the languages of New Guinea, which are very numerous.

It is not surprising that the first languages of speakers have some kind of influence on the pidgin as it emerges. There are various theories about the form this takes. For example, one famous description of Haitian Creole is that it is 'an Ewe [West African] language with French vocabulary' (Sylvain, 1936). Nowadays hardly anyone would support this view, in which the substrate provides everything apart from the lexicon. A more balanced view is that of Roger Keesing, who suggests that pidgins and creoles tend to adopt features of the substrate when these are widely shared by the substrate languages. So, for example, many West African languages have a type of verb construction called 'serialization', where two verbs occur together in a sentence and have a combined meaning. Just this kind of structure is also found in the Creole Sranan, which is known to have been 'created' by slaves brought mainly from West Africa, see the example below.

SRANAN: A tyari mi kon
            He carry me come
ENGLISH: 'He brought me'

Another example comes from the South Pacific region, where many languages have a distinction between 'inclusive' *we* (= me and you) and 'exclusive' *we* (= me and some other(s) but not you). English, and apparently a majority of other languages, do not make this distinction but many of the substrate languages of Tok Pisin do. Sure enough, Tok Pisin makes the distinction too:

yumi   'we = me and you'
mipela   'we = me and others'

Role of the substrate and superstrate in later development of creoles

The substrate and superstrate may have different degrees of influence on the pidgin/creole at different stages of development. An interesting contrast emerges between two creoles which have rather similar early histories, but different later histories. Sranan Tongo, as has already been mentioned, emerged among slaves in Surinam in the mid-seventeenth century. In much the same period Jamaican Creole developed in another English colony in the same region – Jamaica – among slaves who came from very similar origins to the Surinam slaves.

Evidence suggests that the early Jamaican and Surinamese creoles were very similar. However, as mentioned earlier, the English presence in Surinam was very brief – it soon became a Dutch colony. Dutch provided some vocabulary for the creole, but it remained mainly English in its lexicon. However, new slaves were constantly being imported from Africa over the next two centuries (a consequence of the appallingly short lives of the slaves after their arrival on the plantations). Thus the influence of the substrate languages was constantly being renewed and reinforced in the creole.

In Jamaica, on the other hand, the English (later the British) remained the colonial masters until the twentieth century, and Standard English was the language of administration, justice and formal education throughout. This probably had relatively little effect upon the slave population (few of whom went to school, for example) until emancipation in the mid-nineteenth century. After this, however, some social mobility became possible for the ex-slaves and with it, some exposure to Standard English in its local varieties. The creole was thus kept in contact with its lexifier, which also was the language associated with prestige and economic success.

If we compare Sranan with Jamaican Creole today, we find two languages which are very unlike each other. Sranan in some ways resembles an African language; on hearing it spoken, one might never guess the connection with English. Jamaican Creole, on the other hand, shows much more influence from English (although even then, it is more different than you might at first think), and may be thought of as 'bad English' by some of its own speakers.

21.2.5 Attitudes towards pidgins and creoles

Both pidgins and creoles tend to attract negative attitudes from the speakers of their lexifier languages, and sometimes from their own speakers as well. Why is this so? A common mistake is to assume that the speaker of a pidgin or creole is trying to speak the lexifier language, and failing very badly. In this view, a pidgin may be despised as being 'bad English' or 'bad French' when, in fact, it is perfectly grammatical in its own terms; it is only 'wrong' when compared to something which it is not meant to be. The simplified grammar of a pidgin or creole may sound, to hearers who know the lexifier language, like the grammar of a child who has not yet mastered the adult language; hence pidgins and creoles are sometimes derided as 'baby talk'. Also, as we have seen, some of the vocabulary of pidgins derives from 'rude' or 'coarse' language (or slang) in the lexifier. It is easy to make fun of a Tok Pisin speaker who says *as bilong diwai i bagarap* but all this means is 'the base of the tree (*diwai*) has been damaged'.

It must be said that these views were more widely held in colonial times, and were part of a racist attitude towards the indigenous people who were the speakers of pidgins and creoles. In some parts of the world, pidgin and creole languages are highly valued in society; for example, Tok Pisin is an official language in the Republic of Papua New Guinea, and a related pidgin, Bislama,

ILLUSTRATION BOX 21.4

A sample of Jamaican Creole

This is an extract from a thread on a web forum where Jamaicans discuss health issues. The thread is titled **A dyam migraine** (a damn migraine) and the contributors use a mixture of JC and Standard English. The creole portions are spelt using English spelling conventions as there is currently no standard way of spelling JC in common use. Creole parts of the text have been printed in _underlined italic_.

M: well _mi nuh know_ if is a migraine but it's been killing me since Monday.
[Well, I don't know if it is a migraine but it's been killing me since Monday.]

T: _u drinking_ enough water...
[Are you drinking enough water?]

A: one weeks headache... _daht nuh good man._
how you pressure?
[One week's headache... that's no good, man. How is your (blood) pressure?]

M: _mi nuh know how mi pressure_ A and yes Mrs. T I get lots and lots of water.
[I don't know how my blood pressure is A and yes Mrs T. I get lots and lots of water.]

Z: I have had a headache since March 7th went to the Dr on Monday and that was a waste of time \:\(
Him seh is either
[He said it is either]

Pressure (yes mine is high but it is always high)
or
Pinched nerve
or
Unknown cause

wi narrow it down now to pinched nerve.....and I am waiting till after the holidays to get in for a massage \:\(

A: _naw man, you fi always know daht._
go get check out please
[No, man, you always have to know that. Go and get checked out please.]

N: buy a pressure cuff and keep at home just to be sure.
for a quick fix, drink a cup of coffee and take an ibuprofen at the same time. that will help ease the pain in your head.

K: _mine yu stressing yuself out too much enuh_
[Mind, you are stressing yourself out too much you know]

M: and I'm doing such a good job eliminating all stressors. \:\(

K: good for you and _mek_ sure Mr. M.. _a give yu_ regular 'medicine' during the week and _ova dose you pon_ weekend.
[Good for you, and make sure Mr. M.. gives you regular 'medicine' during the week and overdoses you at the weekend.]

is official in the neighbouring Republic of Vanuatu. A number of countries have a creole as an official language, including Haiti (Haitian Creole is official alongside Standard French) and the Seychelles (the French-lexicon creole Seselwa (Seychellois) is official along with French and English). These are relatively recent developments, made possible by a better understanding of what creole languages really are.

21.3 Case study: Jamaican Creole

In Section 21.2.4 there is some brief historical background to Jamaican Creole (hereafter JC). JC (also called *Patwa* or *Patois*) is the vernacular language of most Jamaicans, although the official language is Standard English. Standard English is also 'officially' the language of education and the mainstream print and broadcast media. However, JC has a lively existence in everyday life and in various forms of cultural expression – oral poetry, proverbs and song lyrics, for example. Many of the most popular song and rap lyrics by Jamaican artists are in Creole, and some of these are also reproduced in written form in various places. Since the advent of email and the Internet, JC is also used (often mixed with English) for personal email communications, contributions to forum discussions, chatrooms, etc. Thus despite lack of any official status, and despite disapproval by many 'educated' Jamaicans who regard the Creole as an inferior form of English, it is widely spoken and written, though mainly in more private, personal and leisure contexts.

In this section we will focus on the features of the 'broadest' JC, in other words the form of the language which is most **unlike** English or most 'true to its roots'. In Chapter 22 we will discuss how JC and Jamaican English coexist in a 'Creole Continuum'.

21.3.1 A comparison of some features of Standard English and Jamaican Creole grammar

The pronouns of Jamaican Creole can take any of the three functions: subject, object and possessor, for which English usually has distinct forms (e.g., *we, us, our* would all be rendered *wi* in JC). However, JC has distinct forms for second-person singular and plural, as can be seen in Table 21.3, where English has just *you*.

Pronouns of Jamaican Creole   *Table 21.3*

	singular	plural
1	mi	wi
2	yu	unu*
3	im (m/f)	dem
	i (n)	

*This item is likely to be of African origin.

Table 21.4

Grammatical feature	Standard English form	JC form	JC example
Nouns			
Noun plural	–s etc.	none	
Noun possessor	X's Y, e.g., *Mary's book*	XY fi-XY	*Di man buk* 'the man's book' *fi-mi buk* 'my book'
Verbs			
Present continuous tense	BE + V–*ing*	*a* V	*mi a go* 'I am going'
Past	V + –*ed*	V *bin* V *did* V	*mi luk* 'I looked' *mi bin/did luk* 'I looked'
Copula (*to be*)*			
(1) joining nouns A,B	BE	*a*	*mi a di man* 'I am the man'
(2) location		*de*	*mi de ina di haus* 'I am in the house'
(3) with an adjective		—	*mi sik* 'I am sick'
Negation			
	not, n't	*no* *neva*	*mi no sik* 'I am not sick' *mi neva se dat* 'I didn't say that'

*Jamaican Creole has three possible equivalents of *to be*, depending on the function.

Some other features of Jamaican Creole grammar are displayed in Table 21.4.

In conclusion, it is clear that Jamaican Creole shares much of its vocabulary and some of its grammar with English but is nevertheless a very different language. As the two are often mixed in everyday usage (as in the Internet forum example) the dividing line is not always easy to draw.

Recommended readings

There are several introductory level books on pidgins and creoles, of which the most recent is Singh (2000). Todd (1991, first published 1974) is a classic description suited to beginners, but now out of date. Todd (1984) is restricted to English-lexicon pidgins and creoles. Sebba (1997) is at intermediate level, while Romaine (1988) is an advanced introduction requiring some specialist knowledge of linguistics. Holm (2000) is likewise advanced and fairly comprehensive. Arends, Muysken and Smith (1995) is an edited work covering a range of topics at an advanced level. Siegel (2008) is an advanced book which reviews and re-evaluates research on the theories of pidgin and creole origins.

Information about individual pidgins and creoles, with one or two exceptions, tends to be in books too specialized to be widely available. However there are some accessible Internet resources, such as a page on Tok Pisin written by Jeff Siegel (http://www.une.edu.au/langnet/definitions/tokpisin.html) and Mark Sebba's British Creole Resources page (http://www.ling.lancs. ac.uk/staff/mark/resource/resourcs.htm). Generally it is necessary to evaluate the quality of web pages on pidgins and creoles by determining who wrote them and/or whether they are based on serious scholarly research.

CHAPTER 22

World Englishes[1]

MARK SEBBA

> **ILLUSTRATION BOX 22.1**
>
> **Diverse Englishes**
>
> HOBI,
> RAMPE,
> SAMI,
> TEMPO,
> ROOPE
> I ♥YOU ALL VERY MUTCH
> MUT ENITEN
> ON IKÄVÄ TEITÄ!?
> (Graffiti seen in a playground in Finland, 2007)
>
> Translation: Hobi, Rampe, Sami, Tempo, Roope
>   I love you all very much but [Rampe] most of all
>   I miss you all!?
>
> I'm always beside
> you.
> when istretc my
> hand. Somewhere
> near to touch
> believe forever!
> (Text on pocket of boy's jacket, China, 2003)

22.1   Introduction: diverse Englishes

When teenage girls in Finland (and many other places) write graffiti in English mixed with their own native language, and texts in English (or what is meant to be English) are incorporated into the design of children's clothing in China to make them more desirable fashion items, we can surely say that English has become, in some sense, a 'world language'(see Illustration Box 22.1 above).

In this chapter we will look at how this has come about, and investigate some of the processes involved.

What are World Englishes? English is sometimes called a 'world language' (also *World English, Global English* or *International English*), meaning that English is conceived as a language for world-wide communication, either as an existing form of Standard English or as a modification of it which eliminates features which might be difficult or confusing for people who have learnt it as a foreign language. Although this 'English as a world language' would certainly have its place among 'World Englishes', the term **World Englishes** refers to a whole range of languages which are forms of, or related to, English. Among these are many geographical varieties of Standard English, but also other, non-standard forms of English such as the pidgin and creole varieties spoken in certain countries. World Englishes is thus a cover term for a diverse group of languages spread around the globe and which are all, in some sense, 'English'. (See Chapter 12 for a further discussion of the 'boundaries' of English.)

Clearly, English as a distinct language has its original home and birthplace in the British Isles. Over several centuries, it found additional 'homes' where its speakers settled – initially in the North America and the Caribbean, and later in British colonies in many other parts of the world. In some of these colonies, nearly all of which are now independent states, English became the majority language: this is true of the United States, the country with the largest population of first-language speakers of English, and also of Australia and New Zealand, which were settled mainly by people from Great Britain. The influential scholar of World Englishes Braj Kachru (1986, 2005), himself born in India, but working in the United States, calls this group of countries the **Inner Circle** of English-speaking countries, the ones with communities of native speakers of English who are themselves of British ethnic origin. According to Kachru, the countries in this group are traditionally 'norm-providing' for Standard English around the world; in other words, it is these countries (and especially Britain and the USA) which provide the models – of pronunciation, grammar and vocabulary – which are followed by users of English in the rest of the world. In terms of the way English is taught, these countries can be categorized as **English as a Native Language (ENL)** countries, where (even though it is not true for many people) it is assumed that English is a first language and is already known by children when they start school.

In other British (and US) colonies, English became an important language in education and administration, but never was the first language for most people. In most of these, it had and still has the role of a *second* language – in other words, although most people do not speak it as a first language, it is widely used for administrative and commercial purposes and in education. In these countries, it may even be the main medium of education, with the result that most people who have been through the school system can speak and understand it to a greater or lesser extent. Kachru calls this group of countries the **Outer Circle** – a region where, for historical reasons, English is familiar and in everyday use by *some* parts of the population. According to Kachru, the countries and regions in this group are 'norm-developing'; after a period during which they closely followed the norms of the 'mother country', they are now developing their own local standards of pronunciation, grammar and vocabulary. From the language teaching point of view, these are **English as a Second Language (ESL)** countries: in practice this often means that English is taught as a school subject in the early years, but later stages of education are taught *through* English (with varying degrees of success), though in some ESL countries all schooling is in English.

In the rest of the world, English is mainly a 'foreign language' – a language which does not have a local base of first-language speakers, nor a particularly strong role in administration or education. However, in most of these countries, it would be wrong to regard English as 'just one of many foreign languages'. If we look at what English is actually used for and where it is found in these countries, we will find that it has functions and roles that other foreign languages do not have, though these vary from country to country. In many places, for example, it has some role in the local media (you can buy a local English-language newspaper in Beijing or Buenos Aires, and listen to interviews in English on Swedish television) and is the main foreign language learned at school – often as a compulsory subject. These countries are said by Kachru to belong to the **Expanding Circle** – countries where English does

Table 22.1   Kachru's 'three circles' of English and their characteristics

Kachru's categorization	Language teaching orientation to English	Examples (countries)	Typical functions of English	Historical connection with English
Inner Circle: *norm providing*	English as a first/native language	Britain, USA, New Zealand	all functions	Countries settled by first-language speakers of English
Outer Circle: *norm developing*	English as a second language (ESL)	Nigeria, Kenya, India, Singapore, Philippines	administration, media, law, education (as medium of instruction), literature (varies from country to country)	Countries colonized by Britain or USA
Expanding Circle: *norm dependent*	English as a foreign language (EFL)	Sweden, Japan, Russia, Taiwan	education (as a school subject), scientific research, business and diplomatic communications with English-speaking countries; communications with individuals and institutions in non-English-speaking countries (English as a Lingua Franca – see text)	No colonial connections, though trade connections may go back centuries (Russia, Japan)

not have a strong historical connection through colonialism, but is increasingly important in various aspects of life. In Kachru's terms, these countries are 'norm-dependent': they lack the speaker base which would allow them to develop their own English norms, and therefore look to other countries, especially those of the Inner Circle, to provide models. For language teaching purposes, these are **English as a Foreign Language (EFL)** countries, where educators must make the assumption that English is not used outside certain limited settings, and children learning the language will be encountering it at school for the first time.

Table 22.1 above summarizes the position of English in these three groups of countries.

The countries of Kachru's Expanding Circle are also very likely to use English for 'outward-looking' purposes – for example in commercial and diplomatic dealings with foreign countries, and in their own tourist industries. Studies have shown that in some countries the language most likely to be used with tourists is English, even where this is not a native language for either speaker. This is an example of another major role of English in the world today – **English as a Lingua Franca**, or **ELF**. In this role, English serves as a means of communication between people *none of whom* are first-language speakers of it.

22.2 Diverse ways of learning English: three types of acquisition

Kachru's 'three circles' categorization of World Englishes could be described as a **sociohistorical** approach: it classifies and labels the varieties in terms of their historical and social relationship with the 'original' English, that of Britain. An alternative way of looking at World Englishes is in terms of their *acquisition*, in other words how a variety comes to be learned and used by a particular group of speakers.

22.2.1 Normal transmission

This may become clearer if we consider the most straightforward case, what we may call, following Thomason and Kaufman (1988) normal transmission. This is the way most of us learnt our first language – in infancy, from our main carers who were probably our parents. **Normal transmission** simply means that the language is acquired in early childhood from adults who speak it to the child; the result is that the child speaks the language in an almost identical form to that of the parents. It is necessary here to say 'almost identical' because we know that language change across generations is not only possible but common; it is itself part of 'normal transmission'. However, the pace of change through 'normal transmission' is usually very slow.

It is worth noting that of the many millions of people around the world who speak English as a first language, only a minority acquire *Standard* English through normal transmission. Most will *first* learn a different variety such as a local dialect. For most of these, if they acquire Standard English at all it will be through *school acquisition* (see below).

22.2.2 Abnormal transmission: pidginization, creolization, restructuring

Abnormal transmission (Thomason and Kaufman 1988) refers to a situation where for some reason the language of the parents or carers is not passed on to the child in the usual way. The language which the child learns is therefore different, perhaps very different, from that of the parents.

Pidginization and creolization are two processes which involve abnormal transmission of language. In **pidginization**, a version of a language which is grammatically simplified and reduced in vocabulary is learned informally, usually in adulthood (though it can be learned in childhood) as a lingua franca. Through the process of pidginization a number of 'Pidgin Englishes' have arisen in different parts of the world, which are discussed in Chapter 21.

In **creolization**, a pidgin becomes the first language of some group of speakers – typically through children growing up in an environment where the pidgin is the main language of communication (e.g., a community where the adults come from a variety of language backgrounds and have the pidgin as a lingua franca). The creole comes into being through abnormal transmission because children are learning a language from their parents and carers, but it is a language which the adults do not speak natively, and may even be a language without stable rules. The first generation of creole speakers will transform this pidgin into a first language with more functions, more stylistic nuances and more stable norms. Note that although creoles come into being initially through a process of abnormal transmission, after that they are transmitted normally from generation to generation like any other language.

The outcome of both pidginization and creolization is a **restructured** language, one which has superficial resemblances to English but is in fact radically different in its structure.

22.2.3 School and peer group transmission

Since English is a second or foreign language in many places, it is often acquired through formal education rather than in the family setting. We could call this **indirect transmission**. Clearly, this is different from 'normal transmission' and may lead to changes in the language brought about by the **model**, that is, the teachers whose pronunciation and grammar the learners try to copy. In most cases, these teachers are themselves local and have a local language as their first language; as a result, some features of this language (especially features of pronunciation) may be transferred to their English and, over time, may become the local norm. Thus Hong Kong English shows some influence from Chinese, East African English has some features of indigenous East African languages, and Indian English has certain features which can be traced to languages of India. Once these features have become sufficiently established as local norms, they will be passed down the generations even by first-language speakers of the local variety.

In some places indirect types of transmission have led to the establishment of two distinct local varieties of English. Singapore is one such place. Singaporean English – the local standard – is Standard English with some local features of pronunciation and vocabulary. On the other hand, Singlish (Singapore Colloquial English) is a widely used but stigmatized restructured form of English, with heavy influence from the local languages – Malay and Chinese. Singlish is frowned on in schools, but spoken informally everywhere, suggesting that peer groups could play a big role in its transmission.

22.2.4   Acquisition types and variation

Variation in language is one of the topics of great interest to linguists, one which is dealt with throughout this book, particularly Chapter 12 onwards. Some of the main parameters of variation are geography, social class, and register: in other words, we find that a language can take slightly different forms depending on where it is spoken, who is speaking it, and the topic of the communication. Looking at the different world Englishes, we can see that the mode of acquisition of a particular form of English is related to the type and extent of variation which it can undergo. Thus in places where English is acquired through normal transmission as a native language, we find the full range of variation: geographical and social varieties, and a wide range of styles and registers, from the most informal to the most formal, encompassing slang, in-group varieties and professional registers.

Where English is learnt primarily through school (as a second, and particularly as a foreign language), we are likely to find variation from the model, but not the kind of variation we find in natively learnt varieties. For example, about two-thirds of the population of Finland are able to speak some English. However, we do not find regional dialects of English in Finland; the English spoken in Helsinki in the south is not systematically different from the English of Oulu in the north. Rather, what we find in situations like this is variation along the spectrum of second-language learning, so that some people will acquire large vocabularies while others will acquire small ones; some people will have pronunciation which is very close or identical to the model while others will show strong influence from their first language in their accent. Most people who learn English through formal schooling will learn the more formal registers of English; they are less likely to need – or to acquire – colloquial, slangy registers which are probably not needed in the contexts where they use English.[2]

22.3   More about world Englishes

22.3.1   English of the British Isles

While English in the British Isles is of course the 'original' or 'source' English, it is important to see it also as a World English itself. There are several reasons for this. First of all, English within the British Isles is itself diverse – there are many dialects and socially differentiated varieties, just as there are in other parts of the world. Secondly, some of these varieties have themselves been sources of the varieties of English found in other parts of the world – for example, Irish varieties of English have been important influences in the formation of English varieties in Canada and the Caribbean. Thirdly, in the

British Isles we can see a trend which we might call the 'westward march' of English which has been in progress for more than 1000 years (see the historical description in Chapter 12). By this I mean the movement in which English, from its 'heartland' in the more central and eastern parts of Britain and lowlands of Scotland, gradually moved westward, displacing the older indigenous languages. Hence today in Wales, Cornwall, the Scottish Highlands, Isle of Man and Ireland, the indigenous Celtic languages are minority languages (as in Ireland, Scotland and Wales), recovering from the brink of extinction (as with Manx) or officially dead, but reviving uncertainly (Cornish). In the Channel Islands, Norman French has also been all but replaced by English. However, all these languages have left their mark on the locally spoken varieties of English – perhaps most noticeably in Ireland, where Irish English, especially in some rural areas, is very different from Standard English in grammar as well as in vocabulary and pronunciation.

The westward movement of English within the British Isles did not necessarily involve the large-scale *displacement* of the original population, but mainly was the result of language *shift* in which the local population encouraged their children to learn and use English in preference to the indigenous language: for example, in Ireland the proportion of Irish speakers suffered a very sharp decline (about 50 per cent between 1830 and 1870) and all of these will have become speakers of English instead.

22.3.2 English in the Inner Circle – countries settled by speakers of English from Britain

On the other hand, the next westward movement – into North America and the Caribbean – involved the movement of people who were mostly already speakers of English to settle in areas where English speakers had not lived before. Through the settlement of North America from Britain during the 1600s, English became the dominant language there. Later waves of colonization by people from Britain led to the establishment of colonies of British English speakers and the development of distinctive English varieties in Australia, New Zealand and South Africa at slightly different stages of the nineteenth century. Thus the major countries today where English is spoken as an *only first* language are Great Britain, Ireland, the United States, Canada, Australia, New Zealand and South Africa.

The varieties of English spoken in these Inner Circle countries have had, at the most, about four centuries (and at the least, less than two) in which to diverge from their 'mother dialects'. Given that language change is generally quite a slow process, it is not surprising that they remain fairly close to British English (which has, of course, changed as well). Regarding the written standard, the differences are extremely small; differences in grammar and style can be detected stylistically using corpus methods, which deploy computers to interrogate vast collections of text in electronic form (see Chapter 26, Section 26.3.2, for a brief demonstration of how a corpus might be used to address a stylistic issue, and Chapter 15, Section 15.5, for a demonstration of how it can reveal social characteristics). But the reader is only likely to notice slightly different spelling conventions (e.g., US *–ize* for British *–ize/–ise*, US *tire, cozy* for British *tyre, cosy*) and different choices in vocabulary (e.g., US *elevator, diaper, gasoline* for British *lift, nappy, petrol*). Vocabulary differences are much more prevalent in the colloquial, slang and taboo areas of language use, where there are likely to be regional and local words which are not shared with any other varieties. Variation in the spoken language is most noticeable in terms of accent: all the varieties mentioned here have distinctive accents. (Chapter 12 elaborates on some of the points mentioned here.)

Within the different countries of this group, regional and social dialects have developed much as they have in Britain itself. Thus there are several major dialect areas within North America, and identifiable regional accents in Australia, New Zealand and South Africa. Social variation (by class and gender) is also present and has been studied extensively in all these countries.

Each of these 'inner circle' varieties of English has developed in a slightly different context in terms of the other languages in its environment. In the United States, the indigenous people and their languages were pushed westward or wiped out for the most part; they have had relatively little impact on the development of English there, except in vocabulary where indigenous words were borrowed for some native flora and fauna, such as *squash* and *racoon*. Two other European languages, French and Spanish, have substantial numbers of speakers in North America, and this has impacted on local forms of English in various ways. In Canada, not only French but also native American and Inuit (Eskimo) languages continue to coexist with English. As in American English, the main impact of indigenous languages on Canadian English has probably been in terms of vocabulary.

In Australia, English predominated as the indigenous population declined through disease, dispossession of land and aggression by the colonists, with some of the remaining Aboriginals shifting to English or creolized varieties of English. In New Zealand, English existed alongside the indigenous Maori language, which has contributed a large amount of vocabulary to New Zealand English – see the box below. While Maori continues to be spoken, most Maori speak English (as a first or second language) and a distinctive variety, *Maori English*, has been recognized by linguists. In South Africa, English has coexisted with another language of partly European origin, Afrikaans, as well as ten or so indigenous languages. These have influenced South African English mainly in terms of vocabulary, but also in other subtle respects, like word formation (e.g., *play-play* 'pretend' and *now-now* 'in a moment/a moment ago' are modelled on Afrikaans), and discourse markers (e.g., the Afrikaans *ja* is very widely used for *yes* in South African English, though it is stigmatized).

In Kachru's classification, these Inner Circle countries are described as being 'norm-providing' – in other words they provide the norms of grammar and pronunciation which are followed by users of English in other countries. But this is more complex than it might seem at first. While clearly this is true for the United States, which provides a model for English Language teaching in many countries, it is less clear for Australia, New Zealand and South Africa, which until recently tended to follow the British norms themselves. In South Africa and New Zealand, for example, 'BBC English' (Received Pronunciation) was the required standard for newsreaders and 'serious' radio presenters even in the last quarter of the twentieth century. South African

ADVANCES BOX 22.1

New dialect formation in New Zealand

European settlement of New Zealand started in a small way in the 1770s. By the time of the large-scale immigration of (almost exclusively) British and Irish people from 1840 onwards, the territory already known as New Zealand (Maori: Aotearoa) had a population of some 70,000–80,000 descendants of Polynesians who had settled some 7–800 years earlier (Belich, 1996: 120). These people called themselves the Maori, and spoke a language nowadays referred to by the same name. By 1850, the European population already exceeded that of the Maori (Gordon et al., 2004: 42), whose numbers had been drastically reduced by disease. By the 1871 census, the non-Maori population numbered 256,393, the vast majority from the British Isles. Of these, 51 per cent came from England, 27 per cent from Scotland and 22 per cent from Ireland (Hay *et al.* 2008: 6). Today, some 14 per cent of the population identify as Maori and, of these, 26 per cent claim to speak the language (Hay, Maclagan and Gordon 2008: 10, 11).

We can, then, expect input from all these three national varieties, as well as from Maori, in New Zealand English (NZE). Let us take the Maori influence first: New Zealanders routinely use words such as *pukeko, tui* and *kiwi* (species of bird), and are often unaware of European equivalents even where they exist. Perhaps more surprisingly, words referring to Maori culture and kinship relations are used without explanation, e.g., *mana* ('authority' or 'prestige'), *whānau* ('extended family') and *iwi* ('tribe'). In text, these are written without special marking, such as italics or inverted commas, indicating that they are regarded as a normal part of English. Maori has arguably affected the **prosody** of NZE, too. Warren (1998) finds that Maori speakers of English are often more **syllable-timed** than non-Maori (i.e., their syllables are more equal in length, as in French or Spanish), and that NZE generally is more syllable-timed than Received Pronunciation. What of the original English-speaking settlers? Since the proportions of people from Scotland and Ireland in the mix were greater than their proportions in the British Isles, we might expect to be able to trace many features (words, pronunciations, grammar) back to these two countries. And so it proves: unlike Australians, New Zealanders use *wee* meaning 'small', as in Scotland, and the originally Scottish *pinkie* means 'little finger' (also used by Australians). In Southland (in the far south), the local accent is **rhotic** (see Chapter 18), reflecting the heavy Scottish migration to the region. Unlike most of England, but like Scotland and Ireland, NZE preserves initial /h/ as in *hammer* or *hospital*, reflecting, according to Trudgill (2004: 116), the likelihood that a majority of settlers – all the Irish and Scottish, but also some of the English – did so. Even so, English speakers from the Northern Hemisphere generally perceive NZE as sounding rather like London English. The reason for this lies mainly in the diphthongs, which are strongly 'shifted', in Wells's (1982) sense. This is discussed, for London English, in Chapter 14 – and it turns out that NZE diphthongs are *even more* shifted.

How can it be that NZE is both south-eastern and Scottish/Irish in character? Peter Trudgill (2004) provides a possible answer. He claims that the features (especially pronunciations) that 'won out' did so as a direct consequence of the proportions in which they were heard among the early settlers, and that there was a competition between features with the result that (usually) only one could win. Thus, although plenty of the original settlers did 'drop their aitches' (as Trudgill was able to observe in a bank of recordings made of elderly New Zealanders in the 1940s), none of their descendants do. As for the preponderance of southern English (or London) features more generally, these survive simply because a high proportion of the settlers came from this region. That said, many commentators (e.g. Kerswill, 2007c) argue that Trudgill's theory, while able to account for a great deal of what we know must have happened, is too mechanistic in that it explicitly excludes the influence of social factors in the early stages.

English was barely acceptable in broadcasting at one time as local accents were considered too 'bad' to broadcast. More recently local or regional norms in this group of countries have acquired enough prestige to be accepted in broadcasting and these may also be used in teaching English as a second or foreign language in the region.

22.3.3   English as an elite first language or second language in the British Empire – the Outer Circle

In the eighteenth and nineteenth centuries, Britain had an extensive colonial empire which included parts of North America, the Caribbean, Africa, Asia and the Pacific region. In all these parts of the Empire, there existed an English-speaking elite, who were typically the administrators, professionals, major landowners and business people. In most parts of the empire, Standard English was the language of education and administration, and this led to the development of local or regional standard varieties of English even where English was not used by the majority of people – for example, in parts of East and West Africa, in parts of the Caribbean, in the Indian subcontinent, Malaya and Sri Lanka.

Even though English as a **first** language may have been the property of a very small elite in these countries, it came to be used as a **second** language by a much larger group of people, for whom it was the language of education and economic advancement. This situation has continued in many countries of the former British Empire, where English remains the official language and in some cases the only language of administration and education, at least beyond the primary levels. In India, the long British imperial involvement resulted in a class of Anglo-Indians for whom English was a first, or an everyday second language: English remains a major language of India although only a minority of Indians can use it for daily communication. In most of these countries, a local or regional Standard English has emerged, and in many cases also, a local English-language literature. There are very prominent English-language novelists and playwrights from India, Kenya, Nigeria and St Lucia, for example, as well as important writers of non-fiction in English (such as economists, historians and social scientists) from this group of English-speaking countries.

ILLUSTRATION BOX 22.2

English in Ghana

Ghana, like many countries which gained independence from European coloni-alism in the period after the Second World War, has chosen to keep the language of the former colonial power for all official purposes. Ghana belongs to what Kachru (1986; 2005) calls the Outer Circle of countries using English. It is used as the medium of instruction in virtually all schools (though sometimes a local language is used in the first two years in primary school). It is universally used by government, the law courts, the press and commerce, though local languages are used in smaller-scale trade and may be encountered on shop signs. Ghana is highly multilingual, with some 79 languages distributed across a population of 23 million. Most people regularly use two or more African languages, and with literacy (in English) now at 77 per cent among the young, English is a major **lingua franca** (language used by people who do not have a language in common), alongside Ghanaian Pidgin English, Hausa (a major trade and military language which is also the language of the Hausa in Nigeria), and Akan (the language spoken natively by half the population and which dominates the capital, Accra). Given all this complexity, it comes as no surprise that Ghanaian English has a dis-tinctive flavour on all levels – pronunciation, grammar, vocabulary and usage.

Vowels

The vowel system has fewer phonemes than Inner Circle Englishes. It is similar to those found elsewhere in West Africa:

/i/	bid, bee
/e/	bay
/ɛ/	bed, bird
/a/	bad, bud, bard, _father_, b_utte_r
/ɔ/	pot, paw, port
/o/	boat
/u/	boot, put
/ai/	buy
/ɔi/	boy
/au/	bout

(Trudgill and Hannah, 2002: 125; modified for Ghana)

Consonants

Ghanaians tend to use /t/ (or sometimes /f/) and /d/ for Inner Circle /θ/ and /ð/. Even some fluent speakers of English may use /l/ for /r/, especially in clusters, giving rise to the following spelling in an email:

If we get good _glades_ we will continue our education.

Grammar

Key features which differentiate Ghanaian English from Inner Circle English include:

(i)   Stative verbs (which describe permanent or long-term states) may be used with the progressive aspect:

_She is _having_ a child with a certain man from Ho_

(Huber and Dako, 2008: 369)

(ii) Non-count nouns are often treated as count-nouns:

You should have seen the <u>furnitures!</u>

(Huber and Dako, 2008: 376)

(iii) Reduplication may be used for emphasis:

I must do some <u>small small</u> jobs today
Things are going on <u>small small</u> (i.e. moving slowly)

Vocabulary – new words to describe Ghanaian institutions and culture

Enstoolment	The installation of an Akan chief. The 'stool' element refers to the associated ceremonial stool
Outdooring	The ceremonial presentation of a new-born child to the community after seven days

Vocabulary – new meanings for old words

Brutal American film (seen on a billboard outside a local cinema)	*Brutal* translates as 'exciting' in Inner Circle English
Tea	Milo (brand of malt-based hot milk drink), or other hot drink

Idiomatic usage

I met your absence	You were not there
My junior brother	My younger brother
I'm coming	Wait a moment
"	I'll be back in a minute

Culturally determined usages – an example

Scene: British visitor on a long-distance bus, sitting next to a Ghanaian stranger. After some time, the Ghanaian gets out a banana, peels it, and says to the visitor: "You are invited". The visitor replies: "Thank you!". The Ghanaian eats the banana, and no further communication ensues.

Explanation: As a matter of etiquette, Ghanaians do not eat in the presence of others without offering some of the food. In this instance, the offer was probably ritualistic, and in any case, in Ghanaian English *thank you* as a response to an offer translates as "No thank you" in Inner Circle English.

Sources: UNESCO: http://stats.uis.unesco.org/unesco/TableViewer/document.
aspx?ReportId=121&IF_Language=eng&BR_Country=2880&BR_Region=40540
(accessed 12 October 2008).

Ethnologue: http://www.ethnologue.com/show_country.asp?
name=ghana (accessed 12 October 2008).

Although the United States did not have an empire as large as the British one, American involvement in a small number of countries has similarly produced communities of first- and second-language English speakers, most notably in the Philippines.

Two European countries where English has a major role are Gibraltar and Malta. Gibraltar is a British dependency, while Malta was a British colony for about 150 years, and English is well established in daily life and in administration in both. However, in both places the local communities have another well-established language: Spanish in Gibraltar, and Maltese in Malta. Both have high levels of bilingualism, and the mixing of languages is common in colloquial speech.

22.3.4   Restructured and creolized Englishes in West Africa, Caribbean, South Pacific and elsewhere

In slavery and plantation labour lie the origins of many of the non-standard varieties of English used in some parts of the world. The slave trade along the coast of West Africa from the sixteenth century onwards gave rise to a number of pidgins based on European languages, including English. West African Pidgin English continues to be used in several countries along the coast of West Africa, and is used as a first or community language (i.e., is a creole) in parts of Nigeria.

During the seventeenth century English slave plantations were set up in the Caribbean area – in islands like Jamaica and Trinidad, and on the South American mainland in the Guianas. This led to the development of local varieties of Standard English among the elite, but also to the existence of English-lexicon creoles which are the vernacular language of many parts of the Caribbean. Through migration some of these creoles have come to be spoken elsewhere – in Costa Rica and Nicaragua in Central America, and more recently in Britain, the United States and Canada.

The plantation labour system in the South Pacific region in the nineteenth century led to the spread of an already-established local pidgin which has now split into several varieties and become a national language in Papua New Guinea (under the name **Tok Pisin**), Vanuatu (**Bislama**) and the Solomon Islands (**Pijin**). In parts of Papua New Guinea Tok Pisin is now used as a first language. Elsewhere in the region, Hawaii is home to **Hawaiian Creole English**, a legacy of the plantation labour system there.

22.3.5   English as a foreign language

Beyond the former British Empire or the modern Commonwealth, English has become an important language for education and commerce in many parts of the world. As a result, more and more people are learning English as a foreign language, and more and countries are incorporating English in their educational curricula as a compulsory subject, at earlier and earlier stages of education. We thus have the phenomenon of the huge world-wide growth of English as a **foreign** language. The knowledge of English is particularly widespread in some of the countries of northern and western Europe, to the extent that its position begins to resemble that of English in some of the former British colonies. While English is rarely a feature of family life or small workplaces in these countries, it may be used regularly in some large international businesses and many people will need it in order to practise a profession. Academics and non-fiction writers from these countries have already for a long time been publishing their work in English, and recently some literary writers have begun to use English as the language for their original works (rather than having them translated into English).

22.4   Changing trends in English as a world language

An important aspect of the current expansion of English is its growth as a lingua franca, that is, for use as a common language between speakers or writers for all of whom it is a second or foreign language. When a doctor from Hungary communicates with a doctor from Thailand, whether through speech or in writing, there is a good chance that their discussion will be in English. Likewise, two tourists or students from different parts of the world. In other words, while English at one time was mainly learnt as a foreign language in order to communicate with first-language speakers of English, like British or American business people or tourists, people who speak English as a foreign language now use it largely to communicate with *other* people who speak it as a foreign language. This is undoubtedly one of the main functions of English today, and is found in all sorts of different areas of human activity, for example:

- international diplomacy
- academic conferences
- business meetings
- university courses (courses taught in English in 'Expanding Circle' countries)
- amateur sports and games
- internet chatrooms, discussion forums etc.

The mention of English as a lingua franca on the internet brings us to another important use of English in the world at the moment. Even in countries where there are hardly any first-language speakers of English, English enters people's lives through technology. While of course use of the new technologies is not by any means confined to younger people, it seems that English has a special role among the youth in many countries. For adolescents in many countries, English comes into their daily lives through genres like pop music, hip-hop, advertising (which often incorporates English even in Expanding Circle countries) and computer games. Much of this is passive (i.e., 'hearing' English rather than 'speaking' it) but it is not completely so. Studies have shown, for example, that adolescents may use English among themselves while playing computer games even though for them English is a 'school language', one which they would be expected to use only in English classes. Furthermore, while in other functions Standard English (in a relatively formal register) is the variety most likely to be used, recreational uses of English often involve non-standard and informal varieties of English, or even restructured Englishes like Jamaican Creole (in Reggae and Hip-Hop), African-American Vernacular English (mainly in Hip-Hop) or West African Pidgin English (Afrobeat music). See Pennycook (2007) for a discussion of this.

In addition to these informal uses, English is increasingly used for formal functions where national languages would formerly have been used routinely. This is particularly true in higher education in Continental Europe, where certain courses, or even whole degree programmes, particularly in areas such as business administration, are delivered in English. In Norway, over 80 per cent of doctoral theses are now written in English (Mæhlum, 2008: 22) – a situation which is common in much of northern Europe. Some people see this kind of high-status use of English as a threat to the national languages.

In fact, many people around the world are speaking English as one part of their repertoire of languages in daily use. In some speech communities, mixing of languages or **code-switching** between a variety of English and another local language is a normal practice. This is very common in communities where English is well-established alongside another language (Welsh in Wales, Maltese in Malta, Spanish in Gibraltar, Chinese in Hong Kong) and is one of the main ways in which English (in one of its local varieties) is used outside the Inner circle.

22.5 Case study: Jamaica

On the Caribbean island of Jamaica, the slavery system resulted in the development of a creole, called **Jamaican Creole** by linguists although it is often called **Patois** or **Patwa** by its speakers. This language is described in more detail in Chapter 21 on Pidgin and Creole Englishes. Also in Jamaica, the existence of an English-speaking elite led to the development of a Jamaican form of **Standard** English, which was and is the language of administration, education and the print media. Jamaican Standard English, like other Outer Circle Englishes, is basically very similar to Standard British English but is different in its pronunciation and includes vocabulary of local origin (in particular words of Creole, African and Spanish origin).

22.5.1 The creole continuum

One of the things which has made the Jamaican situation interesting to linguists is the observation (first made by David De Camp) that in Jamaica, there is what appears to be a **continuum** linking the broadest Creole (i.e., the form of Creole which is most different from English) with the local Standard English. In other words, although it is possible to identify a broad creole (the **basilect**) and a locally prestigious standard form (the **acrolect**) which are spoken by some people, we can also find speakers – the majority – who speak neither, but something in between. As De Camp put it (1971: 350): 'Each Jamaican speaker commands a span of this continuum, the breadth of the span depending on the breadth of his social contacts.' We thus have a situation of two languages, each with its own distinct grammar, linked by a continuum of intermediate varieties. Furthermore, these varieties have

Acrolect (Jamaican Standard)

	/ - /	*I am eating*	
	/ - /	/aɪ æm i:tɪn/	
	/ - /		
	/ - /	/a ɪz i:tɪn/	*I is eatin'*
Mesolect	/ - /		
(the middle)	/ - /	/a iitɪn/	*I eatin'*
	/ - /		
	/ - /	/mi i:tɪn/	*me eatin'*
	/ - /		
	/ - /	/mi a i:t/	*me a eat*
	/ - /		
Basilect (Broadest Creole)		/mi a nyam/	*me a nyam*

The Jamaican Creole continuum FIGURE 22.1

strong social associations: the acrolect or standard would be used by educated speakers – professionals, for example – while the basilect is associated with rural people and the urban poor. The **mesolect** or range of intermediate varieties is associated with speakers who lie somewhere in-between on the social scale.

Figure 22.1, taken from Sebba (1997: 211), illustrates the continuum as a 'ladder' joining the basilect and the acrolect. The example sentence 'I am eating' in Standard English differs from British or American English only in terms of accent. The corresponding sentence in the basilect or broadest Creole, *mi a nyam*, differs from it in several important ways: it has the pronoun *mi* where SE has *I*, it has a verbal tense/aspect particle *a* instead of *am* (which is a part of the verb *to be*) and it has a different vocabulary item, *nyam* (probably of African origin) where SE has *eat*. All this just shows that SE and JC are two languages with their own grammar and lexicon. What is more remarkable is that the intermediate combinations of these forms can be found as well; thus most people in Jamaica in fact speak something which is 'more Creole-like' or 'more Standard English-like' but is not really either.

Although the 'post-creole' continuum depicted above is a feature only of Jamaica and other creole-speaking parts of the Caribbean, and resulted from a particular set of social and historical circumstances, a similar continuum between a local vernacular form of English and Standard English may exist elsewhere. For example, it has been claimed that there may be such a continuum linking Scots and Scottish English, Singlish and Singaporean Standard English, West African Pidgin English and Standard English in Nigeria, and Hawaiian Creole English and Standard English in Hawaii. In each case, the local Standard English has connotations of prestige and education, while the vernacular is stigmatized and viewed as illegitimate, though it may be an important symbol of identity for its speakers.

ADVANCES BOX 22.2

London Jamaican

In the early 1980s, schoolchildren of Caribbean descent in London were observed to be using a variety of Jamaican Creole, mixed with English, in their everyday conversation among themselves. This variety was given the name **London Jamaican** by linguists (see Sebba, 1993). What was surprising about this was that only some of these children had parents who were from Jamaica; others had no connection with Jamaica itself; one or both parents may have come from elsewhere in the Caribbean and used a different creole altogether. This was of importance for several reasons.

Firstly, it showed that in this case – and probably in many other cases as well – language was transmitted through peer groups and not just from parents to children. In other words, these Jamaican Creole speakers had learned their Jamaican Creole from their age-mates or slightly older children, not from their parents (in fact, some parents deliberately tried to prevent their children from speaking Creole because of the stigma it bore).

Secondly, London Jamaican seemed to have great importance as a badge of identity. In fact, it contained many of the more stigmatized basilectal or 'deep creole' features: this was unexpected, given that the parents of the children probably spoke mesolectal varieties themselves. London Jamaican seemed to be the product of an 'act of identity' (Le Page and Tabouret-Keller, 1985) in which its speakers intentionally distanced themselves from British English by using a language variety maximally different from it.

In spite of the fact just mentioned, most speakers of London Jamaican did not speak 'pure' London Jamaican for long stretches at a time, but mixed it frequently through code-switching with London English (see end of Section 22.4 above). Sebba (1993) found that although many London-born Caribbeans could speak and understand Creole well, they used London English much more than they used Creole. Creole had special functions in conversation, for example to emphasize a point or to mark something intended as a joke.

Recommended readings

There are numerous books covering the topic of World Englishes from different perspectives. Two accessible general overviews are Crystal (2003) and Svartvik and Leech (2006). Some books, like Melchers and Shaw (2003) provide descriptions and illustrations of individual varieties of English, while others like Mair (2003) and Pennycook (2007) concern themselves more with the social, political and pedagogical issues relating to the use of English around the world. A book which successfully deals with both these aspects at a beginner level and provides useful resources is Jenkins (2003). Schmied (1991) and Mesthrie (2008) cover Outer Circle English in particular regions. Bauer (2002) is concerned with the main Inner Circle varieties (USA, Canada, Australia, New Zealand and South Africa), while Trudgill and Hannah (2002) has Standard English as its main focus, with most detail on the Inner Circle and some coverage of the Outer and Expanding Circles. Huber (1999) is an in-depth study of Ghanaian Pidgin English. Kachru, Kachru and Nelson (2006) is an advanced resource covering the important theoretical and pedagogical issues in this field.

Notes

1 I am grateful to Paul Kerswill for providing the material on English in New Zealand and in Ghana.
2 This may be less true where computer-mediated communication and interactions such as gaming are concerned.

PART 4

English Writing: Style, Genre and Practice

EDITED BY JONATHAN CULPEPER

CHAPTER 23

Speech, Writing and Discourse Type

ANDREW WILSON

23.1 Medium versus discourse type in language variation

We all probably have an intuition that people tend, on the whole, to write differently from the way that they speak. But how far can we account for this in terms of the **medium** itself (i.e., speech vs. writing) and how far is it a consequence of situational features (e.g., the level of formality or the overall purpose of the text)? Consider first of all the following extract from a real-life conversation between two teenage girls (the markers <ol> and </ol> bracket stretches of overlapping speech):

> KATH: We were having a sly fag in the ladies. I thought oh my God, my God, my God he's gonna smell it on me. He knows I smoke anyway so it's not a prob <pause> well not really <ol>anyway.</ol>
>
> CLAIRE: <ol>He must know.</ol>
>
> KATH: I know he knows. We were having a massive a-- er conversation the other night <pause> about smoking, he was going oh well you know, you smoking are you, I went why, he goes oh we found, found a box of matches in your er top I went oh no no no, it's just for, for the joss sticks, yeah. He went yeah alright. <laugh> I mean I've, I've smoked <pause> cos I was in France with him last year erm sitting at the erm dinner table smoking a cigar with him <ol>and my uncle</ol>
>
> CLAIRE: <ol>Urgh!</ol>
>
> KATH: I like cigars.
>
> CLAIRE: Rough.
>
> KATH: Only the thin ones, the massive chunky ones are rough.
>
> (BNC Text KPH 1216)

The most characteristic features of this spoken text can be summarized under three broad headings.

(i) Degree of fluency and planning

Many of the features in the text are connected with the fact that it is composed in **real time** – what we might also call the stream of consciousness.

This means that each word is uttered only shortly after being called to mind: pre-planning of stretches of language is minimal, and the speaker has no possibility to go back and edit them before placing them into the awareness of the hearer. Consequently, we see various types of retraction – that is, going back on what has just been said – such as postposed hedging phrases (*well not really*) and incomplete words (as in the phrase *a massive a-- er conversation*, where we guess that the speaker was originally going to say *argument* rather than *conversation*). When the speaker needs time to think, she may make use of pauses, either silent ones (marked by *<pause>* in the transcript) or what we call **filled pauses** (particles such as *er* and *erm*). Alternatively, she may, so to speak, 'go into autopilot' and keep repeating the same word whilst she thinks of what to say next: we see several examples of this in the extract. In grammatical terms, we see relatively little in the way of complex sentence structures but mostly a sequence of very short independent clauses. (On planning and fluency see, for example, Goldman-Eisler, 1968; and a very thorough recent review by Eklund, 2004.)

(ii) Level of formality

A second, rather smaller set of features concerns the level of **formality** of the text. We can judge it to be quite an informal text. It tends to make use of contractions rather than full forms – for example, *gonna* rather than *going to* and *cos* in place of *because* – and it also employs mostly informal vocabulary: *fag* (instead of *cigarette*), *to go* (instead of *to say*), and *yeah*.

(iii) Interactional features

The final set of features are a direct result of the fact that this is an **interactive** text. The most of important of these are the presence of **turn-taking** between the two speakers and the two occurrences of overlapping speech.

Now consider the following piece of written language, taken from an unpublished short story:

> Sara was a heavy smoker and after twenty minutes' ride she was longing for another cigarette. Reaching a quiet glade, she dismounted, took out her silver cigarette case, and lit up one of her Turkish cigarettes. As she inhaled the smoke deeply into her lungs, she heard a low moaning noise coming from the trees. What could it be? She dropped her cigarette on the ground, crushed it out with her shiny riding boot, and removed from her pocket the small pistol she always carried with her for protection. The risk from petty criminals was ever present in this industrial metropolis...

This clearly feels quite different in style from the conversation, so let us look at what exactly is distinctive in it. To help systematize the comparison, we shall use the same set of headings.

(i) Degree of fluency and planning

This text contains no examples of filled or silent pauses, nor does it contain any incomplete words or retraction. There is some degree of repetition – for example, the word *cigarette(s)* is repeated four times. Here, however, the repeated words do not come immediately after one another, as they did in the first passage. In other words, this repetition does not seem to serve the purpose of 'playing for time' as the author gathers his thoughts, but is simply a device for continuing the progression of a theme across several sentences. The grammatical structures are also more complex. For instance, we have examples of subordinate clauses being fronted before the main clause (e.g., *as she inhaled...*), which requires a certain amount of advance planning. Two sentences also exhibit the 'tricolon' structure from formal rhetoric: they are made up of three main clauses of increasing length, for example: *she dismounted* (2 words), *took out her silver cigarette case* (6 words), *and lit up one of her Turkish cigarettes* (8 words). (See Chapter 8, Section 8.6 for discussion of grammar and spoken language).

(ii) Level of formality

The vocabulary is more formal than that of the conversation. For example, we encounter some relatively obscure words such as *glade* and *metropolis*. There is, furthermore, a preference for more formal Latinate synonyms in cases where there are also informal alternatives – for example, *dismounted* (rather than *got off*), *removed* (instead of *took out*).

(iii) Interactional features

In comparison with the first extract, this text is non-interactive: it involves a single narrator and does not have any turn-taking.

So, we can certainly see a number of differences between the spoken and written texts. However, we must ask ourselves: how many of these differences are the result of a difference in medium? How far would it have made a difference if the conversation had been carried on in writing by means of an online chat-room and the story had been made up and told orally to an assembled group of people? The simple answer to this is: probably very little. Leaving aside deliberate attempts to represent speech within written texts (e.g., play scripts and dialogue in novels), nearly all of the features which we noted in respect of the conversational extract can also occur in certain types of written language. (The only real exceptions to this are filled pauses, incomplete words and immediate repetition in the service of planning.) The discourse type in which these features are most strongly present is online chat-room discourse, where two or more participants are writing messages to each other on the computer screen in real time (Yates, 1996). So, it seems that factors other than the medium must be responsible for most of the things that we may intuitively think of as 'spoken' language features, as exemplified in the conversational extract. These factors can probably be reduced down to three, of which the first is by far the most important: (1) the psychological constraints of composition in 'real time'; (2) informality, which is a feature of many spoken discourse types; and (3) interactivity, which is also very common in speech.

However, we should also note that there are some genuinely unique features of spoken language which are not visible in the transcribed extract. Of greatest relevance to a comparison with writing are those that come under the general heading of **prosody** – stress, loudness, pauses, syllable duration and intonation – and we will consider below how these affect spoken versus written expression. It is also important to emphasize that, although this particular transcript contains punctuation, the notion of punctuation belongs solely to written language, as we shall see in Section 23.2.3.

23.2 Medium

23.2.1 The primacy of speech or the primacy of writing?

If you pick up an introductory book about language, it is quite likely that it will make some reference to the 'primacy of speech'. What linguists mean by this is that language was originally a purely spoken phenomenon. It was not for a long time after humans were able to speak that they started to write things down (Wildgen, 2004), and even today, children learn to speak before they learn to write. The upshot of this, it is claimed, is that, if we want to understand how language works, we should focus our attention on its spoken form, without importing any assumptions that are based on the written medium. However, there are good grounds for questioning whether speech is any longer independent of writing and whether we should therefore nowadays talk about the 'primacy of writing'.[1]

Because most contemporary speakers of English are capable of reading and writing, and have undergone formal schooling in which these skills play a key part, it is arguable that we no longer think about language in purely spoken terms, but that our notions of usage are suffused by concepts from writing. For example, if you ask almost anyone, they will say that language contains sentences. However, if you look at an unpunctuated transcript of spontaneous speech, it can sometimes be very difficult to identify where sentence breaks should be placed. In fact, you may be surprised to know that there are occasionally no identifiable gaps of silence at all between 'sentences' in speech (cf. O'Connell and Kowal, 2002: 94). The thing is that most people's notion of 'sentence' comes largely from written language, where sentences are entities delineated by full stops (or by question or exclamation marks). Indeed, even early examples of writing (such as ancient Greek and Latin manuscripts) may have little or no punctuation (cf. Finegan, 2001: 32–3), and this can sometimes make it difficult for a modern scholar to work out the grammar of the text. In Old and Middle English texts also (roughly covering the period 700–1500), there tended to be very little punctuation, and what did appear was often unsystematic. The systematic punctuation of sentences, broadly as it exists today, dates only from the seventeenth century (see, for example, Treip, 1970; Lennard, 1995; Robinson, 1998).

Similarly, the problem of deciding what constitutes a **word** in English is also very much grounded in writing (for a discussion of this, see Chapter 5, especially Table 5.2; also Katamba, 1994: ch. 2). For example, both English and German have a class of compound nouns. In German, the elements of the compound noun are always written together as a single word – for example, *Bahnkarte* (where *Bahn* = 'rail' and *Karte* = 'card'); but, in English, there is frequently a choice: we can choose to write *rail card*, *rail-card*, or *railcard*. Occasionally, however, we have to write something as two separate words, for instance: *riding boots*. This raises the question: if we can have *railcard* as a single word, why can't we also have *ridingboots*? In speech, the issue hardly arises, because the pronunciation is the same, regardless of orthography; however, in writing, it is a major issue, because present-day written usage is codified in terms of 'correctness' in a way that is not the case for spoken language. The whole question hinges on definitions that are grounded in writing.

23.2.2 Things that you can't do in writing but you can do in speech

The two key meaning-bearing elements that are present in speech but not in writing are **prosody** (i.e., stress, loudness, intonation, syllable duration, pauses, etc.) and – at least as far as face-to-face communication is concerned – **non-verbal communication** or 'body language'. Although these frequently do not contribute hugely to the verbal message, there are nevertheless instances where they are crucial in acting as cues for the disambiguation of pragmatic meaning or **force**. For instance, someone once wrote in an e-mail:

Do you think it is worth spending 60 pounds on this? (That's a genuine question – not a negative comment!!)

In spoken language, he would not have needed to include the sentence in brackets, because his intonation would have distinguished between an unmarked question (asking for information) and an evaluative comment (implying that the thing was not worth 60 pounds). In writing, however, these clues are absent, and there is consequently a greater danger that an ambiguous speech act will be wrongly interpreted. To compensate, it is necessary to use this form of **metapragmatic comment** (cf. Thomas, 1995).

Similar cases occur when someone wants to emphasize an element in a sentence (Quirk et al., 1985). Take, for example, the following:

Sara didn't tread mud into the carpet.

In ordinary writing, this looks like just a straightforward informative sentence about what Sara has (not) done. However, in speech, the same sentence structure could be used to imply that, although Sara had not trodden mud into the carpet, somebody else had done so. This effect is achieved by adding extra stress and a fall-rise intonation to the word *Sara*; but to get across the same message in writing, it would be necessary to change the sentence structure to something like:

It wasn't Sara who trod mud into the carpet.

or to add extra information to make a contrast explicit:

Sara didn't tread mud into the carpet: Lizzie did.

An alternative strategy would be to use a different typeface for *Sara* (such as capitals, bold, italics or underlining), and we will consider this in the next section.

23.2.3 Features unique to written language

Although written communication lacks prosody and body language, this does not mean that it is, in some sense, the 'poor cousin' of spoken language. In fact, it has a number of valuable features of its own, which spoken language does not share. The most important of these are punctuation, typeface, and what I shall call font shifts (i.e., the use of bold, italics, capitalization, etc.)

Punctuation serves primarily as an aid to the reader in distinguishing the grammatical structure of the text and helping to resolve any ambiguities.

ILLUSTRATION BOX 23.1

Creative punctuation

The following extracts are from a magazine advertisement for holidays in the Bahamas:

> *Our sea averages 77°F all year round. No wonder people take to it. To snorkel, scuba dive, sail, kayak or fish.*

> *After soaking up the sun, there's nothing better than a long, relaxing bath. In the sea.*

In the first extract, *take to* is ambiguous: it can mean either to get to like something or to embark onto something (as in the idiom *take to the road*). Following a positive statement about the water temperature, and with a full stop afterwards suggesting that the sentence is complete, our first instinct is to understand it in its 'get to like' sense. But then we see the incomplete sentence fragment *To snorkel, scuba dive, sail, kayak or fish* and we must reconsider our interpretation: clearly, the 'embark' sense is also intended.

In the second extract, once we reach the first full stop, we assume again that the information package of the sentence is complete: we imagine going back to our hotel to take a bath. But we then read on and see an incomplete sentence fragment, *In the sea*, which we must tack on to what has gone before. Immediately, our assumption is shattered and we realize that we are to bathe in the sea...

These creative effects would not have been possible without punctuation, nor if the advertisers had punctuated the sentences 'correctly' so that no fragments remained without a finite verb in them. So, although punctuation often serves to resolve ambiguities, sometimes it can be used deliberately to introduce them.

However, it also enables a writer to do things which are possible in speech only by changing the wording or sentence structure (in a similar way to the speech-to-writing example above). For instance, the use of quote marks can have two main functions: (a) to mark something out as direct speech or a quotation without needing a speech act verb or other explicit marker (e.g., *N said; according to N*), and (b) in an attitudinal function, to distance oneself from a word or statement or to question its meaning. We could, for example, write *This 'improvement' in conditions* (questioning whether it was really an improvement), whilst in speech we would have to say something like *This so called improvement in conditions*. Quote marks are so useful for the latter purpose that the 1980s chat-show host Russell Harty took them over into his body language and often used his fingers to 'draw' quote marks in the air.

Typeface plays an important role in suggesting an overall ethos for a text. For example, German 'Fraktur'-style printing on beer-bottle labels is used to emphasize the national origin of the beer. More generally, the so called serif typefaces (such as Times New Roman, which is offered as a default by most word-processing programs) suggest a traditional ethos, whilst sans serif typefaces (such as Arial, another common typeface in word-processing) are more suggestive of modernity. (Figure 23.1 explains the difference between a serif and sans serif typeface.) Advertising, in particular, makes creative use of typefaces: advertisements that draw on themes from science, medicine and engineering will tend to use sans serif typefaces or typefaces which mimic a computer screen, whilst advertisements for luxury goods will often use serif typefaces and typefaces that imitate old-fashioned copperplate handwriting.

Font shifts again can have multiple roles. Italics can, of course, be used for emphasis (another way round the problem discussed in Section 23.2.2) but also, for instance, to indicate that a word belongs properly to a language other than English – for example, 'One of the features of *fin-de-siècle* Paris was ...'. Word-initial capitals may be used to distinguish between general and specific uses of a word –for example, *the University* versus *a university*. In the case of words which started out their life as acronyms, such as *LASER* (= Light Amplified by Stimulated Emission of Radiation), the point at which they began to be written more commonly in lower case can help linguists to determine when they changed from being thought of as acronyms and became accepted words in the language (cf. Katamba, 1994: 182).

This	This
This is an example of a serif typeface. The 'serifs' are the little embellishments at the ends of bars – for example at the bottom of the vertical bar of the T and on the left and right embellishments of the horizontal bar of the T.	This is a sans serif typeface. ('Sans' is French for 'without'.) Notice that the T consists of two simple straight lines, without any (or 'serifs').

Serif and sans serif typefaces   *FIGURE 23.1*

ILLUSTRATION BOX 23.2

Cross-linguistic variation in written language

Some European languages (such as French and German) have peculiarities in writing practices that set them apart from English.

Capitalization

Nowadays – unless something is being written entirely in capital letters – English only uses capital letters at the beginnings of sentences and proper names. In German, however, a capital letter is used at the beginning of *every* noun, regardless of whether or not it is a name. This practice is also commonly encountered in eighteenth-century English texts, but it then quite rapidly dropped out of use, leaving us with the convention that we use today.

Emphasis

When we want to emphasize something in English, we normally write it in bold or italic type. Failing that, we may underline it or write it entirely in capitals. In German, however, at least until around the 1940s, it could be very difficult to use these conventions, because a lot of things were printed in a special kind of typeface known as 'Fraktur'. Instead, a space was often inserted between each letter of the word. For example:

Der V o r s ch l a g von M e y e r i s t gut.

This practice was also used in typewriting and persisted in print even after Fraktur was mostly abandoned. It is only comparatively recently that German has widely adopted the practice of using bold and italics, like English does.

Writing people's names

In English, we do not normally give any special emphasis to people's names. We begin them with capital letters, but that is it. However, in both German and French, there is a cultural tendency to give added emphasis to surnames in certain written texts. German traditionally used the spacing method referred to above, but sometimes printed the whole name in capitals; French just uses capitals. The deeper reasons for giving this emphasis to names are not entirely clear, but they may be tied up with notions of politeness (cf. Myers, 1989).

Indicating special discourse types

Vachek (1989) has pointed out that newspapers in Germany use font shifts as a way of indicating different discourse types. Whilst the main body of the newspaper is printed in ordinary type, 'lighter' material is printed completely in italics, to distinguish it from the more serious reporting and topical commentary.

23.3 Discourse type

We began this chapter by looking at two examples – one written and one spoken – and concluded that many of the differences between them had more to do with situational features such as formality and purpose than with the medium itself. Once we get onto considering factors such as these, we are no longer talking about variation according to medium but about variation according to discourse type.

23.3.1 Classifying texts: text-internal and text-external criteria

Discourse type (sometimes also called **register**) is a generic term for systematic variation between different kinds of texts, which avoids some of the complexities introduced by other terms in the area of language variation (see also Section 23.3.2). One of the reasons that the terminology is so complex is that there are two ways of approaching variation according to discourse type: one by referring to features external to the text and one by referring to features internal to the text.

A text-external approach draws on features such as the characteristics of the anticipated audience (e.g., age, social class, educational level, gender, etc.), the characteristics of the author, the nature of the relationship between the author and the audience (e.g., formal or informal), the overall purpose of the text (e.g., to inform, to instruct, to entertain), and so on.

A text-internal approach examines which linguistic features predominate. For instance, are most sentences long and complex or short and simple? To what extent are nouns modified by adjectives? Which verb tenses are used the most often? By comparing check-lists of features such as these, it is possible to group texts according to similarities in their use of language, without considering any text-external criteria.

23.3.2 Genre, text-type, style and sublanguage

As we just noted, the terminology of discourse types is quite complicated. Another reason for this is that it is used inconsistently by different authors, perhaps more so than terminology in other areas of language study. The terms and definitions that I shall introduce here are based mainly on those proposed by Fairclough (1992), but you should be aware in your reading that the same terms may be used to mean different things.

On the one hand, **genre** is a very common way of referring to a discourse type. We talk, for example, about the genre of the novel, or of the newspaper editorial, or of political speeches. More narrowly, however, genre is best used to describe a classification of texts where text-external criteria have a decisive role. Fairclough (1992: 126) defines it as 'a relatively stable set of conventions that is associated with…a socially ratified type of activity'. So, when we talk about the newspaper editorial as a genre, we refer both to its conditions of production, distribution and consumption, and to its characteristic linguistic features.

The term **text type**, on the other hand, is normally reserved for a description of discourse types based solely on text-internal features, without any reference to social practices.

ILLUSTRATION BOX 23.3

A suggested checklist for discourse type analysis (adapted from Weise (1993) and Hoffmann (1991))

1 Situational criteria
1.1 **Address** (source, author(s), time of publication)
1.2 **Standard** (e.g., American English, British English)
1.3 **Subject field** (general area and special area)
1.4 **Degree of professionalism** (e.g., whether addressed to experts or lay-people)
1.5 **Medium** (written v. spoken; special forms such as radio, TV, etc.)
1.6 **Degree of formality** (formal v. informal; prepared v. spontaneous)

2 Interactional criteria
2.1 **Participation** (monologue, dialogue, polylogue (e.g., a round-table discussion))
2.2 **Social roles** (kind of interaction; differences in status between participants)
2.3 **Spatial and temporal contact** (proximity v. distance)

3 Pragmatic criteria
3.1 **Communicative function** (What is the overall function of the text? (e.g., to establish contact; to convey information; to exercise control))
3.2 **Speech act configuration** (Which speech acts are used to convey the communicative function of the text? Do they occur in particular sequences? Which predominate?)

4 Semantic and syntactic criteria
4.1 **Macrostructure** (What is the overall structural plan of the text?)
4.2 **Coherence** (How are the elements of the text linked together? Repetition of key words; use of conjunctions; linking adverbs (*therefore, so, thus, then, next,* etc.); deictic determiners (*this, that, those, these*); pronouns)
4.3 **Grammar** (What sentence types predominate – statements, questions, commands, exclamations? Are sentences mostly short or long? Are they simple or complex? Coordinated or subordinated? Do nouns occur on their own or are they typically modified by adjectives or postmodifying phrases/clauses? Are adjectives typically modified by adverbs? Do verbs occur on their own or are they modified by adverbials? Are these adverbials single words or phrases/clauses? Are contracted verb forms used?)
4.4 **Vocabulary** (Is it formal or informal? Are specialized technical terms used? Are they explained or is it assumed people know what they mean? What are the main semantic fields involved? How varied are the choices of wording within these semantic fields?)
4.5 **Grammatical categories** (What voices/tenses/persons of the verb are used? Are nouns mostly proper or common; abstract or concrete; human, animate or inanimate? Are pronouns mostly first, second, or third person; singular or plural?)

ADVANCES BOX 23.1

Multidimensional analysis

An important advance in the way that we classify texts according to text-internal features has been enabled by the use of large computer-readable databanks of naturally occurring texts. We call these databanks **corpora** (singular: **corpus**). When twinned with advanced statistical methods, corpora are a powerful way of discovering or confirming fundamental patterns of variation between texts. Looking at both spoken and written texts, Biber (1988) uncovered several dimensions of variation. The most important of these is the dimension 'informational' versus 'interactive', which incorporates many of the features hitherto often called 'written' vs. 'spoken'. Other dimensions include 'narrative' vs. 'non-narrative' and 'impersonal' vs. 'non-impersonal'. The basic idea is that any text can be positioned somewhere on each of these dimensions by adding up the frequencies of characteristic linguistic features. Although the replicability of dimensions other than 'informational-interactive' has been questioned (e.g., by Lee, 2000), Biber's work is important because it shifts the focus from classifying texts in terms of a typology (so that a text either belongs to type X or it does not) to thinking of discourse type variation in terms of gradients (so that any text is more or less of X). This ties in well with ideas such as interdiscursivity (see Section 23.3.3 in the main text), which questions whether there are (m)any 'pure' discourse types. Similar work has been carried out by Nakamura (e.g., 1992), who has suggested that we can classify written texts mostly according to a single dimension 'informative-imaginative', and by Takahashi (2006), who focused especially on spoken language and revealed the importance of the dimension 'formal-informal'.

A job interview is a good example for distinguishing between genre and text-type approaches. In approaching this discourse type from a genre perspective, we would make reference to features such as its purpose (getting a job), its setting (commercial), the participants involved (applicant, manager, etc.), its place in a larger pattern of social behaviour (the whole process of advertising and applying for a job), and so on. We might choose to group it, using these criteria, with functionally related discourse types such as job descriptions, application letters, interview report forms, etc. In approaching the job interview from a text-type perspective, however, we would focus solely on linguistic features such as the lengths of turns, predominant speech act types and their sequences (e.g., question followed by report), level of formality of vocabulary, pronouns (we would expect mostly first- and second-person forms), verb tenses and so on. In this case, we would probably end up grouping it with other conversations involving unequal roles, in so far as they would tend to show a similar distribution of linguistic features – for instance, doctor–patient interactions and the exchanges between experts and members of the public on the TV show *The Antiques Roadshow*.

Related to discourse types is also the notion of **style**. Fairclough considers style to be describable as a combination of three components: tenor (the relationship between participants – e.g., formal, informal, intimate, casual); mode (what we have been calling medium – i.e., spoken, written, written to be spoken, etc.); and rhetorical mode (i.e., the overall communicative function of the text – to describe, argue, explain, etc.). However, this is – unusually for Fairclough – a rather peculiar use of the term. A more widely agreed definition might be to consider style as the set of characteristic linguistic features that distinguish one textual entity from another – be it one text-type from another or the writing of one author from that of another. (We commonly talk, for example, about the style of Jane Austen or Charles Dickens. See also Chapter 26 for further elaboration of the notion of style).

Finally, a **sublanguage** is a rather special discourse type, in that it constitutes a very restricted variety of language. To understand what this implies, it is helpful to think about its opposite. If we read a novel from start to finish, we will constantly come across words being used for the first time in that text: the last page may well contain at least one, and possibly several words that have not been used in the text up to that point. New sentence structures will also continue to crop up as the text progresses. In contrast, the main defining characteristic of a sublanguage is that it reaches what we call **closure** (i.e., an absence of new words or structures) very quickly (McEnery and Wilson, 1996: ch. 6). For instance, if you watch a whole series of television weather forecasts, you will quite soon reach a point at which rather few new words or grammatical constructions are starting to crop up. This is what defines a sublanguage. Examples of sublanguages, in addition to weather forecasts, include such things as pathology and radiology reports in hospitals (cf. Friedman, Kra and Rzhetsky 2002).

23.3.3 Interdiscursivity

Although we typically have a fairly shrewd idea of what a particular discourse type looks like, there are, in fact, rather few 'pure' types. For example, we might think that a typical full-page magazine advertisement consists of a big colour picture, a main slogan in large type, a longer piece of text in smaller type, and then the brand logo, possibly with a further short slogan. However, some magazine advertisements deliberately disguise themselves as other discourse types such as news reporting, cookery recipes and so on, borrowing both their physical appearance and their linguistic characteristics. This mixing of discourse types is known either as **generic intertextuality** (Cook, 2001) or, more simply, as **interdiscursivity** (Fairclough, 1992). Although advertising is a major everyday user of interdiscursivity, we encounter it in many other contexts: for instance, newspaper opinion pieces that draw on the discourse type of court judgements, university prospectuses that draw on prototypical features of advertising, and so on.

23.4 Bringing it all together: medium and discourse type variation in the British National Corpus

The British National Corpus (hereafter: BNC) is a very large computer databank of British English, containing approximately one hundred million running words of text and over 4000 individual text samples. Ninety per cent of these texts are written texts and 10 per cent are spoken texts. Most of the texts in the BNC date from the late 1980s and early 1990s, which means that, whilst it is not bang up to date, it does represent a very recent stage in the history of English and is therefore an excellent test-bed for exploring ideas about variation according to medium and discourse type.

The BNC is divided into four main sections – two written and two spoken. The written element is divided into imaginative texts (i.e., fiction and poetry) and informative texts (i.e., non-fiction); the spoken element is divided into conversational speech and task-oriented speech. Task-oriented speech refers to speech events such as lectures, church services, doctor–patient consultations, business meetings, etc. – that is, anything except everyday conversation.

Using a 2,000,000 word subsample of the BNC, Rayson, Wilson and Leech (2002) looked at the frequencies of different grammatical word categories (e.g., adjective, past tense verb, subordinating conjunction, etc.) in each of the four sections. For each word category, they placed the corpus sections on a gradient from the one which had the lowest frequency of use of the category to the one with the highest frequency. Their working hypothesis was that, with most word categories examined, there would be a clear distinction between the two spoken sections on the one hand and the two written sections on the other.

In some cases – for example, with adjectives – it turned out that the distinction between speech and writing was indeed the most important one. These cases tended to show the following gradient:

conversational speech – task-oriented speech – imaginative writing – informative writing

where both the spoken corpus sections are at one end and both the written sections are at the other. However, in other cases – for example, with the preposition *of* – it was evident that the discourse function was a more strongly distinguishing factor than the medium. In these cases, the gradient was as follows:

conversational speech – imaginative writing – task-oriented speech – informative writing

The fact that neither a medium-based nor a discourse-type gradient dominates overall in the BNC is likely to be down partly to the mixing of varied situational features within the corpus sections – that is, they turn out to be not particularly homogeneous. For instance, the section of task-oriented speech mixes quite informal, spontaneous and interactive speech events (such as meetings) with comparatively formal, planned and non-interactive ones (such as church sermons). Indeed, even a better defined section such as imaginative writing, which consists predominantly of fictional prose, is subject to the effects of interdiscursivity: fictional prose often contains extensive amounts of invented dialogue, which give it an immediate partial affinity with conversational speech.

'There is always more to it' (DeLillo, 1988: 321, quoted in Hogenraad, McKenzie and Péladeau, 2003: 234), and such is certainly often the case with variation between texts. However, two overriding morals are clear, which you should bear in mind when undertaking analyses. First, avoid excessively broad generalizations about the grounds for variation, especially when these are cast in terms of the medium rather than situational features: genuinely medium-specific features make up only a very small proportion of what distinguishes between texts. Second, beware of any pre-imposed classifications of variation, which may be disguising other possible reasons for what is observable in the form of text-internal features. New discourse types, such as those which have emerged in computer-mediated and mobile phone communication, can be of considerable use in revealing other factors that lay hidden behind previous assumptions.

Recommended readings

For a general overview of spoken and written English, you might consult Hughes (1996). On the terminology of discourse types, and especially on the notion of interdiscursivity, see Chapter 4 of Fairclough (1992). The most accessible account of Biber's multidimensional work and its applications can be found in Biber, Conrad and Reppen (1998). Vachek (1989) is one of the few scholars who have looked comprehensively at writing as a system in its own right, whilst Nunberg (1990) has undertaken a more narrowly focused study of punctuation. McEnery and Wilson (1996) devote a whole chapter to sublanguages. Biber and Finegan (1994) is a good general collection of essays on discourse-type variation. Useful checklists for classifying texts according to both external and internal criteria are provided by Weise (1993) and Hoffmann (1991), on which the checklist in the current chapter is based.

Note

1 The philosopher Jacques Derrida (1976) also argued for the 'primacy of writing', though on very different grounds to those outlined here.

CHAPTER 24

Language in Newspapers

ELENA SEMINO

24.1 Introduction

In the twenty-first century, news and information are easily available 24 hours a day via television, the Internet, mobile phones and so on. You may therefore wonder whether it is still relevant to study the language of newspapers. Recent statistics suggest that it is: in 2007, 45 per cent of all adults in the United Kingdom read a national newspaper every day, 73 per cent read a national newspaper every week, and 81 per cent read a national newspaper every four weeks (www.nmauk.co.uk).

Newspaper language, however, is not a single, homogeneous object of study. This is mainly because (a) there are many different types of newspapers, and (b) newspapers include a variety of different genres. In the next two sections of this chapter, I consider each of these aspects of variation in turn. I then focus particularly on the language of news reports, and compare two reports of the same event from two different newspapers. I finish by discussing in detail the presentation of speech in news reports.

24.2 Newspapers and news values

Newspapers differ primarily in terms of their geographical reach and the readership they address. A visit to your local newsagent will reveal a difference between regional newspapers (e.g., the *Yorkshire Post*) and national newspapers (e.g., *The Times*). The former are based locally and target a local readership, while the latter are based in major cities and target a national readership. A further distinction, which is particularly relevant to the United Kingdom, can be made between 'quality' or 'elite' newspapers on the one hand (e.g., *The Guardian*, *The Independent*), and 'popular' newspapers on the other (e.g., *The Sun*, the *Daily Mirror*). This distinction concerns the interests, social class, level of education and income of a newspaper's target readership. Until recently, in the United Kingdom, the elite/popular opposition was also reflected in the physical size of the newspaper: popular newspapers were printed on tabloid-size paper (A3), and were known as 'the tabloids'; elite newspapers were printed on larger broadsheet-size pages (A2), and were known as 'the broadsheets'. However, elite newspapers are now increasingly adopting the smaller tabloid size, which is easier for readers to handle.

All newspapers are supposed to deal primarily with 'news'. However, a glance at the front pages of different (kinds of) newspapers on any individual day will reveal that 'news' is a highly elusive and relative notion. Out of all the events that happen within, usually, a 24-hour time span, newspaper editors select a subset for inclusion in the next edition of their newspaper. This selection is based on an assessment of what will interest the newspaper's intended audience, and therefore varies considerably from newspaper to newspaper. As an example, I reproduce in Illustration Box 24.1 the main front-page headlines of four national daily newspapers published in the United Kingdom on Tuesday, 17 July 2007. The four newspapers include two elite publications (*The Daily Telegraph* and *The Guardian*), and two popular publications (*The Sun* and the *Daily Mirror*).

On that particular day, no single item of news made all the front-page headlines in those four newspapers. One item was, however, included in three out

---

ILLUSTRATION BOX 24.1

The main front-page headlines of four UK national daily newspapers on 17 July 2007

(NB: headlines have been numbered for ease of reference; an attempt has been made to reflect the original size and font).

The Daily Telegraph

1. **Putin vows revenge as Britain expels four diplomats**
2. **Britain warming to idea of 'Queen Camilla'**
3. **Income divide at widest for 40 years**
4. **SAS chief quits to take security job**

the guardian

5. **Cold war diplomacy is back as UK expels spies**
   Moscow vows retaliation after four agents thrown out over Litvinenko case
6. Mr Njini lived to 45. He was an old man

THE Sun

7. **WHO DARES IS BINNED**
   SAS head axed for being too brave
8. **COPS SWOOP ON 3 FOOTIE CLUBS**
9. **Kerry and tot held hostage**

DAILY Mirror

10. **MADDY POTTER**
    JK asks for Madeleine poster in EVERY shop selling her new book
11. **KERRY'S ARMED ROBBERY AT HOME**
12. **GORD SLAMS VLAD**

of the four newspapers: the diplomatic clash between Britain and Russia over the expulsion of four Russian diplomats after Russia refused to extradite the main suspect in the murder of ex-KGB agent Alexander Litvinenko in London in 2006 (headlines 1, 5 and 12). Two further news items made the headlines in two out of the four newspapers: the resignation of the commanding officer of the SAS (headlines 4 and 7); and the armed robbery at the home of Kerry Katona, a former member of the pop group Atomic Kitten (headlines 9 and 11). The other front-page articles in the *Telegraph* and *Guardian* include, amongst others, reports on social issues in the United Kingdom and abroad (headlines 3 and 6). In contrast, *The Sun* gives prominence to a story about an anti-corruption police raid on some major football clubs (headline 8), while the *Daily Mirror* reports an initiative on the part of J. K. Rowling, the author of the *Harry Potter* novels, to help with the search for four-year-old Madeleine McCann, who had gone missing while on holiday in Portugal (headline 10).

Taken together, these headlines show that the events and issues that make the headlines share some general characteristics: they are overwhelmingly negative; they tend to concern prominent individuals, such as politicians, royalty and celebrities, or, alternatively, ordinary individuals who go through negative or extraordinary experiences; they tend to be the subject of series of stories on different days. The differences among the four different front pages, however, reflect different news values, that is, different criteria that are applied by reporters and editors in selecting relevant stories from the large number of news items reported by news agencies, or, more rarely, experienced first hand by their own journalists. These news values reflect primarily the news workers' perceptions of the interests and priorities of their readerships. The elite newspapers, for example, give priority to international politics (headlines 1 and 5) and, in one case, humanitarian crises (headline 6). The popular newspapers concentrate more on celebrities (headlines 9 and 11) and on heart-tugging personal stories (headline 10). These distinctions are not totally clear-cut, of course. For example, the *Daily Mirror* includes a (small and humorous) headline on the diplomatic stand-off between the United Kingdom and Russia (headline 12), and both *The Daily Telegraph* and *The Sun* give front-page coverage to the departure of the SAS chief (headlines 4 and 7), albeit with rather different emphases (voluntary resignation in the *Telegraph* vs. unjust dismissal in *The Sun*). In other words, what we call 'news' is the result of a selection process that reflects and reinforces different interests, values and world-views, which may be described as different ideologies.

24.3 Genres in newspapers

The prototypical type of text in the press is the news report: a relatively short piece which consists of a 'factual' account of events that have occurred since the last edition of the newspaper. News reports are concerned with what are known as **hard news**: crimes, accidents, disasters, wars, political and diplomatic events, and so on. Most of the headlines included in Illustration Box 24.1 introduce reports that fall into this category. A more specific type of news report concerns special-topic news, such as sports and business, which often occupy particular sections of newspapers.

Since hard news is the 'staple product' of newsworkers (Bell, 1991: 14), this chapter will focus particularly on the language of news reports. This should not, however, obscure the fact that news reports are only one of many genres that are included in newspapers. Alongside hard news, newspapers also contain **soft news**, which can be described as issues or events that are generally relevant but not as time-bound as hard news (e.g., racism, failing schools, climate change, etc.). Soft news is typically presented in feature articles: longer pieces which combine accounts of events with commentary, analysis and background information. An example is the article from *The Guardian* introduced by headline 6, which is concerned with low life-expectancy in Zimbabwe. Another major genre in the press is the editorial: a lengthy opinion piece that provides the official view of the newspaper on particular issues, and that may be written by the editor him/herself.

Newspapers also contain texts belonging to a variety of other genres, some of which are not concerned with news at all. These include, for example, letters, personal advertisements, reviews, obituaries and commercial advertisements. Advertisements are one of the genres in the press that combine verbal and visual elements, as is also the case with photographs and cartoons.

24.4   The language of news reports

In discussing the language of news reports I will refer to two concrete examples: the *Guardian* front-page article on the difficulties in diplomatic relations between the United Kingdom and Russia introduced by headline 5 above (635 words), and a report on the same topic that appeared on page 2 of *The*

ILLUSTRATION BOX 24.2

Opening of front-page article from *The Guardian*, 17 July 2007

Cold war diplomacy is back as UK expels spies

Moscow vows retaliation after four agents thrown out over Litvinenko case

Luke Harding in Moscow
Ian Cobain and Julian Borger

The British government was last night bracing itself for an inevitable diplomatic backlash after expelling four Russian intelligence officers in protest at the Kremlin's refusal to hand over the prime suspect in the polonium-210 poisoning affair.

(NB: 13 further paragraphs have been omitted)

ILLUSTRATION BOX 24.3

Opening of page 2 article from *The Sun*, 17 July 2007

I AM NOT SORRY FOR EXPELLING RUSSIANS

Brown blasts Putin in row over Litvinenko's poisoning

By George Pascoe-Watson and Andrew Porter

FURIOUS Gordon Brown last night stood up to Vladimir Putin — saying he had no apologies for expelling four Russian diplomats.

(NB: nine further paragraphs have been omitted)

Sun on the same day (286 words). The headlines and opening paragraphs of the two articles are reproduced in Illustration Boxes 24.2 and 24.3.

News reports typically consist of the following main elements:

- **Headline** (which may consist of a main headline and a subheadline);
- **Attribution**: one or more bylines crediting a news agency and/or the journalist(s) who wrote the piece; an indication of time and place may also be included.
- **Lead**: a paragraph that provides a summary of the story, and that may be graphologically distinct from the rest of the article (e.g., in bold type).
- The **main body** of the report itself.

The report from *The Sun*, for example, includes all these elements: a headline (*I am not sorry for expelling Russians*) and subheadline (*Brown blasts Putin in row over Litvinenko's poisoning*); attribution to two named reporters (*By George Pascoe-Watson and Andrew Porter*); a lead paragraph in bold (beginning *Furious Gordon Brown ...*); and the body of the report itself consisting of nine further paragraphs.

Before I consider headlines, leads and news stories in more detail, two general points need to be made. First, news reports are the result of the work of several different individuals, who are involved at various stages in the production of the newspaper. In addition to the two reporters named in the *Sun* article, for example, editors and sub-editors will have revised the text and devised the headline, which is normally added last. Second, news reports appear to be the most 'factual' genre of reporting in terms of style, since overt comment and opinion are absent or kept to a minimum. However, like any linguistic representation of events, they are not at all neutral or objective, but reflect the general ideology of the newspaper and the particular slant that the journalist and editors will have chosen for the story. This will be shown in the next sections via a comparison of the two reports from *The Guardian* and *The Sun*.

24.4.1   Headlines

Newspaper headlines are associated with three main functions: they have to attract the attention of potential readers; they indicate the topic of the story, usually by providing a short summary; and they may suggest the approach that will be taken to the relevant event, in terms of tone, evaluation, ideological slant and so on. The fact that all this has to be achieved in a small amount of space explains the peculiar linguistic characteristics of headlines, which I will discuss with reference to the examples in Illustration Box 24.1.

Graphologically, headlines are printed in larger characters than the body of the story, and their relative size and position on the page reflects the newspaper's view of the relative importance of different news items. Because of space constraints, headlines have very distinct grammatical characteristics, which they share with other types of **block language** such as notices, titles, advertising slogans and so on (Quirk et al., 1985: 845ff.). Any dispensable grammatical words tend to be omitted, such as auxiliary verbs and the definite and indefinite articles. In headline 2, for example, no auxiliary verb is used to precede the progressive form of the verb *warming*. In headline 4, no article is used in the noun phrase *SAS chief*. Similarly, the main verb *to be* is often left out, as in headline 3, where the third-person singular form *is* could have been placed between *Income divide* and *at widest for 40 years*. As a result, a significant proportion of headlines are noun phrases or elliptical clauses. In many other cases main verbs **are** used, but typically in the present tense or the infinitive form, in order to avoid the need for suffixes.

As far as lexis is concerned, headlines are characterized by relatively short, dramatic words, which combine brevity with effectiveness. Monosyllabic lexical items are favoured over polysyllabic ones (e.g., *quits* instead of *resigns* in headline 4); numerical information is expressed in digits rather than words (e.g., headlines 3 and 8); and acronyms and abbreviations are often employed (e.g., *UK* in headline 5 and *footie* in headline 8). In addition, the news value of the story and the reporter's slant are conveyed via the selection of lexical items that are often hyperbolic, emotive and evaluative. For example, in *The Guardian* and *The Telegraph,* the problems in British–Russian diplomatic relations are conveyed via expressions such as *Cold war* and *vows revenge*, which emphasize, and, possibly, exaggerate, the seriousness of the situation. The headlines from *The Sun* and *The Mirror* make an even more obvious use of sensationalist and value-laden vocabulary, which is often associated with the popular press. Headline 7 from *The Sun*, for example, contrasts *dares* with *binned* in order to convey the paper's outrage at the dismissal of someone who is presented as a hero. Similarly, in headline 9, *tot* is used in reference to Kerry Katona's baby daughter to convey emotional involvement.

Words such as *tot* and *cops* are in fact commonly used in the popular press: they are not just conveniently short, but they potentially suggest sympathy and contribute to a general tone of informality and orality, which implies a close bond with the newspaper's readership. This is also emphasized by the use of first names or nicknames for people who are assumed to be familiar to the audience, as in the case of *JK* and *Madeleine* in headline 10.

In addition, headlines often exploit a range of stylistic and rhetorical devices to attract and intrigue readers. These include puns and word play generally, alliteration, rhyme, metaphor, proverbs and intertextual references. For example, headline 10 exploits the phonetic and graphological similarities between 'Maddie' and 'Harry' to produce *Maddy*, and combine it with the surname of J. K. Rowling's famous character. In headline 7, the final word of the proverbial expression 'Who dares wins' is replaced with *is binned*, which is phonetically similar to the original, but very different in meaning. In headline 12, the first names of the British Prime Minister (Gordon Brown) and Russian President (Vladimir Putin) are shortened to monosyllabic nick-names consisting of four letters (*Gord* and *Vlad*), so that they form a sym-metrical structure with the verb *slams* in the middle (the headline was also flanked by photos of the two politicians, one on each side, in such a way that they appear to be scowling at each other). More generally, a number of conventional metaphorical expressions are used in several of the headlines to increase their impact, such as *binned* and *axed* in headline 7 and *slams* in headline 12. Headlines may also purport to present the 'voice' of one of the protagonists, as in the case of the *Sun* article in Illustration Box 24.2, which appears to present a statement made by UK Prime Minister Gordon Brown.

While all these linguistic devices are intended to attract, involve and, to some extent, inform audiences, it is also of course possible for some headlines to be perceived as ambiguous or obscure. Newspapers, however, aim their headlines at their own readerships, who are likely to be familiar with their language, running stories and main personalities.

24.4.2 Leads and news stories

The word *stories* in the heading above is an important one. In news reports, issues and events are presented in **narrative** mode, that is, as interconnected sequences of actions or happenings that are worth telling from the perspec-tive of the newspaper and of its intended readership. It is well known that narratives play an important role in the construction of personal identities, interpersonal relationships, and shared cultures. News reports contain stories that contribute to present a particular view of the world for the readership of a particular newspaper.

While the headline provides a minimal summary of the story that will follow, the rest of the news report tells the story itself. A distinctive char-acteristic of news reports, however, is that stories are not normally told in chronological order; that is, starting from earlier events and finishing with the most recent events. Rather, events tend to be ordered in terms of their recency and perceived importance, with major recent events preceding earl-ier events and minor details. Another characteristic of news reports is that first-person narration is usually banned. This is one of the characteristics that contributes to the impression that news reports are written in a neutral and factual manner.

The lead, which is the first paragraph below the headline, has been described as a 'micro-story' (Bell, 1991: 176): it provides the gist of the issues or events that are the subject of the report, as well as an indication of their newsworthiness. Leads usually include details that relate to what are known as the journalist's 'five Ws', namely the story's 'who', 'when', 'where', 'what' and 'why'. To these may be added an 'H', which stands for the 'how' elements of the story. However, leads have to be short (usually less than 30 words), so that only a selection of details can be provided. This selection is important because many readers may well not read beyond the lead, or may decide whether or not to carry on reading on the basis of the headline and lead.

In the *Sun* article reproduced in Illustration Box 24.3, the lead paragraph is graphologically marked out from the rest of the report by the use of bold letters and a larger font size. It consists of 20 words and includes details of 'who' is involved (Brown and Putin), 'when' the main event occurred (*last night*), and 'what' happened (Brown *standing up* to Putin and saying he *had no apologies*). In the *Guardian* article, the lead paragraph is not graphologically distinct from the rest of the article, but provides in 36 words the main details of the story, including 'who' (*The British government, four Russian intelligence officers, the Kremlin, the prime suspect*), 'when' (*last night*), and 'what' (the British mood, the expected Russian backlash, the expulsion on the part of the British, the refusal on the part of the Russians, the poisoning affair). These details are presented in reverse chronological order, starting from the most recent event (the Government *bracing itself* for something that has not yet happened), and ending with the original event that started the whole diplomatic case.

Both newspapers use emotive and evaluative vocabulary to emphasize the news value of the story, and to present the various events from the perspective of the British side. In the *Sun* article, Gordon Brown is described as *furious* and as *standing up* to Putin. In the *Guardian* article, the Russian reaction is presented as an *inevitable backlash* and the British government current attitude as *bracing itself*. The two leads differ, however, in the amount of detail they provide, and, more crucially, in the way they handle the 'who' and 'what' aspects of the story. In the *Guardian* lead, the two main 'actors' in the dispute are referred to via the collective noun *(The British) government* and the expression *the Kremlin*, which refers to the Russian government by mentioning the building where it is based (this phenomenon is known as 'metonymy'; for more detail, see Chapter 16, Section 16.3). In contrast, the *Sun* lead personalizes the dispute by presenting Prime Minister Brown and President Putin as the two main actors in the confrontation. As for the 'what' of the story, in the *Guardian* lead the main event is the government's expectation of a hostile diplomatic reaction from Russia, while in the *Sun* lead, the main event is that Gordon Brown has recently said things that amount to *standing up* to Mr Putin.

The remainder of each story continues in the same vein. In both cases a summary of the most recent and important events is followed by increasingly more detailed information concerning the background to the story and the statements made by various individuals. Similarly, in both cases, different choices and patterns in lexis and grammar construct the topic of the story in a particular way, reflecting the newspaper's general stand on foreign policy and international relations. This results in the presentation of two rather different kinds of 'news': in the *Guardian*, the main news involves increasingly tense relationships between the two governments, while in *The Sun* the main news involves tense relationships between two individuals, with 'our guy' standing up to 'their guy' in a show of strength.

More generally, a number of areas of language have been shown to be particularly important in how people and events are mentioned, presented, evaluated and, in some cases, obscured in news reporting. These include:

- the use of noun phrases to refer to people and groups (e.g., *rebels* vs. *resistance fighters*);
- the use of different kinds of verbs to refer to actions and events (e.g., *protesting* vs. *rioting*);
- the use of nouns instead of verbs to refer to actions and events; this phenomenon is known as 'nominalization' and allows the omission of the main agent in an action (e.g., *the killing of a Palestinian child*);
- the use of the passive voice, which also allows the omission of the agent (e.g., 'a Palestinian child was killed');
- the use of metaphorical expressions, which describe one thing in terms of another (e.g., *a flood of immigrants*);
- the use of figures to back up claims;
- the use of vague or exaggerated expressions (e.g., the adjective *huge* as a description of the knock-on effect of recent events in the *Sun* article).

In the remainder of this chapter, I focus particularly on the presentation of speech in news reports.

24.4.3   The presentation of speech in news reports

The presentation of others' words is central to news reporting for two main reasons. First, journalists are seldom present to witness directly the events they write about. In most cases, their stories rely on texts produced by news agencies and on what is said by eye-witnesses or by the participants in the stories themselves. Journalists then decide what material to attribute explicitly to their sources and what material to present without attribution. Second, what counts as 'news' is often what people **say** rather than what they **do**. This applies, for example, to announcements, declarations, political debates, speeches, meetings, negotiations, rows and so on. The two articles I have selected are a case in point. The British expulsion of the Russian officials is a verbal act, as is Russia's refusal to extradite the murder suspect. In addition, the most recent events in the story are the statements on the part of several prominent individuals on both sides of the dispute.

In discussing the forms and functions of **speech presentation** in the press, I will rely on the model proposed by Semino and Short (2004) in a corpus-based study that involved, among other things, the analysis of approximately 83,000 words of British news reports, equally divided between the elite and popular press (this model was a development of the one proposed in Leech and Short, 1981). Semino and Short's main categories of speech presentation are defined and exemplified in Table 24.1.

Table 24.1   *Semino and Short's (2004) categories of speech presentation*

Category	Brief description	Example
Narrator's representation of voice (NV)	Minimal reference to speech or speech event taking place.	*talks in Germany* (from the *Guardian* article)
Narrator's representation of speech acts (NRSA)	Reference to the speech-act value or illocutionary force of an utterance (often with an indication of the topic)	*as Mr Putin threatened retaliation* (from the *Sun* article)
Indirect speech (IS)	Presentation of an utterance or utterances via a reporting clause (e.g., 'she said') followed by a (grammatically subordinated) reported clause. The language used in the reported clause is appropriate to the reporter (in terms of pronouns, tense, deixis generally, lexis, etc.)	*the Foreign Office announced it was ceasing cooperation with Russia on a range of issues…* (from the *Guardian* article)
Free indirect speech (FIS)	In news reports, a stretch of text that (a) follows a report of what someone said in DS or IS, (b) continues or expand on the same topic, (c) does not include a reporting clause in the same sentence, and (d) includes the use of, for example, the past tense where the tense appropriate to the journalist's own narrative would be the present. (See underlined sentence in the example.)	*The Bishop of Wakefield […] said that […] such practices were "utterly disgusting and blasphemous". They were not recognizable as part of any Anglican creed.* (from Semino and Short's corpus; *The Guardian*, 5 December 1994)
Direct speech (DS)	Presentation of an utterance or utterances typically via a reporting clause (e.g., 'she said') and a (grammatically independent) reported clause, which is typically enclosed within quotation marks. The language used in the reported clause is appropriate to the original speaker (in terms of pronouns, tense, deixis generally, lexis, etc.). The reporting clause may be omitted.	*Foreign Secretary David Milliband told MPs: "The heinous crime of murder requires justice."* (from the *Sun* article)

Semino and Short found, in their press corpus, that the presentation of speech accounts for almost half of all words (approximately 47 per cent). In cases where the news being reported consists wholly or in part of verbal activity, this proportion can be higher of course. By applying Semino and Short's method of analysis to the two articles considered in this chapter, I found that speech presentation accounts for 53 per cent of the words in the *Sun* report and for 80 per cent of the words in the *Guardian* report.

An important aspect of speech presentation in the press is decisions about whose voices are important enough to be reported, and how the various speakers are identified. For example, a random sample of 100 instances of speech presentation in Semino and Short's corpus revealed a large gender imbalance in reported voices. In 31 cases, the gender of the speaker was not specified (e.g., *British sources*). Out of the remaining 69 instances of speech presentation, 60 involved male voices and only nine involved female voices. In the vast majority of cases (79 out of 100), speech was attributed to a singular individual speaker (e.g., John Major). There was variation, however, in how speakers were identified, such as for example via their first name, their name and surname, their title and surname, their status or role (e.g., *the Home Secretary*), or a description that might be more or less specific and evaluative (e.g., *a woman, Tory toff Boris Johnson*). This variation reflects reporters' assumptions about readers' familiarity with different speakers, and also affects the way in which speakers are presented, particularly with respect to the authority and reliability of what they say. A variety of strategies were also used in the sample to avoid identifying with any precision the person or people whose words are being presented. These strategies include the use of the passive voice (e.g., *is said to be*), the use of nominalization (e.g., *allegations that*), the use of the conventional metaphorical expression *source* (e.g., *Security sources*), and the use of metonymy (e.g., the use of *Britain* to refer to some unspecified members of the British government).

The *Guardian* article includes a roughly equal number of voices from the British and Russian sides of the dispute. For both sides, there are cases where speech is attributed to unnamed officials (e.g., *the Russian Foreign Ministry, British counter-intelligence officers*), as well as cases where speakers are identified by name. Crucially, the *Guardian* article mentions an authoritative Russian source who argues that the refusal to extradite the suspect, Mr Lugovoy, is due to constraints on extradition imposed by the Russian Constitution. The *Sun* article does not mention this, and predominantly focuses on the voices of representatives of the British side in the dispute. The only exceptions are two references to Russia's refusal to comply with the extradition request, and the use of DS to present a threat issued by Mr Lugovoy in the final paragraph of the article:

> Mr Lugovoy, who denies the murder, blasted Mr Miliband, saying: "If they blame me directly, I will take that minister to court."
>
> (The *Sun*, 17 July 2007)

It is also worth noting that the only case in which a female voice is explicitly presented in both articles is the following stretch of text from the *Sun* report, where a series of statements are attributed to Mr Litvinenko's widow:

> Mr Litvinenko's widow Marina said she was "very grateful" for the expulsions — adding she was "proud to be a UK citizen".
>
> (The *Sun*, 17 July 2007)

The woman's status in the story, however, is not that of an active participant but that of a victim, and the words that are attributed to her reinforce the nationalistic slant of the report as a whole.

Another crucial aspect of variation in speech presentation is the choice of how to present the various voices that have been chosen for inclusion. Semino and Short (2004) found, in their press corpus, that the most frequently used categories were NRSA, IS and DS. This general pattern is reflected in the two articles under analysis. The *Guardian* article includes 29 instances of speech presentation; of these, ten are NRSA, nine IS and six DS. The *Sun* article includes 16 instances of speech presentation; of these, five are NRSA, four IS and six DS. Bearing in mind that the *Guardian* article is over twice as long as the *Sun* article, the two reports also reflect Semino and Short's finding that DS is used more frequently in the popular than the elite press, largely due to its effects of dramatization and vividness.

Generally speaking, NRSA and IS are used to provide concise summaries of long utterances or series of utterances. DS, in contrast, is used to present (parts of) utterances that are regarded as particularly important, or that the reporter wants to include without being held responsible for their content or wording. DS can also be used to dramatize the reporting of speech events or debates, and to provide a flavour of the original speaker's voice and verbal repertoire. Although DS is typically associated with a faithful word-by-word reproduction of the original utterance, the material that is included within quotation marks in news reports has usually undergone a number of changes: minimally, it has been polished (e.g., by omitting repetitions, false starts and verbal fillers) and turned into written language (by adding punctuation). In addition, it might have also been significantly edited, and, in some cases, transformed.

In news reports, the most glaring transformations tend to occur in headlines, where DS is often used (without quotation marks) to provide a brief and sensationalized version of an utterance that is then reported again in the body of the story in a different, more plausible, form (see Short, 1988). For example, the main headline of the *Sun* article is a DS presentation of the voice of someone who was directly involved in the decision to expel the Russian diplomats (*I am not sorry for expelling Russians*). In reading the body of the report, it becomes clear that the relevant speaker is Prime Minister Gordon Brown, but DS is used again to attribute to Brown a different version of the utterance:

> The PM said: "I have no apology to make for this action. When a murder has been committed on British soil, and hundreds of innocent civilians' lives have been put at risk, we expect authorities in other parts of the world to bring that person to justice.

Failure to recognize that has led to this action."

(The Sun, 17 July 2007)

The expression I have no apology to make is not just more formal than that presented in the headline, but also has a slightly different meaning. Most importantly, it does not necessarily imply that Brown is not sorry that he had to make the decision to expel the Russian diplomats. In other words, the headline attributes to Brown a much stronger and 'gung ho' statement and attitude than he actually appears to have expressed.

The Guardian article also includes a DS presentation of statements made by Brown, but the words that are quoted express a slightly different attitude:

Last night Gordon Brown, arriving for talks in Germany, said Britain wanted a constructive relationship with Russia, but added: "When a murder is committed on British soil, action has to be taken."

"We believe there should be cooperation from the Russian authorities in this. We are sad that cooperation is not forthcoming. We have therefore had to take the action we have taken and we hope we can have a resolution of this matter shortly."

(The Guardian, 17 July 2007)

The DS stretches included in The Sun stress the responsibility of the Russian authorities and the decisiveness of the British reaction, while the DS stretches attributed to Brown in The Guardian include the expression of sadness for the lack of cooperation and the hope for a speedy resolution of the dispute. In other words, the use of DS may contribute to the overall impression of factuality of news reporting, but is in fact itself the result of a number of choices that affect the overall representation of the relevant events and participants.

Because of its association with verbatim reproduction, DS tends to foreground the represented utterances more than other forms of speech presentation, and, other things being equal, to bring the original speakers closer to the readers. This may explain why, in both articles, DS is primarily reserved for the voices of the representatives of the British side, and particularly Prime Minister Brown and Foreign Secretary David Milliband. Apart from one case in each article, the Russian side is presented via nondirect forms of speech presentation (e.g., Mr Putin threatened retaliation, from the Sun article). This means that the relevant utterances are summarized and backgrounded in comparison with those from the British side. In a number of cases, however, short stretches of direct quotation are included within instances of nondirect forms of speech presentation in order to foreground the most important parts of the utterances. This is the case in the report of Mrs Litvinenko's utterances reproduced above, and in the following extract from the Guardian article, where an instance of IS includes four words that are enclosed within quotation marks:

with a spokesman warning it would have "the most serious consequences" for relations between the two countries.

(The Guardian, 17 July 2007)

Semino and Short call this phenomenon **embedded quotations** and point out that it can be found in all forms of nondirect speech presentation apart from NV. In their corpus, approximately 20 per cent of all instances of NRSA, IS and FIS include an embedded quotation. This is a distinctive stylistic characteristic of news reporting and can be seen as the result of attempting to achieve maximum effectiveness and vividness in the shortest space possible. The use of embedded quotations is also particularly conducive to biased or partial reporting, not just because of the brevity of the quotations but also because the quoted material has to be fitted both grammatically and semantically into the reporters' own sentence structures.

The articles from *The Guardian* and *The Sun* contain, respectively, eight and three instances of embedded quotations. In *The Sun*, they are used as part of representations of voices from the British side, alongside all instances of DS apart from the concluding (and rather self-damning) quotation from Mr Lugovoy's statement. In *The Guardian*, five of the nine embedded quotations are included within representations of voices from the Russian side. This could be described as a compromise between a more distanced nondirect presentation and a closer but lengthier DS presentation, which is primarily reserved for the British side.

Overall, an analysis of speech presentation in the two articles shows how both rely significantly on material that is attributed to other voices, and both privilege the perspective of the British side in the dispute. However, this tendency is much more marked in *The Sun*, where the dispute is represented as a personal affair involving primarily Brown and Putin, and where speech activity is presented metaphorically in terms of physical violence and aggression via the use of expressions such as *blasts* and *stood up to*. The metaphorical construction of verbal communication as physical aggression is a well-known phenomenon in English generally and the press in particular, but has been found to be particularly pervasive in the popular press (see Semino, 2008: 207–16).

ADVANCES BOX 24.1

Among the further phenomena discussed in Semino and Short (2004) is the inclusion, in the press, of representations of the thoughts and internal states of participants in news stories – a phenomenon that has traditionally been studied only in relation to literature. For example, the *Sun* article describes Gordon Brown as *furious*, and the *Guardian* article reports that *British government officials* **believe** *extradition may have been possible*. While the presentation of speech involves a phenomenon that is perceptible through hearing and potentially recordable, the presentation of internal processes and states involves private phenomena that cannot be accessed directly. This raises the issue of the basis for such reports of mental phenomena in the press, and of how they are interpreted by readers.

Semino and Short (2004) provide an account of thought presentation in the press, but do not exhaust all possible issues and complexities. This area needs further investigation, both by analysing more press data and by eliciting readers' responses to them.

24.5 Conclusions

The language of newspapers is a heterogeneous and complex object of analysis which is worthy of investigation because of its sheer reach in terms of readership. In particular, news reports are the main vehicle for the provision of information about recent events in what may appear to be a neutral and objective manner. However, news reporting is characterized by a number of linguistics techniques that are exploited to present 'facts' briefly and without overt comment, while at the same time providing a particular perspective and evaluation. This applies, amongst other things, to the presentation of speech, which constitutes, on average, about half of the material included in news reports.

Recommended readings

The most accessible and comprehensive account of the language of the press remains the one provided in Bell (1991). Reah (1998) is a useful introductory textbook. A number of books have analysed media language generally and press language in particular from the perspective of Critical Discourse Analysis. Classic books in this tradition include van Dijk (1988), Fowler (1991) and Fairclough (1995). For more recent contributions, see Conboy (2007) and Richardson (2007). The interdisciplinary work of the *Glasgow Media Group* has also been influential (e.g., see Eldridge, 1995; Philo, 1995). Keeble (2001) provides a useful introduction to newspapers from the journalist's perspective.

CHAPTER 25

Language in Advertisements

GREG MYERS

25.1 Why study advertisements?

Advertisements do not have a register of their own, special grammatical features or lexis; everything they do with language is found in other genres. There is no separate academic approach to advertising language, with its own concepts; the concepts throughout this book all apply to 'ads'. But we are devoting a chapter to ads in this book because the analysis can serve as an approach for all sorts of other everyday texts (Delin, 2000) that you might come across: a newspaper column, a letter from the local council, a university prospectus, the back of a cereal packet. The issues of textual analysis, contextual interpretation and placement that arise in ads also arise in any of these other texts. An advertisement is usually more fun than a cereal packet (and certainly more fun than a university prospectus), largely because the genre promotes innovative use of language. This chapter starts with those innovative uses, and moves out to analysis of the texts of ads in a wider context.

25.2 Advertising texts foreground unusual stylistic choices

The innovation and playfulness that we often (but do not always) find in advertising language does not mean that the purpose of the ad is to entertain; it is often pointed out that boring ads may better serve the client. But in an environment saturated with advertising, an ad that makes clever use of language (or visuals or sound) is more likely to stand out, to engage the reader/viewer, and to be talked about and recycled in popular culture. Consider the example in Illustration Box 25.1.

This fairly typical advertisement foregrounds language forms on several levels by making unexpected choices:

- **Orthographic:** The ad spells out *bodyfor-orm-bodyform* the way it sounds as sung (for those who miss the intended allusion, there is an explanation in Section 25.5 below).
- **Morphological:** The ad first caught my attention because of the huge adjectives; instead of saying, for instance, 'youthful happiness' and 'domestic happiness', the copywriters make up new hyphenated compounds that

---

ILLUSTRATION BOX 25.1

Skoda advertisement

(Agency: Fallon London)

Not so much a roller-blading-down-the-sea-front-in-tight-shorts-woooaa-hoooaaah-bodyfor-orm-bodyform-for-you happiness. But more of a the-kids-won't-ever-kick-the-back-of-Dad's-seat-again happiness.

If you've ever driven any distance with a child's size 7 swinging repeatedly into your coccyx, you'll appreciate the Roomster's twenty different seating options. One of which is happily sliding your little darlings 6 inches backwards, and all from £9,920RRP.

The New, surprisingly roomy Roomster, from Skoda. Manufacturer of happy drivers.

Now available with 6.9% APR typical finance.

---

modify *happiness* with a whole phrase in the first instance and a whole clause in the second.

- **Lexical:** The brand name *Roomster* itself is an invention (as are many brand names), containing *room* with a suffix *–ster* found in words like *youngster* and *hipster* (also gangster, but let's assume that didn't come up when the name was coined). So the apparent tautology, *the surprisingly roomy Roomster,* is built into the brand name.
- **Syntactic:** Written English usually uses complete sentences, while corpus studies show that minor sentences, or what are sometimes called sentence fragments, are common in conversation. Ads tend to have more minor sentences; here there are seven 'sentences', only one of which (the third) is an independent clause.
- **Pragmatic:** Nearly all ads flout Grice's Conversational Maxims (see Chapter 11, Section 11.5). The slogan *Manufacturer of happy drivers* flouts the Maxim of Quality; one possible implicature is that they make the cars that make drivers happy. The headline violates the Maxim of Manner, making for very difficult processing, with the implicature that these situations are themselves familiar enough to be lexicalized.

I will argue that the innovation in language use, the constant foregrounding of unexpected language choices, even in some relatively dull ads, follows from the purpose and audience of advertising.

25.3 Advertising texts have a purpose

In one possible definition, advertisements are texts that have been paid for in order to associate meanings with brands (Myers, 1998: 216). You might think that's a bit long winded – surely ads just try to sell us things. An index card put up on a bulletin board in a shop, or a classified ad in a newspaper, try to sell us furniture or a puppy. But the Skoda ad, and most ads we see and hear in the course of a day, are trying to do something rather more complicated; they have to place that brand in systems of linguistic and visual symbols, place the ad where the right people see it, and engage those people in the process of interpreting the ad. That is why this ad does not just say 'Skoda Roomster £9,920.'

A **brand** is not the same as a product; a brand is a cluster of meanings associated with a label, such as Nokia, Levi's, or British Airways. The brand usually covers a range of products that change constantly to suit the market, while the meanings of the brand (such as Apple or Burberry or Coke) may remain fairly consistent. A single brand, such as Virgin, may apply to a rail line, an airline, a recording label, financial services and mobile phones. One can increase the sales of a given product in many ways, by lowering the price, getting it displayed more prominently in shops or adding features, not just by ads. Ads are usually directed more at positioning the brand in a crowded field of other competing brands, each with somewhat different meanings. The Skoda ad, for example, is not, in the first instance, trying to get you to buy a Skoda; it is trying to get you to think about the Skoda brand in a somewhat different way, so that when you do buy a car, it might be on the list. Recent Skoda advertising in the United Kingdom has been spectacularly successful in changing the meaning of the brand, from associations with cheap and unreliable East European cars left over from communist days, a joke brand, to associations with practical, well-made and stylish cars, like those of the parent company, Volkswagen. (We will see this campaign in a later example.) The more recent campaigns no longer need to confront bad associations with the product, so they can use this rather more positive slogan.

25.4 Advertising texts address an audience

One of the most frequently seen words in any ad is *you*. But it is a complex word to use, because of course the readers of the ad, the readers projected by the ad, and the target audience of the brief could be quite different. Very few ads are really directed at the whole population; even ads for products that we all need (such as loo rolls) are directed at the most likely shopper. In the Skoda ad, the *you* picks out someone of a particular age and family status:

[25.1]   If you've ever driven any distance with a child's size 7 swinging repeatedly into your coccyx

And it is presupposed in the headline that Dad is driving. I can say, 'hey, our daughter no longer wears size 7 shoes', but the point has been made; I have tried to imagine the sort of person they are addressing, and I have responded by taking on, however temporarily, that position (Williamson, 1978). The ad need not use *you* to make us feel addressed; it can use shared knowledge (such as UK shoe sizes) or shared evaluations (the ironic *little darlings*), or a picture of someone staring out of the page at us (see Section 25.5). An ad can cut out some readers by its form of address and references (see, for instance, ads for Diesel or Benetton or some computer games), but it will be all the more effective if, by showing some people it **wasn't** addressing them, it affirms the sense of recognition in those it **was** addressing.

Ads can also project a response from the audience. We will see later an ad using the slogan, *It's a Skoda. Honest.* This only makes sense if we assume that the reader/viewer has seen the beautiful car, and decided it did not fit with his/her negative preconceptions about Skodas. The *honest* then serves as a response to our projected expression of surprise. So the audience is not so much addressed as enacted, with our response made for us by the punctuation. Ads are more effective when they promote this kind of active response, engaging readers/viewers in interpreting them.

25.5 Advertising texts work in relation to other texts

This ad assumes we know other ads. The phrase *roller-blading-down-the-sea-front-in-tight-shorts-woooaa-hoooaaah-bodyfor-orm-bodyform-for-you* is an allusion to a mid-1990s campaign for Bodyform sanitary towels. In one of the TV commercials, a thin young woman is rollerblading with a dog on a lead, to a tune that ends with a woman's voice singing this slogan (the creative team are now in the special circle of Hell for writers of jingles that stick in your head for decades). The target reader recognizes the ad, recognizes it is a naff ad (unlike this one) and recognizes it was aimed at a younger audience, or at themselves when they were younger. (Our daughter, then 8, pointed at the screen and said she wanted one of those.) Ads delight in alluding to ads because that can position the advertiser on our side. Not for you such superficial, clichéd pleasures, or such euphemistic advertising, or such an awful jingle.

Advertisements can allude to other texts, from literature, movies, news or the visual arts. They can take on almost any register, varieties of language associated with almost any field. A cosmetics ad will be full of pseudo-scientific jargon; a cooker will send up romantic novels, a bank or jeans or a mobile phone will use the style of Soviet era posters. An advertising break on UK television poses repeated puzzles as one tries to figure out what this elaborate 30-second Gothic or science fiction or historical short could possibly be advertising, with the answer revealed typically only in the last five seconds. Part of the wit of the Skoda ad is in the use of slightly too specific lexis: *child's size 7* for shoes, *coccyx* for back. Then it switches to the ironic *little darlings.* And the bottom of the ad is entirely full of a different kind of language (see Section 25.8).

As ads allude to other texts, specific ads and advertising language in general can be picked up in other discourses. One might recall, for instance the way the hero's flat in the movie *Fight Club* is labelled like an Ikea catalogue, or the way another film is entitled *Batteries Not Included*, or a US Presidential candidate can mock his opponent by quoting a hamburger ad: *where's the beef?* This particular Skoda ad and slogan have not, as far as I know, entered into popular culture, but Skoda UK's earlier slogan, *It's a Skoda. Honest* can be found echoed in such uses on the web as *It's a New Web Application...Honest,* and in a parody ad using the slogan with an old, rusted communist era Skoda. I will return to the ways that other texts can pick up advertising language.

25.6   Advertising texts are placed in space and time

Since ads target specific audiences for specific purposes, an enormous amount of thought (and money) goes into placing them where they are most likely to be effective. The Skoda ad appeared in the first pages of a weekend newspaper supplement, where many of the other ads are devoted to home, food and family concerns. Television ads would appear in the evening during programmes watched by a young, middle-class, family-oriented audience. Direct mail would target existing owners of Skodas or cars from other manufacturers in the same class. Ads try to give us the message at just the time and place it will work. Discourse analysis has only recently taken up issues of the placement of a text (Scollon, 1998; Scollon and Scollon, 2003); advertising media buyers have been thinking about it for much longer.

25.7   Advertising texts are regulated

Advertisers are constrained in their choices of words, not just by the client's brief, its specification of the effect it wants, but by various kinds of regulations. The Skoda ad, for instance, has in the crowd of text at the bottom of the page the words:

[25.2]   Official fuel consumption for Roomster range in mpg [litres/100km]: Urban 27.2 (10.4) – 46.3 (6.1); Extra Urban 45.6 (6.2) – 64.2 (4.4); Combined 36.7(7.7) – 55.4 (5.1). CO_2 emissions for Roomster range [g/km]: 135–185.

Not very snappy copywriting, that. The mileage figures (not the point of this particular ad) are included because they **have** to be included under UK legislation, following a European directive on fuel consumption (Vehicle Certification Agency, 2004). The regulations also specify that the figures must be legible (black on white here, so that's fine) and the font size must be no smaller than the font of the main text (the font here is the same size). This particular information is distinct in legal terms from the other information and disclaimers in the text box, that is, about the model to which the price applies, the conditions of the financing offer, and the status of the trademark; these are all different areas of regulation, involving different agencies and enforcement.

As there are legal requirements on what the text **must** say, there are also rules saying what they ad **can't** say. The Advertising Standards Authority enforces a voluntary code of practice in print advertising; four of the eight guidelines on automotive ads deal with suggestions of unsafe practices or illegal speeds (Advertising Standards Authority, 2003: paragraph 48). No such suggestion is made here, of course, but other car ads regularly fall foul of this regulation. There is a rule that the model shown must correspond to the price given; this rule is addressed in the Skoda ad with a disclaimer at the bottom: *Model shown is Roomster 3 1.4 16v 85 bhp at £12,885 RRP inc. metallic paint at £350.*

Other categories of products will have other kinds of regulatory constraints, for instance on advertising to children, or claims for diets, and legal constraints in such areas as financial services, pharmaceuticals and alcohol or tobacco products. As discourse analysts, we might see this as part of a wider issue, that authors of everyday texts are seldom given a blank page on which to write; they must work with lawyers and bureaucrats and regulators looking over their shoulders, and skilled professionals learn to incorporate these constraints as part of their work practices.

25.8 Advertising texts use all modes available

Linguists may forget that ads tend to rely at least as much on the image as on the words, and often there is a complex relation between them, in which neither the words nor the picture convey the whole message. Like almost all car ads, the Skoda ad shows the car (in this case, going through a blurred green rural scene at sunset). There is no reference to the picture in the text, and the picture does not show explicitly the extra six inches in the back seat. But the picture is still dominant, taking up the top two-thirds of the page. The form of the text is also part of the message, a modern, sans serif, variable width font that goes with the witty, understated tone of the message.

Print ads can be ingenious in suggesting modes beyond written text: gestures, movements, even smells. But we will see the multimodality more easily in a television commercial, so let us take as an example an earlier ad for Skoda(Illustration Box 25.2).

- **Text:** If one simply read the script for this ad, one might think it rather conventional; the Guide gets in three Unique Selling Points in his lines. But he is saying these things, not to us, but to another character, so we have to look, not just at what is said, but **how** it is said.
- **Accent:** The two speakers are characterized by their accents as much as by their appearance. The Guide is not a native speaker of English, fluent but with a slight accent and frequent pauses. The Visitor speaks in RP (see Chapter 12), and with a kind of exaggerated enthusiasm, mixed with boredom, that conveys a sense that he is being patronizing.
- **Gesture:** The relation of the Visitor to the others is also conveyed by non-verbal means: his leading the group, holding them back at the barrier, looking away while the guide is talking, leading the clapping at the car, and then finally patting the Guide on the shoulder. More subtly, in the long silence at the end, as the slogan appears, the Guide looks slightly away, to the rest of the party who are apparently his colleagues, and they also avoid eye contact with each other, conveying that the Visitor's comment is a gaffe.
- **Deixis:** The script has seven deictic words, pointing to the car and plant around them: *this* (x 5), *that*, *here*. So it only makes sense in relation to the activities around the characters, and it draws our attention to these activities.

ILLUSTRATION BOX 25.2

Skoda 'Factory Tour' (2001)

Director: Laurence Green Writer: Andrew McLeod
Agency: Fallon London (http:www.fallon.co.uk)
LS: Long Shot; MS: Medium Shot
G: Guide; V: Visitor

LS of racks of car bodies on racks, with a group of half a dozen people emerging from between rows	**Guide:**	*this is where the body parts are made sir*
	Visitor:	*this is absolutely enormous*
LS of the group behind a conveyor belt of shining car bodies moving past	**Guide:**	*the car has a 10-year anti-corrosion warranty*
MS of G and V		*we have uh 240 robots here*
LS of group with robots working in the background	**Visitor:**	*marvellous . oh*
MS of V by barrier raising		*look at that . incredible*
MS of V waving to off-screen left		*oh stand back get back*
		hello:
LS of G and V coming down steps	**Guide:**	*this is the first car in its class to meet the new European emissions standards for the year 2005*
LS of group moving across the factory floor	**Visitor:**	*I must say this is very impressive*
MS of V looking away	**Guide:**	*every single car is individually tested before we can uh leave the factory*
	Visitor:	*every car*
	Guide:	*yes*
LS of group approaching a single car		*and this sir . is the finished article*
V walks up to car, followed by group, and applauds	**Visitor:**	*I sa:y . wonderful . well done uh .*
MS of V and G		*and I hear you also made those funny little Skoda cars here as well*
G looks to the rest of the group		
LS of whole group looking away		
V pats G on shoulder	**text:**	*'The new Fabia. It's a Skoda. Honest.'*

- **Visuals:** The central irony intended in this and all other commercials in this campaign is that the car at the end is supposed to be obviously desirable; that is why the badly informed Visitor/Trade Fair Supervisor/ Parking Attendant doesn't think it is a Skoda. Here the conventional beauty of the car is emphasized by the more unconventional visual beauty of the factory, with its rows of car bodies, flow of conveyor belts, and balletic movements of robots. The plant is gleaming, mostly white, the very opposite of what people might think of as an Eastern European car factory.

- **Sound:** Unlike most car ads, the Skoda ad dispenses with music. Instead, there is the hum of the factory; not the deafening roar we might expect of conventional heavy machinery, but the steady sound of activity. The last embarrassed moment, without speech, plays against this sound.

The whole effect of the ad might be summarized as follows: a patronizing British boss figure is touring a very modern Eastern European car factory, showing little interest because it is, for him, a routine trip, while we in the audience notice the efficiency and beauty of the plant and, by implication, the reliable construction of the car. In the end the visitor is revealed to be both uninformed and tactless, while we, the British audience, identify with the hard-working plant employees. All this is conveyed, not just by the script, but by performances and visuals that have a sometimes ironic relation to what is said.

A current award-winning Skoda television ad has no spoken language in it at all. Instead, there are shots of gleaming factory robots assembling the cars, to sound effects such as giggles, sighs and squeals. Since there are no spoken words, it might seem a rather hard text for a linguist, but the same sort of analysis applies. It is all very puzzling until one gets to the slogan, and sees it is taking literally the idea that Skoda is a 'Manufacturer of happy drivers.' The wit comes, not just from the visual and aural channels, but from the sudden reinterpretation of what one has seen in terms of the written text.

25.9 Advertising texts are changing

The 'Factory Tour' (2001) ad can be seen on the Fallon London web site. The more recent 'Giggles' (2007) ad can be seen there and in lots of other places on the web, including YouTube. That's because, since 2001, a whole distribution system of short video clips has developed. Advertisers have for the most part been happy to play their part, with their ads reproduced at no cost by enthusiastic fans. **Viral advertising** like this may have little place in the marketing strategy of an automotive brand (I don't picture the Skoda Roomster's target audience spending much time on YouTube), but it helps support the general image of the brand as hip, ironic and self-aware.

Viral advertising is just one aspect of a rapidly changing media environment for advertising:

- The traditional mass media are fragmenting, so there is no one television programme or magazine that can deliver a large proportion of the population. So ads have to be more carefully targeted, and links have to be made between broadcast, web, cinema, press, poster and direct mail aspects of the campaign.
- Ads can be more easily avoided, with digital TV services and web ad blockers existing that enable audiences to skip to the content. So some ads engage the viewer as interesting and entertaining in themselves.

- 'Above-the-line' advertising, the creating of advertisements for a percentage of the costs, is becoming relatively less important, while 'below-the-line' advertising, paid services including public relations and direct mail, have become more important. (The 'It's a Skoda. Honest' campaign was carefully planned with direct mail as part of the strategy from the beginning). Discourse analysts tend to miss this shift, because they focus on advertising texts (but see Cook, forthcoming).
- Brands are, if anything, more important than ever. With cars, phones and computers perceived as more or less the same in their construction and functionality across producers, brands give distinctive meanings.
- Web 2.0 content, as on YouTube, blurs the boundary between producer and consumer. YouTube not only has (pirated) versions of the Skoda ads, it has various amateur videos of the cars, including an odd genre with videos of the speed indicator showing that one is going far over the speed limit (which would, of course, be against the regulations in paid advertising). And YouTube not only includes old Bodyform ads, it includes parodies with roller-bladers and little films of guys singing the song. So Fallon can have the satisfaction that their ads are reproduced free all over the web, but also the anxiety that the brand image of Skoda is not entirely in their control.

Critics of advertising in the 1950s, 1960s and 1970s saw it as a dangerous monolith, the 'hidden persuaders' (Packard, 1957). Now we are in a period in which the single advertising text published or broadcast in the single mass-media outlet has much less impact; no longer do tens of millions of people see an expensive and carefully crafted ad at once. Instead, marketing involves a complex network of genres, often practised by different kinds of professionals. And at the same time, promotional discourse has entered into almost all other areas of society, including higher education, religion, local government and the arts. Linguistic analysis of promotional texts remains relevant, but it can no longer just be the specimen critique of an ad; it needs to start from that ad to consider other interpretations, practices and media.

Recommended readings

The best introduction to advertising language remains Guy Cook, *The Discourse of Advertising* (2001). The first, and still classic, study was Geoff Leech's *English in Advertising* (1966). More introductory texts include those by Vestergaard and Schrøder (1985), Myers (1994; 1998) and Goddard (2002). Specialized and advanced monographs include comparative studies on cross-cultural issues by Kelly-Holmes (2004), Martin (2006) and Freitas (2007) and pragmatic studies by Tanaka (1994) and Forceville (1998). Kress and van Leeuwen have developed a research programme in multimodality that has direct application to ads (Kress and van Leeuwen, 1996, 2001; van Leeuwen and Jewitt 2001; van Leeuwen 2004). Often such semiotic approaches start with Roland Barthes's analysis of a past advertisement in 'The Rhetoric of the Image' (Barthes 1977a [1964]). Cook has edited a collection of writings on the language of advertising (Cook, forthcoming).

Most of the huge literature on advertising has surprisingly little to say in detail on language. From sociology, Cronin (2003) provides useful links to cultural studies, and Schudson (1984) makes a detailed analysis of claims for the effects of advertising, based on detailed study of the field. Preston deals with the legal issues surrounding advertising language from a US perspective (Preston, 1994). Of the many, many memoirs and how-to books by famous advertisers, *Ogilvy on Advertising* probably has the most useful comments on language (Ogilvy, 1983). And of the many journalistic accounts of advertising life, my favourite is Rothenberg (Rothenberg, 1994); it makes an interesting comparison to the UK work on the Skoda account by Fallon London, analysed here, since it is about work on an equally difficult car account (Subaru) by an equally imaginative US agency (Weiden and Kennedy).

CHAPTER 26

Language in Literature: Stylistics

MICK SHORT

26.1 What is stylistics and how will this chapter work?

Stylistics is mainly concerned with trying to explain how, when we read texts, particularly (but not exclusively) literary texts, we get from the words on the page to an understanding of the text, and how the words on the page affect us in the way they do. Stylisticians do this by analysing the language of texts and relating that analysis to what we know about how readers interact with texts. This means that just about every aspect of language analysis discussed in this book will have some relevance for stylistics, as we use what all kinds of descriptive linguists have shown us in our analyses of texts. That said, no single text will make significant use of every aspect of language: particular texts exploit particular aspects of language in particular ways, and so we always need to see which linguistic features are stylistically relevant in each particular text.

In this chapter I will introduce you to some basic notions in stylistics, which, as we shall see, also apply generally to other areas of our experience as well as to texts. Indeed, I will first illustrate the general concepts I want to explore by using non-linguistic examples as well as linguistic ones, to help make this general point clear. Then I will explore the basic ideas I have sketched out in relation to a particular text, through a concentrated examination of a short poem, 'Flying Crooked' by Robert Graves. Hopefully, this process will help you to understand the poem well and also appreciate how it works in more detail, as well as understanding a bit better the kind of work that stylisticians do, and why.

26.2 Style and meaning: choice, foregrounding and appropriateness

26.2.1 Style, meaning and choice

The first general things we need to notice are that (i) style and meaning are not exclusively linguistic phenomena – they are important for non-linguistic activity too, and (ii) we can't have style or meaning unless we can choose what we say (or do), and how we say (or do) it. Two different tennis players will have different playing styles because they do the same thing in consistently different ways. **Styles** thus depend on consistent particular choices.

For example, a particular tennis player might play backhand shots double handed and this choice will become part of that player's overall playing style. Without playing choices it would not be possible to have different styles of playing tennis. Similarly, different singers will sing the same song in typically different ways (e.g., using different speeds, different intonations, different voice qualities) and so have different singing styles. The same is true of language. Some people seem to use swear words in practically every sentence, and so this becomes part of their speech style. Others may typically speak very fast and animatedly or very slowly and carefully, which thus begins to characterize their speech styles, and so on.

Choosing particular ways of saying something also makes for differences in meaning. Obvious examples would be the differences created by choosing different synonyms to refer to the same object – for example the words *terrorist* and *freedom fighter* can refer to the same person but represent very different attitudes to that person. Similarly, choosing different ways of doing the same thing (e.g., wearing clothes) also makes meaning. Choosing to wear casual jeans or 'smart trousers' makes a difference to how people perceive you, and so how they classify and react to you. I often wear a tie when I teach. So I may well be seen, at first sight at least, as being a bit more formal and unapproachable than my colleagues who wear T-shirts.

26.2.2 Unusual choices and their effects: deviation, parallelism, foregrounding and appropriateness

These days, there are many more men in Britain who hardly ever wear ties than those who wear them often. So choosing to wear a tie deviates from the norm in terms of male dress habits. But when I wear a tie, I don't just wear any tie. I wear a bow tie. This behaviour is even more deviant because most tie wearers wear a 'normal' tie! As a consequence, my deviant dress behaviour (which can be seen in every lecture I give, and so is part of my personal dress style) is highly noticeable, or **foregrounded**. And because my behaviour is foregrounded it also becomes highly **interpretable**, as the fact that people often ask me about my bow ties, and why I wear them, shows. But I could make my behaviour even more foregrounded, and so increase your felt need to interpret it, if I wore a bow tie carved out of wood. This is because the choice I would be making would not be 'within the tie-wearing system', as it would be for standard bow ties. I would have chosen to deviate in an even more flagrant way by making a choice **outside the normal system of choices**. My behaviour would be more flagrant still if I turned up for my lecture wearing nothing but a bow tie, because it would break a more strongly felt social norm. Indeed, you may well think this highly deviant and foregrounded behaviour as so meaningful that you would feel the need to consult the local psychiatric unit. The same is true of language choices. Imagine the effect if I decided to sing one of my lectures, or alternate one sentence at a time between English and Chinese. The general point is that **deviation**, linguistic or otherwise, produces the psychological effect of foregrounding for the observer, which in turn induces a felt need to interpret the deviant behaviour or language involved.

Another way in which the psychological effect of foregrounding can be achieved is through parallelistic behaviour. A clear non-linguistic example of this occurred when my wife and I visited Japan recently. Most Japanese people do not wear kimonos any more, and so we definitely noticed kimono wearers when we came across them because they were statistically deviant. But one particular kimono-wearing activity stood out for us much more than any other. One Sunday we saw a Japanese family – husband, wife, son and daughter, all wearing kimonos. What is more, the two males wore kimonos of one colour and design and the two females wore kimonos of another colour and design. So the kimono-wearing behaviours of the man and his son paralleled one another, as did that of the woman and her daughter. The behaviour of the male pair was also parallel to that of the female pair. This clear set of clothing-behaviour parallels increased the foregrounding effect for my wife and I, and we immediately started discussing it. The parents seemed to be wanting to show themselves as traditional by having all the family wear the kimonos. The fact that man and son, and woman and daughter, wore closely parallel kimonos suggested that they wanted to display special sex-related closeness between the males on the one hand and the females on the other. And the fact that the male behaviour paralleled the female behaviour suggested that they saw their sex-related pairs as being similar, and so close-knit in familial terms.

The same is true of linguistic behaviour, as can be seen in the way that members of the same social group talk in similar ways, using similar grammar, pronunciation, lexical choice and discoursal behaviour. More text-specifically, note how the long-lasting, highly memorable and effective advertising slogan *A Mars a day helps you work, rest and play* depends on **parallelism** to catch our attention and help us remember it (an important reason for poetry being easier to learn than prose, note, is that the phonetic parallelism – e.g., rhyme, alliteration, assonance – aids memorability). The rhyming words *day* and *play* at the end of the subject and the predicate of the slogan are phonetically parallel, and here the parallelism links inextricably the complex iterative idea of *a Mars a day* with the pleasant associations of *play* (and also the other verbs before *play* in the list (grammatical parallelism) that it is part of). *A Mars* is also grammatically parallel to *a day* and pushes the idea of eating a Mars bar every day (which is clearly advantageous for the manufacturers), and the grammatically parallel list of verbs, *work, rest and play*, conveniently provides a general characterization of the waking components of a typical day.

The last general point I want to make is that we can choose to make our linguistic and non-linguistic choices **appropriate** to something else if we want. Formal occasions often lead people to dress more formally than normal, and also to speak or write more formally (and so appropriately) than normal. An over-chatty style seems inappropriate for an essay, and even more so for a dissertation, a thesis or an academic book. This idea of appropriateness actually goes against an important general characteristic of language, which is often referred to as the arbitrariness of the linguistic sign. The sounds which make up most words, for example, are **arbitrary** with respect to what the word refers to: there is nothing particularly 'doggy' about the phonetic make-up of the word *dog*, otherwise we would expect all languages to have very similar-sounding words for the same concept, something which clearly is not true (cf. French *chien* and German *hund* for dog — see also the discussion in Chapter 5, Section 5.2). But although most linguistic signs are arbitrary, some are not. There are a small set of words in each language which are compositionally appropriate to what they refer to. This is most easily seen in words which are described as **onomatopoeic** – that is, the phonetic composition of the word matches fairly closely the sound characteristics of the sound they refer to in the world. The sound that ducks make is phonetically close to the word *quack* (/kwæk/) which we use to refer to it, and in this case French and German, although they don't have the same word as English, do have words which are similar phonetically, *coin* (/kwæ̃/) and *qwark* (/kwa:k/). This kind of 'form to meaning' appropriateness is often referred to as **iconicity**. Sometimes particular texts make a point of being linguistically **iconic** in relation to what they are describing, and towards the end of this chapter we will explore how this is true of the poem we are going to concentrate on.

ADVANCES BOX 26.1

More on stylistics

If, after reading this chapter, you want to explore stylistic analysis in more detail, I suggest you try Leech (1969), Fowler (1996 [1986]), Short (1996 and 2002), Simpson (1997) or my free web-based course at <http://www.lancs.ac.uk/fass/projects/stylistics/start.htm>. Leech (1969) is devoted entirely to poetry and includes extended discussion of foregrounding, deviation and parallelism. Short (1996) is an introductory book with work on each of the three major literary genres, as are Simpson (1997), Fowler (1996 [1986]) and the web-based course. Short (2002) is an introductory article with poetry and prose examples discussed. Verdonk (1993), Verdonk and Weber (1995) and Culpeper, Short and Verdonk (1998) are collections of essays for students on the stylistics of poetry, prose fiction and drama respectively. More advanced books on foregrounding theory are van Peer (1986), which describes research to predict foregrounding in poetry and test empirically whether readers respond to the phenomenon, and Douthwaite (2000) which describes work on foregrounding more generally and concentrates on prose fiction. If you are interested in foregrounding effects in advertising, try Leech (1966), Myers (1994) or Cook (2001 [1992]). Wales (2001 [1989]) is a useful and sometimes entertaining dictionary of terms and concepts relevant to stylistics.

If you are interested in following up on the notion of iconicity, see Nänny and Fischer (2006).

26.3 Stylistic choice in 'Flying Crooked'[1]

Now that we have explored the general points above about choice within and outside language, we will examine them in more detail through discussing one particular text, 'Flying Crooked' by Robert Graves. We will first look at some foregrounded parts of the poem in terms of how they contribute to our understanding of the poem. Then we will move on to consider ways in which the grammatical form of the poem is iconic of its subject matter.

First, though, read the poem in Illustration Box 26.1 carefully a few times to familiarize yourself with it, noting down anything interesting that occurs to you. It is not a difficult poem. After you have read it, jot down brief answers to the general questions about the poem which I ask below it. I will then use my own responses to the questions as the beginning of a 'way into' the language choices that have been made in the poem. I have numbered the lines below for ease of reference.

ILLUSTRATION BOX 26.1

'Flying Crooked' by Robert Graves

Flying Crooked

1. The butterfly, a cabbage-white,
2. (His honest idiocy of flight)
3. Will never now, it is too late,
4. Master the art of flying straight,
5. Yet has – who knows so well as I? –
6. A just sense of how not to fly:
7. He lurches here and here by guess
8. And God and hope and hopelessness.
9. Even the aerobatic swift
10. Has not his flying-crooked gift.

Question

(i)   Why in line 1 does Graves use the definite article in his first noun phrase referring to the butterfly but the indefinite article in the second one?
(ii)   Is flying crooked a good thing or a bad thing in the poem? What evidence can you point to in order to support your view?
(iii)   Why are *honest idiocy* in line 2 and *flying-crooked gift* in line 10 foregrounded?
(iv)   What, if anything, is odd about *here and here* in line 7?
(v)   How is *by guess / And God and hope and hopelessness* in lines 7–8 deviant?
(vi)   In what ways does the same phrase exhibit parallelism?
(vii)   Is the poem just about butterflies? If not, what else is it about, and why? Consider line 5 and the pronouns in lines 2, 7 and 10.
(viii)   In what ways could the linguistic form of the poem be said to be iconic of its content?

Now let's try answering the above questions, using the linguistic choices Graves has made in the poem to help us out.

26.3.1 Why the change from definite to indefinite reference in line 1?

Note that if both the articles in the two noun phrases had been indefinite, as in 'a butterfly, a cabbage white', we would have assumed that the poet is describing a particular butterfly that he happens to see at the moment the poem begins. But the change from *the butterfly* to *a cabbage-white* changes these assumptions. First of all, psychologically the definite reference suggests that he has already seen the butterfly before the moment he is evoking. It is being presented as 'old' information, and the use of the indefinite article (suggesting 'new' information) for the more precise reference to the specific kind of butterfly suggests that he has only just realized that it is a cabbage-white, as opposed to some other kind of butterfly. This **psychological sequencing** of information, along with the use of the present tense throughout the poem, helps us to feel that we are with the poet in the scene as he evokes it, witnessing what he sees and reacting to it as he does. Graves's use of the definite article in the first noun phrase, while allowing for the idea of particular reference to a particular butterfly also allows an interpretation for the phrase which is generic. The phrase *the American red Indian*, for example, can be seen, depending on the particular context it occurs in, as referring to red Indians in general or to some particular red Indian who has already been mentioned by the speaker or writer. The same is true here, and because the poem is fairly decontextualized (e.g., we don't know anything about where the butterfly is) it becomes rather unclear whether Graves is describing a specific butterfly or butterflies in general. So Graves seems to be having his 'referential cake' and eating it too, in referring to one butterfly and all butterflies at the same time. In this case it is grammatical choice within the normal article system in English which is being used to create these meanings and effects in us as we read.

26.3.2 Is flying crooked a good thing or a bad thing in the poem?

Again, the evidence suggests both at the same time. Let's begin with the title 'Flying Crooked'. Most people will see this phrase as having negative associations, I think. Why? Well, first of all flying is primarily a mode of getting from A to B for us, and the default assumption is that arriving straightforwardly without delays or detours is to be preferred to getting there 'crookedly' (e.g., by having to change planes *en route*), and so taking longer. What I have just said is not much more than the statement of an intuition of normality, of course, but one way in which we can test it is by using the British National Corpus (BNC), an electronic corpus of 100 million English words, 90 million written and ten million spoken, collected around 1990, to check. If we search for the various grammatical variants of the word *fly* (*fly*, *flies*, *flew*, *flying* – which together are usually referred to as the **lemma** *<fly>*, we find that there are a total of 45 examples of *<fly>* + *straight*, but no examples at all of *<fly>* + *crooked*. So we begin in the title of the poem with negative associations for *flying crooked*, and that view seems to hold true for lines 1–4 too. But from line 5 onwards things change, with the final 6 lines (the larger part of the poem) containing more positive associations. This is first signalled by the contrastive conjunction *yet* at the beginning of line 5 and becomes most obvious in the reference to *his flying-crooked gift* at the very end of the poem. Here *flying-crooked* has to be seen positively because it modifies the positive noun *gift*, and the fact that *his flying-crooked gift* comes at the very end of the poem suggests that we are meant to see this positive association as the most salient in the poem. If we consult the BNC for evidence, it is very difficult to find any examples of negative gifts in the 2877 instances, whereas positive examples abound. Here is a representative selection (see Table 26.1).

Table 26.1   *Examples of* gift *phrases from the BNC*

Phrase	Number of occurrences
gift shop	95
gift aid	57
precious gift	20
great gift	21
perfect gift	19
new gift	18
generous gift	16
rare gift	12

It is clear, then, that the modification of *gift* by *flying-crooked* gives *flying-crooked* the positive associations it has at the end of the poem. In addition, in line 6 we are told that the butterfly has *a just sense of how not to fly*. Here, the clause *how not to fly*, rather like *flying crooked*, would seem negative on its own, but when combined with *a just sense of* it takes on positive associations. This is because *a sense of* tends to have positive collocates (i.e., the words and phrases which occur close to that phrase in texts) rather than negative ones and *just* when modifying *sense* means 'exact', 'precise', 'due' or 'accurate', which is also positive. The phrase *just sense of* does not appear in the BNC and so instead I looked at the first 200 examples of the 9422 cases of *sense of*. Of these, 63 had clearly positive connotations and 28 negative (roughly a 2:1 ratio in favour of positive connotations), the rest being neither obviously negative or positive (e.g., *sense of the word*). Moreover, if we look at phrases with the *X sense of* pattern, where *X* is represented by one of the above synonyms for *just*, we get the following results (see Table 26.2).

Table 26.2   X sense *of phrases where* X *is a synonym for 'just'*

Phrase	Number of positive phrases
due sense of	4 out of a total of 4
exact sense of	3 out of a total of 3
precise sense of	4 out of a total of 4
accurate sense of	2 out of a total of 4

So again the evidence from the BNC shows that the deviant and foregrounded textual context in which an originally semantically negative clause occurs changes the negative associations to positive ones.

26.3.3 Why are *honest idiocy of flight* in line 2 and *flying-crooked gift* in line 10 foregrounded?

We have already seen in Section 26.3.2 why *flying-crooked gift* is deviant. A phrase which typically occurs with negative associations modifies a word which typically turns up in positive contexts, and so the whole phrase is foregrounded and the associations for *flying crooked* are changed from negative to positive. Something similar is happening with *honest idiocy*. Idiocy is almost always a negative semantic attribute and so *idiocy of flight* should be negative, as it suggests flight which is not well carried out. But *honest*, which modifies it, is almost always positive. This foregrounding via semantic deviation again suggests that an apparent disadvantage may not be so much of a disadvantage after all. Note how the associations for the modifier change in the first case, but those for the headword change in the second instance. Which part of the phrase changes its associations clearly depends upon inferring the change which is most relevant contextually.

26.3.4 What, if anything, is odd about *here and here* in line 7?

You probably contrasted *here and here* with *here and there*, which you thought of as somehow more normal. How could we support this assumption? Firstly, *here* and *there* are adverbs which are **deictic** (see Chapter 11, Section 11.2). That is, they form a contrasting pair (in the same way that the demonstrative pronouns *this* and *that* and the prepositions *toward* and *away from* do) in terms of whether they are close (**proximal**) or remote (**distal**) from the speaker. It would appear that *here and here* is much more unusual in terms of frequency, and so more foregrounded than *here and there*. The BNC has 673 instances of the latter, but only 11 of the former, of which six instances come from the spoken part of the BNC, suggesting a colloquial tone for the poem. *Here and there* clearly marks the locations referred to as proximal and then distal, whereas *here and here* seems more unusual because the locations, though not apparently identical, are both proximal to the speaker. Both phrases can be seen as related to the apparently uncontrolled flight of the butterfly, but the unusual choice which Graves makes suggests that the 'speaker' (the poet himself?) has the person he is speaking to (the reader?) physically close to him as he describes (and physically points to?) what, from a human viewpoint at least, is erratic behaviour.

26.3.5 How is *by guess / And God and hope and hopelessness* in lines 7–8 deviant and in what ways does it exhibit parallelism?

I will consider questions 4 and 5 from Illustration Box 26.1 together as they concern the same prepositional phrase, a phrase which tells us about how (or the manner in which) the butterfly flies. The preposition *by* has a list of noun phrases acting as its complement. All lists are examples of grammatical parallelism, but this list is deviant because it is **polysyndetic**: that is, each of the items in the list is linked to its neighbour by the conjunction *and*. In writing, only the last two items in a list are normally linked by *and*, the rest being separated by commas.

If we put a series of items (usually nouns or noun phrases) together in a list, we are effectively presenting them as being the same as one another (e.g., 'things I have to buy' in a shopping list), even though they are different (otherwise we would not need the different nouns or noun phrases to refer to them). Using the polysyndetic construction emphases the 'differentness' factor a bit more in the 'same but different' characterization, suggesting that the manner or instrumentality of the butterfly's flight changes continuously as it lurches along the various parts of his journey. Another way in which the list is unusual is that it consists of two pairs of apparently contrasting nouns. This is made clear by the word-initial phonetic parallelisms (alliteration) that link the first two nouns (*guess* and *God*) and the last two (*hope* and *hopelessness*) together. In the examples of parallelism we discussed in Section 26.2.2, the parallels promoted the idea of same meaning, but here we see another common function of parallelism, promoting the idea of opposing meanings. This is perhaps obvious enough for *hope* and *hopelessness* (though note that, outside this poem, *hopelessness* is the absence of hope, not its opposite, which is usually thought to be fear or despair – this helps us to see that it must be the parallelism which is pushing us to see the two words as **antonymical** in this context). *Guess* and *God* would not, at first sight, seem to be connected at all. However, the parallelism makes us search for a 'same or opposite' relation between the two nouns and so helps us to remember that the Christian God in the cultural tradition to which Graves belonged is all-knowing, and so would never need to guess. Overall, then, we have two pairs of contrasting opposites, none of which can normally be related to the manner or operation of flight (deviation, and so foregrounding, again). Each pair of parallel opposites is thus effectively the same (much as we saw with the kimono wearers we discussed in Section 26.2.2). But as they each contain an opposed pair of *how*s we still end up with dramatic lack of control over all.

26.3.6 Is the poem just about butterflies? If not, what else is it about, and why?

The poem is explicitly about the flight of an individual butterfly and butterflies in general, for the reasons I gave in Section 26.3.1. But I think that implicitly it is also about people, in spite of the fact that no people are described in the poem. Did you feel that too? If so, we need an explanation for how that idea gets into the poem, and also a characterization of exactly how the butterfly's flight is relevant to the human condition.

First of all, as readers we expect literature in general, and poems in particular, to have human relevance, whether or not humans are present in the 'world of the poem'. So we are likely to want to interpret this poem as relevant to the human condition, even though it is ostensibly about butterflies and the only humans in the poem are (i) the 'I-narrator' who describes the flight of the butterfly, and possibly (ii) the reader, who can imagine him- or herself to be 'in the scene', observing the butterfly as the narrator/speaker describes its erratic flight.

Secondly, the pronouns used to refer to the butterfly are consistently human. In lines 2 and 10, the possessive pronoun used is *his*, not 'its' and in line 10 we get the *he* subject pronoun, not 'it'. So the poet consistently anthropomorphizes the butterfly. Thirdly, an explicit comparison is made between the butterfly and the human poet/narrator/speaker in lines 5–6, where we are told that [*the butterfly*] *has– who knows so well as I? – / A just sense of how not to fly*. The foregrounded rhetorical question which is embedded in the middle of the other clause, holding up, or arresting, the specification of the object of *knows* makes it clear that the poet, like the butterfly, somehow possesses the Janus-faced, positive and negative at the same time, gift of *flying crooked*.

By providing an explanation of how the 'I' in the poem can be said to have the gift of flying crooked we can come finally to an interpretation of the poem. We need to find a way of characterizing human behaviour in such a way that it is apparently erratic, like that of the butterfly, and is both negative (from the viewpoint of others) and at the same time positive (from the viewpoint of the 'I'). I can certainly characterize my own behaviour like that, and I suspect that you will be able to do so as well. I am forever being deflected from what I am doing (writing this chapter, for example) by other things. So everything I do takes longer to do than it takes my more focused friends and colleagues, who sometimes see my butterfly-like behaviour as inefficient. But I don't see it quite like that. Sometimes I stop writing to help others (stopping to help a colleague or student with a problem, for example). Sometimes the reasons for changing direction are 'pre-programmed' (preparing the classes I have to teach, for instance). This sort of erratic behaviour is rather like the butterfly's *by guess and God* flight, and although I sometimes get irritated with not getting to the end of my chapter as fast as I might otherwise have done, I also think that the other things I do are worthwhile, and that helping others when they need it (rather than saying 'sorry, I am busy', for example) is a good thing. I also think that flying *here and here* sometimes has advantages for me too – helping me to see connections between different activities – research, writing and teaching, for example – that I may well not have been able to see if I finished one task completely before moving on to the next.

You may be able to think of ways in which your behaviour is both butterfly-like and negative-and-positive at the same time, depending on the viewpoint. If so, you will feel that the poem we have been exploring is especially relevant to you. If my discussion of the linguistic choices in the poem and their stylistic effects has helped you understand the poem in a detailed way and relate what it says to your own behaviour and human behaviour more generally, then I will have helped you to **appreciate** the poem better, as well, which will please me considerably.

26.3.7 In what ways could the linguistic form of the poem be said to be iconic of its content?

Some critics use the more transparent term **enactment** (see Wales, 2001 [1989]: 125) to describe the way in which some texts have linguistic forms which are iconic of what they describe, and so 'do what they say'. Below I use this term to bring out how Graves's poem 'does what it describes'. 'Flying Crooked' does not seem to have much in the way of onomatopoeia, which is the most obvious kind of linguistic iconicity, but it does look as if the grammar of the poem, in particular, enacts the 'clumsy' flight of the butterfly in various ways. In other words, it enacts the idea of flying crooked by 'talking crooked'. We have already partly discussed two examples of this when we examined lines 7–8 in Sections 26.3.4 and 26.3.5:

> He lurches here and here by guess
> And God and hope and hopelessness.

The polysyndetic nature of the *by*-phrase list separates out the four nouns and so can be seen as mirroring the lurching of the butterfly referred to by the verb. In addition, the *here and here* phrase can be seen as an example of flying crooked, as the butterfly's flight does not seem to get it very far from where it starts.

The first six lines also have grammatical structurings which seem to enact the butterfly's awkward flight pattern. The first two lines have two appositional phrases related to the initial subject phrase (*the butterfly*) which delay, or 'get in the way' of, the onset of the main clause verb phrase, *will...master.*

> The butterfly, a cabbage-white,
> (His honest idiocy of flight)
> Will never now, it is too late,
> Master the art of flying straight,
> Yet has – who knows so well as I? –
> A just sense of how not to fly:

ADVANCES BOX 26.2

More on iconicity/enactment

Nänny and Fischer (2006) is a good general account of iconicity in literature. When talking of iconicity or enactment via sound structure, some linguists and stylisticians have used the term **sound symbolism**. Topic 5 of my web-based course at: <http://www.lancs.ac.uk/fass/projects/stylistics/topic5a/begin5.htm> explores onomatopoeia and other aspects of sound symbolism. Leech (1969: 6.4.2–3) discusses onomatopoeia in some detail. Short (1996: ch. 4) discusses sound, meaning and effect in poetry and Knowles (1987: 38–42, 60–3, 84–8, 113–14) explores sound symbolism and related matters. Epstein (1978: ch. 3) explores iconicity in poetry and Bolinger (1980) examines iconicity in language structure more generally.

Sinclair (1966, 1968, 1972) uses the term 'arrest' for what I have called 'delay' in Section 26.3.7 as part of an account, at various language levels, of delay and release phenomena in poems.

The appositions in lines 1 and 2 also seem to change the focus of what is being referred to, which thus amounts to 'crooked viewpoint'. Graves changes his reference to a particular butterfly to specify its genus, and then changes the reference to the flight of the butterfly, rather than the butterfly itself. The appositional delaying of the onset of the modal auxiliary *will* is matched by another delay, in the onset of the main verb which *will* modifies. This is achieved by the positioning of the adverb *now* immediately after *will*, which in turn is followed by a whole main clause *it is too late* before the main verb. Finally, lines 5–6 also contain a delay – achieved this time by inserting another main clause, separated by dashes (which also suggest delay), in-between the verb *has* and its object *a just sense of how not to fly*.

This heavy use of grammatical delay is clearly iconic too, and so enacts the butterfly's crooked flight, which is then contrasted with that of the *aerobatic swift* in line 9, which, unlike the butterfly, is apparently capable of putting on sophisticated and highly organized flying displays (of the 83 instances of *aerobatic* in the BNC, 82 of them refer to aerobatic displays of planes and man-made kites, the other referring to the flight of bats).

26.4 Conclusions and prospects

What I hope to have shown is how, if we examine carefully the linguistic choices in texts (whether those choices are within the normal paradigm of choice or, as they so often are in poetry, from outside the normal range), we can reveal their stylistic effects, and so how we arrive at the impressions we do when we read. I also hope that the detailed discussion I have taken you through, even though it does not cover everything which could be said about Graves's apparently rather simple poem, has helped you to understand 'Flying Crooked' in more detail and appreciate the ways in which it affects us when we read. If I have managed this, I will have helped you appreciate the poem in a more exact way and also helped you to see why stylisticians go to all this analytical bother, rather than just recording their intuitions and supporting those intuitions merely by pointing to or quoting relevant parts of the text. Being carefully analytical helps us to understand better how particular interesting texts, and texts in general, affect us in the ways that they do and how we infer non-obvious meanings in them.

Recommended readings: more advanced work in stylistics

Introductory and key readings in stylistics have already been given in Advances Box 26.1. More advanced work includes the following. Semino (1997) is an exploration of how fictional worlds are created in poems and other texts and Leech (2008) brings together revised versions of his earlier seminal articles and some interesting new material. Leech and Short (2007 [1981]) and Toolan (2001 [1988]) are influential accounts of stylistic choice in prose fiction. Culpeper (2001) explores how language contributes to characterization in drama and other texts and McIntyre (2006) discusses point of view in drama, a concept which is usually discussed in relation to prose fiction. Simpson (2003) is a resource book for stylistics students, containing extracts from seminal articles, discussions of texts and tasks. Carter and Stockwell (2007) contains many seminal articles in stylistics and also gives a flavour of new directions in the field. The journals *Language and Literature* and *Style* are good sources of articles on stylistics theory and practice.

Note

1 A brief discussion of this poem, with which I largely agree, can be found in Cluysenaar (1976: 33, 57–9). My account will be a more detailed exploration of the poem, and so, I hope, more explanatory.

CHAPTER 27

Literacy Practices

DAVID BARTON

27.1 Introduction

This chapter is about how people use language, their language practices; it focuses on how people and institutions use language to get things done. It continues on from earlier chapters in this section which examine the structure of texts; here we look at how texts are used, the practices associated with them, with examples from different domains of life.

27.2 Everyday literacies

If you go into someone's house, where would you expect to find the language? What forms would it take and what purposes does it serve in people's lives? It is likely that you would see evidence of language in the form of writing all around you. In fact most everyday activities use literacy in some way. There is a great deal of print in the average house: it is on packaging, notice boards, instructions, junk mail, as well as in magazines and books and can be found in every room. Even in households with few books there is still other environmental print. The activities of cooking, eating, shopping, keeping records and celebrating all make use of literacy in some way. Literacy is not the aim of these activities, their aim is something else, to survive, to consume, to act in the world, but literacy is an integral part of achieving these other aims.

Literacy is an essential part of these everyday activities and, in many ways, in mainstream culture the household is structured around literacy, that is, literacy mediates family activities. There are many ways of putting this. Shirley Brice Heath locates literacy in the ways families use space and time and describes how literate traditions:

> ...are interwoven in different ways with oral uses of language, ways of negotiating meaning, deciding on action, and achieving status. Patterns of using reading and writing in each community are interdependent with ways of using space (having bookshelves, decorating walls, displaying telephone numbers), and using time (bedtime, meal hours, and homework sessions).
>
> (1983: 234)

People are surrounded by literacy. Hope Jensen Leichter (1984: 41) lists the artefacts associated with literacy which she identified in an extensive observational study of literacy in the home. Her litany of some of the arte-facts extends to 50 items, making a prose poem. They include:

> Books; dictionaries; atlases and maps; encyclopaedias; school work books, reports and tests...postcards; political fliers; coupons; laundry slips; cook-books...diaries; Christmas cards; gift lists; record albums; sewing patterns; baseball cards; sweatshirts; photograph albums; identification cards; and tickets.

This is one of those lists which never seems to be complete, as each study finds more examples, and it was compiled before computers were widespread in people's homes. The home is a particularly important domain in that it is the site for such a wide range of activities and it is the place from which peo-ple go out to other domains such as education and work. The household is an ecological niche in which literacy survives, is sustained, and flourishes.

The examples so far have been of households where literacy has a clear role. Even in seemingly less literate households, literacy has a significant role. Where researchers have taken very simple measures, such as the number of books in the home, it is very easy to find wide disparities – and to be shaken in one's literate world by the high number of homes containing almost no books. However, all homes in contemporary society are touched by literacy. There is still consumer packaging to get through, bills to pay, junk mail to sort and various official forms and notices to deal with. Junk mail is difficult to avoid; you have to do something with it and people develop individual solutions to cope with the continuous tide. There is also the vision of literacy flowing through the household, it pours in through the letterbox and goes out through the waste bin, hopefully to be recycled; in-between, people act on it, use it and change it (see Leichter, 1984: 40).

It is not a question of households being literate or not. It is not adequate to characterize this as a simple dimension of amount of literacy. What we have seen in several studies and most clearly in Heath's work is that households are part of whole communities which are oriented to literacy differently. This is not just to do with literacy but is part of the whole dynamics of households. Nevertheless, people in all households engage with texts. When we look at a range of everyday activities, it becomes apparent that most activities in con-temporary life involve literacy in some way: we live in a textually mediated world and literacy is a central part of participating in most social activities.

A useful concept for understanding and researching this is the idea of **liter-acy events**. Put simply, literacy events are activities where literacy has a role. Many literacy events in life are regular, repeated activities, such as paying bills, sending greetings cards, reading bedtime stories. In fact the original idea of a literacy event was the bedtime story (see Heath, 1983) with the idea of a parent and a child sitting down and sharing a book between them and it has spread from this to cover all activities involving texts. Identifying such activities can often be a useful starting point for practical research into lit-eracy. Some events are linked into routine sequences and these may be part of the formal procedures and expectations of social institutions like work-places, schools and welfare agencies. Some events are structured by the more informal expectations and pressures of the home or peer group. Events are observable episodes and the notion of events stresses the situated nature of literacy, that it always exists in a social context and gets part of its meaning and value from that context.

Usually there is a written text, or texts, central to a literacy event and there may be talk around the text. Texts may be a focal point of the event, as with the bedtime story example, or they may exist in the background. Texts include rapidly scribbled notes, calendars, books, web pages, text messages, signs, instruction leaflets; there is a seemingly limitless list of possible text types. In whatever form they appear and however they are used, texts are a crucial part of literacy events and often they provide some stability to activities and across different settings. How such texts are produced and used is a central part of the study of literacy.

27.3   Literacy events and literacy practices in cooking

A second central term is the idea of **literacy practices**. This offers a powerful way of conceptualizing the link between the activities of reading and writing and the social structures in which they are embedded and which they help shape. Literacy practices are the general cultural ways of utilizing written language which people draw upon in their lives. In the simplest sense, literacy practices are what people do with literacy. However, practices are not observable units of behaviour since they also involve values, attitudes, feelings and social relationships. This includes people's awareness of literacy, constructions of literacy and discourses of literacy, demonstrated in how people talk about and make sense of literacy. At the same time, practices are the social processes which connect people with one another, and they include shared cognitions represented in ideologies and social identities. Practices are shaped by social rules which regulate the use and distribution of texts, prescribing who may produce and have access to them. They straddle the distinction between individual and social worlds.

The starting point for this approach to literacy is to examine the things people do in their lives, ranging from routine household activities and leisure activities through to political participation, working and pursuing education. In this approach, we take people's activities and ask what is the role of reading, writing and texts in the activities. We then see that literacy is best understood as a set of social practices; these can be inferred from events which are mediated by written texts. The situated literacies case studies at the end of this chapter are concerned with identifying the events and texts in people's everyday lives and describing their associated practices. The aim of the studies was to analyse events in order to learn about practices. Illustration Box 27.1 presents an example of an everyday literacy event taken from one of the case studies, that of someone following a recipe when making a pudding (and is discussed further in Barton and Hamilton, 1998: 8). It is a simple example where one can imagine a straightforward text, a recipe, and how it might be used.

This example can be used to illustrate various points about literacy. Firstly, once one begins to think in terms of literacy events there are certain things

---

ILLUSTRATION BOX 27.1

Cooking literacies

When baking a lemon pie in her kitchen, Rita follows a recipe. She uses it to check the amounts of the ingredients. She estimates the approximate amounts, using teacups and spoons chosen specially for this purpose. The recipe is hand-written on a piece of note-paper; it was written out from a book by a friend more than ten years ago. The first time she read the recipe carefully at each stage, but now she only looks at it once or twice. The piece of paper is marked and greasy by having been near the cooking surface on many occasions. It is kept in an envelope with other handwritten recipes and ones cut out of magazines and newspapers. The envelope and some cookery books are on a shelf in the kitchen. The books range in age and condition and include some nationally known ones full of illustrations, alongside plain locally produced ones. Sometimes she sits and reads them for pleasure.

Rita does not always go through the same set of activities in making the pie. Sometimes she makes double the amount described in the recipe if more people will be eating it. Sometimes she cooks the pie with her daughter Hayley helping her where necessary. Sometimes she enjoys cooking it, at other times it is more of a chore, when time is limited or she has other things she would rather do. Rita has passed the recipe on to several friends who have enjoyed the pie.

Rita does not always follow recipes exactly, but will add herbs and spices to taste; sometimes she makes up recipes; at one point she describes making a vegetable and pasta dish similar to one she had had as a take-away meal. She exchanges recipes with other people, although she does not lend her books.

---

about the nature of reading and writing which become apparent. For instance, in many literacy events there is a mixture of written and spoken language. Many studies of literacy practices have print literacy and written texts as their starting point, but it is clear that in literacy events people use written language in an integrated way as part of a range of symbolic resources and communicative resources; these resources include mathematical systems, graphics, maps and other non-text based images. The cookery text has numeracy mixed with print literacy and the recipes come from books, magazines, the Internet, television, as well as orally from friends and relatives. By identifying literacy as one of a range of communicative resources available to members of a community, we can see some of the ways in which it is located in relation to other mass media and new technologies.

Looking more closely at different literacy events, it becomes clear that literacy is not the same in all contexts; rather, there are different literacies. The notion of there being different literacies has proved very useful and has been used by people in several senses: for example, practices which involve different media or symbolic systems, such as a film or computer, can be regarded as different literacies, as in **film literacy** and **computer literacy** (along with the more metaphorical **emotional literacy** and **political literacy**). Another sense is that practices in different cultures and languages can be regarded as different literacies, often involving different writing systems (as in **Arabic literacy** or **Chinese literacy**). While accepting these senses of the term, the main way in which the term is used here is to say that literacies are coherent configurations of literacy practices within a culture; often these sets of practices are identifiable and named, as **academic literacies** and **workplace literacies**, and they are associated with particular aspects of cultural life.

Education has distinct literacy practices in that literacy is central to teaching and learning itself and there are specific **literacies for learning**, the ways in which teachers and students use reading and writing to learn. And, alongside literacies for learning, there are distinct literacies for assessment and literacies for accountability in education. At the same time there also specific literacies associated with subject areas so that on a cookery course, learning to be a cook involves learning to read and write like a cook, learning the literacies of cooking (and these are distinct from the literacies of being a geographer, a nurse, a plumber or a journalist.) In education, literacy is central to both what is taught and the way in which it is taught.

The first illustration has dealt with an example of literacy practices in the home, an important domain in people's lives. Work is another identifiable domain, where relationships and resources are often structured quite differently from in the home. We might expect the practices associated with cooking, for example, to be quite different in the home and in the workplace – they may be supported, learned and carried out in different ways. The division of labour is different in institutional kitchens, the scale of the operations, the clothing people wear when cooking, the health and safety precautions they are required to take, and so on. Education can also be seen as a distinct domain and the ways in which cooking is taught within education will, again, be a set of distinct practices, although drawing upon and overlapping with both home and work.

Within these domains there are various institutions which support and structure activities. These include family, religion and government. They can be seen as sponsors of literacy and they support and promote different forms of literacy (Brandt, 1998). Some of these institutions are more formally structured than others, with explicit rules for procedures, documentation and legal penalties for infringement, whilst others are regulated more by the pressure of social conventions and attitudes. Particular literacies have been created by and are structured and sustained by such institutions. However, domains, and the discourse communities associated with them, are not in any way clear-cut: there is a great deal of overlap between domains and there are questions of the permeability of boundaries, of leakages and movement between boundaries.

27.4 Office literacies

To provide an example of workplace literacies, Illustration Box 27.2 draws upon a 17-page vignette in a book about communities of practice (Wenger, 1998: 18–34, as discussed in Barton and Hamilton, 2005: 15–24). It is a composite example based upon detailed ethnographic work in the claims department of a health insurance company. The vignette consists of a chronological

---

ILLUSTRATION BOX 27.2

Office literacies

Ariel works in the claims department of an insurance company. She leaves home and drives to work, thinking about traffic congestion and her physical appearance. She meets colleagues at the elevator and travels up to her workplace. When she arrives at work, Ariel signs in, checks her mail, logs on and works at her desk. Her work of dealing with insurance claims is a mixture of using computer databases and forms, using print-based documents, talking on the phone and talking to colleagues. Her activities are a mixture of informal activities and formal procedures. Her reading and writing activities go across print and screen and her writing appears to be mainly form filling and manipulating pre-written 'pattern paragraphs'.

She attends a meeting with colleagues of different status which has a formal agenda and where new procedures are explained. She has to fill out forms at the meeting and is invited to express her opinions on new work plans. There are also informal activities, such as celebrating a birthday by sharing a cake. Colleagues order their lunch ahead of time by phone and then leave the office to take their lunch break together. Work passes more slowly in the afternoon, punctuated by a visit by senior staff. There is a description of training, where new procedures are taught. The workers joke about how formal procedures taught in training have to be backed up by the informal knowledge which workers pass on to each other.

Ariel keeps track of her activities throughout the day and her work is then checked by the supervisor; she finishes the work day by filling in a production report detailing the work she has done and that she has achieved her targets. Then she leaves work, talks to colleagues in the elevator and drives home alone, worrying about traffic congestion and pollution.

---

description of a day in the life of Ariel, a claims processor, documenting her activities and with a running commentary of her thoughts and feelings. It is part ethnographic description, part fictional narrative. It follows her from leaving home in the morning, through her working day and finishes with her driving home. The vignette provides a clear description of the working lives of a group of people in a certain workplace at a particular point in time. It was not written with literacy practices in mind, but it provides a powerful example of workplace literacies.

In Illustration Box 27.2 we can clearly see the role of texts in this workplace. As with the cooking example earlier, it is immediately apparent that there is a range of literacy events. Whilst human social interaction may appear to be based upon spoken language, most contemporary interactions are, at the same time, literacy events. The interactions are about written texts. This is in two senses. Much spoken language is in the presence of texts and a large amount of spoken language makes reference to texts. This can be seen in the vignette where, even when the workers go off to lunch, and although they are away from the workplace, they talk about texts. The existence of these mediating texts changes what is said and how it is said. Ordinary everyday spoken interaction which is usually referred to as face-to-face and somehow viewed as 'natural' and unmediated is in fact highly mediated, most often by texts but also by other artefacts (and in fact there is no clear distinction between face-to-face and mediated).

The literacy events in the illustration can be clearly identified. The work activities which are described can be seen as a chain of discrete literacy events. Ariel signs in, checks her mail, ignores some phone messages, logs on. The events may overlap but there is often clear signalling of the beginning and end of each one. Each literacy event is nested and can be broken down into a set of smaller activities like reading from a screen, entering a number on a form, signing a document. These go together to make up the meaningful event.

The second point is that specific events are made up of more general practices, there are distinct, coherent configurations of practices which can be identified and named. In terms of the illustration, the specific activities of signing in, checking the mail and logging on are all identifiable, nameable, culturally recognizable practices with a cultural significance beyond the individual activities. Many of the activities are typical of workplaces and it is thus helpful to talk in terms of workplace literacies. The vignette provides a clear example of specific practices associated with this sort of workplace. The writing, for example, is often the filling in of forms and using pre-written paragraphs. It is routine and repetitive. The writing can also be seen as collaborative, where several people have been involved in the writing at different stages and there is no identifiable author. Similarly, the range of reading activities in the workplace is formulaic, limited and constrained. In terms of the language used, this workplace has its own specific discourses, ways of talking and writing, including a specialized vocabulary, such as *a pre-exist*, *junk claims*, etc. Other examples of workplace literacies described within a literacy studies framework can be found in Belfiore and colleagues (2004).

These are typical workplace literacies and they can be contrasted, for example, with the domain of education, where such activities of sharing, copying and collaborating are tightly controlled and policed, and often punished as plagiarism. We can identify distinct practices in different domains of life, so that the set of practices associated with writing an assignment in education are distinct from those associated with filing a safety report in a workplace, or writing a personal diary in the home. In real life, such practices are hybrid and overlapping, with blurred edges, and people apply practices learned in one situation in new situations. This means that boundaries themselves are significant, generative spaces where resources may be combined in new ways or for new purposes.

When examining practices at a particular point in time, as in Illustration Box 27.2, it is clear that literacy practices are **situated**. They exist within a cultural context and are built up from existing practices. Often a key to understanding contemporary practices is to see what they are built upon. The literacy events in the illustration are strongly anchored in a specific place and time. It is in the United States with a privatized medical system at a point in the 1990s when computers were beginning to revolutionize office work. Since then, probably much of the work has been changed to being carried out online, maybe Ariel's workplace has been restructured with the work sub-contracted to another company and she has lost her job, or perhaps the whole claim centre has been moved by the parent company to another country.

An important aspect of people's 'meaning making', or **semiosis**, is that it is **multimodal**. Print literacy always exists alongside a range of other modes of meaning making, in particular visual meaning making; literacy is but one part of a range of semiotic resources (Kress and van Leeuwen, 2001). Each has its specific **affordances**, the perceived possibilities for action available to a person. The work of claims processing is highly multimodal, involving as it does an ever-shifting combination of speech, visuals, numerical information and other symbolic systems. Ariel is constantly bringing together written information, spoken information and visual information from printed material, computer screens, face-to-face conversations and phone conversations.

The illustration also provides examples of the ways in which spoken language is constantly mediated by the written word, as mentioned above. Much of the talk is about texts, and much of the workplace's spoken language, such as answering the phone, is scripted text-based language. There is also a subtle interplay of what is orally communicated and what gets written down. For example, when workers receive warnings about not meeting their targets these are often delivered orally and therefore are off the public record, whereas there are certain things within the claims process that for legal purposes they have to receive 'in writing'. Again these practices may be changing, with, for example, computer interactions and the routine recording of phone conversations at work.

One important aspect of multimodality is that the **materiality** of literacy is undergoing change. The affordances of literacy are associated with its material aspects; this includes the materiality of texts and the range of literacy artefacts which exist, their availability and expense. Focusing on literacy is particularly salient as the artefacts of paper, pen and printing provided a fairly stable set of textual affordances for 500 years which have been disrupted by changes in technologies. New technologies shift the materiality of literacy, profoundly changing the semiotic landscape (see Chapter 28).

The last specific point to be made about texts is that they move across contexts, often changing their meanings and functions, but nevertheless providing a fixed reference point in different events. We refer to this as **recontextualization** and it is central to the activity of claims processing. Texts provide constancy across events; for example, in the ways in which medical documents are put to new uses when they are used as evidence for medical claims. This workplace is held together in many ways by the texts which cross events. All the forms have different purposes as they pass through different events. For instance, Ariel fills in a form recording her output. This has another purpose when it is checked by her supervisor. In this way, texts can be a reference point for shared meanings and can synchronize activities. The same form is used to make a calculation; it is checked with colleagues; it is then a record of that calculation; it is used to explain the benefits to customers; and it is also used in training.

27.5   Case study: situated literacies

A key empirical study carried out at Lancaster was the Local Literacies research (Barton and Hamilton, 1998), where we examined the role of reading and writing in the local community of the town in which we lived. The study identified key areas of everyday life where reading and wring were significant for people and it contrasted these vernacular literacies, which were often voluntary, self-generated and learned informally, with more dominant literacies which were often more formalized and defined in terms of the needs of institutions.

The research also demonstrated the importance of social networks and relationships in these practices, with literacy being used for social communication. People also drew on these social networks to help them with particular literacy requirements. So, for example, we saw the ways in which literacy is significant in terms of local democratic participation in a range of community activities. This data shows the importance of literacy as a communal resource, rather than just as an attribute of individual people. Literacy was used by people to make sense of events in their lives and resolve a variety of problems, such as those related to health, legal problems, employment-related problems and issues around schooling. Often this involved confrontation with professional experts and specialized systems of knowledge, and people often drew on their networks for support and knowledge, thereby becoming expert in a particular domain and becoming a resource for other community members themselves. Literacy was also used for personal change and transformation, both within and outside education-related domains, for accessing information relating to people's interests, for asserting or creating personal identity, and for self-directed learning.

Further examples of local and community literacy research can be found in the later edited volume, *Situated Literacies* (Barton, Hamilton and Ivanič, 2000), which brought together a number of studies of reading and writing in a variety of different local contexts, informed by the same theoretical perspective outlined above. Many of the studies in this collection show how qualitative methods and detailed local studies can deepen our understanding of literacy. A study of literacy in prisons by Anita Wilson demonstrated the role of literacies in the struggle against institutionalization and 'losing your mind', the importance of literacy in attempts to maintain an individual identity within a bureaucratic controlling institution, and how people used literacy to construct a 'third space' between prison and Outside. This resistant use of literacy contrasts with work by Kathryn Jones with bilingual Welsh farmers at an auction market, where literacy inscribed the people's lives into a broader social order, how the local and the global are linked by textual activity. Jones focuses on the process of filling in a particular form, showing how the individual farmers are incorporated into the agricultural bureaucratic system through a complex process of locally-situated talk around texts and the interweaving of spoken Welsh with written English. A study by Karin Tusting on the role of literacy practices within a Catholic congregation shows how literacy is used to manage time in a variety of ways: how literacy artefacts are produced within a preparation class both as tangible evidence

> ### ADVANCES BOX 27.1
>
> **Literacies across time and space**
>
> The examples in this chapter are of one culture at a specific point in time. If we look across cultures and across time, we see some very different practices. And the examples given here may contrast with your own experiences. There has now been a range of studies across cultures. These have been both within societies (as in Moss, 1994; Perez, 2004; Purcell-Gates, 2007) and across the world, covering very different societies, languages and scripts (e.g., Prinsloo and Breier, 1996; Kalman, 1999; Rogers, 2005). Many of these instances are multilingual contexts where the contrasts, mixing and hybridity of literacy practices can be seen in the different languages; a wide range of such studies is reported in Martin-Jones and Jones (2000). In addition, historical studies show the development of practices over time and the different practices, beliefs and attitudes to literacy in earlier historical periods (as in Clanchy, 1993; Vincent, 2000; Brandt, 1998).

of commitment through showing investment of significant amounts of time, and to serve as a permanent historical record of a fleeting set of events; and how the parish bulletin is used to synchronize events in time, both locally within the parish community and globally in relation to the Catholic Church as a whole, thereby maintaining community identity. As a set of studies, these pieces demonstrate distinct practices in different domains of life. They also show links between local and global phenomena.

27.6 Concluding remarks

This chapter has provided snapshots of literacy practices in different domains of life. It has outlined a theory about the significance of language in the lives of people and institutions. The methods used for researching the familiar, by standing back and examining people's practices in detail, can be very revealing about how language is used at a time of great social and technological change.

Recommended reading

The books and articles cited in the chapter can be used for further reading. In particular Barton (2007) provides a broad overview of the field of literacy studies. For ideas of how to carry out practical projects investigating literacy practices, click through to student projects on http://www.literacy.lancs. ac.uk.

CHAPTER 28

New Technologies: Literacies in Cyberspace

UTA PAPEN

28.1 What do we mean by literacies in cyberspace?

Electronic literacies, digital literacies, silicon literacies, cyberliteracies – how many of these literacies are there? What is the difference between **computer literacy** (a term that is widely used and which you may be familiar with) and **literacies in cyberspace** (a phrase you probably have not heard before)?

Electronic literacies (or silicon literacies, digital literacies, cyberliteracies) refer to reading and writing activities that use computer technology rather than pen and paper (or other materials). In the previous chapter, David Barton has introduced a social view of literacy. A social or socio-cultural definition of literacy (Lankshear and Knobel, 2007) believes that reading and writing is never simply coding and decoding letters, words and sentences. Reading and writing are activities that always have particular purposes. Reading is always reading something and reading and writing are always part of a broader social activity. We write an email to a friend because we want to tell her about our Saturday evening and because by writing to her we want to let her know that she is on our minds. Writing emails, text messages, electronic postcards or conventional paper-based letters to friends is part of a more general social activity that we could call relating to others (who are not physically present) or maintaining social relationships. We can only understand the act of composing the message (the literacy event, see previous chapter), if we look at this broader practice that gives meaning to our writing.

The arrival of computer technologies in our lives has extended the forms of reading and writing available to us. New practices of writing have emerged. Other 'old' practices have become a lot easier or can be used for new purposes thanks to new technologies. Many of us make use of these technologies in a variety of ways, inventing new practices (e.g., sharing personal photographs through websites such as Flickr or Facebook) and creating new forms of language (e.g., the emoticons used in SMS and instant messaging). Writing a weblog – blog – is not the same as keeping a conventional paper-based diary. Blogs are to be shared and discussed with others, while diaries were traditionally kept secret.

We can see from the above that people do different things with digital technologies. Therefore, it is best to describe these in the plural, as different electronic or silicon literacies (Snyder, 2002), not one single 'computer literacy'. The term computer literacy is commonly used to refer to the skills needed to use a computer. We describe people as being more or less computer literate. If, instead, we talk about electronic literacies or literacy **practices**, this means that we are first of all interested in what people do with computer technologies, not how well they are at doing this. This is also my focus in this chapter.

The variety of electronic literacies that exist these days not only places a question mark on our idea of literacy as a single set of abilities. The new digital literacies many of us use so regularly these days also pose a challenge to the conventional idea of literacy as being about 'letters' (as in letters of the alphabet). Kress (2003; Kress and van Leeuwen, 2001) has suggested that in our current societies everyday forms of texts no longer primarily consist of written language. He claims that the image has taken over from writing as the primary mode of expression. Think for a moment about your own writing and the kind of texts you come across every day. To what extent are your own texts a mixture of letters, images and other modes? For example, you may use emoticons regularly. Websites draw on a variety of modes: visual, audio, written, etc. We do not need to possess sophisticated software or highly specialized knowledge to produce and distribute our own multimodal creations. Thus writing these days (and reading) is not limited to writing words and sentences, but often involves images and sounds.

The arrival in our lives of new electronic literacies requires us to change fundamentally how we think about literacy. Public views on literacy (as well as many teachers' attitudes) are lagging somewhat behind when it comes to understanding contemporary forms of communication. Just ask a 15-year-old girl or a 12-year-old boy about their reading and writing at home and they will easily convince you that for them digital writing is just 'normal' (Alvermann, 2002). Sam, a 14-year-old girl participating in a study of instant messaging (IM), explained that 'Everybody does it. It's like I've grown up on it' (Lewis and Fabos, 2005: 470). For young people like Sam, IM, a form of synchronous **computer-mediated communication**, is a taken for granted part of their lives and it is also very much part of their identities, a point I will come back to later in this chapter. Electronic literacies have become central to how our lives are textually mediated (see Chapter 27, Section 27.2). In addition to the new 'cool' literacies (such as MySpace and Facebook), there are more mundane electronic literacies; for example, online banking and shopping. Many of us will send an SMS rather than phone a friend. You may email your tutor rather than visit her in her office hour. These days, job applications can often be made online. The widespread use of digital literacies is part of how our literacy practices are changing, a point referred to already in the previous chapter. But what drives these changes in reading and writing practices?

You may want to say that the recent dramatic changes in our literacy practices are a result of the new technologies available to us. But this is only partly true. Computers are made by people – they are a product of particular people's inventions. Different types of software and technologies (e.g., software to upload photographs on an Internet site or synchronous (real-time) talk in IM) have been designed by particular people for particular purposes (Hine, 2000). So people have ideas about computers and other digital technologies.

This is the case for the users of such technologies too. They have views on the Internet and what it might be good for. Thus, people, not technologies, are the driving force behind changes in our literacy practices. This also means that the effects of new technologies cannot simply be predicted. SMS is a case in point. Its popularity had not been foreseen by mobile phone companies when they first introduced the service.

All technologies have potentials as well as constraints. Kress (2003) refers to these as **affordances**, a term introduced in Chapter 27, Section 27.4. For example, much of the new writing we engage with on the computer is highly interactive: it allows us to involve others directly in the process of writing or composing a text. Affordances, however, are not simply there: they need to be picked up or identified. Because as users of technologies we need to be able to see what we can do with them, Lee (2007), who has studied the IM practices of young people in Hong Kong, prefers the term **perceived affordances** (Norman, 1990). To give an example, two of her informants explained that IM allowed them to look at a website together. Sending each other photos and MP3 files was also seen as an affordance of IM – such files can be shared and talked about at the same time.

The following is not a comprehensive account of all electronic literacies and what they are about. It is impossible to provide such an overview. Whatever I'd say now, unavoidably, by the time this chapter is published, would already be out of date and incomplete (Tusting, 2007). Electronic literacies are constantly changing. Instead, the following sections focus on three aspects of electronic literacies: literacies and social relations; the role of identity in electronic writing and the Internet as a new source of knowledge.

28.2 We no longer knock at each others' doors, but we chat with people in New Zealand: literacy and new social relations

The above heading is meant as a question not a statement. Do we really no longer knock at each others' doors? And do we no longer have friends nearby but only 'cyberfriends' across the world. The answer, of course, is no.

Talking to people, enjoying company, being in touch and in tune with others and their lives – these are things we all care about and there is nothing new about human beings being 'social'. But 'being connected' with others has gained new meaning these days. We can be connected with others in new ways. Instant messaging allows for instant connection with people who are not physically present. This is one of its main affordances, to use the term introduced above. SMS, another of the new digital literacy practices, allows us to stay in almost constant connection even while on the move. Before the arrival of computer technologies, instant desires to talk had to be fulfilled in other ways. We had to walk round the bloc to visit our friends in their house or we had to get to the phone. Today much of this relational work can be done electronically, in writing. Digital literacies such as IM are central to the way these days we relate to others and to the kinds of social networks we engage in.

Instant Messaging (IM) is a synchronous (real-time) chat. According to Lewis and Fabos (2005), IM became popular in 2000, when America Online introduced the Buddy List. It allows IM users to maintain several conversations with different 'buddies' simultaneously. Since then, IM has taken off with rapid speed, in particular amongst young people. Popular IM programmes are AOL, which had 53 million users world-wide in March 2006, MSN/Windows Live Messanger with 27 million and Yahoo with 22 million (Arstechnica, citing Nielson/Netratings).

Contrary to what is often claimed in the media, IM (and other online networking facilities) is not so much about the search for cyberfriends, but it serves to maintain and deepen friendships between offline friends. Two recent studies of IM have confirmed this. Lewis and Fabos (2005), who studied the IM practices of a group of young people aged 14–17 in the United States, have found that their IM activities are a form of socializing that extends and at times replaces the offline social contacts of school friends and acquaintances (see also Leander and McKim, 2003). IM peaks in winter evenings, when meeting outside is less fun than in summer. Knowing what was talked about in IM the previous night was crucial to being able to join in the conversations in the school yard the next morning. Lee (2007) has found that university students in Hong Kong use IM to socialize, but also to organize their work, for example to prepare presentations.

While IM appears to be mostly used by people who also know each other and meet offline, other new Internet sites bring together people who have not and may never meet in 'real life'. Davies (2006) has researched the photosharing site www.flickr.com and how it promotes the development of communities of people sharing and commenting on each others' photos. She highlights that the people using flickr learn and teach from each other (see also Lee, 2007). That people share knowledge and learn from each other has also been

---

ADVANCES BOX 28.1

How to research IM and other cyberliteracies

Both Lewis and Fabos (2005) and Lee (2007) have studied IM from a perspective of literacy as social practice. But how did they do this? All three researchers adopted an ethnographic perspective. This means they studied IM in 'real life' and 'in context': they looked at IM as it is used by real people and taking account of their personal situations and social context. Both studies involved a small number of young people. In Lewis and Fabos's case, these were seven high school students, several of whom were close friends. Lee worked closely with 19 people. The advantage of working with a relatively small number of people is that it allowed the researchers to spend considerable time with the young people in interviews and informal conversations (often carried out through IM). This enabled them to get a good understanding of what role IM played in their lives. Lee has also asked her participants to keep a log-book of their IM activities. Her study looks in particular on how writing in IM is done. As a linguist, she paid much attention to how the group of students she worked with used different languages (Chinese, Cantonese and English) and different scripts (Chinese and Roman characters) to compose their messages. She calls this the multilingual and multiscriptual 'text-making practices' of her informants.

highlighted by Gee (2004, 2005, 2007), who has studied the practices of young people playing video games. He has introduced the idea of **affinity** spaces to describe the ways people gather around a shared liking or purpose. In Gee's example, this is to play video games. In affinity spaces, people share practices – ways of doing things – including literacy practices and they learn from each other. They may, for example, invent non-standard spellings and share these with each other. Affinity spaces can be created by fans of movies, comic books or TV shows. Writing fanfiction is another new literacy practice that brings together people in an affinity space or group, as I call it (Thomas, 2007). Affinity groups can be more or less close and more or less stable. Buying and selling on eBay requires people to develop new forms of trust in a new type of community. But this is much looser and less stable than other online communities. eBaying involves a variety of literacy practices, the most interesting one perhaps the ratings and writings of commentaries (netgrrl * (12) and chicoboy26 * (32) 2002).

ILLUSTRATION BOX 28.1

Socializing online – Facebook

IM is not the only way people these days stay in touch electronically. Among young people, social networking facilities such as MySpace and Facebook are very popular. According to the BBC's Radio 4 Today programme (25.7.07), Facebook is 'the Internet story of the year' with 50,000 new members signing up every day. The site presents itself as 'a social utility that connects you with the people around you' (www.facebook. com). On Facebook, participants create a sketch of themselves, called a 'Profile', and they interact with others via the 'Friends' function. Users invite each other to become friends and once the other has accepted, a photo of them is displayed on the user's profile. Facebook affords various ways of people communicating with each other, for example through a public commenting feature called 'the Wall'. Each user has a wall, which others can write on. Socializing also includes sharing photos, asking 'questions' and participating in quizzes and surveys. Needless to say that all this socializing requires Facebook users to engage in a range of multimodal literacy practices. Such regular use of new forms of 'writing' affords mutual learning (Boyd, 2007a).

Social networking sites such as Facebook can be described as 'mediated publics' or more specifically as 'networked mediated publics' (Boyd, 2007b). These are environments where people can meet in public and which are mediated – bound together – by networking technology. To talk about networked publics might suggest that we are referring here to something that never existed before. But while much about Facebook is truly new, in many ways it's an old-age practice: Social networking sites are about young people hanging out with their friends and acquaintances. What used to be done in parks, shopping centres, cafes and other (unmediated) public spaces, can now also be done online.

28.3 From diaries to blogs: identity, performance and new forms of writing

Weblogs or blogs can best be described as a form of online journal or commentary with regular updates. The most recent post is shown at the top of the screen, previous posts are listed below and older posts are archived and can be assessed through hyperlink. Blogging is very popular. In April 2007, 70m blogs were estimated to exist (Guardian, 7.4. 07, quoting www.technorati.com). Blogs first started to appear in the early 1990 as websites which individuals used to list hyperlinks to other sites that they found useful or interesting (see Knobel and Lankshear, 2006). Today's blogs are easy to use: bloggers do not need to know web programming language. Various types of blogs exist, for example personal blogs, business blogs (that serve advertising purposes), blogs on specific hobbies or even obsessions, travel blogs, blogs that comment on news, political (pressure groups, etc.) and campaigning blogs and academic blogs (for a typology of blogs, see Knobel and Lankshear, 2006).

Another way of categorizing blogs is by thinking about the number of readers they attract. Through the comments and hyperlink functions, many bloggers form a blogger community and often this is a network of people who comment on each others' blogs regularly. These blogs are mainly addressing a limited audience. Other blogs are written for and attract a much wider audience. Such blogs, the 'big catchers' offer comments on topics of wider interest. Many of these are news focused and they can add new political voices to the established newspaper, radio and TV commentators. Such blogs, if read and distributed by many, have the potential to influence public opinion and to challenge the dominance of the mass media (Lankshear and Knobel, 2007; Tusting, 2007). In order to do so, blogs need to be read regularly, they need

---

ILLUSTRATION BOX 28.2

A popular blog entry

To be popular a blog doesn't have to tackle big societal or political questions. Much more mundane stuff can attract readers and invite comments. Holidays, for example, are a much loved topic. I recently read through the blog entry of a Chinese-American blogger about to set out for a family visit in Hong Kong. To my surprise, his entry had attracted a large number of comments. Most of these dealt with just one topic: Multivitamins! Seeking his mother's advice for what presents to get for his family in Hong Kong, our blogger had been told that he had to buy multivitamins. According to his mum, they were the number one present Americans had to bring their families in Asia. Off he went to buy his pills. On his blog, he expressed his surprise at this very odd request and he wondered what his relatives would say to their gifts. Multivitamins, of the same type and brand he got in the States, can be bought everywhere in Asia. He must have felt reassured by the many comments and responses he received to his musings. As bizarre as it seemed, he was told by his readers, multivitamins really were the 'new crack' in Asia and they had to come from the States!

to receive comments and figure as hyperlinks on other people's blogs. There aren't, however, any clear rules as to what counts as a good blog and there aren't any experts (such as the editors of newspapers) who judge what can be published and what counts as good blogging. In the bloggosphere, not only can everybody be a published author or journalist, we can also all be reviewers and editors. It's the community of active bloggers and passive consumers of blogs that decides what is or isn't a good blog (Knobel and Lankshear, 2006).

Blogs differ a great deal from paper-based texts. As texts, blogs don't stand alone in the same way a book does. The blog itself is a complex body of texts written by different people. Hypertext needs to be read laterally. It has no prescribed reading path, but has each reader creating her own text. We can see from this that the literacy practices of blogging differ significantly

"On the Internet, nobody knows you're a dog."

'On the Internet, nobody knows you're a dog' © Peter Steiner/Condenast   *FIGURE 28.1* from other more conventional reading and writing practices. Most importantly, in the blogosphere, writing and reading is no longer a fully individual practice, but more of a collaborative act which is made possible through the affordances of hyperlinks, tags and the comments functions. Blogs are frequently multimodal and they can be very creative. Some bloggers use visual images to a greater extent than written language. Others use a lot of audio and video files. Blogging allows writers to experiment with various styles and genres and there are few, if any rules and conventions that prescribe how to write and what to say.

Several researchers have discussed the role of blogs in relation to how we construct and present our identities (see, for example, Bortree, 2005; Huffaker and Calvert, 2005). Lankshear and Knobel (2007) point out that the content of a blog has much to do with what its writer wants others to know about themselves: what they are like, what they enjoy and care about, etc. It has been suggested that the Internet allows people to experiment and play with different identities. On the web, nobody knows that you are a dog, whether you have a long nose or a silly laugh. You can reinvent yourself completely on the web. In multi-user domains anonymity is a common experience and participants of chat rooms may present themselves in ways that have little to

ADVANCES BOX 28.2

More on identity

Bloggers can never be certain of their audience, as theoretically their writings can be read by anybody with access to the Internet (Bortree, 2005; Davies and Merchant, 2007). This has an impact on how they present themselves in their blogs and it makes self-disclosure problematic. Identities can be thought of as positions we take up in particular social situations (Woodward, 2002). We present ourselves differently depending on who is around and where we find ourselves. Thus our identities are multiple and shifting and this is the same whether we talk about online or offline contexts. We all are constantly working on our identities. Changing circumstances in our lives need to be integrated with the image we have of ourselves and which we want to project to the outside world. Thus there is a need to create, and keep going, a narrative of oneself (Giddens, 1991). This narrative is constructed through conversations with others. Hypertext is ideal for this process. Davies and Merchant (2007), both academics who write blogs, explain that blogging can induce feelings of pride but also embarrassment and worries about how others react to what one has written and how one has presented oneself. Writing (as well as talking) to a public is always to some extent a performance and blogs are places of repeated public performance (Lewis, 2007). Blogs provide a new medium to discover and present (or 'perform') our identities. This is a therapeutic process, aimed to make us feel good about ourselves and our relations with others. The power of writing a blog therefore is not only for the big catchers whose views are read and received by millions. Writing can be a powerful act if my story of my Saturday night written up on my blog has pleased the three close friends who read it.

do with their real personae. But as with many of the ideas about electronic literacies floating around in the media, the Internet is not necessarily the place where one pretends. Blogs, often, are authentic presentations of people's selves. Huffaker and Calvert (2005), who have studied 70 teenage blogs, have found that the writers of these blogs revealed a lot of personal information about themselves, including demographical information that made them easily identifiable.

28.4   Endless choices: the World Wide Web as a new source of information and advice

I have already said that the new electronic literacy practices change our notion of the author. But they also change how we think about knowledge and what counts as legitimate understandings and reliable information. The World Wide Web is an enormous source of knowledge. But what do we do with all this information? Who can we trust? This is of course a question we also might want to ask about blogs. But, true or fictional, does it matter?

In some social contexts, it does. In health care, for example, whether information is trustworthy and can be relied on for guidance is essential. The Internet allows lay patients to access health information, including articles in medical journals which are written for medical scientists, not the lay public. But what do patients make of this information? How do they know that what they have read about a specific treatment for their migraines is reliable and not just a hoax or the money-making project of a pharmaceutical company? Between 2003 and 2006, a colleague and I have conducted research that aimed to find out how ordinary people access and make use of health information (Papen and Walters, 2008). We interviewed 44 adults (who were students in adult education classes) about their reading and information searching practices in relation to their health. Several of them regularly used the Internet as a source of information. This is what one of our informants said about the Internet:

> And it's telling you, I mean you can go to the doctor, and be told you have got that and you can have that, but they don't tell you everything, but this gives you much more information, you know, why have you been sent for this test and what are they looking for, what are they going to do and...

Here is what Anna, another informant, said in response to my question about how she decides which sites to look at:

> Ah, what I believe or not, then I would say it's probably after I checked several out, I just see information, if it is more or less the same, then I believe.

Other people told us that they tended to trust web-based information if it confirmed what they had been told by other people, including their doctor. This indicates that the professional's opinion is still trusted. But because the Internet is open to many non-experts, it has the potential to help create and

---

ILLUSTRATION BOX 28.3

On the Internet, 'no one laughs at you'

For Pamela, another participant in our study, the Internet was a lifeline. It offered anonymity (Orgad, 2000; Henwood et al., 2003) and it allowed her to talk about a topic nobody liked to discuss with her. Pamela had had several miscarriages. She wanted to know why these had happened and what she could do to prevent herself from having another one. But she struggled to get her doctor and midwives to talk to her about the subject. Her own friends didn't know what to say and preferred not to broach the topic. In the library, Pamela didn't find the information she was looking for and she was too embarrassed to ask. In the end, she turned to the Internet. There, she told us, she wasn't turned away, nobody thought she was mad and nobody laughed at her.

---

distribute knowledge beyond what is legitimated by conventional professional expertise. Writing also plays a role in this. There are many interactive health websites, where patients share their experiences. These affinity spaces (see above) bring together non-experts who share knowledge and in so doing create their own expertise (see, for example, Drentea and Moren-Cross, 2005). Potentially, here the Internet can support the democratization of knowledge and it can help patients challenge their doctors' views.

So there is plenty of information, it's readily available and confidential. Not uncommon these days, our doctor may even invite us to look for it. But do we always want it? Not everybody in our study wanted to know. Searching the Internet can be frustrating, because it's time-consuming and laborious, some people told us. And it can be frightening. There is too much information and as a patient it is easy to get scared by all the worst case scenarios we can find while searching for a seemingly benign and common infection.

28.5 New wine in old bottles: new technologies = new practices = new ethos?

In the previous sections, I have discussed several of the new digital literacy practices which in recent years have become part of many people's lives. But how new are these new electronic literacies? What I mean by 'new' here refers to the technology (its newness) and the practices (what we do with the technology).

I have already said that for most of the people who use them, they are not that new at all. They are a 'normal' part of their lives (Tusting, 2007). I also explained that what people do with cyberliteracies may be 'new' in some ways, but 'old' in others. But there is undoubtedly something new, exiting and appealing about cyberliteracies. There is a new ethos to these new electronic literacy practices (Knobel and Lankshear, 2007). Some researchers (e.g., Kress) believe that the new multimodal and interactive forms of communication allow for more democracy, for greater participation and for greater creativity. This counts in particular for the new type of Internet applications known as 'Web 2.0': interactive and sharing facilities such as blogs or Wikipedia, an online encyclopaedia everyone can add to and edit. But other researchers are more cautious and point out that electronic literacies can be used in different ways, not all of which are necessarily inclusive, democratic and empowering (Freebody, 2001; Knobel and Lankshear, 2007). Others remind us that computers and Internet access are not available to everybody (Snyder and Prinsloo, 2007) and that we need to be careful about the impact they are supposed to have on our societies.

It is often researchers who are enthusiastic about cyberliteracies. But ask a parent, a teacher or a member of the general public. They are likely to be critical of the new literacies. They may express their dismay at what they think is happening to our language. Teachers and parents may show signs of panic in the face of what they believe to be the dangers of the Internet for young people: the weakening of old social ties and the declining standards of grammar (Carrington, 2005; Thurlow, 2006). But are digital literacies dangerous, dull and damaging to our social lives? Literacy researchers have begun to challenge the assumptions many people make about these new literacy practices. Contrary to what public opinion makes us believe, electronic writing is not necessarily full of non-standard language (Jacobs, 2004; Baron, 2005). Research has also found that on the Internet, people can engage with very complex texts (Stone 2007) and that young people using IM and other chat programmes are in the know about the dangers these might entail (Lewis and Fabos, 2005). Finally, as mentioned earlier, online communication systems do not seem to ruin but to support and complement our offline relations.

So views on cyberliteracies are highly divided and this in itself makes them a great topic for research. Much still needs to be found out about how, why and what for people of different backgrounds and ages use digital literacies, what role they play in the workplace, in communities and institutions. Ideally, such research should be carried out by 'insiders': those for whom the practices are second nature (Markham, 1998; Lankshear and Knobel 2003). Thus the ideal researcher of cyberliteracies are young people, not academics my age or older. This is an invitation to you, the readers of this chapter, to get involved! And while you learn the tricks of the (research) trade, plenty of new cyberliteracies are likely to appear, ready and waiting for you to study them.

Recommended readings

You may want to start with Lee (2007). She offers a good introduction to how we can understand digital literacies from a social practices perspective and she also gives a detailed account of her research methodology. Lankshear and Knobel (2003, 2006 and 2007) have written a lot about cyberliteracies, in particular blogs. They have recently published their 'New Literacies Sampler' (Knobel and Lankshear, 2007), a collection of studies on different digital literacies (available online). Lewis and Fabos (2005) is best for an insight into IM and if you are interested in social networking sites such as Facebook, look for the home page of Dannah Boyd, an Internet sociologist.

PART 5

English: Communication and Interaction

EDITED BY RUTH WODAK

CHAPTER 29

Structures of Conversation

GREG MYERS

29.1 Defining 'conversation'

Sometimes people who aren't studying language, and even some who are, express puzzlement that there is academic study of conversation. After all, most people feel they can talk pretty well, even if they can't parse a sentence, write sonnets or give after-dinner speeches, so they don't see much need for anyone to ask how conversation works. But the structure of talk is crucial to many areas of language study: most chapters in this book touch on it in one way or another. And talk is crucial to many social processes, from getting a job, to trying a criminal, to making friends. Talk is apparently loosely structured and even careless. But studies show that it is in fact very orderly, among the most precisely ordered things we do.

At the outset we come to the problem that the word **conversation** has two different meanings, in popular use and in academic study. It can mean all interaction using language, including institutional talk such as teachers talking to students or lawyers questioning witnesses. Or it can mean just those everyday uses of talk such as a family talking about the events of the day at the dinner table, or two acquaintances passing time on a bus. These uses, which some analysts call **mundane conversation**, are crucially different from institutional uses, because there are typically no constraints on who can speak next, for how long or about what. This chapter is using the word in the first sense, to cover any kind of talk. But some researchers who study conversation in this sense call it **talk-in-interaction,** to avoid this confusion, and to stress that their interest is in what people do together with talk.

29.2 Different approaches

There are many different academic approaches to everyday talk, in linguistics, social psychology, anthropology, communication studies and computer science. I will be introducing an approach first developed, not by linguists, but by the sociologists Harvey Sacks, Emanuel Schegloff and Gail Jefferson, who saw conversation as one example of the ways people create social structure in their everyday interactions (for background, see Silverman, 1998; Peräkylä, 2004). Their approach, called **Conversation Analysis** or CA, starts with detailed analysis of the transitions from one person speaking to another; it stays very close to what participants do and show in the data, and does not allow for inferences about what they are thinking, or why they do what they do, or assumptions about their roles and the wider social context. Other approaches, which may be called Discourse Analysis, Interactional Sociolinguistics or Ethnography of Speaking, may start with what we know about the context and purposes, and look for features of language that illustrate or enact this situation. There is often controversy between researchers from different schools (see Recommended readings). But they also agree in most of their descriptions of what goes on in talk; they disagree about what one should do with these descriptions.

29.3   Key concepts

29.3.1   Turn-taking, gaps and overlaps

Conversation analysis begins with the observation that people who are talking to each other do not generally talk at the same time, or leave gaps. The issue for conversation analysis is how people signal to each other when they can talk, and what can come next. This example comes from near the beginning of a phone call (the colons show that that vowel is drawn out):

[29.1]   Mum: Helloo:
         Les: Oh hello how're you?
        Mum: Very well thank you love and you?
         Les: Yes tha:nk you
        Mum: That's good
                 (0.5)
        Mum: We had torrential rain today
(Drew and Chilton, 2000: 145)

As usually happens at the beginnings of phone calls, the participants follow a regular routine of greetings and inquiries. Of course conversation analysts are not saying that people **don't** ever leave gaps or overlap. For instance, here there is a half-second pause, indicated by (0.5). In this case, Drew and Chilton point out, it is more typical for the caller (Les) to introduce the first topic. Mum concludes the opening greetings, waits a bit, and only then introduces the first topic herself.

Conversation analysts argue that any variation from the expectation will be **accountable**; participants may interpret it, comment on it, justify or criticize it. Participants, not just analysts, are aware of the patterns as they talk. Here the (1.0) in the transcription indicates a second of silence between the turns:

[29.2]   Roger: well it struck me funny
                 (1.0)
          Al: ha, ha-ha-ha
        Ken: hh
       Roger: thank you

(Jefferson, 1979)

Roger has apparently told what he thought was a joke, and has then pointed out that it was a joke. Normally laughter would follow. When it doesn't, Al makes an issue of the lack of laughter by doing a mock laugh, and Ken laughs at that. Roger then responds as if they had indeed laughed as they were prompted to do. Similar silences after invitations or statements of opinion can also be interpreted as meaningful in themselves, as we will see.

Similarly, overlapping talk may occur in any conversation, but the participants, as well as the analyst, pay attention to it. The overlapping can be heard as competitive, each speaker trying to get the floor, but in some cases it can be collaborative, showing that each participant is following very closely what the others are saying. In this example, a group of young people who had been arrested for racing cars are welcoming a newcomer to the group. The [indicates that these two turns overlap from this point:

[29.3] Joe: we were in an automobile discussion,
        Henry: discussin' the psychological motives fer
        ?:   hhh   [hhhh hh
        Mel: [drag racing on the streets
                            (Sacks, 1992: I. 175 and II.71)

Here Joe, Henry and Mel together produce a complete sentence, Henry adding on the adverbial that specifies what 'automobile discussion' means, and Mel completing the prepositional phrase, while another participant laughs. This sort of collaboration is a normal feature of fast-paced group talk among acquaintances; it indicates that other participants can project how an utterance might continue, and time their contributions so that they all come together as if one person had said it.

29.3.2 Adjacency pairs and preference

Conversation analysis does not just say that one turn follows another, but that some kinds of turns are typically followed by others. In example [29.1], a drawn out *Helloo:* is followed by an *Oh hello*. A greeting leads to a greeting, a question is followed by an answer, an invitation is followed by acceptance or rejection. Again, this seems obvious enough. The interesting aspects start when we see what people do with these patterns. If a greeting is followed by a greeting, the failure to return a greeting will lead to inference, and maybe a repetition of the greeting. A question produces a slot for an answer, so that almost anything said in that slot might be taken as an answer. These patterns where a turn of one type is predictably followed by a turn of another specific type, one after the other, are called **adjacency pairs.**

For adjacency pairs where there are two possible responses (acceptance/rejection, agreement/disagreement), one kind of next turn is treated differently from the other. For instance, after an invitation, an acceptance will typically come quickly, even overlapping, and will possibly be emphatic:

[29.4] B: Why don't you come up and <u>see</u> me some //times
       A: I would like to.
       B: I would like you to

(Heritage, 1984: 258)

A rejection, on the other hand, may be marked by delay, particles such as *well*, and explanations or justifications before the response is given:

[29.5] B: Uh if you'd like to come over and visit a little while this morn-
          ing I'll give you a cup of coffee.
       A: hehh Well
          that's awfully sweet of you,
          I don't think I can make it this morning
          hh uhm I'm running an ad in the paper and-and uh I have to
          stay near the phone.

(Pomerantz, 1984: 101)

Here A gives laughter, a particle, a favourable comment, a hedged (*I don't think*) refusal, and then an account, an explanation and justification of the behaviour. The quick, unmarked, simple response is called **preferred**, and the delayed, marked, sometimes complicated response is called **dispreferred**, not because anyone necessarily wants it to happen (it could be that neither the inviter nor the invitee really wants to go), but simply to indicate this asymmetry, this difference between the ways the two responses are treated.

One common form of adjacency pair is an assessment – an evaluative statement followed by another assessment. There is a preference for agreement in the next turn after an assessment; if one is going to agree, one does it simply, quickly, and often in upgraded form:

[29.6] A: Isn't he cute
       B: O::h he::s a::DORable

(Pomerantz, 1984)

The exception to this general rule, as one might think, is when the first person is saying something unfavourable about themselves; it is <u>not</u> the preferred second turn to agree:

[29.7] A: I was just wondering if I'd ruined <u>yer</u> weekend [by uh
       B: [no. no. hm
                                              mh . I just
              loved to have -

(Pomerantz, 1984)

Here B has to disagree (whatever he or she might really feel about the weekend), and does it in the way preferred turns are done, quickly (even overlapping), simply and emphatically. The imagined alternative, where B admits his or her weekend **was** ruined by A, would typically involve some delay, particles, hedging or accounts.

29.3.3 Managing the flow of conversation

Since participants typically share these expectations about how one turn is followed by another, they can use the turn-taking system to signal possible problems, project what is coming, and review what has been said. These actions are potentially problematic, and participants make them carefully, with openings for the other to respond. For instance, talk is susceptible to many problems of noise, not just literal sounds blocking what is said, face to face or on the phone, but all the problems of pronunciation and processing that characterize rapid speech. So it is not surprising that talkers have developed ways of checking and correcting possible misunderstandings. In this example, the caller to an emergency help line has not given enough information for the dispatcher to know where to send help:

[29.8]   CT: Mid-City police and Fi:re
         C: Yes. Um: I'm at fifty three twenty seven Nelson
         CT: Fifty three twenty seven Nelson what
         C: North
         CT: Yeah:
         C: An:d uh there's been uh [continues]

                                        (Zimmerman, 1992: 451)

This example illustrates the most common pattern of what is called **repair**: the person who uttered the trouble source turn (C's first turn) is prompted by the other person (CT), in the next turn, to repair it. The prompt could be a repetition of what was just said, or a question about it, or a silence where a response might be expected. In this case, CT repeats the whole utterance, to show what he or she did receive correctly, and then appends *what*, showing that an additional piece of information is needed. (Simply saying *what* would have left C wondering whether the problem was the number, or the street name or general audibility). C then provides just the bit that needed repairing, and CT acknowledges the repair. Since this highly efficient routine is so well established for sorting out misspeaking, mishearing, misunderstanding and inaudibility, one can use it to project doubt or disapproval, for instance just by repeating back what someone has just said.

Many common sequences have developed **pre-sequences** that enable other participants to tell that what follows will be a story (*did you hear what happened to ...*), a request (*do you have five quid?*) or an announcement (*I have good news today!*). These pre-sequences can become so ritualized that the actual sequence is hardly needed (if someone asks if you have five quid, you may just say you can't lend them anything, without waiting for an actual request for a loan). Here the turns lead up to an announcement of news:

> [29.9] D: I-I-I had something <u>terr</u>ible t'tell you.
> So [uh
> R: [How terrible <u>is</u> it.
> D: Uh, th- as worse it could <u>be</u>.
> (0.8)
> R: W-y'mean Edna?
> D: Uh yah.
> R: Whad she do, die?
> D: mm:hm,
>
> (Levinson, 1983: 356)

D hints and delays, while R guesses at the scale of the news, its object and the event, until R supplies the news that is to be announced, and D just confirms it. This indirection suggests that both sides accept there is reason to treat the announcement as sensitive; if D has simply said *Edna's dead* in the first turn, it could have been seen as inappropriately abrupt. R must play along with the hinting strategy for it to work, signalling that he or she can project how the conversation will develop.

As pre-sequences look forward, **formulation** looks back. In formulation, one speaker repeats in other words what they think the previous speaker has said or meant:

> [29.10] A: I was just gonna say come out
> and come over here and talk this evening
> But if you're going out [you can't very well do that
> B: [Talk you mean get drunk, don't you
> A: what?
>
> (Lerner, 1996: 253)

B has rephrased what A has said; *talk* means **get drunk**. There is typically then a slot in which the formulated speaker can accept the formulation or reject it. Just as pre-sequences work because both parties are constantly monitoring the way that the conversation could go forward from this turn, formulations work because both parties are assessing the relevance of the previous turn. In both cases, the issue is not the accuracy of the prediction or the summary, as judged by the analyst, but how the other participant responds in the next turn, whether they are willing to allow this to be the meaning of the next turn, or the last turn, for present purposes.

29.4 An example of talk in a group

The patterns discussed so far are just a few of the many that have been discussed by conversation analysts. The key feature of any analysis is that they look at how one turn is followed by another, asking 'why did this come just after that?' When another analyst disagrees about an interpretation, they don't raise issues of what the participant must have been thinking, or trying to do, or who he or she was; they look ahead to the next turn, to see how the other participant took it. This deliberately narrow window on the text means conversation analysis if often attacked by other analysts, but it also means it provides a rigorous way of analysing and discussing talk. We can see how one might begin to apply it in the extended example presented in Illustration Box 29.1.

ILLUSTRATION BOX 29.1

Telling a story

re-transcribed from the BBC Voices Project http://www.bbc.co.uk/voices/recordings/individual/sheffield-burngreave-kaggwa-nasreen.shtml

NASREEN: uh uh I was uh about to walk through . I think it was somewhere at the airport or something and I knew where I were going but I were just fiddling with something that I had in my hand and this uh guy came up to me and said you dis way   [like that
                                                            [hhh (6) [hh

NASREEN: [yeah you dis way like that . you know he was trying to use ((slows down)) limited language to try
                    ( )

NASREEN: 'cos he thought I was standing in the middle . of nowhere . which I was I was kinda like standing in the middle   [( )

MONA: [he was white [English?

NASREEN: [yeah so I was I was just fiddling with something
                    ( )

NASREEN: maybe in my purse or something like that so he said you dis way and that and I said I know where I'm goin
                    hhh hhh

MIRIAM: (mate)

NASREEN: yeah and then he looked and like he was so embarrassed

MONA: how disgusting [is that!

NASREEN: [yeah and he says I'm really I'm really really sorry it's just that we get a lot of people that end up wandering in the wrong place

MONA: [( )

NASREEN: [because they don't know where they're going

MONA: [( )

NASREEN: [yeah I says I'M JUST TRYING to put abc together whatever it were that I were holding on to . so: I thought that were a bit cheeky

We could of course start from the context: who are Nasreen, Mona and their friends? What is their relation to each other? Why are they talking? What is the necessary structure of stories, and why is she telling this one? But from a conversation analysis approach, we need to look first at the sequence of turns. We see then that Nasreen keeps taking turns, even when others break in. She can do this because she has signalled that she is telling a story, that whatever others say, she is not done (has not given up the floor (Edelsky, 1981)), until she signals the end of the story. The BBC clip starts with her setting the scene for a story, and ends with her giving her evaluation of her participation in it, providing an opening for others to come in. Along the way, Mona and maybe others overlap with her talk. But this overlapping is not heard as interruption; we know this because Nasreen keeps acknowledging them as part of her story, before continuing. The others offer their own views of what facts are relevant (*was he white English?*) and their own evaluations of events (*how disgusting is that?*), but Nasreen does not give her own evaluation until the end.

This example is not just talk, it is talk about talk. Nasreen does not just say *I met an airport employee who was condescending to me because the colour of my skin made him take a British native for a foreigner*, she enacts how he said it, and how she responded. His simplified way of talking to her, and her colloquial response, is the point. And it is a point the others take, because Mona carries it one step further, projecting a possible completion for Nasreen's remark (*mate*) that would have been consistent with her demonstrating that she was British and was rejecting his interference, and Nasreen says *yeah*. After this point is made, Nasreen continues the conversation, but it is clearly not important that she give the exact words, even though it is in direct speech; she says *trying to put abc together whatever* because it doesn't matter, for this story, just what it was she was fiddling with; what matters is that her fiddling was mistaken for confusion. It is possible to analyse the structure of this story (see Labov and Fanshel, 1977; Eggins and Slade, 1997), but the point here is that it is carefully constructed in the course of interaction (Georgakopoulou, 2006).

29.5 Mediated conversation

The approach of conversation analysis starts with everyday talk, what they sometimes call mundane conversation, where the roles, the next speaker and the content of adjacency pairs is left to the participants. In many institutional contexts, these aspects are not left to the participants to work out; for instance, in many school contexts, the teacher chooses the next speaker, so there is no point in following the turn-taking mechanism, and the teacher determines whether a response counts as an answer to a question, or not. Conversation analysts have applied their approach to some of these institutional contexts; for instance, example [29.3] above was from a therapeutic group, and example [29.8] from a call to an emergency help line. Conversation analysis applies to all these situations, but one has to look closely at the actual talk to see how it is different from everyday talk. One cannot, in this approach, just assume that a doctor controls talk with a patient, or a lawyer controls talk with a witness on the stand. Participants have whatever effect they have on each other, and on overhearing participants, by drawing on conventions that they take for granted from everyday talk, and modifying them in terms of the institution.

Let us take one example from a kind of institutional talk, a White House Press Briefing. These briefings are held by the US President's office almost every day, and are attended by reporters from the press and broadcast news organizations who have White House press credentials. The Press Secretary typically reads out a list of events of the day, and then answers questions. In this excerpt, from about ten minutes into a rather tense session mainly focused on one issue, Tony Snow is the Press Secretary (PS).

ILLUSTRATION BOX 29.2

White House Press Briefing

re-transcribed from the streaming video available at http://www.whitehouse. gov/news/releases/2007/03/20070319-1.html

Q1   Tony you've said that the uh President retains confidence in the Attorney General but is he fully satisfied with the job that the Attorney General has been doing? does he think that uh Gonzales maybe needs to be more involved in some of the day-to-day decisions =

PS: = I'm I'm not- I'm not going to parse that

Q 1   why not? I mean why [

Q 2   [parse away.

Q 1   [is he [

PS: [because it's such a vague question that I'm not sure it's answerable

Q 1   well what's vague about . you know [

PS: [is there something you don't like about management in some area and some [

Q1   [well okay let's be more specific . has he told him that he . specifically . Gonzales . has he expressed any unhappiness to him . with how he's doing the job . or say that he needs to improve something?

PS: again that's that's too vague . I'm not [

Q1   [that's not vague

PS: sure it is it's a fishing question . I mean . the fact is the President has said he's got confidence in the Attorney General .the other thing he's- and I heard him say that . furthermore he's also said that on this issue, it's going to be important he said it publicly . that the Attorney General explain what went on in the process

In analysing this excerpt, we might start with the observations in research broadcast political interviews that shows they are not like everyday talk: the Interviewer asks only questions, the Interviewee gives only answers, the Interviewer decides who the next speaker will be, and both perform as if they were not really talking for the other, but for an overhearing broadcast audience (for more on these patterns, see Heritage, 1985; Greatbatch, 1988; Clayman and Heritage, 2002). But when we, in that overhearing audience, watch and listen, we do not entirely suspend our expectations about questions and answers, formulations, overlaps or silences; we use our knowledge of what is usual to evaluate the speakers and interpret their contributions.

Let us consider the way that Tony Snow doesn't answer this question. The grounds on which a PS can reject a question as inappropriate are not formally stated (as they might be, say, in parliamentary questions); they are worked out by the participants over time and as they go along. Here Q1 frames his question as following on from something the PS has already said, and therefore as immediately relevant. He then reformulates his own question (*does he think that maybe Gonzales needs to be more involved* ...). But the PS interrupts him before the reformulated question is finished: *I'm not going to parse that*. Readers of this book will be familiar with parsing sentences (see Chapter 8). Here *parsing* seems to mean taking the question apart; the implication is that there is some ambiguity or alternative possible meaning. (The joking call from another Questioner suggests that they take the term *parse* as fairly odd and striking language). When Q1 challenges this, PS rejects the question again: *it's such a vague question*. When Q1 asks what is vague, PS formulates the question in a way that makes it seem vague (and waving his hands in a way that suggests irony): *is there something you don't like about management in some area or some*. Q1 rephrases the question, with an introduction presenting this as a dispreferred response to the previous turn: *well okay let's be more specific*. The PS rejects it as vague again: *it's a fishing question*. 'Fishing questions', asked without a definite end in view, are ruled out of courtroom questioning; here he applies it to the Press Briefing. And then he shifts back to his previous answer: *The fact is* ....

Conversation analysis does not enable us to say if the question is or is not vague, and if the response is or is not evasive. But it does tell us about the resources we as audience bring from everyday conversation when we try to interpret what is going on here. The first interruption projects the question as entirely out of line; otherwise the Press Secretary (like a politician in a political interview) would wait until the question is over. Similarly, Q1's interruption to reformulate his question projects the response as insufficient and unreasonable. The PS can, in the end, always decide which questions to answer (and whom to call on), but it is moments like this that project him or her as confident, defensive, open or evasive.

29.6 Transcription

Conversation analysts have developed a form of transcription that tries to record on the page as much as possible of the information in a tape recording, especially the issues of pauses and overlaps that are important in CA.

Readers coming to CA for the first time are often put off by the difficulty of reading this level of detail (see example [29.9]). But the details can be crucial to the point one is making about the data (for instance the half-second pause in example [29.1]). Early conversation analysts made transcriptions in this detailed form (usually associated with Gail Jefferson), so that other analysts could use them for other purposes if they wanted. The symbols can be found in almost any of the introductions under 'Further Reading', or you can find useful introductions online from Charles Antaki: http://www-staff.lboro.ac.uk/%7Esscal/antaki1.htm or Emanuel Schegloff: http://www.sscnet.ucla.edu/soc/faculty/schegloff/. But for most language courses, it is probably best to use just as much detail as you need for your purposes, and no more, and to use any of the standard forms of transcription (for instance [or // for onset of overlap).

Recommended readings

As noted in the Introduction, Conversation Analysis is just one approach to analysing talk. For fairly even-handed overviews of a range of approaches, see Schiffrin (1994), Tischer, Meyer, Wodak and Vetter (2000), Cameron (2001), Wetherell, Taylor and Simeon (2002), and Johnstone (2008). For standard introductions to CA by noted practitioners, see Psathas (1995), Hutchby and Wooffitt (1998), and ten Have (1999). Of the many chapter-length introductions, the best is probably Peräkylä (2004); see also the influential early overview by Levinson (1983). For intellectual background to the approach, see Heritage (1984) and Silverman (1998). Edited collections are often the first publications of key CA research (for examples, see Sudnow, 1972; Atkinson and Heritage, 1984; Button and Lee, 1987; Boden and Zimmerman, 1991; Duranti and Goodwin, 1992; Ochs and Thompson, 1996). But for intellectual stimulation, nothing beats the sprawling and repetitive but lively, accessible and far-ranging undergraduate lectures between 1964 and 1968 in which Harvey Sacks first explored the ideas underlying what later became CA; they are now available in transcribed form, with an essential index (Sacks, 1992).

There have been several influential collections on institutional talk (Drew and Heritage, 1992; Sarangi and Roberts, 1999; McHoul and Rapley, 2001); on broadcast talk see Scannell (1991), Clayman and Heritage (2002), Thornborrow (2002), Hutchby (2006) and Tolson (2006).

CHAPTER 30

Language, Reality and Power

NORMAN FAIRCLOUGH

30.1   Introduction

How do inequalities of power affect which of the many available ways of construing the real world in language become the dominant ones? The 'dominant' ones are the most widespread, the most influential, those with the most impact on:

- how people see the world
- how they act within and upon the world
- how the world changes

This is the main question I shall address. I shall suggest that addressing it requires a **critical** approach to language analysis (Fairclough and Wodak, 1997). I shall first discuss construing reality (and why I prefer 'construe' to the more obvious term 'represent'), power and the relationship between them (Section 30.1), then critical approaches to language analysis (Section 30.2), and finally how critical analysis of language can contribute to social research (Section 30.3).

30.1.1   Construing reality

I am actually using **construe** in preference to two other widely used terms, **represent** but also **construct**. Most of you will have come across the latter – it is very fashionable these days to insist that the language people choose to use not only represents the world in a particular way; it also constructs it in a particular way. For instance, if I were to suggest that you are not just a university student but also a **customer** of your university, or a **consumer** of the **products** it offers, this would not (so the argument goes) just be a particular – and, you might think, peculiar – way of representing students and universities, it would also construct them in non-traditional and (at least until recently) unconventional ways. It would contribute to changing and remaking this bit of the real world, changing what students and universities are.

   For this example, I see no difficulty with the argument. I agree with the claim that the term 'represent' suggests an overly simple picture of the relationship between language and the real world, and with the claim that language can contribute to changing reality. But I do have a difficulty when this argument is over-generalized in a general claim that **language constructs the world**. Language **can** contribute to constructing and changing the real world, but it does so only under certain conditions, and it is misleading to claim that **everything** we say or write changes the real world. That is why I prefer construe to construct (on the distinction, see Sayer, 2000). There are many ways of construing aspects of the real world, but few of them have the effect of constructing, that is, changing it. Construing students as customers and consumers of a university's products does seem to be having constructive effects on Higher Education (HE) in Britain and other countries – it seems to be contributing to change in the nature of HE – but this is because this particular construal is supported and promoted by people who have power in and over HE (including government, business and university managers). Construing also has the advantage of suggesting that adequately grasping the world in language can sometimes be a process fraught with difficulty. Let me illustrate.

ILLUSTRATION BOX 30.1

An example of construing

How can we determine when people can be adequately construed as *terrorists*? This is currently sometimes a real problem, for journalists, politicians and ordinary citizens. We need some sense of what counts as *terrorism*, e.g., 'violence with a political and social intention, whether or not intended to put people in general in fear, and raising a question of its moral justification' (Honderich, 2003: 98–9), though not everyone will agree with this definition; and it helps to find clear cases most people could agree on – those who attacked the World Trade Centre in New York in 2001 and the London Underground in July 2006 are perhaps pretty uncontentiously *terrorists*.

In some cases we might recognize that people use *terrorist* methods in something like Honderich's sense, and are *terrorists* in some sense, yet feel reluctant because of particular features of the context of their violence to leave it at that and so implicitly equate them with people who are *terrorists* in an unmitigated sense. This might be so with certain acts of extreme violence (e.g., suicide bombings) against Israeli civilians by Palestinians within the *intifada* (though I would unhesitatingly say that, for example, the Palestinians who murdered members of the Israeli team at the Munich Olympics in 1972 were *terrorists*) or by Iraqis in the aftermath of the Iraq War. This is because these actions can be seen as part of a war or insurgency, and are matched by and are responding to acts of comparable violence against civilians by military or paramilitary forces. Note that Honderich's definition is consistent with *state terrorism*, and we might ask why these Palestinians or Iraqis are widely called *terrorists* in the media whereas soldiers using *terrorist* methods are not. I sometimes feel that while such people are *terrorists* in a sense, this is not a fully adequate construal because they are resisting extreme violence, carried out by others who might equally be called *terrorists* but are generally not, so it is also inequitable, but I feel unsure what other word to use, what an adequate construal would be. It's difficult to grasp this bit of the world in language – that's the sort of difficulty we quite often have in construing the world, even if this is an extreme example of it.

30.1.2 Power

Power is clearly part of the problem in this example. In the news media (press, television, etc.) *terrorist* is widely used as a sufficient and adequate construal of Palestinian fighters, but Israeli or American armed forces are rarely construed in this way (though widely condemned in other terms). This inadequate – and I would argue unjust – habit of construing seems to be explicable in terms of power. The news media are far from being the mere plaything of the rich and powerful, yet the balance of power in British national and indeed international and 'global' news media is clearly in favour of the most powerful states and governments, business corporations, military establishments, and so forth – what we might for short call 'vested interests'. Generalizing the point, certain habits or practices of construing various significant aspects of the real world are dominant or (to use a political term) **hegemonic** in news and other fields of social life (politics, government, education, entertainment, etc.), certain 'alternative' habits or practices are subordinate or marginalized (e.g., construing the Palestinians and Iraqis in question as 'fighters' or 'soldiers'), and these patterns of dominance and subordination in practices of construing are an effect of relations and inequalities of power.

Power is a complex concept, there are various conflicting theories, and the word **power** is used in various senses (Lukes, 1974; Fairclough, 2001). Let me distinguish just three: **power to, power over** and **power behind**. The first appertains to power in its most general sense: the capacity or ability to bring about change. We can say that all human beings have some measure of power in this sense – the power to change their own ways of acting and behaving, aspects of the environment within which and upon which they act, the actions and behaviour of other people, and so forth.

But it is obvious that human beings have different measures of power, and this leads us to **power over**, relations of power between people. An important aspect of differences in power is that some people have a greater capacity than others to bring about change by using the capacities and agency of other people. They have, or they try to have, power over other people. Language is an important aspect of power over, both in the sense what we might call **communicative power** (the power to control others in communication, in conversations or interviews or the media, is a form of power over), and in the sense that communicative power is a means of exercising power over people in a more general way (controlling their behaviour and actions). For example, imagine being interviewed by your boss or Head of Department about inadequacies in your work. Your interviewer will have the communicative power to ask the questions and to make you not only answer them but give the sort of answers s/he requires (if the question is 'Why did you not meet the deadline for your report?', a reason or explanation is required, not, for example, your reflections on what a wonderful company or department it is), but will also seek to use this communicative power to control your future behaviour.

Communicative power is power that is exercised, sought for and indeed often fought for – and fought against – in actual communicative events such as interviews. Questions of what I am calling **power behind** arise when we consider not actual events but the habitual, often institutionalized, forms or practices which shape or influence what people actually do – for instance the conventional forms of various institutionally recognized types of interview (e.g., job interviews, interviews to assess entitlement to social security benefits, political interviews) – and ask who has the power to determine these forms, to police compliance with them, etc. These types of interviews have characteristic linguistic features (e.g., features typical for job interview questions) which, taken together, define them as **genres**, conventionalized ways of interacting linguistically. In broad terms, those who have most power within an institution (e.g., a particular type of workplace) exercise or seek to exercise the power behind its practices, forms and genres.

ILLUSTRATION BOX 30.2

Classroom interaction

Taken from Coulthard (1977: 94). 'T' stands for 'teacher' and 'P' for 'pupil'.

T: Where does it go before it reaches your lungs?
P: Your windpipe, Miss.
T: Down your windpipe...Now can anyone remember the other word for windpipe?
P: The trachea.
T. The trachea...good.

This is a conventional form of interaction between teachers and pupils – you have almost certainly experienced something of the sort, but you may well have also experienced rather more open forms of dialogue. It's a particular genre with a predictable structure and certain 'rules' (which are not always strictly adhered to): only T asks questions, Ps are required to answer questions and to do so appropriately (e.g., an appropriate answer to a **where?** question identifies a place), following an answer T gives some sort of feedback which evaluates the answer (repeating the answer e.g., *the trachea* is a way of implicitly accepting it as adequate, *good* is an explicit evaluation, but *Down your windpipe* combines acceptance through repetition with a subtle correction).

One aspect of such an example is T's and Ps' **power to** communicate within this format, based on knowledge and training – both demonstrate in practice that they know what to do – their power to interact within this genre. Another aspect is T's **power over** Ps – T is controlling and constraining Ps' contributions to the event. A perhaps rather less obvious aspect is the **power behind** the conventions of classroom communication, part of institutional power in the educational system. Teachers are subject to this power no less than pupils. But the fact that this is no longer the overwhelmingly dominant form of classroom communication is an indicator that institutional power is open to challenge and change.

30.1.3   How does power affect the construal of reality?

It takes a brave interviewee in a job interview to diverge too obviously from the ways in which aspects of the job are construed by the interviewers. For instance, if my interviewers for an academic job were to ask me (heaven forbid!) how I would ensure that the **products** I offer meet the **needs** of my **consumers**, I might think it rash not to use this market language in my answer. I might decide nevertheless not to and – given the game-playing which goes on in interviews – it may even turn out to be what the interviewers wanted. The example illustrates that one aspect of communicative power (as a form of power over) is the power to choose and try to control how particular aspects of reality are construed.

I suggested earlier that certain groups are generally construed in news media as 'terrorists' while others (like the military) are not, and that this is a matter of the power of 'vested interests'. This is an example of power behind –how those with institutional power control habits and practices of construal. I referred above to the power behind genres, but here it is a matter of the power behind **discourses** – conventionalized ways of construing particular aspects of the real world. Those with most power within an institution (news media or education) seek to control its discourses, how the world is generally construed.

ADVANCES BOX 30.1

Globalization

The examples so far might suggest that construing is just a matter of selecting particular vocabulary. But different discourses also differ in other linguistic features, including grammatical features. Take, for instance, the processes of **globalization** which are endlessly referred to in contemporary texts. We can say that globalization is a real set of (highly complex) processes which are creating a global scale of social life in economy, politics and even culture. But there are also various discourses of globalization, various ways of construing it. In some discourses, globalization frequently appears as the subject of verbs which construe actions (e.g., *globalization is creating new markets, globalization destroys jobs*). You will find this in Tony Blair's speeches, for instance (Fairclough, 2000), and it can be regarded as a feature of the dominant discourse of globalization (Fairclough, 2006; Weiss and Wodak, 2000). From the perspective of other discourses, such claims are objectionable – 'how can a highly complex, diverse and uneven set of processes possibly be an agent of change? Globalization cannot *do* anything!' And, as this suggests, discourses also differ in the sorts of arguments that are used to support or undermine claims about the world. These other discourses also have their own distinctive ways of using the word *globalization*, e.g., they categorize it to distinguish different (acceptable and unacceptable) forms of globalization – e.g., *neo-liberal globalization, progressive globalization* – which the dominant discourse does not.

30.2   Why should we analyse language critically?

In a book based on remarkable diaries secretly kept throughout Nazi rule in Germany (1933–45), the Romance philologist Victor Klemperer (a Jew who only survived thanks to having a non-Jewish wife) comments on the word *Entnazifizierung* ('denazification'), that one day it will 'fade away' but not for some time, 'because it isn't only Nazi actions that have to vanish, but also the Nazi cast of mind, the typical Nazi way of thinking and its breeding-ground: the language of Nazism' (Klemperer, 2000 [1946]: 2). In fact he calls it a 'dreadful word', because it is formed like many words with 'the dissociating prefix' *ent–* (English *de–*) which were coined or given new meanings during the Nazi period. This links to a major conclusion of Klemperer's analysis of 'the language of the Third Reich' – it was used by everyone, irrespective of age, educational level, region, and 'enmity towards or resolute faith in the Führer', and people were often unaware of the import of the language they unselfconsciously used, even quite a time after the Third Reich had collapsed. If language is the 'breeding ground' for ways of thinking, and we are often unaware of these effects, this is one good reason for analysing language critically.

Klemperer draws attention to what we might call the **soft power** of language as well as the **hard power** of language, such as the brutal abusive terms which the Nazis used to refer to and address Jews, Roma and gays. An example of the soft power of language is the way in which people he taught after the war were 'seduced and confused' by words like *heroisch* ('heroic'), which they used without being aware of it in a Nazi way – exclusively for people in uniforms, as Klemperer strikingly puts it! Aldous Huxley, the author of the novel *Brave New World* (1931), also emphasizes the importance of the soft power of language when he argues, in a later book 'revisiting' the Brave New World (Huxley, 1959), that his own dystopia imagined the way the world is actually going more accurately than George Orwell in his novel *1984* (1948), because 'government through terror works on the whole less well than government through the non-violent manipulation of the environment and of the thoughts and feelings of individual men, women and children'. Huxley discusses 'propaganda in a democratic society', how the 'mass communications industry' manipulates people through feeding their 'appetite for distractions', relying on 'the repetition of catchwords which they wish to be accepted as true, the suppression of facts which they wish to be ignored, the arousal and rationalization of passions' (1959: 13, 54–6).

Noam Chomsky, equally famous for his contributions to Linguistics and his political writings, also stresses the importance of 'distractions', tracing the emergence of the 'public relations industry' in the United States from the 1920s, noting that it was 'all very consciously committed to the belief that you must control attitudes and opinions, because the people are otherwise just too dangerous' (Chomsky, 2005: 21). Chomsky in fact chooses to de-emphasize language as such, perhaps because his approach to language is a-socially centred on language form (see Section 30.2.3).

30.2.1   How can construals of reality be evaluated?

One central concern of critical approaches to language is to not only describe but also evaluate ways of construing the world in terms of relations of power, and this involves considering the **adequacy** of construals. What sort of considerations enter into judging construals as more or less (in)adequate? We cannot answer this question in a vacuum, claiming to stand outside the complicated business of construing the world. We can never do that. We need some sort of theory of the real world and of the relationships of social life to other parts of it, and of how language figures within these relationships. Since theories are just construals of a special sort, we need to have made certain decisions – of course open to challenge and revision – about the relative adequacy of ways of construing the world. There is a circularity here, but it only becomes a vicious circle if we try to disguise our prior assumptions or treat them as beyond question.

For instance, I would argue (though I don't have space to do so here) that reality is most adequately construed as constituted primarily not of objects or individuals but **relations**, which are generally not immediately obvious but have to be discovered through experience and research. Given this assumption, construals of reality are adequate to the extent that they grasp such 'underlying' relations rather than just the **forms of appearance** in which such relations are manifested in a more easily observable form. For instance, the trouble with *terrorist* (and many other words) is that while it may more or less adequately construe forms of appearance (after all, terrorism and terrorists are real enough), it tends to obscure underlying relations and to be unhistorical – those who are generally construed as 'terrorists' in the news media are in complex historical relations with those they target and those who aim to 'eradicate' them which are generally missing in media coverage of 'the war on terror'.

30.2.2   How can we assess constructive effects of language?

I suggested above that particular ways of construing reality may have constructive effects in changing reality, the main sorts being on (a) how people see the world (beliefs, attitudes), (b) how people act and behave, and (c) changes in the world beyond changes in thought and action, including physical changes. One concern of critical approaches to language is to describe and assess such constructive effects – the dialectical process in which language is **operationalized** (made operative, put into practice) in the world (Fairclough, 2003, 2006).

Investigating such effects amounts to investigating a causal relation: language as a cause of change in the world. We can say that language has causal power, the power to bring about change. But we have to be careful how we understand causality. We can say in a general way that language has causal power, but that does not tell us whether specific uses of language bring about change. We have to say something like: they **may** do so, other things being equal. That is, there are always various factors in assessing whether concrete events change the world and how, and language is only one of them. And the fact that certain ways of using language **may** have certain effects does not mean that they always or regularly **do**, it depends on other factors.

What sort of other factors? Well, let's go back to construing students as 'consumers' or 'customers'. We can say in an abstract way that such a construal **may** change the world in certain ways (e.g., how students and lecturers think and see each other and act towards each other). But the factors which condition whether it **does** include: how much power do the people who promote this construal have in universities? What other construals are in circulation, how much power do the people who promote those have? How well does this way of construing students fit in with other discourses and practices (e.g., construals and practices of teaching and learning)? How well does it fit in with the beliefs, values, experiences and discourses of students themselves – for example, with discourses through which students construe their identities, aspirations, hopes for and fears about the world? And so forth.

Given all these factors, it is often difficult to say exactly what the effects of language are, even where it seems pretty obvious – as in this case – that particular ways of construing have contributed to change in thinking, action, and the character of institutions and organizations. But the difficulty in being precise goes with the territory – social science is not (or only rarely) exact science – and, since the constructive effects of language are now probably beyond question for most social researchers (not just linguists), we should not let the difficulty put us off.

ADVANCES BOX 30.2

Chomsky's position

Chomsky is a fascinating exception to this claim about social researchers, and given his influence in Linguistics it is worth considering his position. Chomsky (2005) is a set of interviews, and one interesting feature is that the interviewer repeatedly invites Chomsky to comment on the language associated with American foreign policy (e.g., 'Talk about the role of language in shaping and forming people's understanding of events'), but Chomsky repeatedly avoids doing so, sometimes saying why: 'It has nothing much to do with language … naturally, people use the means of communication to try to shape attitudes and opinions and to induce conformity and subordination. This has been true forever, but propaganda became an organized and very self-conscious industry only in the last century' (2005: 18–19). In short, the role of language is a historical constant which is therefore of little value in understanding the recent development which really matters – a propaganda industry.

But why does he not see this development as constituted to a significant extent by change in the social use of language? Surely the industrialization of propaganda amounts to an important set of changes in public language, for instance the extension of advertising language into politics? The basis of his position becomes clearer when he discusses what people need to do in response to propaganda: 'Instead of repeating ideological fanaticism, dismantle it, try to find out the truth, and tell the truth. It's something any one of us can do' (2005: 63–4). There are, he says, 'no special techniques'.

This seems to amount to discounting constructive effects of language – people have the intelligence to cut through the crap, so to speak, and find the truth, if they make the effort. The crap **can** be cut through (we are not passive victims), but I don't see it as a mere act of will, nor is the truth something that is transparent if only we look for it (sometimes it may be, more often it isn't). Take again the example of *terrorists*. I suggested that calling people *terrorists* is not always adequate (the truth) but not wholly inadequate (part of the truth), and that finding an adequate construal is not that easy. Actually it is much easier finding an adequate construal in an essay than an alternative word to *terrorists*, but 'telling the truth' effectively in public does depend on finding a language in which to do it succinctly. What this suggests is that, *pace* Chomsky, 'dismantling' the 'ideological fanaticism' and 'telling the truth' has a great deal to do with language – critical analysis of inadequate construals, and the difficult search for more adequate construals.

30.3   What can critical analysis of language contribute to social research?

My own research develops a version of **critical discourse analysis** designed for researching relations between language and other social elements in interdisciplinary research (van Dijk, 1993; Fairclough and Wodak, 1997; Wodak and Meyer, 2001). It seeks a systematic framework for focusing specifically on the language aspects of aspects of social life and change which social researchers are concerned with. Such language aspects are widely recognized by sociologists, political scientists and other social scientists. Generally, however, they deal with them at a relatively superficial level. Critical discourse analysis contributes more developed theories of language and ways of analysing language which can be integrated into interdisciplinary research (Fairclough, 2003).

These resources can be used to address various concerns for social researchers. The significance of language in relations of power, as well as in resistance to abusive power and struggles for power, is one issue. Another is language aspects of the emergence, enactment and change of social and personal identities, including national identities and gender identities. And critical analysis of language allows social research to move from general statements about language as a dimension of social life to detailed statements about particular sets of key texts or genres of spoken interaction such as interviews. For instance, social scientists stress that the exercise of power depends upon systems of power and power-holders having **legitimacy**, and often recognize that they are actively legitimized through particular forms of argument. Critical analysis of language can go one step further and actually analyse legitimizing argumentation in texts and interactions. Another example is that research on social identity commonly sees the stories (narratives) that people or social groups tell about themselves as a crucial part of enacting and constructing identity, but often fail to carry out analyses of actual narratives.

30.3.1 An example – *we thank you for your understanding*

A number of years ago I introduced the term **synthetic personalization** for giving the impression of treating people individually when 'handling' them *en masse*, including the **conversationalization** of public language, making public language (in politics, advertising, etc.) more like ordinary conversation (Fairclough, 1989/2001, 1992). An interesting recent development within this longer-term tendency is the proliferation of **apologizing** and **thanking** in public discourse. All sorts of public organizations and persons that used to publicly apologize and thank rarely, now constantly do so. Governments and leaders now readily apologize not only for their own actions but even for those of their predecessors; for example, German and Japanese apologies for war-crimes in the Second World War, and British apologies for the slave trade. Companies routinely apologize for deficiencies in their goods and services and thank the public not only for their enquiries and their interest but even for their understanding and patience.

These changes in language can be seen as a part of social changes investigated by social researchers. One is the growth of the public relations industry (which Chomsky alluded to) which has profoundly affected not only business but politics and government, and progressively, virtually all public fields (religion, education, the arts, etc.). Another closely associated tendency is for the capitalist **market model** to be extended from the buying and selling of goods to services, politics, education, etc., which has included the extension of market language (which, notably in advertising, has long been conversationalized and synthetically personalized). You might, for instance, look for some old prospectuses for your university and compare them with its current website. Another is cultural analysis of the tendency for the values and ethics of the private sphere ('ordinary life') to colonize the public sphere – think of how politicians try hard to pass themselves off as just ordinary people with ordinary concerns and values.

Such social research often recognizes the important language dimension of these social changes, but generally does not analyse it in any detail. Critical analysis of language can help fill this gap.

ILLUSTRATION BOX 30.3

Thanking

Let me illustrate this with just one very specific example – public use by various organizations of expressions like *we thank you for your understanding*. This is personal rather than impersonal ('third-person') language (c.f. *the understanding of the public is appreciated*), and it is direct address rather than indirect address, i.e., the public are directly addressed (as *you*). Furthermore, although this sort of speech act is actually addressed to a mass audience (e.g., all the passengers on a train), it uses the standard advertising conceit of apparently addressing people individually (*you* is to be understood as singular). And the organization which actually 'owns' the speech act is also personalized, as *we*. We can't be precise about who *we* are, it's inherently vague and doesn't bear much analysis.

A notable semantic feature is that whereas people are usually thanked for something they have actually done (e.g., an *enquiry* or some practical assistance) or some quality of what they have done (e.g., their *generosity*), in this case they are thanked for a quality they haven't manifested (*understanding*) but which is rather anticipated or hoped for. Pragmatically, there is an oddity in terms of pragmatic presuppositions (see Chapter 11, Section 11.3): the speech act presupposes (takes as a matter of fact) that they **are** understanding, but since they may not be, it is an invalid presupposition.

Corpus linguistics would be helpful in clarifying the **contexts** in which speech acts of this sort appear (*we thank you for your patience, we appreciate your cooperation*, are other examples) (see Chapter 23, Section 23.4; Chapter 26, Section 26.3.2; and Chapter 34, Section 34.5, for demonstrations of corpus linguistics in action). Even the rough-and-ready results of a *Google* search (in October 2007) are revealing: out of approximately 29,500 instances of *we thank you for your understanding and,* the following word in 850 cases was *apologize.* Speech acts of this sort are commonly used when an organization has something to apologize for (the delay of a train, 'all our operators are busy' in a call centre, etc.).

This 'small practice' can be seen as part of a new means for governmental, business and other organizations to govern and manage the public, and as such a new way of exercising and seeking power through language. It has the paradoxical property of apparently conceding and spreading power to more effectively maintain and concentrate it – being considerate and polite to the public, bowing to the practices and values of ordinary life, admitting and apologizing for mistakes and showing gratitude, yet effectively using these gestures of concession to manipulate situations and people and control them. Questions of construal do not seem to immediately arise, but they are implicit: behind the practice is a way of construing relations between organizations and the public as more equal, open and convivial than arguably they actually are, and the practice can be seen as enacting this discourse.

Recommended readings

Fairclough (2001) provides a general introduction to relations between language and power, and Fairclough (2003) focuses on analysing texts within interdisciplinary research. Both adopt versions of critical discourse analysis, and there is a review of various approaches to it in Fairclough and Wodak (1997), and of methods of critical discourse analysis in Wodak and Meyer (2001). Cameron (2000) is a lively critical discussion of contemporary preoccupations with 'communication' in work, education and private life. Particularly relevant journals include: *Critical Discourse Studies, Discourse & Society*, and the *Journal of Language and Politics*.

CHAPTER 31

Politeness in Interaction[1]

JONATHAN CULPEPER

31.1 What is politeness?

Need the question be asked? We all know what politeness is, don't we? Imagine you are ensconced at a dinner table in England: politeness might include remembering to use *please* when you want something passed, saying something nice about the food and definitely not burping. In fact, all of these particular things are somewhat more complex – even problematic – than they first appear. The word *please* is the 'magic word' that British parents impress upon their children to use with all requests, and it looms large in the British psyche. But how is it actually used by adults? Aijmer (1996: 166–8) provides some evidence. It matters how the rest of the request is worded: *please* is most likely to be used in conjunction with an imperative (e.g., please <u>make</u> me a cup of tea) or with *could you* (e.g., <u>could you</u> please make me a cup of tea), but much less likely to be used with *can you* or *will you*. You will note that I failed to specify whether you were ensconced at a family meal or had been invited to dinner. Differences in situation would influence whether you use the word *please*. *Please* tends to be used in relatively formal situations, and in business letters and written notices. It is particularly frequent in service encounters, notably via the telephone (all too often we hear 'can you hold the line please'!). So, if the dinner were a formal invitation, *please* would more likely be used. Complimenting the cook on the food may seem a straightforwardly nice thing to do, but it is not straightforward: you place the recipient of the compliment in a rather tricky position. If they simply accept the compliment, they may sound rather immodest, but if they simply reject it, they may offend the person who made it. Consequently, responses to compliments tend to weave a path between these two positions. A response such as 'it's kind of you to say that' suggests that the compliment is (at least in part) a product of the complimenter's kindness and not necessarily a true reflection of the value of the food. Finally, even burping cannot always with certainty be seen as the antithesis of politeness. Cultural considerations come into play here. In some cultures, burping may be acceptable, or even a sign of appreciation of the food – a compliment! Needless to say, culture also keenly influences politeness too. The use of the word *please* is more typical of British culture than North American, being used about twice as frequently (Biber et al., 1999: 1098). This is not to say that American culture is less polite. There are other ways of doing politeness, and those other ways might be evaluated as polite by North Americans, just as using *please* in certain contexts might be evaluated as polite by British English people. (Im)politeness is in the eyes and ears of the beholder.

Politeness, then, involves 'polite' behaviours. What those behaviours, linguistic and non-linguistic, consist of, how they vary in context, and why they are considered 'polite' are some of the key areas of politeness study. This does not mean that academics who do those studies can easily define politeness. Bargiela-Chiappini (2003: 1464) remarks: '[d]espite the variety of studies which focus on linguistic politeness...the field still lacks an agreed definition of what "politeness" is.' However, understanding the different ways of defining or approaching politeness can help deepen one's appreciation of the issues. The first part of this chapter introduces two different approaches to politeness. The middle part of the chapter focuses on the most popular politeness framework, namely that of Brown and Levinson (1987[1978]) (hereafter B&L). The chapter concludes with a look at relatively recent work arguing that the notion of politeness be reconsidered, and also at a new, rapidly developing area closely related to politeness, namely impoliteness.

31.2 Two general approaches to politeness

31.2.1 The social-norm view of politeness

Social norms are of two types. A **prescriptive social norm** is a rule of behaviour enforced by social sanctions. Thus, throwing litter on the floor breaks a social norm. Social norms are driven by social rules ('do not litter'), and breaking those rules incurs sanctions. Impolite language – that is, abusive, threatening, aggressive language – is often explicitly outlawed by signs displayed in public places (e.g., hospitals, airport check-in desks). Sanctions are underpinned by social institutions and structures (e.g., a legal system) and enforced by those in power. Also, if social norms become internalized by members of society, sanctions can take the form of disapproval from others or guilt emanating from oneself. Thus, they take on a moral dimension. The social-norm view of politeness is neatly summed up by Fraser:

> Briefly stated, [the social-norm view] assumes that each society has a particular set of social norms consisting of more or less explicit rules that prescribe a certain behavior, a state of affairs, or a way of thinking in context. A positive evaluation (politeness) arises when an action is in congruence with the norm, a negative evaluation (impoliteness = rudeness) when action is to the contrary.
>
> (1990: 220)

Politeness, in this sense, subsumes notions such as 'good manners', 'social etiquette', 'social graces' and 'minding your Ps and Qs'. Parents teaching their children to say *please* typically proscribe requests that are not accompanied by that word. Note that social norms are sensitive to context: the social politeness norms that pertain to a family dinner are rather different from those pertaining to an invited formal dinner occasion. In fact, there are some situations where communicative behaviours are not subject to politeness prescriptions; in other words, situations in which behaviours which might be viewed as 'impolite' are unrestricted and licensed. Often, such situations are characterized by a huge power imbalance, as might be the case in army recruit training. But not necessarily so: Harris (2001), for example, describes the sanctioned impoliteness that takes place in the UK's House of Commons, giving Opposition MPs opportunities to attack the Government that they might not have had in other contexts.

Discussions of the social-norm view of politeness would normally stop here. However, there is another sense in which social norms underpin much research on politeness. **Experiential or descriptive social norms** have their basis in an individual's experience of social situations. Repeated experience of social situations may lead one to expect certain kinds of interaction to happen, to be able to hypothesize what others' expectations are and to know how to meet them. Etiquette books and parental instruction are simply not detailed enough to help us through the mass of social occasions we will tackle in our lives. We acquire politeness routines from our experience of social interactions. Politeness routines and markers are expressions which are conventionally associated with politeness. Linguistic politeness here can be taken to mean the use of expressions that are both contextually appropriate and understood as socially positive by the target (some researchers take 'socially positive' to mean showing 'consideration' to the target). Remember the use of *please*. It is not used by anybody to anybody, or in any context, and when it is used, it is generally considered socially positive. The point about politeness routines/markers is that knowledge of both their appropriate context and their positive social meaning has become conventionally associated with the word-meaning. Of course, this does not mean that simply using a politeness routine/marker will result in politeness being achieved. Politeness always involves an overall **contextual** judgment. Thus, 'Go to hell please', said to get rid of somebody, might well be considered socially negative, despite the fact that a conventional politeness marker has been used. In fact, this particular utterance achieves its power, because politeness is part of the conventional word-meaning of *please*. The contexts of usage and socially positive meanings of that word clash with its actual usage on this occasion – they lend a note of sarcasm (i.e., mock politeness).

In practice, prescriptive social norms and experiential social norms can – and often do – coincide and interact. Thanking a host for dinner, for example, involves both: it is something we are under social pressure to do and we often do do it.

31.2.2   The pragmatic view of politeness

The classic, and most frequently cited, politeness studies lean heavily towards a pragmatic view. Over the last 20 or so years politeness theories have concentrated on how we employ communicative strategies to maintain or promote social harmony (Leech, 1983: 82; B&L, 1987: 1; Lakoff, 1989: 102).

Thomas neatly summarizes the research agenda of scholars engaged in the study of pragmatic politeness:

> All that is really being claimed is that people employ certain strategies (including the 50+ strategies described by Leech, B&L, and others) for reasons of expediency – experience has taught us that particular strategies are likely to succeed in given circumstances, so we use them.
>
> (Thomas, 1995: 179)

In our dinner table scenario, an example would be the choice of linguistic strategy in order to achieve the goals of both being passed something *and* maintaining harmonious social relations despite inconveniencing the target of our request. For example, 'could you pass the salt please' may be more expedient in this sense at a formal dinner event than 'pass the salt'. As the quotation from Thomas (1995) makes clear, the pragmatic approach to politeness involves experiential social norms, as outlined in the previous section.

31.3 The two classic pragmatic politeness theories

31.3.1 A note on the conversational-maxim view: Leech (1983)

The classic theories of politeness draw, as one might guess, on the classic pragmatic theories. So, this might be the point to refresh your memories on Conversational Implicature and Speech Act Theory, as outlined in Chapter 11. The bulk of the work in politeness studies has been based on or related to Brown and Levinson (1987), which I will outline in the following section. Here, I will briefly note an alternative theory, mainly as a way of illustrating how politeness can interact with the Cooperative Principle (Grice, 1975). Lakoff (1973) was the first to posit a maxim-based view of politeness, but Leech (1983) is much more developed. Leech (1983) posits the Politeness Principle, which is involved in 'trade-offs' with the Cooperative Principle. As an illustration, consider this event from my past. At the annual general meeting of a university society of which I was a member, I had been witness to the fact that a candidate for the presidency had gained only one vote from the 40 people present in the room. I was asked to summon this candidate from where she had been waiting outside. Upon meeting her, she immediately asked me how many votes she had gained. I clearly remember the machinations of my brain: I could not reveal the truth, since that would upset her; on the other hand, I did not want to be seen to be lying. Cornered by her question, I decided to be vague and replied, 'Not many'. My response thus avoided both a lie and the upset to the hearer that would have accompanied a more cooperative – in Grice's sense (1975) – reply. By flouting Grice's Maxim of Quantity (1975), I hoped that she would draw the implicature that a more cooperative reply would have been more damaging to her, and that I had been uncooperative in order to soften the potential for damage. In Leech's (1983) terms, the reason why I had expressed myself uncooperatively was to uphold the Politeness Principle, which he defines as: ' "Minimize (other things being equal) the expression of impolite beliefs…Maximize (other things being equal) the expression of polite beliefs" ' (1983: 81). More specifically, I had abided by the Approbation Maxim (minimize dispraise of other/maximize praise of other), by minimizing 'dispraise' of the candidate. The other maxims of the Politeness Principle are: Tact, Generosity, Modesty, Agreement and Sympathy (see Leech, 1983: 131–9, for details). The key point is that the Cooperative Principle accounts for *how* people convey indirect meanings, the Politeness Principle accounts for *why* people convey indirect meanings.

31.3.2   The face saving view: Brown and Levinson (1987)

The main proponent of the face-saving view is B&L (1987). Their theory consists of the following inter-related components: face, facework and face threatening acts, parameters affecting face threat and pragmatic and linguistic output strategies. I shall deal with each in turn.

Face

What is **face**? Notions such as reputation, prestige and self-esteem, all involve an element of face. The term is perhaps most commonly used in the idiom 'losing face', meaning that one's public image suffers some damage, often resulting in humiliation or embarrassment. Such reactions are suggestive of the emotional investment in face. Much modern writing on face draws upon the work of Goffman (e.g., 1967). Goffman defines it thus: 'the positive social value a person effectively claims for himself by the line others assume he has taken during a particular contact. Face is an image of self delineated in terms of approved social attributes' (1967: 5). B&L's conception of face consists of two related components, which they assume are universal: '*every* member wants to claim for himself' (1987: 61) [my italics]. One component is labelled **positive face**, and appears to be close to Goffman's definition of face. It is defined as: 'the want of every member that his wants be desirable to at least some others...in particular, it includes the desire to be ratified, understood, approved of, liked or admired' (1987: 62). I may assume, for example, that you want me to acknowledge your existence (e.g., say, *Hello*), approve of your opinions (e.g., *You're right about that student*), or express admiration (e.g., *I thought you did a good job*). The other component, **negative face**, is defined as: 'the want of every "competent adult member" that his actions be unimpeded by others' (1987: 62). I may assume, for example, that you want me to let you attend to what you want, do what you want, and say what you want (hence, requests that inconvenience you are tentatively worded).

Face threatening acts (FTAs)

Facework, according to Goffman, is made up of 'the actions taken by a person to make whatever he is doing consistent with face' (1967: 12). Any action – though B&L almost always discuss speech acts – that impinges in some degree upon a person's face (e.g., orders, insults, criticisms) is a **face threatening act** (hereafter, FTA). Facework can be designed to maintain or support face by counteracting threats, or potential threats, to face. This kind of facework is often referred to as redressive facework, since it involves the redress of an

ADVANCES BOX 31.1

More on face

Recent discussion has focused on the precise definition of 'face' (see, in particular, Bargiela-Chiappini, 2003). Much of this has been a reaction to B&L's (1987) idea that face can be described in terms of universal individualistic psychological 'wants'. B&L (1987: 61) claim that their notion of face is 'derived from that of Goffman and from the English folk term'. Compare the definitions above. That of B&L is a very reductive version of Goffman's. With Goffman, it is not just the positive values that you yourself want, but what you can claim about yourself from what *others* assume about you – much more complicated! The point is that how you feel about yourself is dependent on how others feel about you. Hence, when you lose face you feel bad about how you are seen in other people's eyes. This social interdependence has been stripped out of B&L's definition. Furthermore, some researchers have criticized the **individualism** reflected in B&L's definitions, particularly in negative face. Positive face is about what you as an individual find positive; negative face is about not imposing upon you as an individual. But this seems to ignore cases where the positive attributes apply to a group of people (e.g., a winning team), or where an imposition on yourself is not the main concern, but rather it is how you stand in relation to a group (e.g., whether you are afforded the respect associated with your position in the team). From a cultural perspective, researchers have argued that B&L's emphasis on individualism is a reflection of Anglo-Saxon culture, and not at all a universal feature. Matsumoto (1988) and Gu (1990), for example, point out that Japanese and Chinese cultures stress the group more than the individual. Recent approaches to politeness (e.g., Arundale, 2006) have tended to shift back towards Goffman.

FTA. Facework, in B&L's (1987) model, can be distinguished according to the type of face addressed, positive or negative. One might say that positive facework provides the pill with a sugar coating in that one affirms that in **general** one wants to support the other's positive face (e.g., in saying, *Make me a cup of tea, sweetie*, the term of endearment expresses in-group solidarity with and affection for the hearer, thereby counterbalancing the FTA). In contrast, negative facework softens the blow in that one **specifically** addresses the FTA (typically, in British culture, this is achieved by being less direct, as in *I wondered if I could trouble you to make me a cup of tea*).

Variables affecting face threat

B&L argue that an assessment of the amount of face threat of a particular act involves three sociological variables: the **social distance** between participants, the **relative power** of the hearer over the speaker, and the **absolute ranking** of the imposition involved of in the act (see, in particular, 1987: 74–8). For example, B&L would predict that asking a new colleague for a cup of tea is more face threatening than asking a long-standing colleague (the distance variable); asking one's employer for a cup of tea is more face threatening than

ADVANCES BOX 31.2

Beyond FTAs

It is important to note that B&L's work is limited to acts that *threaten* face, and facework that attempts to *redress* those threatening acts. What about acts that simply *enhance* face? An important merit of Leech's Politeness Principle is that it is not confined to the management of potentially 'impolite' acts (i.e., FTAs), such as asking somebody to do something for you, but also involves potentially 'polite' acts (Leech, 1983: 83) (i.e., face enhancing acts), such as a compliment out of the blue. Leech's Politeness Principle allows for the minimization of impolite beliefs and the maximization of polite beliefs. This helps account for why, for example, the direct command *Have a drink* at a social occasion, which would appear to be impolite in brusquely restricting the hearer's freedom of action, in fact maximizes the polite belief that the hearer would like and would benefit from a drink but might be too polite to just take one. And what about acts that simply attack face – threats, insults, put-downs, sarcasm, mimicry and so on? Goffman (1967: 24–6) mentions 'aggressive facework'. Clearly, politeness is not the issue here but rather 'impoliteness', an area I will attend to in Section 31.4.2. Recent 'relational' approaches (e.g., Locher and Watts, 2005; but see also Spencer-Oatey, 2008) within politeness studies are based on the full range of facework, and locate potentially polite behaviours within that framework.

asking a colleague (the power variable); and asking for a glass of vintage port is more face threatening than asking for a glass of water (the ranking variable). They claim that these three variables subsume all other factors that can influence an assessment of face threat, and also that numerical values could be attached to each variable, so that the degree of face threat can be summed according to a formula (see 1987: 76). The point of calculating face threat, according to B&L, is that it will lead to 'a determination of the level of politeness with which, other things being equal, an FTA will be communicated' (1987: 76). They do not, however, attempt to apply this formula in a quantitative analysis of face threat.

ADVANCES BOX 31.3

More on sociological variables

Note that B&L's book was published in a sociolinguistics series, exemplifying **interactional sociolinguistics**. It is no surprise, then, that the methodological flavour of the dominant sociolinguistics paradigm, that of Labov, with its emphasis on quantification, affected subsequent politeness studies. Numerous researchers began administering questionnaires (a favourite though not the only methodology) to quantify the kind of politeness strategies used by people of different relative power, social distance and so on (see Spencer-Oatey, 1996, for many references). In general, the studies confirmed B&L's predictions for power and to a lesser extent social distance, but generally avoided testing ranking. However, the basis of these studies is now being questioned. Spencer-Oatey (1996) demonstrated that researchers varied widely in what is understood by power or social distance. In fact, these variables were subsuming other independent variables. Baxter (1984), for example, showed that **affect** (i.e., whether there is liking or disliking between participants) was getting muddled up with social distance, but in fact was an independent variable. More fundamentally, research on **social context** has moved on. Social values, it is argued, are not static values but dynamic, and they are not given values (i.e., automatically known by participants) but negotiated in interaction (e.g., I may start by assuming that somebody is more powerful than me but re-evaluate that in the course of an interaction). To be fair to B&L, they did acknowledge this vision, stating that values on their variables 'are not intended as *sociologists'* ratings of *actual* power, distance, etc., but only as *actors'* assumptions of such ratings, assumed to be mutually assumed, at least within certain limits' (1987: 74–6, original emphasis). But they did not back this vision up with a suitable methodology (one which is more qualitative in nature and thus able to handle the complexity), and certainly subsequent researchers chose to ignore it.

Pragmatic and linguistic politeness output strategies

B&L (1987) suggest that there are five pragmatic super-strategies for doing politeness, the selection of which is determined by the degree of face threat. I summarize these below (the examples are mine). They are ordered from least to most face threat, and include examples of linguistic output strategies.

Bald On Record: The speaker performs the FTA efficiently in a direct, concise and perspicuous manner, or, in other words, in accordance with Grice's Maxims (1975). Typically used in emergency situations, or when the face threat is very small, or when the speaker has great power over the hearer.

Positive Politeness: The speaker performs the FTA in such a way that attention is paid to the hearer's positive face wants. Includes such strategies as paying attention to the hearer (*Hello*), expressing interest, approval or sympathy (*That was so awful, my heart bled for you*), using in-group identity markers (*Liz, darling, ...*), seeking agreement (*Nice weather today*), avoiding disagreement (*Yes, it's kind of nice*), assuming common ground (*I know how you feel*) and so on.

Negative Politeness: The speaker performs the FTA in such a way that attention is paid to the hearer's negative face wants. Includes such strategies as mollifying the force of an utterance with questions and hedges (*Actually, I wondered if you could help?*), being pessimistic (*I don't suppose there would be any chance of a cup of tea?*), giving deference that is, treating the addressee as a superior and thereby emphasizing rights to immunity (*I've been a real fool, could you help me out?*), apologizing (*I'm sorry, I don't want to trouble you but ...*), impersonalizing the speaker and the hearer (*It would be appreciated, if this were done*), and so on.

Off-Record: The speaker performs the FTA in such a way that he can avoid responsibility for performing it. The speaker's face threatening intention can only be worked out by means of an inference triggered by the flouting of a Maxim.

Don't Do The FTA: The speaker simply refrains from performing the FTA because it is so serious.

ILLUSTRATION BOX 31.1

Brown and Levinson (1987) applied

Data taken from Candlin and Lucas (1986), where politeness issues are only very briefly touched on. The lineation has been slightly changed. Context: An interview at a family planning clinic in the United States. CR is a 'counsellor', who interviews clients before they see the doctor. CT is a client, who is pregnant.

(1) CR: have you ever thought about discontinuing smoking?

(2) CT: uh. I've thought about it (*laughs*)

(3) CR: do you think you'd be able to do it?

(4) CT: I don't know (*laughs*) I guess if I really wanted to .. I've been smoking for a long time.

(5) CR: are you under more stress now?

(6) CT: um. I guess you could say so. yeah, because it was last year that I started smoking more.

(7) CR: do you think if you worked on those things you might be able to cut down?

(8) CT: on the stress you mean?

(9) CR: well. I don't know what the stress is and I don't know if you're open to talking about that but .. from your facial expressions .. it seems like you're really hesitant to make a decision to discontinuing smoke. I mean smoking, that gonna have to be something up to you .. do you think if the stress was eliminated that maybe ..

(10) CT: I could cut down.

(11) CR: or quit

[A few more turns elapse, with minimal contributions from CT]

(12) CR: well. you know its not easy. cause everybody. well I've got my bad habits too. so I know it's not easy .. I smoked for eight years too so I know it's not easy.

(13) CT: Did you quit?

(14) CR: yeah.

CR's goal is to get CT to stop smoking. She repeatedly uses the speech act of request. However, this request is realized indirectly. A very direct request might be 'cut smoking'. In contrast, in (1) her request is couched as a question about whether CT has *ever thought* about stopping, and in (2) it is a question about what CT thinks of her ability to stop. This does not meet with success, so in (5) CR tries another tack, engaging CT in talk about a possible cause of the smoking, rather than directly talking about stopping. Then in (7) CR links the cause to cutting down. Note how indirect this is: it is phrased as a question about whether she has thought about whether she would be able to *cut down*.

CR's strategy thus far is largely **Off-Record Politeness**: by flouting the Maxim of Relation (it is improbable in this context that CR is only inquiring about CT's thoughts) and the Maxim of Quantity (what is to be *cut down* is not specified), she leaves it to CT to infer that she is requesting her to stop smoking (i.e., CR's implicature). (7) is further modified by hedging the possibility that she has the ability to cut down (cf. *might*), and making it conditional (cf. *if you worked on those things*). These linguistic strategies – conditionals and hedges – are the stuff of **Negative Politeness**. Note that a downside of this kind of indirectness is the loss of pragmatic clarity. In (2) CT either chooses to ignore or possibly was not aware of CR's implicature requesting her to stop, and just replies to the literal question (*I've thought about it*). Similarly, after (7) CT either exploits or is simply confused by the lack of clarity regarding what she should *cut down* (*on the stress you mean*). In (9) CR probes what the reasons for not giving up might be. The frequent hesitations signal tentativeness, a reluctance to impose, and thus can be considered a Negative Politeness strategy. In the final part of that turn, she again uses a question, but notably she refrains from completing the question and spelling out the other half of the if-structure (i.e., if the stress is eliminated, the smoking will be). This could be considered an example of **Don't do the FTA**. Thus far, CR does not seem to be making much progress with her goal, and in the following turns (not presented in the text above) she makes only minimal responses. In (12) CR tries a completely different tack. She not only self-discloses (*I've got my bad habits too … I've smoked for eight years too so I know it's not easy*), but reveals information that (a) is negative about herself, and (b) is something that she has in common with CT. The kind of strategy in (a) is not well covered in B&L, but could be accounted for by Leech's **Modesty Maxim** (minimize praise of self/maximize dispraise of self); the strategy in (b), claiming common ground, is an example of **Positive Politeness**. Importantly, note the effect of this on CT. For the first time, CT has engaged CR in conversation: instead of simply responding in a fairly minimal way, she asks a question (*Did you quit?*).

31.4 Recent developments

31.4.1 The notion of politeness

Generally, recent work on politeness has usefully stressed that politeness is not inherent in linguistic forms but is a contextual judgment (see also comments at the end of Section 31.2.1). More fundamentally, Eelen (2001) and Watts (e.g., 2005) argue vigorously that the classic pragmatic approaches articulate a pseudo-scientific theory of particular social behaviours and label it politeness, whilst ignoring the focus of the social discursive approach, namely the lay person's conception of politeness as revealed through the use of the terms *polite* and *politeness* to refer to particular social behaviours. The key issue here is: who decides that some language counts as polite? Is it the analyst applying a politeness theory to a recording of language or is it the actual user of the language making comments about it? The first approach is fraught with difficulties regarding the definition of politeness and proving that it really did occur; the second approach addresses those problems, but has others of its own, not least the fact that people often do not provide (or provide insufficient) discussion of their own language use. Note that the social discursive approach is concerned with 'developing a theory of social politeness' (Watts, 2003: 9, *et passim*). A pragmatic approach has a different agenda:

> The starting point of pragmatics is primarily in language: explaining communicative behaviour. By studying this we keep our feet firmly on the ground, and avoid getting lost too easily in abstractions such as 'face' or 'culture'. The basic question is: what did s mean [to convey] by saying X?. It is useful to postulate the Politeness Principle (PP), I claim, not because it explains what we mean by the word 'politeness' (an English word which in any case doesn't quite match similar words in other languages), but because it explains certain pragmatic phenomena...
>
> (Leech, 2003: 104–5)

Bearing in mind Section 31.2.1, one can see that the social discursive approach is more sympathetic to the prescriptive social norm view (etiquette manuals, for example, provide insight into what the lay person would label *polite*). In contrast, the pragmatic approach is more sympathetic to the experiential social-norm view, given that it often focuses on regular usages in context – usages which usually have become regular because they are expedient.

Eelen's and Watts's work highlights important distinctions with respect to how one relates to the notion of politeness. My own view is not to see the pragmatic and the social discursive approaches to politeness as mutually exclusive. On the one hand, pragmatics, as we saw in Chapter 11, is very much to do with linguistic choice, and understanding prescriptive social norms and how the terms *polite* and *politeness* are used will help us to understand those choices. On the other hand, the social discursive approach lacks the power to explain the very language that the lay person might label as polite, and so it needs to take on board some theoretical apparatus from pragmatics.

31.4.2 Impoliteness

As far as pragmatic approaches are concerned, politeness relates to how we use linguistic strategies to maintain or promote harmonious social relations. However, there are times when people engage in **aggressive facework** (Goffman, 1967: 24–6) and use linguistic strategies to attack face – to **strengthen** rather than redress the face threat of an act. For most people, the majority of our everyday encounters are unlikely to be dominated by such facework (society could hardly function if they were). However, it plays a central role in a number of contexts. A few minutes watching television will furnish you with many examples (consider: *The Weakest Link, Pop Idol, The Dame Edna Everage Experience*, documentaries on traffic wardens and army recruit training). I have defined impoliteness as follows:

> Impoliteness comes about when: (1) the speaker communicates face-attack intentionally, or (2) the hearer perceives behaviour as intentionally face-attacking, or a combination of (1) and (2).
>
> (simplified from Culpeper, 2005b:38)

A key point to note here is that impoliteness is not dependent on participants' actual intentions. The second part of the definition accommodates the fact that if you think that someone intends to offend you, you are likely to take that as an offensive attack. Also, note that the definition rules out cases of mock impoliteness, where speakers use impolite expressions to each other (e.g., *come here you old bastard*), but in contexts (e.g., between close friends) where they are likely to be interpreted not as sincere attacks on face but as expressions of solidarity.

To conclude this chapter, I will present, in brief, a framework for analysing impoliteness strategies (adapted from Culpeper, 2005b; examples are among the most frequent in my data). Of course, no act or linguistic expression is inherently impolite, though some, I would argue, have a more stable relationship with impolite effects than others. This means that the strategies below need to be carefully assessed in context in order to establish whether they really are achieving *impoliteness*:

(i) **Situational impoliteness** (the impolite effect is based on contextual expectations)

    (a) **Bald on record impoliteness** (e.g., *be quiet* said by child to parent, defendant to a judge)

    (b) **Withhold politeness** (e.g., withhold thanks where it is very clearly required in the context)

(ii) **Conventional or semi-conventional impolite expressions** (the impolite effect is based on conventional meanings associated with the expression) (Square brackets indicate common structures)

    (a) **Positive impoliteness**
    Vocatives
        twat / wanker / dickhead / etc.
        [you] [[fucking/rotten/dirty/fat/ etc.*] [berk/pig/shit/bastard/loser/ cunt/* etc.*]]*

        Personal evaluations (with negatively marked lexis or structures)
        you're [nuts/nuttier than a fruit cake/ etc.*]*
        you can't do anything right

    (b) **Negative impoliteness**
    Dismissals
        get [lost/out]
        [fuck/piss] off
        go fuck yourself

Silencers

> *Shut [it/your mouth/face/ etc.]*
> *shut [the fuck] up*

Threats

> *[I'll/I'm/we're] [gonna] [smash your face in/beat the shit out of*
> *you/ box your ears/bust your fucking head off/ etc.]*

Condescensions

> *that's [being babyish/stupid/ etc.]*
> *little [mouth/act/ass/body/ etc.]*

(iii)   **Implicated impoliteness** (the impolite effect is based on a conversational implicature)

(a)   *Off-record impoliteness* (the impolite belief is implicated but cannot be easily denied)

> *Are you running on empty?* (Anne Robinson, *The Weakest Link*)

(b)   *Sarcasm* (mock politeness, i.e., insincere politeness)

[Letter in Lancaster University's electronic staff bulletin]

> *I would just like to say thank you to the person who backed*
> *into my car on the perimeter road yesterday. It was a wonderful*
> *surprise... As a single parent and part-time member of staff on*
> *a clerical grade, I look forward to receiving an obscene quote*
> *from my local garage and then not eating for a week! Thank you*
> *SO VERY MUCH.*

Recommended readings

Two excellent and accessible, though somewhat dated, politeness reviews are Fraser (1990) and Kasper (1990). Spencer-Oatey (2008) provides an excellent overview, as well as her own developments of the area, and Watts (2005) provides a provocative critical discussion of classic politeness theories, as well as introducing the social discursive approach to which he has contributed himself. Readings on impoliteness include my own work (e.g., Culpeper, 1996, 2005b; Culpeper, Bousfield and Wichmann, 2003), and also Bousfield (2008), the papers in Bousfield and Locher (2007) and the 2008 special issue of the *Journal of Politeness Research: Language, Behaviour, Culture* on impoliteness, edited by Bousfield and Culpeper. More generally, the *Journal of Politeness Research: Language, Behaviour, Culture* is a key source of highly relevant papers (and note that the first issue is available for free on the internet).

Note

1   This publication is part of a project funded by the UK's Economic and Social Research Council (ESRC) (RES-063–27-0015).

CHAPTER 32

Gender and Language

JANE SUNDERLAND

32.1 Introduction

To talk about gender and language, we need to consider language in both of its theoretical senses: what the early twentieth-century linguist Ferdinand de Saussure called *langue* (language as a code, the words available to us) and *parole* (language in use, what people actually say or write). When we look at *langue*, we can see how the English language is changing: we can look at relatively new coinages such as *Ms*, *chairperson* and *s/he*, for example. Here we are concerned with gender **in** the language, what is **available** for our use. When we look at *parole*, we can consider how people use words such as *Ms*, and we can also question whether women and men really do speak differently from each other. But we can in addition look at **discourse**, which brings *langue* and *parole* together: 'discourse' refers to what is said (or written), in relation to those aspects of the language which are (more or less) available in the language (for a full definition and discussion of the term 'discourse', see Chapter 35, Advances Box 35.2). All this will become clear in the sections that follow.

Much of what is written below refers to the English language – the examples are in English, and indeed most research on language and gender has been done on English. But the issues and concepts are relevant to all languages.

32.2 Gender 'in' the English language

To refer to gender **in** a language is misleading, as it suggests that language is something fixed and unchanging. I am using the phrase 'in the English language' here simply to suggest that the English language is a resource (of which gender is a part) for communication and interaction. Included in the notion of gender **in** a language (*langue*) is the third-person singular pronoun (e.g., whether there is a distinction between *he* and *she* in a given language, and, if there is, whether the distinction is made in both speaking and writing) (see, for example, Corbett, 2004). But this resource, of course, is changing, as are all languages. Languages change not only in their vocabulary (as a look at a nineteenth-century English language novel will soon tell you), but also in their grammar, and in the ways words are pronounced. Gender is relevant to all these.

Sexist language: issues and intervention

It was the notion of **sexist language** that ushered in the language and gender field in the (very) late 1960s and 1970s – the advent of the 'second wave' Women's Movement. Feminist linguists were concerned not so much with what English grammatically **allowed** in terms of gender, but what was prescribed (e.g., in grammars and dictionaries) and practised. So, for example, *he* and *man* were prescribed as masculine generics (i.e., words including males and females) – but were they truly generic? (The oddity of the example: *Man breastfeeds his young* suggests not.) Other problematic generics included words such as *chairman* and *spokesman* to refer to women. Still other issues were 'male firstness', in the phrase *he or she*; female **diminutives** and gender marking – such as *usherette* and *lady doctor/authoress*; the imbalance between *Mr* as an honorific for men (which does not indicate his marital status) and *Mrs* or *Miss* for women (which do); derogatory lexis such as *a blonde* (used of women but rarely of men); and **overlexicalization** in, for example, the excessive number of derogatory terms to describe sexually active or elderly women (compared with those which could be used of men). Underlying these concerns was a belief that language not only reflected but also shaped thought and social action.

The feminist response to the above is now history: there was a range of interventions to make the English language at least potentially more gender-inclusive, which had different degrees of success (see Sunderland, 2004: 202–9 on intervention; see Pauwels (1998) and Kotthoff and Wodak (1997) on evidence for language change as regards gender in a range of languages). As a result, **generic** usage of *he* and *man* has observably reduced, although it is probably more accurate to say that expressions such as *he or she* have become more frequent, as unremarkable alternatives. Similarly, *chairperson* and *spokesperson* are now familiar, if minority usages. *Ms* (intended to be the equivalent of *Mr*), rather than replacing *Mrs* and *Miss*, is, instead, also an alternative, third honorific – though, in the United Kingdom (in contrast to the USA), definitely a minority one. Interestingly, much more successful has been the linguistic strategy in German of making all women *Frau* (originally the equivalent of *Mrs*), and abandoning *Fräulein* (*Miss*), rather than using a **neologism** (new term) such as *Ms*.

Dictionaries and grammar books

What is (and was) the role of dictionaries and grammars in the above? Dictionaries and lexicography have long been a focus of gender and language study (e.g., Hoey 1996), and explicitly non-sexist (Graham 1975) and feminist (Kramarae and Treichler 1985) dictionaries have been created. Dictionaries and grammars both **encode** given languages – but, these days, linguists see their role as primarily **descriptive** rather than **prescriptive**. They encode standard usage, of course. However, rather than telling people how they should speak and write, they also reflect what people actually do, that is, they reflect change in language use. Good grammars and dictionaries also point out what is informal, colloquial or offensive, so that the language user can make an informed choice.

The situation is a little more complex, and perhaps more relevant, for learners of English as a second or – particularly – a foreign language. Learners of EFL are not surrounded by English, and therefore may see dictionaries and grammars (as well as textbooks) as particularly authoritative. So how did pedagogic grammars and dictionaries (i.e., those designed for learners of English) respond to the challenge of representing non- and anti-sexist language items in the 1970s and 1980s?

Many pedagogic grammars did not mention non- and anti-sexist items at all – for example, in one study, of 11 grammars with sections on titles, *Ms* was not mentioned in five (Sunderland, 1994). *They* as an alternative to the **generic** *he* was mentioned frequently (not surprisingly, as this is not a recent phenomenon in spoken English), but non-*they* alternatives (*he or she, s/he*) less frequently (and these were sometimes represented as stylistically inferior). On the whole, emphasis remained on the traditional forms, and grammars varied in the amount of encouragement they offered users as regards alternative forms (see again Sunderland, 1994). A specific study of the *University Grammar of English* also found a considerable amount of gender stereotyping in examples, for instance, females cast in passive roles, and males 'pulling the strings' (Stephens, 1990).

As regards learners' dictionaries (in particular, the Collins *COBUILD English Language Dictionary* (1987), the *Longman Dictionary of Contemporary English* (1987) and the *Oxford Advanced Learners' Dictionary of Current English* (1989)), Hennessy found that items considered as sexist by some were not flagged as such, and that there was 'little in the way of guidelines and models which would encourage learners to develop non-sexist idiolects akin to those of many of their native-speaking peers' (1994: 110–11). Prechter (1999) more recently noted that the *Longman Dictionary of Contemporary English* did have a policy of challenging gender stereotypes, but more widely reports no positive developments towards 'gender-fairness' in learners' dictionaries of English, even those which use invented (rather than spoken corpus) examples.

32.3 Gender and language use

Gender and language use (*parole*) in general, and **gender differences** in language use in particular, are what many people think the study of **gender and language** is all about. And certainly there is a range of relevant issues here.

Folklinguistic views

Across the globe, a wide range of **folklinguistic** views about women's talk exists. Most are decidedly uncomplimentary to women: for example, that women gossip, nag, have vicious tongues and, in particular, talk a lot (compared to men). These views are often enshrined in proverbs, for example, from traditional China: 'Men talk like books, women lose themselves in details.'

Anthropological studies

More academically, some early anthropological studies were also concerned with gender and language. Famously, Jespersen (1922) reported the early findings of Rochefort who, in the seventeenth century, documented the Carib Indians of the Lesser Antilles speaking in different ways, in the sense that some of their words and phrases were **only** used by women, others **only** by men. Later, the anthropologist Mary Haas found gender differences in Koasati (a Native American language spoken in Louisiana) in word forms, pronunciation and stress among the older generation (Haas, 1944). Both these sets of differences were what can be called **sex-exclusive** in that there was no gender overlap.

Variationist studies

Although feminist linguists did much to advance the study of gender and language, it was already of some concern to sociolinguists (Labov, 1966; Trudgill, 1972; Gal, 1978), as well as to those concerned with first language acquisition (Gleason, 1973). For early sociolinguistics, **gender** was an independent variable (actually, **biological sex**), and the focus was on gender differences in certain aspects of talk (largely pronunciation) across large numbers of speakers. Controversially, Trudgill, who found women tended to use more 'prestige' forms, claimed this was because of women's greater status-consciousness (see Cameron, 1992, for a critique). Gal's (1978) work, however, contributed to later gender and language study more generally: she showed how women in Oberwart (on the Austrian/Hungarian border) tended to speak German more than their male counterparts (with a view to marrying German men and getting away from farm-work). This illustrated how any gender differences are highly context-specific, or 'contingent', and hence not generalizable. And Milroy (1980), looking at women and men in three areas of Belfast, also from a non-feminist sociolinguistic perspective, found that in the Clonard, where women worked and socialized together, women used **more** vernacular language than did those of their 'menfolk' who were unemployed. In this she in effect challenged the notion that women's talk was always more prestigious than that of men.

Gender, language and the Second Wave Women's Movement: mixed-sex talk, women's talk, men's talk

With the advent of the second wave of the (Western) women's movement, language and gender study was given a new impetus through feminist linguists seeking to reveal men's dominance over women in talk. This was done through small-scale, interactional studies of largely private conversations which examined amount of talk, questions, interruptions, 'backchannelling' (e.g., one speaker's use of *yeah* while the other is talking) and tag questions (e.g., *isn't it?*). The overall picture was that women were interrupted more, and that women did more of the supportive work in talk; for example, asking questions and back-channelling. (Studies of tag questions proved more equivocal.) These tendencies were **sex-preferential** (in contrast to 'sex-exclusive') – simply because they were tendencies rather than differences. But what came through most clearly was that women were **not** the talkative sex: men almost always talked more.

Such studies fell into what has been retrospectively named the (**male**) **dominance** paradigm. They were, however, criticized by other feminist linguists, in part for portraying women as passive victims, in part for confusing male dominance with what might actually be a form of **cultural difference** (see, for example, Coates, 1989; Tannen, 1991), and in part for looking at mixed-sex rather than single-sex talk. In some contrast, the '(cultural) difference' approach extended to a focus on women's talk in single-sex groups, and also, to an extent, to a **celebration** of women's talk (Wodak and Schulz, 1986; Kotthoff, 1997; Wetschanow, 1999). Not surprisingly, there followed work on men's talk (Coates, 2003), and, more generally, on language and masculinity (Johnson and Meinhof, 1997), which dovetailed with the wider focus in the social sciences on masculinity in general.

Private talk, public talk: the case of classroom interaction

Early study of private, domestic talk gradually gave way to studies of public, institutional talk, for example, in the church and parliament, and talk at work (in which what is **private** and what **public** is more problematic). One public **site** of language and gender, which was studied early on, was the mixed-sex classroom. This has been a focus of interest for feminist linguists for many reasons, all of which are potentially gendered:

- classrooms are characterized by talk
- children are presumed to be at a more critical stage of social development than adults
- classroom interaction may be related to learning
- academic achievement (or lack of it) is seen as socially important

Classroom interaction includes both teacher-talk and student-talk (student–teacher and student–student).

Teacher talk

Studies of teacher talk have found that teachers talk far more to the male students. Dale Spender audio recorded her own lessons and noted that, in contradiction to her intention, and indeed her perception that she had spent most time with the girls, 'the maximum time I spent interacting with girls was 42% and on average 38%, and the minimum time with boys 58%' (1982: 56) (see also Howe, 1997).

A **meta-analysis** of 81 such studies found this phenomenon to be widespread, operating 'across all subjects in the curriculum' (Kelly, 1988: 20). Teachers giving male students more attention is, however, unlikely to be intentional, rather a **collaborative**, unrecognized process between teacher and students (Swann and Graddol, 1988). Such talk is, accordingly, best referred to as 'differential teacher treatment by gender' rather than **discrimination** or **favouritism**.

Kind of attention may however be more relevant than amount. Here are some findings (which are of course context-specific):

- boys received more response opportunities, in the form of a range of question types from the teacher (Good, Sykes and Brophy, 1973)
- there were significant differences in 'wait-time' in mathematics classes, boys being given longer to answer a question (Gore and Roumagoux, 1983)
- in 'Language Arts' lessons, teachers reprimanded girls for calling out more than boys who did the same (Sadker and Sadker, 1985)
- there were differences in types of questions, girls being asked 'challenging and open' questions less often than boys (Swann and Graddol, 1988)

Kelly concluded that boys get 'more instructional contacts, more high-level questions, more academic criticism and slightly more praise than girls', but also that 'The discrepancy is most marked for behavioural criticism' (1988: 29), that is, a lot of the extra attention boys get is due to their being told off more than girls.

In my own study of gender and interaction in a German as a Foreign Language classroom (Sunderland, 1996), **similarities** were the norm. However:

- The teacher paid more attention to the boys in terms of number of 'solicit words', i.e., getting someone to do/say something (statistically significant at 5 per cent level) and proportion of 'non-academic solicits', i.e., solicits not concerned with academic content (approaching significance).
- The girls were asked a greater proportion of academic solicits, to which they were expected to respond in German, than were boys (approaching significance) and a greater proportion of questions which required an answer of more than one word (significant at 5 per cent level).

These findings suggest that the teacher was actually treating – or, arguably, **constructing** – the girls as the more academic students. Many of the non-academic solicits addressed to boys were in fact (as Kelly, 1988 had found) disciplinary ones.

There is little evidence of male teachers treating students differently from female teachers (e.g., Powell and Batters, 1986). Good, Sykes and Brophy note, 'sex differences in classroom interaction patterns are mostly due to students... teachers are primarily *reactive* to the different pressures that boys and girls present' (1973: 85). Female and male teachers may differentiate by student gender – but in the same way.

Student talk

Studies of student talk in mixed-sex classrooms largely found boys talking more than girls (French and French, 1984; Swann and Graddol, 1988). In her meta-analysis, Kelly concluded 'Girls are just as likely as boys to volunteer answers in class, but boys are much more likely to call out the answers' (1984: 29) and Alcón (1994) found that in pairwork with Spanish learners of EFL, the boys interrupted both girls and other boys more than the girls interrupted each other. In relation to this, Baxter observes how even though boys' talk might be seen as disruptive, it may develop their confidence to 'seize and hold the "floor", to control topics … and, obliquely, to prepare them for the skills of competitive, public speaking' (1999: 86).

In my own study (Sunderland, 1996, 1998), despite overwhelming gender similarities, the **average girl** produced shorter academic solicits than the **average boy**. However, one statistically significant difference was that when the teacher asked a question without naming a student, the **average girl** volunteered more answers in German than did the **average boy**.

Gender may interact with other aspects of identity, including ethnicity. Grant (1985), for example, found that boys, especially black boys, approached teachers less often than most girls, and that white girls approached most often. Male students were more likely to challenge the teacher, but 'white males challenged statements of fact … black males more typically challenged application of rules, or … the teacher's right to impose rules' (1985: 69, 70).

ADVANCES BOX 32.1

Diversity

Male dominance of classrooms may not on the surface sit well with female students' often superior academic achievement (e.g., in 2006, in the UK 32 per cent more girls than boys got an A or B at A-level, qualifications taken when pupils are approximately 18 years old). However, girls' higher achievement in a given subject does not refute boys' dominance in classrooms, or its importance: it is logically possible for female learners to do better despite speaking less than male learners. Without male dominance, they may do even better!

In the 1970s and 1980s, studies tended to downplay **diversity**. Yet this is crucial (and evident to any classroom observer). In Sunderland (2000), I reported on how two boys in a German classroom received the lion's share of teacher attention. If they are excluded from the figures, the boys as a group and the girls as a group get broadly the same range of attention (see also French and French, 1984). Generalizations about 'boys' taking all the teacher's attention are usually simply inaccurate.

It is, however, equally important not to lose sight of gender amid acknowledgement of diversity. In contrast to findings about teacher attention, the findings about the greater amount of talk produced by the girls reported in Sunderland (2000) were due to the contributions of half the girls – more than just a 'small subset'. In this classroom, gender was thus arguably a more important factor in student talk than in teacher talk.

There is a danger in seeing findings of gender tendencies as how girls and boys, somehow, just 'are'. Rather, we need to remember that humans always have a measure of agency, and to consider the possibility that both girls and boys may intentionally construct themselves as more or less academic, in ways which may vary with school subject.

32.4   Gender, language and discourse

You may have noticed that the focus so far has been very much on male–female differences. Of course we are not talking about absolute differences – there will always be a large overlap between male talk and female talk in any arena of life. Differences among males and differences among females in any context are likely to be greater than cross-gender differences. So really we are again talking about **tendencies**. Further 'nuancing' of gender tendencies will come from context (and what is referred to as a **Community of Practice**), and the interplay between gender and other identities, such as age and ethnicity (as shown above).

You may also have noticed that we seem to have been assuming that somehow language use reflects a person's gender. What I am asking you to do now is to consider the reverse possibility: that gender is **constructed** by language. By this I mean that by talking and writing about gender (e.g., about women and/or men, boys and or/girls), a language user is constructing ideas about gender, both in the words that she or he uses and, beyond them, in people's minds and perhaps practices. Similarly, as suggested in the section above on classroom interaction, girls and boys can construct themselves in certain ways, ways which may themselves be gendered. What makes this clearer is the notion of **discourse**. This provides a counterpoint to our focus to date, which has been on **who** (the speaker, and whether s/he is male or female). A 'discourse' approach is less concerned with who is speaking (or writing), and more with the language (or discourse) they are articulating (the 'what').

Discourse analysis of talk and written texts

Whereas much early gender and language study (e.g., that which analysed talk through a '(male) dominance' or '(cultural) difference' paradigm) focused on talk, studies of gender and discourse have tended to focus on written texts (often of a broadly political nature, but of many sorts, including fiction). Discourse analysis of a written text may consider:

- lexical features (vocabulary)
- syntactic features (grammar)
- 'voices' (e.g., of the writer (in fiction, the narrator), of people quoted in the text)

and an analysis focusing on gender may also identify **linguistic traces** of what we might call **gendered discourses** (Sunderland, 2004). In all of the above, something to be considered is what is **not** said, that potentially could have been said, that is, authorial choices. A classic example here is whether a political writer writing of a given political struggle refers to *guerrillas/terrorists* or *freedom fighters*, but syntax is relevant too. To say, for example, that *a woman was sexually harassed on the underground* is very different from saying that *she was sexually harassed by Peter Brown on the underground*. Discourse analysts who use 'discourse' in this sense, then, are often very vigilant when it comes to the use of passive verb forms as to whether an 'agent' (here, Peter Brown) is supplied (see Chapter 24, Section 24.4.2, and Chapter 35, Section 35.4).

The case of parenting magazines

Over the last decade or so, magazines which used to have titles such as *Mother and Baby* have largely been replaced with magazines with titles such as *Parents, Parenting* and *Practical Parenting*. This is presumably in response to changing ideas about the value of active, hands-on fathers, and perhaps to target male as well as female readers. But does the content of these magazines live up to their titles? Magazines with such titles should surely be expected to represent and address mothers and fathers alike. We might reasonably expect to find, for example, few verbs describing the father's actions in terms of the *helping out* variety – verbs which might be seen as linguistic 'traces' of what I call the 'Part-time father discourse' (Sunderland, 2000, 2002). The father's role in breastfeeding, that is, in providing support, would be frequently mentioned, as would the alternative or supplementary practice of expressing milk (since this milk can then be given to a baby by the father).

Genuine 'Parenting' magazines would also be expected to address fathers and mothers equally. Here, Althusser's (1984) notion of **interpellation** is useful. Usually glossed as 'hailing', the most frequently cited example of interpellation is someone hearing a police officer call out *Hey, you!*, who then turns round. The police officer has constructed (or **subject positioned**) the person in a particular way (i.e., subject to authority, and possibly guilty of something), and the person who turns round (assuming she is not simply curious) can be seen as sharing that recognition, and even constructing/positioning herself as guilty.

If shared parenting is being encouraged, we would thus expect recurring plural *you* (and few occurrences of *your husband*, for example). But linguistic features other than pronouns can also interpellate (see Mills, 1992: 186) indirectly; for example, noun phrases – here, those which **lexicalize** or **reference** parents. If shared parenting is being encouraged, we would expect recurrences of *parent/s, Mom and Dad*, and their equivalents. There would be no 'slippage' here (i.e., where, despite being in principle 'common gender', *parent* may start off meaning either parent, but later mean *mum/mom* or *dad*).

Whether these magazines live up to their titles is then an appropriate question for a discourse analysis carried out within the field of gender and language study, the broad research question being whether the magazines constitute a 'shared parenting' environment, or at least a 'father-friendly' one. The magazines sampled for the study cited here were issues of the American *Parents* (November 2002), *Parenting* (November 2002) and *Baby Years* (October/November 2002) (referenced by PS, P and BY, respectively).

I chose to focus on *advice* features that concerned parental *childcare*. The features were mostly **multivoiced**, not only in terms of multiple authorship, but also in the sense that they are sometimes populated by various characters. Voices included not only that of the writer, but also of quoted 'experts' and parents.

Analysis of these parenting magazines required looking at interpellation/ referencing and these different voices, as well as references to breastfeeding, gender stereotyping, representations of shared parenting and salient textual absences of fathers. (Visuals were also analysed, but not discussed here.)

Starting with formal linguistic features, pronouns and referents to parents, phrases such as *you, your baby, your tot, your doctor, your child, your children, your kids, your newborn* were commonplace, most articles allowing readings of *you* as male parent, female parent or both. 'Common gender' phrases involving <u>parent(s)</u> were also frequent. There were, however, instances of what can charitably be interpreted as slippage: *Parenting's* 'Work and Family: How your working affects your child' opens with *For working <u>mothers</u>....* Similarly, *Parents'* '0–12 months: Pucker up!' begins: *You've undoubtedly been smooching your baby and saying things like 'Give <u>mommy</u> a kiss!' ...'*

References to fathers occurred in several features, though somewhat problematically, for example, from *Parents*:

'Massage may help new fathers bond with their babies'
'Putting an open mouth on daddy's face shows just how scruffy his cheek is; placing it on Mommy's reveals her skin's softness'

However, the linguistic absence of father was salient (i.e., often he was not interpellated at all!). Explicit occurrences of *father, Dad* and equivalents were relatively rare (both alone and as part of *Mum and Dad* phrases), occurring in around only one in three of the advice articles. (In contrast, *Mom* and equivalents could be found in almost every article.) This only makes sense against a dominant 'Part-time father discourse'. Consider, for example: ' "*If you wash the pacifier every time the baby drops it, you are going to be too tired to be a good mother," says Dr Margaret Byers Smith'*. This would presumably be true of fathers too. But, given a 'Part-time father discourse', the omission of *father* does not read oddly. Father **not** being interpellated, either with *you, Dad* or equivalent, is a 'missing trace' characterizing the 'Part-time father discourse'.

There were also several **lexical** manifestations of this discourse – *step in, help out*, give Mum a *break* – as well as linguistic accumulations. For example (my underlining):

Include your partner. <u>After *you*</u>'ve performed <u>your regular</u> nighttime ritual, for instance, <u>he might</u> <u>give your child a massage</u> or <u>sing her a song</u>.
(*Parenting*)

Again, this makes sense only within the context of a 'Mother as main parent/ Part-time father discourse'.

What contributed most to the mother-friendly environment of these magazines, however, was probably the array of different female voices. These include those of 'experts' (who are also often mothers): '*Dr Margaret Byers Smith, a mom and retired social psychologist from Fayetteville, Arizona'*, as well as non-experts: parents, almost always mothers. We read, for example, that '"*I got all choked up and teary when they had their first shots,*" *says Heather M. Haapoja, a <u>mom</u> from Duluth, Minn.*' The mother-friendly environment is also achieved through fleeting, but reiterated references to breastfeeding. For example:

> Don't smoke or allow your children to spend time around smokers. And, just as importantly, breastfeed as long as possible...
>
> (*Baby Years*)

Injunctions to breastfeed clearly directly interpellate mothers, and make clear that *you*, here, does not have a plural referent. It is surprising that fathers are not explicitly included. Fathers can provide support (by burping the baby after their feed), by feeding the baby expressed milk (at no cost to nutritional value). The father does not **need** to be textually absent – but he is.

Many traditional gender stereotypes can also be found, and these 'traces' help to recycle familiar, traditionally gendered discourses. For example:

> At some point, if you're a mom to a toddler, you must face the inevitable tantrum in the supermarket, in the restaurant, or wherever you'd least like it to happen...
>
> (*Baby Years*)

One might expect that in a 'parenting' magazine the reference would have been to a *mom or dad* to a toddler. Then there are the predictable female stereotypes:

> Most of us at some point in life have been either the toddler or the <u>frustrated mom</u>,' says Douglas [expert]. 'We just have to hope that we don't end up turning into the <u>annoyed little old lady</u> down the road...
>
> (*Baby Years*; my underlining)

which provide support for the use of one gendered stereotype by adding another. Another example:

> Dr. Humiston...suggests that Dad or Grandma take the baby to that first appointment [for an inoculation] if Mom doesn't feel like she can handle it
>
> (*Baby Years*)

stereotypes the mother as the default carer **and** a potentially over-emotional one, and dad as someone who will 'step in' – and be rational! We can, however, find some progressive representations of fatherhood. In 'Talking to kids about sex' [P], for example, we read *If your little boy feels cheated [at not being able to have a baby], that's a cue to sit him down and tell him all the ways <u>a father helps</u> take care of an infant.* While we are back with the predictable *help*, it is interesting that this problem and 'solution' were chosen. And, in that these magazines do include some explicit 'shared parenting' lexis *(Mom or Dad, moms and dads)*, we can see a limited 'shared parenting' discourse in these articles – and this may be magazine policy.

A 'Shared parenting discourse' was never **explicitly** articulated, however, in the sense that, somewhat bizarrely (given the titles of the magazines), shared parenting itself was neither actively encouraged nor discussed. The only feature to come close to doing so was 'Parenting as a team' [P], and this was particularly disappointing. Written by a father, 'Dr Sears', at first sight it was encouraging. There are frequent occurrences of *parents* and *mom and dad*, and we learn that

> '[Hayden] helped us discover how necessary it is to share parenting responsibilities – from changing diapers to telling bedtime stories – both for our sanity and for the good of our children.'

However, the word *share* here is less impressive than it might have been given that in reality the couple do not share the parenting at all! Dr Sears writes '*... I'd often <u>step in</u> and say, "I'll comfort the baby. You need <u>a break</u>"'. Step in* and *break* both index **atypical** parts of any childcare regime, and, with *comfort the baby* (a non-survival-oriented, fun-related activity), are 'classic' traces of the 'Part-time father discourse'. Shared parenting could also have been talked about in *Parenting*'s 'Work and family: how your working affects your child'. However, not only does *your* refer only to the child's mother, there is also no discussion of how paid work and childcare might be shared between two (working) parents, to the advantage of all – another notable absence.

32.5   Third wave feminism and 'subtle sexism'

In less than half a century, the position of women world-wide has improved immensely and radically: in many countries, overt, gross discrimination against and maltreatment of women has been made illegal. Talk of 'equal opportunities' is fairly standard. This improvement is not, of course, the case everywhere – and, even where it is, this does not mean that we live in a utopia as far as gender is concerned. In many contexts we can now talk of **subtle sexism** (e.g., Lazar, 2005). An example: I have a responsible and pretty well-paid job; I earn more than many of my male colleagues. Yet when some construction work was done on my office recently, in response to a written request of mine to the decorators about which wall should be painted, amazingly quickly I found the response *OK baby* pinned up on my noticeboard. Trivial, minor, presumably not illegal and even amusing – but it's hard to imagine a request from a male academic resulting in such a response. Sexist thinking and practices have not disappeared with anti-sexist legislation. Hence the need for what can be called 'Third Wave Feminism' (see Advances Box 32.2, below). If the first wave was the suffrage movement and the struggle for votes for women, and the second a fight for issues such as equal pay and equal opportunities in many other areas, the third wave addresses not only 'subtle sexism' but also takes fully on board the notion of meaning as context-specific and contingent, and as multiple. For example, *OK baby* was, to me, offensive in the context in which it occurred, but one can imagine other, non-offensive uses. And is there more than one reading of even the contextualized use of *OK baby*? For example, a sense of 'camaraderie' and no hint that the job might be done more slowly, just because it had been requested by a woman? (admittedly a rather strained 'positive' reading).

This is relevant to the sexist language debate in the twenty-first century, which is ongoing but has taken different turns. A concern with inclusive language use of any sort is now often dismissed as **political correctness**, *PC* being used as a slur and a strategy to reject the need for speakers to think about the words they use. This makes the use of, say, *chairperson*, an unattractive option for some. Rather differently, for feminist linguists, what might be described as **post-structuralist** thinking in combination with an increasing use and appreciation of irony, and an awareness that word-meaning is highly context-dependent, makes it hard to label a word as 'sexist'. Social and linguistic developments mean that we now hear about *lads* and *ladettes* – is this a cause for concern? What about a man being referred to as a *bitch*? And although *guys* may be used of groups of women, why is *this guy* not used of an individual woman?

I will conclude with the notion of power. Given 'subtle sexism' (and even gross sexism), power can be seen to fluctuate – different people having and using different forms of power at different points in time. This is partly a matter of language and of discourse. Drawing on a dominant discourse in the right context may render a woman at least momentarily powerful. For example, in the current 'Western' climate, use of a discourse of 'equal opportunities' in a tribunal may render powerful a woman who is being denied promotion in the workplace because of her gender, at least in that place and at that time. Even intentional silence may constitute a form of power for

---

ADVANCES BOX 32.2

Third wave feminism, subject positioning, agency and resistance

Third Wave Feminism is concerned with a notion of identity in which gender is just one facet – sexuality, class and ethnicity being other facets. Gender may not be relevant at all times or may be less relevant than other factors:e.g., in educational achievement, class may play a greater role. Having said this, the notion of identity itself has been challenged (e.g., Butler, 1999 [1990]), as it suggests something that we 'are'. More important, Butler claims, is what we 'do', i.e., we 'perform' in different ways in different situations, largely through language. We 'subject position' ourselves, and others as certain sorts of people, and do so in continually shifting ways.

Related to this are the notions of agency and resistance. We can go beyond the old dichotomy of 'heredity' or 'environment' and add 'agency'. Of course we cannot do exactly what we please whenever and wherever we choose, but in almost all situations we **can decide**: we have a measure of agency in what we say and in the way we use language to achieve what we want. Similarly, we have the ability to resist, and resistance may come into play when we are 'subject positioned' in ways we reject (e.g., as _naturally_ maternal, or as _superwoman_) (see also Mills, 2008).

women, for a while. But such fleeting moments of power still need to be located against a broader backdrop of overall powerlessness of women in the many contexts where this is still the case.

Recommended readings

A recent and very accessible book is Lia Litosseliti's (2006) *Gender and Language: Theory and Practice*; an up-to-date book on sexism in language is Sara Mills (2008) *Language and Sexism*. For a 'resource book', which contains extracts from a range of important articles on language and gender, as well as related tasks, see my own *Language and Gender: An Advanced Resource Book* (2006). There is now a new journal for the field, *Gender and Language*, in which cutting-edge articles can be found. Interesting articles on or related to language and gender can also be found in the journals *Discourse and Society*, and the *Journal of Pragmatics*. Those interested in language, gender and sexuality should read Paul Baker's *Sexed Texts: Language, Gender and Sexuality* (2008), while I would direct those interested in different research approaches within language and gender to *Gender and Language Research Methodologies* (2008), edited by Kate Harrington, Lia Litosseliti, Helen Sauntson and Jane Sunderland. A classic work in the field, still very worth reading, is Deborah Cameron's (1992) *Feminism and Linguistic Theory*.

CHAPTER 33

Language and Sexuality

PAUL BAKER

33.1 Introduction

This chapter considers a number of overlapping fields of linguistics (**gay and lesbian language**, **lavender linguistics**, **queer linguistics** and **language and sexuality**) which all place the sociolinguistic analysis of sexuality at their centre. Although these fields often refer to similar types of research and can sometimes be used as synonyms of each other, they also embody differences regarding theoretical stance, scope and foci of analysis. This chapter is called 'language and sexuality' because that label suggests a wider stance which potentially encompasses the others.

The chapter begins by considering some early studies, probably best retrospectively classed under **gay and lesbian language**. Whereas early research on gender and language initially focused on **women's language** (or more accurately, language used by and about women), with **men's language** assumed as a general default and therefore covered by all other branches of linguistics, early research on language and sexuality tended to be centred around gay men (and to a much lesser extent, lesbians) with the language of heterosexuals seen as the default. I go on to consider how researchers struggled to define what was meant by terms like *gay language* or the *gay voice* in ways which often reflected the same problems that feminist linguists had in defining **women's language**. I then look at how focus shifted from lexical and stylistic analyses to the conceptualization of lavender linguistics based around social interaction and, in particular, the concepts of community and cooperation. I then show how two post-structuralist concepts – *performativity* and *queer* – impacted on the field, presenting a simple yet sophisticated response to the difficulties in defining *gay language*. Additionally these concepts broadened and blurred the subject of enquiry, to take into account all sexual identities that societies consider to be 'deviant' as well as those viewed as 'normal', rather than just gay men and lesbians.

The later sections of this chapter consider the related post-structuralist concepts of heteronormativity and erasure, focusing on how sexual identities are discursively constructed and regulated via language use in different settings. I end by examining some more recent developments in the field, including the impact of globalization and marketization on the field of language and sexuality. I also argue that an understanding of how non-Western (and non-current) sexual identities are constructed helps us to move beyond the concept of reified sexual identities, which could ultimately lead to a greater focus on sexual desire rather than identity. Suggestions for further reading are given at the end of the chapter.

33.2 Early work

33.2.1 Gay lexicons

The majority of early writing (mainly from the 1940s to the 1970s) on language and sexuality had a narrow focus – focusing on the language use of homosexual men (and to a lesser extent, lesbians). In the countries (mainly the UK and the USA) where this research was carried out, homosexuality was criminalized and homosexuals had therefore developed a number of covert ways to recognize and communicate with each other. Legman (1941), Burgess (1949: 234) and Westwood (1952: 126) identified secret homosexual languages that had been established around the beginning of the twentieth century. In 1950, slang lexicographer Eric Partridge wrote about a secret, spoken form of language called *Parlyaree*, which eventually evolved into *Polari*, used mainly by gay men and lesbians (see Baker, 2002). With origins in Italian, Yiddish and the slang of numerous subcultures (sailors, prostitutes, beggars, costermongers, theatre people), it consisted of a reduced lexicon mainly referring to body parts, sexual acts and people. Polari speakers made use of a telegraphic grammatical structure, double entendre, euphemism and humour (see the Polari joke in Illustration Box 33.1).

The most ambitious study was carried out by Rodgers (1972) who collected over 7000 terms, many of them appearing to suggest that gay men were bitchy, feminizing and obsessed with (anonymous) sex. Unfortunately, such lexica tended to overlook context, and it is unlikely that every man who identified as homosexual would have known or used these terms, or they may have been employed ironically or in limited circumstances.

33.2.2 GaySpeak

A later approach, which did consider gay male language use from a context-based perspective, was developed by Hayes (1976, reprinted 1981). Moving

---

ILLUSTRATION BOX 33.1

Polari joke

A gay man becomes Pope. He sees a gay friend from his past who admires his vestments. The pontiff replies 'Nante the drag – vada the bijou!'

The punchline translates to 'Never mind the clothes, look at the ring!' The term *bijou* means ring in Polari. The humour in the joke comes from the fact that *ring* itself (and hence *bijou*) is also a slang term for anus (via the term *ringpiece*). So the Pope's instruction here could be viewed as a risqué double entendre.

away from lexicon collecting, Hayes attempted to make sense of the functions of gay male speech, which he called **GaySpeak**. His theory took into account the fact that people, including gay men, modify their behaviour (and language) according to the social context that they are placed in at any given time. Thus, for Hayes (1981: 46), GaySpeak had three distinct branches, according to whether a gay man was in a **secret** setting, a **social** setting, or a **radical-activist** setting. Each setting required a different use of language, for example, in public places, gay men would modify their use of language, speaking in agreed-upon codes (such as pronoun-switching or euphemisms) so that strangers in the same vicinity would not be able to identify them as gay – *Secret GaySpeak*. The social setting is where the large gay lexicon established by Rodgers is more likely to be heard, with language used humorously and theatrically as a way of establishing camaraderie or negotiating hierarchies. Hayes points out that Social GaySpeak was a form of acting within acting; a language of irony where gossip and trivia were lampooned and exaggerated for comic effect. Finally, *Radical-Activist GaySpeak* was a more politicized use of language which Hayes (1981: 51) described as the 'rhetoric of gay liberation'.

GaySpeak was criticized by Darsey, who argued that 'Hayes fails to provide us with any words or word patterns that have a constant function and usage across settings which might indeed illuminate something uniquely and universally gay' (1981: 63). In the two decades following, researchers attempted to identify 'something uniquely and universally gay', but as the following section on the gay voice shows, this proved to be a difficult task.

33.3   Lavender linguistics

33.3.1   The gay voice

In the 1990s a notable amount of work was carried out by phoneticians attempting to chart features of the so-called **gay voice**, relating to beliefs that gay men can be identified because they sound different to heterosexual men. While some researchers (e.g., Gaudio, 1994) did not find that pitch range or pitch variability correlated with the sexual identity of speakers, other researchers, for example, Crist (1997), found that certain segments such as /s/ and /l/ were longer in stereotypically gay speech. However, such studies could be criticized because they have tended to rely on small numbers of speakers. Podesva and colleagues (2002) also note that the context of speech production is likely to have an impact on language use; they analysed the speech of a gay man who was speaking on a radio programme about gay rights, and surmised that 'Gay identity is highly salient for representatives of gay political organizations, especially in public discussions. But at the same time, participants are frequently warned against sounding "too gay"' (2002: 181).

Other studies, however, have found that people tend to make assumptions about sexuality based on features such as large pitch range (e.g., Jacobs, Rogers and Smyth 1999). It therefore appears that many speakers possess some sort of shared understanding of what constitutes a stereotypically 'gay voice', based on features used by some gay men, but not all of them, and additionally also used by some heterosexual men. As Cameron and Kulick (2003: 90) point out, 'Not all gay men have "the voice" and not everyone who has "the voice" is gay'. Additionally, as the research by Podvesa and colleagues (2002) suggests, 'the voice' can come and go in different contexts.

33.3.2   Cooperation and communities

In the 1990s, researchers developed newer conceptualizations of gay and lesbian language use that were based around the notions of community and cooperation rather than lexicon collecting. The 1990s also saw the emergence of **lavender linguistics** as an academic field, with the first Lavender Languages conference held in Washington DC in 1993. Leap published an edited collection of papers about gay and lesbian language, arguing:

> If there is no lesbian/gay language, there is no reason for this book. What the authors present in these chapters is a celebration of lesbian and gay experience as revealed and displayed through the practice of spoken and written communication. All of us assume that there is something unique about this discourse.
>
> (1995: xiv)

The concept of gay and lesbian discourse as co-constructing and cooperative was developed by Morgan and Wood (1995) and Leap (1996). Morgan and Wood analysed lesbians in conversation, noting that they worked together to build

> a sort of temporary conversational community, for the purpose of creating solidarity, tying us to a collective past as well as to each other within this conversation...This unrehearsed, rhythmic collusion was another tool, which worked to connect us as lesbians to a perceived, shared past.
>
> (1995: 245)

Leap (1996) examined conversations where gay male strangers successfully or unsuccessfully attempted to establish common ground with **suspect gays**, also noting the cooperative nature of this kind of communication.

A related community-based position was taken by Queen (1997), who drew on the idea of **imagined communities**, a term coined by Anderson (1983) who used it in order to explain how the concept of nationhood is socially constructed. Anderson theorized that communities are 'imagined because the members of even the smallest nation will never know most of their fellow-members, meet them, or even hear of them, yet in the minds of each lives the image of their communion' (1983: 6). Queen (1997: 233, 254) wrote that lesbian identities were constructed from a number of such imagined communities:

> The few studies that exist on lesbian language either centre on lexical or topic issues...or come to the conclusion that there are no unique linguistic features used by lesbians...The characterization of lesbian language does

not revolve around a simple binary choice: either we speak like women or we speak like men. Instead lesbians have a rather broad range from which to draw their linguistic choices. Elements of these choices incorporate the construction and enactment of a lesbian identity, a queer identity, a female identity, an ethnic identity and a class identity, in addition to a variety of other kinds of identity...I propose that it is through the combination of the linguistic resources available from each of the 'imagined' communities to which lesbians 'belong' that we get a lesbian speech style.

Similarly, Barrett (1997) employs Pratt's notion of **linguistics of contact** in order to theorize issues of sexual orientation and gender identification. One problem with traditional community-based approaches to language, according to Pratt, is that they tend to assume that speakers are monolingual, even monodialectal – therefore the focus is on homogenous communities, with linguistic idiosyncrasies being passed down from one member to another as a kind of 'inheritance'. However, Pratt argues that communities do not work in this way: people can belong to numerous communities at any given time, particularly because their identities are multiple and changing:

> Imagine then a linguistics that decentered community, that placed at its centre the operation of language across lines of social differentiation, a linguistics that focused on modes and zones of contact between dominant and dominated groups, between persons of different and multiple identities, speakers of different languages...Let us call this enterprise a linguistics of contact.
>
> (Pratt, 1987: 60)

Pratt's contact framework was applied by Barrett in his study of Texas 'bar queens'. Barrett noted that the bar queens in his study used a variety of language features such as lexical items from Lakoff's (1975) 'women's language' including precise colour terms, but also empty adjectives, a wider range of intonational contours, lexical items specific to gay subcultures (such as those noted by Rodgers) and hypercorrect pronunciation. Barrett argues that it is possible to view gay men's use of these features as cases of 'borrowing' from one community by another – for example, gay men are borrowing stereotypical features of women's language or African American vernacular English when using phrases like *work it, girlfriend* or *Miss Thang*. However, Barrett argues that such cases should not be understood as being traditional borrowings, but cites that the linguistics of contact theory

> in which community boundaries are not assumed to be static and rigid, allows for an analysis in which bar queen speech may be composed from the speech of a variety of individuals (or groups of individuals) with different linguistic backgrounds who participate in mutual acts of identity (Le Page and Tabouret-Keller 1985) to create shared linguistic markers of social identity...In a situation where gay men from various backgrounds come together in the setting of a bar, stereotypes of effeminate linguistic behaviour from white English and African American English, as well as

from other ethnic and regional varieties, come together to create a unified stereotype of what constitutes gay English.

(1997: 194)

33.3.3 Performativity and queer theory

Related to the concept of community is Butler's theory of **gender performativity**, which resulted in a large shift in the way that researchers made sense of the relationship between language and identities (see Chapter 32, Advances Box 32.2). Butler argued that language can be used in order to **construct** gender. Additionally, though, gender itself is performative, a socially constructed and never-ending process, a 'work-in-progress and in-practice', which we are continuously engaged in. Gender therefore becomes something that we do, rather than who we are: 'Gender is the repeated stylization of the body, a set of repeated acts within a highly rigid regulatory frame that congeal over time to produce the appearance of substance of a natural sort of being' (Butler, 1999 [1990]: 33).

As Lloyd (1999: 200) writes, the construction and maintenance of gender is always 'repetition with a difference'. In the same way, gendered behaviours (such as language) are appropriated. So a female impersonator or drag queen may appropriate uses of language that are considered to constitute a feminine gender performance (calling people *honey* or using adjectives like *gorgeous* or *fabulous* for example). But additionally a 'real' biological woman is also performing a feminine gender when she uses such words – she is consciously (or more often unconsciously) replicating the performance of other women that she has seen and heard, who in turn have replicated other women, creating a seemingly endless series of reflections, stretching back over time, yet differing from each other in minor ways.

Butler's research was also important in that it made an explicit link between gender and sexuality. She argued that the idea of there being two distinct genders was dependent on heterosexuality, referring to a **heterosexual matrix** (1990: 5). She outlines the relationship between sex, gender and sexuality as follows:

for bodies to cohere and make sense there must be a stable sex expressed through a stable gender (masculine expresses male, feminine expresses female) that is oppositionally and hierarchically defined through the compulsory practice of heterosexuality.

(Butler, 1999 [1990]: 151)

Sexuality, gender and biological sex are therefore mapped onto each other, fixed and the relationship between the three phenomena is made to appear somehow 'natural', unchanging and having been that way forever.

Theories of community and gender performativity offered solutions for the problem that some researchers came up against when they tried to identify universal features of gay language. While societies had attempted to reify heterosexual and homosexual identities, in particular suggesting that all gay men were similar to each other in a number of ways (and would therefore use language in the same ways), it is actually the case that such identities are social constructs, fluid and unstable. An examination of historical data shows how, in the past, sexual categories such as *homosexual*, *gay* and *heterosexual* did not exist as we understand them today. See, for example, Halperin (1990: 301) and Spencer (1995) who write about sexuality in Ancient Greece or Trumbach's (1991) distinction between fops and rakes in seventeenth- and early eighteenth-century Britain. So different societies construct different configurations of sexual categories at different points in time, which are presented as 'natural'. And it is through gender performance that we appear to have a particular stable identity. However, because gender performance is only one type of performance we can engage in (we all possess many other components of identity or belong to many other 'imagined communities'), and because it is also performed in relation to social context (such as who is present to witness our performance), it becomes difficult to identify linguistic features that are universally gay – for the simple reason that sexual identities are context-specific and subject to change over time both within a person's lifetime and across the course of history, as well as varying according to culture. Stable, universal sexual identities do not exist.

Gender performativity also became a key concept in the field of queer theory (which included queer linguistics) which built on post-structuralist approaches to knowledge popularized by Barthes (1977b [1968]), Derrida (1974) and

ADVANCES BOX 33.1

Criticisms of queer theory

Seidman (1993: 133) raises a note of concern about queer theory: its refusal to 'name the subject' or anchor experience in identification could result in 'denying differences by either submerging them in an undifferentiated oppositional mass or by blocking the development of individual and social differences through the disciplining compulsory imperative to remain undifferentiated'. While movements such as gay liberation could be said to unwittingly reify and essentialize the sexual and gender categories constructed by the hegemonic majority, they have at least led to political advances for such people who identify as gay or lesbian. On the other hand, queer theory disrupts such categories, but leaves us with questions – where do we go from here, and how can we attain improved social and political conditions for people who **are** currently oppressed because most of society accepts the categories of gay and lesbian as real and discriminates against them accordingly? Butler (1999 [1990]: 19) refers to a concept called **strategic provisionality**, which allows us to preserve sexual identities (such as 'lesbian') as signs, enabling them to function as a site of contest, revision and re-articulation. Gayatri Spivak uses a similar phrase – 'strategic essentialism' – referring to the strategy by which groups sometimes find it advantageous to temporarily 'essentialize' themselves and bring forward their group identity in a relatively simplified way in order to achieve certain goals (Landry and MacLean, 1996: 214). *Queer* perhaps should therefore be implemented as an additional perspective to those which already exist.

Foucault (1976). A central aspect of queer theory is deconstruction. Instead of concentrating on constructing a 'gay subject' (e.g., by asking 'how do gay people use language?') a queer approach would focus on deconstructing the underlying logic or rules of a gay subject by examining how the identity itself is constructed through language ('how is language used to construct the category of gay people?'). Queer theory therefore has the political goal of showing how sexual identities are unstable, fluid and subject to disruption. And, as Cameron and Kulick (2003: 149) write, 'Queer theory is not exclusively concerned with people designed as "queer"...Many heterosexuals are also queer, men and women who never marry, women with lovers or husbands who are much younger than themselves, women who openly reject motherhood as an option, men who purchase sex from women, women who sell sex to men ...' This definition of *queer* is useful in that it enables different sets of people to find common ground, and it also emphasizes that a wide range of heterosexual identities can also be problematized or viewed as deviant.

33.4 Sexuality and discourse

33.4.1 Heteronormativity and subtle homophobia

Since the 1990s there has been a growing focus within the field of language and sexuality on showing how language is used in order to construct discourses or 'ways of seeing the world, often with reference to relations of power' (Sunderland, 2004: 6) (see also Chapter 30). Many of our interactions with others are heteronormative (Warner, 1993), whereby people are often assumed to be heterosexual. For example, Kitzinger (2005) examined the ways that sexual identity was disclosed in a number of spoken conversations, mainly looking at the speech of heterosexual people. She points out that that the speech of heterosexuals has tended to receive much less attention than the speech of more marginalized groups like homosexuals, and advocates treating 'the language through which heterosexuality is displayed with the same "outsiders'" curiosity that has animated the analysis of the subcultural argot of pickpockets...drug addicts...or dance musicians' (2005: 224). Her analysis reveals a number of strategies which are used by heterosexuals in order to reinforce the presumption of universal heterosexuality. For example, people engage in sexual joking, banter and reports of (hetero)sexual activity. They regularly use terms like *husband*, *wife* and *in-law* or talk about heterosexual relationships. What is interesting about these conversations is that heterosexuality is routinely deployed as a taken-for-granted resource: 'nowhere in the data is heterosexuality itself treated as problematic' (2005: 231).

On the other hand, homosexuality **has** been regularly treated as problematic in societies. For example, Chirrey (2003) looked at the word choices in British newspaper reporting of the pop star Will Young's 'coming out'. She noted that the *Daily Express* wrote, *Will admits he's gay*, while the *Daily Mail* wrote of Will's *frank admission* and *his secret*. The Mirror claimed that Young was *in hiding yesterday after telling the world he is gay*. Chirrey (2003: 32) suggests that the choice of lexis in these newspapers 'resonates with a sense of acknowledging criminality, sinfulness and blame, while phrases such as "his secret" and "in hiding" suggest that being gay is characterized by clandestine activity, presumably due to its supposedly shameful nature'.

My own research (Baker, 2005) found that while British tabloid newspapers regularly used a 'shame and secrecy' discourse in relation to homosexuality, on the other hand, they also employed a related discourse of 'shamelessness' which was used in reference to a set of people who did not appear to be ashamed of their sexuality. In such cases, these people:

> don't *confess* their sexuality, but they *declare* or *proclaim* it, like a town-crier with a piece of important news. Such people are *infamous*, *visible* and *famously* homosexual. Their sexuality is *well-known* by everyone and prefaced by adverbs that suggest that the person being talked about purposefully seeks attention. Such people have no compunction not just in being *openly* gay but *flagrantly*, *flamboyantly*, *outrageously* or *unbelievably* gay...phrases like *proudly gay*, *happily gay* or *assuredly gay* never occur in the tabloid corpus. The emphasis on these types of people is not to do with pride, but to do with showing off (Baker, 2005: 79)

The language of such newspaper articles suggests a subtly homophobic stance, where it is not openly stated that writers believe homosexuality to be wrong, but, discursively, through connotation or presupposition, gay people are constructed as notable because they are **anything but** ashamed.

33.4.2 Hegemony and erasure

Again, linking sexuality to gender, Connell's (1987, 1995) framework of hegemonic masculinity has been used in order to explain why gay identities are subordinated, while bisexual identities are erased almost completely. As Frosh, Phoenix and Pattman point out, the dominant mode of 'being a man' (**hegemonic masculinity**) is typically associated with 'heterosexuality, toughness, power and authority, competitiveness and the subordination of gay men' (2002: 75–6). Connell describes gender as a hierarchy, with hegemonic masculinity having dominance not only over femininity (or more rightly, femininities), but over **non-hegemonic masculinities** (such as gay men, nerds, hippies, wimps, etc).

Connell notes that although only a small number of men embody hegemonic masculinity, most men benefit from it indirectly, and the majority of people (including women and gay men) are complicit in it to an extent. Studies such as Cameron (1997) show how masculine heterosexual identity is carefully policed in conversation, with its boundaries firmly fixed. Cameron (1997) examined a number of conversations between (nominally heterosexual) male college students where they criticized other male students who were not present as being gay. She notes that, oddly, it was unclear whether the students being talked about **were** actually gay. For example, in one case, the men talked about *four homos* who were continually *hitting on* (making sexual overtures) towards a woman who was described as *the ugliest-ass bitch in the history of the world*. Clearly, men who 'hit on' women are not engaging in stereotypically homosexual behaviour, yet none of the speakers noted this apparent irony. Cameron (1997: 52–3) suggests that the contradiction can be resolved if the term *gay* is understood not in terms of sexual deviance, but gender deviance for these speakers. The four male students who hit on the *ugliest-ass bitch* were failing to live up to gender norms – hegemonic masculinity requires the object of desire not just to be female but to be physically attractive as well.

Sexuality and gender are therefore often conflated so as to appear indistinguishable. For men, masculinity must equate with heterosexuality and vice versa. If gender and sexuality are framed as separate and independent entities, then we could conceive of the existence of a masculine gay man, or an effeminate heterosexual man. Such people would potentially confuse and threaten the status quo and blur the hard boundaries between the hegemonic in-group and the subordinate and marginalized out-groups.

Additionally, identities must be linguistically and discursively constructed in ways that emphasize their difference while underplaying any similarities. For example, men must be constructed as different to women, heterosexual people different to homosexuals. However, a potential problem, for the maintenance of binary identity systems, is that sometimes there are people who do not fit easily into one category or the other, but rather fall somewhere in between or outside the system. These people may therefore threaten group solidarity, which is often based around defining oneself as belonging to a group which is different to others.

Bisexuality, for example, tends to be erased in society. While sex researchers such as Kinsey and colleagues (1948, 1953) found that many people have the capacity to be attracted to either sex, if we examine frequency data from the hundred million word British National Corpus we find that references to bisexuality are extremely rare, occurring much less frequently than references to homosexuality, heterosexuality and transsexuality (see Table 33.1). And on the rare occasions that they are mentioned, bisexuals are often referred to problematically – for example, in Illustration Box 33.2 which gives examples from the BNC, bisexuals are linked to spreading sexual diseases (example (1)), sexual voracity (example (2)), being the cause of relationship problems (example (3)), and even equated with paedophila (example (4)).

Frequencies of words relating to sexual identity in the hundred million word British National Corpus for general British English   Table 33.1

Terms	Collective frequency
gay, gays, homosexual, homosexuality, homosexuals, homo	3423
lesbian, lesbians, lesbianism	1156
heterosexual, heterosexuals, heterosexuality, hetero, straight, straights	570
transsexual, transsexuals, transsexuality,	120
bisexual, bi, bisexuality	111

ILLUSTRATION BOX 33.2

Examples of *bisexual* from the British National Corpus

1. *Tom has in turn infected Mary and Sam – he's <u>bisexual</u>.*
2. *he says he was an enthusiastic <u>bisexual</u> who involved J Edgar Hoover in sexual orgies just as the Kennedys were trying to make him take action against the Mob.*
3. *To learn that he is <u>bisexual</u> is enough to plunge his wife into an abyss of torment, anger, pain and fear.*
4. *I wondered what would have happened if I had told him that I was <u>bisexual</u> or that I liked little girls.*
5. *The first meeting of Focus, the new name for the re-formed Chester Lesbian, Gay and <u>Bisexual</u> Group, takes place this evening*
6. *Still, he was 'absolutely very aware' that '<u>bisexual</u>' is often taken as some strange pop-code for 'gay' and is keen to point out that, as it happens, he is indeed <u>bisexual</u>.*
7. *The transvestite serial killer in Silence of the Lambs, or the <u>bisexual</u> anti-heroine of Basic Instinct, are both examples of homophobia; of negative stereotyping.*

Examples (5)–(7) show ways that bisexuality is conflated with or 'tagged on to' homosexuality: in (5) bisexuals are grouped with gay men and lesbians (this happened 25 per cent of the time that bisexuals were mentioned in the corpus, but there were no cases in the corpus of bisexuals being grouped with heterosexuals). In (6) there is reference that *bisexual* is 'code' for *gay*, whereas in (7) negative stereotyping of bisexuals is referred to as *homophobia* (rather than *biphobia*).

33.5   New directions

33.5.1   Rethinking power: marketization of sexual identity

While more recent theories of language and sexuality have examined power relations, it should be borne in mind that post-structuralism does not view power as a simple all or nothing binary. Instead, as Baxter writes, 'individuals are rarely consistently positioned as powerful across all discourses at work within a given context – they are often located simultaneously as both powerful and powerless' (2003: 9). For example, gay men and, to a lesser extent, lesbians are perceived to have large disposable incomes and few financial responsibilities, leading to the notion of the 'pink pound' in the United Kingdom. This has resulted in advertising targeted at gay and lesbian people which incorporates gay-specific buzz-words and ideas into their advertising (see Illustration Box 33.3).

It could be more cynically argued, however, that such advertising is actually a marketing technique, and it is therefore in the interests of advertisers

---

ILLUSTRATION BOX 33.3

Advertising targeted at gay and lesbian people

Come out smiling (Fleet Street Dental Centre)
We take Pride (British Airways)
A Break with Tradition (Holiday in Piedmont)
Something Fabulous is Happening in Soho (Prowler Store)
Whatever you do, do it with Respect (Respect Holidays)

(Gay Times, July 2006)

ILLUSTRATION BOX 33.4

Gay personal adverts

Good-looking, 32, 6' tall, slim, straight-acting. Interests: keep fit, weights, badminton, squash, other sports and interests. Non-scene, genuine person, wanting to meet similar, straight-acting with similar interests. 21–34. Photo please. ALA. Box 9333

Normally straight? Just happened to be looking at these pages? Clean-shaven, non-smoking, young-looking guy (21+) wanted by straight-acting totally non-scene male 28. Fun/friendship. London Box 6611

(Baker, 2005: 140, 142)

---

to construct and reify a fixed gay identity. Additionally, even within subordinated or marginalized identities, hierarchies can exist, which orient to hegemonic masculinity. As Chasin (2000: 131–42) also notes, adverts aimed at gay communities often involve exclusions which reproduce traditional power relations. For example, in an advert for a watch in a brochure aimed at the gay community by the catalogue company, Tzabaco, the text reads 'Not a limp-wristed watch or one to be hidden in a pocket, this original hangs proudly from your belt loop'. Here, the use of the term *limp-wristed* (pejoratively used on camp or effeminate gay men) suggests a disavowal of such identities in favour of a gay identity which maps more closely onto traditional hegemonic masculinity.

Similarly, my analysis (Baker, 2005) of gay personal adverts (a form of self-marketization) found that many advertisers oriented to an idealized, desirable gay identity (both in terms of their self-presentation and their description of the desired other), consisting of stereotypically masculine qualities, as shown by the advertisements in Illustration Box 33.4.

Here, terms like *non-scene* and *straight-acting* indicate a disavowal of the gay subculture or 'scene'. In the first advert, interest in a variety of sports is given as a further indicator of an authentic masculine identity, whereas in the second, the advertiser is paradoxically seeking someone who *normally* identifies as straight but *just happened to be looking at these pages*. Such men are viewed as desirable because of their association with 'authentic' hegemonic masculinity and because they are not 'tainted' by contact with the gay sub-culture. Both Chasin's and Baker's research shows how gay men ultimately orient to, and are to an extent complicit with, hegemonic masculinity.

33.5.2   Global and local approaches

A more recent direction in language and sexuality has moved the field beyond the confines of westernized societies, to consider how language is used by and about holders of sexual identities who do not necessarily exist within English-speaking countries like the United Kingdom, the United States and Australia (Leap and Boellstorff, 2005). Studies of language use surrounding identities such as the Hijra in India (Hall, 1997) and the Tongzhi in Hong Kong and China (Wong, 2002) help to confirm the post-modern argument that sexual identities are specific to time and place, rather than fixed. According to Hall, '*heterosexual* and *homosexual* are terms that do not capture the complexity of most human lives when viewed diachronically for past behaviours and always inherent future potentials' (2003: 101; my italics).

With that said, the spread of Western discourses to other cultures via glo-balization (McLuhan, 1964) or Americanization is also worth addressing. Graddol (1997) and Ross (1995) have demonstrated the impact of American media, modernization and global economies on non-Western cultures. The proliferation of Western or American media is likely to ensure that the dis-courses of gender and sexuality which originate in the West will continue to make a strong impression on the rest of the world. For example, the decline of the language variety Polari (see Section 33.2.1) during the twentieth century has been linked to an increasing Americanization of the British gay subcul-ture (Baker, 2002: 121–2), with Polari being replaced by words and phrases originating from the United States (e.g., *come out of the closet*).

It could also be asked whether the configuration of sexuality and sex-ual relations which currently exists in the West will replace those in other cultures. And will the 'pink pound' translate into other currencies, influen-cing eventual reification and acceptance of gay and lesbian identities around the world, yet at the same time, presenting such communities with problems relating to stereotyped expectations and the creation of competitive sexual hierarchies?

Finally, it will be interesting to see whether the field of language and sexu-ality widens further to examine other facets of sexuality other than the homo/hetero continuum. Queer theory offers the capacity for academic enquiry into a wide range of sexual identities, and Cameron and Kulick (2003: 137–42) have suggested that the concept of desire ought to be foregrounded, rather than identity itself, particularly as desire is not always conscious. We might want to consider language use based around a range of sexual desires – par-ticular fetishes for example, or consider discourses surrounding an alterna-tive sexual continuum, such as monogamy/polygamy. And we should also continue to bear in mind that sexuality is one aspect of identity, warrant-ing study of how it intersects with a wide range of other components; for example, gender, age, social class, ethnicity, religion. The field of language and sexuality has come a long way from its early collections of lexicons, but it still has the potential to go much further.

Recommended readings

Leap (1995), Livia and Hall (1997) and Cameron and Kulick (2006) are edited collections of key papers. Cameron and Kulick (2003) and Baker (2008) are textbooks taking a critical look at language and sexuality. Leap (1996) considers gay men and cooperative discourse, while Baker (2005) takes a corpus-based analysis of discourses surrounding the construction of male homosexuality. Finally Leap and Boellstroff (2003) is a collection of papers focusing on the issue of globalization and gay uses of language, and Baker (2002) is a monograph about Polari.

CHAPTER 34

Bad Language

Tony McEnery

34.1   Introduction

Bad language, like many things in linguistics, sounds as though it is probably easy to define and study. Once again, as with many things in linguistics, this is far from being the case. People disagree on what words, idioms or utterances constitute bad language. As will be discussed in this chapter, even where they might agree in any one situation, as the situation shifts, so may the perceived 'badness' of the language. Also, even where we may find one word which all people in a speech community agree at a given point in time is a good example of bad language, it is almost certainly the case that, at points in the past and the future, others would disagree with them. Let me illustrate the statements that I have made so that we can begin a study of bad language with a reasonable appreciation of how difficult the study of it is.

34.2   What is bad language?

Firstly, there are plentiful examples of how people find different words to be either bad language or not – in Modern British English (ModBE from now on) words relating to religion provide a very good example of this. There are people who are still genuinely offended to hear expressions such as *Oh God* and *Damn it* used in everyday speech. The majority of speakers of ModBE would not now find such language offensive. Indeed, they would probably need a crash course in history and religious studies to understand how such phrases could prove to be offensive. Yet offensive they remain to some. For the second point, let us stay with this example. While very few people would find the use of these phrases offensive in everyday speech in contexts such as the home, on the street or out shopping, I would hazard to guess that a larger number of people might find these phrases to be inappropriate in the context of a church service, when talking to a member of the clergy or, perhaps, even when simply in a religious building. Hence words which one would be prepared to hear an infant utter, without note, in the context of everyday speech, may be ones that one might avoid in a different social and physical context.

For the third point, let us consider the difficulty that must have been faced by Wowbagger the Infinitely Prolonged. Wowbagger appears in the *Hitchhiker's Guide to the Galaxy* novels of Douglas Adams. Wowbagger becomes immortal by mistake and, though initially happy with this state, he eventually becomes so bitter that he decides to spend his infinite life on the task of insulting everyone in the Universe, past, present and future. Setting the scientific challenges aside, he would have had a difficult task linguistically. Wowbagger's task would have led him to the frequent use of bad language. But as he travelled through time, he would have found that not only the physical universe, but also the linguistic universe would change around him. While he may well have been able to effectively insult a regency dandy in early nineteenth-century Bath by saying *damn you!* he would probably only have raised a smile if he had tried this insult on somebody in twenty-first-century Bath. Similarly, while he may have scored a success by saying *Fuck you* to someone in twenty-first-century Bath, had he travelled to the thirteenth century and said that to someone, then it is likely that again they would not have been insulted – the word *fuck* was not at all a common word at that time, and linguistically it does not appear that it had the form of an insult – it had only its literal meaning of coitus. At best, if he had found someone who knew the word, it may be that Wowbagger's insult would have been misinterpreted as a request to engage in sexual intercourse. While that would quite possibly have caused offence, it would not have insulted in the way Wowbagger had intended. Wowbagger must have experienced at first hand quite how difficult it would be to try to keep track of what language is likely to be an effective insult in one language – let alone all languages ever spoken or to be spoken.

So the perception of what is bad language varies by individual, by context and over time. It also differs by variety. So far I have limited myself to ModBE, which for the purposes of this chapter I will assume to be relatively homogeneous. If we consider other varieties of English, then again we find significant variation in what is considered to be bad language. Consider the word *bloody*. This is not current in American English, it is mild to the point of being innocuous in Australian English yet it still has potency in ModBE. So bad language varies by variety of language also.

While the focus of this book is English, we do need to consider the contrastive dimension of bad language, for here another area of uncertainty arises. Different cultures find different things offensive. Consider what you would do if you dropped a cup of coffee – in all likelihood you may utter an imprecation such as *God*, *Oh shit* or *Fuck* – you would call upon a stock of swearwords to express your anger, annoyance or pain. The aborigines of the Cape York peninsula in Australia would call out the name of a long dead relative. Naming dead relatives is taboo among the tribes of this region. When a relative dies saying their names is taboo for a certain period of time. After that time has passed their names may be used to express anger or annoyance. The name retains the memory of the taboo once attached to it, hence allowing it to function in a way that *shit*, *God* or *fuck* does in English. This adds a further level of complexity to the study of bad language which, while we will not pursue it in the context of this book, should not be forgotten.

34.3 Bad language, insult and taboo

Having established the difficulty that one has in studying bad language, let us now turn to another area of difficulty – defining it. Bad language might simply be defined as language which, when used in polite company, would be likely to cause offence. To this extent it clearly links very closely to the concept of politeness. Politeness, as discussed in Chapter 31 of this book, is clearly highly relevant to the study of bad language. Assuming for the moment that we can easily define what polite company may be (most people think of their grandmother or a vicar if asked) we cannot assume that the words and phrases which we can identify using this definition are an undifferentiated mass. They are not. Bad language has many clear subcategories. It includes blasphemy – bad language which is to some degree disrespectful of a religion or supposed deity. Amazingly, blasphemy in the context of Christianity is still an offence in English law. It also includes obscenity – language which is obscene, often in sexual terms. Yet increasingly in twenty-first-century society certain subcategories of swearing are losing their potency, while others are growing in potency. Blasphemy is, at least with respect to Christianity, clearly in decline as a source of offence. Disability, homophobia and racism, however, are all very strong sources of words and phrases which are deemed deeply offensive. The processes changing the status of words such as *nigger*, *queer* and *spazzy* are social – significant changes in the politics and social make-up behind ModBE have had a major impact upon the language. Take the word *nigger*, for example. This existed for a long time as a word which was not deemed to be especially offensive, though it could doubtless be viewed as such on occasion. However, the word was also clearly used at times with a degree of affection – the title of Debussy's *Little Nigger* would be difficult to explain in relation to the jolly tone of the music associated with it if the word *nigger* was not, to some degree, positive or at least neutral in the nineteenth century. Further evidence of the positive connotations associated with *nigger* by speakers of English in the nineteenth and early twentieth centuries comes from the use of the word as a common pet's name. It is difficult to conceive of an abusive word being used by many people to name their pet. However, changes in social attitudes in Britain, especially in the wake of large-scale immigration from the Caribbean to the United Kingdom in the 1950s and 1960s, has led to race becoming a sensitive issue in the United Kingdom and *nigger* undergoing a very significant shift along the spectrum of offence to being a word that is so offensive that it is now rarely uttered. It is certainly not a name that one would call a pet any more. The same is true, though the social processes are slightly different, of words which are associated with negative attitudes to disability and homosexuals. Yet in all three cases a point made earlier is relevant – in certain contexts even a word such a *nigger* or *queer* can be acceptable. Both may be used in-group – it is much more acceptable for a person of Afro-Caribbean heritage to call another such person *nigger*. Readers should look at Section 31.2 of *Politeness in Interaction* (Chapter 31 in this book) – the discussion there of social norms is of use in understanding how and when the use of certain words may be licensed in context.

Analogously to the in-group acceptability of the use of the word *nigger*, homosexuals may refer to one another as *queer* with a markedly diminished likelihood of offence. The social process behind such a use of language is closely linked to reclamation – the process of a group using a derogatory word which is aimed at them as a term of familiarity of reference in in-group discussion. This provides evidence of the fluidity of the concept of bad language, but also powerful evidence of why bad language is difficult to study – it is subject to linguistic and social pressures that are many, varied and complex. These pressures give rise to concerns about the use of bad language. For centuries it has been thought, in the English-speaking world, that such language has the power to corrupt people morally. Bad language has, over time, become closely associated in the psychology of the English-speaking world with both sex and violence. Unsurprisingly, therefore, it has along been claimed that such language is especially dangerous to children. Nonetheless, bad language is something which seems to be closely associated with younger speakers, as will be explored later in this chapter.

The examples of homophobic and racist speech also show well how closely taboo, insults and bad language are related. Taboo concepts are influenced

---

ILLUSTRATION BOX 34.1

The corrupting power of bad language

Following is a letter from a magazine, *The National Viewer and Listener*, published in 1999. The magazine is published by the National Viewers' and Listeners' Association in the UK, a pressure group seeking to 'clean up' the media in the UK. It is reproduced here as an illustration of the nature and form of public claims that bad language has the power to corrupt.

The power of television first impressed me when I lived near a school. Every morning as a stream of children passed by I was treated to advertising jingles, catch-phrases, unarmed combat play-acting or 'bang, bang, you're dead' dialogue with bad language from the previous nights' TV programmes. I began to take a closer look at what I was watching. Did the playground echo an escalation of violence, sex and language? It led me to National VALA with its world-wide findings, the concerns of others like myself and the fight to maintain common-sense standards of good behaviour, decency and moral values in public communications.

Ten years on the pattern has become clear. 'Adult' television material with its rise in violence, increasing sexual explicitness and filthy expressions has abandoned responsibility for viewers of every age. Too extreme a view? Films like *Natural Born Killers*, *Reservoir Dogs*, *Pulp Fiction* and *Trainspotting* (and hundreds of similar examples shown since 1988) all on television must give any responsible citizen cause for worry.

If on-screen assaults, beatings, killings, shootings, woundings and brutal behaviour accompanied by revolting language and profanity and often linked with explicit sexual detail, female degradation and drugs are not considered to have a debasing influence on viewers, then monitoring is pointless. But I do not think so. Knowledge has fuelled my indignation with the irresponsible response from broadcasting channels, weak regulation laid down by Government and excuses from public bodies who should know better.

Good positive thinking will ensure that decency, morality and good standards return to the screen when you, the viewer, insist. After all, it is the nation and our children at risk.

powerfully by social processes. In turn, words associated with taboos become charged with a degree of offence that allows them, potentially, to become bad language. Bad language in its turn is so charged that it may be used for a range of speech acts, including insult. However, though connected, taboo, bad language and insults are not always easily linked. Some taboos do not give rise to bad language. For example, there is little doubt that paedophilia is taboo in the United Kingdom. However, words such as *paedophile*, while not a label one would be happy with, are clearly not in the category of bad language – they remain firmly in the category of professional language, technical terms for unpleasant objects or actions that make reference to them acceptable. Typically such words have a bad language equivalent which is not acceptable as we see in the oppositions between *vagina/cunt*, *penis/cock* and *coitus/fucking*. Interestingly, an opposition for paedophile which has wide currency and is used with some frequency in spoken English has yet to be established. There are phrases such as *kiddy fiddler* and words such as *paedo* but both of these are infrequent, with paedophile still being used widely and generally in preference to either of these words. This bucks the trend for such oppositions, where the professional word tends to be confined to professional contexts with the bad language word being much more typical of general ModBE. *Paedo* has also failed to shift beyond its literal meaning – the word is used to refer to a paedophile, not in any other way. This marks it apart from a bad language word like *cunt* which, although it can have its literal meaning, is also a very powerful insult when used in a non-literal context. In short, *paedo* is simply a clipped form of *paedophile* – it has not become a general insult and it is not bad language. Hence paedophilia is an interesting example of a taboo which has yet to give rise to a stock of bad language words and phrases in spite of its clear potential to do so.

The link between bad language and insult – while strong – is not ineluctable. Bad language, as we will explore shortly, does not always have to be used as an insult. Similarly, Wowbagger would be pleased to note that bad language – while of great utility in insulting people – is not the only way in which people can be insulted. To exemplify both points, if I drop a hammer on my toe and cry *Oh Christ* to myself in a locked room, I have clearly insulted nobody. Indeed, even if someone were present and were insulted in some way by my language use, my intention in saying *Oh Christ* was clearly not to insult – it was to express anger or annoyance at experiencing pain. However, if someone were present when this happened and laughed at my pain, I may well feel like insulting them. I would not need to resort to bad language in order to do so. I could say *you have a laugh like a hyena* and they would almost certainly be insulted. Even if they were not, it is fairly clear that in saying this I had the intention of insulting them. The sentence, however, is clearly devoid of anything that one might call bad language. This insult could reasonably be uttered in front of a grandmother or the vicar, though they may admonish you for being so uncharitable.

34.4 Types of bad language

If not all insults contain bad language it is also the case, as noted, that not all uses of bad language entail insulting someone. What is bad language used

Types of swearing   *Table 34.1*

Category	Description
1	Predicative negative adjective: e.g., *the film is <u>shit</u>*
2	Adverbial booster: e.g., *<u>Fucking</u> marvellous/<u>Fucking</u> awful*
3	Cursing Expletive: e.g., *<u>Fuck</u> You!/Me!/Him!/It!*
4	Destinational usage: e.g., *<u>Fuck</u> off!/He <u>fucked</u> off*
5	Emphatic adverb/adjective: e.g., *He <u>fucking</u> did it/in the <u>fucking</u> car*
6	Figurative extension of literal meaning: e.g., *to <u>fuck</u> about*
7	General expletive e.g., *(Oh) <u>Fuck!</u>*
8	Idiomatic 'set phrase': e.g., *<u>fuck</u> all/give a <u>fuck</u>*
9	Literal usage denoting taboo referent: e.g., *We <u>fucked</u>*
10	Imagery based on literal meaning: e.g., *kick <u>shit</u> out of*
11	Premodifying intensifying negative adjective: e.g., *the <u>fucking</u> idiot*
12	Pronominal form with undefined referent: e.g., *got <u>shit</u> to do*
13	Personal insult referring to defined entity: e.g., *You <u>fuck</u>!/That <u>fuck</u>*
14	Reclaimed usage – no negative intent e.g., *Niggers/Niggaz* as used by African American rappers.
15	Religious oath used for emphasis: e.g., *by God*

for? Table 34.1 below gives a range of uses of bad language which is a good guide to the analysis of any given example of bad language.

In short, bad language is very versatile indeed. Yet some words are more versatile than others. Not all bad language words exist in all of the categories above.

Consider *shit* and *fuck*. Both may clearly be nouns (*the fuck I had last night was marvellous, I have just had a shit*) or verbs (*I was shitting when the cat came in, I fucked him*). Morphosyntactically the words are very similar. However, their distribution across the bad language categories differs – *shit* occurs only in categories (1), (2), (6), (7), (8), (9), (10), (11), (12) and (13). *Fuck* occurs in a larger number of categories – (2), (3), (4), (5), (6), (7), (8), (9), (11), (12), (13). While morphosyntactically similar, the words respond to these categories in different ways – while their functions overlap, they are not identical. There are some categories in which *shit* can be placed which do not apply to fuck (e.g., (1)) and some categories *fuck* can be placed in which do not apply to *shit* (e.g., (4)).

Consequently, while we may be able to produce a catch-all characterization of bad language, we should not be blind to the very real differences that may exist between the subcategories of bad language, noting that these may differ markedly in terms of strength They may decline in offensiveness to the extent that they may only quite nominally be bad language or they may shift from being acceptable general English to being markedly bad language. We also need to be aware that the words themselves may have markedly different behaviours which are controlled by linguistic conventions in the community of ModBE speakers – there is no particular reason that we cannot say *shit off*. We just don't do so by convention at this moment in time.

> **ADVANCES BOX 34.1**
>
> **Morphosyntax and types of swearing**
>
> There is, quite clearly, a link between morphosyntax and the classification scheme outlined in Table 34.1. At times, a given word is classified partly because of its part of speech, e.g., when a word is acting as an adverbial booster it receives one label, when the same word form is acting as a premodifying adjectival intensifier it receives another label. One cannot, however, simply replace the labels with part-of-speech categories. For example, (1), (4), (7) and (9) are all examples where, for the word *fuck*, the word is most likely to be a verb, as is shown in the examples given in the table for this word. Yet in each case the use of the words, in functional terms, clearly differs. In cursing there is a clear insult intended, with a very clear target for the word. With (4), while once again the intention to some degree is to insult, there is also an imperative involved, typically with a demand being made that the target go away. When used as a general expletive, *fuck* is used as an expression of general anger, annoyance or frustration. In the case of its literal use, there is no clear intention to insult, merely an intent to describe an act of coitus. Parts of speech are clearly important to the categorization scheme, but the scheme itself is not simply a relabelling of parts of speech. It should also be noted that the distribution of examples across these categories is different – for example, *fuck* as an emphatic adverb/adjective accounts for 55 per cent of the uses of the word, while for *shit* most of its occurrences (44.6 per cent) are general expletives. Swearwords do not act the same just because they share similar parts of speech. The range of classifications the word may express can differ, and their affinities for different categories in quantitative terms may differ radically, even where two words can appear in the same category

The picture that has been painted of bad language so far is that it is difficult to analyse. In large part this difficulty links to the fluidity of the use and categorization of bad language. It even relates to uncertainty about membership of this class of words. In addition to the complexities discussed so far, however, a further set of complexities can be added – those complexities focused around how different types of speakers engage with bad language. It has long been argued that a number of sociolinguistic variables interact with bad language. Formal linguistics aside, speakers of ModBE have strong prejudices about who does and who does not swear. It is thought that women swear less than men. Older adults less than younger adults. The lower class more than the upper classes. In the next section I will summarize findings related to each of these claims. Before doing so, however, note that the claims will be explored purely in the context of swearing and blasphemy. The data on which the findings are presented contained so little data relating to racist language, for example, that no real conclusions could be drawn.

34.5 Swearing in Modern British English

The findings reported in the rest of this chapter are taken from a study I did quite recently (McEnery, 2005). I used a corpus of spontaneous spoken English to explore patterns of swearing in ModBE. A **corpus** is a body of language data which can be searched using computer programs called **concordancers**. These programs allow researchers to scan millions of words of data rapidly and reliably, looking at words in context and exploring how they interact with one another. If the corpus has been enriched with information which allows the program to determine where and by whom the language in the corpus was produced, it is also possible to look at the interaction between words and variables such as age, gender and social class in speech data, and genre and year of publication in written data. My study used a ten-million word corpus of spoken data, called the **British National Corpus**, collected in the early 1990s. This data was collected by people recording the conversations they had over a 24-hour period. These conversations were naturally occurring – they were not scripted and they were not explicitly elicited. This data was then orthographically transcribed, producing a written form of the data that concordance programs could search easily. Importantly, in the process of producing the transcription the corpus data was encoded with information that allowed the concordance program to know, in most cases, the age, gender and social class of the speakers. It is on the basis of this data that, for the first time, a large-scale study of swearing in English in everyday conversation was undertaken.

34.5.1   Gender of speaker

Through the analysis it was possible to explore widely held folk beliefs such as 'men swear more often than women'. This is not the case. Bad language is as likely to be used by a male as by a female. Real differences between male and female swearing do occur, however, if we look at the preferences males and females have for specific swearwords. There is a set of words significantly overused by males and a set of words significantly overused by females. If we look only at those words where a highly significant difference in use by males and females occurs (i.e., where there is a one in 100 chance or less that the result we have observed is attributable to chance) then 15 words emerge as being those which distinguish male and female swearing apart – *fucking, fuck, Jesus, cunt* and *fucker* are, in descending order of significance, more typical of males, *God, bloody, pig, hell, bugger, bitch, pissed, arsed, shit* and *pissy* are, once again in descending order of significance, more typical of females. Looking at the words, it looks as though males may have a preference for stronger swearwords than females – *cunt* is a very strong swearword while *bloody* is a very weak one. Generally speaking, then, while males and females seem to use a similar number of swearwords in their speech, there are words which each group favour, with the words which are strongly associated with male speech being stronger, by and large, than those strongly associated with female speech.

Given these differences, is there anything more to say about the differences between male and female swearing? Yes – they have preferences for different types of swearing. Table 34.2 below outlines in detail which types of swearing are strongly associated with male and female speech.

Another way in which we might think of speaker sex and gender interacting relates to the gender of speaker and hearer. Might it be the case that there

---

ADVANCES BOX 34.2

The strength of particular swearwords

It was beyond the scope of my work to conduct a large-scale survey to determine the strength of particular swearwords. Fortunately there was no need to do so as such reviews have been commissioned by various media watchdogs in the UK. I combined together the results of two such surveys – those of Millwood-Hargrave (2000) and the British Board of Film Classification Guidelines to the certification of films in the UK – in order to provide a fiv- part scale of offence with which to classify the use of swearwords. The scale itself is borrowed from the British Board of Film Classification. The scale is given below, with examples of words in each category:

Very mild	*bird, bloody, crap, damn, God, hell, hussy, idiot, pig, pillock, sod, son-of-a-bitch, tart*
Mild	*arse, balls, bitch, bugger, Christ, cow, dickhead, git, Jesus, Jew, moron, pissed off, screw, shit, slag, slut, sod, tit, tits, tosser*
Moderate	*arsehole, bastard, bollocks, gay, nigger, piss, Paki, poofter, prick, shag, spastic, twat, wanker, whore*
Strong	*fuck*
Very strong	*cunt, motherfucker*

Using this scale it was possible to explore the relationship between the strength of the words and such matters as gendered direction and speaker gender.

Table 34.2 *Gender and swearing type*

Type of word	Strong association with
General expletive e.g., *(Oh) <u>God</u>!*	Females
Emphatic adverb/adjective: e.g., *He <u>fucking</u> did it/in the <u>fucking</u> car*	Males
Adverbial booster: e.g., *<u>Fucking</u> marvellous/<u>Fucking</u> awful*	Males
Premodifying intensifying negative adjective: e.g., *the <u>bloody</u> idiot*	Females
Idiomatic 'set phrase': *<u>fuck</u> all/give a <u>fuck</u>*	Females

is a difference in how the sexes speak if they are speaking to one another as opposed to somebody of the same sex? Table 34.3 outlines how intrasex and intersex swearing works.

Interestingly, intrasex swearing is higher for both males and females than intersex swearing. It seems that we are more likely to swear if the hearer is someone of the same sex than we would be if the hearer is someone of the opposite sex.

Consequently, we can say, to add to the complexities of the use of bad language that have been discussed so far, that when a simple sociolinguistic variable is considered, sex, the use of bad language, in this case swearing, seems

Intersex and intrasex swearing   *Table 34.3*

	Male directed	Female directed
Male speaker	High	Low
Female speaker	Low	High

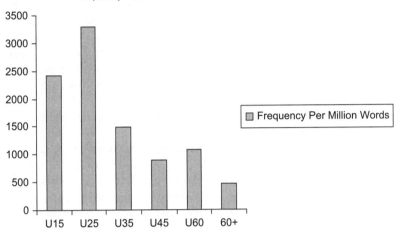

Frequency of swearing per million words of speech produced by different age   *FIGURE 34.1*
groups.

to be complex and can be analysed in a number of ways, revealing similarities
and differences in the use of swearing by males at females that challenge the
assumptions that we may make of the use of swearing by those groups. The
situation becomes more complex still if we take another sociolinguistic variable, age, into account.

34.5.2 Age of speaker

The literature would lead one to believe that age is an important variable in
the use of swearing. For example, Cheshire (1982: 101) claimed that swearing has a particular value for teenagers, as it is a 'major symbol of vernacular
identity' for this age group. Hence one would expect to find more swearing
in that group. This is indeed the case. There is a positive correlation between
age and the production of swearwords, though the pattern is not quite as
straightforward as it at first appears. Below is Figure 34.1 gives the profile of
the use of swearwords by speakers of different ages. For ease of analysis the
speakers have been grouped into six age bands, u15 (0–14 years of age), u25
(15–24 years of age), u35 (25–34 years of age), u45 (35015044 years of age),
u60 (45–59 years of age) and 60+ (60 years of age and upwards).

This figure shows that swearing increases into the age range u25 and thereafter generally steadily declines. This result holds for both males and females.

As the strength of swearwords had a role to play in the discussion of sex, the next obvious question one may ask is: Will the order reported here change if we take the strength of the swearwords produced by speakers of different ages into account? The answer is no; when one calculates the average strength of a swearword produced by speakers in the different age groups, the results powerfully reinforce the negative correlation of age with swearing. The results show a fairly steady decline in average strength of swearword used from u15 through to 60+. Considering that males and females seemed to prefer different categories of swearing, might the same be true of people in different age groups? For each age group the picture is remarkably similar – they use emphatic adverbial/adjectival swearing, general expletives, personal insults and premodifying intensifying negative adjectives most frequently. The exception is the 60+ age group, where personal insults do not feature in the top four types of swearing, being usurped by the much weaker idiomatic type of swearing. While the ordering of the four types of swearing varies somewhat age group by age group, it is clearly in the 60+ age group that the major change occurs. However, one might claim again that age and strength interact – personal insults, the strongest category of swearing, declines steadily in the rank ordering as the speakers grow older, with the rank profile being (2), (3), (3), (4), (4) before the personal insult type of swearing exits the top four in the 60+ age group. So with specific reference to personal insults, we might suggest that age and strength of swearing is negatively correlated.

34.5.3   Social class of speaker

Let us now consider social class. Figure 34.2 below shows how it is indeed the case that swearing and social class are closely related – the upper classes swear less, the lower classes swear more. In this figure, the social classes run from AB (highest) in order through to DE (lowest).

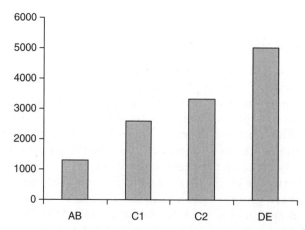

FIGURE 34.2   *Frequency of swearing per million words of speech produced by different social classes.*

What of the strength of this swearing? A slightly different picture emerges if we rank the social classes in terms of the average strength of the swearword that they use. ABs use slightly stronger words than C1s. The rank order for average strength of swearword usage is DE>C2>AB>C1. The rank order no longer aligns itself neatly with the social class hierarchy. So the picture is slightly more complex than one might expect. It may be that the C1s are engaging in a process called hypercorrection – they are modelling their speech on a class they seek to emulate, the ABs, and in doing so are engaging in a behaviour which they see as emblematic of that class, an aversion to swearing, so much that they actually emphasize that behaviour even more markedly than the ABs, that is, they suppress their swearing more than the ABs do.

34.6 Conclusion

As a result of studies such as this we now know a great deal more about swearing. As noted earlier in this chapter, bad language is a complex object of study. What we know about swearing bears this out. While we may have strong views about swearing, when we look at swearing in action the simple blanket statements that we may want to make about bad language, such as 'men swear more than women', begin to appear very difficult to make. Swearing in particular, and bad language in general, is a complex social and linguistic phenomenon. When looked at from different perspectives, the possibility of making or supporting general blanket statements about bad language begins to recede. Men may swear more than women in different ways and on different occasions. But under certain circumstances – females talking to females as opposed to makes talking to females – females will swear more. So while our intuitions may be of help in a study of bad language, we must accept that they are a faulty guide. Bad language requires careful and informed study. Our prejudices in approaching it may be just as strong as the prejudices at times encoded in the bad language we seek to study.

Recommended reading

The main results presented in this chapter come from McEnery (2005). This is a good source of information on patterns of swearing in modern British English as well as being a good source of information on the historical development of attitudes to bad language in English. Beyond this work, there is relatively little – swearing had been studied infrequently, though some recent work on swearing in American English (e.g., Jay, 1992), British English (Stenström, 1991) and Australian English (e.g., Kidman, 1993) has addressed the topic. Montagu (1967) is a rich source of examples of the use of bad language by other cultures, not only in the present but also in antiquity. In terms of approaches, swearing has been approached from the points of view of history (e.g., Montagu, 1967; Hughes 1991), lexicography (Sheidlower, 1995), psycholinguistics (e.g., Jay, 1992) and semantics (Kidman, 1993). Andersson and Trudgill (1992), while brief, is also informative.

CHAPTER 35

Language and Politics

RUTH WODAK

35.1 Performing politics

When thinking or talking about politics and political discourse, we usually regard political speeches as being the most salient genre (Ensink and Sauer, 2003; Chilton, 2004; Fairclough, 2006; Reisigl, 2006; 2008a, b; Wodak and De Cillia, 2007). Many speeches have become famous throughout the centuries (e.g., *I have a dream*, delivered by Martin Luther King, Jr. on 28 August 1963, at the Lincoln Memorial, Washington, DC (available at http://www.americanrhetoric.com/speeches/mlkihaveadream.htm) or *Blood, Sweat and Tears*, one of the most famous calls-to-arms in history, delivered on 13 May 1940 by Sir Winston Churchill (available at: http://www.historyplace.com/speeches/churchill.htm).

Speeches are usually written by 'spin-doctors', but performed by the politicians themselves. Therefore, the audience and the media identify the particular speech with the speaker and her/his style (Pels and Corner, 2003), and usually do not ask who the author is (Goffman, 1981). Spin doctors have become ever more important, both as speech writers and in their role as 'mediators' (Laux and Schütz, 1996), linking the fields of politics, administration, media, and so forth. **Spin** is not a new phenomenon – politicians have always used persuasive strategies and tactics; in opposition, however, to British Prime Minister Tony Blair's policies relating to the war in Iraq, the notion of **spin** acquired negative connotations in the sense that politicians could not be trusted anymore (e.g., Alastair Campbell was said to have had huge power as a spin doctor when advising Tony Blair); indeed, if one believes recent opinion polls in the United Kingdom, a **politics without spin** is demanded by the majority of the population – a pipe dream!

In our daily lives, we are confronted with many other genres of political discourse apart from speeches, foir example, in televised press conferences, in broadcast or televised interviews with politicians, in snippets on the Internet (e.g., YouTube), or in reports on political events in the press. Moreover, slogans and advertisements confront us when we are walking down the street, leaflets from political parties or interest groups are delivered by mail, and during election campaigns we are able to listen to politicians campaigning in town halls or at election rallies. Political parties have their own home pages, logos and brands; we are thus able to download relevant documents and photos as well as party programmes (Blasch, 2007). We are even able to listen to particular pop songs which politicians (or their ghost writers) have created to promote themselves (e.g., H. C. Strache, an extreme right wing Austrian politician: http://www.hcstrache.at/index.php?style=13andPHPSESSID=bb29df0f70fc 6279cb6336a571ab1724). If we wish to contact members of parliament or even the President of the United States, we are able to email them or chat with them on discussion forums specifically constructed for such purposes (Wright, 2005).

The BBC and other national broadcasting organizations transmit special programmes dedicated to bringing parliamentary debates right into our living rooms (BBC Parliament); such programmes convey the impression of allowing the listener or viewer to be part of decision-making processes and debates although only a few snapshots of the politicians' life are actually represented in the media:

> And after spending an entire day campaigning with the Conservative leader William Hague, the presenter of *Channel Four News*, Jon Snow, calculated that the total amount of time spent with members of the 'public' was a mere forty minutes.
>
> (Paxman, 2003: 93)

Weblogs of individual politicians give insight into daily and *quasi* private thoughts (Myers, Chapter 25 in this volume); and fictional films about important political events ('which nobody will ever forget') construct plausible narratives to keep memories alive or to offer explanations of unsolved cases (e.g., *JFK* by Oliver Stone or *The Life of a President* by Aaron Sorkin).

The above examples all shed light on the life and work of politicians from the outside. These are official genres, designed for the public and demonstrating the many ways in which politicians want to present themselves, stage their work and 'perform', and therefore how they like to be perceived by their various audiences ('frontstage'; see Goffman, 1981):

> A correctly staged and performed character leads the audience to impute a self to a performed character, but this imputation – this self – is a *product* of a scene that comes off, and not the *cause* of it. The self, then, as a performed character, is not an organic thing that has a specific location, whose fundamental fate is to be born, to mature, and to die; it is a dramatic effect arising diffusely from a scene that is presented, and the characteristic issue, the crucial concern, is whether it will be credited or discredited.
>
> (Goffman, 1959: 252–3)

These activities follow specific norms and rules, are part of the 'field of politics' (in Pierre Bourdieu's sense; see below) and are ritualized, as Murray Edelman claimed in his seminal book *The Symbolic Use of Politics* (Edelman, 1967). However, we have no access to the 'backstage', to the 'politics *du couloir*', and to the many conversations and gossip in the corridors when politicians meet informally (Krzyżanowski and Oberhuber, 2007; Wodak, 2009).

> **ADVANCES BOX 35.1**
>
> ### Politics and critical discourse analysis
>
> Politics necessarily includes persuasion, rhetoric, deceptive devices, and so forth. It is wishful thinking and indeed wrong to believe that politics as a profession could be imagined without strategies or tactics, always depending on the interests of the respective political party. Hence it is not surprising that politicians make use of such discursive strategies. Critical researchers describe and deconstruct which devices are used in which function and in which way, where and when, and possibly why. It is obviously an issue of grading and scales, not a decision to either employ strategies or to not employ them. We also encounter a debate about the notion of 'lying' in politics. Research in pragmatics, **critical discourse analysis** and political science is tackling these important phenomena; e.g., Wodak (2007a, c) and Heywood (2004) for more information.
>
> In the context of discourse and text analysis, critical certainly does not mean 'negative' (Wodak, 2007b). Critical social research and critical discourse analysis do not take common knowledge for granted but rather challenge such assumptions, thus opening up many more readings and options for interpretation, e.g., when analysing media texts or political discourses. Reisigl and Wodak (2001) distinguish between three levels of critique: **Text or discourse immanent critique** which detects inconsistencies, contradictions and fragmentations in the text itself; **socio-diagnostic critique** which relates the text to the text producers, their respective interests and the context of the text; and **prospective critique** which aims at proposing changes in discourse related to the two other levels (e.g., suggesting guidelines for non-discriminatory language) (see Fairclough, Chapter 30 in this volume). Below, I point to specific levels of critique when analysing extracts of political speeches.

In the image in Figure 35.1, we see (from left to right) President Abbas (Palestine), Prime Minister Blair (UK), and President Barroso (European Commission), responding to questions posed by journalists. All three have their own style related to a typical *habitus* of politicians when they are on *front stage* (eager, smiling, alert, serious and attentive). Observe the body gestures and mimics of the three politicians, which demonstrate all these mentioned characteristics.

35.2 Defining the field

35.2.1 Two definitions of 'politics'

The approaches of Aristotle and Machiavelli can be regarded as the two primary roots for the meaning of **politics**: ethics and morals, on the one hand, violence and hegemony, on the other:

> Our purpose is to consider what form of political community is best of all for those who are most able to realize their ideal in life. We must therefore

examine not only this but other constitutions, both such as actually exist in well-governed states, and any theoretical forms which are held in esteem, so that what is good and useful may be brought to light.

(Aristotle, 1999, book II.1: 301)

The Aristotelian goal, to discover the best form of government, is thus clearly linked to definitions of ethics and morals, that is, values for a given society: what is believed to be 'good' or 'bad'. The definition of values always depends on the context and the political system: what might have been 'good' for a totalitarian state like Nazi Germany was certainly experienced as 'bad' for democratic systems. On the other hand, we find 'the dark view of political power'. All politics is of necessity driven by a quest for power, but power is inherently unpredictable, irresponsible, irrational and persuasive. This view has been articulated most prominently by Michel Foucault, yet its roots can be detected in many authors from Niccolò Machiavelli to Antonio Gramsci.

Paul Chilton has summarized the two opposing views very succinctly:

On the one hand, politics is viewed as a struggle for power, between those who seek to assert their power and those who seek to resist it. On the other hand, politics is viewed as cooperation, as the practices and institutions that a society has for resolving clashes of interest over money, influence, liberty, and the like.

(Chilton, 2004: 3)

Press conference, Barcelona, 25 November 2005, EMEDIATE Project Archive   *FIGURE 35.1*

35.2.2   A brief history of the field

Research in the field of language and politics has expanded enormously in recent years. Although this kind of research may seem to be quite 'young', rhetoric is one of the oldest academic disciplines and was already concerned with aspects of political communication in ancient times (see Holly, 1990: 6ff.) After the Second World War, Harold Lasswell and Nathan Leites (1949) published one of the most important studies on quantitative semantics in the field of language and politics, developing approaches from communication and mass media research. The famous economist Friedrich von Hayek (1968) discussed the impact of language on politics during his stay at the London School of Economics. In the late 1940s, research on the intricate links between language and politics began throughout Central Europe, though mainly in Germany (see below). The novel *1984* by George Orwell was a significant point of departure for the development of the entire field (see Chilton, 2006). Of course, all this research was influenced by the massive use of propaganda during the Second World War and in the emerging Cold War era, in the 1950s.

Political linguistics (*Politolinguistik*) was the first attempt to create an academic discipline for the research of political discourse (see Wodak and De Cillia, 2006, for an extensive overview). Klein (1998) argued that the 'linguistic study of political communication' should be defined as a subdiscipline of linguistics. He cited the critical linguistic research that began in the wake of National Socialism and which was conducted primarily by Victor Klemperer (1947; 2005) and Rolf Sternberger, Storz and Sußkind (1957) as having paved the way for the new discipline (Schmitz-Berning, 2000; Fairclough, Chapter 30 in this volume). Both Klemperer and Sternberger sampled, categorized and described the words used during the Nazi regime: many words had acquired new meanings, other words were forbidden (borrowed words from other languages, like *cigarette*), and neologisms (new words) were created; similar language policies were adopted by former communist totalitarian regimes (Wodak and Kirsch, 1995). Controlling language in this way implies an attempt to control (the minds and thoughts of) people. Because these early studies provoked criticism for being inadequate from the perspective of linguistic theory, a new methodological approach, '*Politolinguistik*', emerged in the late 1960s. It drew on various linguistic subdisciplines (pragmatics, text linguistics, media research).

Burkhardt (1996) proposed the use of 'political language' as the generic term comprising 'all types of public, institutional and private talks on political issues, all types of texts typical of politics as well as the use of lexical and stylistic linguistic instruments characterizing talks about political contexts'. From 1990 onwards, research on **political discourse** expanded, drawing on sociological approaches (Goffman) and sociolinguistic research (e.g., on the functions of pronouns like *we, us, them*) (Wilson, 1990). Research was carried out into communication within political organizations (e.g., the European Union (Muntigl, Weiss and Wodak, 2000)), as well as on the unique (charismatic) style of politicians (Tony Blair; Fairclough, 2000), on political speeches (commemorative speeches; Ensink and Sauer,

ADVANCES BOX 35.2

What does the term **discourse** mean?

In the following section, you will see the term **discourse** used several times. Indeed, this is a term that has been often used in the chapters of this section. But what does it mean? The term **discourse analysis** has in recent decades penetrated many disciplines, such as sociology, philosophy, history, literary studies, cultural studies, anthropology, psychology and linguistics. In all these disciplines the term carries distinct meanings, including a social science methodology, the label for a whole field, a subdiscipline of linguistics, a critical paradigm and so forth. Reisigl (2004) lists 23 meanings of *discourse* used by Michel Foucault throughout his famous lecture in the Collège de France on 'orders of discourse'. In his lecture, Foucault formulates a number of crucial axioms about the nature and contexts of discursive events (*énoncés*):

> I make the assumption that the production of discourse is at once controlled, selected, organized and canalized in every society – and that this is done by way of certain procedures whose task it is to subdue the powers and dangers of discourse, to evade its heavy and threatening materiality.
>
> (Foucault, 1984: 10–11)

Although Foucault refers to many definitions of *discourse* in the course of his lecture, it is equally important to note what discourse is not supposed to mean in Foucault's work – specifically, that it is neither defined thematically nor by a strict system of concepts, and that it is not an object but rather a set of relationships existing between discursive events. These stipulations open the door to a dedicated functional approach, enabling the cultural critic to identify both static and dynamic relationships between discursive events and to address the causes and consequences of historical change.

However, and in contrast with Foucault's more abstract notion, in the tradition of Wittgenstein's **language games** (1967) and Austin's **speech acts** (1960), *discourse* is mainly understood as 'linguistic action', be it written, visual, or oral communication, verbal or non-verbal, undertaken by social actors in a specific setting determined by social rules, norms and conventions. Furthermore, language-specific meanings exist as well as distinct uses within the Anglo-American academic community on the one hand, and European scholarship on the other. For example, in British research, the term *discourse* is frequently used synonymously with *text*, meaning authentic, everyday linguistic communication. The French '*discours*', however, is more focused on the connection between language and thought, for instance meaning 'creation and societal maintenance of complex knowledge systems' (Ehlich, 2000: 162). In German, in functional pragmatics '*Diskurs*' denotes 'structured sets of speech acts' (ibid.). In the analysis of discourse, the meaning of *discourse* is therefore closely linked to the particular research context and theoretical approach.

Following the most important traditions in text linguistics and Discourse Studies, I distinguish between 'discourse' and 'text' in my chapter, and take Jay Lemke's definition (1995, 7ff.) as a starting point:

> When I speak about *discourse* in general, I will usually mean the social activity of making meanings with language and other symbolic systems in some

particular kind of situation or setting ... On each occasion when the particular meaning characteristic of these discourses is being made, a specific *text* is produced. Discourses, as social actions more or less governed by social habits, produce texts that will in some ways be alike in their meanings ... When we want to focus on the specifics of an event or occasion, we speak of the text; when we want to look at patterns, commonality, relationships that embrace different texts and occasions, we can speak of discourses.

In other words, 'discourse' is defined on a different, more abstract level as 'text'. 'Discourse' implies patterns and commonalities of knowledge and structures whereas a 'text' is a specific and unique realization of a discourse. Texts belong to genres. Thus a discourse on New Labour could be realized in a potentially huge range of genres and texts; for example, in a TV debate on the politics of New Labour, in a New Labour manifesto, in a speech by one of New Labour's representatives, and so forth.

2003; Martin and Wodak, 2003), on right wing political rhetoric (Wodak and Pelinka, 2002), on strategies of manipulation and persuasion (the 2003 Iraq war; Van Dijk, 2006; Chouliaraki, 2007), on interviews with politicians in the media (Clayman and Heritage, 2002), and so forth. Nowadays, many refereed journals publish research from this area (e.g., *Discourse and Society*; *Journal of Language and Politics*).

35.3   Frameworks and methods

Chilton (2004: 201–5) lists 12 propositions which could serve as a possible framework for the field of language and politics. I will discuss the most important five, briefly, in the following and will then focus on **positive self- and negative other-presentation** in the use of political speeches as one of many genres in the field of language and politics:

- **Political discourse operates indexically,** which implies that one's choice of language (a politician's choice or a layperson's choice) will always – implicitly or explicitly – signal some political distinction. This might be the choice of using a specific accent, of including certain lexical items, or the choice of which address forms to use, and so forth.
- **Political discourse operates as interaction.** Here Chilton states that many features of interaction such as interruptions or overlaps might indicate hierarchy or rank. Moreover, interactions of any kind (such as dialogues, negotiations or debates) serve to find common representations of the world and to mark agreements or disagreements.
- **Modal properties of language subserve political interaction.** Many claims put forward by politicians remain vague; others are claims for truth, confidence, trust, credibility or even legitimization (of actions or positions). Hence, in English, the use of *can, must, should, could*, and so forth implies such statements.

- **Binary conceptualizations are frequent in political discourse.** Most politicians attempt to present themselves in positive ways and to portray their political opponents negatively (van Dijk, 1984; Reisigl and Wodak, 2001). The construction of **us** and **them** lies at the core of persuasive discourse. Binary concepts are also used in attributing a range of characteristics to **us** and **them** (see below) which emphasize positive or negative connotations.
- **Political discourse involves metaphorical reasoning.** Metaphors serve as arguments, for example to legitimize restrictions on immigration, which is often depicted as occurring in *floods* or *waves*, and so forth. Other spatial metaphors (the *path schema*) are regularly used in indicating actions or positions which a political group endorses (*being at cross roads, boarding the train, choosing directions*, and so forth) (Musolff, 2004).

Chilton's framework could be related to Burkhardt's (1996) dimensions of concrete textual analysis (see Advances Box 35.3 below). For example, modality can be analysed through lexical or visual analysis. Binarity involves lexical choices, rhetorical structures, the analysis of pronouns, of arguments and of address forms, and so forth.

An important claim missing in Chilton's framework relates to the dimension of **persuasion**. Political language and discourse serve to convince hearers/viewers/readers of a specific ideological position, of actions that are to be implemented or of a programme which needs to be endorsed. Hence, all genres in the field of politics necessarily involve persuasive elements which serve to enhance the position and opinion of the text producer in a televised interview, in a parliamentary debate or in a speech given for a specific occasion.

35.3.1   Binarity: *us* and *them* (positive self- and negative other- presentation)

Let us focus a bit more on **binarity**, 'the discursive construction of 'us' and 'them''. This necessarily reduces the complexity of actions and events to two

---

ADVANCES BOX 35.3

Burkhardt's procedures

Burkhardt (1996) lists four different procedures as being particularly promising methods and techniques to be used for 'ideological reconstruction' (the various technical terms used here are explained in this volume in Chapters 9–11 on semantics, pragmatics and text linguistics): **lexical-semantic techniques** (analysis of catchwords and value words, of euphemisms, and of ideological polysemy); **sentence and text-semantic procedures** (e.g., analysis of tropes, of 'semantic isotopes', and of integration and exclusion strategies); **pragmatic text-linguistic techniques** (e.g., analysis of forms of address, speech acts, allusions, presuppositions, argumentation, rhetoric, quotations, genres and intertextuality); and finally **semiotic techniques** (icon, symbol and semiotic analysis).

ILLUSTRATION BOX 35.1

President's address

I just completed a meeting with <u>our</u> national security team, and <u>we</u>'ve received the latest intelligence updates. The <u>deliberate</u> and <u>deadly</u> attacks, which were carried out yesterday against <u>our</u> country, were more than <u>acts of terror</u>. <u>They</u> were <u>acts of war</u>. This will require <u>our</u> country to <u>unite in steadfast determination and resolve</u>. <u>Freedom and democracy</u> are under attack. The <u>American people</u> need to know <u>we</u>'re facing a <u>different enemy</u> than <u>we</u> have ever faced. This <u>enemy</u> hides in <u>shadows</u> and has <u>no regard for human life</u>. This is an <u>enemy who preys on innocent and unsuspecting people</u>, then <u>runs for cover</u>, but it <u>won't be able to run for cover forever</u>. This is an <u>enemy</u> that tries to hide, but <u>it won't be able to hide forever</u>. This is an <u>enemy</u> that thinks its harbors are safe, <u>but they won't be safe forever</u>. <u>This enemy</u> attacked not just <u>our</u> people but <u>all freedom-loving people everywhere in the world</u>.

The <u>United States of America</u> will use all <u>our</u> resources to conquer <u>this enemy</u>. <u>We</u> will rally the world. <u>We</u> will be <u>patient</u>. <u>We</u>'ll be <u>focused</u>, and <u>we</u> will be <u>steadfast</u> in <u>our</u> determination. This battle will take time and resolve, but make no mistake about it, <u>we</u> will win. The federal government and all our agencies are conducting business, but it is not business as usual. <u>We</u> are operating on heightened security alert. <u>America</u> is going forward, and as <u>we</u> do so, <u>we</u> must remain keenly aware of the threats to <u>our</u> country (George W. Bush, The Deliberate and Deadly Attacks…Were Acts of War, President's Address from Cabinet Room following Cabinet Meeting, 12 September 2001; underlining by RW; http://www.americanrhetoric.com/speeches/gwbush911cabinetroomaddress.htm)

In a first brief analysis, we can clearly detect the relevant 'social actors' **us** (*we, I, freedom, democracy, America, freedom loving people, our country, United States of America*) and **them** (*enemy, preys on the innocent, runs for cover*; note that the impersonal neutral pronoun *it* is being used, not *they* which would clearly indicate human beings). *We* are active and willing to confront the enemy ('material verbs'), whereas *the enemy* is described as being cowardly, hiding, immoral, a threat to all values of democracy and freedom. Once the opposing groups have been categorized, we can also observe several 'rhetorical techniques' (repetitions of syntactic structures as well as lexical items), the use of **metaphors** to depict 'the enemy' (*hiding in the shadows*), while *us* is attributed by very positive 'flag-words' (*patient, steadfast, freedom-loving*). A **discursive contrast** between light and dark is constructed: the light relates to democracy, freedom, patience, and the whole freedom-loving world; the dark relates to a small group of enemies who are hiding and have *no regard for human life* and who commit *acts of terror* or even *acts of war*. The construction of the contrast serves **argumentative-rhetorical means**: to **convince** the in-group (us, all Americans, the freedom-loving world) that acts of war (thus **redefining** *acts of terror*) were committed against America (which is rhetorically **equated** with the *freedom loving world*), and therefore, a war seems a necessary measure against *the enemy*. This speech marks the preparation for a 'calls-to-arms' (see also Young and Fitzgerald, 2006: 10–33).

distinct groups, one of which – **us** – is deemed to be good, the other – **them** – bad. Thus, binarity serves important functions in politics by including some and excluding others ('Othering') and/or by defining a distinct group of victims and a group of perpetrators who can be blamed for something ('Scapegoating').

In the brief analysis of positive self- and negative other-presentation above, I applied the following five questions as guidelines (Reisigl and Wodak, 2001: 44) which have proved very useful:

(i)   How are social actors – either individual persons or groups – linguistically constructed by being named (**nomination**)?

(ii) What positive or negative traits, qualities and features are attributed to the linguistically constructed social actors (**predication**)?

(iii) Through what arguments and **argumentation schemes** do specific persons or social groups try to justify or de-legitimize claims containing specific nominations and predications (e.g., claims of discrimination of others)?

(iv) From what perspective or point of view are these nominations, predications and argumentations expressed (**perspectivation**)?

(v)   Are the respective utterances (nominations, predications and argumentations) articulated overtly, are they intensified or are they mitigated (**mitigation versus intensification**)?

Discursive strategies for positive self- and negative other-representation (Wodak, 2001)   **Table 35.1**

Strategy	Objectives	Devices
Referential / nomination	Construction of in-groups and out-groups	• membership categorization • biological, naturalizing and depersonalizing metaphors and metonymies • synecdoches (whole for part, part for whole)
Predication	Labelling social actors positively or negatively	• stereotypical, evaluative attributions of negative or positive traits • implicit and explicit predicates
Argumentation	Justification of positive or negative attributions	• topoi used to justify inclusion or exclusion
Perspectivation, framing or discourse representation	Expressing involvement Positioning speaker's point of view	• reporting, description, narration or quotation of events and utterances
Intensification, mitigation	Modifying the epistemic status of a proposition	• intensifying or mitigating the illocutionary force of utterances

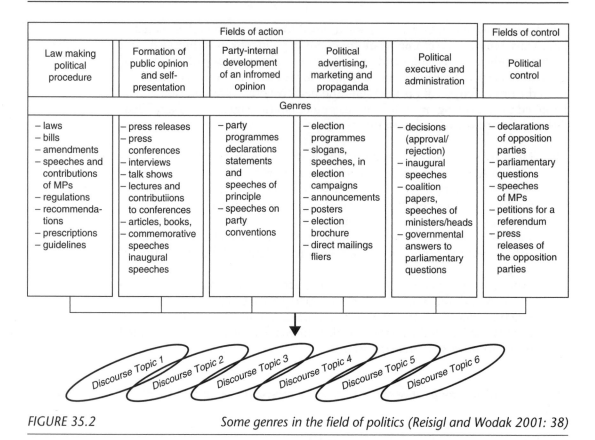

Fields of action					Fields of control
Law making political procedure	Formation of public opinion and self-presentation	Party-internal development of an infromed opinion	Political advertising, marketing and propaganda	Political executive and administration	Political control
Genres					
– laws – bills – amendments – speeches and contributions of MPs – regulations – recommenda-tions – prescriptions – guidelines	– press releases – press conferences – interviews – talk shows – lectures and contributiions to conferences – articles, books, – commemorative speeches inaugural speeches	– party programmes declarations statements and speeches of principle – speeches on party conventions	– election programmes – slogans, speeches, in election campaigns – announcements – posters – election brochure – direct mailings fliers	– decisions (approval/rejection) – inaugural speeches – coalition papers, speeches of ministers/heads – governmental answers to parliamentary questions	– declarations of opposition parties – parliamentary questions – speeches of MPs – petitions for a referendum – press releases of the opposition parties

Discourse Topic 1 Discourse Topic 2 Discourse Topic 3 Discourse Topic 4 Discourse Topic 5 Discourse Topic 6

FIGURE 35.2   *Some genres in the field of politics (Reisigl and Wodak 2001: 38)*

Table 35.1 contains some of the linguistic, pragmatic and rhetorical devices used in political discourse to realize the five discursive strategies mentioned – this list serves as a possible stimulus for further engagement with analysis in the field of political discourse.

35.3.2   Context and genres

Let us now turn to the context of speech events or of interactions. I suggest considering four levels of context in the concrete textual analysis (Wodak 2001):

(i)   the **immediate, language or text internal co-text** (i.e., Bush's speech, 12 September 2001);

(ii)   the **intertextual and interdiscursive** relationship between utterances, texts, genres and discourses (i.e., other speeches and media reporting on the specific speech, reporting on 9/11 or other speeches related to 9/11);

(iii)   **extralinguistic social/sociological variables** and institutional frames of a specific 'context of situation' (the setting, other political parties, TV);

(iv)   **the broader sociopolitical and historical contexts**, which the discursive practices are embedded in and related to (events surrounding and leading up to 9/11).

Hence, a discourse about a specific topic (calls-to-arms after 9/11 or a commemoration of the end of the Second World War, see below) can find its starting point within one field of action and proceed through another one. Discourses and discourse topics **spread** to different fields and discourses. They cross between fields, overlap, refer to each other or are in some other way socio-functionally linked with each other. We can represent the relationship between fields of action, genres and discourse topics with the example of the field of politics (Figure 35.2). In this way, it becomes obvious how many different genres can be employed for political means.

Each genre which relates to one of the macro-functions defined above thus follows conventions defined culturally and politically (see analysis of texts in Illustration Boxes 35.1–35.3).

35.4   A second example: Political speeches at commemorative events

In an extensive and elaborate typology of political speeches, Martin Reisigl (2008a, b) defines a speech as 'a structured verbal chain of coherent speech acts uttered on a special social occasion for a specific purpose by a single person, and addressed to a more or less specific audience'. Speeches may differ from each other in length, and in terms of the respective occasion (including time and place) of the speech, the primary and secondary topics, the speech's manifest and latent functions, the identity and function of the speaker, the addressees, the form of presentation and degree of preparedness, and the speech's style and structure, depending on the respective language, culture and political position or ideology of the speaker and the audience.

Speeches are rarely spontaneous as they are given in formal situations. Classic rhetoric distinguishes three forms of oratory: the judicial (*genus iudiciale*), the deliberative (*genus deliberativum*) and the epideictic (*genus demonstrativum*).[1] According to the standard scheme, judicial oratory is focused temporally on the past, and thematically on justice or injustice. Deliberative oratory is connected with the future, and thematically related to expediency or harmfulness. Epideictic oratory is temporally linked to the present, and thematically concerned with honour and disgrace – commemorative speeches belong to this type (Plett, 2001: 17–18).

Much research, however, has illustrated that the theoretical separation has to be taken as a simplification (Reisigl, 1998; Wodak and De Cillia, 2007). Since the first theory on rhetorical genre by Aristotle, political systems, conditions and circumstances have changed and become increasingly complex. Thus forms, types and functions of political speeches have altered accordingly.

Commemorative speeches are delivered on public days of remembrance, which primarily serve to retrieve the past for the present (e.g., *Remembrance Sunday*, commemorating the First and Second World Wars in the UK). They are often highly epideictic in nature, that is, they assign praise or blame to certain moments of a nation's past or present. However, epideictic oratory does not exclusively serve as a vehicle for the linguistic self-presentation and self-promotion of the speakers; it also has an 'educational' function, that is, it seeks to convey certain political values in order to create consensus and a spirit of community which in turn serve as a model for future political actions (Perelman, 1980: 28ff.). In addition, commemorative speeches contain deliberative elements and/or argumentative insertions. They sometimes even exhibit traces of judicial rhetoric, if a given speech attempts to justify past or present problematic actions and events.

35.4.1 The year 2005

Let us start with the fourth level of context (Section 35.3.2.) – the socio-political and historical circumstances: 2005 marked an important commemorative year in Austria –60 years since the end of the Second World War, 50 years since the signing of the Austrian State Treaty, and ten years since Austria's accession to the European Union, the second of which had made a democratic and free Second Austrian Republic possible (the Allied forces left Austria after its declaration of neutrality in October 1955). In the following, I will consider two extracts of one political speech by the then Austrian chancellor, Dr Wolfgang Schüssel, which attempted to establish a hegemonic stance towards the Nazi past (the one official and accepted version), the widespread participation of Austrians in Nazi war crimes, and the question of 'who the victims were'.

We proceed to the next level of context – the speech event. Chancellor Schüssel's speech was given on 27 April 2005, as part of a commemorative event in the Redoutensäle of the Hofburg (the previous palace of the Habsburg emperors) in Vienna. The occasion was the sixtieth anniversary of the 'birth hour' of the Second Republic, in other words the date of the proclamation of a provisional Austrian state government recognized by the Allied Forces, eight days before the end of the Second World War. The proclamation declared that the Austrian republic was 'reconstituted' and that 'the Anschluss forced on the Austrian people in 1938' was 'null and void'.

The following, very brief, analysis (first level of context) illustrates how the speaker views this history, understands it, presents it and therefore formulates/constructs it anew throughout the whole speech (for an extensive analysis, see Wodak and De Cillia, 2007). I focus primarily on the use of metaphors related to birth, rebirth and birth hours which I deem to be key conceptual metaphors of this commemorative discourse.

This text is clearly marked by the use of **metaphors**. Moreover, the abundance of evaluative adjectives **intensifies** such metaphors and complements the cognitive, conceptual frames with emotions and values. Without being able to present the details of the ongoing debate surrounding the theories about and analysis of metaphors, I would like to emphasize the function of **conceptual frames**, realized in metaphorical expressions, for the discursive construction of national identity through commemorative speeches (Wodak et al., 2009).

Chancellor Schüssel's speech (1)

Mr President, Right Honourable Cardinal, President of the National Assembly! I have come to ... for the initiation of our festive gathering and can put on record that the 27th of April 1945 was, first and foremost, a day of joy. It was the <u>birth hour of the Second Republic,</u> ...

The 27th of April was, in Vienna ... in any case, a spring day 60 years ago, in ten days the Second World War in Europe will have ended, ten days ago the big Austrian parties were founded. Their founders returned from concentration camps and detention, and together with other democrats <u>created the Second Republic</u>. The drama of this six-year war and the trauma of the National Socialist terror regime, however, throw sombre shadows onto the <u>cradle of this red-white-red rebirth</u>, but <u>the child</u> lives. In the midst of ruins, need, hunger and desperation, <u>lives this small, new, Austria</u>, because on this day everyone looks ahead. The nightmare is over. But the horror was not over for everyone, and not every horror was over. The displacements continued, in all of Europe, especially in Central Europe over ten million people were displaced, lost their home; whole convoys of refugees were on the move looking for a new home. (Speech by Austrian Federal Chancellor Wolfgang Schüssel, 27.4.2005, Hofburg, Vienna.)

The ostensible reason for the speech was the Austrian Declaration of Independence on 27 April 1945, which took place before the surrender of the Nazi regime on 8 May 1945. This political event is apparently conducive to descriptions as a 'birth' or 'rebirth': the 27 April *is the birth hour of the Second Republic* and later *The drama of this six-year war and the trauma of the National Socialist terror regime, however, throw sombre shadows onto the cradle of this red-white-red rebirth, but the child lives.* Later still, he speaks of *the birth hour of a new, democratic Austria.*

The re-establishment of the Second Republic is thus expressed in the **conceptual cognitive frame** of a natural, biological event through the **anthropomorphizing metaphor** of birth and rebirth. A political entity thus becomes a child, and the 'founding fathers' of the Second Republic appear as parents. However, there are no mothers present or evoked which causes the metaphor to appear somewhat stilted.

Let us take the five questions (Section 35.3.1) as guideline for a brief analysis: The **political actors** who really made independence possible do not appear, they are absent, **back-grounded** and deleted; i.e., the Allied forces who defeated the Nazi regime and forced its surrender a short time later. The main actors are 'the founders', returning from concentration camps, and 'other democrats', thus in contrast and opposition to the Nazi-regime.

The birth is constructed as **drama** – a further metaphorical perspective which transforms the genre of the speech into a story, with a happy ending (*the child lives* **in spite of** *terror, sombre shadows, ruins, hunger, need and desperation*). The Nazi-regime is labelled as a *nightmare*; the Nazi-regime is thus defined as a static subconscious phenomenon. Active agents exist after the Nazi-regime was over: as *displaced persons* and *refugees* who are nevertheless depicted in passive roles. The rebirth is discursively constructed as a miracle (supported through the genre of a story), in spite of all the negative circumstances.

These labels and attributions serve to construct a new narrative about Austria's history, to position arguments that nobody had been able to do anything against *the nightmare*; and that a new beginning, a *rebirth*, had happened. In this way, perpetrators were backgrounded, and only the victims were made explicit.

ADVANCES BOX 35.4

Scenarios

Musolff introduces the concept of 'metaphor scenarios' to grasp the attempt of (re)defining historical trajectories:

> We can characterize a 'scenario' as a set of assumptions made by competent members of a discourse community about 'typical' aspects of a source situation; e.g., its participants and their roles, the 'dramatic' storylines and outcomes, and conventional evaluations of whether they count as successful or unsuccessful, permissible or illegitimate, etc. These source-based assumptions are mapped onto the respective target concepts.
>
> (Musolff, 2006: 28)

Scenarios relate to collective experiences and assist in constructing coherent representations of the past (e.g. the notion of 'model' or 'frame' in Chapter 9, Advances Box 9.1). These cognitive theories and concepts, however, do not explain the mass-psychological, highly emotional, illocutionary force of such images. To be able to explain why specific narratives succeed and others do not, a **discourse-historical, interdisciplinary analysis** must consider other contextual factors as well. By addressing certain topics or events which are thought to be part of collective experiences or memories, the speakers intentionally trigger hegemonic context models and scenarios.

Let us now look more closely at how the speech presents the victims:

ILLUSTRATION BOX 35.3

Chancellor Schüssel's speech (2)

The victims of this horror must be named: 100,000 Austrians died in the concentration camps or in captivity, most of them Jews. Many had to lose their lives because of their political or religious convictions, also thousands of Roma, Sinti, ill and disabled people were murdered. 50,000 civilians were killed, 100,000 political prisoners lost years of their lives. 250,000 soldiers were killed, 250,000 came back from the war badly injured or mutilated, and in the following years 500,000 prisoners of war had to pay for this criminal war having been started.

Noteworthy here are, among other features, the **lexical means** used to refer to the deaths of victims, the choice of verbs; moreover, which function the numbers might have and how the group of victims is constructed in detail (hence focusing on nomination and predication):

100,000 Austrians <u>died</u> in the concentration camps or in captivity, <u>most of them Jews</u>; many <u>had to lose their lives</u>, Roma, Sinti, ill and disabled people <u>were murdered</u>. Civilians were killed, political prisoners <u>lost years of their lives</u>, soldiers <u>were killed</u> or <u>came back from the war badly injured or mutilated</u>, prisoners of war <u>had to pay</u> for the war.

Only once is *murder* explicitly mentioned. This verbal treatment of the crimes of National Socialism leads to a **euphemization** of the deaths of those murdered in the concentration camps; the use of *had to*, for example, gives the impression that the loss of life was necessary and not the choice of a group of individuals to kill another group of individuals. The perpetrators are not named – **passivization and agent deletion** make it possible to keep the originators of these crimes obscured, and reinforce the impression that the events were unavoidable and fated.

The whole speech of which I only present two brief examples in this chapter constructs a stark contrast: the political event of the Declaration of Independence is represented metaphorically as a *rebirth*; a **metaphorical scenario** which constructs a 'creation myth', contextualized in a story frame. A child, or even better a newborn child, is of course innocent. The metaphor thus carries an additional meaning – not only is Austria newly born, it is also innocent like a newborn child. On the other hand, the historical events before and immediately following are placed in the fateful context of *horror* and *nightmare* of a *dark age*. The cognitive frame is that of natural disasters or fateful events, which thus represents political events as immutable by humans.

This is also shown linguistically in the almost continuous agent deletion. **De-historicization** and **de-politicization** of historical events are the ultimate result, realized through the argumentative strategies presented in this brief analysis. All this makes a communal 'commemoration' possible, including the perpetrators and their families. This is because the perpetrators are not named, and because in the end no one is responsible for the crimes, since the events are constructed using **argumentative fallacies** as apparently fateful and generally unavoidable natural disasters. The shift in genres, combining the epideitic genre with a very simple story frame, reinforces the **dramatic illocutionary effect** and constructs a new **temporal and causal sequence** of facts. Such speeches construct consensus and do not alienate possible political opponents; in this way the official purpose of commemoration is ultimately well fulfilled.

This analysis illustrates that political meanings are always created in contexts. Hence text analysis necessarily includes context analysis on the four levels mentioned. All dimensions of language can be used in persuasive and manipulative ways, depending on the respective context, language, culture, ideologies, topic, functions, speakers, audience and occasion.

To conclude, consider the extract of the speech, and a brief analysis of it, given in Illustration Box 35.4, as additional evidence for the claims made above. This is a speech given in 1986 by Ronald Reagan and delivered at the Arlington Cemetery. It was part of the national Memorial Day commemoration (commemorating the Vietnam War; see Slavickova, forthcoming, for details), at which it is traditional for the sitting US president to address the nation. This text extract illustrates similar but also different discursive strategies, like the text extracts above from the Austrian context. The similarity is created through the fact that the Vietnam War and its consequences present a huge trauma for the US population which is frequently tabooed or silenced. The differences are due to the significantly different culture of rhetoric in the United States (see Young and Fitzgerald, 2006).

ILLUSTRATION BOX 35.4

Ronald Reagan's speech (1986)

I know that <u>many veterans</u> of Vietnam will gather today, <u>some of them</u> perhaps by the wall. And <u>they're</u> still helping each other on. <u>They were</u> quite a group, the <u>boys of Vietnam</u> – <u>boys</u> who fought a terrible and vicious war without enough support from home, <u>boys</u> who were dodging bullets while <u>we</u> debated the efficacy of the battle. It was often <u>our poor</u> who fought in that war; it was the <u>unpampered boys</u> of the working class who picked up the rifles and went on the march. <u>They</u> learned not to rely on <u>us</u>; <u>they</u> learned to rely on <u>each other</u>. And <u>they</u> were special in another way: <u>They</u> chose to be faithful. <u>They</u> chose to reject the fashionable scepticism of <u>their</u> time. <u>They</u> chose to believe and answer the call of duty. <u>They</u> had the wild, wild courage of youth. <u>They</u> seized certainty from the heart of an ambivalent age; <u>they</u> stood for something.

And <u>we</u> owe them something, <u>those boys</u>. <u>We</u> owe <u>them</u> first a promise: That just as <u>they</u> did not forget their missing comrades, neither, ever, will <u>we</u>. And there are other promises. <u>We</u> must always remember that peace is a fragile thing that needs constant vigilance. <u>We</u> owe them a promise to look at the world with a steady gaze and, perhaps, a resigned toughness, knowing that <u>we</u> have <u>adversaries</u> in the world and challenges and the only way to meet <u>them</u> and maintain the peace is by staying strong.

Generally speaking, similar to the Austrian text, there is strong use of third-person pronouns to refer to the dead which creates a sense of **vagueness and distance**. The stylistic shifts from *we/our* to *they/their* evoke a stark dichotomy of the living vis-à-vis the dead. The psychological effect is further reinforced by the sharp shift in **anaphora** from paragraph 1 to paragraph 2: the experience of *they* implies the moral obligation of *we*, and the intensity of their use highlights the discursively constructed **contrast** between the two sections. Also foregrounded is the shift in **tense**, from past in most of paragraph 1 to present. Significantly, however, while the word *they* is clearly attributed (Vietnam casualties and veterans), the word *we* remains vague and lacks a specified referent in both paragraphs.

Indeed, it seems that the first-person plural of paragraph 1 implies a different **subject** than that of paragraph 2. The *we* here seems to be the Washington political elite, i.e., Reagan's presidential predecessors. Reagan ventures an implicit reproach, by weak implication, also reproaching himself as a member of that elite, in keeping with Wodak and de Cillia's (2007) claim, that commemorative speeches 'assign praise or blame to certain moments of a nation's past or present' (see also extracts in Illustration Boxes 35.2 and 35.3: **historical** *we*). However, the attribution of the first-person plural remains ambiguous: its referent could be the American public in general, or possibly the mass media, or both. In any case, Reagan appears to be using – for rhetorical purposes – the point of view of many war veterans who accused their leaders of neglect (and who still need to be *helped on*), and/or of those who at the time accused non-combatant Americans of inadequate moral support. Thus distinct groups are constructed via **nomination** and **predication strategies**. Moreover, he is lending **voice** to *our poor*, i.e., the *unpampered boys of the working class*. Such 'critique' is only achieved, however, through the engendering of **distance**. Reagan's discourse sets up a relatively safe point of view **(strategy of perspectivation)** for one who is in a position to distance himself both spatially and temporally, and hence ideologically, from the subject of his mild rebuke. (Reagan was governor of California for much of the Vietnam War, which had ended a decade before this speech.)

The speech **collectivizes** the armed forces (volunteers and conscripts) in to a group as *the boys in Vietnam, working class boys* with a monopoly on good and honourable values: with a unified faith, beliefs, courage, and sense of certainty in *an ambivalent age*, who *stood for something*. The **declarative style** is reinforced by the use of **definite articles** which present potentially contentious assertions as non-negotiable or objective, thus employing **epistemic modality**; the **predication through (intensified) attributes** is also salient here: *the unpampered boys, the fashionable scepticism of their time, the wild wild courage of youth*.

In sum, a glorious, homogeneous identity, resting on selfless sacrifice, is discursively related to the burden of debt such *sacrifice* entails for future generations. The **language of war** thereby **presupposes** the inevitability of debt and repayment through further conflict and death which is maintained via the familiar amnesiac **tropes** and **topoi** (for more detail, see Slavickova, forthcoming, who analyses the Memorial Day commorative speeches of three US presidents, i.e., Bill Clinton, Georg W. Bush and Ronald Reagan).

Recommended readings

Reisigl and Wodak's *Discourse and Discrimination* (2001) presents the Discourse-Historical Approach in CDA in much detail, with many, different examples of 'Language and/in Politics' (news reports, TV interviews, manifestos, spontaneous conversations at election rallies, etc.). Chilton (2004), *Analyzing Political Discourse*, is an excellent introduction to the field, with a focus on British politics, while employing a cognitive approach to (Critical) Discourse Analysis. *The Discursive Construction of History: Remembering the Wehrmacht's War of Annihilation* (Heer et al., 2008) allows insight into the complex debates about Germany's and Austria's post-war history and related narratives. Many different genres are analyzed in an interdisciplinary way to be able to provide a multi-faceted picture of events and positionings. Krzyżanowski and Oberhuber (2007) provides us with a detailed case study of the many debates and controversies at the European Convention 200203 which allows insight into the 'functioning and staging' of politics. Wodak (2009) presents a comprehensive overview of the state of art of research on language and politics, as well as an analysis of everyday discourses in the European Parliament which are juxtaposed with a multimodal analysis of the US TV soap *The West Wing*.

Note

1 'Rhetoric' is here intended to denote both the *ars bene dicendi et scribendi*, i.e., the practical art of speaking and writing well in public, and the theory of eloquence.

Chapter 36

Business Communication

Veronika Koller

36.1   What is business communication?

Business communication, also known as corporate communication, is language use in and by companies. As such, it is part of a wider area often referred to as **organizational communication** or **institutional communication**, which also includes communication in and by not-for-profit organizations such as hospitals, schools, universities and charities. Instead of the term 'communication', we also find **discourse**, as in 'corporate discourse', 'business discourse' or 'organizational discourse'. For our purposes, we can treat **communication**, that is, using mostly language to interact with others, and **discourse**, that is, language use as social practice, as having the same meaning (for further definition of the term 'discourse', see Chapter 35, Advances Box 35.2).

Even small companies are often very complex entities that operate as part of a network of people and organizations, using language to do so. Take the example of a pub: The owner of the pub can run it him- or herself or as a franchisee, that is, effectively run a branch of a chain. In either case, they will be in touch with their local council about building regulations and licences before they can pull the first pint. The owner also has to negotiate contracts with suppliers and landlords, and, crucially, has to find and keep employees and customers. Finally, they have to keep an eye on the competition and invest in advertising. All these multiple and complex relationships involve communication, within the company (in our example: between the owner and employees), with other companies (e.g., suppliers), with not-for-profit organizations (here: the council), with potential and actual customers, and with the general public (e.g., neighbours complaining about disorderly behaviour outside the pub). The overall aims of communicating with all these so-called 'stakeholders' are to keep the business running smoothly and to make a profit. However, relations are with very different groups and individuals who have very different interests and agendas: suppliers wishing to sell at a price that pays for them, customers expecting a range of food and beverages, and employees wanting decent working conditions and decent pay, so clearly there is no one-size-fits-all solution to business communication. At every stage, the owner of our imaginary pub has to decide how to address their different stakeholders.

This starts with the choice of the medium in which to communicate: To draw on the pub example once more, communication with suppliers and the council is likely to be by email, fax or phone, while customer and employee contact is almost always face to face. Cutting across all this is the decision of whether to use written or spoken forms of language (i.e., genres), and which one: Will a short phone call do in answer to an enraged letter from a complaining neighbour or does the occasion require a formal written apology? Can suppliers best be reached by phone or do they prefer to be contacted by email? Do customers just want to chat at the bar or would they like to receive a newsletter about live music and other events? Once those decisions about medium and genre have been made, communicators need to find the appropriate form of the language itself, including issues of formality and politeness. And finally, all these decisions need to take into account that different stakeholders are of different social and cultural backgrounds, which may lead to particular expectations about what kind of communication is appropriate in each situation. The following section addresses these considerations in more detail, by looking at research interests in business communication studies.

36.2   Research interests in business communication

In this section, I outline some recent literature on business communication, distinguishing between internal and external communication and, within these, between spoken and written genres. I also mention particular research interests for each area of business communication, e.g., story-telling in spoken internal communication. Figure 36.1 summarizes the interests of researchers in business communication studies and the methods they have used. (Methods are dealt with in Section 36.3.)

The area of business communication that has received most attention from linguists is companies' internal spoken and written communication (Jablin and Putnam, 2001; Grant et al., 2004; Iedema and Wodak, 2005). The study of so-called organizational discourse combines concepts from sociology,

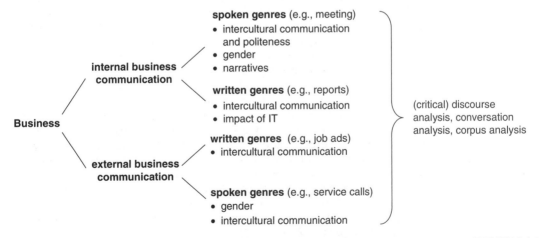

Research interests and methods in business communication studies   *FIGURE 36.1*

philosophy, psychology and semiotics at a rather abstract theoretical level. By contrast, work with a specific research interest such as intercultural business communication (Candlin and Gotti, 2004) or gendered discourse in business (Holmes, 2006; Mullany, 2007) typically analyses a broad range of real-life data. When we look at the subdivision into spoken and written genres in business communication, we see that research into spoken genres continues to be influenced by two seminal works (Boden and Zimmerman, 1991; Drew and Heritage 1992). These early anthologies provided an influential tool-kit for researchers interested in talk in professional settings and its various aspects such as intercultural communication (Yuling, Scollon and Scollon, 2002) (see Chapter 1, Section 1.6), politeness (Holmes and Stubbe, 2003) (see Chapter 31) or gendered talk in the workplace (Baxter, 2003: 128–80) (see Chapter 32). A particular genre that has been studied extensively is that of business meetings, especially those involving participants from different

---

ADVANCES BOX 36.1

Critical views on business communication

Some recent studies of the discourse of companies and organizations have adopted a critical stance that takes into account the historical development of capitalism. Such an approach seeks to reveal how particular forms of language use and communication serve to reinforce corporate power in society and hierarchical power structures within companies (e.g., Iedema and Scheeres, 2003) (see Chapter 30). Studies on gender in particular have gone beyond conversation analysis to include a critical discussion of the construction of gendered social roles in institutional settings by means of language, and of the communicative restrictions that are placed on some employees because of their gender. Examples range from the – almost always female – secretary whose job it is to take minutes at a meeting but who is not expected to join the discussion, although it may directly affect her, to the female senior executive who tries to develop styles of communication that go beyond adhering to a masculine norm (Holmes, 2006).

The ongoing redefinition of various areas of life along the lines of the market means that especially promotional language colonizes, and is appropriated in, other areas of language use (Fairclough, 2003: 32–3). One example is the redefinition of citizens as consumers, with some councils now explicitly offering 'customer services', striving for 'customer satisfaction' and having drawn up 'customer charters' (Koller, 2008). Furthermore, many social fields, and the language use found in them, have become increasingly promotional. This is indicated by all the typical features of advertising, such as persuasive rhetoric, explicit positive evaluation and direct address, which reconstruct consumers as the close friends of product and service providers. This trend recasts many genres that used to be mostly informative as hybrid genres that now combine information and self-promotion. Evidence of this trend can, for example, be found in companies' annual reports to shareholders, where the writers react to the increased pressure that comes with shareholder value by including promotional features such as persuasive narratives (Jameson, 2000) or positive description and evaluation (Bhatia, 2004: 81–4).

ADVANCES BOX 36.2

Outlook

It is clear that research interests in business communication are as broad and multi-faceted as the field they investigate. If I were to hazard a guess about the future direction of the field, I would say that studies on diversity in organizations are here to stay. In terms of language studies, these can address the use of different languages in global corporations, efficient communication in organizations with flat hierarchies and self-managed teams, and the impact that employees' different cultural backgrounds have on business communication.

---

cultures (Poncini, 2004) and of different genders (Martín-Rojo and Gómes-Esteban, 2003). A final research interest into spoken internal business communication is narratives, that is, stories and their function in institutional contexts (Czarniawska and Gagliardi, 2003; Hopkinson, 2003).

Research has also been conducted on written genres of internal business communication (Bargiela-Chiappini and Nickerson, 1999). Again, crucial foci are gender (Kessapidou and Makri-Tsilipakou, 2001), intercultural written communication (Zhu, 2005; Garzone and Ilie, 2007), as well as the impact that new technologies have made on communicative practices within organizations (Ducheneaut, 2002; Gimenez, 2002) (see Chapter 28). The persistent focus on culture and gender bears witness to the growing importance of diversity management in companies nowadays.

It is not always clear where internal communication within companies ends and communication between the company and the outside world begins. Van de Mieroop's (2005) study on how managers construct and communicate their companies' corporate identity is a case in point. The speech situations she investigated were seminars involving academic and corporate experts, but not the general public, that is, representatives of different companies were talking to each other, taking communication beyond the internal sphere, but not making it public. Also, genres such as mission statements have multiple internal and external audiences (employees, shareholders, customers), leading to shifts in **address** and **reference** (see Section 36.4). Research into some text types of outwardly directed communication includes studies of spoken genres such as call centre interaction (Cameron, 2000) and other service encounters (Ventola, 2005). Externally oriented specimens of written business communication are press releases (Jacobs, 1999: ch. 7) as well as company profiles and mission statements (Swales and Rogers, 1995; Gurau and McLaren, 2003; Isaksson, 2005; see also Section 36.4).

36.3 How to do research into business communication

36.3.1 Collecting business communication data

Depending on the topic of the study, data collection can be the greatest obstacle to researching business communication. There are usually few problems for the researcher who wants to look at how a company presents itself in the public sphere, because companies put many texts, such as their company history and financial results, online. However, the data that shows the organization at work, that is, informal conversations, internal emails and meetings, are often inaccessible due to reasons of confidentiality. Corporate decision-makers are extremely wary of sensitive information such as the development of a new product, the relaunch of a brand or a new strategy for increased productivity being disclosed, which would put them at a disadvantage vis-à-vis their competitors. Even if all details are omitted and all participants of a study are made anonymous, researchers into internal corporate communication still report often high levels of distrust. Undoubtedly, it helps to know a decision-maker in the company, but in any case, management will have to be persuaded that the 'intrusion' of a researcher ultimately serves a corporate interest, for example, by optimizing decision-making processes or reducing conflict and misunderstandings. (Even then, anecdotal evidence suggests that some managers try to dictate to the researcher what the findings of their study will have to be!) The advice resulting from the investigation may never, or only partially, be implemented, but in order to gain access to internal data in the first place, it will be necessary to persuade the decision-makers in the company that the research represents a potential benefit rather than a threat. The research question and subsequent decision of whether to look at publicly available or at internal data also influences to some extent the methods used to analyse the data, once this has been collected.

36.3.2   Methods in researching business communication

Research into business communication research utilizes a variety of methods and in essence, every project, whether large or small, requires its own set of methods for data analysis, in line with the problem or question that the analyst is interested in answering. In this section, I will restrict myself to two basic approaches, namely **conversation analysis** and the ethnography of communication (see Chapter 29) on the one hand and **corpus linguistics** on the other (see Chapter 34, Section 34.5, for a demonstration of this methodology). These two basic approaches are predominantly used to look at spoken and written data respectively, and represent two basic ways of doing linguistic research in general. Conversation analysis, especially when drawing on ethnography (literally 'description of the people'), starts out from a particular speech community, such as a project team in a company, and describes the social relations and identities within that community. Only then do ethnographers of communication go on to describe the (spoken) texts by means of which members of the community interact, and explain how those texts reproduce or challenge the relations in that community. For example, as a first step, an ethnographic researcher might investigate communication in a project team by identifying what the background of the people in the team is, who is more or less powerful and what personal histories influence communication within the team. Our hypothetical researcher would then use a number of tools from conversation analysis to describe what they observe in the spoken interaction in team meetings, such as turn-taking (i.e., the sequence of utterances, including interruptions and silences), speech acts (e.g., looking at who tends to issue commands, how question–answer pairs are organized between speakers and if stories are told by one person or collaboratively) and topic management (i.e., who introduces or elicits their own or other people's topics and concerns). Description would then be followed by explanation in light of what the researcher knows about the speech community; for example, one finding could be that people from different departments within the company are competitive towards each other, using specific technical jargon to exclude others. A relatively powerful person may tend to use direct speech acts to voice requests, while other members of the team tend to formulate questions to ask for something. Finally, the personal histories of and between team members can surface in more or less collaborative speech behaviour such as eliciting others' topics, co-telling a story or alluding to shared knowledge and experience.

Corpus linguistics on the other hand is a computer-assisted method of analysing large databases of language, and as such generally starts with (mostly written) text. (For the application of this method in business communication research, see Bargiela-Chiappini, Nickerson and Planken 2007: 87–109.) Specific software packages such as Wordsmith Tools or AntConc can analyse text collections of up to several million words for phrases and words that are significantly over- or underused in comparison to another corpus (key words), for statistically significant co-occurrences of words (**collocations**), for the use of different word classes and for a range of **statistical features** such as average sentence length or the variety of words used in a text or text collections. Other programs, such as Wmatrix,[1] investigate not only the word and sentence patterns in a corpus but also the concepts that writers (and speakers) express in the text, by allocating a so-called semantic domain to each word and then again analysing which concepts are over- or underused in comparison with another corpus. Such a large-scale analysis allows for the description of different genres in business communication, by detailing, for example, the linguistic features of mission statements as compared to annual reports. Because the researcher building the corpus can include information on the text producers, corpus linguistic investigations can also be linked back to the people behind the text, for example, by looking at specific features in business texts of the same genre as written by people in junior or senior positions. To complement the **quantitative method** that is corpus linguistics, a **qualitative method** to analyse written business texts will be presented in the case study in Section 36.4.

36.3.3 Commercial applications of business communication research

Given the general trend in the 'Western' world away from manufacturing things to building and managing brands, it is obvious that communication plays an ever more important role. Indeed, branding has arguably become one of the main areas of activity not only for large multinationals, but also for small and medium-sized enterprises wishing to move their products and services in saturated markets, where people already have everything they need.

ILLUSTRATION BOX 36.1

Negotiating refusals and achieving compliance at work

Context: Senior manager (Ros) and policy analyst (Bea) in a government department discussing strategies for dealing with a problem.

1	Ros:	Is there anyone else we can talk to?
2	Bea:	Tim Halligan
3	Ros:	Talk to him couldn't we couldn't you?
4	Bea:	[laughs] oh: I suppose
5	Ros:	I thought we had an okay relationship with-
6	Bea:	I've been fairly grumpy about stuff
7	Ros:	About this study oh some of their criticisms of our our work
8	Bea:	Oh no I've really been [laughs] criticizing an article of theirs [laughs]
9	Ros:	Of theirs well they were quite critical of ours remember their review their external review was a bit-
10	Bea:	ah: yeah but that was because he thought it was too narrow
11	Ros:	yeah
12	Bea:	and I we renamed it so that it wasn't you know
13	Ros:	It was more reflective of what it was about
14	Bea:	we were at- yeah mm
15	Ros:	Well we haven't received any criticisms of ours that it's not analytically sound
16	Bea:	No
17	Ros:	So okay
18	Bea:	Rightio I'll ring him then

(adapted from Holmes, 2006: 158–9; reproduced with permission)

In the above data extract, the senior manager makes a request to an employee (*talk to him*), which is rendered less direct, i.e., more polite, by the addition of the negated modal verb in the tag question (*couldn't we couldn't you*). Despite this cushioning, Ros switches the personal pronoun from *we* to *you* to make clear who is supposed to make the call. Bea shows reluctance by drawing out her response (*oh:*) and not directly saying that she will follow the request. This can be read as an indirect refusal, and indeed her manager understands it thus, enquiring if there are problems between departments (5). Bea interrupts her to explain the cause for her reluctance. Although giving reasons is a politeness strategy, the interruption is not, and Bea interrupts Ros again later (10). Bea goes on to explain the perceived problem with the person she has been asked to contact ((10)–(14)), and her manager, despite having been interrupted twice, shows a collaborative communication style through minimal responses (*yeah*) and supporting explanations (13). Bea's explanation finally peters out when she self-interrupts and closes her turn on an undecided note (*we were at w- yeah mm*). This continued reluctance despite having no legitimate reasons to refuse then prompts Ros to make a decisive statement (15), introduced by *well* to signal a shift away from her employee's reasoning. The senior manager's statement implicitly dismisses Bea's concerns, and Bea's monosyllabic admittance that there are actually no serious problems between her and the other person (16) gives Ros the possibility to implicitly repeat her request (*so okay*). This time, Bea complies (18).

The excerpt represents one strategy of dealing with an employee's refusal and ensuring their compliance. The manager here uses a mixture of polite indirectness (negated tag questions, modal verbs, implicit requests), support (minimal responses, supportive statements) and, despite interruptions from the employee, ultimate control over turn-taking (direct address, shifting topics) to have her request met. In corporate communications consulting for senior managers, this excerpt could therefore be used as an example of a successful strategy to achieve compliance without bullying.

Branding is thus no longer restricted to advertising, but pervades all sorts of corporate communication, from sponsoring and investor relations to supply chain management and customer services. Linguists and other business communication experts have a vital role to play in helping companies communicate their brands through various channels. To quote but one example, Delin (2005) has looked at the layout and tone of voice used in bills issued by British telephone and utilities companies. Going beyond description and explanation alone, she has complemented her analysis by suggesting ways to extend branding to less obvious instances of corporate communication. Thus the layout and wording of bills can be used to communicate particular brand values and address particular target groups of a certain age or social background. As a positive side-effect, changing instances of corporate communication such as bills also made them easier to read and was thus empowering for the customer.

However, it is not only in the area of branding that linguists can act as consultants. Communication pervades all areas of organizations; we could even say that companies are brought into being mainly through people communicating. As a downside, miscommunication, misunderstanding and inefficient communication can have negative impacts on employee motivation and, ultimately, productivity. Consultancy with regard to crisis, conflict and change communication is thus increasingly sought after by corporate decision-makers. Illustration Box 36.1 presents a brief 'good practice' example that could be drawn upon when training employees and managers with regard to their communicative behaviour.

36.4 Case study: Porsche

In this final section, I will provide a brief sample analysis of a corporate mission statement to introduce one way of qualitatively analysing written business discourse. My starting point in doing so is the question of how a particular company presents itself in the public sphere and what this self-presentation tells us about the relations between the company and its stakeholders and, in more general terms, about the role of companies in 'Western' countries. The three related questions – about the text, the relations between writers and readers, and the wider socio-economic context – place this case study in the area of **critical discourse analysis** (CDA) (see Fairclough, 2003, and Chapters 30 and 35). It is important to note that CDA is not a method by which to analyse texts. Rather, it is an approach that researchers take when they analyse texts to explain and raise awareness about social problems. What methods the researcher then chooses to analyse the text with very much depends on the text itself as well as the specific question and will therefore vary from one study to the next. The following sample analysis will proceed along the parameters of actors and processes, modality, evaluation and metaphor.

The text in question, automobile manufacturer Porsche's 'philosophy', represents a hybrid genre that blurs the boundaries between mission statement (the reason why the company exists), value statement (its guiding principles) and brand proposition (the cluster of mental associations that are communicated about the company). Published on the corporate website in 2005,[2] the text is a translation from the German original. It can be divided into three parts: The first addresses an implicit audience of customers in outlining the company's history and values, while the second part is directed at investors in pointing out the advantages of an independent small company and thereby implicitly fending off a potential takeover. The closing lines return the focus onto the customers.

The most prominent actor is represented by the first-person plural pronoun, *we*, which can in our text be linked to *Porsche* and *our company*. As collectives, these referents are rather unspecified, and it does not become clear which group in the company is actually the author's voice in the text. The prominent but vague use of *we* is a common feature of most corporate mission statements. In the Porsche text, the *we* is set in contrast to *other manufacturers* and *other companies*, which are epitomized in two references to *David against Goliath*. This opposition potentially serves both audiences in that it makes customers feel special as drivers of an exclusive brand. Moreover, it persuades investors that the company can go it alone and they should therefore refuse any offers from larger companies to sell their shares.

The collective actors *Porsche/our company/we* is not only the most frequent one in the text, it also features in an exclusively active role. Figure 36.2 shows the percentages of how often various actors occur.

The dominance of *Porsche/our company/we* also shows in the fact that, as an actor, it engages in the widest range of different processes and is therefore not only quantitatively most frequent but also qualitatively most differentiated, as shown in Figure 36.3.

Without going into detail here about process types (see Thompson, 1996), it is interesting to note that Porsche also features in mental-affective processes, that is, it is depicted as having thoughts and feelings (e.g., *our company thinks and plans, Porsche relishes its role*). The brand is thus given a very prominent role in the text, up to the point where it is personified and therefore made more tangible for the reader.

Use of **modality** is again typical of genres that fall under the umbrella term 'corporate mission statements', in that we find high-affinity deontic and epistemic modality, that is, high degrees of both obligation and likelihood being associated with the central actor. Examples of deontic modality include

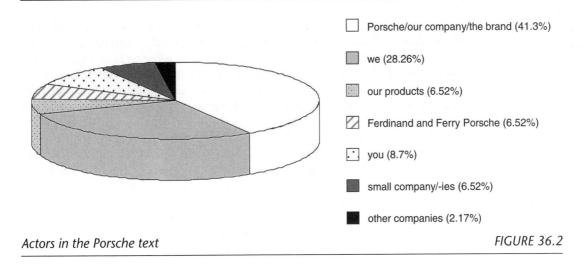

Actors in the Porsche text

FIGURE 36.2

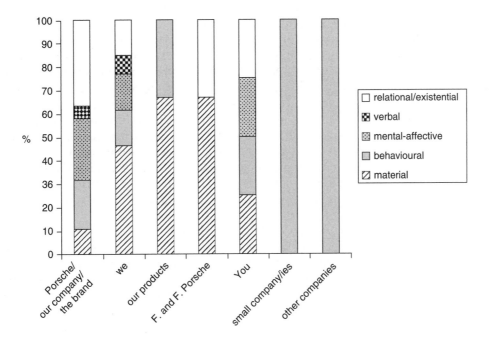

Actors and processes in the Porsche text

FIGURE 36.3

Porsche must grow and *Porsche and its staff must live up to [the company's heritage]*, the latter being reinforced by the adverbial *every day*. Such strong obligation is balanced by equally high degrees of likelihood, which communicate not only the company's ambitious goals, but also the confidence that it will reach those goals (e.g., we *will adhere to [this claim] in the future*). This confident stance is mitigated in the second part of the text, where adverbially modified phrases such as '*[e]ven apparently small companies*', '*[i]t is not generally wrong*' and '*[s]o far nobody has proven*' serve to refute the conventional wisdom that independent companies will struggle to survive.

Evaluation can be subdivided into the affect (i.e., emotional response) of typically human actors, the judgment of, again, typically human actors, and the appreciation of typically non-human entities (Martin and White, 2005). In the Porsche text, affect is linked to a collectivized feeling actor (*Porsche relishes*) and is also expressed in nouns such as *emotion, delight* and *fascination*. The customer as the implicit audience of the final part of the text is referred to in *you [can] feel the power that is unique to Porsche*. Unsurprisingly in a promotional genre, affect is exclusively positive, as indeed is judgement (e.g., *we possess the necessary decisiveness* or *the power that is unique to Porsche*). It should be noted that judgement is here passed on a non-human, even abstract actor. Appreciation, which we would normally expect to be used for non-human actors, hardly features at all, the only instance being the neutral *it is also a sports car*. It seems that the features of the tangible product have become less important than the intangible brand, which has in turn taken on features of a sentient human actor.

This is also reflected in a LIVING ORGANISM metaphor that sees Porsche embroiled in an evolutionary struggle to *survive*. The metaphor is elaborated when Porsche is said to be *ready to pounce*, which may also be a passing shot at competitor Jaguar. Metaphors of LIVING ORGANISM and EVOLUTIONARY STRUGGLE are typical features of the language used to report on mergers and acquisitions (Koller, 2004: 114–71) and it is therefore no surprise to find them in the second part of the text, which implicitly addresses investors. Elsewhere, the text is dominated by a JOURNEY metaphor, which is likely to be triggered by the topic of cars and driving (e.g., *driving the future*). As such, it is elaborated (*our route, path, new direction* and *turn around*) and even extended to related domains (*our guiding light*) and so lends coherence to the text.

To sum up, the writers of the text present Porsche as a quasi-human being that can think, feel and be judged like a person. This being is put under a strong obligation to be successful but is also endowed with the confidence to meet that goal. The concept of the company as a living, possibly human, being also shows in the use of metaphors that depict Porsche as involved in an evolutionary struggle for survival and growth. It is the company as a quasi-human being that facilitates the relations between the writers of the text and its readers. Indeed, Porsche as a being is very much in the foreground both quantitatively and qualitatively, while the writers of the text stay undefined and vague, hiding behind the ambiguous corporate *we*. The writers use the text to address two key stakeholder groups, customers and shareholders. These two groups are central as it is in their power to spend or invest their money on or in the company, ensuring its metaphorical survival, or to withhold it. They are therefore flattered and persuaded, at the expense of other stakeholders such as employees or suppliers. Still, even central stakeholders are only positioned in relation to that mysterious being, Porsche, not

to actual human executives. Both the reluctance of senior executives to identify themselves, and the focus on some stakeholders at the expense of others, can be seen as typical of contemporary capitalism: Corporations seem
to have taken on a life of their own – in fact, they *are* legal persons – while
actual decision-makers avoid personal responsibility. Likewise, in a culture
of American-style shareholder values, the interests of shareholders are often
prioritized over employee satisfaction or wider social, political and environmental concerns.

Recommended readings

A good book for novices in the field of business communication is Bargiela,
Nickerson and Planken's (2007) volume, simply titled *Business Discourse*.
Rather than presenting a research study in its own right, the authors provide a detailed overview of interests and methods in business communication
research, as well as its applications in teaching and consulting. The book
includes brief presentations of seminal studies and portraits of influential
researchers in the field. It also provides a list of resources ranging from the
titles of journals and contact details for professional organizations to conferences, corpora and degree courses. For those who would like to learn
more, Bargiela-Chiappini's (2009) edited volume *The Handbook of Business
Discourse* combines a number of original contributions that outline the state
of the art in business discourse research, provide overviews of methodological
approaches and disciplines that business communication research draws on,
as well as taking a closer look at business discourse in various parts of the
world, especially Europe and Asia.

For anyone interested in analysing spoken business communication –
meetings, phone conversations, etc. – the seminal volume on *Talk at Work* by
Drew and Heritage (1992) is still highly relevant, while the more theoretically inclined reader will find a wealth of original research in the latest edition
of *The Sage Handbook of Organisational Discourse* (Grant et al., 2004). It
was pointed out above that intercultural business communication and the
role that gender plays in professional discourse continue to attract a lot of
research interest. As for the former, Bargiela-Chiappini and Harris's (1997)
edited volume on *The Languages of Business* presents research studies from a
host of intercultural business settings, while Holmes's (2006) and Mullany's
(2007) works on *Gendered Talk at Work* and *Gendered Discourse in the
Professional Workplace*, respectively, represent recent contributions to the
field of gender and business discourse.

Some readers may be surprised to have found nothing on advertising in
this chapter. Although advertising is of course a form of external business
communication, it has received so much attention from scholars in linguistics, marketing, psychology, semiotics, sociology and other areas, that it can
be seen as a topic in its own right – hence it is treated in a separate chapter of
this volume. I have therefore deliberately focused on other forms of business
communication. Chapter 25 and Myers's (1994, 1998) and Cook's (2001)
works provide a good introduction to research into advertising from a linguistic point of view.

Finally, in a chapter on business communication, I may perhaps be permitted a little self-marketing and mention that the volume *Handbook of Communication in the Public Sphere*, edited by Wodak and Koller (2008), also includes five chapters dedicated to business communication.

Notes

1 See http://ucrel.lancs.ac.uk/wmatrix/
2 The text has since been changed, see: http://www.porsche.com/uk/aboutporsche/porschephilosophy/ (accessed 25 September 2008) for the current version.

PART 6

English: Learning and Teaching

EDITED BY TONY MCENERY

CHAPTER 37

Language Acquisition

ANDREW HARDIE

37.1 Language learning versus language acquisition

Learning a first language is unlike most other forms of learning. One obvious reason for this is that a lot of the learning we do – for instance at school – is done via the medium of language. Obviously, language itself cannot be learned in this way. So, for a long time there has been a sense that language learning requires, in some respects, a special explanation. In particular, since often there is no conscious effort on the part of parents and caregivers to teach children language – and where there is such an effort, there is little evidence that it has much effect – the term **language acquisition** is often preferred to **language learning**, when discussing a child's first language. There have been many different accounts for language acquisition; much of the difference between them relates to one key question. Is language acquisition primarily due to innate abilities possessed by human beings, or is it more a result of learning from the environment? In (over-)simplified terms, is language acquisition a process of 'nature' or 'nurture'? In this chapter, we will take a general overview of the process of language acquisition, and then go on to consider two examples of theories for language acquisition. The student of the English language is particularly fortunate in that the vast majority of research into language acquisition has been done on English-speaking children. For this reason, although the discussion below covers many points that are relevant to the acquisition of any language, the particular details of this chapter all relate to English.

37.2 Checkpoints in language learning

In this section, we will look at an overview of some of the major transitions that take place as a child learns English, covering between them the most important developments in the course of language learning. They include the transition from natural, 'biological' sounds to phonetic sounds, the transition from non-meaningful vocalization to words with meaning, and the transition from single words to grammatical structure.

37.2.1 From sounds to speech sounds

The earliest sounds that children produce are non-linguistic in nature. Crying is present from birth, stimulated by physical or psychological discomfort or distress. A baby may cry for a variety of reasons – when it is hungry, in pain, angry, or when it desires attention from a caregiver. There are other very early sounds that children make, such as burping, swallowing and sneezing. A child has little or no conscious control over the production of these sounds. By the age of two months, cooing and laughter are added to this repertoire of sounds. It is within the production of these non-linguistic sounds that we can discern the earliest consonants and vowels.

The famous Russian linguist Roman Jakobson (1941) suggested that in the earliest stage of acquiring consonants, children would produce a very wide range of consonant sounds – in fact, all the possible sounds of all the languages of the world. So, for example, Jakobson's theory suggested that a baby in an English-speaking environment might produce click consonants, or pharyngeal consonants, at the outset, even though these sounds are not found in English. However, it is very hard to support this view when we look at children's actual production. The raw fact seems to be that children don't produce as wide a variety of sounds as Jakobson suggested they would. In fact, it is probable that they **cannot**: the vocal tracts of very young babies are shaped more like those of non-human apes than those of adult humans.

For this reason the earliest consonant sounds are most likely to be velar or glottal consonants (such as [h], [w], [k] or [g]). However, although these consonants are **produced** first, children may not be able to **make distinctions** among these consonants – that is, use them to indicate differences between words – at the earliest stages. The consonant distinctions that children find easiest to make are those among the front oral plosives such as [p], [b], [t] and [d], and nasals such as [n] and [m]. Other consonant distinctions appear to be more difficult and may be learnt later. The last distinctions to be learnt are usually distinctions between fricatives (e.g., [s] versus [ʃ] or [f] versus [θ]) and those involving affricates ([tʃ] and [dʒ]) and the 'liquid' sounds [ɹ] and [l]. Indeed, children can continue to have problems with some of these consonants long after they have otherwise finished learning the language, up to the age of ten or so in some cases. The sounds that children have difficulty distinguishing in their production seem to be those that require the finest control of the vocal tract.

It is harder to investigate the order in which vowels are learnt, for several reasons. Firstly, vowels are acquired within a much shorter period of time. While it can take until the age of five or six before all the consonants of English are mastered, vowels are typically mastered much earlier, by about age three. Secondly, vowels are in any case much less discrete than consonants: while consonants are clearly distinguishable in terms of place of articulation and manner of articulation, vowels exist on a continuum. So studying the distinctions that the child makes at any given point is much harder for this reason. However, some work has been done to investigate what distinctions among vowels the child gets control over first. For example, Jakobsen suggested that the first vowel contrasts are between low front [a] and high front [i].

37.2.2   From pre-words to words

Babbling

When speech sounds are first connected together into larger phonetic units, it takes the form of **babbling** (also known as 'vocal play'). Babbling is the production of repeating strings of alternating consonants and vowels, such as [bababa] or [gəgəgə], and occurs in children from around the third or fourth month of life. Even deaf children have been found to babble – this aspect of language acquisition, at least, is clearly an innate part of development. Babbling arises as children get greater control over their vocal tract. It also seems that children enjoy this form of vocal play! At first, babbling tends to involve glottal, velar and labial consonants, but later the sounds [b], [d], [m] and [n] will become more important. This fits with the general picture of the development of consonants. The main difference between babbling and speech is that babbling is not meaningful. Children are not intending to communicate when they babble, and in particular they are not using the strings of speech sounds as communicative symbols that have meaning to others. That is not to say that adults do not sometimes attribute meaning to the babble that a child produces. In some cases a child's 'first words' may actually be babble that has been interpreted as meaningful by a caregiver, for example, such words as *Dada*, *Mama* or *Baba*.

Vocal gestures

So how does the child move from this type of pre-word phonetic string to the use of meaningful words? A number of researchers have suggested that there is a 'halfway' point in this transition. At this stage, the child becomes capable of using precursors to words – phonetic units which are more stable in form than babbling, and which seem to have some kind of meaning. The meaning is, however, rather vague. Rather than them having a specific reference, we tend to observe children using these phonetic units consistently in the context of performing a particular action. They are more like a gesture than a word. So we could describe these precursors as 'vocal gestures', although different researchers have used a range of terminology to describe them. For instance, Dore and colleagues (1976) describe these units as **phonetically consistent forms**, whereas Halliday (1975) describes the same things as **proto-words**. The meaning of a vocal gesture is restricted to the context in which it is used. When a vocalization takes on a meaning that is independent of its context, we can actually begin to class them as linguistic symbols – early words.

First words

Once a child is capable of using words with meaning – although they may still not pronounce them precisely in an adult manner – they will start learning words for things in their immediate environment. In fact, most of a child's very early vocabulary will be made up of terms for things they are likely to encounter in their everyday lives. So words for people, body-parts (especially those associated with the face), food, clothing, pets, toys and household items are all prominent in the first couple of hundred words that a child learns. As we will see below, these earliest words do tend overwhelmingly to be content words, not grammatical words – grammatical words emerge later. It has been claimed that nouns especially are very prominent in the early vocabulary, with verbs being somewhat less frequent. The nouns in question are almost always concrete rather than abstract nouns.

37.2.3 From words to sentences

When children produce their first words, at around the age of nine months to a year, they initially produce these words one at a time. Over time, they begin to put words together to produce longer utterances; at this point, we begin to see evidence that they are using basic (but increasingly complex) morphology and syntax.

The notion of holophrase

The earliest utterances consist of a single word. These utterances are some-times called **holophrases**, a term which means 'whole sentence'. This raises the question of the degree to which the child possesses the concept of the sentence. One view of holophrase utterances is that they are partial represen-tations of adult sentences – sentences with all but one of the words 'missed out'. This implies that the structure of a sentence is understood by the child, but left unspoken, due to the child's limited abilities. For example, if the child says *Clock*, what they really have in mind is something like *There's a clock!* or *Where's the clock?*, but they are only able to produce the most important word. It is difficult to support this view. Of course, adults frequently produce one-word utterances that can be interpreted as abbreviations of full sentences – but with an adult speaker, we have good evidence that they are capable of producing the full sentence if they wish. We don't have such evidence for child speakers. So on balance, it is better to see grammatical development as a process which builds up complicated structures from the initial one-word utterances, rather than as a process of gradually leaving out fewer words from a sentence structure which the child has in mind from the start.

Two-word utterances

Somewhere around 18 months old, children move on to what is sometimes called the **two-word stage** of grammatical development. This is not an over-night change. Firstly, children of course do not cease to produce single-word utterances when they acquire the ability to produce longer utterances. Even adult language contains many one-word sentences! Secondly, because there is a grey area in telling the difference between two one-word utterances pro-duced in quick succession, and an actual two-word utterance, there cannot be a sharp division between the stages. This **juxtaposition** of separate utter-ances may in fact be an important intermediate step.

The two-word stage has been of great interest to many researchers because it is only with multi-word utterances that there is scope to investigate the early emergence of syntax. However, it has proven very difficult to provide a single characterization for all the utterances produced at the two-word stage. Different theories have been proposed. For example, Brown and Fraser (1964) suggested that early multi-word utterances are basically **telegraphic** – adult utterances with grammatical words like *of*, *and* or *the* missed out. This explains utterances like *Sweater chair*, *Mommy sock* or *Baby table*, but not the many two-word utterances that *do* contain grammatical words, such as *No down*, *She here*, *There high* or *More noise*. The alternative theory of 'pivot grammar', proposed by Braine (1963) and McNeill (1966), hypothesizes that children have two classes of words: pivot words and open words. Pivot words are restricted to one position in the utterance – first or second – and cannot occur alone. Instead, they occur with open words, which can occur in either position, or alone. So a child might produce a set of utterances such as *More milk*, *More juice*, *More read* and *More teddy*, where each utterance 'pivots' around the fixed first word *more*. A comparable set with a second-place pivot might be *Juice gone*, *All gone*, *Daddy gone*. But again, this theory does not account for all the utterances produced by children in the two-word stage (you might be able to see why utterances like *Outside more* and *No more*[1] are problematic for this approach). There is also the problem that it is not clear how a child would transition from using a pivot grammar to using adult grammar. So the theory of pivot grammar is not ultimately satisfying as an explanation for usage by young children. However, a recent account by Tomasello (2003: 114–17) of early utterances based upon *pivot schemas* seems promising as an explanation for children's utterances at this stage. Tomasello's account is important as it preserves the insights of the pivot grammar approach, without the difficulty of a strict separation between pivots and open-class words. Tomasello's ideas on language acquisition are discussed further in Advances Box 37.1 below.

Grammatical morphemes

After the two-word stage, longer and longer utterances are produced by children. However, there is not just an increase in length – there is also an increase in grammatical complexity, as grammatical morphemes (including inflectional affixes and closed-class grammatical words) begin to occur in children's utterances. Brown (1973) investigated the order in which the grammatical morphemes were acquired in different children. He found that the order was fairly consistent in all three children that he looked at; the average order of acquisition that Brown reports is given in Table 37.1.

The reason that the grammatical morphemes appear in children's speech in that particular order seems to be related to complexity. Some morphemes are more complex than others because they represent, in cognitive terms, more difficult ideas. For instance, the shades of meaning represented by the past tense morpheme or a definite article are cognitively more complex than the straightforward locational meanings indicated by the prepositions *in* and *on*. Arguments of this sort can be made to explain many of the relative orderings that Brown observed. So the easiest morphemes are acquired first. By contrast, the frequency of the different morphemes in the child's input does not seem to have much effect on the order of acquisition: more frequent morphemes are not acquired earlier.

Table 37.1   *Order of acquisition of 14 grammatical morphemes (adapted from Brown 1973: 274)*

	Type of grammatical morpheme
1	present progressive (*–ing*)
=2	the preposition *in*
=2	the preposition *on*
4	plural inflection (*–s, –es*)
5	irregular past tense verbs
6	possessive *'s*
7	uncontractible copula (*is, am* and *are*)
8	articles (*the, a* and *an*)
9	regular past tense verbs (*–ed*)
10	regular third person forms (*–s, –es*)
11	irregular third person forms (*has, does*)
12	uncontractible auxiliary verb *be* (*is, am* and *are*)
13	contractible copula (clitic forms like *–'s* and *–'re*)
14	contractible auxiliary verb *be* (clitic forms like *–'s* and *–'re*)

Questions and negatives

There are numerous types of questions (interrogatives) in English. The simplest type, which is the earliest to develop in children, consists solely of using a declarative sentence with a rising intonation. The other types – use of subject-auxiliary inversion and then use of *wh*-words – develop later, in stages. McNeill (1970) described the stages by which questions develop as follows. First is the use of rising intonation alone. Then, in a second stage, children begin to use *wh*-words at the beginning of an utterance to form a question such as *Where my shoes?* It is at the third stage that subject-auxiliary inversion emerges; but there might still be problems in the ordering of auxiliary verbs in *wh*-questions, with utterances such as *Where my shoes are?* instead of *Where are my shoes?* being produced. Finally, fully adult interrogatives are produced. Concerning the order of acquisition of the different *wh*-words, Tyack and Ingram (1977) found that *what* and *where* were used comparatively early on, but *why* and *how* were more likely to be used as a child grows older. This seems to be related to complexity: **things** and **places** are concrete notions and thus conceptually much simpler than abstractions such as **reasons** or **manners**.

Klima and Bellugi (1966) found that, as with interrogatives, children learn to use negatives by starting off with simple forms and gradually moving on to more complex forms. The first stage of using negatives is to place the word *not* or *no* outside of an utterance, in utterances such as *No go movies, No sit down* or *Not sleepy*. In the second stage, the child starts to include the negative inside the sentence in utterances such as *I no want book* or *I no like it*. It is also at this stage that negative auxiliary forms such as *can't* start to appear. In the final stage of development, the remaining differences between the child's usage and adult negatives disappear.

One thing which emerges from looking at the acquisition of both questions and negatives is the importance of juxtaposition as a step towards the acquisition of a complex grammatical structure. As we saw before, the very origin of multi-word utterances may be in the juxtaposition of single-word utterances. Here, we see that the juxtaposition of a question word or a negative word with an utterance is often an initial step towards the integrated interrogative and negative sentence-types.

37.3 Theories of language learning

In this section, we will look at two important theories explaining the process of language acquisition which was described in outline above.

37.3.1 Chomsky's Universal Grammar

Without question, the most broadly influential theory of language acquisition is the one originally proposed in the late 1950s by linguist Noam Chomsky. Chomsky proposes that large parts of the human language capacity are, in fact, not learned from experience but **innate**: built into the human brain from birth. This type of theory is often called a **nativist** theory.

The overturning of behaviourism

Chomsky's theory first came to wide attention when he wrote a very critical review (Chomsky, 1959) of a book supporting another theory. This was the psychologist B. F. Skinner's book *Verbal Behavior*, which presented a **behaviourist** approach to language acquisition. Behaviourism is a school of psychology which seeks to explain how animals and humans behave in terms of a small number of very basic learning mechanisms. In this approach to language acquisition, everything (not just language) is learned from exposure to the environment. The child is **conditioned** to associate a particular environmental **stimulus** – let's say, a chair – with a particular **response** – let's say, the sound [tʃeə] – by repeatedly encountering them together. A parent could **reinforce** this association by rewarding the child for producing the right response (i.e., the correct word), or punishing them for producing the wrong response. Environment-based theories such as this were widely thought, at the time, to explain language learning completely. But in his 1959 review, and subsequent works, Chomsky developed an argument that not only behaviourism, but any approach relying solely on learning from the environment, cannot account for language acquisition. For instance, in arguing against behaviourism, Chomsky pointed out that language is not produced simply as responses to predictable stimuli. When we encounter a chair, we **might** say *chair*, but we might also say *The upholstery needs cleaning, Oh, I fancy a nice sit down, It doesn't go with the décor of this room*, or any number of other things, and this is not predictable in the way that behaviourist stimulus–response links are. This is a major flaw in Skinner's account. Chomsky's proposed alternative to a behaviourist approach is that important components of language are **not** learned from the environment but rather are innate.

Evidence for innate grammar

The elements of language that Chomsky believes simply cannot be learned are, primarily, the abstract rules of grammar that underlie sentence structure. Chomsky proposes that there exists, within the mind, a module devoted specifically to grammar, which contains the core elements of human syntax. It is this module, which Chomsky calls **Universal Grammar** or UG, which allows a child to learn grammatical structures which would be impossible to learn just by the behaviourist learning mechanisms of association, conditioning and imitation. What evidence is there for the existence of UG? Chomsky is a syntactician, and Chomsky's theory of language acquisition is the same theory as his theory of syntax: that is, his proposal that there is an innate UG is mostly based on his analysis of the grammar of adult language, and likewise the innate UG explains why adult syntax is the way it is. So, much of Chomsky's evidence for UG is drawn from analyses of syntax, rather than the study of children's language use. See Illustration Box 37.1 for a detailed explanation of the **Argument from Poverty of the Stimulus**, one of the most important arguments for the idea that grammar cannot be learned from the environment; another syntax-based argument is the idea that certain aspects of syntax are universal, found in every language, and this cannot be explained unless those aspects of syntax are innate. However, other researchers have supplied other lines of evidence. For example, Bickerton's research on the creation of creoles from pidgins has been used as evidence for a UG. When the children of speakers of a pidgin language – which is not a 'proper', grammatical language – expand it into a creole, they do it by adding grammar to the vocabulary of the pidgin. Since they could not have learnt that grammar from their parents' pidgin – which doesn't have a grammar – they must have got the grammar from their UG (pidgins and creoles are explored further in Chapter 21). Pinker (1994) has also presented evidence for UG. For example, Pinker points out that there are developmental disorders, including some known to be genetic, that affect linguistic development but not non-linguistic cognition (e.g., non-verbal IQ); there are also disorders that impede general cognition without affecting language use. This suggests that language is a distinct system within the brain, controlled by distinct genes in the human DNA code.

UG and the acquisition process

As we noted, for Chomsky it is grammar that is impossible to learn: the words of a language must be learned from the environment, naturally. However, not all languages have exactly the same grammar. So there must be some environmental effects on grammar as well. To explain this, Chomsky proposes that the linguistic knowledge contained in the UG is split into principles and parameters. **Principles** are the universal elements that are the same in all languages; **parameters** are like 'switches' which can be set to either on or off. The grammar of any given language depends on the interaction of its parameter settings with the principles. When a child is acquiring language, they absorb example sentences from the speech around them. This **primary linguistic data** is then processed by the UG module in the mind: it is used to

ILLUSTRATION BOX 37.1

How poor is the stimulus?

One of the most important arguments for an innate UG is that the grammars of actual adult languages **cannot** be learned. One aspect of grammar that Chomsky has claimed cannot be learned is structure dependency. This is the idea that all syntactic rules are based on the structure of the sentence, not just on the order of the words. Chomsky has often exemplified this with English question formation. In English questions, the auxiliary verb is moved to the beginning of the clause. Compare the declarative sentence in [37.1], and the corresponding interrogative in [37.2]: you will see that the auxiliary *is* has moved from its original position, indicated by ___:

[37.1]   This man is insane.
[37.2]   Is this man ___ insane?

However, a declarative sentence might contain a subordinate clause, as in example [37.3], where [square brackets] indicate the subordinate clause. In this case, it is always the auxiliary verb of the main clause that is moved, not the auxiliary verb of the subordinate clause. So [37.4] is a grammatical sentence of English, but [37.5] is not:

[37.3]   The man [who is insane] is smiling.
[37.4]   Is the man [who is insane] ___ smiling?
[37.5]   *Is the man [who ___ insane] is smiling?

This is an example of **structure dependency**, because knowing which auxiliary verb should be moved requires an awareness of the syntactic structure of the sentence – which bits are the main clause, which parts are the subordinate clause, and so on. Chomsky argues that children learning English have no way of learning that the formation of questions is structure-dependent in this way, because the examples they would need to learn it – sentences like [37.4] – are incredibly rare. Chomsky has even said that a person might go their entire life without being exposed to such examples (Piattelli-Palmorini, 1980: 40). But adult speakers of English clearly **do** know that question formation follows this structure-dependent rule. If adults know it, but children can't possibly learn it, then it follows, in Chomsky's argument, that this aspect of grammar – like many others – is innate. This, in brief, is what is called the **Argument from Poverty of the Stimulus**: at least some key aspects of language must be innate, because the **stimulus** (language input) that we have to learn it from is not sufficient to learn it (it is **impoverished**).

This argument has not gone uncriticized. In particular, Chomsky's assertion that sentences like [37.4] are incredibly rare has been scrutinized by Pullum and Scholtz (2002), who found many example sentences of exactly this type in a range of different text corpora. For example, they found the following three examples in a corpus of utterances addressed to a child between the ages of one and three:

[37.6]   Where 's the little blue crib [that was in the house before] ___ ?
[37.7]   Where 's the other dolly [that was in here] ___ ?
[37.8]   Where 's the other doll [that goes in there] ___ ?

In examples [37.6] to [37.8], the question is marked by a *wh*-word as well as by the movement of the auxiliary, but the sentences illustrate the same grammatical principle. Pullum and Scholtz cite other examples, both with and without *wh*-words, found in corpora of genres such as news text and drama. They calculate that a child could potentially hear around 7500 questions like those in [37.4], [37.6], [37.7] and [37.8] before they reach the age of three. This is obviously far more than Chomsky's argument allows for.

We might ask, does the argument from poverty of stimulus stand up in the light of evidence like this? Pullum and Scholtz's results are not unique: Sampson (2005: 77–89) has found additional corpus examples of the relevant type of sentence. The debate over this, and many other aspects of Chomsky's controversial theory, continues.

learn the words of the language, and it is used to set the UG parameters to the right settings for the grammar of the language the child is learning. The result of the UG processing the input data is an adult grammar. For Chomsky, this is the end-point of language acquisition.

37.3.2 Learning through interaction

In strong contrast to Chomsky's theory is the approach sometimes called **interactionist** or **social constructivist**. This is, in fact, a range of approaches to the study of language learning, linked by a shared emphasis on the social environment of the child – in other words, their interactions with their caregivers and others around them. One of the earliest examples of a theory of this type is that of psychologist Lev Vygotsky.

Vygotsky and social learning

Vygotsky lived and worked in the Soviet Union, and his ideas did not become widely known in the West until decades after his death in 1934. Vygotsky stresses the importance of the social environment for cognitive development, including the development of language. Vygotsky proposed the notion of the **Zone of Proximal Development (ZPD)**. This is the idea that, at any given stage in a child's development, there are some things that the child can accomplish unaided, and there are other things that they cannot accomplish at all. Between these, however, is the 'zone' of things that the child cannot accomplish alone, but can accomplish if helped by a more knowledgeable person. In terms of language, for instance, a child at the one-word stage is capable, unaided, of producing single-word utterances; they are not capable, in any way, of producing long stretches of coherent, cohesive language; but with appropriate support and assistance from an adult speaker, they can participate in a structured conversational interaction. So, for a child at this stage, such an interaction is within the ZPD. Crucially, it is by this very process of participating in interactions that they are not capable of coping with alone that a child **becomes** capable of managing such interactions on their own.

Another important aspect of Vygotsky's view of language is that it implies that aspects of a child's cognitive development – including language – initially take place not within the child's mind, but within the child's social context. Only later do they take root within the child's mind. As Vygotsky puts it, 'any function in the child's cultural development appears on the stage twice, on two planes, first on the social plane and then on the psychological' (1966: 44). In terms of language, this means that the crucial site of activity for language acquisition is not the brain of the child – as proposed by nativist theories such as Chomsky's – but rather the interaction between children and their caregivers. Language within the mind is a later phenomenon: in fact, for Vygotsky, it is the process of internalizing the originally-external language skills that gives rise to our ability to think-in-words.

The role of the caregiver

So what is special about a child's interaction with their caregiver? When we observe how adults typically interact with children in their care, we see that they often behave in such a way as to provide particular kinds of support to the child, shaping the interaction to allow the child to develop gradually as a communicative partner. As Vygotsky suggested, the interaction is usually structured at a level just slightly above what the child is currently capable of. This behaviour on the part of the adult was termed **scaffolding** by Bruner (1979). What might scaffolding consist of? Snow (1977b) observed that when children are very young, and not capable of understanding linguistic communication, adults will still tend to treat them as conversational partners. For example, mothers will very often talk to small babies who cannot understand or respond in any way. Not only this, but they will react to the babies' random movements and vocalizations as though they had communicative intent – mothers may impose a meaning on whatever noise or motion the baby has produced, and incorporate it into the 'conversation' that they are building. This is a form of scaffolding: clearly, at this stage, the mother is doing all the work. As the child learns language, however, the mother has to do less and less scaffolding work – for example, the child's vocalizations come to have intended meaning, so the mother no longer has to impose a meaning.

One important way in which an interaction may be scaffolded involves repetitive or ritualized routines, where sets of events tend to occur in a particular order, such as feeding the child, going to bed, reading a favourite book, and especially games like give-and-take or peekaboo. Because these interactions may be repeated dozens or hundreds of times in a child's early life, the child has the opportunity to learn what happens in these routines by heart. The adult can run these routines in such a way that all the child has to do to participate is produce the appropriate conventional response at the appropriate time. These routines, then, provide a good context for the child to come to understand the way in which interaction works, and observe the relationships between sounds, meanings and actions. This is all made possible by the adult's scaffolding behaviour.

CDS: English for the child

We might also describe as scaffolding, adults' habit of using a special, simplified register when communicating with children. This register is often called **child-directed speech** (CDS) or, more colloquially, **motherese**. What are its

---

ADVANCES BOX 37.1

Tomasello's theory

There is no space here to give a full overview of the different theories of language acquisition that have been suggested over the past half-century. However, new approaches continue to be developed, and existing ideas refined. An example of a recent theoretical proposal is the theory put forward by Tomasello (2003). The key feature of Tomasello's theory is that, like Chomsky's, it relates language acquisition to a general theory of language. But Tomasello uses a very different theory of language, and as a result ends up with a very different view of language acquisition – one that draws on a lot of psychological research into how young children learn.

Tomasello's approach is linked to the linguistic theory of **Construction Grammar**. This is an approach to grammar that argues that grammar consists of a learned collection of **constructions**, which are meaningful units of grammatical patterns that can be combined with each other and with words to build utterances. Tomasello argues that these patterns can be learned from the language that a child observes by a gradual process of abstraction from concrete patterns. First, the child learns to work out what adults mean when they talk to the child, and uses this skill (called 'intention reading') to learn the meanings of utterances they hear. The patterns of grammar are secondary to meaning, and emerge slowly from examples of meaningful utterances they have heard and produced. For instance, the combination of a subject with a verb is learnt initially from concrete examples of utterances containing a subject and verb which the child hears and imitates.

At this stage, the child doesn't know that there is any such thing as a 'subject' or a 'verb' – it is all just words. However, the child will notice that different words can come before the verb, and will come to understand that the verb has a slot in front of it, into which a whole range of words can be inserted. Given time, they will come to possess a range of these 'word-plus-slot' structures, each with a different verb at the core of it. Then, by a process of **analogy**, these structures are grouped together as instances of the same abstract 'verb-plus-subject' structure. At the same time, **distributional analysis** – learning based on the positions in which different words do and do not occur – allows the child to work out categories of words, for example, the category of words that can go into the abstract 'subject' slot.

The innate cognitive skills that are called upon in Tomasello's theory – such as the 'theory of mind' that allows intention reading, or the analogical thinking and distributional analysis that makes the learning of grammar possible – are not specific to language: they are domain-general and we know that human beings have these skills based on psychological research into other aspects of human thought. This allows Tomasello to explain language acquisition without positing an innate ability that is specifically for learning language.

main features? On the level of prosody, CDS has been found to involve the use of a higher pitch than normal, exaggerated intonation using a greater range of pitch, and slower, clearer pronunciation of words. There are also syntactic differences to normal language. Utterances tend to be shorter, and to contain fewer subordinated clauses. Fewer verb forms are used, and there are more utterances without verbs. Finally, there tend to be more content words, and fewer grammatical words, in CDS than in normal speech. And at the level of discourse, it is notable that CDS tends to contain more interrogatives and imperatives, and also more repetition, than normal speech.

CDS clearly constitutes a simplified register, and thus a form of scaffolding; there is, in fact, evidence to suggest that caregivers tailor their use of CDS features to match the abilities of the child they are interacting with (see Snow, 1977a). It would be easy to imagine that the use of CDS is a direct cause of language acquisition: that by providing these samples of simplified language, caregivers provide children with the equivalent of explicit language lessons. However, we must be cautious in drawing any such conclusion. It has actually proven extremely difficult to find empirical evidence directly linking the use of CDS by caregivers – or any other pattern of interaction – to the development of any particular aspect of language acquisition by children.

37.4 Modern methods: large-scale data analysis

Investigating how children learn English is a painstaking and laborious process for the linguist or psychologist. First, access to children of appropriate age and language background must be arranged. Then recordings must be made, which must then be transcribed. Transcription even of adult speech is a difficult process; with child speech, many of the problems are exacerbated because, especially in the earlier stages, children's speech may be wholly or partially unclear. Then the data must be analysed, which (depending on the extent of the transcriptions) may take months or years.

Because of these difficulties, a lot of the basic work on child language acquisition was based on rather few children. The very earliest studies were 'diary studies', typically involving a linguist making regular notes on their own child's language learning. Later studies were based on wider samples, but the numbers were still usually low. For instance, Roger Brown's classic study (Brown, 1973), which – as we saw above – laid much of the foundation of our knowledge of how English grammar is learnt, was based on the analysis of just three children.

However, just as modern computer technology has revolutionized the study of English in general, in the form of corpus linguistics, so too has it revolutionized the study of child language. This revolution has largely been made possible by the CHILDES initiative, pioneered by Brian MacWhinney (2000). CHILDES (*Child Language Data Exchange System*) is a large database of transcripts of children's speech. These transcripts have been contributed by many different researchers over a period of many years. All were created, originally, by the painstaking methods described above. However, by adding their transcripts to the CHILDES database, researchers make it possible for others to use their data. By bringing together data contributed by different researchers, it is possible to investigate child language on a truly massive scale.

The advantage of computer-based investigation is that we can reliably analyse massive amounts of data at high speed. Another important contribution of the CHILDES project has been the creation of a piece of corpus-analysis software, CLAN, which is specifically designed for the analyses that child language researchers most often wish to carry out. It has also been designed to work with the file format of the CHILDES database. In the remainder of this chapter, I will outline a very simple example of the kind of study that can be done using the massive amounts of data in CHILDES and the CLAN program for swift, large-scale analysis of the language of young children.

I took three of the largest datasets from the CHILDES database: the *Manchester* transcripts from Theakston and colleagues' (2001) study, the data from Brown (1973), and the *Providence* transcripts from the study of Demuth, Culbertson and Alter (2006). Between them, these contain 1381 transcripts, based on recordings of 21 different children (some learning British English and some American English). Using the CLAN program, I extracted two measures of a child's level of language production. The first, the 'mean length of utterance' or MLU, was introduced by Brown (1973) and measures the average number of morphemes of a child's utterances in a text. As such it is a good measure of grammatical complexity (as more complex sentences are usually longer). The second measure is a statistic called D, introduced by Malvern and Richards (1997). D indicates how diverse the child's vocabulary is, and thus tells us how advanced their lexical development is. I compiled the results from CLAN into a table like Table 37.2, with one row for each transcript.

I was then able to generate the graph in Figure 37.1, comparing MLU to age. The points form an upward line, as we would expect, but the important thing to note here is how much variation there is in MLU among transcripts of children at the same or similar ages. Remember that there are only 21 different children in the data. What these results suggest is that the MLU of any given child can vary a lot from occasion to occasion! Figure 37.2 is a similar graph comparing vocabulary diversity to age. We can see a similar general upward trend, but with even greater variability, especially at earlier ages. Finally, Figure 37.3 compares MLU and vocabulary diversity. We can see from the way these two measures correlate that these two types of linguistic progress mostly go hand-in-hand – as, perhaps, we would expect. However, again there is much variation, and as the two statistics increase, the variability rises.

Table 37.2   *Example of data extracted for three of the texts*

Mean length of utterance	Vocabulary diversity score	Age in years
2.097	69.63	2.26
2.143	83.73	2.30
2.334	84.04	2.34
...	...	...

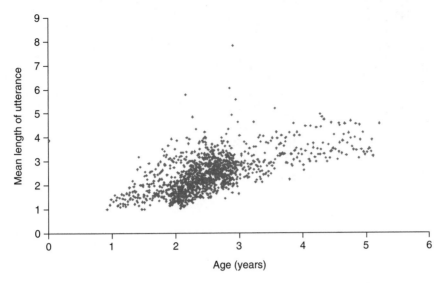

Mean length of utterance and age of child in 1381 CHILDES transcripts FIGURE 37.1

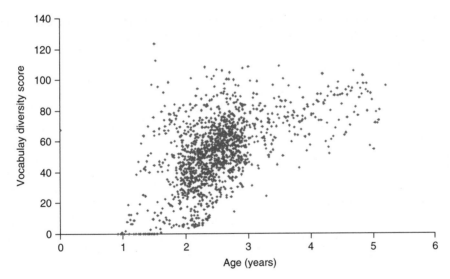

Vocabulary diversity and age of child in 1381 CHILDES transcripts FIGURE 37.2

This analysis is not particularly 'original' in terms of what was measured, or in terms of the findings. But it is 'original' in the sense that I worked out these figures for the first time when writing this chapter. It took a few hours, and if you wanted to do something similar yourself, all you would need is an everyday computer, an Internet connection, and some time to practise.[2] The CLAN tool, and the entire CHILDES database itself, are freely available for download on the Web.[3] Despite its simplicity, however, this analysis clearly

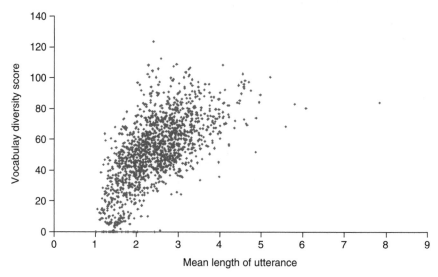

FIGURE 37.3 *Mean length of utterance and vocabulary diversity of child in 1381 CHILDES transcripts*

demonstrates what a great change the CHILDES initiative has wrought to the range of possibilities now open to the child language researcher.

Recommended readings

There is a range of excellent introductions to the field of language acquisition. These include Aitchison (1989), Foster (1990), and Gleason (1993). A more advanced-level account is given by Ingram (1989), a book especially notable for its detail in describing and discussing primary research. Another good advanced volume is Ritchie and Bhatia (1999). Recent collections of key research papers include Lust and Foley (2004), and Tomasello and Bates (2001). The two sides of the (occasionally heated) debate over Chomsky's theory are well-represented by Pinker (1994) and Sampson (2005). For more on the view of language acquisition which emphasizes input from the caregiver, see Snow and Ferguson (1977). Finally, the *Journal of Child Language* is one of the major avenues for the publication of new research in this area.

Notes

1 These two examples are from Braine (1976).
2 CLAN is controlled by typing commands in a special format. The commands used for this analysis were as follows:

    mlu +t*CHI FILENAME
    vocd +t*CHI +r6 +s"*-%%" FILENAME

   where *FILENAME* stands for the name of the computer file containing the transcript being analysed. If you do wish to try this yourself, I recommend starting with just one transcript, then moving on to a group of a dozen or so files.
3 The web address of the CHILDES project is http://childes.psy.cmu.edu/.

CHAPTER 38

Languages and Literacies in Education

Roz Ivanič

38.1 The roles of languages and literacies in education

Language and education are inextricably linked in two ways: language can be not only a **target** of learning but also a **tool** for learning. A central aim of education is to develop and extend learners' language and literacy capabilities, since spoken and written languages are so essential to life, work and study. The idea of language as a target of learning has been the focus of Chapter 37 of this book, and therefore will not be addressed directly here. However, language is also the main medium through which learning, teaching and assessment are conducted, and that is the focus of this chapter. Sections 38.2 and 38.3 look at the ways in which languages and literacies act as tools and resources for learning in formal and informal settings, and in all subjects across the curriculum. Section 38.2 is concerned with the linguistic aspects of the **content** of learning and Section 38.3 is concerned with the **social and interpersonal** aspects of learning.

38.2 Language as a tool for learning

It is very informative to try to imagine learning something without language. Everyone can think of certain very personal and physical aspects of their lives that they have learnt entirely by trial and error, and/or by encounters with others who have more experience. However, even the most physical and personal of these have probably involved language at least indirectly. To take an example which is not too intimate, most people have probably learnt to iron a shirt without a lot of talking or use of written instructions, especially if they live on their own. We learn something like that by facing the need to do it, and then either remembering seeing a family member doing it when we were younger, or by just doing it, and learning by trial and error. However, even in the case of learning to iron a shirt, we don't have to look far to find some recourse to language. Those memories may be mainly visual, but are almost certainly also accompanied by words which help to fix the experience in our minds. Even without talking or writing, we often process our actions through 'words in the mind' which help us to understand what we are doing and remember it. Someone who has to iron a shirt may also have learnt about it vicariously from something they have read in the past. And then there are always the instructions which came with the iron which need reading (as in the examples of literacy practices mentioned in Chapter 27). So even when we think we are not using language as a tool for learning, it may well be playing a part indirectly or subconsciously.

38.2.1 Talking knowledge and understanding into being

However, this sort of learning is far more likely to be done in company, and to involve the person who needs to learn asking for help from someone who already knows how to do it. For people who don't live alone, learning to iron is almost bound to be accompanied by a lot of talk: advice, instructions, criticism (constructive, preferably) and almost certainly lots of jokes. Language is a primary tool for learning, as people talk knowledge and understanding into being. The recognition of this function of language originates in the work of Vygotsky (1962 [1934]) and has been extensively discussed by many educational linguists, for example, Cazden (2001), Mercer (2000). I chose the example of learning how to iron a shirt deliberately, because it is the sort of learning which happens in everyday settings, rather than in educational institutions. There is a lot of language which accompanies learning, both spoken and written language, not only 'teacher talk' or textbook language. Language is a tool for learning in informal, everyday learning contexts, just as much as in classrooms and other official sites for learning.

In more recognizably 'educational' contexts, such as a preschool playgroup, a GCSE science classroom, or an electronics company which takes on apprentices, the same relationships between language and learning can be observed. Some learning takes place without any use of language, but an observer doesn't have to look far to see spoken conversations, explanations and instructions; written guidelines, books, printed sheets and computer screens, all using language as a resource for the development of capabilities, knowledge and understanding. The difference in these settings is that there are usually one or more people who see their role as 'carer', 'teacher', 'trainer' or 'instructor', who almost certainly perform that role through language. People performing these roles may be physically present, and/ or embodied in documents, materials or computer programs. In such settings, spoken and written language are often the major vehicle through which teaching and learning take place. In Section 38.3 below, I will discuss the language of teacher–learner interaction in more detail.

38.2.2 Specialist languages of 'education' and of subject areas/disciplines

A special characteristic of educational settings is that in many of them there is a conscious, explicit emphasis not just on learning **how** but also on learning **what**. Particularly in schools, colleges and universities, there is a focus on 'knowledge': learning facts and information, and on understanding principles, theories, interpretations and opinions. These formal settings do not have a monopoly on knowledge learning – most of us learn a lot of information and ideas in more informal ways, but teachers are entrusted with the duty of imparting knowledge and understanding, and hence in educational settings there is an explicit focus on 'what is to be learned'. This produces a recognizable language of 'facts' and 'information', often expressed in categorical statements about states of affairs, events and processes: the 'objects' of learning. There are also linguistic features which characterize particular views of pedagogy, different approaches to the facilitation of learning, and the social interaction in educational settings, as discussed in Section 38.3.

Each subject area in the curriculum has its own linguistic characteristics, sometimes called 'curriculum literacies' (Wyatt-Smith and Cumming, 2003): not only specialist terminology but often grammatical structures which are typical of the subject area and distinguish it from other subject areas. This differentiation has been called 'diatypic variation' (Stubbs, 1983a, b), meaning variation according to the context and purpose of the language use, rather than according to the social identity of the user. For example, academic disciplines such as geology and history have linguistic features which characterize them. Geology uses a specialist vocabulary including such words as *tectonic system*, *lithosphere*, *mantle* and *seismic activity* which are not likely to appear in connection with any other subjects. Not only that, but it has grammatical features, particularly the use of many present tense **state** verbs with inanimate concrete nouns as subjects to represent states of affairs in the physical world, as in Example 1 in Illustration Box 38.1. This contrasts sharply with the language of history as a subject, which uses a very different specialist vocabulary including words such as *civilization*, *rebellion*, *monarchy* and *settlement*. The grammatical features of history as a subject area differ significantly from geology too, with a great deal of the knowledge in the area carried by past tense **action** verbs with animate nouns as subject, and many expressions of circumstances of time, as in Illustration Box 38.1, Example 2. (For more detail see, for example, Lemke (1990), Halliday and Martin (1993), and for a critical perspective on the gendered nature of such discourses, see Lee (1996).)

Vocational areas also have their specialist language and structures. Catering and hospitality, for example, has its own terminology which distinguishes it from other areas – terms such as *patissier*, *food hazards*, *storage temperatures* and *silver service*. The spoken and written language of learning catering and hospitality has a wider range of grammatical structures than academic subjects such as geology and history, since it encompasses both theoretical and practical aspects of the subject. Some of the theoretical aspects are similar to biology and chemistry, and others have more in common with business management. The language of learning for the practical aspects of the subject is characterized by instructions and sequences of **process** verbs.

The examples In Illustration Box 38.1 come from A-level and equivalent textbooks, but at different levels of the education system, and in different genres, some of these characteristics change. For example, in history, geology, hospitality management and any other subject at university, more and more abstract nouns are used to represent concepts and relationships on the theoretical side of the subjects. Thus, some aspects of the language in education are dependent on the stage of educational development, rather than the subject being studied.

ILLUSTRATION BOX 38.1

Examples of specialist languages of subject areas in education

Example 1   Geology

The margins of plates are sites of considerable geologic activity, such as volcanoes, mountain building, earthquakes, and seafloor spreading.

(from Hamblin, 1994: 41)

Example 2   History

A year later, the [East India] Company took complete control of the administration of Bengal revenues.

(from Smith, 1998: 18)

Example 3   Catering and Hospitality

[You must know] the specific aspects of health and safety, data protection, equal opportunities, disability discrimination and legislation and regulations that affect the way the products or services you deal with can be delivered to your customers.

(from City & Guilds, n.d.: 37)

For a linguist, the study and comparison of such linguistic features is not only of great interest in its own right, but also has a great deal to contribute to educational research and practice.

38.2.3   Linguistic features of assignment and examination prompts

Illustration Box 38.2 provides an overview of a variety of linguistic devices which are used to elicit the demonstration of knowledge. These features are typically found in examination papers or in assignment specifications. In all these ways, teachers and particularly examiners use the resources of the language to indicate what the student is to write about, without giving away any of the content of what they are to write (or say). The devices in (a), (b), (c) and (d) are using the facility of language to refer to areas of knowledge, so that it is the candidate's responsibility to fill in the particulars of what they have learnt. The devices in (e) show the range of linguistic resources available for giving learners more or less help with the structure of their answer, often with the consequence that the prompt is quite hard to interpret. The devices in (f) provide very different ways of wording questions: the 'objective' uses are more suited to testing knowledge of unequivocal facts; the 'subjective' uses are more suited to eliciting understanding and argument. Unfortunately, not all teachers or testers take account of these distinctions when they are preparing exam papers.

ILLUSTRATION BOX 38.2

The variety of linguistic devices used to elicit the demonstration of knowledge

(a) **Questions and commands**

(b) *Wh*–**question words:** (i) in direct questions
(ii) in indirect questions

(c) **Verbs for mental**   **and linguistic processes**

(critically) assess / evaluate	*write about / discuss*
compare	*outline / sketch*
contrast	*describe*
consider	*comment on*
	suggest

(d) **Nouns which don't give away any answers**

comparison / contrast	*issues*	*example(s)*
cause(s) / reason(s) / explanation(s)	*solutions*	*relationship(s)*
difficulties	*aspects*	
differences / similarities	*implication(s)*	

(e) **Simplicity and explicitness**
yes/no questions
structured questions: (i) separate parts;
(ii) coordinated (i.e., with several parts connected with 'and', 'or' and other coordinating conjunctions;
(iii) parallelisms (i.e., with parts which require the reader to understand that previous wording has been omitted to avoid repetition).
long clauses to delimit answers.

(f) **Eliciting objective and subjective answers**

	Objective	Subjective
articles, determiners and quantifiers	*the, four*	*a, one of the, some*
inclusion of the word *you*	No	Yes
main verb type	Categorical (i.e., present tense verbs which suggest that something is unquestionably true)	Modalized (i.e., verbs including modals such as *may, might* or *could*, to suggest there could be alternatives).

38.2.4   Characteristics of communicative practices in educational settings

It is not only the linguistic characteristics of spoken and written language which distinguish one subject area from another, and distinguish educational settings from communication which is not designed with an educational intent. There are also particular ways of reading, writing and engaging with multi-modal semiotic resources which are specific to 'learning'. There are particular kinds of texts – whiteboards, occasionally still blackboards (more common in some subject areas than others), exercise sheets, 'educational' computer programs, CDs and books which provide information in particular ways which are clearly designed for use in educational settings. Learning is also characterized by the writing of particular types of text: notes in exercise books or on sheets of A4, the completion of 'handouts' often designed to test what the learner can or can't do, or does or does not know. Classroom walls are usually covered in texts which are designed specifically for information or instruction – the kinds of posters and displays which are not likely to be found in other contexts. An educational context is usually immediately recognizable by the presence of these types of text and activities associated with them.

There are particular ways of engaging with these texts which characterize educational settings, and different aspects of education have particular communicative and literacy practices, both paper-based and electronic, associated with them. Membership of an educational institution in general is mediated by communicative practices such as the reading and writing associated with enrolment in classes, checking timetables and arranging to meet teachers. A characteristic practice in schools is the storing and distribution of multiple sets of the same book. Learning itself is mediated by communicative practices such as many people reading from a whiteboard and checking a page in a textbook and then writing on A4 paper while one person (a teacher) is talking.

On many courses the learning context might also incorporate many of the literacy practices of the real-life activity the course is preparing people for: for example, the literacies of historical research, of conducting an experiment in physics, of cooking, of restaurant management, of office work, of painting and decorating. The picture in Illustration Box 38.3 on page 632 shows interactive reading and writing on a painting and decorating course. This communicative practice of estimating the nature of the job to be done can be found in actual workplace practice, as well as in a course preparing people for this work. Educational policies and individual courses vary considerably in how far they incorporate such 'real life literacies' into teaching and learning.

Finally, there are many literacy practices associated specifically with assessment and the demonstration of knowledge, understanding and capabilities. Indeed, on some courses the majority of reading and writing is not aimed at learning, but at providing evidence of learning. The most obvious of these practices is the reading of examination papers, often quite a complex reading task in itself, and the writing of answers, either in an examination booklet or on separate paper. On many vocational education courses assessment is based on a 'log-book' recording what has been learnt, and/or a 'portfolio' of

ADVANCES BOX 38.1

The study of the textual mediation of learning

Recent research has focused specifically on the communicative practices of academic and vocational courses in colleges of further education. The Literacies for Learning in Further Education (LfLFE) project aimed to identify literacy practices which enable students to succeed in learning across the curriculum. One of its major objectives was to uncover actual and potential overlaps and connections between the reading and writing students do in their everyday lives for their own purposes, and the literacy demands of their courses. More than 100 students took part in researching 32 units of study across 11 curriculum areas. Childcare was studied in common across all four colleges and the other areas ranged from A-level Social Science to NVQs in Painting and Decorating.

Noticing and collecting texts was a starting-point for research into the literacy practices whereby these texts mediate, potentially mediate, or fail to mediate learning in the curriculum areas in the sample. The collection of texts was supplemented with data on the purposes and processes of reading and/or writing these texts – according to the teachers, according to the learners – on who does what with them, and how. The research showed how texts are to a greater or lesser extent constitutive of curriculum areas, and that texts play an important role even in relatively practical curriculum areas. For example, media studies was a textually saturated curriculum area which involved not only textbooks about the history and theory of the subject, and classroom tasks which required students to read about, write about and discuss the subject, but also the study of a wide range of media texts themselves. However, the National Vocational Qualification in Food and Drink Service, which appeared at first sight to be a curriculum area with minimal textuality, proved on investigation to involve a wide variety of reading and writing, both in the running of the restaurant and in completing evidence of the achievement of attainment targets for the course. When spoken language is also taken into account, the communicative practices on the catering and hospitality course were far more diverse than in media studies, involving learning how to interact with customers as well as classroom talk. (For further details of this comparison, see Satchwell and Ivanič (2007).)

The final year of the research was devoted to developing, implementing and evaluating small changes in practice based on the understandings reached about vernacular and pedagogic literacies. Through the close analysis of these changes, the project found that aspects of the literacy practices from students' everyday lives, for example, their collaborative nature, could be harnessed as resources for learning. The research contributed to linguistic and educational research in particular, and social scientific understanding more generally, by demonstrating how the semiotic (meaning-making) aspects of learning are integral to the cognitive and the practical.

(For examples and further discussion of this research, see the *Literacies for Learning in Further Education* project website (www.lancs.ac.uk/lflfe) and publications, for example, Pardoe and Ivanič (2007), Ivanič and others (2007, 2009), and for discussion of the project methodology, see Mannion and Ivanič (2007)).

ILLUSTRATION BOX 38.3

Interactive reading and writing on a painting and decorating course

evidence of learning. These are practices which are specific to being assessed, and not found in everyday life. (For further discussion of the concepts of communicative and literacy practices, see Chapter 27 by David Barton and Chapter 28 by Uta Papen.)

38.2.5   Multilingualism: what is the language of this class?

Language and communicative practices for learning, and differences in these from one curriculum area to another, can be found in all languages. The best language to serve as a tool for learning curriculum subjects is not necessarily English, even in a school in the United Kingdom. A large number of children in UK schools speak a language other than English as their first language (see, for example, Block, 2006), and multilingualism characterizes most parts of the world (for case studies from Europe, see Kenner and Hickey (2008)).

It is salient to ask 'What is the language of this class?' both in the sense of 'What language(s) do the learners in this class use?', and in the sense of 'What language(s) would be most beneficial for the conduct of learning and teaching in this class?' There has been a great deal of research to show that children benefit from encountering new ideas, concepts and knowledge in their first or best language, which may not be the dominant language of education in the country in question (for discussion of this issue in a range of contexts, see Garcia, Skutnabb-Kangas and Torres-Guzman, 2006; Helot and de Mejia, 2008; Luk and Lin, 2007; Martin-Jones, 2007). This means that a focus on English language and British communicative practices in educational settings in the United Kingdom will not be most productive for some children's all-round educational development.

There has been a variety of policies to take account of this issue in the United Kingdom, one of which has been the employment of bilingual classroom assistants, particularly in primary schools. Bilingual assistants can help children whose first language is not English to access the curriculum through the language and communicative practices in which they are most confident, alongside learning English (for examples, see Martin-Jones and Saxena, 2003; Creese, 2005). In this way, the conceptual and intellectual development of these children is not hampered or delayed, and they are able to make the transition gradually to learning all subjects in English when they are ready. Not only does such a policy help to ensure that children can take up their entitlement to learning of all subjects across the curriculum, but it can also contribute to the maintenance and valuing of their home languages and the communicative practices which are an important resource for their future lives.

In order to operate a fully bilingual education policy, schools would need to ensure that all learning materials and opportunities are available in all the languages and cultures of the school. This is possible in some places. For example, in Wales, there is an active policy of making the whole curriculum available in Welsh as well as in English in as many schools as possible. In other places, a fully bilingual education policy is unrealistic. For example, in some parts of London there may be as many as 37 languages spoken in one school. In such situations, it is impossible for the teacher to serve all the children's multilingual needs, but some imaginative schools and education authorities recognize the value of home languages and are committed to maintaining them and harnessing them as resources for learning wherever possible.

38.3 The language of classroom interaction

In educational settings – classrooms, but not only classrooms – it is not only knowledge that is negotiated, but also social relations. 'Knowledge is power', and by virtue of their roles, carers, teachers and trainers are assumed to have superior knowledge to those in their care, and hence they exercise authority over them. In this section I will discuss the ways in which teachers and learners interact in order to develop each other's knowledge, understanding and capabilities.

Spoken interaction among teachers and learners will be somewhere on the continuum

teacher-led — — teacher-guided — — teacher-free

The stereotype of a classroom is that the teacher will be at the front of the class, controlling what is being done and what is being said. At the other end of the continuum is the situation – often orchestrated by carers, teachers and trainers – in which the learners are working without any immediate control from the teacher. In between these extremes are many more fluid situations in which the learners are working independently of the teacher, but the teacher has a strong influence over what they are doing through designing the task and participating in it occasionally. The extent to which the teacher is taking the role as the main source of knowledge and understanding greatly affects the nature of the spoken interaction between the participants in the learning event. There are plenty of examples of teachers completely dominating the interaction, for example in university lectures in the United Kingdom and many countries of the world. In the majority of educational settings, however, it is believed that learning will be enhanced if learners have the opportunity to engage in two-way interaction with teachers (for further discussion see, for example, Edwards and Mercer, 1987; Barnes and Todd, 1995).

38.3.1   The IRF structure

Educational linguists are interested in patterns of interaction between a teacher and one or more learners. (The original study was Sinclair and Coulthard, 1975. For further developments see Willes, 1983; Wells, 1986; Cazden, 2001; Christie, 2005). Although it is common to call this 'the language of classroom interaction', it can be found elsewhere: whenever someone takes on the role of the 'knower' and tries to help another person learn something that s/he already knows. Recognizable patterns have been identified for different types of class, for different age groups, in different settings, and at various levels of delicacy. However, the most discussed is the so-called **IRF structure**, which stands for 'Initiation – Response – Feedback/ Follow-up': a very common sequence of utterances in classroom interaction. Illustration Box 38.4 shows how the pattern in a stereotypic teaching event differs from a very similar sequence of utterances which are common in an everyday conversation.

ILLUSTRATION BOX 38.4

The IRF structure in everyday conversation and a stereotypic teaching event

The IRF Structure

Conversation				Classroom talk	
A:	What time is it, Sarah?	I		*T:*	What time is it, Sarah?
Sarah:	Half past two	R		*Sarah:*	Half past two
A.	Thanks	F		*T:*	Well done

In an everyday conversation, if person A initiates the interaction with a question, and 'Sarah' answers the question, the initiator (A) is likely to follow this by expressing their appreciation for the information she has supplied. In classroom talk, however, if the same question is asked by a teacher, and the same answer is provided by a learner, the expected 'third turn' is an evaluation of the answer. The teacher's question is understood not as a genuine request for information, but an 'initiation' of a sequence designed to test what learners know. This conveys, and creates, a very different relationship of power between the two speakers. In the conversation, there is nothing in the interlocutors' roles to suggest anything other than a relationship of equality between them. If there is an imbalance of power, it is in favour of the provider of information. In the classroom talk, however, there is an unequal relationship in which the teacher has the authority to judge the correctness or acceptability of Sarah's response. The acronym IRF is usually used only to refer to this type of three-part sequence in classroom talk, even though in principle it is possible to find such sequences in other social settings, particularly if the 'F' is understood to stand just for 'Follow-up'.

One of the features of this sequence is that it gives teachers the prerogative and the responsibility for both the opening and the closing move of the sequence, effectively doubling their contribution to the interaction, and surrounding the learners' words with theirs. The use of the IRF structure is based on, and perpetuates, the assumption that teaching consists of the elicitation and evaluation of what learners know or think, and that learning can be accomplished through learners demonstrating what they know, having it evaluated, and hearing the others go through the same process. The assumption is that a series of such interactions will lead to a group of learners building a joint construction of knowledge and understanding. Needless to say, this benefits some learners more than others.

Some researchers (especially in the USA) call this structure **IRE** in which the 'E' stands for 'Evaluation', emphasizing the way in which this slot in the interaction structure is typically realized. Courtney Cazden says: 'In linguistic terminology, IRE, or IRF, is the *unmarked* pattern; in computer terminology, it is the *default option* – doing what the system is set to do "naturally", unless someone makes a deliberate change' (2001: 31). This means that, if a teacher really is requesting information, s/he would need to indicate this explicitly, because otherwise learners assume that every question is designed to evaluate what they do or don't know. The structure is so prevalent that, whatever sort of utterance a teacher uses to begin a communicative sequence – a statement, or even a single word, learners are likely to interpret this as the 'initiation' of an IRE sequence.

Research on classroom discourse has shown that the IRF/IRE structure is realized in many different ways, has many variations, is used for many different purposes, and combines into many longer sequences involving repeated and nested IRFs. There have been experiments in which teachers have consciously tried to avoid this stereotypical interaction structure, exploring ways of facilitating learning which do not resort to it. In spite of this, the structure does appear to be extraordinarily prevalent, as do the assumptions of the nature of teaching and learning which underlie it.

38.3.2 Types of question in classroom interaction

The 'elicitation' slot in the IRF structure is often realized by a question. Linguists have studied the types of question used by teachers, and found three important distinctions among them. The first of these is the distinction between 'closed' and 'open' questions. 'Closed' questions are those for which there is only one possible answer, and 'open' questions are those for which there is potentially an infinite range of answers. Closely associated with this is the distinction between 'pseudo' and 'real' questions. Pseudo questions are those which are in the form of a question, but to which the questioner already knows the answer, as in the example of the IRF structure in Illustration Box 38.4. Pseudo questions are typical of situations in which teachers are assessing what learners do or don't know, as a starting point for building on their existing knowledge, to recap on what has been previously taught, or to give them the opportunity to demonstrate their knowledge. By contrast, 'real' questions are those in which the questioner doesn't know the answer. In educational settings, these may be used by teachers and, ideally, by learners, in order to find out about each other's knowledge, experience and views, without a pre-ordained 'correct' answer.

The third distinction, which interacts with the other two, is between yes/no questions and *wh*-word questions. Yes/no questions are more likely to be closed, pseudo questions, and *wh*-word questions are more likely to be open and real. However, there is no one-to-one fit among these categories, since a teacher may ask a *wh*– question which is neither open nor real. For example, in Illustration Box 38.5, the teacher asks, 'What is a different form of traffic?', but she is not really interested in all the children's ideas; she is actually waiting for one of them to mention trains.

Questions play an important role in learning and teaching. The pattern of a teacher's questions is likely to be determined to a large extent by her or his philosophy of learning. Teachers who treat learning as the transmission of an established body of objective knowledge from themselves to their learners, and as the assessment of what the learners do or do not know, are likely to use more closed, pseudo questions. In contrast, teachers who treat knowledge as more subjective, and learning as a constructive exploration of experience

---

ILLUSTRATION BOX 38.5

Closed questioning in the classroom

T: What is a different form of traffic can anybody . Philip
Ph: e:m . (unclear)
T: I'm on traffic . I'm on traffic David
Da: the trains (unclear)
T.   trains yes . the trains ....

(Adapted from Open University video-recording for course E262, *Teachers and Pupils Talking*)

are more likely to use more open, real questions. However, these distinctions cannot be made through simple counting of question types, because it all depends on exactly who is asking what, and about what, to identify a more nuanced understanding of the role of questioning in learning and teaching.

38.3.3 Learning through small-group interaction

Many teachers and educational researchers believe that learners learn more 'by discovery' than by teaching, and that many of the goals of education can be achieved by designing activities for learners to carry out in small groups, with little or no direct involvement of the teacher (see, for example, Haworth, 1994). Spoken interaction is thought to provide the opportunity for learners to explore topics and issues in their own terms, and to talk knowledge and understanding into being, as described in Section 38.2.1:

> It is as talkers, questioners, arguers, gossips, chatterboxes, that our pupils do much of their most important learning. Their everyday talking voices are the most subtle and versatile means they possess for making sense of what they do and for making sense of others, including their teachers.
>
> (Rosen, 1969: 127)

> Two heads are better than one.
>
> (Mercer, 1995: 2)

> Benefits derive from listening and thinking before speaking, not just speaking a lot.
>
> (Swann, 1992: ch. 4)

Linguists have been interested in the nature of the spoken interaction in 'teacher-free' groups. Mercer proposed that such talk can be broadly divided into disputational, cumulative and exploratory talk (1995: 104), observing that disputational talk in which learners merely argue over the solution to a task does not enhance learning. By contrast, cumulative talk between pairs or in small groups of learners, in which learners build on each others' contributions, knowledge and ideas, can be very beneficial. Exploratory talk, in which learners collectively make suggestions, constructively challenge and evaluate one another's contributions, and speculate and hypothesize about the completion of a task, is thought to lead to the 'best' learning.

However, again it is not a question of making a simple equation between linguistic features and quality of learning. Responsible researchers have abandoned attempts to count surface features as evidence of 'better' or 'worse' talk:

> We doubt whether there is a consistent relationship between the distribution of cohesion features and the extent to which group members are trying to assimilate one another's viewpoints. ...
>
> the logical relationships in our materials are more often left implicit than given verbal form, so that the logical antecedents of utterances are

frequently ambiguous or diffuse. This indeterminacy, we concluded, was functional in such conversations, and should not be obscured by an idealizing logical analysis.

(Barnes and Todd, 1977: 16–21)

Labov, commenting on attempts to identify exploratory talk by counting expressions of uncertainty, called words like 'might' and 'perhaps'

the benchmarks of hemming and hawing, backing and filling.

(Labov, 1969: 19)

So, as with IRF, research on questions in classroom interaction needs to be sensitive to detail, and not make assumptions as to what counts as 'good' talk for facilitating learning.

38.3.4 Language and identity in educational settings (including language and gender)

Educational linguists have looked at language and identity in the classroom from two perspectives. One approach has been concerned with the way in which interaction and other aspects of language in education vary according to the social identity of the participants. This approach can be called a 'differences' theory of language and identity, based on a belief that children and adults from different social groups use language differently. This research has been particularly focused on gender: ways in which girls behave and are treated differently from boys, but also applies to social class differences, age differences and other differences in the characteristics learners bring with them into the classroom. A more positive variation on the same theory is that children and adults from different social groups bring different kinds of language resources into the classroom. This view, that the language people use reflects their identities, has been criticized as essentialist: that is, stereotyping people and making assumptions that, for example, all females will behave in the same way (see, for example, Swann, 1992; Sunderland, 2003).

A second and, I suggest, more satisfactory theory is that identity is not only reflected in language but also constructed by it. This focus, on the social construction of identity in educational settings, concerns the ways in which learners and teachers are positioned by the discourses they are subject to and participate in. In discussing language and identity, researchers have noted the significance of the use of different terminology:

The term 'identity' is useful, ... but ... it is a misleadingly singular word. The plural word 'identities' is sometimes better, because it captures the idea of people identifying simultaneously with a variety of social groups. One or more of these identities may be foregrounded at different times; they are sometimes contradictory, sometimes related: people's diverse identities constitute the richness and dilemmas of their sense of self.

(Ivanič, 1998: 11)

Some researchers (e.g., Kress, 1996; Scott, 2000) prefer the term **subjectivity** to emphasize that identity is not an essential characteristic, but is something shaped by social factors, and to align themselves with this second, social constructionist approach to the study of identity.

Various aspects of our identities are constructed and reconstructed through the different experiences in our lives, including experience in educational settings. Jane Sunderland and I have proposed the 'three As' to sum up the ways in which language constructs identity:

- by **attribution** – the way we are talked **about** by others
- by **address** – the way we are talked **to** by others
- by **affiliation** – the way we talk **like** others

Of these, the third is perhaps the most insidious, since it refers to the way in which discourses can, without our realizing it, co-opt us into belonging to a certain group or thinking in a certain way:

> ... a social constructionist view of identity ... [proposes that identity] is the result of affiliation to particular beliefs and possibilities which are available to [people] in their social context.
>
> (Ivanič, 1998: 12)

The multiplicity of identities are not fixed but can be seen as continually emerging from one's relationships with others, including those which exist in the classroom. So, for example, if a female learner has encountered a pervasive discourse of 'girls are no good at maths', she is likely to take that discourse to herself and to think of herself as no good at maths. She has been socially constructed by this discourse, but 'being no good at maths' is not an essential feature of her identity. Such subject positioning can be resisted, and the aim of many educational researchers is to make such processes of the social construction of identity more visible so that both teachers and learners can be aware of them, and counter their negative effects, for example, by espousing different discourses. (For discussion and further examples of the social construction of identity in educational settings, see Ivanič, 1998, 2006; Nilan, 2000; Sunderland, 2003.)

38.3.5 The language of evaluation

A key process in the construction of identity in educational settings is the way in which teachers evaluate learners. Evaluation constructs teachers as having power and control over learners, as having the ultimate authority as to what counts as knowledge and what is correct. It constructs learners as relatively powerless and subject to the teacher's judgment. However, with heightened awareness of the power of discourse to construct identity, teachers can significantly vary the effects of evaluation. For example, in evaluating a learner's performance, the teacher can 'say the same thing' in different ways, as shown in the examples in Illustration Box 38.6.

ILLUSTRATION BOX 38.6

Alternative wordings for evaluating a learner's performance

What is being evaluated?

(i)   the learner, or the learner's performance?
compare: *Another example of your sloppy and slapdash attitude to life, eh, Paul?*
with: *I find this letter difficult to read. What can you do to make your writing more legible?*

(ii)   the whole performance, or something specific about the performance?
compare: *You're OK with ladders.*
with: *Well done. I like the way you take your time placing the ladder and testing it by trying to rock it before you put your full weight on it.*

Who is the judge?

compare: *You made a mess of weighing those parcels.*
with: *I think you could have given each parcel more time on the scales to be sure of its weight. What do you think?*

How do positive and negative feedback interact?

compare: *You've got the procedures for accepting payment by cheque and credit card right but you're still not using the cash register properly.*
with: *Well done. You've got the procedures for accepting payment by cheque and credit card right. Now you need to concentrate on how to use the cash register.*

(Adapted from Briscoe, I. (1984) *Developing Curriculum*,
unpublished discussion document, London:
ILEA F/HE Communication Skills Curriculum Development Project)

38.4   Conclusion

This chapter deals with the roles of language in learning across the curriculum: firstly with the relationship between language and the content of what is being learned, and secondly with the social and interpersonal aspects of language in educational settings. I started by discussing the ways in which language and literacy mediate learning, and the central role of talk in the development of knowledge and understanding. I showed how both language and communicative practices differ from one subject area to another, and how there is a particular language for the elicitation of knowledge and understanding which is to be found in examination and assignment prompts. I ended the section on the relationships between language and learning with a brief mention of the place of multilingualism in education, and the importance of maintaining people's first languages for their conceptual development.

In the second half of the chapter I focused on the characteristics of spoken interaction in educational settings. I explained the IRF structure which is very common in teacher–learner interaction, the view of teaching and learning which underpins it, and the ways in which it can be varied. I provided an overview of different types of question in educational settings, and discussed the alternatives provided by small-group 'teacher-free' interaction. I then focused on the construction of identity in educational settings, and pervasive effects of evaluation on learners' self-image, and possible alternative wordings for evaluations.

Throughout the chapter I have drawn attention to the way 'the tail wags the dog': how the focus on assessment and evaluation has a wash-back effect on teaching and learning. More generally, I have emphasized how education professionals in all sectors might benefit from a greater understanding of language and communicative practices. This does not apply just to English teachers or language teaching specialists, but to teachers of every subject in the curriculum.

Recommended readings

The topic of language and literacies in education provides enormous scope for research. The communicative landscape is ever-changing, with fast-moving advances in information, communication and learning technologies, and increasingly multimodal semiotic resources for learning and teaching (see Cope and Kalantzis, 2000; Unsworth, 2001; Lemke, 1998, 2002; Kress and others (2006), and Chapter 28 of this book). These changes provide new affordances for teaching and learning and invite new research agendas for the future.

The most comprehensive and up-to-date source for further reading in the field of educational linguistics is Martin-Jones and Hornberger (2008). A seminal work is Cazden (2001), and a useful, if now somewhat dated, overview is provided by Mercer (1995). Recent collections of key research papers are Goodman and others (2003), and Lillis and McKinney (2003), the latter being unique in its focus on methods of linguistic analysis for educational data. For more advanced reading in the field of curriculum literacies I particularly recommend Halliday and Martin (1993) and Lee (1996). Finally, *Language and Education* and *Linguistics and Education* are two international journals publishing new research in this area.

CHAPTER 39

TESOL and Linguistics

MARTIN BYGATE

39.1   Introduction

The acronym **TESOL** refers to the teaching of English to speakers of other languages. It embraces a wide range of specialist areas – for instance: language teaching methodology, second language acquisition, testing, materials and curriculum development, teacher development, and management and innovation. Given the complexity of this domain, it might seem strange to include a chapter on TESOL in a book largely made up of chapters focusing on the analysis of language. However, despite its multi-dimensionality, it has at its heart issues which are also fundamental to linguistics and which hinge on the nature of language. How do the different domains of a language function – the phonemic, the morpho-syntactic, the lexical or the discoursal? How do they function together? How are the different domains perceived by speakers of other languages? How are those domains learnt, separately or together? And how do different ways of teaching the language affect how they are learnt?

Not surprisingly, given their different backgrounds, different generations have viewed TESOL in somewhat different ways. For example, in the nineteenth century, language was mainly studied for cultural purposes, often for reading or perhaps for translating. It was understandable therefore that language was taught through the mother tongue, that the grammar was described in terms of the grammar of the mother tongue and that vocabulary was presented in bilingual word lists. Activities typically involved reading in the target language, translating from the target language into the mother tongue, and vice versa, and doing grammar exercises. This approach became known as the 'grammar-translation' approach. In the late nineteenth century, more people began to learn languages in order to use them. Reformers argued that since we all learn our first language as children without the help of another language, and since fluent use of a language does not normally work through translation from one's mother tongue, then we should aim to learn languages directly, without reference to the mother tongue. Furthermore, speech should be primary, rather than the medium of the written language. One approach that emerged from this movement was the **Direct Method**. This typically involved the teacher teaching grammar and vocabulary ostensively, that is through the use of objects, pictures and actions in the classroom. Although methods like the Direct Method survive to this day, they seemed to work well only for the early stages of language learning. More complex and abstract grammar and vocabulary is hard to convey through ostensive means!

Meanwhile, however, a new development in learning theory, behaviourism, opened up the possibility that all aspects of language could be made 'learnable', without use of translation, and without depending on explanations of grammatical rules, even the most complex and abstract parts. The teaching approach that was inspired by behaviourism was known as **audiolingualism**. It is useful to have a sense of how this worked. A basic technique of audio-lingualism was the use of drills, consisting of a stimulus or prompt (from teacher or tape), to which the student provided a reply, followed by the correct answer (once again provided by teacher or tape). Audio-lingualism used pictures, especially in the early stages, to introduce relevant vocabulary and grammar. This enabled sequences like the following:

TAPE/TEACHER: Is the mother in the kitchen?
STUDENT: Yes, she is.
TAPE/TEACHER: Yes, she is.

If the mother wasn't in the kitchen, and the student got the reply wrong, then the tape would be primed to say 'No, she isn't'. This would provide a signal to the student that they had misunderstood a part of the prompt. However it wouldn't explain to the student where they had gone wrong – it would leave them to work that out for themselves.

More often, drills would prime learners to produce a particular structure, by providing a sample sentence, and then indicating immediately afterwards how the sentence should be transformed. For instance:

TAPE/TEACHER: The mother is in the kitchen. No....
STUDENT: The mother isn't in the kitchen.
TAPE/TEACHER: The mother isn't in the kitchen.

TAPE/TEACHER: The boy is in the garden.
STUDENT: The boy isn't in the garden.
TAPE/TEACHER: The boy isn't in the garden.

TAPE/TEACHER: The cats are on the bed.
STUDENT: The cats aren't on the bed.
Etc.

A moment's thought shows that by using transformations it must be possible to introduce most, if not all, of the grammar of a language. Affirmative sentences can be transformed into negatives, or interrogatives; actives can be changed into passives; modals can be introduced, as can perfect constructions; singulars and plurals can be practised; gender can be focused on, as can adjective constructions, adverb placement and so on. Furthermore, we wouldn't only be introducing structures, but also ensuring accuracy, and then drilling them, so that learners are able to produce them both fluently and accurately, all without using the mother tongue. The procedure could of course also be used to teach pronunciation and intonation, and indeed the

1970s and 1980s even saw the publication of drills focusing on aspects of pragmatics (such as congratulations, commiserations, requests, apologies, invitations, along with appropriate responses). In many ways, this was perhaps the most ambitious language teaching project up to that time. Its proponents thought that it could cover the entire language, without use of the mother tongue, and that its methods were fail-safe – bound to work for everyone whatever their learning skills.

Unfortunately – or perhaps fortunately – the claims for audio-lingualism were never sustained. Although research suggests that audio-lingualism can be very effective for people needing a crash course for particular uses of a language, it has serious shortcomings, as the reader can probably imagine. In what follows we will take as an example the issue of how to teach speaking in a second language.

39.2 An illustrative case: teaching speaking in a second language

In teaching speaking, plainly a teacher has to provide students with activities which get them speaking. Of course sometimes they may be speaking about something they have had to read or perhaps about something they have written. But it is no good if classroom time intended to develop speaking is used mainly on reading and writing, however important these also may be. Furthermore, it is no good the teacher doing all the talking either. Somehow the teacher needs to choose activities which will lead to (inter)active speaking.

At first sight this might seem straightforward: just ask the students to talk among themselves. But clearly on its own that is not an option. They wouldn't know what to talk about. They need to have a topic. But even then, if they talk among themselves, the teacher won't be able to hear. So a teacher might suggest asking them to stand up and have a conversation in class. Hoey (1991) quotes a case of three students who were asked to do just that. What happened can be seen in Illustration Box 39.1.

Samples of abnormal language are often useful for teaching us about what is normal. For one thing, the reader will have spotted a number of features of talk which appear strange. One set of features revolves around topic development. Topics don't develop. There are no follow-up questions, no clarifications or elaborations, no additions, and no comments. Furthermore, although it is quite normal for speakers to change topic, topic changes are abrupt – speakers make no connections between one topic and another. The general impression is that the speakers are not interested in what they or the others say. Connected to the first set of features, a second group of features concerns the patterns of interaction. The transcript can be easily divided into a series of questions and answers, usually across four turns, occasionally across six. The turns are simple sequences of Initiations and Responses, sometimes without the common third type of turn, the Follow-up. Finally, at a more detailed level of analysis, we can look at the words in each turn. What's quite striking here is that there are virtually none of the kinds of feature we would normally expect in talk. Missing things include pauses, little place holders or acknowledgments, like *well, erm, I see*; no repetitions, no rephrasings or false starts or other kinds

ILLUSTRATION BOX 39.1

Three students in the classroom

A: Good morning.

B: Good morning.

A: I love Tina Turner.

B: Tina Turner?

A: Tina Turner is a famous singer.

B: Singer?

A: Yes.

   (silence for four seconds)

B: What's her nationality?

A: She's American.

B: Where was she performing?

A: At the ….. Canecão.

B: How long was she performing there?

A: Only ….. only three days.

B: How's the weather?

A: It was cloudy.

B: Oh, what time is it?

A: It's twelve o'clock.

B: How are you?

A: Not bad.

B: Uh, Elian…

A: And you?

B: Fine thanks.

A: How, oh what do you live?

B: I live in Passo Manso.

A: And you?

C: I live in Bahia.   *(voices)*

C: What did you do last week?

B: Nothing special.

C: And you?

A: Eh, I went, I went to the beach.

C: How was the weather

A: It was *very* hot.

(Hoey, 1991: 66–7)

of self corrections. There is also little slang, and little of the kind of hedging common in everyday talk – such as *kind of, sort of, like, you know, sort.* When people talk about everyday likes and dislikes and experiences, they will use words like *right, sure, I know.* The question is, why did they speak in this odd way? This is a particularly important question for language teachers. It is also important to consider **why** this is important for language teachers.

It is true that the students who were recorded probably were not used to using these kinds of detailed linguistic features and perhaps did not know some of them. However, they will have learnt enough English to hold a conversation on the kinds of topics that occurred here. And as university students they wouldn't have needed teaching how to hold a conversation. The most obvious explanation for the strangeness of the talk of course is the nature of the activity or task that they were set. Because it wouldn't matter which language we were going to talk in, if told to stand up in class and have an unscheduled conversation in public, unless we were brilliant improvisers, most of us would produce much the same kind of talk. But this still does not really resolve the problem. We need some explanation of what it is about the task that had this dysfunctional effect. For this we need to infer what might have been happening.

The most likely explanation has to do with three main factors. The first is that the students had no purpose of their own for talking. They had been told to talk, so they talked. However, even when chatting on the bus, once we start chatting, we have a number of purposes, such as maintaining contact and being friendly, which push us to introduce topics, and to show interest in other people's topics. The second factor is that usually, when conversing, people have shared roles in maintaining the conversation. People take turns in asking questions, and when answering, they answer cooperatively. In the classroom context, the conversation was being performed to please a teacher, and not to please their interlocutors. The third aspect of the circumstances which may have affected the students was the fact that the context was not informal. Because they were being observed by the whole class as well as the teacher, whatever they might have wished, they would have found it difficult to be informal. That is, they would have found it difficult to produce precisely the kinds of features of informal conversation which the teacher might have wanted them to practise. In all, if the teacher was testing out a teaching technique s/he would have found plenty of evidence that the nature of the classroom activity influences students' language. More usefully, s/he would also have found evidence for the aspects of activities to think about when preparing a lesson, and the ways in which those aspects might relate to learners' language learning.

The kind of issue we are raising here is very much a reflection of approaches to the teaching of language at the start of the twenty-first century. Most language teaching approaches nowadays aim to develop students' ability to use language effectively for real life purposes, what we might call a 'communicative' or 'whole language' (or 'holistic') approach. People using a grammar-translation approach would have seen little point in asking students to 'have a conversation'. 'Having a conversation' does not focus on a specific grammatical agenda, and the students are not being stretched by being asked to work with a difficult passage presented in a piece of writing, whether in their first language or their second. Furthermore, since the students are not asked to translate, we can't be sure that they are saying what they intend to say. Grammar-translation is quite a clever technique for enabling the teacher to control what language puzzles the students have to work on, and for ensuring that the teacher can constantly assess how well they do it: either the translation is 'right' or 'wrong'. It is one kind of technique which enables the syllabus to be steadily pursued.

Proponents of the audio-lingual approach would also be appalled by this kind of activity, unless it were used to get the students to 'transfer' grammatical structures and vocabulary from the drills they had been practising into some kind of 'real life' use. Audio-lingualists were rather like proponents of grammar-translation in wishing to keep a tight control on what the students were doing. Batteries of carefully structured drills were equally carefully sequenced to make sure that the students always had something very precise to do, so that the teacher could constantly monitor their performance. Giving students 'free conversation' practice was generally the kind of thing which was fitted in if there was any time left once the grammar practice activities had been completed. Even in the 1970s, standard language teaching approaches were structured in a similar way, even when they were not strictly audio-lingual. One well-known approach became known as PPP, because it used the sequence 'Presentation-Practice-Production' (see, for example, Byrne, 1976): the teacher first presented the target structure to be taught, through pictures, or an oral or written text; then the structure was studied in more detail through focused exercises and drills; and finally, if there was enough time, students would be allowed to 'produce' the structure freely in pair or group activities. But the 'production' phase was not a central part of language teaching 'technology', and so the question of how best to implement it was rarely discussed.

People working from a communicative approach (such as Brumfit, 1979; Samuda, 2001), take a different angle. As noted above, they start from the assumption that students are learning the language in order to be able to use it. So, they argue that rather than starting from a presentation of a grammatical feature (say, the rule for forming questions or negatives), explaining it and then practising it, teaching and learning activities need to be grounded in learners' actual use of the language. In other words, lessons and cycles of work would do better to start by getting students communicating around a domain where some language is useful (such as getting them to ask questions or use negatives as best they can), so that students come face to face with the meaning they need to communicate. The teacher can then show the students how the target language handles that meaning, and then get them to continue working on their topic, incorporating the new language into what they are doing. Further accuracy work on the language being focused on can be added as needed. That way the chances of its being learned for subsequent use are thought to be much better. This is partly because the procedure should enable the learners to understand the meaning and relevance of what they are being taught. This should also make a difference to their readiness to try to use the new language, and to make sense of any correction they receive. To take an analogy from another domain of learning, that of driving a car, we learn the controls in terms of what they enable us to do (e.g., stop the car, accelerate) in relation to what we can already do. In learning to master the controls, we fit them into our existing ability to control the car (for instance, you can't really learn to use the brakes, and understand the feel of how they work, until you have got the car moving). But learning to drive a car is in many ways quite easy for most people – it is obvious what the controls actually do; and there is no alternative to learning (for instance, you can't put your foot out of the door to stop instead of using the brake pedal).

In contrast, learning a language is a bit more obscure. The basic concept and use of interrogatives and negatives is clear to linguists, but is a bit harder to make obvious to non-linguists. Also, there are alternative ways of expressing interrogatives (such as just using intonation). A further difficulty of course is that grammatical structures usually consist of a lot of little details, which can be hard to learn. Given these problems in learning a language, proponents of CLT argue that if learners first appreciate the purpose and value of the language features to be learnt, and if they are also given the chance to use what they have learnt, all these complicated details will be easier for them at least to begin to digest. It will also make it easier for the teacher to provide meaningful and useful feedback, and work out ways of providing useful practice. Clearly the so-called 'conversation' produced by the students in our first example isn't a very good starting point. To begin with, we need some genuine talk. The first issue is how to get some genuine talk. The second is how the teacher can organize activities so that students and teacher can work on some aspect of their talk. I will now present an example of this.

39.3 A communicative response: a first sample of a learners' talk

Since CLT emerged as an approach in the 1970s, people teaching from and researching this perspective have been using pedagogical activities or 'tasks' that they describe as **communicative**. In all changes of this kind, there is a bit of a leap of faith from what people are used to doing, to the use of the new kinds of activities. Not surprisingly, to being with people focused on the challenge of designing activities that might work (indeed, in 1981, Penny Ur published a book about classroom materials entitled *Discussions that Work*), rather than investigating just how they do in fact work. And indeed, there was an initial very exciting creative period from 1970 to the late 1980s, during which numerous imaginative course books and collections of materials were published, and articles appeared describing different types of activity. It is of course very important to have a rich range of classroom materials. Nonetheless, there are some very interesting questions for linguists surrounding the design and use of materials for language learning. Perhaps the key question is: how can the **design** of an activity, and the ways it is **used**, affect what language is used, and how it is learnt?

In one study, I explored what happens when people tell a story that they have seen on a video. Story-telling is quite a common activity in language classrooms. However, oral story-telling is not well understood, so in a preliminary study I asked a student to watch a 90-second extract from a *Tom and Jerry* video, and then retell it.

She had not had any special preparation for this – for instance, we had not taught her any language to deal with the story; and she had not seen the video before (though of course like most people she was familiar with *Tom and Jerry* cartoons). We recorded her talk, and then transcribed it. As you will see in Illustration Box 39.2, there are some interesting differences between her talk, and that of the students we looked at in the first illustration box.

ILLUSTRATION BOX 39.2

Story-telling

I saw a little film about a cat and a mouse
and the cat would like to eat the mouse
and there was a board covered over and over with plate and bowls
and the mouse put it down
and the cat was afraid that the plates are break damaged
and in the end there was er a big a big er I don't know a big hill with the dishes
and then she took the tail of the cat as a towel
and she gave her erm she touch her with her feet
and all the plates and the bowls break and go g down
and all the things was damaged
and the landlady took the cat
and go to punish to give punishment to the cat
and the mouse were very happy
and she took erm she took a board over her door
who stand er a nice house
so that's all

(from Bygate, 1996)

The reader may have spotted some interesting features of language in this extract. One that is visually very noticeable (especially because of the way the transcript is laid out on the page, but also because of the number of times it is used) is the *and* that appears at the start of each utterance. It marks the sequential connection between one action or element in the scene and the next. This use of *and* signals that the speaker has a number of things to say in order to achieve her purpose. This is related to a broader feature of the transcript, namely that the speaker **structures** the story. This is not just a sample of talk for its own sake: it starts with an introduction of the characters, a quick summary of the general theme of the story (*the cat would like to eat the mouse*), and a bit of initial scene setting (*there was a board covered over and over with plate and bowls*). There is then a series of complicating actions (the mouse does something that makes the cat afraid; the mouse then does something with the cat's tail, which results in the dishes breaking) leading to a conclusion (the cat gets punished), followed by a happy denouement (the mouse is happy). The speaker then actually ends the story explicitly (*so that's all*). All this results in quite a long 'turn' of talk. It is very different from the language in the first extract, in that it shows considerable internal structuring – all by a single speaker. The interest of this is that the structuring of the talk is **motivated** by the nature of the task. In other words, the design of the task can be related to the features of talk that the speaker produces.

Secondly, the reader may also have noticed some features of typical speech. These are what we might call 'editing features', various kinds of self-corrections and hesitations. These features suggest that the speaker is working quite hard on getting her message across. The hesitations are mainly *er, erm*, repetitions like *a big a big, go g down, she took erm she too a board over her door*. The self-corrections are phrases like *are break damaged, she gave her erm she touch her with her feet*, and *to punish to give punishment to the cat*. These are of course features of normal talk, but they are also evidence that the speaker is working on her expression as she goes. Talk here is perhaps unpredictable, but it is not a case of 'anything goes': the speaker is concentrating quite hard to find the right words.

There is a third aspect of the talk that a teacher would be interested in – the errors of various kinds. Some are straight grammatical errors, such as *she touch her* (for *touched*); *all the plates and the bowls break and go g down* (again present instead of past); *all the things was damaged* (singular verb instead of plural); *the mouse were very happy* (plural verb instead of singular); *the mouse put it down* (singular *it* instead of plural *them*). Some of the grammatical errors are more complex – for example *the cat was afraid that the plates are break damaged* would have been better expressed by something like *the plates <u>might</u> (or WOULD) <u>get</u> damaged*.

There are vocabulary errors as well, especially in choice of verb: *the mouse put it down* (instead of *threw*); *a big a big er I don't know a big hill with the dishes* probably means *pile*; *she gave her erm she touch her with her feet* (instead of *kick*); *go g down* (instead of *fell to the floor*); *all the things was damaged* (instead of *broken*); *she took a board over her door*, and *who stand er a nice house*, which do not make a lot of sense, and are hard to correct. Finally there are also some collocational errors involving words or phrases that co-occur differently in the English of native speakers. For instance a native speaker would not say *and the cat would like to eat the mouse*, but more likely something like *wanted to catch*; *there was a board covered over and over with plate and bowls* is a bit odd; in *she took the tail of the cat as a towel*, an English speaker would employ the verb *used*; and a native speaker would probably say *to punish the cat* rather than *to give punishment to the cat*.

Three main things come out of this piece of learner talk. Firstly, there is a direct relationship between the design of the activity and the nature of the language. This is a very important point in TESOL. Other domains of linguistics investigate the nature of language in normal use. TESOL is concerned with the nature of language in the context of pedagogical activities. This is very important, because classrooms are organized around – and through – pedagogical activities: this is what teachers use to structure the language learning experience. The second point concerns the nature of the language: it contains lots of features of normal talk, both in terms of detailed features like pauses and repetitions, and in terms of its overall discourse structure. This puts us in a position to work with the learner on their language in terms of how they use it. The third point concerns the learner's errors: there is a wide range of types of error. Since they all occur within the context of normal use, we have some interesting ways of thinking about what the learner can do to develop her language. In the next section the same speaker returns three days later to do the same task a second time. This involves collecting a second sample of talk entirely comparable to the first, but with one major difference – the fact that the task is repeated. I want to suggest that the results point to some interesting issues for teaching, and illustrate some of the intellectual challenges in working in this area.

39.4 A further sample of the learner's talk

So far we have noted that the design of a task can affect people's language. It seems likely that communication-oriented language offers a much stronger basis for learning, and gives much better information for teaching, than the kind of language found in Illustration Box 39.1. However, using communicative activities raises a number of new and quite important questions. One of these is: what can a learner actually learn from carrying out a communicative task? A second closely related question is: how can this be used by a teacher? Strangely, not many people have so far attempted to answer these questions. In a first attempt to explore these questions, three days after the speaker in Illustration Box 39.2 carried out the Tom and Jerry narrative, without any prior warning, I asked her to repeat the activity. Fortunately she was willing to do this, so she sat down, watched the video extract a second time, and then retold the story.

Now, before looking at the transcript, it can be a good idea to ask ourselves what we would expect to happen when repeating a task like this. Firstly, would we expect her to produce exactly the same language? Well, probably not. As we have seen, one of the criticisms of this kind of activity by people persuaded of the virtues of audio-lingual or grammar-translation approaches is that you can't anticipate what the students will say: there is no control. And we would probably agree with them to the extent that we cannot predict precisely what our student will say the second time around. On the other hand, we might anticipate some similarities. For instance, we would probably expect a sample of language with similar qualities of real-life speech. We would probably also expect similar content. What is harder to predict is whether there will be any changes in how she expresses herself. For instance, might there be any differences in the choice of vocabulary, or in the grammar, or indeed in the collocations? Could there be any differences in the pausing and hesitations?

Here we can start to formulate possible hypotheses. For instance, it is possible that the speaker will introduce a fresh set of problematic expressions, and continue to pause and hesitate in much the same way as on the first occasion. That is, the speaker produces the same overall talk, but composed of different language choices, chopping and changing but without much that looks like progress. A second possibility is that the speaker has a lot more difficulty the second time around, perhaps because she is trying to do too much this time, or because she has 'gone off the boil', as it were – she has done it once, and so doesn't try so hard the second time. This is also quite possible – indeed this is the most common prediction of experienced language teachers, who often suggest that repetition leads to boredom. The third possibility is that the student actually does better when repeating the task. This can happen in everyday life: sometimes our first attempt can be a bit disorganized, whereas having had an initial run at it, we may find we do a better job on the second attempt. Note in passing that each of these three hypotheses has quite different implications for the teacher and the learner in classroom contexts.

Having reflected on the three main possible results, let us now turn to look at our student's second attempt three days later. As you read it, you might like to consider once again the features of her talk, the errors, and this time of course any differences between this and the first version in Illustration Box 39.2.

ILLUSTRATION BOX 39.3

Story-telling (second attempt)

I saw a very nice cartoon about Tom and Jerry
and er the cat tried to catch the mouse
the mouse er run up to a cupboard
and there were a lot of dishes especially plates
and the mouse put up the plates and taked down
because he had fear that the dish will get break
and in the end there is a lot and um very high just like a hill
and after that she used the tail of the cat as a towel
and she kicked the cat
and all the dishes falling down
and all the plates are broken
and she picked up the cat
to give her a terrible punishment
I think so and the cat was smile smiled
and she go to erm to a hole and she put a sign where stand stood
this is a nice home my sweet home

Having already studied the first version, it is probably easy to spot things happening in this second version. Once again we see a story structure with an introduction, a series of events, a denouement and a conclusion. If you look at the different lines, you may also notice that there is at least one explicit descriptive utterance (*there were a lot of dishes especially plates*), and an explicit explanation (*because he had fear that the dish will get break*). This could be seen as a bit of an improvement on the first version, because it makes the circumstances and motives of the actions in the story a bit clearer.

Secondly, we might once again note that there are features of authentic speech: lots of uses of *and* once more; some hesitations (*er, erm*); some repetitions; and some self-corrections. However, there seem to be rather fewer of these features. This may raise the question of whether the speaker is perhaps a bit more fluent second time around.

When we look at the errors, however, we start to note some surprising changes, and strikingly these are mainly for the better. For example, vocabulary is more accurate or target-like – *cartoon, tried to catch, cupboard, dishes, used* (for *took*), *kicked, falling, picked up, a sign*. She still has difficulty with *put up* and *take down* but at least this time the adverbials are correct (what she actually wants are the verb particle combinations *picked up and threw down*). Collocations are also much more target like: *very high just like a hill, a terrible punishment, a nice home my sweet home* (very much closer to the target phrase *Home sweet home*). It is rather as though once the speaker was familiar with the task, she found it much easier to look for appropriate language. This would explain the vocabulary changes, but it also seems to be true for the speaker's grammar. She gets much closer to the target-like form in *he had fear that the dish will get break*. She also self-corrects twice (*smiled, stood*). Although her talk is still not perfect, there is evidence that second time around she makes better choice of vocabulary, collocation and grammar, and is also more fluent.

The general implication of this kind of result is that we can learn through communication simply by being challenged to try to do the same thing on more than one occasion. This is probably because the first time we carry out a task, we are probably busy trying to work out what to say as well as how to say it. Because of this workload, there are at least two difficulties: one is that we may not have the content adequately organized for smooth delivery; the second difficulty is that we don't have the attention or time to express ourselves as well as we can. The result is that the first performance is impoverished. Second time around, on the other hand, the speaker is more in control of the content, and at the same time has more opportunity to find the words needed. This raises some interesting possibilities for teaching.

39.5 Some implications for the practice of TESOL

We noted earlier in the chapter that communicative approaches to language teaching are concerned with teaching and learning through language use. In this section I want briefly to suggest that the preceding analysis of the two performances has some interesting implications for the study and practice of TESOL.

Our first general conclusion was that the design of activities is crucial for effective language teaching and learning. This implies a need to study different designs of activities, and how they impact on students' language. Studying different designs is probably best done by varying some small part of the design of an activity to see what effects the change has. The overall focus, then, is on the systematic interaction between chosen activity and language use.

Our second main conclusion is that performance on an activity is influenced by whether it is the first or a subsequent attempt. In other words, one's performance is influenced by the circumstances. We have only looked at one circumstance – repetition. However, there are other circumstances that can also affect how people use language – for instance, the amount of planning time available, or the formality of the context. Use of activities for a particular purpose would gain from careful thought about the circumstances in which they are used.

The potential impact of repetition raises some interesting empirical possibilities within the context of TESOL, reflecting the kinds of theoretical and practical issues that make up the field. In practical terms first of all, if repetition is pedagogically useful, then it makes sense to think about the ways in which repetition can be implemented in classrooms. This is a design issue. There are two main ways of developing this line of thinking. The first

> **ADVANCES BOX 39.1**
>
> ### Teacher intervention
>
> In addition to activity design, there is the matter of how students' language development can be helped by teacher intervention. For instance, Samuda (2001) describes the way in which a teacher can introduce a meaning-focused oral language activity in which most of the time the students work in groups, in order to be able to give the class a short report. While they are working, Samuda describes the teacher asking the students for interim reports, and using these updates as opportunities to feed language into the talk.
>
> There are also opportunities after the task for students to learn by looking back on what they did. For example, some (e.g., Lynch, 2001, 2007) suggest that learners can gain a lot by transcribing and then trying to correct their own talk. This can be interpreted as another form of repetition, with learners being led back to review their earlier talk, and considering ways it could be rephrased.

is by exploring the ways in which tasks can be re-utilized in a way that learners find motivating. So, for instance, any kind of questionnaire or interview survey task over a population is bound to generate repetition of the same series of questions. Similarly, running a series of interviews for the same job appointment typically involves asking repeatedly the same set of questions. Some kind of cyclical activity would have a similar dynamic, with students telling or presenting the same information to a number of individual colleagues in turn (say information on a poster as in the poster section of a conference, or a personal story). Design issues are also important if we turn to consider how far any given activity has embedded within it a pressure to repeat information orally during the activity as the group works through to a conclusion. Activities involving the sorting and arranging of information may perhaps be more likely to generate repetition when more information is involved: repetition is functionally useful when we find there is so much information that we need to go back over it to make sure we have got things right. I discuss some of these ideas in more detail in Bygate, 2006.

39.6 TESOL and language research

The theoretical implications of these practical issues revolve around clarifying how and why the use and repetition of a task can influence a speaker's use of language, and, in particular, lead to language development, and in what ways. What is at stake here is the extent to which deliberate designs and procedures thought up by professionals can be empirically shown to give rise to consistent patterns of genuine use and learning. If it can be shown that through use of communicative activities learners can be drawn into using language in consistent ways and developing their language, this would justify the claim that language can be effectively learnt without the teacher having to use the kinds of controlling methods that were central to grammar-translation and audio-lingual approaches.

If this could be shown, it would be along the lines that communication activities cannot be foolproof. The relationships that would emerge between activity, language use and language learning would be probabilistic: that is, we could not guarantee particular uses of language arising through a given task. As a result, we wouldn't be able to guarantee their learning. But, working probabilistically, we might be able to say that a particular **domain** of language is almost inevitable for a given activity. This might be enough to enable the teacher to use the activity as the basis not only for getting learners to work with using the language, but also for raising in the learners a sense of the need for the language, and for providing a context for it to be used and mastered.

TESOL might sometimes be seen as a relatively untheoretical specialism, one where the everyday contingencies of classroom contexts dominate, and wash away any empirical rigour. Of course classrooms are real world places, influenced by a wide range of unscheduled factors. However, as I hope this chapter suggests, when we start to study the multiple relationships between activity, language and learning that are at the heart of TESOL, the field turns out to engage with most of the central questions of linguistics. I mentioned several at the start. Maybe they can be best summarized into just two: in what circumstances are the various features of a language used? And how can circumstances lead to people changing their use of those features? These questions are illustrated by the issue of communicative repetition which we have been considering, and show some reasons why linguistics, applied linguistics and TESOL are so closely related.

Recommended readings

The main argument presented in this chapter has been developed through a series of articles, starting with the case study in Bygate, 1996. This was followed by a larger scale study with 32 participants which focused on statistical patterns, and a smaller in-depth study, Bygate and Samuda (2005), which explored the quality of the language. The impact of its use in classrooms was reported in two case studies, by Lynch and Maclean (2000, 2001). More generally the importance of communicative repetition in language acquisition has been discussed in a range of ways: in the context of first language acquisition (Peters, 1983), in first and second language learning (Pawley and Syder, 1983; Cook, 2000; Wray, 2002), in child second language acquisition (Wong-Fillmore, 1979), in the processes of learning language in classroom contexts (Lightbown and Spada, 1999), as a feature of teachers' language in the multilingual or second language classroom (Bernhardt, 1992; Duff, 2000; Wong-Fillmore, 1985), and in the context of foreign language teaching (Johnson, 2001). Finally, communication tasks have become a focus of much interest as a resource for teachers to bring communication and learning into alignment. Two introductory publications on this topic are Samuda and Bygate (2008), and Willis (1996).

Conclusion

Studying the English Language: Reflections

J. Charles Alderson and Jonathan Culpeper

The scope of this book

This book has covered a wide range of topics in the study of the English language, from the analysis of the structural and distributional properties of its sounds, words and sentences, and from the investigation of texts and pragmatic and social meanings, to the study of language variation and change, the historical development of the language, the use of language in political, literary and commercial contexts, the study of first language acquisition, second language teaching, and more. Inevitably, there has not been space to study other topics, including ones that characterize general linguistics degree schemes, such as forensic linguistics – the analysis of language to help solve crimes – or the professional languages such as legal language, areas of applied linguistics (e.g., how language performance and language knowledge are or can be assessed), speech therapy, computer-mediated communication, speech synthesis and speech recognition, machine and human translation and interpretation, and so on. However, in most university courses in which the English language is studied, opportunities exist for students to pursue their own specific interests, both in the areas covered in this book and those not, through independent study and especially through writing a dissertation on a topic of their choosing. This book will provide a solid foundation for such studies, providing numerous frameworks for analysing language and language use, and ways of both approaching and thinking about language.

An area we have not prioritized in this book is the psychology of language – psycholinguistics – how language is processed in the brain, how language and cognition interact, how language perception and use are influenced by factors like memory, attention, intelligence, aptitude, personality, motivation, emotions or by mental disabilities, deafness, blindness, dyslexia and so on. The same might be said for the closely related field of study, cognitive linguistics. One reason why we have not focused much on these areas is that much of the work within them concentrates on cognitive universals (but not all, of course), that is, aspects of the mind that work in the same way for everybody. A book that focuses on the English language is a book about variety, not universals – the English language is, after all, a variety of language itself and characterized by the particular ways it varies. Consequently, many chapters have looked at the English language in contrast with other languages and in various social contexts. Psycholinguistic or cognitive issues have not been ignored, but have played a subsidiary role, often appearing as part of an explanatory account. For example, cognitive aspects are referred to in Chapter 9, in accounting for how people understand texts, and also in Chapters 35 and 36 in accounting for grammatical and semantic change.

Descriptive evidence: quantitative and qualitative

In this volume, and particularly in the chapters that form Part 1, we have relied on the intuitions and introspections of speakers of English to explore aspects of language, including judgements of grammaticality and meaningfulness, the possibilities of word-formation and how sounds can and cannot be combined in English. We can all agree that this sentence in ways ordered is strange, and that the word Englishicity seems odd. However, we also know that intuitions can be idiosyncratic, based on one individual's uses and experiences, and they cannot necessarily be generalized to all users of a language. Indeed, they may simply be inaccurate, often being coloured by beliefs about language – folk linguistics. For example, many folk beliefs about language are based on underlying assumptions about writing. Hence, the belief that 'good', prestigious speech is a close rendering of writing (the claim that 'bad' speech fails to pronounce all the letters of words). Actually, the reality is different. For instance, as we indicated in our very first chapter, an analysis of the current Queen of England's speech – a popular benchmark of social prestige – will discover that even she will say 'fish 'n' chips' in fluent speech rather than 'fish and chips' (all speakers tend to 'drop' word-final alveolar consonants in particular contexts). By analysing actual usage we can support our claims, refine them, reject them or sometimes find evidence for new claims that had not occurred to us.

In recent times, the development of electronic corpora (the singular is 'corpus') – large collections of texts held on computer – has made it possible to complement language users' intuitions with more 'objective' analysis of actual language use. Thus, an individual's beliefs, observations and introspections about language, how it is structured and used, can be tested against language corpora. A concordance (a list of instances of the item along with the contexts from which they came) can be made of the use of target words and phrases in their contexts, so that regularities of use can be attested. Words can be tagged with their form class (nouns, verbs, prepositions, etc) and their patterning and co-occurrences can be studied. The constituent texts in a corpus can be grouped according to their topic, genre and subgenre; their source, whether written or spoken; the date of their production; the age, social background, gender and so on, of their producer, so that their characteristics can be compared and contrasted across groupings. Quite a number of claims made in this book are based on this kind of quantitative evidence, whether it is explicitly acknowledged or not. To take just a few examples, Mick Short, in his stylistic analysis of a poem (Chapter 26), uses a corpus to support his intuitions about the meanings of particular words; Andrew Wilson, in his discussion of spoken/written media and discourse types (Chapter 23), explains how a corpus can be used to identify varieties of language without recourse to intuition; Andrew Hardie shows in Chapter 37 how, in an hour or two, one can use the CHILDES corpus of children's language to test claims about language acquisition, whereas previously days, years or a life-time was required. If you are interested in exploring the corpus-based methodology, try starting with David Lee's website: http://personal.cityu.edu.hk/~davidlee/devotedto-corpora/CBLLinks.htm.

Corpus studies are also used in combination with qualitative text and discourse analysis, methodologies which are described below (see, for example, Baker, 2006). Of course, a corpus is not hotwired to an 'answer' for a research question. The design of the corpus is important (what exactly is in it? is it representative? etc.), and 'results' need interpretation (what does that pattern mean? why is it there?). That interpretation typically relies on understanding what language is doing in context. A corpus provides co-text (the language accompanying an item), but is rather limited with respect to context – the relationships between speaker, the setting, the activity and so on. Other methodologies need to fill this gap. Before noting these, let us briefly consider other methodologies which, like corpus methodologies, may give rise to quantitative results.

Language may be elicited by researchers, either through specially designed tasks hypothesized to give rise to particular linguistic features, or through language judgement or assessment procedures and tests. Regarding elicited data, much of the research on accents reported in Chapters 18, 19 and 20 is based on recordings of many people reading out lists of words, passages or, more naturally, simply being involved in chatting on some topic. With the advent of the digital computer, it is now relatively easy to store those recordings and accurately analyse them with software packages. Elicited data is fairly popular in the field of pragmatics, particularly cross-cultural pragmatics, as illustrated in Chapter 11. Discourse completion tasks are one example, which are a kind of questionnaire in which a short scenario is constructed (e.g., you need to ask a friend for a loan) and then participants produce, usually by writing in the gap provided, specific phenomena (e.g., a request). Such tasks can easily be manipulated to explore, for example, the effect of changing the identity of the person you are talking to (e.g., you need to ask a stranger for a loan, etc.). Some pragmatic phenomena, such as compliments or expressions of gratitude, do not occur that frequently, so finding a few hundred examples could take months, even years – something which elicited data avoids.

Another kind of methodology that can yield quantitative results using questionnaires is the judgement task. For example, one can probe an informant's use of aspects of morphology, syntax or even lexis by asking them to rate on a scale how acceptable they find certain items; one can probe how acceptable certain behaviours are in given contexts; one can gauge respondents' motivations, attitudes, reported behaviours, self-assessments, perceptions of language use and so on. The development of questionnaires is a complex business which can itself be studied to see what affects how informants respond. We must remember, however, that questionnaire data, like elicited data or corpora, are not fully authentic, that is, naturally-occurring, spontaneous and contextualized. It is important to supplement such methods with the qualitative analysis of authentic data.

Many of the chapters in this book, particularly those in Part 5 on Communication and Interaction, do not rely (at least explicitly) on quantitative evidence, but instead seek evidence through qualitative analyses. The general aim here is not so much categorizing linguistic features – a particular grammatical construction, a certain vowel quality, a specific speech act such as a compliment and so on – and then noting regularities that can be used to confirm or disconfirm hypotheses, but rather the aim is to explore how those categories come about in the first place and how they are used in local contexts (e.g., particular situations), with which functions and to what effect. Areas such as Conversation Analysis, Stylistics, Discourse Analysis and Critical Discourse Analysis are dominated by such qualitative analyses. Here what constitutes evidence is not just linguistic forms or structures: the focus is on what language is doing, and how meanings come about through the interaction between language and contexts. To take a brief example, *thank you* may seem to be a straightforward marker of politeness, but in particular contexts it can be used for sarcasm (often additionally signalled with particular intonation), to withhold politeness (' I don't thank you at all!'), for humour, and so on. Note in particular that we are not simply concerned with evidence of language but language and its contexts. Who is speaking to whom? Are they part of a particular social network? What are they doing? What do they want to do? Are they driven by particular social or ideological agendas? What is their attitude towards the situation and the language they are using? What does the specific utterance mean if viewed in a larger socio-political and situational context?

Given the importance of the social context of language, research methods that capture the use of language in context are of particular importance. Careful unobtrusive observation and recording (both audio and video) of language use are common techniques, although they may also raise both technical and ethical issues. Ethnography is one particularly holistic approach. This involves research in natural settings, intimate face-to-face interaction with participants (e.g., the researcher might live with participants), using categories of analysis that are typically used by the participants themselves, being open to any relevant categories, using multiple methods (but emphasizing qualitative and avoiding experimental methods), and attending to historical socio-political and cultural contexts. Ethnographies of communication are increasingly common, including of pilot–air traffic control and doctor–patient interactions, court proceedings, political interviews, classroom activities, dinner conversations and other everyday instances.

One way of collecting evidence about the local contexts of language use is to use questionnaires, which, rather than containing production tasks or rating scales, can be designed with open-ended questions and tasks. Another way is to use interviews or focus-groups to ascertain attitudes to language and language use, beliefs about and interpretations of language-related events, or to probe more deeply into responses to questionnaires. Indeed, responding to questionnaires and taking part in interviews are themselves acts of communication (dialogues) which can be both a method of research, and the topic of research into design issues (e.g., Oppenheim, 2001). There is, however, the danger of questionnaires and interviews getting at either what people think they should say, or what they are thinking now, not yesterday or tomorrow. Meaning and intentions, attitudes and beliefs, are often dynamic, changing and shifting, depending on context or on who else thinks what.

In short, in any aspect of the study of language, it is important to ask the question: 'How do we know this?' It is crucial to explore and establish the empirical basis of linguistic theories, and a critical approach is essential to the evidence presented for one's conclusions. The method we use to research language and language use will inevitably affect the results we get, the theories we develop and the hypotheses we refute or confirm. As we have seen, methods can be both quantitative and qualitative. We can either count occurrences of data, and analyse them statistically, calculating probabilities of occurrence and co-occurrence, or we can analyse discourse in depth, seeking to characterize patterns of use, local (contextual) meanings, and even to identify non-use. Results can be verbal descriptions of meanings, events, rules of use, probabilities of occurrence, frequencies, patterns, correlations or relationships, and so on. Or, we can do both, that is, triangulating data (Wodak and Krzyzanowski, 2008; see below). Table 1 summarizes some of the trends we have dealt with in this section with respect to quantitative and qualitative analysis.

Increasingly, however, researchers consider that the dichotomy between quantitative and qualitative approaches is too simplistic and favour using mixed methods, attempting to triangulate across methods and data sources, in order to get a more rounded, multifaceted understanding of linguistic phenomena. For example, a quantitative analysis may reveal patterns of a

Some characteristics of quantitative and qualitative analysis   *Table 1*

Quantitative characteristics	Qualitative characteristics
Something is counted (often involves statistics)	Something and its context is described
Categories are imposed by the researcher	Categories are found inductively and explored by the researcher
Emphasis on the identification of patterns/norms in the data (often using statistics), as well as exceptions to those norms/patterns	Emphasis on interpretation of the data (often in order to reveal how something works)
Generalizability is claimed (emphasis on representativeness of sample)	Authenticity is claimed (i.e., the ability of the sample to reveal how something works)
Data involves a large sample (sometimes millions of words)	Data involves a small sample (sometimes a short extract)
Data collection methods: corpora of natural language use, elicited data, discourse production tasks, tests, questionnaires with closed questions and rating scales	Data collection methods: analysis of the discourse, ethnography, semi-structured or narrative interviews, focus groups, questionnaires with open-ended questions and tasks

particular linguistic feature, but those patterns have to be interpreted, and this is where qualitative analysis is necessary.

Social and personal agendas

In the previous section, we put forward the idea that the task of linguists is to 'describe' the facts, based on observation, close and systematic analysis, experimentation and argument. And we also briefly touched on the kind of methodologies that might be deployed. We suggested that a descriptive approach stands in contrast to reliance on intuition, and, moreover, intuition coloured by folk beliefs. Many folk beliefs are prescriptive in nature, that is, they espouse the idea that one variety or feature of language has an inherently higher value than others. Value is determined by beliefs about what counts as prestigious (e.g., writing, Latin) and how language works (e.g., following the principles of logic). The prescriptive agenda is that certain varieties/features should be 'prescribed' (i.e., to be followed) and others should be 'proscribed' (i.e., to be avoided) (typically, couched as lists of 'dos' and 'don'ts'). Our earlier example of the belief that the best speech is a close rendering of writing is a case in point, because it assumes that writing has an inherently higher value. (Plato would not have agreed, as, coming from a largely oral culture, he considered writing, which enabled a permanent record to be made, to be conducive to laziness, since people did not have to work so hard to remember all they had to say!). Linguists typically see their agenda as being to describe and not to prescribe/proscribe.

But can linguists really dismiss prescriptivism? Actually, the gap between descriptivism and prescriptivism may not be that big. Both pursue social agendas. As Lippi-Green so neatly put it: 'An extreme representation might be that prescriptivists claim the right to tell people how to talk, and that linguists claim the right to tell prescriptivists what not to say' (1997: 8). In fact, prescriptive attitudes are part of the social fabric of life – we all have them. Moreover, they have considerably more impact in shaping the language than anything descriptively oriented linguists might say. If we take language to be, at least in part, a social phenomenon, then linguists need to take into account attitudes towards, and beliefs about, language as well as their consequences; moreover, all domains in our society are governed by specific norms, rules and conventions by which we all usually abide. In fact, critical discourse analysts do do this, and more – they have a specific social agenda. They aim to reveal how language is used to manipulate and influence; they try to establish the means, functions and motives of the construction of texts and genres within their dependence on contexts, and thereby to raise language users' awareness of the interaction of power, desire for power, and the use of language to achieve personal, institutional, commercial or political aims. This they do by carefully relating the language used to its context, and focusing on the functions and effects. They are particularly concerned with interpretations and understandings. More generally, it is important to remember that many linguists and students of language seek not 'merely' to describe language, but also to explain language behaviour. Prescriptivists also offer accounts of linguistic behaviours ('folk theories'). The key difference is that descriptivists and prescriptivists draw support for those theories from different sources: descriptivists draw on the kind of evidence about language outlined in the previous section, whereas prescriptivists draw on beliefs and assumptions about language.

Hopefully, this book has shown how fascinating it can be to study language, and, moreover, helped you develop a personal agenda for its study and your future. Language is, after all, a unique quality of human beings, and it permeates and pervades our thinking, our belief systems, our attitudes and actions, our social networks. It expresses our identities, it may reflect our gender, our ethnicity, social class, our origins. Language is central to our very existence, and thus studying and understanding language – in this case, English – is central to understanding human beings. Of course, there is a world beyond study. Those who have studied language will hopefully have developed a range of understandings and skills that can serve them throughout their adult and professional lives. The ability to identify problems, to develop or use suitable instruments to address those problems, to analyse results and critically to evaluate their meaning and value, are all important acquisitions. The study of language fosters an awareness of how language can be used to manipulate, to persuade and influence, and to describe accurately, or to obfuscate. Reporting and disseminating research results is an important communication skill one can acquire through the study of language, as is the ability to work in groups, to work independently, to manage one's time and to prioritize. All these affordances (skills) can be the result of the study of language, and thus can contribute to one's career or employability, as well as to one's personality. More specifically, the study of language can lead to any number of careers. Journalists, advertising executives, publishers, editors, product managers and marketing experts, all deal with language. Teachers clearly need to understand language and communication, even if they are not directly teaching language per se. A career in politics can benefit from having studied language, as can careers in counselling, speech therapy, social work, web design, human-machine communication, translation and interpreting, fiction or travel writing, interviewing, developing, conducting and analysing opinion polls, focus groups and the like. And of course, studying language may qualify one to research language, as an academic, and thereby to contribute to an increased understanding of the nature and the complexity of language and language use, and of the social and individual problems and issues which involve language.

A glance at the future for the study of English

It is impossible to predict how the study of English will develop in the future, although no doubt the changing media and the evolving contexts in which English is used, will impact on what is studied and how it is studied. There can be no doubt that technology will both enhance how we can research language, and affect the way we use language. The ability to audio record speech and video record language use in context revolutionized the study of spoken language. Similarly, speech-to-text technologies have already impacted how we can produce and analyse written texts. Speech recognition and analysis technologies have the potential to affect radically how we assess spoken language use; automatic translation tools may one day greatly enhance communication across languages and affect the study of inter-cultural communication, understanding and misunderstanding. Doubtless, the quantity and sophistication of resources for corpus-based study will increase. For example, a recent interesting development is the creation of corpora of the language of learners of English – both first language acquirers, and second and foreign language learners. In the latter case in particular, details of the learner's first language, age, stage of development, etc. can also be recorded. Learners at different stages can be compared, and the development over time of the features of individual learners' language can also be studied to see what changes when. Thus digital technologies have considerable potential in researching the use of language, just as digital technologies have shaped language use and practice (cf. sms, chat rooms, the Internet, email, YouTube).

Appendix: The IPA Chart

THE INTERNATIONAL PHONETIC ALPHABET (revised to 2005)

© 2005 IPA

CONSONANTS (PULMONIC)

	Bilabial	Labiodental	Dental	Alveolar	Postalveolar	Retroflex	Palatal	Velar	Uvular	Pharyngeal	Glottal
Plosive	p b		t d			ʈ ɖ	c ɟ	k ɡ	q ɢ		ʔ
Nasal	m	ɱ	n			ɳ	ɲ	ŋ	N		
Trill	ʙ		r						ʀ		
Tap or Flap		ⱱ	ɾ			ɽ					
Fricative	ɸ β	f v	θ ð	s z	ʃ ʒ	ʂ ʐ	ç ʝ	x ɣ	χ ʁ	ħ ʕ	h ɦ
Lateral fricative			ɬ ɮ								
Approximant		ʋ	ɹ			ɻ	j	ɰ			
Lateral approximant			l			ɭ	ʎ	L			

Where symbols appear in pairs, the one to the right represents a voiced consonant. Shaded areas denote articulations judged impossible.

CONSONANTS (NON-PULMONIC)

Clicks		Voiced implosives		Ejectives	
ʘ	Bilabial	ɓ	Bilabial	ʼ	Examples:
ǀ	Dental	ɗ	Dental/alveolar	pʼ	Bilabial
ǃ	(Post)alveolar	ʄ	Palatal	tʼ	Dental/alveolar
ǂ	Palatoalveolar	ɠ	Velar	kʼ	Velar
ǁ	Alveolar lateral	ʛ	Uvular	sʼ	Alveolar fricative

OTHER SYMBOLS

ʍ	Voiceless labial-velar fricative	ɕ ʑ	Alveolo-palatal fricatives
w	Voiced labial-velar approximant	ɺ	Voiced alveolar lateral flap
ɥ	Voiced labial-palatal approximant	ɧ	Simultaneous ʃ and x
ʜ	Voiceless epiglottal fricative		
ʢ	Voiced epiglottal fricative		Affricates and double articulations can be represented by two symbols joined by a tie bar if necessary.
ʡ	Epiglottal plosive		

k͡p t͡s

VOWELS

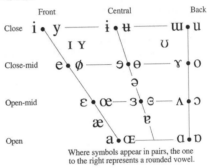

Where symbols appear in pairs, the one to the right represents a rounded vowel.

SUPRASEGMENTALS

ˈ	Primary stress	
ˌ	Secondary stress	ˌfoʊnəˈtɪʃən
ː	Long	eː
ˑ	Half-long	eˑ
˘	Extra-short	ĕ
ǀ	Minor (foot) group	
ǁ	Major (intonation) group	
.	Syllable break	ɹi.ækt
‿	Linking (absence of a break)	

DIACRITICS

Diacritics may be placed above a symbol with a descender, e.g. ŋ̊

◌̥	Voiceless	n̥ d̥	◌̈	Breathy voiced	b̤ a̤	◌̪	Dental	t̪ d̪
◌̬	Voiced	s̬ t̬	◌̰	Creaky voiced	b̰ a̰	◌̺	Apical	t̺ d̺
ʰ	Aspirated	tʰ dʰ	◌̼	Linguolabial	t̼ d̼	◌̻	Laminal	t̻ d̻
◌̹	More rounded	ɔ̹	◌ʷ	Labialized	tʷ dʷ	◌̃	Nasalized	ẽ
◌̜	Less rounded	ɔ̜	◌ʲ	Palatalized	tʲ dʲ	◌ⁿ	Nasal release	dⁿ
◌̟	Advanced	u̟	◌ˠ	Velarized	tˠ dˠ	◌ˡ	Lateral release	dˡ
◌̠	Retracted	e̠	◌ˤ	Pharyngealized	tˤ dˤ	◌̚	No audible release	d̚
◌̈	Centralized	ë	◌̴	Velarized or pharyngealized	ɫ			
◌̽	Mid-centralized	x̽	◌̝	Raised	e̝	(ɹ̝ = voiced alveolar fricative)		
◌̩	Syllabic	n̩	◌̞	Lowered	e̞	(β̞ = voiced bilabial approximant)		
◌̯	Non-syllabic	e̯	◌̘	Advanced Tongue Root	e̘			
◌˞	Rhoticity	ɚ a˞	◌̙	Retracted Tongue Root	e̙			

TONES AND WORD ACCENTS

LEVEL			CONTOUR		
e̋ or ˥	Extra high		ě or ˇ	Rising	
é ˦	High		ê ˆ	Falling	
ē ˧	Mid		e᷄ ᷄	High rising	
è ˨	Low		e᷅ ᷅	Low rising	
ȅ ˩	Extra low		e᷈ ᷈	Rising-falling	
↓	Downstep		↗	Global rise	
↑	Upstep		↘	Global fall	

Bibliography

Advertising Standards Authority (2003) *The CAP Code*. Available at: http://www.asa. org.uk/asa/codes/cap_code/

Aijmer, K. (1996) *Conversational Routines in English: Convention and Creativity*. London and New York: Longman.

Aitchison, J. (1989) *The Articulate Mammal*. London: Routledge.

Alcón, E. (1994) The role of participation and gender in non-native speakers' classroom interaction. *Working Papers on Language, Gender and Sexism*, 4(1): 51–68.

Algeo, J. (ed.), (1991) *Fifty Years Among the New Words: A Dictionary of Neologisms, 1941–1991*. Cambridge: Cambridge University Press.

Allan, K. (2001) *Natural Language Semantics*. Oxford: Basil Blackwell.

Althusser, L. (1984) *Essays on Intertextuality*. London: Verso.

Alvermann, D. E. (ed.), (2002) *Adolescents and Literacies in a Digital World*. New York: Peter Lang.

Anderson, B. (1983) *Imagined Communities: Reflections on the Origins and Spread of Nationalism*. London: Verso.

Andersson, L. and P. Trudgill (1992) *Bad Language*. London: Penguin.

Andrésen, B. S. (1968) *Pre-Glottalization in English Standard Pronunciation*. Oslo: Norwegian Universities Press.

Archer, D. and P. Rayson (2004) Using an historical semantic tagger as a diagnostic tool for variation in spelling. Presented at Thirteenth International Conference on English Historical Linguistics (ICEHL 13), University of Vienna, Austria 23–29 August, 2004.

Arends, J., P. Muysken and N. Smith (eds), (1995) *Pidgins and Creoles: An Introduction*. Amsterdam: John Benjamins.

Argyle, M. (1994) *The Psychology of Social Class*. London: Routledge.

Aristotle (1999) *The Politics and The Constitution of Athens*. Cambridge: Cambridge University Press.

Aronoff, M. and K. Fudeman. (2005) *What is Morphology?* Oxford: Blackwell.

Arstechnica, www.arstechnica.com (accessed 21.09.07).

Arundale, R. B. (2006) Face as relational and interactional: A communication framework for research on face, facework, and politeness. *Journal of Politeness Research*, 2(2): 193–216.

Ash, S. (2002) Social class. In J. K. Chambers, P. Trudgill and N. Schilling-Estes (eds), *The Handbook of Language Variation and Change*. Oxford: Blackwell, 402–22.

AskOxford.com (2008) http://www.askoxford.com/

Atkinson, J. M. and J. Heritage (eds). (1984) *Structures of Social Action: Studies in Conversation Analysis*. Cambridge: Cambridge University Press.

Austin, J. (1960) *How to do Things with Words*. Cambridge: Cambridge University Press.

Austin J. L. (1975 [1955]) *How to Do Things with Words*, 2nd edn, ed. J. O. Urmson and M. Sbisà. Cambridge, MA: Harvard University Press.

Bach, K. (2004) Pragmatics and the philosophy of language. In L. R. Horn and G. Ward (eds), *The Handbook of Pragmatics*. Oxford: Blackwell, 463–87.

Bach, K. and R. M. Harnish (1979) *Linguistic Communication and Speech Acts*. Cambridge, MA: MIT Press.

Back, L. (1996) *New Ethnicities and Urban Culture: Racism and Multiculture in Young Lives.* London: UCL Press.

Back, L. (2003) X Amount of Sat Siri Akal. In R. Harris and B. Rampton (eds), *The Language, Ethnicity and Race Reader.* London: Routledge, 328–45.

Bailey, G. and N. Maynor. (1987) Decreolization. *Language in Society,* 16(3): 449–73.

Bailey, G. and N. Maynor. (1989) The divergence controversy. *American Speech,* 64: 12–39.

Bailey, R. W. (1991) *Images of English: A Cultural History of the Language.* Ann Arbor: University of Michigan Press.

Baker, P. (2002) *Polari: The Lost Language of Gay Men.* London: Routledge.

Baker, P. (2005) *Public Discourses of Gay Men.* London: Routledge.

Baker, P. (2006) *Using Corpora in Discourse Analysis.* London: Continuum.

Baker, P. (2008) *Sexed Texts: Language, Gender and Sexuality.* London: Continuum.

Ballard, K. (2001) *The Frameworks of English: Introducing Language Structures.* Basingstoke and New York: Palgrave Macmillan.

Barber, C. (1993) *The English Language, A Historical Introduction.* Cambridge: Cambridge University Press.

Bardovi-Harlig, K. (2001) Evaluating the empirical evidence: Grounds for instruction in pragmatics. In K. R. Rose and G. Kasper (eds), *Pragmatics in Language Teaching.* Cambridge: Cambridge University Press, 13–32.

Bardovi-Harlig, K. and Z. Dörnyei. (1998) Do language learners recognize pragmatic violations? Pragmatic vs. Grammatical awareness in instructed L2 learning. *TESOL Quarterly,* 32(2): 233–59.

Bargiela-Chiappini, F. (2003) Face and politeness: New (insights) for old (concepts). *Journal of Pragmatics,* 35(10–11): 1453–69.

Bargiela-Chiappini, F. (ed.). (2009) *The Handbook of Business Discourse.* Edinburgh: Edinburgh University Press.

Bargiela-Chiappini, F. and S. Harris. (1997) *The Language of Business: An International Perspective.* Edinburgh: Edinburgh University Press.

Bargiela-Chiappini, F. and C. Nickerson (eds). (1999) *Writing Business: Genres, Media and Discourses.* New York: Longman.

Bargiela-Chiappini, F., C. Nickerson and B. Planken. (2007) *Business Discourse.* Basingstoke: Palgrave Macmillan.

Barnes, D. and F. Todd. (1977) *Communication and Learning in Groups.* London: R.K.P.

Barnes, D. and F. Todd. (1995) *Communication and Learning Revisited: Making Meaning Through Talk.* Portsmouth, NH: Boynton Cook.

Barnes, J. A. (1954) Class and committees in a Norwegian island parish. *Human Relations,* 7: 39–58.

Baron, N. (2005) Instant messaging and the future of language. *Communication and the ACM,* 48(7): 29–31.

Baron, N. S. (1977) *Language Acquisition and Historical Change.* Amsterdam: North-Holland.

Barrett, R. (1997) The 'homo-genius' speech community. In A. Livia and K. Hall (eds), *Queerly Phrased.* Oxford: Oxford Studies in Sociolinguistics, 181–201.

Barth, F. (1969) *Ethnic Groups and Boundaries: The Social Organization of Culture Differences.* Boston, MA: Little Brown.

Barthes, R. (1977a [1964]) The rhetoric of the image. In *Image – Music – Text.* London: Fontana, 32–51.

Barthes, R. (1977b [1968]) *Image, Music, Text,* ed. and trans. S. Heath. New York: Noonday Press.

Barton, D. (2007) *Literacy: An Introduction to the Ecology of Written Language,* 2nd edn. Oxford: Blackwell.

Barton, D. and M. Hamilton. (1998) *Local Literacies – Reading and Writing in One Community*. London: Routledge.

Barton, D. and M. Hamilton. (2005) Literacy, reification and the dynamics of social interaction. In D. Barton and K. Tusting (eds), *Beyond Communities of Practice: Language, Power and Social Context*. Cambridge: Cambridge University Press, 14–35.

Barton, D., M. Hamilton and R. Ivanič (eds). (2000) *Situated Literacies: Reading and Writing in Context*. London: Routledge.

Bauer, L. (1983) *English Word-Formation*. Cambridge: Cambridge University Press.

Bauer, L. (2002) *An Introduction to International Varieties of English*. Edinburgh: Edinburgh University Press.

Bauer, L. M. (2003) *Introducing Morphology*, 2nd edn. Edinburgh: Edinburgh.

Baugh, A. C. (1935) *A History of the English Language*. New York: Appleton-Century-Crofts.

Baugh, A. C. and T. Cable. (1993) *A History of the English Language*, 4th edn. London: Routledge.

Baugh, A. C. and T. Cable. (2002) *A History of the English Language*, 5th edn. London: Routledge.

Baxter, J. (1999) Teaching girls to speak out: The female voice in public contexts. *Language and Education*, 13(2): 81–98.

Baxter, J. (2003) *Positioning Gender in Discourse: A Feminist Methodology*. Basingstoke: Palgrave Macmillan.

Baxter, L. A. (1984) An investigation of compliance-gaining as politeness. *Human Communication Research*, 10(3): 427–56.

Beal, J. C. (2004) The morphology and syntax of English dialects in the North of England. In B. Kortmann (ed.), *A Handbook of Varieties of English*. Berlin: Mouton de Gruyter, 114–41.

Beal, J. C. (2006) *Language and Region*. London: Routledge.

Bedisti, E. (2004) *The Influence of Social Class on the Language of School Children in Greece*. Unpublished PhD Thesis: University of Reading.

Belfiore, M. E., T. Defoe, S. Folinsbee, J. Hunter and N. S. Jackson. (2004) *Reading Work: Literacies in the New Workplace*. London: Lawrence Erlbaum Associates.

Belich, J. (1996) *Making Peoples: A History of the New Zealanders from Polynesian Settlement to the End of the Nineteenth Century*. Honolulu: University of Hawai'i Press.

Bell, A. (1991) *The Language of News Media*. Oxford: Blackwell.

Benskin, M. (1992) Some New Perspectives on the Origins of Standard Written English. In J. A. van Leuvensteijn and J. B. Berns (eds), *Dialect and Standard Language in the English, Dutch, German and Norwegian Language Areas*. Amsterdam: Royal Netherlands Academy of Arts and Sciences, 71–105.

Bernhardt, E. B. (ed.). (1992) *Life in Language Immersion Classrooms*. Clevedon: Multilingual Matters.

Bernstein, B. (1971) *Class, Codes and Control*, Volume 1. London: Routledge & Kegan Paul.

Bhatia, V. K. (2004) *Worlds of Written Discourse: A Genre-Based View*. London: Continuum.

Biber, D. (1988) *Variation across Speech and Writing*. Cambridge: Cambridge University Press.

Biber, D. and E. Finegan (eds). (1994) *Sociolinguistic Perspectives on Register*. New York: Oxford University Press.

Biber, D., S. Conrad and G. Leech. (2002) *Longman Student Grammar of Spoken and Written English*. Harlow: Longman.

Biber, D., S. Conrad and R. Reppen. (1998) *Corpus Linguistics: Investigating Language Structure and Use*. Cambridge: Cambridge University Press.

Biber, D., S. Johansson, G. N. Leech, S. Conrad and E. Finegan. (1999) *Longman Grammar of Spoken and Written English*. Harlow: Pearson Educational.

Bilton, T., K. Bonnett, P. Jones, T. Lawson, D. Skinner, M. Stanworth, A. Webster, L. Bradbury, J. Stayner and P. Stephens. (2002) *Introducing Sociology*. Basingstoke: Palgrave Macmillan.

Blake, N. F. (1996) *Shakespeare's Language: An Introduction*, 2nd edn. Basingstoke: Macmillan.

Blasch, L. (2007) *Die Homepage der ÖVP in der Nationalratswahl 2006*. Unpubl. MA Thesis, University of Vienna.

Block, D. (2006) *Multilingual Identities in a Global City*. Basingstoke: Palgrave Macmillan.

Bloomfield, L. (1935) *Language*. London; Allen & Unwin; New York: Holt Rinehart & Winston. 1933.

Blum-Kulka, S., and J. House. (1989) Cross-cultural and situational variation in requesting behaviour. In S. Blum-Kulka, J. House and G. Kasper (eds), *Cross-Cultural Pragmatics: Requests and Apologies*. Norwood, NJ: Ablex Publishing, 123–54.

Blum-Kulka, S., J. House, and G. Kasper (eds). (1989) *Cross-Cultural Pragmatics: Requests and Apologies*. Norwood, NJ: Ablex Publishing.

Bock, H. (1931) Studien zum präpositionalen Infinitiv und Akkusativ mit dem to-Infinitiv. *Anglia*, 55: 114–249.

Boden, D. and D. H. Zimmerman (eds). (1991) *Talk and Social Structure: Studies in Ethnomethodology and Conversation Analysis*. Cambridge: Polity Press.

Bodman, J., and M. Eisenstein. (1988) May God increase your bounty: The expressions of gratitude in English by native and non-native speakers. *Cross Currents*, 15(1): 1–21.

Bolinger, D. (1980) *Language, the Loaded Weapon*. London: Longman.

Börjars, K. and K. Burridge. (2001) *Introducing English Grammar*. London: Hodder; New York: Oxford University Press.

Bortree, D. S. (2005) Presentation of self on the web: An ethnographic study of teenage girls' weblogs. *Education, Communication and Information*, 5(1): 25–39.

Bourdieu, P. (1988) *Language and Symbolic Power*. Cambridge: Polity.

Bousfield, D. (2008) *Impoliteness in Interaction*. Amsterdam and Philadelphia: John Benjamins.

Bousfield, D. and J. Culpeper. (2008) Impoliteness. Special Issue, *Journal of Politeness Research*, 4(2): 161–337.

Bousfield, D. and M. Locher. (2007) *Impoliteness in Language*. Berlin: Mouton de Gruyter.

Boyd, D. (2007a) Social network sites: Public, private or what? *The Knowledge Tree*. Available at: http://kt.flexiblelearning.net.au/tkt2007.

Boyd, D. (2007b) Why youth ♥ social network sites: The role of networked publics in teenage social life. In D. Buckingham (ed.), *Youth, Identity, and Digital Media*. Cambridge, MA: MIT Press, 119–42.

Braine, M. D. S. (1963) The ontogeny of English phrase structure: The first phase. *Language*, 39: 1–13.

Braine, M. D. S. (1976) *Children's First Word Combinations*. Monographs of the Society for Research in Child Development, Volume 41. Chicago: University of Chicago Press.

Brandt, D. (1998) Sponsors of Literacy. *College Composition and Communication*, 49: 165–85.

Brazil, D. (1995) *A Grammar of Speech*. Oxford: Oxford University Press.

Brinton, L. and E. C. Traugott. (2003) *Lexicalisation and Language Change*. Cambridge: Cambridge University Press.

Britain, D. (2002) Space and spatial diffusion. In J. K. Chambers, P. Trudgill and N. Schilling-Estes (eds), *The Handbook of Language Variation and Change*. Oxford: Blackwell. 601–37.

Britain, D. (ed.). (2007) *Language in the British Isles*. Cambridge: Cambridge University Press.

Broadbent, J. M. (2008). t-to-r in West Yorkshire English. *English Language and Linguistics*, 12(1): 141–68.

Brown, G. and G. Yule. (1983) *Discourse Analysis*. Cambridge: Cambridge University Press.

Brown, P. and S. C. Levinson. (1987 [1978]) *Politeness: Some Universals in Language Usage*. Cambridge: Cambridge University Press.

Brown, R. (1973) *A First Language: The Early Stages*. Cambridge, MA: Harvard University Press.

Brown, R. and C. Fraser. (1964) The acquisition of syntax. In U. Bellugi and R. W. Brown (eds). *The Acquisition of Language*. Monograph of the Society for Research in Child Development. Chicago: University of Chicago Press for SRCD, 29(1): 43–79.

Brown, R. and A. Gilman. (1960) The pronouns of power and solidarity. In T. A. Sebeok (ed.), *Style in Language*. Cambridge, MA: MIT Press, 253–76.

Brumfit, C. J. (1979) 'Communicative' language teaching: An educational perspective. In C. J. Brumfit and K. Johnson (eds), *The Communicative Approach to Language Teaching*. Oxford: Oxford University Press, 183–91.

Brumfit, C. J. (1984) *A Communicative Methodology for Language Teaching*. Cambridge: Cambridge University Press.

Bruner, J. (1979) From communication to language: A psychological perspective. In V. Lee (ed.), *Language Development*. New York: John Wiley & Sons.

Brunner, K. (1963) *An Outline of Middle English Grammar*, trans. G. Johnston. Oxford: Basil Blackwell.

Bucholtz, M. (1995) From Mulatta to Mestiza: Passing and the linguistic reshaping of ethnic identity. In M. Bucholtz and K. Hall (eds), *Gender Articulated: Language and the Socially Constructed Self*. London: Routledge, 351–73.

Burgess, E. W. (1949) The sociological theory of psychosexual behavior. In P. H. Hoch and J. Zubin (eds), *Psychosexual Development in Health and Disease*. New York: Grune & Stratton, 227–43.

Burkhardt, A. (1996) Politolinguistik. Versuch einer Ortsbestimmung. In J. Klein and H. Diekmannshenke (eds), *Sprachstrategien und Dialogblockaden. Linguistische und politikwissenschaftliche Studien zur politischen Kommunikation*. Berlin and New York: de Gruyter, 75–100.

Butler, J. (1999 [1990]) *Gender Trouble: Feminism and the Subversion of Identity*, 2nd edn. New York: Routledge.

Button, G. and J. R. E. Lee (eds). (1987) *Talk and Social Organisation*. Clevedon: Multilingual Matters.

Bygate, M. (1996) Effects of task repetition: Appraising learners' performances on tasks. In D. Willis and J. Willis (eds), *Challenge and Change in Language Teaching*. London: Heinemann, 136–46.

Bygate, M. (2001) Effects of task repetition on the structure and control of language. In M. Bygate, P. Skehan and M. Swain (eds), *Task-Based Learning: Language Teaching, Learning and Assessment*. London: Longman, 23–48.

Bygate, M. (2006) Areas of research that influence L2 speaking instruction. In E. Uso-Juan and A. Martinez-Flor (eds), *Current Trends in the Development and Teaching of the Four Language Skills*. The Hague: Mouton de Gruyter.

Bygate, M. and V. Samuda. (2005) Integrative planning through the use of task repetition. In R. Ellis (ed.), *Planning and Task Performance in a Second Language*. Amsterdam and New York: Benjamins.

Byrne, D. (1976) *Teaching Oral English*. Harlow: Longman.

Cameron, D. (1992) *Feminism and Linguistic Theory*, 2nd edn. London: Macmillan.

Cameron, D. (1997) Performing gender identity: Young men's talk and the construction of heterosexual masculinity. In S. Johnson and U. Meinhof (eds), *Language and Masculinity*. London: Blackwell, 47–64.

Cameron, D. (2000) *Good to Talk? Living and Working in a Communication Culture*. London: Sage.

Cameron, D. (2001) *Working with Spoken Discourse*. London: Sage.

Cameron, D. (2005) Language, gender and sexuality: Current issues and new directions. *Applied Linguistics*, 26(4): 482–502.

Cameron, D. and D. Kulick. (2003) *Language and Sexuality*. Cambridge: Cambridge University Press.

Cameron, D. and D. Kulick (eds). (2006) *The Language and Sexuality Reader*. London and New York: Routledge.

Campbell, A. (1959) *Old English Grammar*. Oxford: Clarendon.

Campbell-Kibler, K., R. J. Podesva, S. J. Roberts and A. Wong. (2002) *Language and Sexuality: Contesting Meaning in Theory and Practice*. Leland Stanford Junior University: CSLI Publications.

Candlin, C. N. and M. Gotti (eds). (2004) *Intercultural Aspects of Specialized Communication*. Linguistic Insights, Volume 14. Bern: Peter Lang.

Candlin, C. N. and J. Lucas. (1986) Interpretations and explanations in discourse: Modes of 'advising' in family planning. In T. Ensink, A. van Essen and T. van der Geest (eds), *Discourse Analysis and Public Life: Papers of the Groningen Conference on Medical and Political Discourse*. Dordrecht: Foris Publications, 13–38.

Cann, R. (1993) *Formal Semantics: An Introduction*. Cambridge: Cambridge University Press.

Cannadine, D. (1998) *Class in Britain*. London: Penguin.

Carney, E. (1994) *A Survey of English Spelling*. London and New York: Routledge.

Carr, P. (1999) *English Phonetics and Phonology: An Introduction*. Oxford: Blackwell.

Carrington, V. (2005) The uncanny, digital texts and literacy. *Language and Education*, 19(6): 467–82.

Carter, R. and M. McCarthy. (1995) Grammar and the spoken language. *Applied Linguistics*, 16(2): 141–58.

Carter, R. and M. McCarthy. (2006) *Cambridge Grammar of English: A Comprehensive Guide*. Cambridge: Cambridge University Press.

Carter, R. and P. Stockwell (eds). (2007) *The Language and Literature Reader*. London: Routledge.

Catford, J. C. (1994) *A Practical Introduction to Phonetics*. Oxford: Oxford University Press.

Cazden, C. (2001 [1988]) *Classroom Discourse: The Language of Teaching and Learning*. Portsmouth, NH: Heinemann Educational.

Cazden, C. and S. W. Beck. (2003) Classroom discourse. In A. C. Graesser, M. A. Gernsbacher and S. R. Goldman (eds), *Handbook of Discourse Processes*. Mahwah, NJ: Lawrence Erlbaum Associates.

Chambers, J. K. (1991) Canada. In J. Cheshire (ed.), *English Around the World: Sociolinguistic Perspectives*. Cambridge: Cambridge University Press, 89–107.

Chambers, J. K. (2003) *Sociolinguistic Theory*, 2nd edn. Oxford: Blackwell.

Chambers, J. K. and P. Trudgill. (1998) *Dialectology*, 2nd edn. Cambridge: Cambridge University Press.

Chambers, J. K., P. Trudgill and N. Schilling-Estes (eds). (2002) *The Handbook of Language Variation and Change*. Oxford: Blackwell.

Chasin, A. (2000) *Selling Out: The Gay and Lesbian Movement Goes to Market*. New York and Basingstoke: Palgrave Macmillan.

Cheshire, J. (1982) *Variation in an English Dialect*. Cambridge: Cambridge University Press.

Cheshire, J. (1991) Variation in the use of 'ain't' in an urban British English dialect. In P. Trudgill and J. Chambers (eds), *Dialects of English: Studies in Grammatical Variation*. New York: Longman. 54–73.

Cheshire, J. (1998) Double negatives are illogical. In L. Bauer and P. Trudgill (eds), *Language Myths*. London: Penguin, 113–22.

Cheshire, J. (2007) Discourse variation, grammaticalisation and stuff like that. *Journal of Sociolinguistics*, 11(2): 155–93.

Cheshire, J., V. Edwards and P. Whittle. (1993) Non-standard English and dialect levelling. In J. Milroy and L. Milroy (eds), *Real English: The Grammar of English Dialects in the British Isle*s. London: Longman, 53–96.

Cheshire, J., P. Kerswill and A. Williams. (2005) On the non-convergence of phonology, grammar and discourse. In P. Auer, F. Hinskens and P. Kerswill (eds), *Dialect Change: Convergence and Divergence in European Languages*. Cambridge: Cambridge University Press, 135–67.

Cheshire, J., S. Fox, P. Kerswill and E. Torgersen. (2008a in press) Ethnicity, friendship network and social practices as the motor of dialect change: Linguistic innovation in London. In A. Lenz and K. Mattheier (eds), *Sociolinguistica*, 22: 1–23.

Cheshire, J., S. Fox, P. Kerswill and E. Torgersen. (2008b) *Linguistic Innovators: The English of Adolescents in London*. Final report submitted to the Economic and Social Research Council, February 2008.

Chilton, P. (2004) *Analysing Political Discourse: Theory and Practice*. London: Routledge.

Chilton, P. (2006) George Orwell. In *Elsevier Encyclopaedia for Language and Linguistics*, 2nd edn. Oxford: Elsevier.

Chirrey, D. (2003) 'I hereby come out': What sort of speech act is coming out?' *Journal of Sociolinguistics*, 7(1): 24–37.

Chomsky, N. (1959) A review of B. F. Skinner's *Verbal Behavior. Language*, 35(1): 26–58.

Chomsky, N. (2005) *Imperial Ambitions*. London: Hamish Hamilton.

Chomsky, N. and M. Halle. (1968) *The Sound Pattern of English*. New York: Harper & Row.

Chouliaraki, L. (2007) *The Soft Power of War*. Amsterdam: John Benjamins.

Christie, F. (1989) *Language and Education*. Oxford: Oxford University Press.

Christie, F. (2005) *Classroom Discourse: A Functional Perspective*. New York: Continuum.

City & Guilds (n.d.) *Level 2 NVQ in Food and Drink Service Candidate Logbook*. London: City & Guilds.

Clanchy, M. T. (1993) *From Memory to Written Record*. Oxford: Blackwell.

Clayman, S. E. and J. Heritage. (2002) *The News Interview: Journalists and Public Figures on the Air*. Cambridge: Cambridge University Press.

Cluysenaar, A. (1976) *Introduction to Literary Stylistics*. London: Batsford.

Coates, J. (1989) Gossip revisited: An analysis of all-female discourse. In J. Coates and D. Cameron (eds), *Women in their Speech Communities*. Harlow: Longman, 94–122.

Coates, J. (2003) *Men Talk*. Oxford: Blackwell.

Cohen, A. (2001) On the generic use of indefinite singulars. *Journal of Semantics*, 18: 183–209.

Collins, B. and I. M. Mees. (2003) *Practical Phonetics and Phonology: A Resource Book for Students*. London: Routledge.

Collins, P. and C. Hollo. (2000) *English Grammar: An Introduction*. Basingstoke: Palgrave Macmillan.

Conboy, M. (2007) *The Language of the News*. London: Routledge.

Connell, R. W. (1987) *Gender and Power*. Stanford, CA: Stanford University Press.

Connell, R. W. (1995) *Masculinities*. Oxford: Polity Press.

Conrad, S., D. Biber and G. Leech. (2002) *Longman Student Grammar of Spoken and Written English*: *Workbook*. Harlow: Longman.

Cook, G. (2000) *Language Play, Language Learning*. Oxford: Oxford University Press.

Cook, G. (2001) *The Discourse of Advertising*, 2nd edn. New York: Routledge.

Cook, G. (2008) Advertising and Public Relations. In R. Wodak and V. Koller (eds), *Handbook of Applied Linguistics. Volume 3: Language and Communication in the Public Sphere*. Berlin: Mouton de Gruyter, 113–30.

Cook, G., (ed.). (forthcoming) *The Language of Advertising*. London: Routledge.

Cook, V. (2004a) *The English Writing System*. London: Arnold.

Cook, V. (2004b) *Accommodating Brocolli in the Cemetary: Or Why Can't Anybody Spell?* London: Profile Books.

Cope, B. and M. Kalantzis (eds). (2000) *Multiliteracies: Literacy Learning and the Design of Social Futures*. London: Routledge.

Corbett, G. (2004) *Gender*. Cambridge: Cambridge University Press.

Coulmas, F. (2005) *Sociolinguistics: The Study of Speakers' Choices*. Cambridge: Cambridge University Press.

Coulthard, M. (1977) *An Introduction to Discourse Analysis*. London: Longman.

Coupland, N. and A. Jaworski (eds). (1997) *Sociolinguistics: A Reader and Coursebook*. Basingstoke: Macmillan.

Coupland, N. and H. Bishop. (2007) Ideologised values for British accents. *Journal of Sociolinguistics*, 11: 74–93.

Creese, A. (2005) *Teacher Collaboration and Talk in Multilingual Classrooms*. Clevedon: Multilingual Matters.

Crist, S. (1997) Duration of onset consonants in gay male stereotyped speech. *University of Pennsylvania Working Papers in Linguistics*, 4(3): 53–70.

Croft, W. (2000) *Explaining Language Change: An Evolutionary Approach*. Harlow: Longman.

Croft, W. (2003) *Typology and Universals*, 2nd edn. Cambridge: Cambridge University Press.

Croft, W. (forthcoming) The origins of grammaticalization in the verbalization of experience. *Linguistics*.

Croft, W. and D. A. Cruse. (2004) *Cognitive Linguistics*. Cambridge: Cambridge University Press.

Cronin, A. (2003) *Advertising Myths: The Strange Half-Lives of Images and Commodities*. London: Routledge.

Crozier, A. (1984) The Scotch-Irish influence on American English. *American Speech*, 59: 310–31.

Cruse, A. (2004) *Meaning in Language*, 2nd edn. Oxford: Oxford University Press.

Cruttenden, A. (1994) *Gimson's Pronunciation of English*. London: Arnold.

Cruttenden, A. (1997) *Intonation*, 2nd edn. Cambridge: Cambridge University Press.

Crystal, D. (2003) *The Cambridge Encyclopedia of the English Language*, 2nd edn. Cambridge: Cambridge University Press.

Crystal, D. (2004) *The Stories of English*. London: Penguin.

Crystal, D. (2005) *Pronouncing Shakespeare*. Cambridge: Cambridge University Press.

Culpeper, J. (1996) Towards an anatomy of impoliteness. *Journal of Pragmatics*, 25(3): 349–67.

Culpeper, J. (2001) *Language and Characterisation: People in Plays and Other Texts*. London: Longman.

Culpeper, J. (2005a) *History of English*. London: Routledge.

Culpeper, J. (2005b) Impoliteness and *The Weakest Link*. *Journal of Politeness Research*, 1(1): 35–72.

Culpeper, J. and P. Clapham. (1996) The borrowing of Classical and Romance words into English: A study based on the electronic Oxford English Dictionary. *International Journal of Corpus Linguistics*, 1(2): 199–218.

Culpeper, J., D. Bousfield and A. Wichmann. (2003) Impoliteness revisited: With special reference to dynamic and prosodic aspects. *Journal of Pragmatics*, 35(10–11): 1545–79.

Culpeper, J., M. Short and P. Verdonk (eds). (1998) *Exploring the Language of Drama: From Text to Context*. London: Routledge.

Czarniawska, B. and P. Gagliardi (eds). (2003) *Narratives We Organize By*. Advances in Organization Studies, vol. 11. Amsterdam: John Benjamins.

Darsey, J. (1981) 'Gayspeak': A response. In J. Chesebro (ed.), *Gayspeak: Gay Male and Lesbian Communication*. New York: Pilgrim Press, 58–67.

Davies, J. (2006). Affinities and beyond! Developing ways of seeing in online spaces. *e-learning, Special Issue: Digital Interfaces*, 3(2): 217–34.

Davies, J. and G. Merchant. (2007) Looking from the inside out: Academic blogging as new literacy. In M. Knobel and C. Lankshear (eds), *A New Literacies Sampler*. New York: Peter Lang, 167–98.

De Beaugrande, R. A. and W. U. Dressler. (1972/1981) *Introduction to Text Linguistics*. London: Longman. The first version appeared in German in 1972. It was digitally reformatted in 2002: http://www.beaugrande.com/introduction_to_text_linguistics. htm

De Camp, D. (1971) Towards a generative analysis of a post-creole speech continuum. In D. Hymes (ed.), *Pidginization and Creolization of Languages: Proceedings of a Conference held at the University of the West Indies, Mona, Jamaica, April 1968*. Cambridge: Cambridge University Press, 349–70.

de Saussure, F. (1916) *Course in General Linguistics* (also, 1974; trans. 1959 by Wade Baskin). London: Fontana/Collins.

DeLillo, D. (1988). *Libra*. Harmondsworth: Penguin.

Delin, J. (2000) *The Language of Everyday Life*. London: Sage.

Delin, J. (2005) Brand tone of voice: A linguistic analysis of brand positions. *Journal of Applied Linguistics*, 2(1): 1–44.

Demuth, K., J. Culbertson and J. Alter. (2006) Word-minimality, epenthesis, and coda licensing in the acquisition of English. *Language & Speech*, 49: 137–74.

Denison, D. (1993) *English Historical Syntax: Verbal Constructions*. London: Longman.

Dent, S. (2004) *Larpers and Shroomers: The Language Report*. Oxford: Oxford University Press.

Derrida, J. (1974) *Of Grammatology*. Baltimore, MD: Johns Hopkins University Press.

Derrida, J. (1976) *Of Grammatology*, trans. G. Spivak. Baltimore, MD: Johns Hopkins University Press.

Dinh-Hoà, N. (2001) Vietnamese, in J. Garry and C. Rubino (eds), *Facts About the World's Languages*. New York: H. W. Wilson, 794–96.

Dobson, E. J. (1968) *English Pronunciation 1500–1700*, 2 vols, 2nd edn. Oxford: Clarendon Press

Dore, J., M. B. Franklin, R. T. Miller and A. L. H. Ramer. (1976) Transitional phenomena in early language acquisition. *Journal of Child Language*, 3: 13–28.

Douthwaite, J. (2000) *Towards a Linguistic Theory of Foregrounding*. Torino: Edizioni dell'Orso.

Drentea, P. and J. L. Moren-Cross. (2005) Social capital and social support on the web: The case of an internet mother site. *Sociology of Health and Illness*, 27(7): 920–43.

Drew, P. and J. Heritage (eds). (1992) *Talk at Work: Studies in Interactional Sociolinguistics.* Cambridge: Cambridge University Press.

Drew, P. and K. Chilton. (2000). Calling just to keep in touch: Regular and habitualised telephone calls as an environment for small talk. In J. Coupland (ed.), *Small Talk.* Harlow: Longman, 137–62.

Dubois, S. and B. Horvath. (1998) Let's tink about dat: Interdental fricatives in Cajun English. *Language Variation and Change,* 10: 245–61.

Ducheneaut, N. (2002) The social impacts of electronic mail in organizations: A case study of electronic power games using communication genres. *Information, Communication and Society,* 5(2): 153–88.

Duff, P. A. (2000) Repetition in foreign language classroom interaction. In J. K. Hall and L. S. Verplaetse (eds), *Second and Foreign Language Learning through Classroom Interaction.* Mahwah, NJ: Lawrence Erlbaum, 91–108.

Duranti, A. and C. Goodwin. (1992) *Rethinking Context: Language as an Interactive Phenomenon.* Cambridge and New York: Cambridge University Press.

Dyer, J. (2002) 'We all speak the same round here': Dialect levelling in a Scottish-English community. *Journal of Sociolinguistics,* 6(1): 99–116.

Eckert, P. (1989) *Jocks and Burnouts: Social Categories and Identity in the High School.* New York: Teachers College Press.

Eckert, P. (2000) *Linguistic Variation as Social Practice.* Oxford: Blackwell.

Edelman, M. (1967) *The Symbolic Uses of Politics.* Urbana and London: University of Illinois Press.

Edelsky, C. (1981) Who's got the floor? *Language in Society,* 10: 283–423.

Edmondson, W., and J. House. (1991) Do learners talk too much? The waffle phenomenon in interlanguage pragmatics. In R. Philipson, E. Kellerman, L. Selinker, M. Sharwood Smith and M. Swain (eds), *Foreign/Second Language Pedagogy Research.* Clevedon: Multilingual Matters, 273–87.

Edwards, A. D. and N. Mercer. (1987) *Common Knowledge: The Development of Understanding in the Classroom.* London: R.K.P.

Edwards, V. (1986) *Language in a Black Community.* Clevedon: Multilingual Matters.

Edwards, V. (1997) Patois and the politics of protest: Black English in British classrooms. In N. Coupland and A. Jaworski (eds), *Sociolinguistics: A Reader and Coursebook.* Basingstoke: Macmillan, 408–15.

Edwards, W. (1992) Sociolinguistic behaviour in a Detroit inner-city black neighborhood. *Language in Society,* 21: 93–115.

Eelen, G. (2001) *A Critique of Politeness Theories.* Manchester: St Jerome.

Eggins, S. and D. Slade. (1997) *Analysing Casual Conversation.* London: Cassell.

Ehlich, K. (2000) Diskurs. In H. Glück (ed.), *Metzler Lexikon Sprache.* Stuttgart: Metzler, 162–3.

Eisenstein, M., and J. Bodman. (1986) 'I very appreciate': Expressions of gratitude by native and non-native speakers of American English. *Applied Linguistics,* 7(2): 167–85.

Eklund, R. (2004) *Disfluency in Swedish Human–Human and Human–Machine Travel Booking Dialogues.* Linköping Studies in Science and Technology, Dissertation No. 882. Linköping University. Retrieved September 29, 2008, from: http://www.ida.liu.se/~g-robek/eklund04thesis_corrected.pdf

Eldridge, J. (ed.). (1995) *Glasgow Media Group Reader, Volume 1: News Content, Language and Visuals.* London: Routledge.

Ellis, A. J. (1889) *On Early English Pronunciation, Part V: The Existing Phonology of English Dialects.* London: Trübner.

Ensink, T. and C. Sauer (eds). (2003) *The Art of Commemoration.* Amsterdam: John Benjamins.

Epstein, E. L. (1978) *Language and Style*. London: Methuen.

Everett, D. L. and B. Kern. (1997) *Wari': The Pacaas Novos Language of Western Brazil*. Routledge Descriptive Series, London: Routledge

Fabricius, A. (2000) *T-Glottalling: Between Stigma and Prestige: A Sociolinguistic Study of Modern RP*. Unpublished PhD Thesis, Copenhagen Business School.

Fabricius, A. (2002) Ongoing change in modern RP: Evidence for the disappearing stigma of t-glottalling. *English Worldwide*, 23(1): 115–36.

Faerch, C., and G. Kasper. (1989) Internal and external modification in interlanguage request realization. In S. Blum-Kulka, J. House and G. Kasper (eds), *Cross-Cultural Pragmatics: Requests and Apologies*. Norwood, NJ: Ablex Publishing, 221–47.

Fairclough, N. (1992) *Discourse and Social Change*. Cambridge: Polity Press.

Fairclough, N. (1993) Critical discourse analysis and the marketization of public discourse: The universities. *Discourse and Society*, 4: 133–68.

Fairclough, N. (1995) *Media Discourse*. London: Arnold.

Fairclough, N. (2000) *New Labour, New Language?* London: Routledge

Fairclough, N. (2001 [1989]) *Language and Power*, 2nd edn.. London: Longman.

Fairclough, N. (2003) *Analysing Discourse: Textual Analysis for Social Research*. London: Routledge.

Fairclough, N. (2006) *Language and Globalization*. London: Routledge.

Fairclough, N. and R. Wodak. (1997) Critical discourse analysis. In T. van Dijk (ed.), *Discourse as Social Interaction*. London: Sage, 258–84.

Fauconnier, G. (1985) *Mental Spaces*. Cambridge, MA: MIT Press.

Fennell, B. (2001) *A History of English: A Sociolinguistic Approach*. Oxford: Blackwell.

Fenton, S. (2003) *Ethnicity*. Cambridge: Polity Press

Fillmore, C. (1982) Frame Semantics. In The Linguistics Society of Korea (ed.), *Linguistics in the Morning Calm*. Seoul: Hanshin Publishing, 111–38.

Finegan, J. (2001) *Encountering New Testament Manuscripts: A Working Introduction to Textual Criticism*. Grand Rapids, MI: Eerdmans.

Fischer, O. (1992) Syntax. In Norman Blake (ed.), *The Cambridge History of the English Language. Volume II: 1066–1476*. Cambridge: Cambridge University Press, 207–408.

Fischer, O. (2006) *Morphosyntactic Change: Functional and Formal Perspectives*. Oxford: Oxford University Press.

Fischer, O. and F. C. van der Leek. (1981) Review of Lightfoot (1979). *Lingua*, 55: 301–49.

Fischer, O., A. van Kemenade, W. Koopman and W. van der Wurff. (2000) *The Syntax of Early English*. Cambridge: Cambridge University Press.

Fishman, J. (1977) Language and ethnicity. In H. Giles (ed.), *Language, Ethnicity and Intergroup Relations*. London: Academic Press, 15–57.

Fishman, J. (1991) *Language and Ethnicity*. Amsterdam and Philadelphia: John Benjamins.

Forceville, C. (1998) *Pictorial Metaphor in Advertising*. London: Routledge.

Foster, S. (1990) *The Communicative Competence of Young Children*. London: Longman.

Foucault, M. (1976) *The History of Sexuality: An Introduction*. Harmondsworth: Penguin.

Foucault, M. (1984) The order of discourse. In M. J. Shapiro (ed.), *Language and Politics*. Oxford: Basil Blackwell, 108–38.

Fought, C. (2002) Ethnicity. In J. K. Chambers, P. Trudgill and N. Schilling-Estes (eds), (2002) *The Handbook of Language Variation and Change*. Oxford: Blackwell, 444–71.

Fought, C. (2006) *Language and Ethnicity*. Cambridge: Cambridge University Press.

Foulkes, P. and G. Docherty (eds). (1999) *Urban Voices: Accent Studies in the British Isles*. London: Arnold.

Foulkes, P. and G. Docherty. (2000) Another chapter in the story of /r/: 'Labiodental' variants in British English. *Journal of Sociolinguistics*, 4: 30–59.

Foulkes, P. and G. Docherty. (2007) Phonological variation in England. In D. Britain (ed.), *Language in the British Isles*. Cambridge: Cambridge University Press, 52–74.

Fowler, R. (1991) *Language in the News: Discourse and Ideology in the Press*. London: Routledge.

Fowler, R. (1996 [1986]) *Linguistic Criticism*. Oxford: Oxford University Press.

Fraser, B. (1990) Perspectives on politeness. *Journal of Pragmatics*, 14(2): 219–36.

Freebody, P. (2001) Theorising new literacies in and out of school. *Language and Education*, 15(2–3): 105–16.

Freitas, E. S. L. (2007) *Taboo in Advertising*. Amsterdam: John Benjamins.

French, J. and P. French. (1984) Gender imbalances in the primary classroom: An interactional account. *Educational Research*, 26(2): 127–36.

Friedman, C., P. Kra and A. Rzhetsky. (2002) Two biomedical sublanguages: A description based on the theories of Zellig Harris. *Journal of Biomedical Informatics*, 35(4): 222–35.

Frosh, S., A. Phoenix and R. Pattman. (2002) *Young Masculinities*. Basingstoke: Palgrave Macmillan.

Gal, S. (1978) Peasant men can't get wives: Language change and sex roles in a bilingual community. *Language in Society*, 7: 1–17.

Garcia, O., Skutnabb-Kangas, T. and M. Torres-Guzman (eds). (2006) *Imagining Multilingual Schools*. Clevedon: Multilingual Matters.

Garzone, G. and C. Ilie (eds). (2007) *The Use of English in Institutional and Business Settings: An Intercultural Perspective*. Bern: Peter Lang.

Gaudio, R. P. (1994) Sounding gay: Pitch properties in the speech of gay and straight men. *American Speech*, 69(1): 30–7.

Gavins, J. (2007) *Text World Theory: An Introduction*. Edinburgh: Edinburgh University Press.

Gee, J. P. (2004) *Situated Language and Learning*. London: Routledge.

Gee, J. P. (2005) Semiotic social spaces and affinity spaces: From 'The Age of Mythology' to today's schools. In D. Barton and K. Tusting. (eds), *Beyond Communities of Practice: Language, Power, and Social Context*. Cambridge: Cambridge University Press, 214–32.

Gee, J. P. (2007) Pleasure, learning, video games, and life: The projective stance. In M. Knobel and C. Lankshear (eds), *A New Literacy Studies Sampler*. New York: Peter Lang, 95–114.

Geeraerts, D. (1997) *Diachronic Prototype Semantics*. Oxford: Clarendon Press.

Geertz, C. (1996) Primordial ties. In J. Hutchinson and A. Smith (eds), *Ethnicity*. Oxford: Oxford University Press, 40–5.

Geis, M. L. (1995) *Speech Acts and Conversational Interaction*. Cambridge: Cambridge University Press.

Georgakopoulou, A. (2006) The other side of the story: Towards a narrative analysis of narratives-in-interaction. *Discourse Studies*, 8(2): 235–57.

Giddens, A. (1991) *Modernity and Self Identity: Self and Society in the Late Modern Age*. Oxford: Polity Press.

Giddens, A. (2001) *Sociology*. Cambridge: Polity Press.

Giddens, A. (2006) *Sociology*, 5th edn. Cambridge: Polity Press.

Giegerich, H. J. (1992) *English Phonology: An Introduction*. Cambridge: Cambridge University Press.

Giles, H. (1970) Evaluative reactions to accents. *Educational Review*, 22: 211–27.

Giles, H. (ed.), (1977) *Language, Ethnicity and Intergroup Relations*. London: Academic Press.

Giles, H. (1979) Ethnicity markers in speech. In K. Scherer and H. Giles (eds), *Social Markers in Speech*. Cambridge: Cambridge University Press, 251–89.

Giles, H., R. Y. Bourhis and D. M. Taylor. (1977) Towards a theory of language in ethnic group relations. In H. Giles (ed.), *Language, Ethnicity and Intergroup Relations*. London: Academic Press, 307–43.

Gimenez, J. C. (2002) New media and conflicting realities in multinational corporate communication: A case study. *International Review of Applied Linguistics in Language Teaching*, 40: 323–43.

Gimson, A. C. (2001) *Gimson's Pronunciation of English*, 6th edn, revised by A. Cruttenden. London: Arnold.

Gleason, J. B. (1973) Code switching in children's language. In T. E. Moore (ed.), *Cognitive Development and the Acquisition of Language*. New York: Academic Press, 159–67.

Gleason, J. B. (ed.). (1993) *The Development of Language*. New York: Macmillan.

Goddard, A. (2002) *The Language of Advertising: Written Texts*. London: Routledge.

Goddard, C. (1998) *Semantic Analysis: A Practical Introduction*. Oxford: Oxford University Press.

Goffman, E. (1959) *The Presentation of Self in Everyday Life*. Garden City, NY: Doubleday, Anchor Books.

Goffman, E. (1967) *Interactional Ritual: Essays on Face-to-face Behavior*. Garden City, NY: Anchor Books.

Goffman, E. (1981) *Forms of Talk*. Philadelphia: University of Pennsylvania Press.

Goldman-Eisler, F. (1968) *Psycholinguistics: Experiments in Spontaneous Speech*. New York: Academic Press.

Good, T., N. Sykes and J. Brophy. (1973) Effects of teacher sex and student sex on classroom interaction. *Journal of Educational Psychology*, 65: 74–87.

Goodman, S, T. Lillis, J. Maybin and N. Mercer. (2003) *Language, Literacy and Education: A Reader*. Stoke-on-Trent: Trentham Books.

Gordon, E., L. Campbell, J. Hay, M. Maclagan, A. Sudbury and P. Trudgill. (2004) *New Zealand English: Its Origins and Evolution*. Cambridge: Cambridge University Press.

Gore, D. and D. Roumagoux. (1983) Wait time as a variable in sex-related differences during fourth grade mathematics instruction. *Journal of Educational Research*, 76(5): 273–5.

Görlach, M. (1991) *Introduction to Early Modern English*. Cambridge: Cambridge University Press.

Graddol, D. (1997) *The Future of English?* London: The British Council.

Graddol, D., D. Leith, J. Swann, M. Rhys and J. Gillen. (2007) *Changing English*. London: Routledge.

Graff, D., W. Labov and W. Harris. (1986) Testing listeners' reactions to phonological markers of ethnic identity: A new method for sociolinguistic research. In D. Sankoff (ed.), *Diversity and Diachrony: Current Issues in Linguistic Theory*, 53. Amsterdam: John Benjamins, 45–58.

Graham, A. (1975) The making of a non-sexist dictionary. In B. Thorne and N. Henley (eds), *Language and Sex: Difference and Dominance*. Rowley, MA: Newbury House, 57–63.

Gramley, S. and K.-M. Pätzold. (1992) *A Survey of Modern English*. London: Routledge.

Grant, D., C. Hardy, C. Oswick and L. Putnam (eds). (2004) *The Sage Handbook of Organizational Discourse*. London: Sage.

Grant, L. (1985) Race-gender status, classroom interaction and children's socialisation in elementary school. In L. C. Wilkinson and C. Marrett (eds), *Gender Influences in Classroom Interaction*. New York: Academic Press, 57–77.

Greatbatch, D. (1988) A turn-taking system for British news interviews. *Language in Society*, 17(3): 401–30.

Green, G. (1996 [1989]) *Pragmatics and Natural Language Understanding*. New Jersey: Lawrence Erlbaum Associates.

Grice, H. P. (1975) Logic and conversation. In P. Cole and J. L. Morgan (eds), *Syntax and Semantics 3: Speech Acts*. New York: Academic, 41–58.

Grice, H. P. (1989) *Studies in the Way of Words*. Cambridge, MA: Harvard University Press.

Grundy, P. (2000) *Doing Pragmatics*. London: Arnold.

Gu, Y. (1990) Politeness phenomena in Modern Chinese. *Journal of Pragmatics*, 14(2): 237–57.

Gudykunst, W. B. and Y. K. Young. (2003) *Communicating with Strangers: An Approach to Intercultural Communication*. Boston, MA: McGraw Hill.

Gumperz, J. J. and R. Wilson. (1971). Convergence and creolization: A case from the Indo-Aryan/Dravidian border. In D. Hymes (ed.), *Pidginization and Creolization of Languages*. Cambridge: Cambridge University Press, 151–68.

Gurau, C. and Y. McLaren. (2003) Corporate reputations in UK biotechnology: An analysis of on-line 'company profile' texts. *Journal of Marketing Communications*, 9(4): 241–56.

Györi, G. (2002) Semantic change and cognition. *Cognitive Linguistics*, 13: 123–66.

Haas, M. (1944) Men's and women's speech in Koasati. *Language*, 20: 142–9.

Hall, D. E. (2003) *Queer Theories*. Basingstoke: Palgrave Macmillan.

Hall, K. (1997) 'Go suck your husband's sugarcane': Hijras and the use of sexual insult. In A. Livia and K. Hall (eds), *Queerly Phrased: Language, Gender and Sexuality*. Oxford: Oxford University Press, 430–60.

Hall, S. (1988) New Ethnicities. *ICA Documents*, 7: 27–31.

Halliday, M. A. K. (1975) *Learning How to Mean: Explorations in the Development of Language*. London: Edward Arnold.

Halliday, M. A. K. and R. Hasan. (1976) *Cohesion in English*. London: Longman.

Halliday, M. A. K. and J. R. Martin. (1993) *Writing Science: Literacy and Discursive Power*. London and Washington, DC: The Falmer Press.

Halperin, D. (1990) *One Hundred Years of Homosexuality and Other Essays on Greek Love*. Routledge: London.

Hamblin, W. K. (1994) *Introduction to Physical Geology*, 2nd edn. New York: MacMillan.

Hancock, I. (1974) Identity, equality and standard language. *Florida FL Reporter*, Spring/Fall.

Haralambos, M. and M. Holborn. (1995) *Sociology: Themes and Perspectives*. London: Collins Educational.

Harrington, K., L. Litosseliti, H. Sauntson and J. Sunderland. (2008) *Gender and Language Research Methodologies*. Basingstoke: Palgrave Macmillan.

Harris, R. and B. Rampton (eds). (2003) *The Language, Ethnicity and Race Reader*. London: Routledge.

Harris, S. (2001) Being politically impolite: Extending politeness theory to adversarial political discourse. *Discourse and Society*, 12(4): 451–72.

Harris, Z. S. (1951) *Methods in Structural Linguistics*. Chicago: University of Chicago Press.

Harris, Zellig S. (1952) Discourse Analysis: A Sample Text. *Language*, 25 (4): 474–494.

Haugen, E. (1972) Dialect, language, nation. In J. B. Pride and J. Holmes (eds), *Sociolinguistics*. Harmondsworth: Penguin, 97–111.

Hawisher, G. and C. Selfe (eds). (2000) *Global Literacies and the World-wide Web*. London: Routledge.

Haworth, A. (1994) Towards a collaborative model of learning. *English in Education*, 26(3): 40–9.

Hay, J., M. Maclagan and E. Gordon. (2008) *New Zealand English*. Edinburgh: Edinburgh University Press.

Hayes, J. (1981 [1976]) Gayspeak. *The Quarterly Journal of Speech*, 62: 256–66. Reprinted in J. W. Chesebro (ed.), *Gayspeak: Gay Male and Lesbian Communication*. New York: Pilgrim Press, 43–57.

Heath, S. B. (1983) *Ways with Words*. Cambridge: Cambridge University Press.

Helot, C. and A. M. de Mejia (eds). (2008) *Forging Multilingual Spaces*. Clevedon: Multilingual Matters

Hennessy, M. (1994) Propagating half a species: Gender in learners' dictionaries. In J. Sunderland (ed.), *Exploring Gender: Questions and Implications for English Language Education*. Hemel Hempstead: Prentice Hall, 104–11.

Henwood, F., S. Wyatt, A. Hart and J. Smith. (2003) 'Ignorance is bliss sometimes': Constraints on the emergence of the 'informed patient' in the changing landscapes of health information. *Sociology of Health and Illness*, 25(6): 589–607.

Heritage, J. (1984) *Garfinkel and Ethnomethodology*. Oxford and New York: Polity Press.

Heritage, J. (1985) Analysing news interviews: Aspects of the production of talk for an overhearing audience. In T. van Dijk (ed.), *Handbook of Discourse Analysis*. New York: Academic Press, 95–117.

Hewitt, R. (1986) *White Talk Black Talk: Inter-Racial Friendship and Communication amongst Adolescents*. Cambridge: Cambridge University Press.

Hewitt, R. (2003) Language, youth and the destabilisation of ethnicity. In R. Harris and B. Rampton (eds), *The Language, Ethnicity and Race Reader*. London: Routledge, 188–98.

Heywood, J. (2004) 'The object of contempt is the object of desire': Representations of masculinity in 'Straight to Hell' magazine. In S. Johnson and U. H. Meinhof. *Language and Masculinity*. Oxford: Blackwell, 188–207.

Hine, C. (2000) *Virtual Ethnography*. London: Sage.

Hjelmslev, L. (1961) *Prolegomena to a Theory of Language*, trans. F. J. Whitfield. Madison: University of Wisconsin Press.

Hoey, M. (1991) Some properties of spoken discourse. In R. Bowers and C. Brumfit (eds), *Applied Linguistics and English Language Teaching*. Basingstoke: Macmillan/MEP.

Hoey, M. (1996) A clause-relational analysis of selected dictionary entries: Contrast and compatibility in the definitions of 'man' and 'woman'. In C. Caldas-Coulthard and M. Coulthard (eds), *Texts and Practices: Readings in Critical Discourse Analysis*. London: Routledge, 150–65.

Hoffmann, L. (1991) Texts and text types in LSP. In H. Schröder (ed.), *Subject-Oriented Texts: Languages for Special Purposes and Text Theory*. Berlin: Mouton de Gruyter, 158–66.

Hoffmann, S. (2007) Processing Internet-derived text – Creating a corpus of Usenet messages. *Literary and Linguistic Computing*, 22(2): 151–65.

Hogenraad, R., D. P. McKenzie and N. Péladeau. (2003) Force and influence in content analysis: The production of new social knowledge. *Quality and Quantity*, 37: 221–38.

Hogg, R. M. (1992a [–2001]) *The Cambridge History of the English Language*. Volume1 of 6: *The Beginnings to 1066*. Cambridge: Cambridge University Press.

Hogg, R. M. (1992b) Phonology and morphology. In R. M. Hogg (ed.), *The Cambridge History of the English Language. Volume I: The Beginnings to 1066.* Cambridge: Cambridge University Press, 67–167

Hogg, R. M. (1992c) Introduction. In Hogg (1992a).

Hogg, R. M. (1992d) Phonology and morphology. In Hogg (1992a).

Hogg, R. M. (2002) *Introduction to Old English.* Edinburgh: Edinburgh University Press.

Hogg, R. M. and D. Denison (eds). (2006) *A History of the English Language.* Cambridge: Cambridge University Press.

Holborn, M., and M. Haralambos. (2000) *Sociology. Themes and perspectives.* London: Collins

Hollmann, W. B. (2003) *Synchrony andDdiachrony of English Periphrastic Causatives: A Cognitive Perspective.* Unpublished PhD thesis. Manchester: University of Manchester.

Hollmann, W. B. and A. Siewierska. (2006). Corpora and (the need for) other methods in a study of Lancashire dialect. *Zeitschrift für Anglistik und Amerikanistik*, 54: 203–16.

Holly, W. (1990) *Politikersprache. Inszenierungen und Rollenkonflikte im informellen Sprachhandeln eines Bundestagsabgeordneten.* Berlin: de Gruyter.

Holm, J. (2000) *An Introduction to Pidgins and Creoles.* Cambridge: Cambridge University Press.

Holmes, J. (2006) *Gendered Talk at Work.* Oxford: Blackwell.

Holmes, J. (2008) *An Introduction to Sociolinguistics*, 3rd edn. London: Arnold.

Holmes, J. and M. Stubbe. (2003) *Power and Politeness in the Workplace: A Sociolinguistic Analysis of Talk at Work.* London: Pearson Education.

Holtgraves, T. M. (1994) Communication in context: Effects of speaker status on the comprehension of indirect requests. *Journal of Experimental Psychology: Learning, Memory and Cognition*, 20: 1205–18.

Honderich, T. (2003) *After the Terror*, expanded, rev. edn. Edinburgh: Edinburgh University Press.

Honeybone, P. (2001) Lenition Inhibition in Liverpool English. *English Language and Linguistics*, 5: 213–49.

Hopkinson, G. (2003) Stories from the front-line: How they construct the organisation. *Journal of Management Studies*, 40(8): 1943–69.

Hopper, P. (1991) On some principles of grammaticalization. In E. C. Traugott and B. Heine (eds), *Approaches to Grammaticalization*, vol. 1. Amsterdam: John Benjamins, 17–35.

Hopper, P. J., and E. C. Traugott. (2003) *Grammaticalization*, 2nd edn. Cambridge: Cambridge University Press.

Horn, L. R. and G. Ward (eds). (2004) *The Handbook of Pragmatics.* Oxford: Blackwell.

Horobin, S. and J. Smith. (2002) *An Introduction to Middle English.* Edinburgh: Edinburgh University Press.

Howard-Hill, T. H. (2006) Early Modern Printers and the Standardization of English Spelling. *Modern Language Review*, 101(1): 16–29.

Howe, C. (1997) *Gender and Classroom Interaction: A Research Review.* Edinburgh: SCRE.

Huang, Y. (2007) *Pragmatics.* Oxford: Oxford University Press.

Huber, M. (1999) *Ghanaian Pidgin English in its West African Context: A Sociohistorical and Structural Analysis.* Amsterdam: John Benjamins.

Huber, M. and K. Dako. (2008) Ghanaian English: Morphology and syntax. In R. Mesthrie (ed.), *Varieties of English 4: Africa, South and Southeast Asia.* Berlin: Mouton de Gruyter, 368–94.

Huddleston, R. and G. Pullum. (2002) *The Cambridge Grammar of the English Language.* Cambridge: Cambridge University Press.

Hudson, R. (2000). The language teacher and descriptive versus prescriptive norms: The educational context. Lecture presented to a workshop in Paris on prescriptivism and foreign-language teaching in March 2000. Available at: http://www.phon.ucl.ac.uk/home/dick/standard.htm, accessed 23 March 2008.

Huffaker, D. A. and S. L. Calvert. (2005) Gender, identity, and language use in teenage blogs. *Journal of Computer-Mediated Communication*, 10(2): Article 1.

Hughes, A. and P. Trudgill. (1996) *English Accents and Dialects*. London: Arnold.

Hughes, A., P. Trudgill and D. Watt. (2005) *English Accents and Dialects*. London: Arnold.

Hughes, G. (1991) *Swearing: A Social History of Foul Language, Oaths and Profanity in English*. London: Blackwell.

Hughes, G. (2000) *A History of English Words*. Oxford: Blackwell.

Hughes, R. (1996) *English in Speech and Writing: Investigating Language and Literature*. London: Longman.

Hurford, J. R. and B. Heasley. (1983). *Semantics: A Coursebook*. Cambridge: Cambridge University Press.

Hutchby, I. (2006) *Media Talk: Conversation Analysis and the Study of Broadcasting*. Maidenhead: Open University Press.

Hutchby, I. and R. Wooffitt. (1998) *Conversation Analysis: Principles, Practices and Applications*. Cambridge: Polity Press.

Hutchinson, J. and A. Smith. (1996) *Ethnicity*. Oxford: Oxford University Press.

Huxley, A. (1959) *Brave New World Revisited*. London: Chatto & Windus.

Iedema, R. and H. Scheeres. (2003) From doing work to talking work: Renegotiating knowing, doing, and identity. *Applied Linguistics*, 24(3): 316–37.

Iedema, R. and R. Wodak. (2005) Communication in institutions. In U. Ammon, N. Dittmar, K. J. Mattheier and P. Trudgill (eds), *Sociolinguistics: An International Handbook of the Science of Language and Society*, Volume 2, 2nd edn. Berlin: Mouton de Gruyter, 1602–15.

Ingram, D. (1989) *First Language Acquisition: Method, Description and Explanation*. Cambridge: Cambridge University Press.

Isajiw, W. (1974) Definitions of Ethnicity. *Ethnicity*, 1: 111–24.

Isaksson, M. (2005) Ethos and pathos representations in mission statements: Identifying virtues and emotions in an emerging business genre. In A. Trosborg and P. E. Flyvholm Jørgersen (eds), *Business Discourse: Texts and Contexts*. Bern: Peter Lang, 111–38.

Ivanič, R. (1998) *Writing and Identity: The Discoursal Construction of Identity in Academic Writing*. Amsterdam: John Benjamins.

Ivanič, R. (2006) Language, learning and identification. In R. Kiely, P. Rea-Dickens, H. Woodfield and G. Clibbon (eds), *Language, Culture and Identity in Applied Linguistics*. Bristol: Equinox.

Ivanič, R., R. Edwards, C. Satchwell and J. Smith. (2007) Possibilities for pedagogy in further education: Harnessing the abundance of literacy. *British Educational Research Journal*, TLRP Special Issue, 33(5): 703–21.

Ivanič, R., R. Edwards, D. Barton, M. Martin Jones, Z. Fowler, B. Hughes, G. Mannion, K. Miller, C. Satchwell and J. Smith. (2009) *Improving Learning in College: Rethinking Literacies across the Curriculum*. London: Routledge.

Jablin, F. M. and L. Putnam. (2001) *The New Handbook of Organizational Communication: Advances in Theory, Research, and Methods*. Thousand Oaks, CA: Sage.

Jacobs, G. (1999) *Preformulating the News: An Analysis of the Metapragmatics of Press Releases*. Amsterdam: John Benjamins.

Jacobs, G. E. (2004) Complicating contexts: Issues of methodology in researching the language and literacies of instant messaging. *Reading Research Quarterly*, 39(4): 394–406.

Jacobs, G., H. Rogers and R. Smyth. (1999) Sounding gay, sounding straight: A search for phonetic correlates. Paper presented at *New Ways of Analysing Variation*, 28, Toronto.

Jakobson, R. (1941) *Kindersprache, Apasie und allgemeine Lautgesetze.* Uppsala: Almqvist & Wiksell. [English translation 1968; by A. R. Keiler, under the title *Child Language, Aphasia and Phonological Universals.* The Hague: Mouton.]

Jameson, D. A. (2000) Telling the investment story: A narrative analysis of shareholder reports. *Journal of Business Communication*, 37(1): 7–38.

Jay, T. (1992) *Cursing in America: A Psycholinguistic Study of Dirty Language in the Courts, in the Movies, in the Schoolyards and on the Streets.* Philadelphia: John Benjamins.

Jefferson, G. (1979) A technique for inviting laughter and its subsequent acceptance/declination. In G. Psathas (ed.), *Everyday Language: Studies in Ethnomethodology.* Hillsdale, NJ: Lawrence Erlbaum Associates, 79–96.

Jenkins, J. (2003) *World Englishes: A Resource Book for Students.* London: Routledge.

Jensen, A. R. (1968) Social class and verbal learning. In M. Deutsch, I. Katz and A. R. Jensen (eds), *Social Class, Race, and Psychological Development.* New York: Holt, Rinehart & Winston, 115–74.

Jespersen, O. (1909–49) *A Modern English Grammar on Historical Principles*, 7 vols. (Reprinted 1954) London: Allen & Unwin.

Jespersen, O. (1922) *Language: Its nature, Development and Origin.* London: Allen & Unwin.

Johnson, K. (2001) *Introduction to Foreign Language Learning and Teaching.* Harlow: Pearson Education

Johnson, S. and U. Meinhof (eds). (1997) *Language and Masculinity.* Oxford: Blackwell.

Johnstone, B. (2008) *Discourse Analysis.* Oxford: Blackwell.

Jones, C. (1989) *A History of English Phonology.* London: Longman.

Jordan, R. (1974) *Handbook of Middle English Grammar: Phonology,* trans. and revised E. J. Crook. The Hague: Mouton.

Joseph, J. (2004) *Language and Identity: National, Ethnic, Religious.* Basingstoke: Palgrave Macmillan.

Kachru, B. B. (1986) *The Alchemy of English: The Spread, Functions, and Models of Non-Native Englishes.* Oxford and New York: Pergamon Institute of English.

Kachru, B. B. (2005) *Asian Englishes: Beyond the Canon.* Hong Kong: Hong Kong University Press.

Kachru, B. B., Y. Kachru and C. L. Nelson (eds). (2006) *The Handbook of World Englishes.* Malden, MA: Blackwell.

Kalman, J. (1999) *Writing on the Plaza: Mediated Literacy Practices among Scribes and Clients in Mexico City.* Creshill, NJ: Hampton Press.

Karttunen, L. and S. Peters. (1979) Conventional implicature. In C. K. Oh and A. D. Dineen (eds), *Syntax and Semantics 11: Presupposition.* London: Academic Press, 1–56.

Kasper, G. (1990) Linguistic politeness: Current research issues. *Journal of Pragmatics*, 14: 193–218.

Kasper, G. (1992) Pragmatic transfer. *Second Language Research*, 8: 203–31.

Kasper, G. (1997) *Can Pragmatic Competence Be Taught?* Honolulu: University of Hawaii, Second Language Teaching and Curriculum Centre. Available at: http://www.nflrc.hawaii.edu/NetWorks/NW06/ [accessed 19/10/2007].

Kasper, G., and K. R. Rose. (2002) *Pragmatic Development in a Second Language.* Oxford: Blackwell.

Katamba, F. (2005) *English Words: Structure, History, Usage,* 2nd edn. London: Routledge.

Katamba, F. X. (1994) *English Words*. London: Routledge.

Keeble, R. (2002) *The Newspaper Handbook*, 3rd edn. London: Routledge.

Keenan, E. O. (1976) The universality of conversational implicature. *Language in Society*, 5: 67–80.

Kelly, A. (1988) Gender differences in teacher-pupil interaction: A meta-analytic review. *Research in Education*, 39: 1–23.

Kelly-Holmes, H. (2004) *Advertising as Multilingual Communication*. Basingstoke: Palgrave Macmillan.

Kemmer, S. (2004) *New Words in English*. Available at: http://www.owlnet.rice.edu/~ling215/NewWords/page1.html

Kenner, C. and T. Hickey (eds). (2008) *Multilingual Europe: Diversity and Learning*. Stoke-on-Trent: Trentham Books.

Kerswill, P. (1996) Milton Keynes and dialect levelling in south-eastern British English In D. Graddol, J. Swann and D. Leith (eds), *English: History, Diversity and Change*. London: Routledge, 292–300. Reproduced in D. Graddol, D. Leith, J. Swann, M. Rhys and J. Gillen (eds), (2007) *Changing English*. London: Routledge. 179–88.

Kerswill, P. (2002) Models of linguistic change and diffusion: New evidence from dialect levelling in British English. *Reading Working Papers in Linguistics*, 6: 187–216.

Kerswill, P. (2003). Dialect levelling and geographical diffusion in British English. In D. Britain and J. Cheshire (eds), *Social Dialectology: In Honour of Peter Trudgill*. Amsterdam: Benjamins, 223–43.

Kerswill, P. (2007a) Social class. In C. Llamas and P. Stockwell (eds), *The Routledge Companion to Sociolinguistics*. London: Routledge, 51–61.

Kerswill, P. (2007b) RP, Standard and non-standard English. In D. Britain (ed.), *Language in the British Isles*, 2nd edn. Cambridge: Cambridge University Press, 34–51.

Kerswill, P. (2007c) Review of Trudgill, P. (2004). *Dialect Contact and New-Dialect Formation: The Inevitability of Colonial Englishes*. Edinburgh: Edinburgh University Press. In *Language*, 83: 657–61.

Kerswill, P. and A. Williams. (1997) Investigating social and linguistic identity in three British schools. In U.-B. Kotsinas, A.-B. Stenström and A.-M. Malin (eds), *Ungdomsspråk i Norden. Föredrag från ett forskarsymposium [Youth language in the Nordic countries. Papers from a research symposium]*. Series: MINS, No. 43. Stockholm: University of Stockholm, Department of Nordic Languages and Literature, 159–76.

Kerswill, P. and A. Williams. (2000a) Creating a new town koine: Children and language change in Milton Keynes. *Language in Society*, 29: 65–115.

Kerswill, P. and A. Williams. (2000b) Mobility and social class in dialect levelling: Evidence from new and old towns in England. In K. Mattheier (ed.), *Dialect and Migration in a Changing Europe*. Frankfurt: Peter Lang, 1–13.

Kerswill, P. and A. Williams. (2005) New towns and koineisation: Linguistic and social correlates. *Linguistics*, 43(5): 1023–48.

Kerswill, P., E. Torgersen and S. Fox. (2008 in press) Reversing 'drift': Innovation and diffusion in the London diphthong system. *Language Variation and Change*, 20.

Kessapidou, S. and M. Makri-Tsilipakou. (2001) Gender and corporate discourse. In E. Kitis (ed.), *The Other Within. Volume II: Aspects of Language and Culture*. Thessaloniki: Athanassios A. Altintzis, 63–86.

Khan, A. (2006) *A Sociolinguistic Study of Birmingham English: Language Variation and Change in a Multi-Ethnic British Community*. PhD Thesis, Lancaster University, UK.

Kidman, A. (1993) *How to do Things with Four-letter Words: A Study of the Semantics of Swearing in Australia*. BA thesis, University of New England.

Kim, Y. (2001) Old English stress: A synchronic analysis with some notes on diachronic development. *Studies in Phonetics, Phonology and Morphology*, 7(1): 21–61.

Kinsey, A. C., B. Pomeroy and C. E. Martin. (1948) *Sexual Behavior in the Human Male.* Philadelphia: W. B. Saunders; Bloomington: Indiana University Press.

Kinsey, A. C., W. B. Pomeroy, C. E. Martin and P. H. Gebhard. (1953) *Sexual Behavior in the Human Female.* Philadelphia: W. B. Saunders; Bloomington: Indiana University Press.

Kiparsky, P. and C. Kiparsky. (1970) Fact. In M. Bierwisch and K. Heidolph (eds), *Progress in Linguistics.* The Hague: Mouton, 143–73.

Kitzinger, C. (2005) 'Speaking as a heterosexual': (How) Does sexuality matter for talk-in-interaction? *Research on Language and Social Interaction*, 38(3): 221–65.

Klein, J. (1998) Politische Kommunikation – Sprachwissenschaftliche Perspektiven. In O. Jarren, U. Sarcinelli and U. Saxer (eds), *Politische Kommunikation in der demokratischen Gesellschaft. Ein Handbuch mit Lexikonteil.* Opladen and Wiesbaden: Westdeutscher Verlag, 186–210.

Klemperer, V. (1947) *LTI. Lingua Tertii Imperii. Die Sprache des Dritten Reiches.* Leipzig: Reclam.

Klemperer, V. (2000 [1946, German edn]) *The Language of the Third Reich.* London: The Athlone Press.

Klemperer, V. (2005) *The Language of the Third Reich: LTI. Lingua Tertii Imperii.* London: Continuum.

Klima, E. S. and U. Bellugi. (1966) Syntactic regulation in the speech of children. In J. Lyons and R. J. Wales (eds), (1966) *Psycholinguistics Papers.* Edinburgh: Edinburgh University Press.

Knobel, M., and C. Lankshear. (2006) Weblog worlds and constructions of effective and powerful writing: Cross with care, and only where signs permit. In K. Pahl and J. Rowsell (eds), *Travel Notes from the New Literacy Studies: Instances of Practice.* Clevedon: Multilingual Matters, 72–92.

Knobel, M. and C. Lankshear (eds). (2007) *A New Literacy Studies Sampler.* New York: Peter Lang

Knowles, G. (1973). *Scouse: The Urban Dialect of Liverpool.* Unpublished PhD thesis, University of Leeds.

Knowles, G. (1987) *Patterns of Spoken English.* London: Longman.

Knowles, G. (1997) *A Cultural History of the English Language.* London: Arnold.

Koller, V. (2004) *Metaphor and Gender in Business Media Discourse: A Critical Cognitive Study.* Basingstoke: Palgrave Macmillan.

Koller, V. (2008) 'The world in one city': Semiotic and cognitive aspects of city branding. Special Issue on Branding Political Entities in a Globalised World, *Journal of Language and Politics*, 7(3): 431–50.

Kortmann, B. and C. Upton. (2008) *Varieties of English. Volume 1: The British Isles.* Berlin: Mouton de Gruyter.

Kortmann, B., T. Herrmann, L. Pietsch and S. Wagner (eds). (2005) *A Comparative Grammar of British English Dialects: Agreegment, Gender, Relative Clauses.* Berlin and New York: Mouton de Gruyter.

Kotthoff, H. (1997) The interactional achievement of expert status: Creating asymmetries by 'teaching conversational lectures' in TV discussions. In H. Kotthoff and R. Wodak (eds), *Communicating Gender in Context.* Amsterdam: Benjamins, 139–78.

Kotthof, H. and R. Wodak (eds). (1997) *Communicating Gender in Context.* Amsterdam: John Benjamins.

Kotthoff, H., C. Kramarae and P. Triechler. (1985) *A Feminist Dictionary.* London: Pandora.

Kramarae, C, and P. Treichler. (1985) *A Feminist Dictionary*. London: Pandora.

Kress, G. (1996) Representational resources and the production of subjectivity. In C. R. Caldas-Coulthard and M. Coulthard (eds), *Texts and Practices: Readings in Critical Discourse Analysis*. London: Routledge.

Kress, G. (2003) *Literacy in the New Media Age*. London: Routledge.

Kress, G. and T. van Leeuwen. (1996) *Reading Images: The Grammar of Visual Design*. London: Routledge.

Kress, G. and T. van Leeuwen. (2001) *Multi-Modal Discourse: The Modes and Media of Contemporary Communication*. London: Arnold.

Kress, G., C. Jewitt, J. Ogborn and C. Tsatsarelis. (2006) *Multimodal Teaching and Learning: The Rhetorics of the Science Classroom* (Advances in Applied Linguistics). London: Continuum.

Krzyżanowski, M. (2007) European identity wanted! On discursive and communicative dimensions of the European convention. In R. Wodak and P. Chilton (eds), *New Research Agenda in CDA: Theory and Multidisciplinarity*. Amsterdam and Philadelphia: John Benjamins, 137–63.

Krzyżanowski, M., and F. Oberhuber. (2007) *(Un)Doing Europe: Discourses and Practices of Negotiating the EU Constitution*. Bruxelles: PIE-Peter Lang.

Kytö, M. and S. Romaine. (1997) Competing forms of adjective comparison in Modern English: What could be more quicker and easier and more effective? In T. Nevalainen and L. Kahlas-Tarkka (eds), *To Explain the Present: Studies in the Changing English Language in Honour of Matti Rissanen*. Helsinki: Mémoires de la Société Néophilologique de Helsinki, 329–52.

Labov, W. (1963) The social motivation of a sound change. *Word*, 19: 273–309. (Reprinted as Chapter 1 of Labov, W. (1972) *Sociolinguistic Patterns*. Philadelphia: University of Pennsylvania Press, 1–42).

Labov, W. (1966) *The Social Stratification of English in New York City*. Washington, DC: Center for Applied Linguistics.

Labov, W. (1969) The logic of non-standard English. In *Georgetown Monographs on Language and Linguistics*, 22 (quoted in Barnes, 1976).

Labov, W. (1972a) *Language in the Inner City: Studies in the Black English Vernacular*. Philadelphia: University of Pennsylvania Press.

Labov, W. (1972b) *Sociolinguistic Patterns*. Oxford: Blackwell; Philadelphia: University of Philadelphia Press.

Labov, W. (1973) The boundaries of words and their meanings. In C.-J. Bailey and R. Shuy (eds), *New Ways of Analyzing Variation in English*. Washington: Georgetown University Press, 340–73.

Labov, W. (2001) *Principles of Linguistic Change: Volume 2: Social Factors*. Oxford: Blackwell.

Labov, W. and D. Fanshel. (1977) *Therapeutic Discourse: Psychotherapy as Conversation*. New York and London: Academic Press.

Labov, W. and W. Harris. (1986) De facto segregation of black and white vernaculars. In D. Sankoff (ed.), *Diversity and Diachrony: Current Issues in Linguistic Theory*, 53. Amsterdam: John Benjamins, 1–24.

Labov, W., S. Ash and C. Boberg. (2005) *Atlas of North American English*. Berlin: Mouton de Gruyter.

Ladefoged, P. (2001) *A Course in Phonetics*. 4th edn, Boston: Heinle & Heinle; Orlando, FL: Harcourt College Publishers.

Ladefoged, P. and D. Everett. (1996) The status of phonetic rarities. *Language* 72(4): 794–800.

Ladefoged, P. and I. Maddieson. (1996) *The Sounds of the World's Languages*. Oxford: Blackwell, ch. 2.

Laferriere, M. (1979) Ethnicity in phonological variation and change. *Language, 55*: 603–17.

Lakoff, R. (1973) The logic of politeness; or, minding your p's and q's. *Papers from the Ninth Regional Meeting of the Chicago Linguistic Society,* 292–305.

Lakoff, R. (1975) *Language and Woman's Place.* New York: Harper Collins.

Lakoff, R. (1989) The limits of politeness: Therapeutic and courtroom discourse. *Multilingua,* 8(2–3): 101–29.

Landry, D. and G. MacLean (eds). (1996) *The Spivak Reader.* New York and London: Routledge.

Lankshear, C. and M. Knobel. (2003) *New Literacies: Changing Knowledge and Classroom Learning.* Buckingham UK: Open University Press.

Lankshear, C. and M. Knobel. (2006) *New Literacies: Everyday Practices and Classroom Learning.* Buckingham: Open University Press.

Lankshear, C. and M. Knobel. (2007) Sampling 'the new' in new literacies. In M. Knobel and C. Lankshear (eds), *A New Literacy Studies Sampler.* New York: Peter Lang, 1–24.

Lass, R. (1976) *English Phonology and Phonological Theory: Synchronic and Diachronic Studies.* Cambridge: Cambridge University Press.

Lass, R. (1988) Vowel Shifts, Great and Otherwise: Remarks on Stockwell and Minkova. In D. Kastovsky and G. Bauer (eds), *Luick Revisited: Papers Read at the Luick-Symposium at Schloss Liechtenstein 15–18.9.1985.* Tubingen: Gunter Narr Verlag, 395–411.

Lass, R. (1992) Phonology and morphology. In Hogg, 1992a, 23–155.

Lass, R. (2000) Language periodization and the concept of 'middle'. In I. Taavitsainen, T. Nevalainen, P. Pahta and M. Rissanen (eds), *Placing Middle English in Context.* Berlin and New York: Mouton de Gruyter, 7–41.

Lass, R. (2006) Phonology and morphology. In Hogg and Denison (2006).

Laux, L. and A. Schütz. (1996). *Wir, die wir gut sind. Die Selbstdarstellung von Politikern zwischen Glorifizierung und Glaubwürdigkeit.* München: DTV.

Laver, J. (1994). *Principles of Phonetics.* Cambridge: Cambridge University Press.

Lazar, M. (2005) *Feminist Critical Discourse Analysis.* Basingstoke: Palgrave Macmillan.

Le Page, R. B. and A. Tabouret-Keller. (1985) *Acts of Identity: Creole-Based Approaches to Language and Ethnicity.* Cambridge: Cambridge University Press.

Leander, K. and K. McKim. (2003) Tracing the everyday 'sitings' of adolescents on the Internet: A strategic adaptation of ethnography across online and offline spaces. *Education, Communication and Information,* 3: 211–40.

Leap, W. L. (ed.). (1995) *Beyond the Lavender Lexicon: Authenticity, Imagination and Appropriation in Lesbian and Gay Languages.* New York: Gordon & Breech Press.

Leap, W. L. (1996) *Word's Out: Gay Men's English.* Minneapolis: University of Minnesota Press.

Leap, W. L. and T. Boellstroff. (2003) *Speaking in Queer Tongues: Globalization and Gay Language.* Urbana: University of Illinois Press.

Lederer, R. (1987) *Anguished English.* London: Robson Books.

Lee, A. (1996) *Gender, Literacy, Curriculum: Re-writing School Geography.* Melbourne: Taylor and Francis

Lee, C. K. M. (2007) Affordances and text-making practices in online instant messaging. *Written Communication,* 24(3): 223–49.

Lee, D. (2000). *Modelling Variation in Spoken and Written Language: The Multi-Dimensional Approach Revisited.* Unpublished PhD Thesis, Lancaster University.

Leech, G. N. (1966) *English in Advertising: A Linguistic Study of Advertising in Great Britain.* London: Longman.

Leech, G. N. (1969) *A Linguistic Guide to English Poetry*. London: Longman.

Leech, G. N. (1983) *Principles of Pragmatics*. Longman: London.

Leech, G. (1998) English grammar in conversation. Available at: http://www.tuchemnitz. de/phil/english/chairs/linguist/real/independent/llc/Conference1998/Papers/Leech/ Leech.htm

Leech, G. N. (2003) Towards an anatomy of politeness in communication. *International Journal of Pragmatics*, 14: 101–23.

Leech, G. N. (2008) *Language in Literature: Style and Foregrounding*. London: Longman.

Leech, G. N. and M. H. Short (2007 [1981]) *Style in Fiction*. London: Longman.

Leech, G., M. Deuchar and R. Hoogenraad (2006) *English Grammar for Today: A New Introduction*, 2nd edn. Basingstoke and New York: Palgrave Macmillan.

Leech, G., M. Hundt, C. Mair. and N. Smith. (forthcoming 2009) *Change in Contemporary English: A Grammatical Study*. Cambridge: Cambridge University Press.

Legman, G. (1941) The language of homosexuality: An American glossary. In G. W. Henry (ed.), *Sex Variants: A Study of Homosexual Patterns: Volume 2*. New York and London: Paul B. Hoeber, 1147–79.

Lehmann, C. (1985) Grammaticalization: Synchronic variation and diachronic change. *Lingua e Stile*, 20: 303–18.

Leichter, H. J. (1984) Families as environments for literacy. In H. A. Goelman, A. Oberg and F. Smith (eds), *Awakening to Literacy*. London: Heinemann, 38–50.

Leith, D. (1983). *A Social History of English*. London: Routledge & Kegan Paul.

Leith, D. (1997). *A Social History of English*, 2nd edn. London: Routledge.

Leith, D., D. Graddol and L. Jackson. (2007) Modernity and English as a national language. In D. Graddol, D. Leith, J. Swann, M. Rhys and J. Gillen, *Changing English*. London: Routledge, 79–116.

Lemke, J. (1990) *Talking Science: Language, Learning, and Values*. Norwood, NJ: Ablex Publishing.

Lemke, J. (1995) *Textual Politics: Discourse and Social Dynamics*. London: Taylor & Francis.

Lemke, J. (1998) Multiplying meaning: Visual and verbal semiotics in scientific text. In J. R. Martin and R. Veel (eds), *Reading Science*. London: Routledge, 87–113.

Lemke, J. (2002) Multimedia genres for scientific wducation and science literacy. In M. J. Schleppegrell and C. Colombi (eds), *Developing Advanced Literacy in First and Second Languages*. Mahwah, NJ: Lawrence Erlbaum, 21–44.

Lennard, J. (1995) Punctuation: And – 'Pragmatics'. In Andreas H. Jucker (ed.), *Historical Pragmatics: Pragmatic Developments in the History of English*. Amsterdam and Philadelphia: John Benjamins, 65–98.

Lerner, G. H. (1996) On the 'semi-permeable' character of grammatical units in conversation: Conditional entry into the turn-space of another speaker. In E. Ochs, E. Schegloff and S. Thompson (eds), *Interaction and Grammar*. Cambridge: Cambridge University Press, 238–76.

Levinson, S. C. (1983) *Pragmatics*. Cambridge: Cambridge University Press.

Lewis, C. (2007) New literacies. In M. Knobel and K. Lankshear (eds), *A New Literacies Sampler*. New York: Peter Lang, 229–37.

Lewis, C. and B. Fabos. (2005) Instant messaging, literacies, and social identities. *Reading Research Quarterly*, 40(4): 470–501.

Lightbown, P. and N. Spada. (1999) *How Languages are Learned*, 2nd edn. Oxford: Oxford University Press.

Lightfoot, D. (1979) *Principles of Historical Syntax*. Cambridge: Cambridge University Press.

Lightfoot, D. (1991) *How to Set Parameters: Arguments from Language Change*. Cambridge, MA: MIT Press.

Lightfoot, D. (1997) Shifting triggers and diachronic reanalyses. In A. van Kemenade and N. Vincent (eds), *Parameters of Morphosyntactic Change*. Cambridge: Cambridge University Press, 253–72.

Lightfoot, D. (1999) *The Development of Language*. Oxford: Blackwell.

Lillis, T. and C. McKinney. (2003) *Analysing Language in Context: A Student Workbook*. Stoke-on-Trent: Trentham Books.

Lippi-Green, R. (1989) Social network integration and language change in progress in a rural alpine village. *Language in Society*, 18: 213–34.

Lippi-Green, R. (1997) *English with an Accent: Language, Ideology and Discrimination in the United States*. London: Routledge

Litosseliti, L. (2006) *Gender and Language: Theory and Practice*. London: Hodder Arnold.

Livia, A. and K. Hall (eds). (1997) *Queerly Phrased: Language, Gender and Sexuality*. Oxford: Oxford University Press.

Llamas, C. (2007) 'A place between places': Language and identities in a border town. *Language in Society*, 36(4): 579–604.

Lloyd, M. (1999) Performativity, parody, politics. *Theory, Culture and Society*, 16(2): 195–213.

Locher, M. A. and R. J. Watts. (2005) Politeness theory and relational work. *Journal of Politeness Research*, 1(1): 9–33.

Luick, K. (1940 [1914]) *Historische Grammatik der englischen Sprache*. Leipzig: Tauchnitz. Reprined, 2 vols, Oxford: Blackwell.

Luk, J. C. M. and A. M. Y. Lin. (2007) *Classroom Interaction as Cross-Cultural Encounters*. Mahwah, NJ: Lawrence Erlbaum.

Lukes, S. (1974) *Power: A Radical View*. London: Macmillan

Lust, B. C. and C. Foley. (2004) *First Language Acquisition: The Essential Readings*. Oxford: Blackwell.

Lynch, T. (1996) *Communication in the Language Classroom*. Cambridge: Cambridge University Press

Lynch, T. (2001) Seeing what they meant: Transcribing as a route to noticing. *ELT Journal*, 55/2: 124–32.

Lynch, T. (2007) Learning from the transcripts of an oral communication task. *ELT Journal*, 61/4: 311–20.

Lynch, T. and J. Maclean. (2000) Exploring the benefits of task repetition and recycling for classroom language learning. *Language Teaching Research*. Special Issue:*Tasks in Language Pedagogy*, 4(3): 221–50.

Lynch, T. and J. Maclean. (2001) 'A case of exercising': Effects of immediate task repetition on learners' performance. In M. Bygate, P. Skehan and M. Swain (eds), *Researching Pedagogical Tasks: Second Language Learning, Teaching, and Testing*. London: Pearson Educational, 141–62.

Lyons, C. (1999). *Definiteness*. Cambridge: Cambridge University Press.

Lyons, J. (1977) *Semantics* (vols 1 and 2) Cambridge: Cambridge University Press.

Macaulay, R. K. S. (2002) Extremely interesting, very interesting, or only quite interesting? Adverbs and social class. *Journal of Sociolinguistics*, 6(3): 398–417.

Macaulay, R. K. S. (2005) *Talk that Counts: Age, Gender and Social Class Differences in Discourse*. Oxford: Oxford University Press.

MacWhinney, B. (2000) *The CHILDES Project: Tools for Analyzing Talk*, 3rd edn. Mahwah, NJ: Lawrence Erlbaum Associates.

Mæhlum, B. (2008). Skal vi la norsk språk være en ulempe – i Norge?. *Språknytt*, 36: 21–4.

Mair, C. (ed.). (2003) *The Politics of English as a World Language: New Horizons in Postcolonial Cultural Studies*. Amsterdam: Rodopi.

Malvern, D. D. and B. J. Richards. (1997) A new measure of lexical diversity. In A. Ryan and A. Wray (eds), *Evolving Models of Language*. Clevedon: Multilingual Matters.

Mannion, G. and R. Ivanič. (2007) Mapping literacy practices: Theory, methodology, methods. *International Journal of Qualitative Studies in Education*, 20(1): 15–30.

Marchand, H. (1969) *Categories and Types of Present-Day English Word-Formation*, 2nd edn. München: C. H. Beck.

Markham, A. (1998) *Life Online: Researching Real Experience in Virtual Space*. London: Sage.

Marshall, G., H. Newby, D. Rose and C. Vogler. (1988) *Social Class in Modern Britain*. London: Hutchinson.

Martin, E. (2006) *Marketing Identities Through Language: English and Global Imagery in French Advertising*. Basingstoke: Palgrave Macmillan.

Martin, J. R. and P. R. R. White. (2005) *The Language of Evaluation: Appraisal in English*. Basingstoke: Palgrave Macmillan.

Martin, J. R. and R. Wodak (eds). (2003) *Re-Reading the Past: Critical and Functional Perspectives on Time and Value*. Amsterdam: John Benjamins.

Martin-Jones, M. (2007) Bilingualism, education and the regulation of access to language resources: Changing research perspectives. In M. Heller (ed.), *Bilingualism: A Social Approach*. Basingstoke: Palgrave Macmillan.

Martin-Jones, M. and N. Hornberger (eds). (2008) *Encyclopedia of Language and Educaton*, 2nd edn, Volume 3: *Discourse and Education*. New York: Springer.

Martin-Jones, M. and K. Jones (eds). (2000) *Multilingual Literacies*. Amsterdam: John Benjamins.

Martin-Jones, M. and M. Saxena. (2003) Bilingual resources and 'funds of knowledge' for teaching and learning in multiethnic classes in Britain. *International Journal of Bilingual Education and Bilingualism*, 6 (3–4).

Martín-Rojo, L. and C. Gómes-Esteban. (2003) Discourse at work: When women take on the role of managers. In G. Weiss and R. Wodak (eds), *Critical Discourse Analysis: Theory and Interdisciplinarity*. Basingstoke: Palgrave Macmillan, 241–71.

Mason, D. (2000) *Race and Ethnicity in Modern Britain*. Oxford: Oxford University Press.

Matsumoto, Y. (1988) Reexamination of the universality of face: Politeness phenomena in Japanese. *Journal of Pragmatics*, 12(4): 403–26.

Matthews, P. H. (1991) *Morphology*. Cambridge: Cambridge University Press.

McCafferty, K. (2001) *Ethnicity and Language Change: English in (London)Derry, Northern Ireland*. Amsterdam and Philadelphia: John Benjamins.

McCarthy, J. (1982) Prosodic Structure and Expletive Infixation. *Language*, 58(3): 574–90.

McEnery, A. (2005) *Swearing in English*. London: Routledge.

McEnery, T. and A. Wilson. (1996) *Corpus Linguistics*. Edinburgh: Edinburgh University Press.

McHoul, A. and M. Rapley (eds). (2001) *How to Analyse Talk in Institutional Settings*. London: Continuum.

McIntyre, D. (2006) *Point of View in Plays: A Cognitive Stylistic Approach to Viewpoint in Drama and Other Text Types*. Amsterdam: John Benjamins.

McLaughlin, J. C. (1970) *Aspects of the History of English*. New York: Holt, Rinehart & Winston.

McLuhan, M. (1964) *Understanding Media*. New York: Mentor.

McMahon, A. M. S. (1994) *Understanding Language Change*. Cambridge: Cambridge University Press.

McMahon, A. (2001) *An Introduction to English Phonology*. Edinburgh: Edinburgh University Press.

McNeill, D. (1966) Developmental psycholinguistics. In F. Smith and G. A. Miller (eds), (1966) *The Genesis of Language*. Cambridge MA: MIT Press.

McNeill, D. (1970) *The Acquisition of Language: The Study of Developmental Psycholinguistics*. New York: Harper & Row.

Meillet, A. (1912) L'évolution des formes grammaticales. *Scientia (Rivista di Scienza)*, 6(12): 384–400.

Melchers, G. and P. Shaw. (2003) *World Englishes: An Introduction*. London: Arnold.

Mercer, N. (1995) *The Guided Construction of Knowledge*. Clevedon: Multilingual Matters.

Mercer, N. (2000) *Words and Minds*. London: Routledge.

Merriam-Webster Online (2008) http://www.merriam-webster.com/shlumpadinka.html

Mesthrie, R. (ed.). (2008) *Varieties of English 4: Africa, South and Southeast Asia*. Berlin: Mouton de Gruyter.

Mesthrie, R., J. Swann, A. Deumert and W. Leap. (2000) *Introducing Sociolinguistics*. Edinburgh: Edinburgh University Press.

Mey, J. L. (1998) (ed.) *Concise Encyclopedia of Pragmatics*. Pergamon Press: Oxford.

Miller, J. (2002) *An Introduction to English Syntax*. Edinburgh: Edinburgh University Press.

Mills, S. (1992) Knowing your place: Marxist feminist contextualised stylistics. In M. Toolan (ed.), *Language, Text and Context: Essays in Stylistics*. London: Routledge, 182–205.

Mills, S. (2008) *Language and Sexism*. Cambridge: Cambridge University Press.

Milroy, J. (1999) The consequences of standardisation in descriptive linguistics. In T. Bex and R. J. Watts (eds), *Standard English: The Widening Debate*. London: Routledge, 16–39.

Milroy, J. (2000) The ideology of the standard language. In L. Wright (ed.), *The Development of Standard English, 1300–1800*. Cambridge: Cambridge University Press, 11–128.

Milroy, J. (2002) The legitimate language: Giving a history to English. In D. Watts and P. Trudgill (eds), *Alternative Histories of English*. London: Routledge, 7–26.

Milroy, J. and L. Milroy. (1987) *Authority in Language: Investigating Standard English*. London: Routledge.

Milroy, J. and L. Milroy. (1997) Network structure and linguistic change. In N. Coupland and A. Jaworski (eds), *Sociolinguistics: A Reader and Coursebook*. Basingstoke: Macmillan, 199–211.

Milroy, L. (1980) *Language and Social Networks* (Language in Society). Oxford: Blackwell.

Milroy, L. (1982) Language and group identity. *Journal of Multilingual and Multicultural Development*, 3(3): 207–16.

Milroy, L. (1987) *Language and Social Networks*, 2nd edn. Oxford: Blackwell.

Milroy, L. (1997) The social categories of race and class: Language ideology and sociolinguistics. In N. Coupland, S. Sarangi and C. Candlin (eds), *Sociolinguistics and Social Theory*. London: Longman, 235–60.

Milroy, L. (2000) Britain and the United States: Two nations divided by the same language (and different language ideologies). *Journal of Linguistic Anthropology*, 10: 56–89.

Milroy, L. (2002) Social networks. In J. K. Chambers, P. Trudgill and N. Schilling-Estes (eds), *The Handbook of Language Variation and Change*. Oxford: Blackwell, 549–72.

Milroy, L. and M. Gordon. (2003) *Sociolinguistics: Method and Interpretation*. Oxford: Blackwell.

Milroy, L. and J. Milroy. (1992) Social network and social class: Towards an Integrated Sociolinguistic Model. *Language in Society*, 21: 1–26.

Minsky, M. (1975) A framework for representing knowledge. In P. Winston (ed.), *The Psychology of Computer Vision*. New York: McGraw-Hill.

Mitchell, B. (1985) *Old English Syntax*. Oxford: Clarendon.

Modood, T., S. Beishon and S. Virdee. (1994) *Changing Ethnic Identities*. London: Policies Studies Institute.

Montagu, A. (1967 [1973]) *The Anatomy of Swearing*, 2nd edn. London: Rapp Whiting, MacMillan & Collier.

Montgomery, M. (1995) *An Introduction to Language and Society*, 2nd edn. London: Routledge.

Morgan, R. and K. Wood. (1995) Lesbians in the living room: Collusion, co-construction and co-narration in conversation. In W. L. Leap (ed.), *Beyond the Lavender Lexicon: Authenticity, Imagination and Appropriation in Lesbian and Gay Languages*. New York: Gordon & Breech Press, 235–48.

Morris, C. W. (1938) *Foundations of the Theory of Signs* (International Encyclopedia of Unified Science, Vol. 1, No. 2). Chicago: The University of Chicago Press. Also published as *Pragmatics*. Amsterdam: John Benjamins, 473–92.

Morrison, K. (1995) *Marx, Durkheim, Weber: Formations of Modern Social Thought*. London: Sage Publications.

Moss, B. J. (ed.), (1994) *Literacy Across Communities*. Creshill, NJ: Hampton Press.

Mufwene, S. (2001) *The Ecology of Language Evolution*. Cambridge: Cambridge University Press.

Mufwene, S., J. Rickford, G. Bailey and J. Baugh (eds). (1998) *African-American English: Structure, History and Use*. London: Routledge.

Mugglestone, L. (2003) *'Talking proper': The Rise of Accent as Social Symbol*, 2nd edn. Oxford: The Clarendon Press.

Mugglestone, L. (2006) *The Oxford History of English*. Oxford: Oxford University Press.

Mugglestone, L. (2007) Accent as social symbol. In D. Graddol, D. Leith, J. Swann, M. Rhys and J. Gillen *Changing English*. London: Routledge, 153–78.

Mullany, L. (2007) *Gendered Discourse in the Professional Workplace*. Basingstoke: Palgrave Macmillan.

Muntigl, P., G. Weiss and R. Wodak. (2000) *European Union Discourses on Un/Employment: An Interdisciplinary Approach to Employment Policy-Making and Organisational Change*. Amsterdam and Philadelphia: John Benjamins.

Musolff, A. (2004) *Metaphor and Political Discourse: Analogical Reasoning in Debates about Europe*. Basingstoke: Palgrave Macmillan.

Myers, G. (1989) The pragmatics of politeness in scientific articles. *Applied Linguistics*, 10: 1–35.

Myers, G. (1994) *Words in Ads*. London and New York: Edward Arnold.

Myers, G. (1998) *Ad Worlds: Brands, Media, Audiences*. London and New York: Arnold.

Nakamura, J. (1992) The comparison of the Brown and the LOB corpora based upon the distribution of grammatical tags. *Journal of Foreign Languages and Literature*, 3: 43–58.

Nänny, M. and O. Fischer. (2006) Iconicity: Literary texts. In K. Brown (ed.), *Encyclopedia of Language and Linguistics*, vol. 5, 2nd edn. Amsterdam: Elsevier, 462–72.

Nash, M. (1996) The core elements of ethnicity. In J. Hutchinson and A. Smith (eds), *Ethnicity*. Oxford: Oxford University Press, 24–8.

Nazroo, J. and S. Karlsen. (2003) Patterns of identity among ethnic minority people: Diversity and commonality. *Ethnic and Racial Studies*, 26(5): 902–30.

Netgrrl * (12) and chicoboy 26 * (32) (2002) What am I bid? Reading, writing and ratings at eBay.com. In I. Snyder (ed.), *Silicon Literacies*. London: Routledge, 15–31.

Nevalainen, T. (2006) *An Introduction to Early Modern English*. Edinburgh: Edinburgh University Press.

Nevalainen, T. and H. Raumolin-Brunberg. (2000) The changing role of London on the linguistic map of Tudor and Stuart England. In D. Kastovsky and A. Mettinger (eds), *The History of English in a Social Context*. Berlin and New York: Mouton de Gruyter, 279–337.

Nevalainen, T. and H. Raumolin-Brunberg. (2003) *Historical Sociolinguistics*. Harlow: Longman.

Nevins, A. and B. Vaux. (2003) *Metalinguistic, Shmetalinguistic: The Phonology of Shm-Reduplication*. The Proceedings of the 39th Chicago Linguistics Society, 702–21. Available at: http://php-dev.imt.uwm.edu/prjs/markj/projects/fll_surveys/shm/

Nilan, P. (2000) 'You're hopeless I swear to God': Shifting masculinities in classroom talk. *Gender in Education*, 12(1): 53–68.

Norman, D. (1990) *The Design of Everyday Things*. New York: Doubleday.

Nunberg, G. (1990) *The Linguistics of Punctuation*. Stanford, CA: CLSI.

O'Connell, D. C. and S. Kowal. (2002) Political eloquence. In V. C. Ottati, R. S. Tindale, J. Edwards, F. B. Bryant, L. Heath, D. C. O'Connell, Y. Suarez-Balcazar and E. J. Posavac (eds), *The Social Psychology of Politics*. Berlin: Springer, 89–103.

Ochs, E. and S. Thompson (eds). (1996) *Interaction and Grammar*. Cambridge: Cambridge University Press.

Office for National Statistics (2001) The National Statistics socio-economic classification. http://www.statistics.gov.uk/methods_quality/ns_sec/, accessed 18/12/2005.

Ogilvy, D. (1983) *Ogilvy on Advertising*. London: Pan Books.

Oppenheim, A. N. (2001) *Questionnaire Design, Interviewing and Attitude Measurement*. London: Continuum.

Orgad, S. (2000) Help yourself: The World Wide Web as a self-help agora. In D. Gauntlett and R. Horsley (eds), *Web studies*, 2nd edn. London: Arnold, 146–58.

Packard, V. (1957) *The Hidden Persuaders*. New York: McKay.

Paisley, W. J. (1969) Studying 'style' as a deviation from encoding norms. In G. Gerbner, O. R. Holsti, K. Krippendorff, W. J. Paisley and P. J. Stone (eds), *The Analysis of Communication Content*. New York: Wiley, 133–46.

Papen, U. and S. Walters. (2008) *Literacy, Learning and Health*. London: NRDC.

Pardoe, S. and R. Ivanič. (2007) Literacies for learning in further education: Making reading and writing practices across the curriculum more useful for learning. DVD and accompanying booklet. Lancaster: PublicSpace (www.publicspace.org.uk).

Partridge, E. (1950) *Here, There, and Everywhere: Essays Upon Language*. London: Hamish Hamilton.

Pauwels, A. (1998) *Women Changing Language*. London: Longman.

Pawley, A. and F. H. Syder. (1983) Two puzzles for linguistic theory: Native-like fluency, and native-like idiomaticity. In J. C. Richards and R. W. Schmidt (eds), *Language and Communication*. Harlow: Longman.

Paxman, J. (2003) *The Political Animal*. London: Penguin.

Pels, D. and J. Corner. (2003) *Media and the Restyling of Politics: Consumerism, Celebrity, and Cynicism*. London: Sage.

Pennycook, A. (2007) *Global Englishes and Transcultural Flows*. London: Routledge.

Peräkylä, A. (2004) Conversation analysis. In J. G. Giampietro Gobo, C. Seale and D. Silverman (eds), *Qualitative Research Practice*. London: Sage, 165–79.

Perelman, C. (1980) *Das Reich der Rhetorik*. Munich: Beck.

Pérez, B. (ed.). (2004) *Sociocultural Contexts of Language and Literacy*, 2nd edn. Mahwah, NJ: Lawrence Erlbaum Associates.

Peters, A. M. (1983) *The Units of Language Acquisition*. Cambridge: Cambridge University Press.

Philo, G. (ed.). (1995) *Glasgow Media Group Reader, Volume 2: Industry, Economy, War and Politics*. London: Routledge.

Piattelli-Palmarini, M. (ed.). (1980) *Language and Learning: The Debate between Jean Piaget and Noam Chomsky*. London: Routledge & Kegan Paul.

Pickles, W. (1949) *Between You and Me*. London: Werner Laurie.

Pinker, S. (1994) *The Language Instinct*. London: Penguin.

Plank, F. (1984) The modals story retold. *Studies in Language*, 8: 305–64.

Plett, H. (2001) Figures of speech. In T. O. Sloane (ed.), *Encyclopedia of Rhetoric*. New York: Oxford University Press, 309–14.

Podesva, R. J., S. J. Roberts and K. Campbell-Kibler. (2002) Sharing resources and indexing meanings in the production of gay styles. In K. Campbell-Kibler, R. J. Podesva, S. J. Roberts and A. Wong (eds), *Language and Sexuality: Contesting Meaning in Theory and Practice*. Stanford, CA: CSLI Publications, 175–90.

Pomerantz, A. (1984) Agreeing and disagreeing with assessments: Some features of preferred/dispreferred turn shapes. In J. M. Atkinson and J. Heritage (eds), *Structures of Social Action*. Cambridge, Cambridge University Press, 57–101.

Poncini, G. (2004) *Discursive Strategies in Multicultural Business Meetings*. Linguistic Insights, vol. 14. Bern: Peter Lang.

Pottier, B. (1963) *Recherches sur l'analyse sémantique en linguistique et en traduction mécanique*. Nancy: Université de Nancy.

Powell, R. C. and J. Batters. (1986) Sex of teacher and the image of foreign languages in schools. *Educational Studies*, 12(3): 245–54.

Pratt, M. L. (1987) Linguistic utopias. In N. Fabb, D. Attridge, A. Durant and C. MacCabe (eds), *The Linguistics of Writing: Arguments between Language and Literature*. Manchester: Manchester University Press, 48–66.

Prechter, S. (1999) Women's rights – children's games: Sexism in learners' dictionaries of English. *Multilingua*, 18(1): 47–68.

Preston, I. L. (1994) *The Tangled Web They Weave: Truth, Falsity, and Advertisers*. Madison, WI: University of Wisconsin Press.

Prinsloo, M. and M. Breier (eds). (1996) *The Social Uses of Literacy: Theory and Practice in Contemporary South Africa*. Amsterdam: John Benjamins.

Psathas, G. (1995) *Conversation Analysis: The Study of Talk-in-Interaction*. Thousand Oaks, CA: Sage.

Pullum, G. K. and B. C. Scholz. (2002) Empirical assessment of stimulus poverty arguments. *The Linguistic Review*, 19: 9–50.

Purcell-Gates, V. (ed.). (2007) *Cultural Practices of Literacy: Case Studies of Language, Literacy, Social Practice, and Power*. Hillsdale, NJ: Lawrence Erlbaum.

Pyles, T. and J. Algeo. (2004) *The Origins and Development of the English Language*, 5th edn. Fort Worth, TX: Harcourt Brace Jovanovich.

Queen, R. M. (1997) 'I don't speak Spritch': locating lesbian language. In A. Livia and K. Hall (eds), *Queerly Phrased*. Oxford: Oxford Studies in Sociolinguistics, 233–56.

Quirk, R., S. Greenbaum, G. Leech and J. Svartvik. (1985) *A Comprehensive Grammar of the English Language*. London: Longman.

Rampton, B. (2005) *Crossing: Language and Ethnicity Among Adolescents*. Manchester: St Jerome Publishing.

Rayson, P., A. Wilson and G. Leech. (2002) Grammatical word class variation within the British National Corpus Sampler. In P. Peters, P. Collins and A. Smith (eds), *New Frontiers of Corpus Research: Papers from the Twenty First International Conference on English Language Research on Computerized Corpora*. Amsterdam: Rodopi, 295–306.

Reah, D. (1998) *The Language of Newspapers*. London: Routledge.

Reid, I. (1989) *Social Class Differences in Britain*, 3rd edn. London: Fontana.

Reisigl, M. (1998) '50 Jahre Zweite Republik' – Zur diskursiven Konstruktion der öster-reichischen Identität in politischen Gedenkreden. In O. Panagl (ed.), *Fahnenwörter in der Politik – Kontinuitäten und Brüche*. Vienna: Böhlau, 217–51.

Reisigl, M. (2004) *Wie man eine Nation herbeiredet. Eine diskursanalytische Untersuchung zur sprachlichen Konstruktion österreichischen Nation und österrei-chischen Identität in politischen Fest- und Gedenkreden*. Unpublished PhD Thesis, University of Vienna.

Reisigl, M. (2008a) Rhetoric of Political Speeches. In R. Wodak and V. Koller (eds), *Analyzing the Public Sphere: Handbook of Applied Linguistics*, Vol. IV. (Series edi-tors G. Antos and K. Knapp.) Berlin: Mouton de Gruyter, 243–69.

Reisigl, M. (2008b) Analyzing political rhetoric. In R. Wodak and M. Krzyzanowski (eds), *Qualitative Discourse Analysis in the Social Sciences*. Basingstoke: Palgrave.

Reisigl, M. and R. Wodak. (2001). *Discourse and Discrimination: Rhetorics of Racism and Antisemitism*. London: Routledge.

Richardson, J. E. (2007) *Analysing Newspapers: An Approach from Critical Discourse Analysis*. Basingstoke: Palgrave Macmillan.

Rickford, J. (1986) The need for new approaches to social class analysis in sociolinguis-tics. *Language and Communication*, 6(3): 215–21.

Rickford, J. (1999) *African American Vernacular English*. Oxford: Blackwell.

Ritchie, W. C. and T. K. Bhatia. (1999) *Handbook of Child Language Acquisition*. San Diego, CA: Academic Press.

Roach, Peter (2001) *English Phonetics and Phonology: A Practical Course*. 2nd edn, Cambridge: Cambridge University Press.

Robinson, I. (1998) *The Establishment of Modern English Prose in the Reformation and the Enlightenment*. Cambridge: Cambridge University Press.

Rodgers, B. (1972) *The Queen's Vernacular*. San Francisco: Straight Arrow Books.

Rogers, A. (ed.). (2005) *Urban Literacy: Communication, Identity and Learning in Development Contexts*. Hamburg: Unesco Institute for Education.

Rogers, H. (2000). *The Sounds of Language: An Introduction to Phonetics*. Harlow: Pearson Education.

Romaine, S (1988) *Pidgin and Creole Languages*. London: Longman.

Romaine, S. (1989) *Bilingualism*. Oxford: Basil Blackwell.

Rosch, E. H. (1973) Natural categories. *Cognitive Psychology*, 4: 328–50.

Rosch, E. H. (1978) Principles of categorization. In E. H. Rosch and B. B. Lloyd (eds), *Cognition and Categorization*. Hillside, NJ: Lawrence Erlbaum Associates, 27–48.

Rosch, E. H., C. B. Mervis, W. D. Gray, D. M. Johnson, and P. Boyes-Braem. (1976) Basic objects in natural categories. *Cognitive Psychology*, 8: 382–439.

Rosen, H. (1969) Towards a language policy across the curriculum. In D. Barnes, J. Britton and H. Rosen (rev. 1986), *Language, the Learner and the School*. Harmondsworth: Penguin.

Rosewarne, D. (1984) Estuary English. *The Times Educational Supplement*, 19 October.

Rosewarne, D. (1994) Estuary English: Tomorrow's RP? *English Today*, 10(1): 3–8.

Ross, N. J. (1995) Dubbing American in Italy. *English Today*, 11: 45–8.

Rothenberg, R. (1994) *Where the Suckers Moon: An Advertising Story*. New York: Knopf.

Sacks, D. (2004) *The Alphabet*. London: Arrow Books.

Sacks, H. (1992) *Lectures on Conversation*. Oxford: Blackwell.

Sadker, M. and D. Sadker. (1985) Sexism in the schoolroom of the '80s. *Psychology Today*, March: 54–7.

Safire, W. (2007) On Language Hotting Up, *New York Times Magazine*, 10 June 2007: http://www.nytimes.com/2007/06/10/magazine/10wwln-safire-t.html?ftay

Sampson, G. (2005) *The 'Language Instinct' Debate*. London: Continuum.

Samuda, V. (2001) Guiding relationships between form and meaning during task perform-ance: The role of the teacher. In M. Bygate, P. Skehan and M. Swain (eds), *Researching Pedagogic Tasks: Second Language Learning, Teaching and Testing.* Harlow: Pearson Education, 119–41.

Samuda, V. and M. Bygate. (2008) *Tasks in Second Language Learning.* Basingstoke: Palgrave Macmillan.

Samuels, M. L. (1963) Some applications of Middle English dialectology. *English Studies*, 44: 81–94.

Sankoff, D. (ed.). (1986) *Diversity and Diachrony: Current Issues in Linguistic Theory*, vol. 53. Amsterdam: John Benjamins.

Sarangi, S. and C. Roberts (eds). (1999) *Talk, Work, and Institutional Order: Discourse in Medical, Mediation, and Management Settings.* Berlin: Mouton de Gruyter.

Satchwell, C. and R. Ivanič. (2007) The textuality of learning contexts in UK Colleges. *Pedagogy, Culture and Society*, Special Issue on *Contexts, Networks and Communities*, 15(3): 303–16

Sayer, A. (2000) *Realism and Social Science.* London: Sage.

Scannell, P. (1991) *Broadcast Talk.* London: Sage Publications.

Schäfer, J. (1980) *Documentation in the OED: Shakespeare and Nashe as Test cases.* Oxford: Clarendon Press.

Schank, R. C. and R. P. Abelson. (1977) *Scripts, Plans, Goals and Understanding.* New York: Lawrence Erlbaum Associates.

Schauer, G. A. (2006) Pragmatic awareness in ESL and EFL contexts: Contrast and devel-opment. *Language Learning*, 56(2): 269–318.

Schauer, G. A., and S. Adolphs. (2006) Expressions of gratitude in corpus and DCT data: Vocabulary, formulaic sequences, and pedagogy. *System*, 34(1): 119–34.

Scheler, M. (1977) *Der englische Wortschatz.* Berlin: Erich Schmidt.

Schiffrin, D. (1994) *Approaches to Discourse.* Oxford: Blackwell.

Schilling-Estes, N. (2004) Constructing ethnicity in interaction. *Journal of Sociolinguistics*, 8(2): 163–95.

Schmied, J. (1991) *English in Africa: An introduction.* London: Longman.

Schmitz-Berning, C. (2000) *Vokabular des Nationalsozialismus.* Berlin: de Gruyter.

Schudson, M. (1984) *Advertising: The Uneasy Persuasion.* New York: Basic Books.

Schwegler, A. (1994) Analysis and synthesis. In R.E. Asher (ed.), *The Encyclopedia of Language and Linguistics.* Oxford: Pergamon Press, 111–14.

Scollon, R. (1998) *Mediated Discourse as Social Interaction: A Study of News Discourse.* Harlow: Longman.

Scollon, R. and S. W. Scollon. (2003) *Discourses in Place: Language in the Material World.* London: Routledge.

Scott, M. (2000) Agency and subjectivity in student writing. In C. Jones, J. Turner and B. Street (eds), *Students Writing in the University: Cultural and Epistemological Issues.* Amsterdam: Benjamins.

Scragg, D. C. (1974) *English Spelling.* Manchester: Manchester University Press.

Searle, J. R. (1969) *Speech Acts: An Essay in the Philosophy of Language.* Cambridge: Cambridge University Press.

Sebba, M. (1993) *London Jamaican: Language Systems in Interaction.* London: Longman.

Sebba, M. (1997) *Contact Languages: Pidgins and Creoles.* Basingstoke: Macmillan.

Seidman, S. (1993) Identity and politics in a 'postmodern' gay culture: Some historical and conceptual notes. In M. Warner (ed.), *Fear of a Queer Planet: Queer Politics and Social Theory.* Minneapolis: University of Minnesota Press, 105–42.

Selkirk, E. O. (1982) *The Syntax of Words.* Cambridge, MA: MIT Press.

Semino, E. (1997) *Language and World Creation in Poems and Other Texts*. London: Longman.

Semino, E. (2008) *Metaphor in Discourse*. Cambridge: Cambridge University Press.

Semino, E. and M. Short. (2004) *Corpus Stylistics: Speech, Writing and Thought Presentation in a Corpus of English Writing*. London: Routledge.

Serjeantson, M. S. (1935) *A History of Foreign Words in English*. London: Routledge & Kegan Paul. Reprinted 1961.

Service, V. (1984) Maternal styles and communicative development. In A. Lock and E. Fisher (eds), *Language Development*. London: Croom Helm.

Sheidlower, J. (1995) *The F Word*. New York: Random House.

Short, M. (1988) Speech presentation, the novel and the press. In W. van Peer (ed.), *The Taming of The Text*. London: Routledge, 61–81.

Short, M. (1996) *Exploring the Language of Poems, Plays and Prose*. London: Longman.

Short, M. (2002) Who is stylistics and what use is she to students of English language and literature? *Poetica*, 58: 33–54.

Siegel, J. (2008) *The Emergence of Pidgin and Creole Languages*. Oxford: Oxford University Press

Silverman, D. (1998) *Harvey Sacks: Social Science and Conversation Analysis*. Cambridge: Polity.

Simpson, J. (2001) Hypocoristics of place-names in Australian English. In P. Collins and D. Blair (eds) *Varieties of English: Australian English*. Amsterdam and Philadelphia: John Benjamins, 89–112.

Simpson, J. Y. M. (1979) *A First Course in Linguistics*. Edinburgh: Edinburgh University Press.

Simpson, P. (1997) *Language through Literature: An Introduction*. London: Routledge.

Simpson, P. (2003) *Stylistics: A Resource Book for Students*. London: Routledge.

Sinclair, J. and M. Coulthard. (1975) *Towards an Analysis of Discourse: The English used by Teachers and Pupils*. Oxford: Oxford University Press.

Sinclair, J. McH. (1966) Taking a poem to pieces. In Roger Fowler (ed.), *Essays on Style and Language: Linguistic Approaches to Literary Style*. London: Routledge & Kegan Paul, 68–81.

Sinclair, J. McH. (1968) A technique of stylistic description. *Language and Style*, 1: 215–42.

Sinclair, J. McH. (1972) Lines about 'lines'. In B. B. Kachru (ed.), *Current Trends in Stylistics*. Alberta: Linguistic Research, 241–62.

Singh, I. (2000) *Pidgins and Creoles: An Introduction*. London: Arnold.

Skeggs, B. (1997) *Formation of Class and Gender: Become Respectable*. London: Sage

Slavíčková, T. (forthcoming) *A CDA/rhetorical analysis of the American Memorial Day Speech Genre*. Unpublished PhD Thesis, Lancaster University.

Smith, J. (1996) *An Historical Study of English: Function, Form and Change*. London: Routledge.

Smith, J. (2005 [1999]) *Essentials of Early English: An Introduction to Old, Middle and EModE*. London: Routledge.

Smith, S. C. (1998) *British Imperialism 1750–1970*. Cambridge: Cambridge University Press.

Smitherman, G. (1986) *Talkin and Testifyin: The Language of Black America*. Michigan: Wayne State University Press.

Snell, J. (2007) 'Give us my shoe back': The pragmatic functions of singular 'us'. *Leeds Working Papers in Linguistics & Phonetics*, 12: 44–60.

Snow, C. E. (1977a) Mother's speech research: From input to interaction. In C. E. Snow and C. A. Ferguson (eds), *Talking to Children: Language Input and Acquisition.* Cambridge: Cambridge University Press, 31–49.

Snow, C. E. (1977b) The development of conversation between mothers and babies. *Journal of Child Language,* 4: 1–22.

Snow, C. E. and C. A. Ferguson (eds). (1977) *Talking to Children: Language Input and Acquisition.* Cambridge: Cambridge University Press.

Snyder, I. (ed.). (2002) *Silicon Literacies.* London: Routledge.

Snyder, I. and M. Prinsloo. (2007) Young people's engagement with digital literacies in marginal contexts in a globalised world. *Language and Education,* 21(3): 171–9.

Spaulding, R. (1966) *Achievement, Creativity and Self-Concept: Correlates of Teacher-Pupil Interactions in Elementary School.* Washington DC: Dept. of Health, Education and Welfare.

Spencer, C. (1995) *Homosexuality: A History.* London: Fourth Estate.

Spencer-Oatey, H. (1996) Reconsidering power and social distance. *Journal of Pragmatics,* 26(1): 1–24.

Spencer-Oatey, H. (2000) Rapport management: A framework for analysis. In H. Spencer-Oatey (ed.), *Culturally Speaking: Managing Rapport through Talk across Cultures.* London and New York: Continuum, 11–45.

Spencer-Oatey, H. (2008 [2000]) *Culturally Speaking: Culture, Communication and Politeness,* 2nd edn. London: Continuum.

Spender, D. (1980) *Man Made Language.* London: Routledge.

Spender, D. (1982) *Invisible Women: The Schooling Scandal.* London: The Women's Press.

Sperber, D. and D. Wilson. (1995) *Relevance: Communication and Cognition,* 2nd edn. Oxford: Blackwell.

Stalnaker, R. C. (1972) Pragmatics. In D. Davidson and G. Harman (eds), *Semantics of Natural Language.* Dordrecht: Reidel, 380–97.

Stenström, A-B. (1991) Expletives in the London-Lund corpus. In K. Aijmer and B. Alternberg (eds), *English Corpus Linguistics.* London: Longman, 230–53.

Stephens, K. (1990) The world of John and Mary Smith: A study of Quirk and Greenbaum's University Grammar of English. *CLE Working Papers,* 1: 91–107.

Sternberger D. G., G. Storz and W. E. Sußkind. (1957) *Aus dem Worterbuch des Unmenschen.* Hamburg: Claassen

Stockwell, P. (2002) *Sociolinguistics: A Resource Book for Students.* London: Routledge.

Stockwell, R. and D. Minkova. (2001) *English Words: History and Structure.* Cambridge: Cambridge University Press.

Stone, J. C. (2007) Popular websites in adolescents' out-of-school lives: Critical lessons on literacy. In M. Knobel and C. Lankshear (eds). *A New Literacy Studies Sampler.* New York: Peter Lang, 49–67.

Strang, B. M. H. (1970) *A History of English.* London: Methuen.

Street, B. (ed.). (1993) *Cross-Cultural Approaches to Literacy.* Cambridge and New York: Cambridge University Press.

Stuart-Smith, J., C. Timmins and F. Tweedie. (2007). 'Talkin' Jockney'? Variation and change in Glaswegian accent. *Journal of Sociolinguistics,* 11: 221–60.

Stubbs, M. (1983a) *Discourse Analysis.* Oxford: Blackwell.

Stubbs, M. (1983b) *Language, Schools and Classrooms,* 2nd edn. London: Methuen.

Stump, G. (2001) *Inflectional Morphology: A Theory of Paradigm Structure.* Cambridge: Cambridge University Press.

Sudnow, D. (ed.). (1972) *Studies in Social Interaction.* New York: Free Press.

Sullivan, A. (1992) *Sound Change in Progress: A Study of Phonological Change and Lexical Diffusion, with Reference to Glottalisation and r-loss in the Speech of some Exeter Schoolchildren.* Exeter: University of Exeter Press.

Sunderland, J. (1994) Pedagogical and other filters: The representation of non-sexist language change in British pedagogical grammars. In J. Sunderland (ed.), *Exploring Gender: Questions and Implications for English Language Education.* Hemel Hempstead: Prentice Hall, 92–103.

Sunderland, J. (1996) *Gendered Discourse in the Foreign Language Classroom: Teacher-student and Student-teacher Talk, and the Social Construction of Children's Femininities and Masculinities.* Unpublished PhD thesis, Lancaster University.

Sunderland, J. (1998) Girls being quiet: a problem for foreign language classrooms? *Language Teaching Research*, 2(1): 48–82.

Sunderland, J. (2000) New understandings of gender and language classroom research: Texts, teacher talk and student talk. *Language Teaching Research*, 4(2): 149–73.

Sunderland, J. (2002) Baby entertainer, bumbling assistant and line manager: Discourses of paternal identity in parentcraft texts. In J. Sunderland and L. Litosseliti (eds), *Gender Identity and Discourse Analysis.* Amsterdam: John Benjamins, 293–324.

Sunderland, J. (2003) Gender and language learning. In B. Norton and K. Toohey (eds), *Critical Pedagogies and Language Learning.* Cambridge: Cambridge University Press, 222–41.

Sunderland, J. (2004) *Gendered Discourses.* Basingstoke: Palgrave Macmillan.

Sunderland, J.(2006) *Language and Gender: An Advanced Resource Book.* Abingdon: Routledge.

Svartvik, J. and G. N. Leech. (2006) *English: One Tongue, Many Voices.* Basingstoke: Palgrave Macmillan.

Swales, J. and P. S. Rogers. (1995) Discourse and the projection of corporate culture: The Mission Statement. *Discourse and Society*, 6(2): 223–42.

Swann, J. (1992) *Girls, Boys and Language.* Oxford: Blackwell, esp. chs 3 and 4.

Swann, J. and D. Graddol. (1988) Gender inequalities in classroom talk. *English in Education*, 22(1): 48–65.

Swann, J., A. Deumert, L. Lillis and R. Mesthrie. (2004) *A Dictionary of Sociolinguistics.* Edinburgh: Edinburgh University Press.

Sweet, H. (1971) *The Indispensable Foundation*, ed. Eugenie Henderson. Oxford: Oxford University Press.

Sylvain, S. (1936) *Le créole haïtien: morphologie et syntaxe.* Port-au-Prince and Wetteren: Imprimerie de Meester.

Tagliamonte, S. A. and H. Lawrence. (2000) I used to dance, but I don't dance now: The habitual past in English. *Journal of English Linguistics*, 28(4): 324–53.

Takahashi, K. (2006) A study of register variation in the British National Corpus. *Literary and Linguistic Computing*, 21: 111–26.

Tanaka, K. (1994) *Advertising Language: A Pragmatic Approach to Advertisements in Britain and Japan.* London: Routledge.

Tannen, D. (1991) *You Just Don't Understand! Women and Men in Conversation.* London: Virago.

Taylor, J. R. (2003) *Linguistic Categorization: Prototypes in Linguistic Theory.* Oxford: Oxford University Press.

ten Have, P. (1999) *Doing Conversation Analysis: A Practical Guide.* London: Sage Publications.

Theakston, A. L., E. V. M. Lieven, J. M. Pine and C. F. Rowland. (2001) The role of performance limitations in the acquisition of verb-argument structure: An alternative account. *Journal of Child Language*, 28: 127–52.

Thomas, A. (2007) Blurring and breaking through the boundaries of narrative, literacy, and identity in adolescent fan fiction. In M. Knobel and C. Lankshear (eds), *A New Literacy Studies Sampler*. New York: Peter Lang, 137–66.

Thomas, J. (1983) Cross-cultural pragmatic failure. *Applied Linguistics*, 4(2): 91–112.

Thomas, J. A. (1995) *Meaning in Interaction: An Introduction to Pragmatics*. London: Longman.

Thomason, S. G. and T. Kaufman. (1988) *Language Contact, Creolization and Genetic Linguistics*. Berkeley: University of California Press.

Thompson, G. (1996) *Introducing Functional Grammar*. London: Edward Arnold.

Thornborrow, J. (2002) *Power Talk: Language and Interaction in Institutional Discourse*. Harlow: Longman.

Thurlow, C. (2006) From statistical panic to moral panic: The metadiscursive construction and popular exaggeration of new media language in the print media. *Journal of Computer-Mediated Communication*, 11(3): article 1.

Titscher, S., M. Meyer et al. (2000) *Methods of Text and Discourse Analysis*. London: Sage.

Todd, L. (1984) *Modern Englishes: Pidgins and Creoles*. London: Routledge & Kegan Paul.

Todd, L. (1991) *Pidgins and Creoles*. London: Routledge & Kegan Paul.

Tolson, A. (2006) *Broadcast Talk: Spoken Discourse on TV and Radio*. Edinburgh: Edinburgh University Press.

Tomasello, M. (2003) *Constructing a Language: A Usage-Based Theory of Language Acquisition*. Harvard, MA: Harvard University Press.

Tomasello, M. and E. Bates (eds). (2001) *Language Development: The Essential Readings*. Oxford: Blackwell.

Toolan, M. (2001 [1988]) *Narrative: A Critical Linguistic Introduction*. London: Routledge.

Torgersen, E. and P. Kerswill. (2004) Internal and external motivation in phonetic change: Dialect levelling outcomes for an English vowel shift. *Journal of Sociolinguistics*, 8: 24–53.

Tottie, G. (2002) *An Introduction to American English*. Oxford: Blackwell.

Traugott, E. C. (1989) On the rise of epistemic meanings in English: An example of subjectification in semantic change. *Language*, 65: 31–55.

Traugott, E. C. (1992) Old English syntax. In R. Hogg (ed.), *The Cambridge History of the English language. Volume I: The Beginnings to 1066*. Cambridge: Cambridge University Press, 168–289.

Traugott, E. C. and R. B. Dasher. (2001) *Regularity in Semantic Change*. Cambridge: Cambridge University Press.

Traugott, E. C. and H. Smith. (1993) Review of Lightfoot (1991). *Journal of Linguistics*, 29: 431–47.

Treip, M. (1970) *Milton's Punctuation and Changing English Usage 1582–1676*. London: Methuen.

Trousdale, G. and D. Adger. (2007) Variation in English syntax: Theoretical implications. *Journal of English Language and Linguistics*, 11(2): 261–78.

Trudgill, P. (1972) Sex, covert prestige and linguistic change in the urban British English of Norwich. *Language in Society*, 1: 179–95.

Trudgill, P. (1974) *The Social Differentiation of English in Norwich*. Cambridge: Cambridge University Press.

Trudgill, P. (1999a) *The Dialects of England*. Oxford: Blackwell.

Trudgill, P. (1999b) Norwich: Endogenous and exogenous linguistic change. In P. Foulkes and G. Docherty (eds), *Urban Voices: Accent Studies in the British Isles*. London: Arnold, 124–40.

Trudgill, P. (1999c) Standard English: What it isn't. In T. Bex and R. J. Watts (eds), *Standard English: The Widening Debate*. London: Routledge, 117–28.

Trudgill, P. (2000) *Sociolinguistics: An Introduction to Language and* Society, 4th edn. London: Penguin.

Trudgill, P. (2002) The sociolinguistics of modern RP. In P. Trudgill, *Sociolinguistic Variation and Change*. Edinburgh: Edinburgh University Press, 171–80.

Trudgill, P. (2004) *New-Dialect Formation: The Inevitability of Colonial Englishes*. Edinburgh: Edinburgh University Press.

Trudgill, P. (2008) The dialect of East Anglia: Phonology. In B. Kortmann and C. Upton (eds), *Varieties of English 1: The British Isles*. Berlin: Mouton de Gruyter, 178–193.

Trudgill, P. and J. Chambers. (1991) Verb systems in English dialects. In P. Trudgill and J. Chambers (eds), *Dialects of English: Studies in Grammatical Variation*. New York: Longman. 49–53.

Trudgill, P. and J. Hannah. (2002) *International English: A Guide to Varieties of Standard English*, 4th edn. London: Arnold.

Trumbach, R. (1991) The birth of the queen: Sodomy and the emergence of gender equality in modern culture, 1660–1750. In M. B. Duberman, M. Vicinus and G. Chauncey (eds), *Hidden From History*. London: Penguin, 129–40.

Tusting, K. (2007) Ecologies of new literacies and their implications for education. In A. Creese, P. Martin and N. H. Hornberger (eds), *Encyclopedia of Language and Education*, Volume 9: *Ecology of Language*, 2nd edn. Berlin: Springer, 1–13.

Tyack, D. and D. Ingram. (1977) Children's production and comprehension of questions. *Journal of Child Language*, 4: 211–24.

Ungerer, F. and H.-J. Schmid. (2006) *An Introduction to Cognitive Linguistics*, 2nd edn. Harlow: Longman

Unsworth, L. (2001) *Teaching Multiliteracies Across the Curriculum: Changing Contexts of Text and Image in Classroom Practice*. Buckingham: Open University Press.

Ur, P. (1981) *Discussions that Work*. Cambridge: Cambridge University Press.

Vachek, J. (1989) *Written Language Revisited*. Amsterdam: John Benjamins.

van de Mieroop, D. (2005) An integrated approach of quantitative and qualitative analysis in the study of identity in speeches. *Discourse and Society*, 16(1): 107–30.

van Dijk, T. (1972) *Some Aspects of Tense Grammars*. The Hague: Mouton.

van Dijk, T. (1980) *Macrostructures: An Interdisciplinary Study of Global Structures in Discourse, Interaction and Cognition*. Hillsdale, NJ: Lawrence Erlbaum Associates.

van Dijk, T. A. (1984) *Prejudice in Discourse*. Amsterdam: John Benjamins.

van Dijk, T. A. (1988) *News as Discourse*. Hillsdale, NJ: Lawrence Erlbaum.

van Dijk, T. A. (1993) Principles of critical discourse analysis *Discourse and Society*, 4(2): 249–83.

van Dijk, T. A. (2004) From text grammar to critical discourse analysis. Version 2.0: http://www.discourses.org/download/articles (accessed 5 January 2009).

van Dijk, T. A. (2006) Discourse and manipulation. *Discourse and Society*, 17(2): 359–83.

van Dijk, T. and W. Kintsch. (1983) *Strategies of Discourse Comprehension*. New York: Academic Press.

van Leeuwen, T. (2004) *Introducing Social Semiotics: An Introductory Textbook*. London: Routledge.

van Leeuwen, T. and C. Jewitt (eds). (2001) *Handbook of Visual Analysis*. London: Sage.

van Peer, Willie (1986) *Stylistics and Psychology: Investigations of Foregrounding*. London: Croom Helm.

Vaux, B. and A. Nevins. (2003) *The shm-Reduplication Survey*. Available at: http://php-dev.imt.uwm.edu/prjs/markj/projects/fll_surveys/shm/

Vehicle Certification Agency (2004) The Passenger Car (Fuel Consumption and CO2 Emissions Information) Regulations, UK Vehicle Certification Agency. 2007. Available at: http://www.vca.gov.uk/additional/files/fcb--co2/enforcement-on-advertising/vca061.pdf

Vennemann, T. (1994) Linguistic reconstruction in the context of European prehistory. *Transactions of the Philological Society*, 92: 215–84.

Ventola, E. (2005) Revisiting service encounter genre: Some reflections. *Folia Linguistica*, 39(1–2): 19–44.

Verdonk, P. (ed.). (1993) *Twentieth-Century Poetry: From Text to Context*. London: Routledge.

Verdonk, P. and J.-J. Weber (eds). (1995) *Twentieth-Century Fiction: From Text To Context*. London: Routledge.

Verschueren, J. (1999) *Understanding Pragmatics*. London: Arnold.

Vestergaard, T. and K. Schrøder. (1985) *The Language of Advertising*. Oxford: Blackwell.

Vincent, D. (2000) *The Rise of Mass Literacy: Reading and Writing in Modern Europe*. Cambridge: Polity.

Vincent, N. (1997) Synthetic and analytic structures. In M. Maiden and M. Parry (eds), *The Dialects of Italy*. London: Routledge, 99–05.

Visser, F. Th. (1973) *An Historical Syntax of the English Language. Part Three, Second Half: Syntactical Units with Two and with More Verbs*. Leiden: E. J. Brill.

Vygotsky, L.S. (1962) [1934]. *Thought and Language*. Cambridge, MA: MIT Press.

Vygotsky, L.S. (1966) Development of the higher mental functions. In A. N. Leontiev (ed.), *Psychological Research in the USSR*. Moscow: Progress Publishers.

Wald, B. (1984) The status of Chicano English as a dialect of American English. In J. Orstein-Galicia and A. Metcalf (eds), *Form and Function in Chicano English*. Rowley, MA: New House, 14–31.

Wales, K. (2001 [1989]) *A Dictionary of Stylistics*. London: Longman.

Wales, K. (2002) 'North of Watford Gap': A cultural history of Northern English (from 1700). In R. Watts and P. Trudgill (eds), *Alternative Histories of English*. London: Routledge, 45–66.

Wales, K. (2006) *Northern English: A Cultural and Social History*. Cambridge: Cambridge University Press.

Warner, A. (1983) Review article on David Lightfoot, 'Principles of diachronic syntax'. *Journal of Linguistics*, 19: 187–209.

Warner, M. (ed.). (1993) *Fear of a Queer Planet*. Minneapolis MN: University of Minnesota Press.

Warren, P. (1998) Timing patterns in New Zealand English rhythm. *Te Reo*, 41: 80–93.

Watson, K. (2006) Phonological resistance and innovation in the North-West of England. *English Today*, 22(2): 55–61.

Watson, K. (2007) Liverpool English. *Journal of the International Phonetics Association*, 37(3): 351–60.

Watt, D. (2002) 'I don't speak with a Geordie accent, I speak, like, the Northern accent': contact induced levelling in the Tyneside vowel system. *Journal of Sociolinguistics*, 6(1): 44–63.

Watt, D. (2007) Variation and the variable. In C. Llamas, L. Mullany and P. Stockwell (eds), *The Routledge Companion to Sociolinguistics*. Oxford: Routledge, 3–11.

Watt, D. and C. Ingham. (2000) Durational evidence of the Scottish Vowel Length Rule in Berwick English. *Leeds Working Papers in Linguistics & Phonetics*, 8: 205–28.

Watts, R. and P. Trudgill (eds). (2002) *Alternative Histories of English*. London: Routledge.

Watts, R. J. (2005) Linguistic politeness research. Quo vadis? In R. J. Watts, I. Sachiko and K. Ehlich (eds), *Politeness in Language: Studies in its History, Theory and Practice*, 2nd edn. Berlin: Mouton, xi–xlvii.

Weale, M. E., D. A. Weiss, R. F. Jager, N. Bradman and M. G. Thomas. (2002) Y chromosome evidence for Anglo-Saxon mass migration. *Molecular Biology and Evolution*, 19: 1008–21.

Weise, G. (1993) Criteria for the classification of ESP texts. *Fachsprache*, 1: 26–31.

Weise, G. and R. Wodak. (2000) European Union discourses on employment: Strategies of depoliticizing and ideologizing employment policies. *Concepts and Transformation*, 5(1): 29–42.

Weise, R. (2000) *The Phonology of German*. Oxford: Oxford University Press.

Wells, G. (1986). *The Meaning Makers*. Portsmouth, NH: Heinemann.

Wells, J. (1982). *Accents of English*, 3 vols. Cambridge: Cambridge University Press.

Wells, J. C. (2002). *Accents of English*, 3 vols. Cambridge: Cambridge University Press.

Wenger, E. (1998) *Communities of Practice: Learning, Meaning and Identity*. Cambridge: Cambridge University Press.

Werth, P. (1999) *Text Worlds: Representing Conceptual Space in Discourse*. London: Longman.

Westwood, G. (1952) *Society and the Homosexual*. London: Victor Gollancz.

Wetherell, M., S. Taylor and J. Y. Simeon (eds). (2002) *Discourse as Data*. London: Sage.

Wetschanow, K. (1999) The private is political. Are daytime talk shows feminist? In R. Gerin and P. Jedlickova (eds), *A Decade of Transformation*. IWM Junior Fellows Conferences, Volume VIII, Vienna (http://univie.ac.at/ www.iwm.at/).

Whinnom, K. (1971) Linguistic hybridization and the 'special case' of pidgins and creoles. In D. Hymes (ed.), *Pidginization and Creolization of Languages*. Cambridge: Cambridge University Press, 91–116.

Whitman, N. (2006) *Literal-Minded*. Linguistic commentary from a guy who takes things too literally, Available at: http://literalminded.wordpress.com/2006/03/13/backformation-roundup/

Widdowson, H. G. (1978) *Teaching Language as Communication*. Oxford: Oxford University Press.

Wierzbicka, A. (2003) *Cross-Cultural Pragmatics*. Berlin and New York: Mouton de Gruyter.

Wiesse, R. (2000) *The Phonology of German*. Oxford: Oxford University Press.

Wildgen, W. (2004) The Paleolithic origins of art, its dynamic and topological aspects, and the transition to writing. In M. Bax, B. van Heusden and W. Wildgen (eds), *Semiotic Evolution and the Dynamics of Culture*. Bern: Peter Lang, 117–53

Willes, M. J. (1983) *Children into Pupils: A Study of Language in Early Schooling*. London: R.K.P.

Williams, A. (2007) Non-standard English and education. In D. Britain (ed.), *Language in the British Isles*. Cambridge: Cambridge University Press, 401–16.

Williams, A. and P. Kerswill. (1999). Dialect levelling: Change and continuity in Milton Keynes, Reading and Hull. In P. Foulkes and G. Docherty (eds), *Urban Voices. Accent Studies in the British Isles*. London: Arnold, 141–62.

Williams, J. M. (1975) *Origins of the English Language*. New York: Free Press.

Williamson, J. (1978) *Decoding Advertisements: Ideology and Meaning in Advertising*. London: Marion Boyars.

Willis, J. (1996) *A Framework for Task-Based Learning*. Harlow: Longman.

Wilson, J. (1990) *Politically Speaking: The Pragmatic Analysis of Political Language*. Oxford: Blackwell.

Wittgenstein, L. (1953) *Philosophical Investigations*, trans G. E. M. Anscombe. Oxford: Blackwell.

Wittgenstein, L. (1967) *Philosophische Untersuchungen*. Frankfurt am Main: Suhrkamp.

Wodak, R. (1996) *Disorders of Discourse*. London: Longman.

Wodak, R. (2001) The discourse-historical approach. In R. Wodak and M. Meyer (eds), *Methods of Critical Discourse Analysis*. London: Sage, 63–95.

Wodak, R. (2007a) Pragmatics and critical discourse analysis. A cross-disciplinary analysis. *Pragmatics and Cognition*, 15(1): 203–25.

Wodak, R. (2007b) Discourses in European Union organizations: Aspects of access, participation, and exclusion. In C. Briggs (ed.), *Four Decades of Epistemological Revolution: Work Inspired by Aaron V. Cicourel*. Special Issue, *TEXT and TALK*, 27(5/6): 655–80.

Wodak, R. (2007c) Editorial: Language and ideology-language in ideology. *Journal of Language and Politics*, 6(1): 1–6.

Wodak, R. (2008) Introduction: Discourse Studies – important concepts and terms. In R. Wodak and M. Krzyżanowski (eds), *Qualitative Discourse Analysis in the Social Sciences*. Basingstoke: Palgrave Macmillan.

Wodak, R. (2009) *The Discourse of Politics in Action: Politics as Usual*. Basingstoke: Palgrave Macmillan.

Wodak, R. and R. de Cillia. (2006) Politics and language: Overview. In K. Brown (Editor-in-Chief) *Encyclopedia of Language and Linguistics*, Volume 9, 2nd edn. Oxford: Elsevier, 707–19.

Wodak, R. and R. de Cillia. (2007) Commemorating the past: The discursive construction of official narratives about the Rebirth of the Second Austrian Republic. *Discourse and Communication*, 1(3): 337–63.

Wodak, R. and P. Kirsch. (1995) *Totalitäre Sprachen – Langue de Bois*. Vienna: Passagen Verlag.

Wodak, R. and V. Koller (eds). (2008) *Handbook of Communication in the Public Sphere*. Berlin: Mouton de Gruyter.

Wodak, R. and M. Krzyzanowski (eds). (2008) *Qualitative Discourse Analysis in the Social Sciences*. Basingstoke: Palgrave Macmillan.

Wodak, R. and M. Meyer. (2001) *Methods of Critical Discourse Analysis*. London: Sage.

Wodak, R. and A. Pelinka (eds). (2002) *The Haider Phenomenon in Austria*. New Brunswick, NJ: Transaction Press.

Wodak, R. and M. Schulz. (1986) *The Language of Love and Guilt*. Amsterdam: Benjamins.

Wodak, R., R. de Cillia, M. Reisigle and K. Liebhart. (2009 [1999]) *The Discursive Construction of National Identity*, 2nd rev. edn. Edinburgh: Edinburgh University Press.

Wolfram, W. and C. Dannenberg. (1999) Dialect identity in a tri-ethnic context: The case of the Lumbee American Indian English. *English World-Wide*, 29: 79–116.

Wolfram, W. and N. Schilling-Estes. (1998) *American English*. Oxford: Oxford University Press.

Wong, A. (2002) The semantic derogation of Tongzhi: A synchronic perspective. In K. Campbell-Kibler, R. J. Podesva, S. J. Roberts and A. Wong (eds), *Language and Sexuality: Contesting Meaning in Theory and Practice*. Leland Stanford Junior University: CSLI Publications, 161–74.

Wong-Fillmore, L. (1979) Individual differences in second language acquisition. In C. J. Fillmore, D. Kempler and W. S.-Y. Wang (eds), *Individual Differences in Language Ability and Language Behaviour*. London: Academic Press, 203–28.

Wong-Fillmore, L. (1985) When does teacher talk work as input? In S. M. Gass and C. G. Madden (eds), *Input in Second Language Acquisition*. Rowley, MA: Newbury House, 17–50.

Woodward, K. (2002) *Understanding Identity*. London: Arnold.

Wray, A. (2002) Formulaic Language and the Lexicon. Cambridge: Cambridge University Press.

Wright, J. (1898) *English Dialect Dictionary*. Oxford: Oxford University Press.

Wright, J. (1905) *The English Dialect Grammar*. Oxford: Frowde.

Wright, S. (2005) Design matters: The political efficacy of government-run discussion boards. In R. Gibson, S. Oates and D. Owen (eds), *Civil Society, Democracy and the Internet: A Comparative Perspective*. London: Routledge.

Wyatt-Smith, C. and J. Cumming. (2003) Curriculum literacies: Expanding domains of assessment. *Assessment in Education*, 10(1): 47–59.

Wyld, H. C. (1914) *A Short History of English*. London: John Murray.

Wyld, H. C. (1927) *A Short History of English*, 3rd edn. London: John Murray.

Yates, S. J. (1996) Oral and written linguistic aspects of computer conferencing. In S. Herring (ed.), *Computer-Mediated Communication: Linguistics, Social, and Cross-Cultural Perspectives*. Amsterdam: John Benjamins, 29–46.

Young, L. and B. Fitzgerald. (2006) *The Power of Language*. Toronto: University of Toronto Press.

Yule, G. (1996) *Pragmatics*. Oxford: Oxford University Press.

Yuling, P., S. W. Scollon and R. Scollon. (2002) *Professional Communication in International Settings*. Malden, MA: Blackwell.

Zhu, Y. (2005) *Written Communication across Cultures: A Sociocognitive Perspective on Business Genres*. Amsterdam: John Benjamins.

Zimmerman, D. H. (1992) The interactional organization of calls for emergency assistance. In P. Drew and J. Heritage (eds), *Talk at Work: Interaction in Institutional Settings*. Cambridge: Cambridge University Press, 418–69.

Index